Psychology Applied to Teaching

Sixth Edition

Robert F. Biehler

Jack Snowman
Southern Illinois University

HOUGHTON MIFFLIN COMPANY   BOSTON

Dallas   Geneva, Illinois   Palo Alto   Princeton, New Jersey

930768

∠ 60

Library of Congress Catalog Card Number: 89-80917

ISBN: 0-395-43201-4

BCDEFGHIJ-VH-9543210

CONTENTS

PREFACE

The hallmark of this text is its usefulness to teachers. It is written for students enrolled in an introductory educational psychology course, and is at once a basic source of information for prospective teachers and a resource for their future use as classroom teachers.

Organization

Psychology Applied to Teaching, sixth edition, retains its arrangement of chapters intended to make readers aware of a model of learning and instruction. As depicted in Figure 1.1 (p.27), four phases of this model serve as the book's organizational frame of reference:

1. Take into account what students are like.
2. Specify what is to be learned.
3. Provide instruction.
4. Determine if students have learned.

Parts 1 through 4 of the text present information and applications related to each of these phases:

Part 1 Considering Student Characteristics
Part 2 Specifying What Is to Be Learned
Part 3 Providing Instruction
Part 4 Evaluating Performance

Part 5 consists of two chapters that apply across all phases of learning and instruction: "Classroom Management" and "Becoming a Better Teacher."

Features of the Revision

Since the appearance of the last edition of *Psychology Applied to Teaching,* education as a whole has undergone dynamic change. This is especially true of the field of educational psychology. In particular, new research on cognitive learning theory, student motivation, multiculturalism, and helping students become effective problem solvers and strategic learners has been reshaping what we know about learning and what teachers can do to enhance it.

The sixth edition has been extensively revised and comprehensively updated to incorporate these and other important new developments. A key change in the sixth edition is the thorough reworking of the three chapters that focus specifically on learning theory in order to reflect the latest research in this area; indeed, much of Chapters 8 and 9 and portions of Chapter 7 are new. Chapter 7, "Behavioral Learning Theory," contains greatly expanded coverage of social learning theory, as well as updated and expanded coverage of computer use in the classroom.

Chapter 8, "Information Processing Theory," includes more information on basic cognitive processes and a major new section on helping students use learning strategies more effectively. Chapter 9, "Cognitive Learning Theories and Problem Solving," contains a wealth of new material on the nature and teaching of problem solving, including a five-step problem-solving sequence that teachers can use to help their students become skillful problem solvers.

In addition to Chapters 7, 8, and 9, other chapters have also been revised, some in a very major way. Chapter 4, "Assessing Pupil Variability," provides new material on the uses and limitations of standardized tests and the nature of intelligence. Chapter 5, "Dealing with Pupil Variability," features a new section on the nature and effects of ability grouping, new coverage of teaching gifted and talented students, and extensive new material on bilingual and culturally diverse students, including new Suggestions for Teaching on "Promoting Multicultural Understanding." Chapter 11, "Motivation," and Chapter 12, "Measurement and Evaluation of Classroom Learning," have been made even more useful to prospective teachers. Chapter 11 now contains a new section on enhancing motivation for classroom learning, as well as new coverage on the effects of cooperative learning on student motivation. Chapter 12 includes a step-by-step explanation (based on Gronlund) of how to conduct test item analysis and a thirteen-point suggestion list to help teachers implement a mastery learning approach in their classrooms.

Throughout the text, additional coverage of multicultural concerns, issues, and perspectives has been integrated wherever relevant to better prepare prospective teachers for the growing cultural diversity of our schools and classrooms.

In developing *Psychology Applied to Teaching,* sixth edition, we were very much aware that this is a book for the 1990s—and beyond.

Pedagogic Features of the Text

For reasons spelled out in the opening pages of Chapter 1, this sixth edition of *Psychology Applied to Teaching* has been written to be used in three ways: (1) as a text that provides a review of scientific information organized and presented so that it will be understood, remembered, and applied; (2) as a source of practical ideas about instructional techniques for student teachers and beginning teachers; and (3) as a means for teachers to improve their effectiveness as they gain experience in the classroom.

The following features, many of which were introduced in various earlier editions, have been selected, improved, and augmented to make this sixth edition more useful and effective than its predecessors.

Key Points   At the beginning of each chapter, Key Points are listed under major headings. They also appear in color in the margins of pages opposite sections in which each point is discussed. The Key Points call attention to sections of the text that are considered to be of special significance to teachers and thus serve as instructional objectives.

Suggestions for Teaching   Most chapters include summaries of research findings and principles relating to a particular topic. These are followed by detailed descriptions of various ways in which the information and concepts might be applied in classrooms. Numerous examples of applications at different grade levels are supplied, and readers are urged to select and record applications that will fit their own particular personality, style, and teaching situation in a Personal Handbook. The Suggestions for Teaching are intended to be read while the book is used as a text *and* referred to by future teachers and in-service teachers after they have completed course work. For ease in reference, these suggestions are printed in a different typeface from that used in other parts of the book and are highlighted by a colored screen background. Suggestions for Teaching are also indexed inside the front cover of the text.

Mid-Chapter Reviews   This feature summarizes research-based information, principles, and theories presented in the first part of most chapters. These reviews strengthen understanding of points that serve as the basis for the Suggestions for Teaching presented in the second part of most chapters. The Mid-Chapter Reviews include coverage of Key Points and are intended to serve as an effective learning aid for students preparing for examinations.

Handbook Headings and Becoming a Better Teacher: Questions and Suggestions   These two features facilitate the preparation and use of a personal handbook for teaching. Readers are urged to use the Handbook Headings, which appear in the margins, to prepare a personal set of guidelines for reference before and during the student teaching experience and during the first years of teaching. The questions and suggestions in the Becoming a Better Teacher section are intended to help in-service teachers to analyze strengths and weaknesses and to plan how to improve their effectiveness as instructors. A guide for setting up and using these resources is included in Chapter 14: "Becoming a Better Teacher."

Suggestions for Further Study   At the end of each chapter an annotated bibliography is presented offering sources of information of topics of interest to teachers. Some chapters also include within these suggestions instructions for carrying out simple scientific and observational studies and experiments.

Summary   New to this edition is a numbered set of summary statements that appear after the Suggestions for Further Study. This feature is intended to help students review the main points of a chapter for upcoming examinations or class discussions.

Key Terms   Also new to this edition, and appearing after the Summary, is a list of topics that are key aspects of the chapter. Understanding these topics is an essential part of understanding the chapter as a whole. To facilitate use of this feature, the page where each term is initially defined and discussed appears in parentheses.

Discussion Questions   Also new to this edition, this feature appears after the Key Terms. Because understanding and retention of new information is enhanced when learners actively relate it to known ideas and experiences,the Discussion Questions ask the reader to reflect on how previous experiences (or possible future experiences) relate to the chapter material. These questions can serve as the focus for in-class discussion and out-of-class discussion.

Glossary   A glossary of key terms and concepts is provided at the back of the book as an aid in reviewing for examinations or classroom discussion.

Indexes   In addition to the detailed name and subject indexes at the end of the book, an Index to Suggestions for Teaching is included inside the front cover. An Index to Suggestions for Further Study is provided on the inside of the back cover.

Instructional Components That Accompany the Text

Study Guide   A new study guide has been developed for students using the sixth edition of *Psychology Applied to Teaching.* It continues to facilitate mastery of Key Points, and now includes a description of how to use the Study Guide as part of a learning strategy. As an integral part of suggested tactics for learning, original "concept maps" are supplied for each chapter. Concept maps are schematic representations of how major topics, subtopics, and Key Points of a chapter relate to each other. Also included in the Study Guide are exercises designed to help students enhance memory and understanding of Key Point material, and two sets of review questions (multiple choice and short answer) to support student efforts at self-monitoring.

Microstudy Plus   This interactive computerized version of the Study Guide includes rejoinders to multiple choice questions to facilitate independent learning.

Instructor's Manual   This teaching aid includes coverage of Key Points, supplementary discussion topics, student activities, extra references, listings of films and videotapes, reproduction of the Study Guide's concept maps, and reproduction of all transparencies.

Lecture Enrichment Manual   This new teaching aid has been developed for the sixth edition of *Psychology Applied to Teaching.* It provides a detailed lecture outline with supplementary teaching suggestions and "Approaches to Teaching Educational Psychology," a compendium of teaching tactics from professors across the country.

Test Bank   The thoroughly revised and expanded version of the Test Bank includes almost fourteen hundred test items consisting of 1000 multiple choice items in alternate forms, 320 short answer questions, and 69 essay questions. Feedback booklets give students opportunity for self-monitoring.

MicroTest   Also new to this edition is an interactive computerized version of the Test Bank.

Transparencies   An extensive set of transparencies in four, two, and one colors consisting of figures, charts, and instructional aids in the text, is available upon adoption of the text.

Acknowledgments

A number of reviewers made constructive suggestions and provided thoughtful reactions at various stages in the development of the manuscript. Thanks go out to the following for their direction and support:

Barbara Anderson, Rhode Island College

Helen Botnarescue, California State University, Hayward

Charles Brochetti, Slippery Rock University of Pennsylvania

Clifford Burgess, Armstrong State College

Richard Craig, Towson State University

Gail Ditkoff, California University of Pennsylvania

J. B. Engel, Willamette University

Richard English, University of Missouri, Columbia

Dean Ginther, East Texas State University

William Gnagey, Illinois State University

Patricia Haensly, Texas A & M University

Walter Hapkiewicz, Michigan State University

Richard Heck, Mansfield University

William Herman, Madonna College

Julian Hertzog, William Woods College

George Leddick, Purdue University

G. Sidney Lester, San Jose State University

Adele Levine, San Jose State University

Bruce McCormick, Northeast Louisiana University

Ethel Migra, National College of Education

Raymond B. Miller, University of Idaho

Lloyd Noppe, University of Wisconsin at Green Bay

Rolando Santos, California State University, San Bernardino

Dale Schunk, University of North Carolina

Naim Sefein, State University of New York, Fredonia

Stuart Silverman, University of South Florida

Walter Skinner, Georgia State University

Roy Smith, Long Island University

Karen Swoope, Washington State University

Carol Takacs, Cleveland State University

Alice Walker, State University of New York, Cortland

Barry Wilson, University of Northern Iowa

Finally, I would like to acknowledge several other individuals for their own invaluable contributions to this book:

I am indebted to Rebecca Lewis, Pamela Odum, and Kristin Prichard,   o typed most of the manuscript, and to Nancy Buckles who so ably supervised their efforts that every deadline was met.

I am indebted to the staff at Houghton Mifflin Company who developed the final manuscript into a text.

I'm also indebted to Rick, Andrea, and Jeff for giving me what every author needs: love, confidence, and time to think.

J.S.

Psychology Applied to Teaching

chapter 1

APPLYING PSYCHOLOGY TO TEACHING

KEY POINTS

The Nature and Values of Science

Unsystematic observation may lead to false conclusions

Grade retention policies influenced by unsystematic observation

Scientific methods: sampling, control, objectivity, publication, replication

Studying Behavior: Complicating Factors

Research focuses on a few aspects of a problem

Differences of opinion due to selection and interpretation of data

Accumulating knowledge leads researchers to revise original ideas

Teaching as an Art and a Science

Teaching as an art: emotions, values, flexibility

Research provides a scientific basis for "artistic" teaching

Good teachers combine "artistic" and "scientific" characteristics

The Teacher-Practitioner and the Teacher-Theorist

Teacher-practitioner: enthusiastic commitment

Teacher-theorist: objective analysis, caution, uncertainty

Test teaching hypotheses enthusiastically, evaluate results critically

As you begin to read this book, you may be asking yourself, "What will this book tell me about teaching that I don't already know?" The answer to that question depends on several factors, including your previous experiences with teaching and the number of psychology courses you have taken. Since you have been actively engaged in the process of formal education for at least twelve years, you already know a great deal about learning and teaching. You have had abundant opportunities to observe and react to over one hundred teachers. You have probably read several hundred texts, finished all kinds of assignments, and taken hundreds if not thousands of examinations. Undoubtedly, you have also established strong likes and dislikes for certain subjects and approaches to teaching.

Yet despite your familiarity with education from the student's point of view, you have probably had limited experience with education from the teacher's point of view. As you read this book (and as you interact with pupils), you will discover that the teacher's perception of what takes place in classrooms is often substantially different from the perception of students. As a student, for example, you have probably resented certain assignments and examinations. You may have brooded about the weakness of a teacher who was unable to inspire students to learn and had to resort to coercion. However, you probably have not had the experience—yet—of attempting to arouse and hold the interest of one or more groups of students, nor have you been faced with the problem of assigning grades that must be backed up by evidence.

One type of information about teaching that you don't already know, therefore, takes the form of descriptions of classroom practice as seen from a professional educator's point of view. Such descriptions make up a substantial part of this book, since its primary purpose is to acquaint you with information about teaching that is derived from the discoveries of psychologists. Psychologists use the methods of science to study behavior, and if you have taken any courses in psychology, you are already familiar with the nature of knowledge in this field. However, this book differs from other books in psychology that you may have read because it stresses ways you might *apply* psychological knowledge to teaching. Psychologists have discovered many things about human behavior, and they have established principles and theories to summarize and clarify their insights. You may already be familiar with many facts and theories in psychology but probably have not tried to convert this knowledge into classroom applications. As you read this book, you will be frequently urged to think of ways you might use what you learn. To grasp how you might make applications, you should become aware at the very outset that this book has been designed to be used in three different ways. The simplest and most direct way to begin to explain why it is different and how it can be used is to relate a frustrating but enlightening experience.

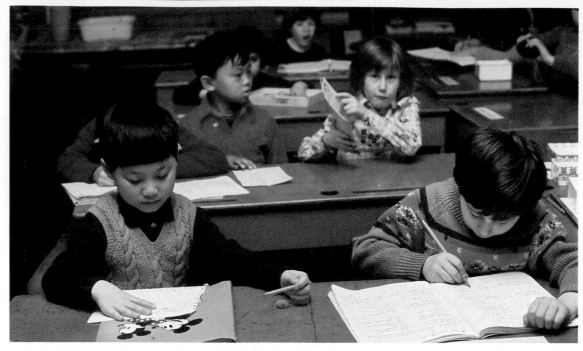

A teacher's perception of what takes place in classrooms is often very different from the perception of students. (Freda Leinwand/Monkmeyer)

"What They Didn't Tell Us"

A few years after the "senior" author of this book began teaching a course in educational psychology, a student-teacher chapter of the state teachers' association was formed on campus. The leaders of this group, who were scheduled to do student teaching the following September, decided to present a panel discussion at the last meeting of the year, in May. They invited five recent graduates who were just completing their first year of teaching to discuss the provocative topic "What They Didn't Tell Us." Since "they" included professors who taught educational psychology and since the professor who is writing these words was just beginning to think about getting to work on a text, he decided to go to the discussion and take notes. The meeting was very well attended, and the panelists had the audience of future student teachers on the edge of their seats much of the evening. When the meeting finally broke up, most of the audience left the room with a sense of satisfaction. They had picked up all sorts of valuable tips straight from the horse's mouth. The professor and would-be author, on the other hand, was bothered and bewildered.

The college the panelists had graduated from was quite small at that time, and all of them had taken his course in educational psychology just two years before. Several of the bits of information that the panelists had told the student teachers to be sure to pick up somehow or other before they entered a classroom had been discussed (directly or indirectly) in the ed psych text they had read. Yet these former students—who had successfully answered test questions and earned high grades in educational psychology—now talked as if they had never heard of such a course.

During the question-and-answer period that followed the panelists' presentations, the professor thought about asking to be recognized, standing up, and saying something like "This discussion really ought to be called 'What We Forgot.' I *did* tell you some of the things you are talking about, but you didn't remember them." Since he tends to be timid about speaking in public, he squirmed silently in his seat in the back row and fumed and brooded. Later that night, after having had time to think things over, he was glad that he hadn't sounded off because he concluded that he (along with the author of the text he had used) was more to blame than the former students for their failure to remember and use what they had learned.

At that early stage of his career, the professor made up tests similar to most of those he had taken all through his college years. After announcing that an exam would be given, he went through the assigned chapters of the text. When he found a section that impressed him as important *or* that looked as if it could easily be converted into a test question, he wrote a multiple-choice item. Much of the time, it must be confessed, information stressed in questions was selected more for testability than for importance or significance. After they had taken the first exam, students figured out that the most sensible way to study for subsequent exams was to try to put themselves in the place of the person writing the questions. That is, they skimmed through the book and selected for study sections that impressed them as likely to appeal to someone making up items for an exam. Since they studied primarily to answer test questions, they naturally assumed that what they had learned had served its purpose as soon as they completed an exam. Since there was no longer any reason to remember it, they forgot it.

While the kinds of test questions used undoubtedly contributed to the tendency for students to fail to remember what they had learned, the text on which the questions were based also deserved part of the blame. The author made no attempt to illustrate how what was discussed might be applied. His philosophy seemed to be "My job is to tell you about facts, principles, and theories. Your job is to figure out what to do with what I tell you." Since the students realized that their primary responsibility during the course was to pass exams, they had no inclination at that time to try to figure out how to apply what they read. And since the book offered no classroom applications that impressed them as being readily accessible for future use, they sold their texts at the end of the semester. Without the book to refer to a year or so later when they engaged in student teaching or two years later when they began to teach on their own, they had to rely on what they remembered. And since they remembered little or nothing about what had been covered in their course in educational psychology that could be converted into classroom applications, it was not surprising that they talked about "What They Didn't Tell Us."

These more or less inescapable conclusions were a source of great dismay to the professor since he was, and continues to be, convinced that educational psychology is potentially the most valuable course in a teacher preparation program. Teachers can benefit in hundreds of ways from the insights and discoveries of behavioral scientists—provided they comprehend, remember, and apply what has been reported and discovered. They can also benefit by frequently functioning as behavioral scientists themselves in their classrooms. So the professor who suffered the agonizing experience at the panel discussion decided to write a book about educational psychology that would correct the limitations of the text he had been using. Taking into account what he had learned from the "What They Didn't Tell Us" experience, the professor-author kept this list of goals on his desk as he wrote:

1. Try to reduce students' tendency to conclude that information about educational psychology should be learned only to answer test questions.
2. Emphasize and illustrate classroom applications of the scientific principles discussed so that students will become aware of the many ways that psychology can be applied to teaching.
3. Organize the book so that it functions, not only as a text, but also as a reference to be kept and used during student-teaching and first year–teaching experiences.

Letters from former students supported the conclusion that *Psychology Applied to Teaching,* as the book came to be called when it was eventually published, often achieved all three goals. Many students reported that they did come to realize that psychological principles can be applied in the classroom. They did keep the book after the course had been completed, and they referred to the book when the time came to student teach and during their first years of teaching.

A survey carried out two years after the book was published provided more-systematic evidence of success. The student-teacher association sent questionnaires to one hundred recent graduates who were just completing their first year of teaching, asking them to evaluate the education courses they had taken. Over 60 percent of the respondents rated educational psychology as the most valuable and useful of all the courses (including general and specific methods) they had taken in their credential programs.

Subsequent editions of *Psychology Applied to Teaching* introduced new features designed to improve its usefulness. This sixth edition incorporates the best features of the previous editions. In order to achieve maximum value from this book, though, you should become aware of its distinguishing characteristics and, before you read any further, understand the three ways of using it.

Uses of This Book

As just noted, this book has been written so that it can be used in three ways. First, it is a text for a course in educational psychology intended to help you master an organized sampling of scientific knowledge about development, learning, objectives, motivation, evaluation, and individual differences. Second, it is a source of practical ideas and suggestions to be converted into specific techniques you might use during the time you serve as a student teacher and during your first years of teaching. Third, it is a reference work to be consulted when you want to analyze certain aspects of instruction as you gain experience as a teacher.

Using This Book to Acquire Scientific Information

A substantial amount of scientific knowledge is of potential value to teachers. This book offers a selection of information from this pool of knowledge, organized so that you can learn and remember what you read as easily and effectively as possible. Chances are that your instructor will present lectures, organize discussions, show films, and perhaps arrange field trips that will tie in with what is discussed in assigned chapters of this text. Depending on the purposes and organization of the educational psychology course you are taking, this book may also serve as the basis for examinations and/or other types of evaluation.

The primary reason for reading this book, then, is to become well acquainted with an organized body of scientific information in the field of educational psychology. Since this book presently functions as the text for a course, you may be asked to learn some sections well enough to be able to answer test questions. Tests function as incentives that motivate students to read with care, and they provide information about how well students understand what they have read. It is particularly desirable for you to read this book carefully during this quarter or semester so that you will become well acquainted with the second way of using the book.

Using This Book as a Source of Practical Ideas

A second way this book can be used is as a source of practical ideas on how to teach. In addition to acquiring knowledge and learning principles that will serve as a general, all-purpose background for teaching, you should think of specific ways in which you might apply what you learn. Sooner or later you will engage in student teaching. You may be a student teaching at the same time you are taking educational psychology. It is more likely, however, that you will student teach after you finish this book and that you will also take one or more additional courses in methods of teaching. Your performance as a student teacher will probably be one of the most important factors to be considered when you apply for a teaching position. Furthermore, once you secure a job as a teacher, your perform-

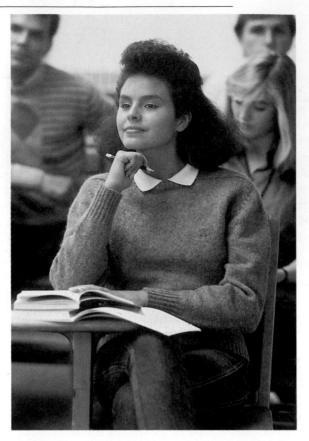

This book has been written so that you can use it as a student in a course in educational psychology, as a student teacher coping with all the new experiences of an "apprentice," and as a first-year teacher interested in perfecting instructional skills. (Left: D. Degnan/ H. Armstrong Roberts; bottom: Paul Conklin/ Monkmeyer. Facing page: Bob Daemmrich/The Image Works)

ance in the classroom will be the major factor considered when your supervisors decide if you will be offered a contract for a second year. Therefore, you will be eager to function as a prepared, confident, resourceful student teacher and first-year teacher. This book has been designed to help you get ready for your first teaching experiences and to make it possible for you to find quick solutions to problems as they occur.

Using This Book to Become a Better Teacher

In addition to getting ready to teach, you will also want to perfect your instructional techniques *as* you gain experience. You will not be able to anticipate all the problems you will encounter in any classroom, so you will continually need to make adjustments and engage in a process of trial and error. To make this process as constructive as possible, you should systematically analyze strengths and weaknesses in your teaching. The third way you can use this book is to analyze specific facets of your instructional techniques and plan how to correct errors and perfect successes.

A description of some of the features of the book further explains the three basic ways you might use this text.

Special Features of This Book

Several distinctive features of this book merit comment since they are intended to be used in rather specialized ways. These features include Key Points, Suggestions for Teaching, Handbook Headings, questions and suggestions for becoming a better teacher, and Suggestions for Further Study. Each feature has been included for reasons explained below.

Key Points

At the beginning of each chapter, you will find a list of *Key Points*. The Key Points also appear within each chapter, printed in bold type in the margins. These points have been selected to help you learn and remember sections of each chapter that are considered to be of special significance to teachers. (They may be stressed on exams, but they were originally selected not to serve as the basis for test items, but because they are important.) If you were to try to learn everything in this book, you would be working against yourself because some of the information you might memorize would interfere with the acquisition of other information. To reduce forgetting due to such interference, you are asked to concentrate on only a few sections in each chapter. To grasp the nature of Key Points, turn to pages 38–39, which list points stressed under the major headings of Chapter 2. Then flip through the chapter to see how their appearance in the margins calls attention to significant sections of the text.

Suggestions for Teaching

In most of the chapters of this book, you will find summaries of research that serve as the basis for related principles or conclusions. These sets of principles or conclusions, in turn, serve as the basis for *Suggestions for Teaching*. Each suggestion is usually followed by a list of examples illustrating how it might be applied. In most cases examples are provided for both elementary and secondary grades since there usually are differences in the way a principle might be applied in dealing with younger and older pupils.

The principles, suggestions, and examples are intended to help you think about how you can apply psychology to teaching. The lists of Suggestions for Teaching and the examples of some ways of applying principles are intended to help you compensate, at least partially, for lack of experience when you begin to teach. Since you will often want to find quick answers with a minimum of difficulty, applications of principles are first listed as sets of related ideas (which you can later refer to as reminders and as an "index" to detailed analyses of each point). Then each point is discussed and illustrated, in most cases by multiple examples. To permit you to find information relating to particular aspects of teaching, an index to the Suggestions for Teaching is printed inside the front cover. To discover the nature of the Suggestions for Teaching, turn to page 55. Read the list of suggestions, and then examine the following pages to become acquainted with the detailed suggestions and examples of applications.

Developing a Personal Handbook of Teaching

The Suggestions for Teaching and the examples of applications are intended to help you prepare for your initial teaching experiences. It is impossible to supply for each point discussed information that will have direct relevance to all teachers. Therefore you should not expect to find under every list of suggestions an example that will be directly applicable to the grade level and subject you hope to teach. Most of the time you will need to devise your own specific applications of principles. To help you do this and to help reduce the pressure and tension of your student-teaching experience and your first years of professional teaching, you are urged to develop your own personal *Handbook of Teaching.* Since you may need to concentrate on learning Key Points in order to demonstrate understanding on exams during the course you are now taking, you may not have time to prepare a Handbook this quarter or semester. But after you have read this book as a text, you might go through it a second time for the purpose of developing a custom-designed Handbook. Record your ideas in a notebook, and leave space for ideas that occur to you during methods courses, during your student teaching, and during your first years as a full-time teacher. To allow room for expansion, you might purchase a three-ring binder so that pages can be added or dropped.

One way to organize your Handbook would be to revise and expand the lists of Suggestions for Teaching presented in each chapter. If you write out your own version of these suggestions, devise your own examples of applications, and prepare an index, you will equip yourself with a custom-designed guidebook that should assist you in coping with many of the problems you will encounter when you first take over a classroom. To further help you organize your Handbook, frequent *Handbook Headings* are inserted in page margins opposite selected points. These headings are intended to serve as an outline you can use to amplify, supplement, and personalize the basic Suggestions for Teaching provided in the text. You might print each heading under the appropriate suggestions for teaching recorded in your Handbook and then list any specific techniques you can remember or invent that relate to that aspect of teaching. On page 544, for instance, you will find "Handbook Heading: Ways to Make Learning Active." That heading is intended to stimulate you to jot down specific ways to motivate your pupils by working activity into lessons. To begin, you might search your memory for techniques used by your former teachers. Did your fifth-grade teacher, for instance, have a clever way of arranging for you and your classmates to move around as you studied? Describe the technique so you will remember to try it yourself. Did a high school teacher have an ingenious way of inducing you to work actively with others on group projects? Exactly how did she or he do it? After you exhaust your own recollections, ask roommates or classmates if they can remember any successful ways that *their* teachers made learning active. Next, look at the examples provided opposite the Handbook Heading. To grasp how you might proceed, turn to page 544 and examine the examples opposite "Handbook Heading: Ways to Make Learning Active." Which ones seem most appropriate for the grade level and subject you will be teaching? Jot them down. Do any of the examples suggest variations you can think of on your own? Write them down before you forget them. Finally, add ideas that you pick up in methods classes or during your student-teaching experience. If you see a film in a methods class that shows how a teacher makes learning active, describe it in your Handbook. If your master teacher uses a successful technique to permit students to move around as they learn, record it.

If you follow some or all of these suggestions for using the Handbook Headings, you will have a rich source of ideas to turn to when you discover that your students seem bored and listless because of inactivity and you find yourself wondering if there is anything you can do about it.

Becoming a Better Teacher

The Suggestions for Teaching and the recommendation that you prepare a personal Handbook are intended to stimulate you to think about how you can apply what you learn. Such preparation for a teaching career may ease some of the trials and tribulations of your first few months in the classroom, but it will not eliminate problems. There are simply too many things to learn and to deal with at once. Furthermore, even if you have thought ahead about what you would like to do in a given situation, you may discover that, for one reason or another, it is extremely difficult or impossible to put your ideas into practice. Or you may become aware that you are so preoccupied with some aspects of teaching that you have slighted other facets of instruction.

For all these reasons, it will be to your advantage during the first months or years of your teaching career to make a systematic effort to evaluate selected aspects of your instructional technique. Otherwise, you may simply "do what comes naturally." Even with the guidance of this text, a personal Handbook, and other books on teaching, you will not be able to think of everything at once. To make it possible for you to analyze selected aspects of your teaching style over a period of time, questions and suggestions you might use to improve your teaching are provided in the last chapter, "Becoming a Better Teacher."

That section of the last chapter is based on points made in the text opposite Handbook Headings printed in the margin. The questions listed call your attention to specific aspects of your teaching technique and should stimulate ideas you might use to improve your instructional skills. To help you relate these questions to appropriate sections of the text, each suggested Handbook Heading printed in the margin is listed in "Becoming a Better Teacher." A question you might ask yourself follows each heading. (The question format is used as the most direct way to call attention to particular facets of instruction.) Then at least one "answer" to the question is provided, written as if it were a specific suggestion you might make to yourself. (Turn to page 000 and examine the questions and suggestions under Handbook Heading: Ways to Make Learning Active.)

You might use the questions and suggestions in "Becoming a Better Teacher" in two ways: (1) as troubleshooting aids when you are confronted with a specific, identifiable problem and (2) as a basis for systematic rotation evaluations. To put the latter procedure into operation, you might make it a habit—at least during the first year of your teaching career—to take a few moments at the end of each school day to examine the questions for one chapter. If you feel that you might improve your teaching by concentrating on techniques highlighted by a particular question, play a step-by-step campaign. The next day peruse the questions for the next chapter, and so on. If you follow this procedure for a few weeks, you should systematically evaluate all aspects of teaching discussed in this book. You will also know where to find information on different facets of teaching. Then, when you see the need to improve some phase of instruction, you will know exactly where to look for help, and you will have your own step-by-step plan for solving a particular problem.

Suggestions for Further Study

In the chapters that follow, you will find suggestions that cover many facets of teaching. You are likely to conclude, however, that information on particular aspects of teaching is not complete enough. Despite the book's attempt to provide at least partial solutions to the most common difficulties faced by teachers, you are bound, sooner or later, to become aware of problems that are not discussed in these pages. To allow for instances where you will need additional information, an annotated bibliography is provided at the end of each chapter. Suggestions for Further Study list articles and books you might consult for detailed information on many topics. To help you locate such sources, an index to the Suggestions for Further Study is printed on the inside of the front cover. You may want additional data on some aspects of teaching, either while you are taking this course or after you are experienced enough to have time for a detailed look at some facet of education, psychology, or instruction. To locate such data, consult the index inside the front cover for a description of topics and use information about suggestion titles and page numbers to find a list of references. Instructions for carrying out simple do-it-yourself studies are also included in the Suggestions for Further Study at the end of many chapters.

The Nature and Values of Science

The Key Points, Suggestions for Teaching, Handbook Headings, questions and suggestions in "Becoming a Better Teacher," and Suggestions for Further Study all summarize information supplied by psychologists. In addition, the observations of individuals not classified as behavioral scientists will sometimes be mentioned. People with many different kinds of backgrounds have taken an interest in education, and their ideas are occasionally noted at appropriate places in the chapters that follow. The primary purpose of this book, however, is to offer suggestions on how *psychology* (the scientific study of behavior) might be applied to teaching. This text is based on the premise that information reported by scientists can be especially valuable for those who plan to teach. Some of the reasons for this conviction become apparent when the characteristics of science are examined.

The values of science become clear when one understands some of the limitations of casual observation (and of unsystematic applications of such observations to behavior) and sees how the scientist tries to correct these weaknesses.

Limitations of Unsystematic Observation

Those who make unsystematic observations of human behavior may be easily misled into drawing false conclusions. The first plausible explanation that comes to mind may be treated as the only possible explanation. A single episode may lead to a generalization that will be mistakenly applied to superficially similar situations. The reactions of an individual in a given situation may be due primarily to unrecognized idiosyncratic factors that may never occur again. The behavior of one person under certain circumstances may not resemble that of other persons in the same circumstances. Unsystematic observers are especially prone to note only evidence that fits their expectations and to ignore evidence that does not. Ignorance of what others have discovered may cause each individual to start at the same point when confronted with a problem—and to make the same mistakes others have made as they struggled to find solutions.

A clear example of the limitation of unsystematic observation is the practice of retaining children for a second year in a given grade because of poor achievement. Grade retention has long been used as a way of dealing with individual differences in learning rate, emotional development, and socialization skills. According to one estimate, 15 to 19 percent of all schoolchildren in the United States are retained in any given year (Smith and Shepard, 1987). The widespread use of retention in the United States and Europe continues despite the fact that most research clearly shows that low-achieving children who are promoted learn more the following year, have a stronger self-concept, and are better adjusted emotionally than similar children who are retained (Bracey, 1988; Bruce, 1988; Smith and Shepard, 1987).

Why is grade retention so popular when the evidence against it is so overwhelming? According to a study conducted by Mary Lee Smith and Lorrie Shepard (1987), teachers invoke one or more of these poorly supported reasons to explain why they retain children:

Unsystematic observation may lead to false conclusions

Grade retention policies influenced by unsystematic observation

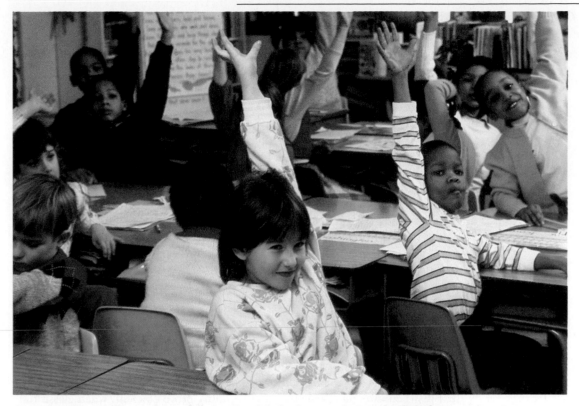

Observing these children raising their hands might lead you to draw a number of conclusions about their teacher's ability to motivate them, but to reach a more trustworthy understanding of their behavior, you would need to study it systematically. (Kevin Horan/Stock, Boston)

1. *Teachers' beliefs about retention.* Many teachers believe that retention allows students to excel academically the following year, that retention in the early grades prevents retention later on, and that retention is free of cost and risk. These beliefs typically are based on personal experiences with one or a few children, limited follow-up, and no knowledge of the fate of similar children who were promoted. Controlled studies with large representative samples of retained and nonretained children clearly show that the effects of retention are seldom positive.

2. *Teachers' beliefs about child development.* Many teachers believe that certain children have not developed sufficiently intellectually, socially, and emotionally to profit from normal classroom instruction. In addition, they believe that changes in the curriculum or in the teacher's instructional methods are not likely to be of much help. The child simply needs time to mature. Research on peer tutoring (high-achieving students teaching low-achieving students of the same age), cross-age tutoring (high-achieving older students teaching low-achieving younger

students), and computer-assisted instruction, to name a few techniques, suggest otherwise.

3. *Teachers' beliefs that children should learn more and learn it sooner.* According to this view, the purpose of kindergarten is to master basic literacy and numeracy skills in preparation for more advanced work. Children who cannot keep up become candidates for retention (instead of the curriculum becoming a candidate for change). As you will see in Chapter 2 when we take up Jean Piaget's theory of cognitive development, the research is not clear about the lasting benefits of pushing five- and six-year-olds to master too many aspects of reading, writing, and arithmetic.

4. *Teachers' beliefs about competitive parents.* This is a variation of the last reason. Here the pressure to learn more earlier and to excel comes from the parents because they think both will give the child a competitive edge later in life. This pressure comes particularly from parents whose children have experienced some form of early educational training, at home or in a preschool. Again, when a child fails to keep up, an oft-mentioned solution is retention.

5. *Teachers' beliefs about homogeneous classrooms.* Most educators believe that instruction is more effective, and certainly more efficient, when classrooms are made up of children who are more alike than they are different. Retention is viewed as one way of producing more homogeneous classes. Once again, however, research findings on the effects of ability grouping are largely negative.

We are not saying here that most teachers are ignorant of or unwilling to accept scientific findings. We know many teachers whose attitudes and actions are informed by research. We are simply trying to illustrate the dangers of basing instructional practices on unscientific observations.

Strengths of Scientific Observation

Scientific methods:

Those who study behavior scientifically are more likely to acquire trustworthy information than a casual observer is, and they are likely to apply what they learn more effectively because they follow certain procedures:

Sampling

In most cases, a representative sample of subjects is studied so that individual idiosyncrasies are canceled out.

Control

An effort is made to note all plausible hypotheses to explain a given type of behavior, and each hypothesis is tested under controlled conditions. If all factors but one can be held constant in an experiment, the researcher may be able to trace the impact of a given condition by comparing the behaviors of those who have been exposed to it and those who have not.

Observers make special efforts to be objective and to guard against being misled by predetermined ideas, wishful thinking, or selected evidence.

Objectivity

Observations are made in a carefully prescribed systematic manner, which makes it possible for observers to compare reactions.

Complete reports of experiments—including descriptions of subjects, methods, results, and conclusions—are published in professional journals. This dissemination makes it possible for other experimenters to replicate a study to discover if they obtain the same results.

Publication

The existence of reports of thousands of experiments makes it possible to discover what others have done. This knowledge can then serve as a starting point for one's own speculations.

Replication

Studying Behavior: Complicating Factors

Although the use of scientific methods makes it possible to overcome many of the limitations of unscientific observation, the application of knowledge acquired in a scientific manner is subject to a number of complicating factors.

The Limited Focus of Research

Behavior is complex, changes with age, and has many causes. A student may perform poorly on a history exam, for example, for one or more of the following reasons: poorly developed study skills, inattentiveness in class, low interest in the subject, a poorly written text, low motivation to achieve high grades, vaguely worded exam questions, and difficulty with a particular type of exam question (compare-and-contrast essays, for example).

In order to understand how these factors affect performance on school-related tasks, research psychologists study at most only a few of them at a time under conditions that may not be terribly realistic. For example, a researcher who is interested in the effect on comprehension of note taking versus rereading may recruit subjects who are equivalent in terms of social class, prior knowledge of the topic of the reading passage, and age; randomly assign them to one of the two experimental groups; give them a brief passage to read; and examine the effects of note taking and rereading on several types of comprehension items. As a consequence, most research studies provide specific information about a particular aspect of behavior. More comprehensive knowledge is acquired by combining and interrelating separate studies that have looked at different aspects of a common problem.

Research focuses on a few aspects of a problem

Selection and Interpretation of Data

The amount of scientific information available on behavior is so extensive that no individual could examine or interpret all of it. Consequently, researchers learn to be highly selective in their reading.

In addition, conclusions about the meaning of scientific results vary from one researcher to another. As you read this book, you will discover that there are differences of opinion among psychologists regarding certain aspects of development, motivation, and intelligence. Opposing views may be based on equally scientific evidence, but the way in which the evidence is selected and interpreted will vary. Just because a topic is studied scientifically does not mean that there will be unanimity of opinion about interpretations of data.

Differences of opinion due to selection and interpretation of data

New Findings Mean Revised Ideas

In addition to being voluminous and subject to different interpretations, scientific information also is constantly revised. A series of experiments may lead to the development of a new concept or pedagogical technique that is highly successful when it is first tried out. Subsequent studies, however, may reveal that the original research was incomplete, or repeated applications of a technique may show that it is less effective once the novelty has worn off. But frequent shifts in emphasis in education are also a function of the basic nature of science. A quality of science that sets it apart from other intellectual processes is that the discoveries of one generation of scientists set the stage for more complete and far-reaching discoveries by the next. More researchers are studying aspects of psychology and education now than at any previous time in history. Thousands of reports of scientific research are published every month. As our knowledge accumulates, it is inevitable that interpretations of how children learn and how we should teach will continually change. For this reason, occasional "fads" in education are not necessarily evidence of confusion; they may simply reflect the fact that thousands of individuals are engaged in a continual search for something better. We know more about development, learning, and teaching today than ever before, but because of the nature of some of the factors just discussed—and the complexity of human behavior—answers to many questions are tentative and incomplete.

Accumulating knowledge leads researchers to revise original ideas

The last few pages have asked you to consider some of the values of science, the strengths of scientific observation, and a few of the factors that complicate the scientific study of behavior and lead to frequent changes of emphasis in teaching techniques. These considerations help to explain why this book stresses how psychology might be applied to teaching and to support the position that information reported by scientists can be especially valuable for those who plan to teach. At the same time, the intention has been to acquaint you with a few of the limitations and sometimes unsettling by-products of science.

The science of psychology has much to offer educators, but a scientific approach to teaching does have its limits. Research on teaching and learning gives you a systematic, objective framework for making instructional decisions. But, for the reasons cited above, it cannot give you a prescription or a set of rules that specify how you should handle every situation. Often you will have to make on-the-spot subjective decisions about how to present a lesson, explain a concept, handle mass boredom, or reprimand a student. This contrast between an objective, systematic approach to planning instruction and the need to make immediate (yet appropriate) applications and modifications of those plans calls attention to a question that has been debated for years: Is teaching primarily an art or a science—or a combination of both?

Teaching as an Art and a Science

Some educators have argued that teaching is an art that cannot be practiced—or even studied—in an objective or scientific manner (Highet, 1957; Dawe, 1984; Rubin; 1985). For example, Gilbert Highet, a distinguished critic and professor of literature, wrote a book titled *The Art of Teaching.* He explains the title and the rationale of the book as follows:

> [This book] is called *The Art of Teaching* because I believe that teaching is an art, not a science. It seems to me very dangerous to apply the aims and methods of science to human beings as individuals, although a statistical principle can often be used to explain their behavior in large groups and a scientific diagnosis of their physical structure is always valuable. But a "scientific" relationship between human beings is bound to be inadequate and perhaps distorted. Of course it is necessary for any teacher to be orderly in planning his work and precise in his dealing with facts. But that does not make his teaching "scientific." Teaching involves emotions, which cannot be systematically appraised and employed, and human values, which are quite outside the grasp of science. . . . "Scientific" teaching, even of scientific subjects, will be inadequate as long as both teachers and pupils are human beings. Teaching is not like inducing a chemical reaction: it is much more like painting a picture or making a piece of music, . . . like planting a garden or writing a friendly letter. You must throw your heart into it, you must realize that it cannot all be done by formulas, or you will spoil your work, and your pupils, and yourself. (1957, pp. vii–viii)

Examples of the emotions and values referred to by Highet include believing that teaching is one of society's most valuable and rewarding activities, that it must be done as well as possible every day, that it is important to get students excited about learning, and that there is no such thing as an unteachable student. When Highet states that teaching cannot all be done by formulas, he is urging you to be flexible. Flexibility can be thought of as a "feel" for doing the right thing at

Creativity and flexibility will always be important parts of the art of good teaching. (Elizabeth Crews)

the right time. In one sense it means using all the knowledge and techniques at one's disposal to formulate effective lesson plans. Knowing, for example, when to present a formal lesson and when to let students discover things for themselves, when to be demanding and when to make few demands, when to be encouraging and when to criticize, when to give direct help and when to give indirect help. Another aspect of flexibility is the ability to improvise. When a lesson plan falls flat, the flexible teacher immediately thinks of an alternative presentation that recaptures the students' interest. A third aspect of flexibility is the willingness and resourcefulness to work around impediments. Teaching does not always occur under ideal circumstances, and teachers must sometimes cope with inadequate facilities, insufficient materials, interruptions, and other difficulties.

Teaching as an art: emotions, values, flexibility

In summary, teaching as an art involves emotions, values, and flexibility. Because these characteristics are intangible, they can be very difficult, if not impossible, to teach. Teachers must find these qualities within themselves.

The argument for teaching as a science is equally persuasive. Scholars like Paul Woodring (1957), Nathaniel Gage (1984), David Berliner (1986), and Lee Shulman (1986) agree that there is no science of teaching at this point. But they contend that it is possible and good to have a *scientific basis* for the art of teaching. By drawing on established research findings, prospective and practicing teachers can be taught many of the prerequisites that make "artistic" teaching possible. This argument, of course, rests on the existence of a usable body of research findings, which educational psychologists believe does exist. As evidence, you might look at an article entitled "The Quiet Revolution in Educational Research" (Walberg, Schiller, and Haertel, 1979). The authors reviewed research on learning and instruction that was carried out in elementary, secondary, and college classrooms. From this collection they were able to identify about sixty-five practices that repeatedly produce positive or negative effects. For example, twenty-four of twenty-five studies found that giving teachers more instructional time or giving students more time to learn leads to higher achievement. At the other end of the spectrum, only one of seventeen studies found teacher disorganization positively related to student achievement. Another example of usable research can be found in the work of Berliner (1986) and Shulman (1986) on the characteristics of expert teachers. One reason why some teachers are experts is that they can quickly and accurately recall relevant knowledge from two large areas: subject-matter knowledge and knowledge of classroom organization and management. From the research being done in this area, we are learning how expert teachers acquire this knowledge, recall it, and use it appropriately.

Research provides a scientific basis for "artistic" teaching

Look back at the heading of this section. Notice that it reads "Teaching as an Art *and* a Science," not "Teaching as an Art *Versus* Teaching as a Science." Our choice of wording indicates that we believe good teaching is a skillful blend of "artistic" and "scientific" elements. The teacher who attempts to base every action on scientific evidence is likely to come across as rigid, mechanical, and indecisive (where that evidence is lacking or unclear). On the other hand, the teacher who ignores scientific knowledge about teaching and learning and focuses only on the need to excite and inspire students runs the risk of using methods and principles of teaching that are ineffective.

Good teachers combine "artistic" and "scientific" characteristics

As was pointed out earlier, the nature of teaching as an art and as a science has been under discussion for some time. One of the clearest and most useful examinations of these two aspects of teaching was offered almost thirty-five years ago by J. M. Stephens (1956). Stephens talked about the need for teachers to play two roles: *teacher-practitioner* and *teacher-theorist*.

The Teacher-Practitioner and the Teacher-Theorist

In the introduction to a text in educational psychology, Stephens made these observations:

> The requirements of the teacher-practitioner and of the teacher-theorist are both very real and very important. They are, however, somewhat different, and the differences in these requirements are nowhere more striking than in the matter of

Teacher-practitioner: enthusiastic commitment

caution versus confidence. There are times, unquestionably, when the teacher-practitioner should not be assailed by doubts or qualifications, when he should carry out with confidence and with decision any course of action that he has undertaken. At these times, any large measure of doubt, uncertainty, or hesitation may seriously reduce his effectiveness.

The hesitation or uncertainty which might work against the practitioner presents no handicap to the theorist. On the contrary, caution, admission of uncertainty, willingness to withhold judgment are of the utmost importance when the teacher-theorist is forming his opinions about the nature of the educational process. The teacher-theorist, therefore, must receive training in this very necessary practice of entertaining doubts and qualifications. (1956, pp. v–vi)

Teacher-theorist: objective analysis, caution, uncertainty

Caution as a Theorist, Commitment as a Practitioner

Awareness of the roles of **teacher-theorist** (the scientific aspect of teaching) and **teacher-practitioner** (the artistic aspect of teaching) will be of value to you, not only as you read this book (and other books and journals), but also when you begin to teach. You have just been acquainted with the nature of scientific methods, as well as some of the complications faced by those who study human behavior. Because they are well aware of the difficulties of scientific study, psychologists typically are cautious about drawing conclusions until initial findings have been corroborated. As Stephens notes, the theorist often should admit uncertainty, withhold judgment, and be assailed by doubts and qualifications. Such attitudes are appropriate not only because it is virtually impossible to carry out a perfect, definitive study (or series of studies), but also because of the cumulative nature of scientific knowledge. As just noted, the accumulation of scientific information leads to constant reinterpretation and revision of earlier conclusions. Therefore, when you read research reports and speculations about types of behavior of relevance to teachers, you should play the role of a reflective, skeptical, but open-minded, theorist. This last point was nicely illustrated in a study of teachers of youngsters who are gifted (Berliner, 1986). The average time taken by novice teachers to read through a hypothetical scenario about a gifted child and begin writing about ways to deal with that child was 2.6 minutes. Experienced teachers with no background in gifted education took an average of 3.0 minutes. Experienced teachers of gifted children, however, took more than three times as long, 9.8 minutes on average, to read and think about the problem.

When the time comes to put teaching techniques into practice, think and act with confidence and commitment. Have faith in the value of methods you use and convey the impression that you know what you are doing and that you are convinced it is worthwhile. If your students sense that you are not convinced that a particular classroom exercise is worth the trouble, they are likely to respond accordingly. If you act enthusiastic, however, and communicate the attitude that you really believe in what you are doing, your enthusiasm may be contagious.

When you evaluate the effectiveness of the techniques you have used, however, play the role of the teacher-theorist. Be honest with yourself in assessing successes and failures. (Pages 000–000 in Chapter 14 include some specific procedures you might use to carry out self-analysis systematically and efficiently.) Suppose you try out a technique for teaching spelling you read about in a teacher's journal. As you think back at the end of the day to the enthusiastic response of your pupils and look over their spelling papers, you conclude that the technique really worked and is worth using again. On the other hand, when you analyze your students' responses to the discussion topic that impressed you as such a terrific idea when you thought of it the night before, you ruefully admit to yourself that it was a disaster when you actually tried it out. Furthermore, you make a mental note that the methods you used to organize the class into discussion groups were ineffective. Once you have acknowledged that something you tried simply did not work out, despite your faith and enthusiasm in putting it into practice, you are in a position to isolate causes and think about revisions, alternatives, and improvements in your teaching techniques.

Test teaching hypotheses enthusiastically, evaluate results critically

J. M. Stephens urges you to play two roles in the classroom. When interacting with pupils or presenting subject matter, you should be a teacher-practitioner—enthusiastic and committed. When analyzing your performance and student behavior, you should be a teacher-theorist—objective and unemotional. (Susan Lapides)

The Teacher as Hypothesis Tester

Perhaps the best way to function as a teacher-theorist is to think of yourself as a practicing behavioral scientist. As you try out various teaching techniques or wonder why certain pupils fail to respond to instruction, formulate hypotheses (tentative explanations) and then try to test them. You will rarely be able to do this in a completely controlled way, of course, but you can often set up what amount to simple experiments. If most of the students in your class tend to act restless and bored whenever you present a particular topic, for instance, you might list some hypotheses such as these to test in an effort to do something about it:

Students will be less bored and restless if I arrange for them to be more active as they learn.

Providing a list of specific objectives to be achieved by the end of a thirty-minute study period will lead to more concentrated effort than simply telling students to read the text until the bell rings.

Once you establish one or more hypotheses, you can test them by trying out appropriate techniques listed in your Handbook. As you use the techniques, be a teacher-practitioner—enthusiastic and committed. Then function as a teacher-theorist: Be objective when analyzing the results. If you find that your students respond more positively, or that test scores go up, or that projects improve, you have evidence to substantiate your hypothesis. If student behavior remains unchanged or deteriorates, formulate another hypothesis and test it. The questions listed in Chapter 14 might be thought of as hypotheses, and the suggestions that follow each question might be thought of as ways to test them.

Because this book is concerned with both scientific knowledge and classroom applications, you are urged to switch back and forth between the roles of theorist and practitioner. The first part of most chapters (or sections of chapters) is usually devoted to a review of research on selected topics. As you read this material, think of yourself as a theorist. In the absence of information about subjects, methods, and treatment of results, you will not be able to evaluate specific studies. You can, however, be cautious about accepting current interpretations of the significance of research as absolute or final answers. Keep in mind that the subjects of many studies may be atypical and that researchers are not able to control all relevant variables. Allow for the possibility that some conclusions reported in the present edition of this book may be revised when the next edition is published. Don't be surprised if your instructor or the authors of a different book disagree with interpretations of research presented in this text. When you read analyses of research in this or other books, think of yourself as a theorist. As Stephens put it, "Entertain doubts and qualifications."

The second part of most chapters (or sections of chapters) in this book is devoted to Suggestions for Teaching. Some of these are based directly on research, some are derived from the implications of research, and some are simply proven methods that are related to research findings. When you begin to teach and refer to the Suggestions for Teaching for ideas to try out in the classroom, play the role of the teacher-practitioner. Whenever you actually put a suggestion into practice, act confident, committed, and enthusiastic.

This book has been written to equip you with information you will be able to use in a great variety of ways as you function as both a teacher-practitioner and a teacher-theorist. It is also designed to help you find information with a minimum of difficulty. Even though specific concepts and interpretations may change as scientific knowledge accumulates and as world and local conditions fluctuate, certain basic kinds of information will always be of value to teachers. This basic core of knowledge is reflected by the contents of this book.

The Contents of This Book

In speculating about ways psychology might be applied to teaching, a number of theorists have proposed what are often referred to as theories of instruction or models of learning (for example, see Mager, 1975; Carroll, 1963; Glaser, 1976; Bloom, 1976). The purpose of such theories or models is to provide a basic strategy for instruction, and several of them will be discussed in subsequent chapters of this book. While details of various theories of instruction will be presented later, at this point it should be noted that they emphasize a basic sequence teachers might follow. To make instruction as effective as possible, it is suggested that teachers follow these four steps:

1. Take into account what students are like and how much they know.
2. Specify what is to be learned.
3. Provide instruction by taking advantage of what has been discovered about learning, cognitive strategies, and motivation.
4. Determine if students *have* learned.

(In some models of learning, it is suggested that the first step is to specify what is to be learned. While this is often a logical place to begin when dealing with college students, it may not be the best first step when dealing with younger students of various ages. Before teachers below the college level begin to formulate instructional objectives, they should consider the characteristics of the students they will be teaching—how much they already know, their cognitive characteristics, how they behave in classrooms, and so forth. Accordingly, it seems most logical to consider student characteristics as the first step in putting into practice a model of learning.)

The contents of this book are arranged with reference to the sequence just described. Chapters 2 through 12 are grouped (as described below and diagrammed in Figure 1.1) to reflect and illustrate the four phases of the model of learning featured in this text. Chapters 13 and 14 provide additional helpful material on effective classroom management and improving teaching skills.

Part 1 Considering Students' Characteristics

Chapter 2, "Stage Theories of Development," outlines and analyzes the most highly respected stage theories of development.

Chapter 3, "Age-level Characteristics," describes the nature and pedagogical significance of selected characteristics of pupils at different grade levels.

Chapter 4, "Assessing Pupil Variability," discusses the nature of pupil variability and the role of standardized tests in its assessment.

Chapter 5, "Dealing with Pupil Variability," examines recent developments in the education of exceptional pupils and describes techniques for teaching types of pupils who require special educational provisions.

Part 2 Specifying What Is To Be Learned

Chapter 6, "Devising and Using Objectives," offers suggestions for devising and using various kinds of instructional objectives.

Part 3 Providing Instruction

Chapter 7, "Behavioral Learning Theories," analyzes learning theories proposed by theorists who prefer to base their conclusions on observations of overt behavior, and describes variations of programmed instructional techniques.

Chapter 8, "Information Processing Theory," analyzes ways humans encode, store, and retrieve information from memory.

Chapter 9, "Cognitive Learning Theories and Problem Solving," outlines concepts proposed by psychologists who have speculated about ways humans solve problems, and describes problem-solving techniques for different types of problems.

Chapter 10, "Humanistic Approaches to Education," discusses techniques of instruction intended to make teachers and pupils aware of feelings, interpersonal relationships, and values.

Chapter 11, "Motivation," examines several theories of motivation as background for developing a variety of ways to arouse and sustain student interest in learning.

Part 4 Evaluating Performance

Chapter 12, "Measurement and Evaluation of Classroom Learning," describes a variety of techniques for objectively and constructively determining if instructional objectives have been met.

Figure 1.1   The Model of Learning Used in Organizing This Book

Part 5 Maintaining an Effective Learning Environment

Chapter 13, "Classroom Management," discusses approaches to classroom management and presents dozens of specific techniques for establishing and maintaining classroom control.

Chapter 14, "Becoming a Better Teacher," describes ways to cope with frustrations and provides suggestions for constantly improving your teaching effectiveness.

Suggestions for Further Study

Professional Journals

In order to gain some direct experience with the raw material of psychology—the building blocks that are eventually combined to establish a principle or theory— you might examine one or more of the professional journals in psychology. These journals consist primarily of reports of experiments. The following journals are likely to be found in a typical college library:

American Educational Research Journal

Behavioral Science

Child Development

Developmental Psychology

Educational and Psychological Measurement

Exceptional Child

Genetic Psychology Monographs

Harvard Educational Review

Journal of Abnormal and Social Psychology

Journal of Applied Behavior Analysis

Journal of Educational Psychology

Journal of Educational Research

Journal of Educational Sociology

Journal of Experimental Child Psychology

Journal of Experimental Education

Journal of Experimental Psychology

Journal of Teacher Education

Mental Hygiene

Merrill-Palmer Quarterly of Behavior and Development

Psychological Monographs

Psychological Review

Psychology in the Schools

Society for Research in Child Development Monographs

To develop awareness of the nature of research in psychology, examine recent issues of some of these journals. To gain some experience as a teacher-theorist, you might select an article describing an experiment that intrigues you or that appears relevant to your own interests, grade level, and subject. Then write an abstract (a brief summary of results) of the article, including the following information:

Author of article

Title of article

Journal in which article appears (including date, volume number, and page numbers)

Purpose (or description of problem)

Subjects

Procedure (or methods)

Treatment of data

Results

Conclusions

Are there any criticisms that you can make of the procedure or of the conclusions?

What inferences for your own teaching can you draw from this experiment?

Would you be willing to change your methods of teaching on the strength of this one article?

Journals of Abstracts and Reviews

Unless you are familiar with research in a particular aspect of educational psychology, you may find it difficult to fit an individual study reported in a journal into a general framework or relate it to other similar research. In most cases, it is prudent to find out what other experiments of a similar type have revealed about a particular point before making generalizations from the results of a single study. A variety of journals and reference works exist to assist you in doing this. The following journals consist of abstracts of articles that appear in the type of journal listed in the preceding section.

Child Development Abstracts and Bibliography

Exceptional Child Education Abstracts

Psychological Abstracts

Psyc SCAN

The journal *Contemporary Psychology* reviews new books in psychology, and the *Annual Review of Psychology* provides information reflected by the title—a specialist in each of several areas of psychology reviews significant studies that have appeared during a given year.

The *Review of Educational Research* features articles that describe, relate, and analyze reports of studies on a particular theme.

To discover the nature of these journals and reference works, examine some of them and perhaps prepare a brief description of the most promising titles to save for future reference. Or select a topic of interest, search for reports of experiments, and summarize the conclusions you reach.

Journals That Describe Trends and Techniques

In addition to descriptions of actual experiments, "discussion" articles are published in some professional journals and in many teachers' magazines. Listed below are journals of this type.

Journals Consisting of General Discussions of Trends, Developments, and Techniques   The following journals describe trends, developments, and techniques and also interpret research data. Some articles cite research studies; others offer interpretations of approaches to teaching without reference to specific data. Many of these journals also feature sections on tricks of the trade, and most provide book reviews.

Change (higher education)

Clearing House (junior and senior high school teaching)

Elementary School Journal

Exceptional Children

Journal of General Education

Journal of Higher Education (college and university teaching)

Junior College Journal

Phi Delta Kappa

Teachers College Journal

Teachers College Record

Theory into Practice

Journals Consisting of Brief Commentaries on Trends, Developments, and Techniques   The following journals consist of short (usually less than five pages) articles on trends, developments, and techniques in education.

Childhood Education

Education

Educational Forum

Educational Leadership

Educational Record (college and university teaching)

Educational Technology (programmed instruction, behavior modification)

High School Journal

Journal of Education

School Review

   Note: *Education Digest* is made up of condensations of articles selected from the types of journals listed in this and the preceding section.

Magazines for Teachers   The following publications provide articles, usually in magazine format, with emphasis on journalistic style, abundant illustrations, and colorful graphic design:

Grade Teacher

Instructor

Learning

Psychology Today

Today's Education

If you look through some recent issues of several of these journals, you will find typical trend and technique articles on psychology and education. For future reference, you might read an article that is relevant to your own interests, grade level, and subject and then write a synopsis of the author's arguments. If any of these arguments are pertinent to your own theorizing about teaching, briefly analyze your thoughts, perhaps by using the following outline:

Author of article

Name of article

Journal in which article appeared (including date, volume number, and page numbers)

Synopsis of arguments presented

Your reaction to the arguments

Specialized Publications for Teachers

Almost every field of study in education has one or more journals devoted to reports of research, reviews of related experimental studies, discussions of teaching techniques, descriptions of tricks of the trade, and analyses of subject matter. The following list of journals may help you discover what is available in your area or areas of interest:

African Studies Bulletin

Agricultural Education Magazine

American Biology Teacher

American Business Education

American Music Teacher

American Speech

American String Teacher

American Vocational Journal

Arithmetic Teacher

Art Education

Athletic Journal

Audiovisual Instructor

Business Education World

Coach and Athlete

Coaching Clinic

Educational Theatre Journal

Education and Training in Mental Retardation

Elementary School Guidance and Counseling

English Language Teaching

English Studies

Forecast for Home Economics

French Review

Geographical Teacher

German Review

Gifted Child Quarterly

Hearing and Speech News

History Today

Improving College and University Teaching

Industrial Arts and Vocational Education

Industrial Arts Teacher

Instrumentalist

Journal of Industrial Teacher Education

Journal of Negro Education

Journal of Nursing

Journal of Reading

Journal of Research on Science Teaching

Journal of School Health

Journal of Secondary Education

Journal of Special Education

Language Arts

Marriage and Family Living

Mathematics Teacher

Music Education Journal

Music in Education

Music Journal

National Business Education Quarterly

National Elementary Principal

Physical Educator

Physics Teacher

Reading Specialist

Recreation

Safety Education

Scholastic Coach

School Arts

School Counselor

School Musician

School Musician Director and Teacher

School Science and Mathematics

School Shop

Science Educator

Science Teacher

Swimming Technique

Teaching Exceptional Children

Tennis

Theatre Arts

Theatre World

Today's Speech

Track Technique

To discover what is available, check titles that sound promising, spend some time in the periodicals section of your college library, and examine some recent issues. You might select an article you find interesting and write an abstract of it, together with your own interpretation. Or you might prepare a brief description of journals that impress you as worthy of attention. This list could serve as a source of information on what journals to consult after you begin your teaching career.

Educational Resources Information Center (ERIC)

As a number of journals listed on the preceding pages indicate, thousands of articles are published each year on every conceivable aspect of educational psychology and education. To assist psychologists and educators to discover what has been published on a specific topic, the Educational Resources Information Center (ERIC) has been established by the U.S. Office of Education. ERIC publishes three sources of information:

Current Index to Journals in Education—Annual Cumulation contains an index of articles in over three hundred education and education-oriented journals published in a given year. There are four sections in each volume: Subject Index (which lists titles of articles organized under hundreds of subject headings), Author Index, Journal Contents Index (which lists the table of contents for each issue of journals published that year), and Main Entry Section (which provides the title, author, journal reference, and a brief abstract of articles published in journals covered by the index).

Research in Education lists curriculum guides, catalogues, and the like, as well as papers, reports, and monographs not published in journals. The Document Résumé section presents descriptions of the documents arranged according to the ERIC classification scheme, together with information about where each can be obtained. There is also a Subject Index (titles of documents listed according to the ERIC classification), an Author Index, and an Institution Index (titles of articles listed with reference to source).

ERIC Educational Documents Index lists titles of documents noted and abstracted in *Research in Education* and in *Office of Education Research Reports.* Each document is classified under up to five *Major Descriptors* (general categories) and perhaps also under *Minor Descriptors* (more specific categories).

For information on what is available in journals, you should refer to *Current Index to Journals in Education—Annual Cumulation.* For information about curriculum guides, pamphlets, and reports not published in journals, consult the *ERIC Educational Documents Index* for titles. Consult *Research in Education* for descriptions and information about how to obtain such documents.

You are urged to examine a recent issue of these publications to discover what is available in the ERIC network and how you might obtain information.

Summary

1. Unsystematic observations of students may lead teachers to draw false conclusions because of limited cases, unrecognized unusual factors, and a tendency to ignore contrary evidence.
2. Even though scientific evidence does not support the practice of grade retention, it remains popular among teachers and parents because of unsystematic observations about its effectiveness.

3. Scientifically gathered evidence is more trustworthy than casual observation because it involves sampling, control, objectivity, publication, and replication.
4. The scientific study of education is complicated by the limited focus of research, the inability of researchers to keep up with all published research, different interpretations of findings, and the ongoing accumulation of new knowledge.
5. Research on teaching and learning gives you a systematic, objective basis for making instructional decisions, but cannot tell you how to handle every classroom situation. Many classroom decisions must be made on the spot. This contrast represents the science and art of teaching.
6. Those who argue that teaching is an art point to emotions, values, and flexibility as qualities that good teachers must possess which are not easily taught.
7. Certain scholars contend that there is a scientific basis for the art of teaching that can be taught by drawing on established research findings.
8. Good teachers strike a balance between the art and science of teaching.
9. Another way of looking at the difference between the art and science of teaching is the distinction between the teacher-practitioner and the teacher-theorist.
10. The teacher-practitioner approaches every lesson with enthusiasm and commitment. The teacher-theorist analyzes every instructional action objectively and critically in order to be more effective in the future.

Key Terms

art and science of teaching *(19)*
teacher-theorist *(22)*
teacher-practitioner *(22)*

Discussion Questions

1. Imagine that you are a second-grade teacher at the end of the school year. You have just finished telling your principal about a student who performed so poorly during the year that you question whether the student is adequately prepared for third grade. The principal suggests that the child should repeat second grade next year. Given what you know about the research on retention, how would you respond to the principal's suggestion?
2. Think of or identify a popular instructional practice. Would you classify that practice as a fad or as the outgrowth of accumulated scientific knowledge? Why? How can you tell the difference between the two?
3. To play effectively the role of teacher-practitioner, you need to display enthusiasm and a sense of "worthwhileness" about the content you cover and the methods you use. At some point, however, you may be asked to teach a

grade level or a subject for which you have little enthusiasm, or you may grow bored teaching the same grade level or subject in the same way year after year. How will you fulfill the role of teacher-practitioner if faced with these conditions?

4. To play the role of teacher-theorist effectively, you would need to set aside regular blocks of time to think about your actions and make new plans. Most teachers complain about not having enough time to reflect and plan. What would you do to make this time available?

5. The point was made in this chapter that good teachers strike a balance between the art and science of teaching. How do they do it? Are they born with the right type of personality? Are they the product of good teacher education programs? Or is some combination of these elements at work? If you believe that both factors play a role, which do you feel is most important?

PART

1

CONSIDERING STUDENT CHARACTERISTICS

STAGE THEORIES
OF DEVELOPMENT

KEY POINTS

A Brief Outline of Theories of Development

Theories organize facts and guide research

Erikson: Psychosocial Development

Personality development based on epigenetic principle

Personality grows out of successful resolution of dichotomies

2 to 3 years: autonomy vs. shame and doubt

4 to 5 years: initiative vs. guilt

6 to 11 years: industry vs. inferiority

12 to 18 years: identity vs. role confusion

Identity: acceptance of body, having goals, getting recognition

Role confusion: not sure what behaviors others will react to favorably

Traditionally, male identity linked to job, female identity linked to husband

Female identity linked to job more now than in past

American boys encouraged to be independent, active, exploratory; girls encouraged to be dependent, quiet

Sex-typed individuals less flexible than those high in psychological androgyny

Occupational choice is a major commitment

Psychosocial moratorium delays commitment

Negative identity: rejection of accepted roles

Identity diffusion types avoid thinking about jobs, roles, values

Moratorium types suffer identity crises of various kinds

Identity achievement types have made their own commitments

Foreclosure types unquestioningly endorse parents' goals and values

Piaget: Cognitive Development

Scheme: organized pattern of behavior or thought

Assimilation: new experience is fitted into existing scheme

Accommodation: scheme is created or revised to fit new experience

Equilibration: tendency to construct schemes that allow better understanding of experiences

Sensorimotor stage: schemes reflect sensory and motor experiences

Preoperational stage: forms many new schemes but does not think logically

Perceptual centration, irreversibility, egocentrism: barriers to logical thought

Egocentrism: assumption that others see things the same way

Concrete operational stage: capable of mentally reversing actions but generalizes only from concrete experiences

Formal operational stage: able to deal with abstractions, form hypotheses, engage in mental manipulations

Instruction can accelerate development of schemes that have begun to form

Adolescent egocentrism: one's thoughts and actions are as central to others as to oneself

Piaget's theory underestimates children's abilities

Most adolescents are not formal operational thinkers

Piaget and Kohlberg: Moral Development

Moral realism: sacred rules, no exceptions, no allowance for intentions, consequences determine guilt

Moral relativism: rules are flexible, intent important in determining guilt

Preconventional morality: avoid punishment, receive benefits in return

Conventional morality: impress others, respect authority

Postconventional morality: mutual agreements, consistent principles

Moral education programs may produce modest acceleration in moral development

Males and females may use different approaches to resolve real-life moral dilemmas

Moral behavior depends on circumstances

In describing theories of instruction and models of learning in Chapter 1, the point was made that a logical first step for teachers planning instruction is to take into account what students are like and how much they know. The term *entering behavior* is sometimes used to refer to the characteristics and knowledge that students possess at the beginning of a sequence of instruction. The types of behavior students exhibit when they enter a learning situation are obviously important for

39

a teacher to know, and that is why the four chapters that make up this first part are devoted to descriptions of typical and variant children.

Because the field of developmental psychology includes so many topics that have been studied intensively, separate courses are often given on infancy, early childhood, childhood, adolescence, and adulthood. If you have taken (or plan to take) one or more such courses, you will gain understanding of the process of development and become familiar with the direction and significance of current research. You may not, however, be inclined or be able to relate a great deal of what you learn to teaching. The four chapters that make up this first part are intended to call your attention to aspects of human development that particularly concern teachers and to encourage you to make use of that knowledge. Even if you have already taken a course in development, or are taking one this semester or quarter, or plan to take one in the future, you can still benefit from reading these first four chapters.

To prove this point, see how many of the following questions you can answer quickly and completely.

What psychosocial stages of development described by Erik Erikson are significant at the preschool, elementary, and secondary school levels?

What are two key factors that contribute to an adolescent's sense of identity?

What cognitive stages of development described by Jean Piaget are significant at the preschool, elementary, and secondary school levels?

How does the moral reasoning of primary grade pupils differ from that of secondary grade students?

How does the rate of physical development influence the behavior of boys and girls?

What are some differences in the aptitudes and attitudes toward school of boys and girls?

What sorts of emotional disorders are most common in male and female secondary school students?

What is Public Law 94–142, and what significance does it have for teachers?

Even if you have already taken one or more courses in human development, it is likely that you were unable to answer all of these questions completely and accurately. Even what you *do* remember may not be of maximum value if you have not thought about how it can be applied in a classroom. Regardless of your previous exposure to courses about development, therefore, you should benefit from a careful reading of these four chapters.

Human development is a difficult topic to discuss because, in addition to analyzing many different forms of behavior (as in an introductory psychology course), it is necessary to trace how each type of behavior changes as a child matures. Authors of books on development have adopted different strategies to cope with this problem. Some have described theories outlining stages in the emergence of aspects of particular forms of behavior. Others have written books that summarize significant types of behavior at successive age levels. Still others have written books made up of chapters devoted to specific types of behavior, noting age changes for every topic. Each approach has advantages and disadvantages.

Theories call attention to the overall sequence, continuity, and interrelatedness of aspects of development, but typically account for only limited facets of behavior. Texts organized in terms of age levels make the reader aware of varied aspects of children's behavior at a given age but sometimes tend to obscure how particular types of behavior emerge and change. Although texts organized according to types of behavior do not have the limitation of the age-level approach, they may make it difficult for the reader to grasp the overall pattern of behavior at a particular stage of development.

In an effort to profit from the advantages and to minimize the disadvantages of each approach, Chapters 2 and 3 present discussions of development that combine all three. Chapter 2 summarizes four stage theories of development. Psychosocial stages described by Erik Erikson, cognitive stages described by Jean Piaget, and stages of moral development described by Piaget and by Lawrence Kohlberg provide an overview of the sequence and continuity of these important aspects of behavior. Chapter 3 describes age-level characteristics of pupils at five levels— preschool, primary and elementary grades, and junior high and high school. Discussion at each age level focuses on four types of behavior. The information in these chapters will help you adapt teaching techniques to the pupils who are in the age range that you expect to teach. The first two chapters in this part describe patterns of behavior exhibited by typical children and adolescents. The following two chapters are devoted to student variability. Chapter 4 discusses the assessment of variability; Chapter 5 describes types of students who vary from their classmates to such an extent they may require special kinds of education.

In order to understand the reasons for featuring Erikson and Piaget in this chapter, a brief outline of theories of development will be presented by way of introduction.

A Brief Outline of Theories of Development

To better comprehend what they have learned and to impose at least a degree of order on related types of information, scientists propose theories. In a book on theories of development, Patricia Miller (1983) notes that theories perform two valuable functions: They organize and give meaning to facts, and they guide research. In another book on developmental theories, Alfred Baldwin (1980) observes that *ideally* a theory should be logical and supply clear definitions. It

Theories organize facts and guide research

should make specific predictions about behavior that are publicly verifiable. Finally, a theory of *development* should call attention to changes in types of behavior that occur as a child develops.

Between them, Miller and Baldwin describe about ten theoretical interpretations of development. While all these interpretations have made it possible to organize facts and have guided research, none of them meets all the criteria for an ideal theory listed by Baldwin. Some views come closer than others to functioning as ideal theories, however. Theories given greatest emphasis by Miller and Baldwin are those proposed by Sigmund Freud, Erik Erikson, and Jean Piaget.

Erikson and Piaget are featured in this chapter for reasons revealed by the results of a study conducted by Norman Endler, J. Phillipe Rushton, and Henry Roediger III (1978). By tallying the number of times the Social Sciences Citation Index mentions different psychologists, Endler and his associates drew up a list of the one hundred most frequently noted behavioral scientists.[1] Sigmund Freud topped the list with 1,426 mentions, and Jean Piaget was second with 1,070. They were the only individuals mentioned over 1,000 times. Most of the psychologists on the list had 200 or 300 citations.

While Freud's theory has had a great impact on speculations about human behavior, it is difficult to explain concisely. As an alternative to an outline of Freudian theory, the opening pages of this chapter will offer an account of the speculations of Erikson, one of Freud's pupils. Erikson studied with Freud but eventually emigrated to America, where he developed a theory to explain personality development in our culture. His theory is thus derived from the work of Freud, but it is directly applicable to children and adolescents in our society.

Jean Piaget has dominated an area of specialization in psychology more than any other individual since Freud. Starting in the 1920s and continuing up to the time of his death in 1980, Piaget published hundreds of books and articles on cognitive development. These works stimulated thousands of studies by others. Furthermore, Piaget's views on cognitive development served as the inspiration for many variations of open education. Any discussion of human development written for teachers should therefore contain an analysis of the work of Piaget.

Erikson: Psychosocial Development

Factors That Influenced Erikson

Erik Erikson was born in Germany of Danish parents. He was an indifferent student, and after leaving high school, without graduating, he spent several years wandering around Europe attending various art schools. At the age of twenty-

---

1. This index supplies data regarding individuals mentioned in articles appearing in 180 psychology journals.

Erik H. Erikson.
(Sarah Putnam/The
Picture Cube)

five, he became friends with someone who later secured a job tutoring the children of an American woman who was being psychoanalyzed by Sigmund Freud.
When some acquaintances of the woman asked if their children might also receive instruction, the friend decided to start a school and asked Erikson to come
to Vienna to assist him. Eventually, Erikson was introduced to Freud, who was
impressed by the young man and invited him to prepare for a career as a psychoanalyst. Erikson completed his training just at the time Hitler came to power, and
to escape from the tension building up in Europe, he decided to come to America.
He taught at Harvard, Yale, and the University of California at Berkeley, did private counseling, and became interested in studying American Indian tribes. He
also did research on normal and abnormal children and served as a psychotherapist for soldiers during World War II. These experiences led Erikson to conclude
that Freud's tendency to stay in Vienna and interact with only a small and very
select group of individuals had prevented the founder of psychoanalyis from fully
appreciating how social and cultural factors influence behavior. Erikson decided
to formulate a theory of development that would be based on psychoanalytic
principles but could take into account such influences.

Erikson bases his description of personality development on the **epigenetic
principle.** In fetal development, certain organs of the body appear at certain specified times and eventually "combine" to form a child. Erikson hypothesizes that
just as the parts of the body develop in interrelated ways in a human fetus, so the
personality of an individual forms as the ego progresses through a series of interrelated stages. All these ego stages exist in the beginning in some form, but each
has a critical period of development.

**Personality develop-
ment based on
epigenetic principle**

Personality grows out
of successful resolu-
tion of dichotomies

In Erikson's view, personality development is a series of turning points, which he describes in terms of dichotomies of desirable qualities and dangers. Erikson does not mean to imply by this scheme that only positive qualities should emerge and that any manifestation of potentially dangerous traits is undesirable. He emphasizes that people adapt to their world best when they possess both the positive and negative qualities of a particular stage provided the positive quality is significantly stronger than the negative quality. Try to imagine, for example, what an individual would be like who was never mistrustful (stage 1) or who never felt guilt (stage 3). Only when the positive quality is outweighed by the negative for any given stage or when the outcome for most stages is negative do difficulties in development and adjustment arise (Hall, 1983).

Stages of Psychosocial Development

The following designations, age ranges, and essential characteristics of the stages of personality development are proposed by Erikson in *Childhood and Society* (1963).[2]

Trust vs. Mistrust (Birth to 1 Year)   The basic psychosocial attitude to be learned by infants is that they can trust their world. Trust is fostered by "consistency, continuity, and sameness of experience" in the satisfaction of the infant's basic needs by the parents. If the needs of infants are met and if parents communicate genuine affection, children will think of their world as safe and dependable. If care is inadequate, inconsistent, or negative, children will approach their world with fear and suspicion.

2 to 3 years:
autonomy vs. shame
and doubt

Autonomy vs. Shame and Doubt (2 to 3 Years)   Just when children have learned to trust (or mistrust) their parents, they must exert a degree of independence. If toddlers are permitted and encouraged to do what they are capable of doing at their own pace and in their own way—but with judicious supervision by parents and teachers—they will develop a sense of autonomy. If parents and teachers are impatient and do too many things for young children, two- and three-year-olds may doubt their ability to deal with the environment. Furthermore, adults should avoid shaming young children for unacceptable behavior since this is likely to contribute to feelings of self-doubt.

4 to 5 years:
initiative vs. guilt

Initiative vs. Guilt (4 to 5 Years)   Being able to participate in many physical activities and to use language sets the stage for initiative, which "adds to autonomy the quality of undertaking, planning, and 'attacking' a task for the sake of being active and on the move." If four- and five-year-olds are given freedom to explore and experiment and if parents and teachers take time to answer questions, ten-

2. All quotations under "Stages of Psychosocial Development" are from Chapter 7 of *Childhood and Society.*

dencies toward initiative will be encouraged. If children of this age are restricted and made to feel their activities and questions are pointless or a nuisance, they will feel guilty about doing things on their own.

Industry vs. Inferiority (6 to 11 years)   A child entering school is at a point in development when behavior is dominated by intellectual curiosity and perform-ance. "He now learns to win recognition by producing things . . . he develops a sense of industry." The danger at this stage is that the child may experience feel-ings of inadequacy or inferiority. If the child is encouraged to make and do things well, helped to persevere, allowed to finish tasks, and praised for trying, industry results. If the child's efforts are unsuccessful or if they are derided or treated as bothersome, a feeling of inferiority results. Children who feel inferior may never learn to enjoy intellectual work and take pride in doing at least one kind of thing really well. At worst, they may feel they will never excel at anything.

6 to 11 years: industry vs. inferiority

Identity vs. Role Confusion (12 to 18 Years)   As young adults approach inde-pendence from parents and achieve physical maturity, they are concerned about what kind of person they are becoming. The goal at this stage is development of ego identity, "the accrued confidence of sameness and continuity." The danger at this stage is role confusion, particularly doubt about sexual and occupational identity. If adolescents succeed (as reflected by the reactions of others) in inte-grating roles in different situations to the point of experiencing continuity in their perception of self, identity develops. If they are unable to establish a sense of sta-bility in various aspects of their lives, role confusion results.

12 to 18 years: identity vs. role confusion

Intimacy vs. Isolation (Young Adulthood)   To experience satisfying develop-ment at this stage, the young adult needs to establish an intimate relationship with another person. Failure to do this will lead to a sense of isolation.

Generativity vs. Stagnation (Middle Age)   "Generativity . . . is primarily the concern of establishing and guiding the next generation." Erikson's use of the term *generativity* is purposely broad. It refers, of course, to having children and raising them. In addition, it refers to the productive and creative efforts in which adults take part that have a positive effect on younger generations (for example, teaching, doing medical research, supporting political and social policies that will benefit future generations). Those unable or unwilling to "establish" and "guide" the next generation become victims of stagnation and self-absorption.

Integrity vs. Despair (Old Age)   Integrity is "the acceptance of one's one and only life cycle as something that had to be and that, by necessity, permitted of no substitutions. . . . Despair expresses the feeling that the time is now short, too short for the attempt to start another life and to try out alternate roads to integrity."

Factors Affecting Identity

The most complex and misunderstood of Erikson's stages is identity vs. role confusion. Erikson has written more extensively about this stage than any other. His observations and those of researchers stimulated by his work can be very instructive, not only to those who will be teaching adolescents, but also to young adults who are in the process of establishing their own identity. Even if you do not plan to teach high school students, careful consideration of what Erikson and other psychologists have to say about identity may help you understand your own behavior better.

The terms *identity* and *identity crisis* have become so popularized that it is important to review Erikson's original meanings. Here is how he describes the concept of **identity:** "An optimal sense of identity . . . is experienced merely as a sense of psychosocial well-being. Its most obvious concomitants are a feeling of being at home in one's body, a sense of 'knowing where one is going' and an inner assuredness of anticipated recognition from those who count" (1968, p. 165).

The danger in adolescence is **role confusion:** having no clear conception of appropriate types of behavior that others will react to favorably. Erikson suggests that adolescence is a critical period in development because "new identifications are no longer characterized by the playfulness of childhood; . . . with dire urgency they force the young individual into choices and decisions which will, with increasing immediacy, lead to commitments 'for life' " (1968, p. 155).

Clearly, then, the task of forming a stable identity and avoiding role confusion is a difficult one for adolescents under the best of circumstances. When social values begin to change, identity formation is made even more difficult. Beliefs about appropriate sex role behavior is one area where changes are affecting identity formation.

Changes in Sex Roles   Erikson believes that sex roles are particularly important in the development of identity because they establish a pattern for many types of behaviors. Until relatively recently (the early 1960s), there was little confusion about appropriate characteristics and activities for males and females in our society. Almost all adult males and females were expected to marry. Husband and wife would then take on well-defined and clearly established responsibilities: The man would function as the breadwinner, the woman would serve as the homemaker and child rearer. This certainty provided a clear code of behavior for those who had or were eager to develop those characteristics, but it created problems for those who did not, especially for adolescent girls.

The typical female adolescent in the America of the 1950s did not formulate as clear a sense of identity as the typical male adolescent because she assumed that what she would become as an adult would depend to a large extent on the man she would marry. The kind of job he secured after marriage and his success at that job would influence her conception of herself perhaps more than her own behavior (Douvan and Adelson, 1966).

Identity: acceptance of body, having goals, getting recognition

Role confusion: not sure what behaviors others will react to favorably

Sex roles establish patterns for many behaviors

Traditionally, male identity linked to job, female identity linked to husband

Identity, as Erikson defines it, involves acceptance of one's body, knowing where one is going, and recognition from those who count. A high school graduate who is pleased with his or her appearance, who has already decided on a college major, and who is admired by parents, relatives, and friends is likely to experience a sense of psychosocial well-being. (Ellis Herwig/The Picture Cube)

Over the last thirty years, interpretations of appropriate behavior for men and women have changed dramatically. Over 60 percent of all mothers of school-age children now work outside the home. The high rate of divorce has led to a significant number of single-parent households. There also are a growing number of families in which both parents hold jobs. Several factors seem to be responsible for these trends: the need for increased family income to meet current lifestyles and future goals; a large increase in the number of jobs traditionally held by women (clerical workers, secretaries, telephone operators, teachers); increased opportunities for women in occupations that have been dominated by men; and a change in women's attitudes about the nature of the female sex role. A 1985 survey of women's attitudes found that 63 percent felt that combining marriage, career, and child rearing was the best alternative for a satisfying and interesting life (Borker, 1987).

Female identity linked to job more now than in past

Because of the changing attitude toward the role of women in our society, the young woman of the 1990s is more likely to feel that her destiny is in her own hands than her mother did when she was the same age. The opportunity for self-fulfillment obviously opens up many other opportunities. But change in social values is a gradual process. There are still many people who hold traditional views of male and female roles and believe in traditional approaches to child rearing. The end product can be confusion and problems, especially for the adolescent who is trying to develop a clear sense of what it means to be a male or female in our society.

Factors That Perpetuate Sex Roles   Inge Broverman and several associates (1972) analyzed perceptions of "typical" masculine and feminine traits. There was considerable unanimity of opinion from respondents of both sexes, all age levels, and all types of backgrounds: Men were pictured as competent, rational, and assertive; women were thought of as warm and expressive.

What gives rise to these stereotypes is still an open question, although parenting behaviors are thought to be very influential. Parents, particularly fathers, emphasize achievement and exploration more for boys than for girls. Girls tend to be kept under closer supervision and given more help in solving problems. As a consequence, they are much more likely than boys to ask for help—a tendency that is strengthened by the positive responses of adults. Boys, on the other hand, often are told directly or indirectly to handle things themselves. In the area of play, boys generally are given toys or are encouraged to participate in activities that involve exploration of the physical world (baseball, Lego blocks, Tinker Toys, cars, science kits); girls are encouraged to participate in activities that involve quiet play and imitation of interpersonal behavior (doll play, dressing up, drawing, painting) (Block, 1973; Carter, 1987; Fagot, 1978; Fagot and Leinbach, 1987).

> American boys encouraged to be independent, active, exploratory; girls encouraged to be dependent, quiet

A major aspect of male-female sex role stereotypes is aggressive behavior. Contrary to earlier research findings, boys exhibit more physical *and* verbal aggression, although the difference is more pronounced for physical aggression. In addition, boys act more aggressively than girls following exposure to an aggressive model. Although the exact influence of parenting and exposure to other models (for example, cartoon and movie characters) on aggressive behavior is unknown at this point, the influence of social factors can be seen in the fact that gender differences in aggression decrease with age (Hyde, 1986).

For those who believe sex role stereotyping is an obstacle to identity formation, one solution is to change the way in which parents raise their children. This is more difficult to accomplish than you realize. Beverly Fagot (1978) found that parents of preschoolers often are not aware that they are responding differently to boys and girls. It is possible, then, that although contemporary parents may *think* they have rejected traditional conceptions of sex roles, they are still encouraging girls to be dependent and passive and boys to be independent and active.

We can look at the results of the studies cited above in both negative and positive lights. On the negative side, even though many young women of the 1990s believe they have unlimited career opportunities, they may still be socialized to prefer working with people and helping others. Furthermore, when girls display independent and competitive behaviors, they may be deliberately or unconsciously discouraged by parents and teachers. On the positive side, greater sensitivity to and understanding of interpersonal relationships may help women in certain personal and professional situations.

Given the ways in which society maintains sex role stereotypes and the difficulties they create for some adolescents in establishing an identity, many researchers have suggested that children and adolescents acquire a sex role that *combines* traditional masculine and feminine traits. This idea is called **psychological androgyny**.

Sex Typing and Psychological Androgyny   Broverman and her colleagues (1972) reveal the extent to which traditional conceptions of sex roles are ingrained in the minds of many Americans. But not all individuals react the same way, as indicated in studies by Sandra Bem (1975, 1976). She found that adults vary in the extent to which they can be classified as *sex typed* or as high in *psychological androgyny*. (*Androgyny* means possessing both male and female characteristics.) Sex-typed females (who endorse stereotyped conceptions of femininity) may refuse to nail two boards together because they feel it is a "masculine" rather than a "feminine" form of behavior. Sex-typed males may refuse to handle a baby or do household chores presumably because they feel that engaging in such behavior will make them appear less masculine. Only adults rated high in psychological androgyny appear able to move between masculine and feminine roles without difficulty or self-consciousness.

Because of this increased flexibility, proponents of androgyny argue that androgynous individuals are better adjusted than those who identify with traditional sex roles. Research findings reported by James Dusek (1987) seem to support this argument. In two studies, college students responded to a series of written questions designed to measure the first six stages of Erikson's theory. Androgynous students scored higher than sex-typed students for trust vs. mistrust, initiative vs. guilt, identity vs. role confusion, and intimacy vs. isolation. In terms of Erikson's theory, at least, these results suggest that androgynous individuals are better adjusted than sex-typed individuals.

How do you help students develop more flexible conceptions of sex roles. In general, you can encourage girls to be more competitive and achievement oriented, particularly in math and science (two areas in which women are seriously underrepresented). Boys can be encouraged to be more sensitive to the feelings of others and to take part in other than traditional masculine activities without being self-conscious. The study by Fagot (1978) and an analysis of research by Jeanne Block (1973) call attention to the extent to which sex-typed behavior is shaped by the responses of parents and teachers. Furthermore, observation of

Sex-typed individuals less flexible than those high in psychological androgyny

Boys who observe their fathers engaging in traditionally "feminine" activities (such as infant care) are likely to develop a flexible view of sex roles and be rated high in psychological androgyny. (Peter Vandermar/Stock, Boston)

models has a significant impact on sex-typed behavior. A boy who watches his father unself-consciously care for an infant or wash the dishes would seem more likely to acquire a flexible view of sex roles than a boy whose father is a sex-typed male. And a girl who sees her mother go off to work should be less inclined to picture women solely as mothers and homemakers.

The Significance of Occupational Choice According to Erikson, occupational choice also has great impact on adolescents' sense of identity. The occupation we choose influences other aspects of our lives perhaps more than any other single factor. Our job determines how we will spend a sizable proportion of our time; it determines how much money we earn; and our income, in turn, determines where and how we live. The last two factors determine, to a considerable extent, the people we interact with socially. All these factors together influence the reactions of others, and these reactions lead us to develop perceptions of ourselves. The choice of a career, therefore, may be the biggest commitment of a person's life. Erikson notes that occupational choice is particularly difficult in America because of our belief in technology, the efficiency of the assembly line, and corporate organization, all of which limit individuality. Other complicating factors are the amount of training needed for many jobs in a technological society, the rapidly changing job market, and the fact that many individuals compete against one another for desirable jobs.

Occupational choice is a major commitment

Dealing with Role Confusion Confronted with the realization that the time has come to make a career choice, that many careers pose a threat to personal identity, and that the job market fluctuates rapidly, the young person seeking to avoid role confusion by making a firm vocational choice may feel overwhelmed and unable to act. Because of this, Erikson suggests that for many young people a **psychosocial moratorium** may be desirable. A psychosocial moratorium is a period marked by a delay of commitment. Such a postponement occurred in Erikson's own life. After leaving high school, Erikson spent several years wandering around Europe without making any firm decision about the sort of job he would seek. Under ideal circumstances, a psychosocial moratorium should be a period of adventure and exploration, having a positive, or at least neutral, impact on the individual and society.

Psychosocial moratorium delays commitment

In some cases, however, the young person may engage in defiant or destructive behavior. A young person who is unable to overcome role confusion—or to postpone choices leading to identity formation by engaging in a positive psychosocial moratorium—may attempt to resolve inner conflict by choosing what Erikson refers to as a **negative identity**.

Negative identity: rejection of accepted roles

> The loss of a sense of identity is often expressed in a scornful and snobbish hostility toward the roles offered as proper and desirable in one's family or immediate community. Any aspect of the required role, or all of it—be it masculinity or femininity, nationality or class membership—can become the main focus of the young person's acid disdain. (1968, pp. 172–173)

For example, an adolescent boy whose parents have constantly stressed how important it is to do well in school may deliberately act in an unscholarly way or quit school and join a religious cult. Erikson explains such choices by suggesting that the young person finds it easier to "derive a sense of identity out of total identification with that which he is least supposed to be than to struggle for a feeling of reality in acceptable roles which are unattainable with his inner means" (1968, p. 176). If the young person who chooses a negative identity plays the role only long enough to gain greater self-insight, the experience may be positive. In some cases the negative identity may be "confirmed" by the way the adolescent is treated by those in authority. If forms of behavior adopted to express a negative identity bring the teenager into contact with excessively punitive parents, teachers, or law enforcement agencies, for example, the "young person may well put his energy into becoming exactly what the careless and fearful community expects him to be—and make a total job of it" (1968, p. 196).

Erikson notes that one reason for the tendency to develop a negative identity is that the adolescent is capable of imagining many possibilities. The number of possible choices of groups, interests, and activities available to the contemporary American teenager may seem overwhelming to a young person who lacks a sense

Adolescents who are dissatisfied with themselves and unable to focus on constructive goals may fashion a negative identity by engaging in forms of behavior that their parents oppose. (Lawrence Migdale/Stock, Boston)

of identity. When confronted with so many choices, the adolescent may develop what Erikson refers to as a *historical perspective,* the fear that earlier events in one's life are irreversible and may limit the choices available.

Erikson's observations on identity and role confusion may help you understand several aspects of adolescent behavior. Many high school students are probably bothered by the realization that they must make important decisions. They may be confused about sex roles and reluctant to make a specific career choice. Disinterest in class work may be interpreted in some cases as evidence that a student is engaging in a psychosocial moratorium and lacks enthusiasm for school because of a sense of aimlessness about preparing for a specific career (or even just graduating). Some types of impertinent or disruptive behavior may be less likely to arouse you to counterattack if you allow for the possibility that those involved are acting out a negative identity.

Adolescent Identity Statuses   The usefulness of Erikson's observations on identity may be increased if you take into account different types of identity. James Marcia (1966, 1980) has proposed the concept of *identity statuses,* which he developed "as a device by means of which Erikson's theoretical notions about identity might be subjected to empirical study. The identity statuses are four modes of dealing with the identity issue characteristic of late adolescents" (1980, p. 161).

Marcia established the four identity statuses after he had conducted semistructured interviews with a selected sample of male youth. The interviewees were asked their thoughts about a career, their personal value system, sexual attitudes, and religious beliefs. Marcia proposed that the criteria for the attainment of a mature identity are based on two variables: crisis and commitment. "Crisis refers to times during adolescence when the individual seems to be actively involved in choosing among alternative occupations and beliefs. Commitment refers to the degree of personal investment the individual expresses in an occupation or belief" (1967, p. 119). After analyzing interview records with these two criteria in mind, Marcia established four identity statuses that vary in their degree of crisis and commitment: identity diffusion, moratorium, identity achievement, and foreclosure.

Identity diffusion types have yet to experience a crisis because they have not given much serious thought to an occupation, sex roles, or values. They may give the impression that they are trying to distract themselves from confronting such issues. They have little self-direction, are disorganized and impulsive, and tend to avoid getting involved in either schoolwork or interpersonal relationships.

Moratorium types have given a certain amount of thought to identity questions, but they have not come up with any satisfactory answers. They are aware that they are "in crisis." They are dissatisfied with school or college, change majors often, daydream a great deal, and engage in intense but short-lived relationships with others. They may also temporarily reject parental values. After a period of experimentation and restless searching, most moratorium types come to grips with themselves and take on characteristics of identity achievement types. (Notice that Marcia's use of *moratorium* stresses an identity crisis, while Erikson's use of *psychosocial moratorium* stresses delay of commitment.)

Identity achievement types have made self-chosen commitments in at least some aspects of their identity. Because of the variety of factors that make up identity, however, it is not likely that too many individuals experience a triumphant sense of having "put it all together." An adolescent may have made a firm occupational choice, to cite just one example, but be indecisive about sex role or religious values. Furthermore, identity achievement is not a once-and-for-all accomplishment. If an ego-shattering event (loss of a job, divorce) later occurs, identity achievement types may be propelled back into a crisis and be faced with the task of rebuilding self-esteem. Because they have already accomplished it once, however, they might be expected to achieve a satisfactory identity again.

Foreclosure types are not experiencing a crisis and may never suffer any doubts about occupational choice, sex roles, and values. The main reason for this lack of doubt about identity issues is that foreclosure types accept and endorse the occu-

Identity diffusion types avoid thinking about jobs, roles, values

Moratorium types suffer identity crises of various kinds

Identity achievement types have made their own commitments

Foreclosure types unquestioningly endorse parents' goals and values pational choices and values of their parents. Such individuals may make up their minds early in high school about the kind of job they want to seek and willingly accept their parents' views on sex roles and religious and political issues.

The percentage of individuals in each of the four categories changes over time. According to Marcia (cited in Scarr, Weinberg, and Levine, 1986), moratorium types were more numerous during the 1960s and 1970s than during the 1980s. And foreclosure and identity diffusion types are more prevalent now than in past years.

A relevant question to ask about Marcia's identity statuses, particularly if you plan to teach in a foreign country or if you plan to teach students with different cultural backgrounds, is whether these identity statuses occur only in the United States. The answer appears to be no. Researchers in such diverse countries as Korea, India, Nigeria, Japan, Denmark, and Holland report finding the same patterns (Scarr, Weinberg, & Levine, 1986).

Marcia's description of identity statuses applies most directly to college youth, but awareness of the various types may help you understand aspects of the behavior of high school students. Some adolescents who seek to establish a sense of identity, for instance, may experience little difficulty because they accept their parents' ideas regarding occupational choice, sex roles, and values. Other high school students, however, may have a diffuse identity and try to distract themselves from thinking about values or about what they intend to do after graduation. Still others may be preoccupied with career and sexual identity problems to the point that they are openly dissatisfied. A few students may resolve identity conflicts before they leave high school, accomplishing in the adolescent years what many youth need another four years to achieve. The identity status concept may also help you understand differences between some college preparatory and vocationally oriented high school students. A high school senior who has definitely decided to seek a particular type of job after graduation is likely to confront different identity issues than a classmate who plans to go to college but who is indecisive about a major.

Criticisms of Erikson's Theory

Erikson occasionally carried out research investigations, but most of his conclusions are based on personal and subjective interpretations that have not been substantiated by controlled investigations of the type that are valued by American psychologists. As a result, there have been no checks on the tendency to generalize from personal experiences. Some of his observations on identity, for example, reflect his own indecision about occupational choice.

Some critics argue that Erikson's stages reflect the personality development of males more accurately than the personality development of females. Marcia (1986) contends that beginning in about fourth grade (the industry vs. inferiority stage), girls are as concerned with the nature of interpersonal relationships as they are with achievement, whereas boys focus mainly on achievement. During adolescence, many young women seem to work through the crises of identity *and* intimacy simultaneously, whereas most young men follow the sequence described by Erikson—identity vs. role confusion, then intimacy vs. isolation (Gilligan, 1982; Scarr, Weinberg, and Levine, 1986).

Erikson has also been criticized because he does not clearly describe the mechanisms that explain *how* a child moves from one stage to the next (Miller, 1983).

A final criticism is that Erikson's early stages, those covering ages two through eleven, seem to stress the same basic qualities. Autonomy, initiative, and industry all emphasize the desirability of permitting and encouraging children to do things on their own. Doubt, guilt, and inferiority all focus on the need for parents and teachers to provide sympathetic support.

If you keep these reservations in mind, however, you are likely to discover that Erikson's observations (as well as the identity status types described by Marcia) will clarify important aspects of development. Suggestions you might refer to in order to take advantage of Erikson's observations are listed below. These suggestions might also serve as the nucleus of a section to be inserted in your Handbook. Possible Handbook Headings are indicated in the margins.

SUGGESTIONS FOR TEACHING

Applying Erikson's Theory in the Classroom

1. Keep in mind that certain types of behaviors and relationships may be of special significance at different age levels.

Handbook Heading: Ways to Apply Erikson's Theory (Preschool and Kindergarten)

2. With younger preschool children, allow plenty of opportunities for free play and experimentation to encourage the development of autonomy, but provide guidance to reduce the possibility that the child will experience doubt. Avoid shaming children for unacceptable behavior.

3. With older preschool children, encourage activities that will permit the use of initiative and provide a sense of accomplishment. Avoid making children feel guilty about well-motivated but inconvenient (to you) questions or actions, and try to help jealous children gain satisfaction from their own behavior.

4. During the elementary school years, help children experience a sense of industry by presenting tasks they can complete successfully. Arrange

Handbook Heading:
Ways to Apply Erikson's
Theory (Elementary
Grades)

Handbook Heading:
Ways to Apply
Erikson's Theory
(Secondary Grades)

such tasks so that students will *know* they have been successful. Play down comparisons and encourage cooperation and self-competition to limit feelings of inferiority. (Specific ways to accomplish these goals will be described in several later chapters.)

5. At the secondary school level, remember the significance of each pupil's search for a sense of identity. The components of identity stressed by Erikson are acceptance of one's appearance, recognition from those who count, and knowing where one is going. Role confusion is most frequently caused by failure to formulate clear ideas about sex roles and indecision about occupational choice.

If you will be teaching secondary school subjects such as health, biology, psychology, or home economics, you may be able to help students accept or improve their appearance. For example, explaining that acne is usually due to physiological changes accompanying puberty and that such changes are temporary may provide a degree of solace for those afflicted with this condition. You might also mention that researchers have found that by the time they reach college, most young people report that they have become quite satisfied with their appearance (Berscheid, Walster, and Bohrnstedt, 1973).

If you are "someone who counts" to your pupils, your recognition of them as individuals and your praise for their accomplishments will contribute to their sense of positive identity. If you become aware that particular pupils lack recognition from peers because of abrasive qualities or ineptness and if you have the time and opportunity, you might attempt to encourage social skills. An excellent book to consult for this purpose is *Skill-streaming the Adolescent: A Structured Learning Approach to Teaching Prosocial Skills* (Goldstein et al., 1980). This volume describes fifty specific skills that fall into five general categories: social skills, skills for dealing with feelings, skill alternatives to aggression, skills for dealing with stress, and planning skills. Each skill is taught by a four-step method:

1. Modeling (or imitating those who use social skills effectively)
2. Role playing (gaining practice in social skills in simulated situations)
3. Performance feedback (improving techniques by noting their effectiveness or ineffectiveness)
4. Transfer of training (applying a technique that was learned in role-playing situations to everyday interactions with others).

Since the techniques are preplanned and structured, you will probably obtain the best results by following the procedures outlined in the book. But remember our discussion in Chapter 1 about the teacher-theorist and the teacher-practitioner. Don't be afraid to experiment or make spontaneous changes.

You might be able to reduce identity problems that are due to indecisiveness about sex roles by having class discussions (in social science courses, for instance) centering on changes in attitudes regarding masculinity, femininity, and family responsibilities. Following the suggestions of Block (1973), boys might be encouraged to become more sensitive to the needs of others and girls to be more achievement oriented. Members of both sexes might be acquainted with the concept of psychological androgyny and made aware of the advantages of possessing both "masculine" and "feminine" characteristics.

Working with your school counselor, in some cases you may be able, directly or indirectly, to help students make decisions about occupational choice. Or you may be able to assist students to decide whether to apply for admission to a college instead of entering the job market just after graduation. There are many ways to enable students to work toward short-term goals, particularly in your classroom. These will be described in detail in Chapters 6 and 11, which deal with instructional objectives and motivation.

6. Keep in mind that the aimlessness of some students may be evidence that they are engaging in a psychosocial moratorium. If possible, encourage such individuals to focus on short-term goals while they continue to search for long-term goals.

7. Try to be patient if you suspect that disruptive behavior on the part of some students may be due to acting out a negative identity. When you must control negative behavior in order to preserve a satisfactory learning environment for other students, try to do it in such a way that the troublemaker is not "confirmed" as a troublemaker. One way is to make clear that you do not hold a grudge and that you have confidence in the student's ability to make positive contributions in class. (If possible, arrange opportunities for troublemakers to carry out assignments that will be positive and constructive.)

8. Remain aware that adolescents may exhibit characteristics of different identity status types. Some may drift aimlessly; others may be distressed because they realize they lack goals and values. A few high school students may have arrived at self-chosen commitments; others may have accepted the goals and values of their parents.

If you become aware that certain pupils seem depressed or bothered because they are unable to develop a satisfactory set of personal values, consult your school psychologist or counselor. In addition, you might use the techniques just summarized to try to help them experience at least a degree of identity achievement. You might also use the technique of *values clarification* (discussed in Chapter 10 in a section on affective goals) to help students become aware of attitudes they wish to prize and act on. Perhaps the main value of the identity status concept is that it calls attention to individual differences in the formation of identity. Foreclosure types will pose few, if any, problems. Identity diffusion and moratorium types may be so bothered by role confusion that they are unwilling to carry out even simple assignments—unless you supply support and incentives.

Piaget: Cognitive Development

Factors That Influenced Piaget

Piaget was born in the small university town of Neuchatel, Switzerland, in 1896. His father was a professor of history who specialized in medieval literature, and young Jean was brought up in a scholarly atmosphere. His main boyhood interest was observation of animals in their natural habitat, an interest he pursued with considerable energy and sophistication. He published his first "professional" paper at the age of eleven. (He had seen an albino sparrow in a park and reported this in a nature magazine.)

When he entered school, Piaget concentrated on the biological sciences. A series of articles on shellfish so impressed the director of the natural history museum in Geneva that fifteen-year-old Jean was offered the post of curator of the mollusk collection. Since he had not finished high school, he felt obliged to decline this offer. Piaget's fascination with the study of knowledge can be traced to a vacation with his godfather, a scholar specializing in philosophy, who urged Jean to broaden his horizons and to study philosophy and logic.

After graduating from high school, Piaget entered the University of Neuchatel and earned undergraduate and graduate degrees in natural science—he was awarded the Ph.D. at the age of twenty-one. At that point he became intrigued with psychology, which he studied in Zurich, where he was introduced to Freudian theory and wrote a paper relating psychoanalysis to child psychology. From Zurich he went to Paris to study abnormal psychology. Shortly after he arrived, he obtained a position preparing a French version of some reasoning tests developed in England. As he recorded the responses of his subjects, Piaget found that he was much more intrigued with wrong answers than with correct ones. He became convinced that the thought processes of younger children are basically different from those of older children and adults. His lifelong fascination with biology and his interest in studying the nature of knowledge led him to speculate about the development of thinking in children.

In 1921 an appointment as director of research at the Jean Jacques Rousseau Institute in Geneva permitted Piaget to concentrate full time on the study of cognitive development. He engaged in active study at the Institute until 1975, and he continued to analyze cognitive development in "retirement" until his death in 1980.

Basic Principles of Piaget's Theory

Piaget's conception of intellectual development reflects his basic interest in biology and knowledge. He postulates that human beings inherit two basic tendencies: **organization** (the tendency to systematize and combine processes into coherent general systems) and **adaptation** (the tendency to adjust to the environment). For Piaget, these tendencies govern both physiological functioning and mental functioning. Just as the biological process of digestion transforms food into a form that the body can use, so intellectual processes transform experiences into a form that the child can use in dealing with new situations. Just as biological processes must be kept in a state of balance (through homeostasis), intellectual processes seek a balance through the process of **equilibration** (a form of self-regulation that all individuals use to bring coherence and stability to their conception of the world).

Organization   As we just stated, *organization* refers to the tendency of all individuals to systematize or combine processes into coherent (logically interrelated) systems. When we think of tulips and roses as subcategories of the more general category "flowers," instead of as two unrelated categories, we are using organization to aid our thinking process. This organizational capacity makes those thinking processes efficient and powerful, and allows for a better "fit" or adaptation of the individual to the environment.

Organization: tendency to systematize processes

Schemes   **Schemes** are organized patterns of behavior or thought that children formulate as they interact with their environment, parents, teachers, and age-mates. Schemes can be behavioral (for example, how to throw a ball) or cognitive (realizing that there are many different kinds of balls). Whenever a child encounters a new experience that does not easily fit into an existing scheme, adaptation is necessary.

Scheme: organized pattern of behavior or thought

Adaptation   This is the process of creating a good "fit" or match between one's conception of reality (one's schemes) and the real-life experiences one encounters. Adaptation, as described by Piaget, is accomplished by two subprocesses: **assimilation** and **accommodation.** A child may adapt either by interpreting the experience so that it *does* fit an existing scheme (assimilation) or by changing an existing scheme to incorporate the experience (accommodation). Imagine a six-year-old who goes to an aquarium for the first time and calls the sea horses

Adaptation: tendency to adjust to environment

Assimilation: new experience is fitted into existing scheme

Jean Piaget. (Yves De Braine/Black Star)

"little fish" and the whales "big fish." In both cases the child is assimilating—attempting to fit a new experience into an existing scheme (in this case, that all animals that live in the water are fish). When her parents point out that even though whales live in the water, they are mammals, not fish, the six-year-old begins to accommodate—to modify her existing scheme to fit the new experience she has encountered. Gradually (and it is important to realize that accommodations are made slowly, over repeated experiences), a new scheme forms that contains nonfish animals that live in the water.

Accommodation: scheme is created or revised to fit new experience

Relationships Among Organization, Adaptation, and Schemes In order to give you a basic understanding of Piaget's ideas, we have talked about them as distinct elements. But the concepts of organization, adaptation, and schemes are all related. In their drive to be organized, individuals try to have a place for everything (accommodation) so they can put everything in its place (assimilation). The product of organizing and adapting is the creation of new schemes that allow us to organize at a higher level and to adapt more effectively.

Equilibration   Before moving on, we should take a closer look at one more basic principle of Piaget's theory—equilibration. It is unfortunate but true that some teachers and parents see children as passive containers waiting to be filled with knowledge. Piaget's view is radically different. He believes children are always thinking and learning. The goal of this mental activity is to reconcile new knowledge and experiences with the schemes they currently have for understanding and interacting with the world. As children develop, the problems they encounter become more complex and abstract, but so does the nature of their schemes. *Equilibration* is the label Piaget gave to the process of working toward better forms of knowledge.

> **Equilibration: tendency to construct schemes that allow better understanding of experiences**

At this point you may be feeling a little overwhelmed by Piaget's ideas. Recognize, as Piaget did, that accommodating to new, complex, and abstract ideas takes time. You may need to think about organization, adaptation, schemes, equilibration, and their interrelationships several times before they become clear to you. Having an example to refer to can help.

Picture a child who has attended a small preschool and kindergarten with a very warm, supportive teacher who permits a maximum amount of pupil self-direction. When the child enters the first grade and encounters a rather business-like teacher who believes in close supervision and methodical instruction, adaptation will take place. The child may relate some aspects of first-grade routine (for example, lining up to get materials) to similar features already experienced as part of the preschool routine, assimilating new experiences so that they mesh with existing schemes. The child is, however, also likely to revise other schemes, accommodating (or altering) the scheme for teacher, for instance, to include the characteristics of the first-grade teacher, who differs substantially from the preschool instructor.

A primary grade child, who is experiencing school for the first time and is being asked to learn many new things, must continually supplement and revise schemes. But even sophisticated college students with a dozen or more years of schooling behind them engage in the process of adaptation. We have had students who were disappointed and confused by a lower-than-expected grade on a classroom exam that surprised them by demanding comprehension and application, not memorization. With some coaching and practice, however, most developed a scheme for coping with tests that reflect higher-level thinking. As you read these words, you should try to assimilate Piaget's ideas so that they relate to schemes you have already formed (perhaps in other courses in psychology). At the same time, if you hope to acquire new insights into cognitive development and behavior, you should accommodate by revising existing conceptions about thinking so that they incorporate Piaget's views.

Stages of Cognitive Development

Organization and adaptation are what Piaget calls *invariant functions*. This means that these thought processes function the same way for infants, children, adolescents, and adults. Schemes, on the other hand, are not invariant. They undergo systematic change at particular points in time. As a result, there are real differences between the ways younger and older children think, and between the ways children and adults think. The schemes of infants and toddlers, for example, are sensory and motor in nature. They often are referred to as *habits* or *reflexes*. In early childhood, schemes gradually become more mental in nature; here they are called *concepts* or *categories*. By late adolescence or early adulthood, schemes are very complex and result in what we call *strategic* or *planful* behavior.

On the basis of his studies, Piaget concluded that schemes evolve through four stages. These stages follow a continuous, but often zig-zag, pattern. That is to say, children do not suddenly "jump" from one stage to the next. Their cognitive development follows a definite sequence, but they may occasionally use a more advanced kind of thinking or revert to a more primitive form. The *rate* at which a particular child proceeds through these stages varies, but Piaget believes the *sequence* is the same in all children.

Piaget's four stages are described below. To help you grasp the sequence of these stages, Table 2.1 briefly outlines the range of ages to which they generally apply and their distinguishing characteristics.

Sensorimotor Stage   Infants and children up to the age of two years acquire understanding primarily through sensory impressions and motor activities. Therefore, Piaget calls this the *sensorimotor stage*. Because they are unable to move around much on their own during the first months of postnatal existence, infants develop schemes primarily by exploring their own bodies and senses. After they learn to walk and manipulate things, however, toddlers get into everything and build up a sizable repertoire of schemes involving external objects and situations.

Most children under two are able to use schemes they have mastered to engage in mental, as well as physical, trial and error behavior. By age two, toddlers' schemes have become more mental in nature. You can see this in the way toddlers imitate the behavior of others. They imitate people they have not previously observed, they imitate the behavior of animals, and, most important, they imitate even when the model is no longer present (this is called *deferred imitation*). These types of imitative behaviors show the child's increasing ability to think in terms of symbols.

Preoperational Stage   The thinking of preschool children (roughly two to five years old) centers on mastery of symbols (such as words), which permits them to benefit much more from past experiences. Piaget believes that many symbols are derived from mental imitation and involve both visual images and bodily sensa-

Sensorimotor stage: schemes reflect sensory and motor experiences

Table 2.1   Stages of Cognitive Development

Stage	Age Range	Characteristics
Sensorimotor	Birth to two years	Develops schemes primarily through sense and motor activities.
Preoperational	Two to seven years	Gradually acquires ability to conserve and decenter, but not capable of operations and unable to mentally reverse actions.
Concrete operational	Seven to eleven years	Capable of operations, but solves problems by generalizing from concrete experiences. Not able to manipulate conditions mentally unless they have been experienced.
Formal operational	Eleven years and older	Able to deal with abstractions, form hypotheses, solve problems systematically, engage in mental manipulations.

tions (notice how the schemes of this stage incorporate and build on the schemes of the previous stage). Even though their thinking is much more sophisticated than that of one- and two-year-olds, preschool children are limited in their ability to use their new symbol-oriented schemes. From an adult perspective, their thinking and behavior is illogical. When Piaget uses the term *operation,* he means an action carried out through logical thinking. *Preoperational,* then, means prelogical. The main impediments to logical thinking that preschoolers have to overcome are *perceptual centration, irreversibility,* and *egocentrism.* You can see these impediments at work most clearly when children attempt to solve **conservation** problems, problems that test their ability to recognize that properties stay the same despite a change in appearance.

One of the best known conservation problems is conservation of continuous quantity. A child is taken to a quiet place by an experimenter, who then pours water (or juice, or beans, or whatever) into identical short glasses until the child agrees that each contains an equal amount. Then the water is poured from one of these glasses into a tall thin glass. At that point the child is asked, "Is there more water in this glass (the experimenter points to the tall thin glass) or this one?" Immediately after the child answers, the experimenter asks, "Why do you think so?" If the child's response is evasive or vague, the experimenter continues to probe until the underlying thought processes become clear.

In carrying out this experiment (and many others similar to it) with children of different ages, Piaget discovered that children below the age of six or so maintain

Preoperational stage: forms many new schemes but does not think logically

Perceptual centration, irreversibility, egocentrism: barriers to logical thought

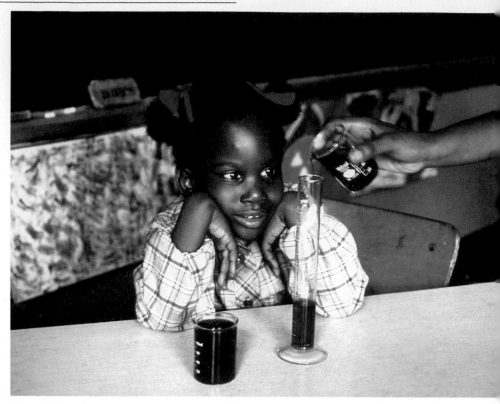

One of Piaget's best-known experiments involves asking children to explain what happens when water is poured back and forth between containers of different sizes and shapes. The preoperational child is unable to consider more than one feature at a time and is unable to mentally reverse the action of pouring. He or she is likely to maintain, therefore, that a tall container holds more water than a squat container, even if the amount is the same. (Marcia Weinstein)

that there is more water in the tall thin glass than in the short squat glass. Even though they agree at the beginning of the experiment that the water in the two identical glasses is equal, young children stoutly insist that after the water has been poured the taller glass contains more. When asked "Why do you think so?" many preschool children immediately and confidently reply, "Because it's taller." Children over the age of six or so, by contrast, are more likely to reply, "Well, it *looks* as if there's more water in this one because it's taller, but they're really the same."

One reason why preoperational stage children have difficulty solving conservation problems (as well as other problems that require logical thinking) is **perceptual centration.** This is the very strong tendency to focus attention on only one characteristic of an object or aspect of a problem or event at a time. The young child focuses only on the height of the water in the two containers and ignores the differences in width and volume.

The second impediment to logical thinking is **irreversibility.** This means that young children cannot mentally pour the water from the tall thin glass back into the short squat one (thereby proving that the glasses contain the same amount of water). For the same reason, these youngsters do not understand the logic behind simple mathematical reversals (4 + 5 = 9; 9 − 5 = 4).

The third major impediment is **egocentrism.** When applied to preschool children, *egocentric* does not mean selfish or conceited. It means that youngsters find it difficult, if not impossible, to take another person's point of view. In their conversations and in experimental situations in which they are asked to describe how something would look if viewed by someone else, preschool children reveal that they often have difficulty seeing things from another person's perspective (Piaget and Inhelder, 1956). They seem to assume that others see things the same way they see them. As a result, attempts to explain the logic behind conservation are usually met with quizzical looks and the insistence (some would mistakenly call it stubbornness) that the tall thin glass contains more water.

Concrete Operational Stage Through formal instruction, informal experiences, and maturation, children over the age of seven gradually become less influenced by perceptual centration, irreversibility, and egocentrism. Schemes are developing that allow a greater understanding of such logic-based tasks as conservation (matter is neither created nor destroyed but simply changes shape or form), class inclusion (constructing hierarchical relationships among related classes of items), and seriation (arranging items in a particular order). But operational thinking is limited to objects that are actually present or that children have experienced concretely and directly. For this reason, Piaget describes the stage from about seven to about eleven years as that of *concrete operations.* The nature of the concrete operational stage can be illustrated by the child's mastery of different kinds of conservation.

By the age of seven most children are able to correctly explain that water poured from a short squat glass into a tall thin glass is still the same amount of water. Being able to solve the water-pouring problem, however, does not guarantee that a seven-year-old will be able to solve a similar problem involving two balls of clay. A child who has just explained why a tall glass of water contains the same amount as a short one may inconsistently maintain a few moments later that rolling one of two equal-sized balls of clay into an elongated shape causes it to become bigger. Children in the primary grades tend to react to each situation in terms of concrete experiences. The tendency to solve problems by generalizing from one situation to a similar but identical situation does not occur with any degree of consistency until the end of the elementary school years. Furthermore, if asked to deal with a hypothetical problem, the concrete operational child is likely to be stymied. Seven-year-olds are not likely to be able to solve abstract problems by engaging in mental explorations. They usually need to manipulate concrete objects physically or to recollect specific past experiences in order to explain things to themselves and others.

Egocentrism: assumption that others see things the same way

Concrete operational stage: capable of mentally reversing actions but generalizes only from concrete experiences

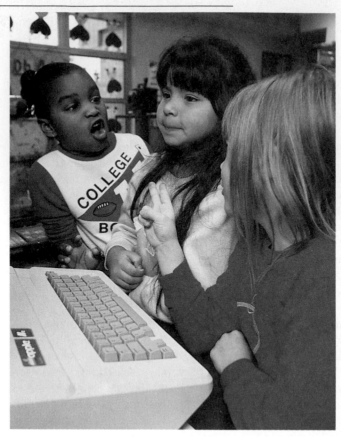

Elementary school teachers who take into account Piaget's description of cognitive development may encourage their pupils to engage in small-group interactions. As children interact with each other they may not only learn from peers but also overcome the tendency to function as *egocentric thinkers*—convinced that everyone else sees things as they do. (Bob Daemmrich/The Image Works)

Formal operational stage: able to deal with abstractions, form hypotheses, engage in mental manipulations

Formal Operational Stage   When children *do* reach the point of being able to generalize and to engage in mental trial and error by thinking up hypotheses and testing them "in their heads," Piaget says they have reached the stage of *formal operations.* The term *formal* reflects the ability to respond to the *form* of a problem rather than its content, and to *form* hypotheses. For example, the formal operational thinker can read the analogies "5 is to 15 as 1 is to 3" and "penny is to dollar as year is to century" and realize that despite the different content, the form of the two problems is identical (both analogies are based on ratios). In the same way, the formal thinker can understand and use complex language forms: proverbs ("strike while the iron is hot"), metaphor ("procrastination is the thief of time"), sarcasm, and satire.

We can see the nature of formal operational thinking and how it differs from concrete operational thinking by looking at a simplified version of Piaget's rod-bending experiment. In the original experiment, adolescents were given a basin filled with water, a set of rods, and a set of weights. The rods could be attached to the edge of the basin and the weights to the ends of the rods. The rods were of different material (steel, brass, wood), length, thickness, and shape (round, square, rectangular). The subject's task was to figure out how much weight was required to bend a rod just enough to touch the water.

To make things a little simpler, imagine this experiment is being conducted with metal rods that vary only in length. Let's say that our hypothetical subject picks out the longest rod in the set (which is 9 inches long), attaches it to the edge of the basin, and puts just enough weight on the end of it (say, 6 ounces) to get it to touch the water. This observation is then recorded. Successively shorter rods are selected and the same procedure is carried out. At some point the subject comes to the 4-inch rod. This rod does not touch the water even when all of the weights have been attached to it. That result is duly noted. There are, however, three more rods, all of which are shorter than the last one tested. This is where the formal and concrete operators part company. The formal operational thinker reasons that if all of the available weights are not sufficient to bend the 4-inch rod enough to touch the water, the same will be true of the remaining rods. In essence, the rest of the experiment is done mentally and symbolically. The concrete operational thinker continues trying out each rod and recording each observation independently of the others. Although both subjects reach the same conclusions, the formal operator does so through a more powerful, efficient process.

But remember that new schemes develop gradually. Even though adolescents can sometimes deal with mental abstractions representing concrete objects, most twelve-year-olds solve problems haphazardly, using trial and error. It is not until the end of the high school years that adolescents are likely to attack a problem by forming hypotheses, mentally sorting out solutions, and systematically testing the most promising leads.

Accelerating Cognitive Development: Mission Impossible?

Piaget believed that cognitive development is caused by two general factors: heredity and environmental experience. *Heredity* establishes the basic nature of physical structures (the brain, for example), the development of physical structures, the existence of reflexes (sucking, grasping, crying), and the tendency to organize experiences and adapt to the environment (through assimilation, accommodation, and equilibration). *Experience* refers to the variety of interactions we have with the world. These interactions can be classified in three ways: physical experiences, mental experiences, and social experiences. Picking up a bunch of rocks and estimating their size and weight is a physical experience. Arranging the rocks in sequence from smallest to largest or lightest to heaviest is a mental experience. (Piaget uses the term *logico-mathematical knowledge* because this type of knowledge is created from schemes based on logic and mathematics). Watching other people behave, listening to other people's ideas, and discussing ideas with others are examples of social experience.

Piaget believed that the amount and quality of environmental experiences could alter the details of cognitive development for better or worse, but could not affect such basic tendencies as organization and adaptation, tendencies that are governed by heredity. Consequently, he maintained that the rate of cognitive development cannot be accelerated through formal instruction. Many American psychologists are not willing to accept this conclusion at face value. Over the past twenty years, dozens of experiments have been conducted to see if it is possible to teach preoperational stage children to understand and use concrete operational schemes or to teach students in the concrete operational stage to grasp formal operational reasoning.

The main conclusion of psychologists who have analyzed and evaluated this body of research is, unfortunately, one of uncertainty (see, for example, Case, 1975; Nagy and Griffiths, 1982; Slavin, 1988; Sprinthall and Sprinthall, 1987). Because of shortcomings in the way some studies were carried out and disagreements about what constitutes evidence of true concrete operational or formal operational thinking, a decisive answer to this question is just not available. Still, something of value can be gleaned from the research on cognitive acceleration. In a useful analysis, Norman and Richard Sprinthall (1987) concluded that children who are *in the process of developing the schemes* that will govern the next stage of cognitive functioning can, with good quality instruction, be helped to refine those schemes a bit faster than would normally be the case. For example, the principle of conservation can be taught by using simple explanations and concrete materials, and allowing children to manipulate the materials. This means that teachers should nurture the process of cognitive growth at any particular stage by presenting lessons in a form that is consistent with but slightly more advanced than the student's existing schemes. The objective here is to help the student assimilate and accommodate new and different experiences as efficiently as possible.

> **Instruction can accelerate development of schemes that have begun to form**

Educational Implications of Piaget's Theory

Some specific educational implications of Piaget's theory are noted in the following sections. The implications are arranged with reference to different grade levels.

Preschool, Kindergarten, Primary Grades   Preschool and kindergarten children (and most first- and some second-graders as well) are at the *preoperational level.* They are capable of using symbols to stand for objects, which makes mental manipulation possible. Their use of language is egocentric, however. Words often have different meanings for different children, and most kindergartners are not able to take into account the fact that other people have different points of view. During the preoperational period, the child gradually becomes capable of **decentration,** thinking of more than one quality at a time.

In order to grasp the fact that the language and thought of the preoperational child are qualitatively different from your own, you might ask kindergarten pupils to explain more fully what they mean by certain words—particularly if you are a bit baffled by their statements. To gain insight into the impact of lack of ability to decenter, try some of Piaget's simple experiments with individual pupils. (Detailed instructions are provided in the Suggestions for Further Study at the end of this chapter.) As background for your experiments, you should bear in mind that children typically go through a three-stage process in their understanding of any aspect of conservation: At first, they simply do not grasp the concept. Then they pass through a transition period in which they can understand it only in some situations. Finally, they grasp the idea well enough to supply correct answers in all situations involving a particular kind of conservation.

The child's earliest awareness of conservation is of mass or substance. If you show four-year-olds two clay balls of the same size and then flatten one of them as they watch, they are likely to indicate that the flattened piece of clay has greater volume. By age five most children comprehend that the mass is the same regardless of the shape, but they may reveal incomplete comprehension when faced with even a slight change of procedure. For example, if instead of flattening one of the balls, you roll it into a sausage shape, you may find yourself explaining again that the two balls have the same mass.

Grades 2 to 4   Awareness of conservation of weight typically takes place between the ages of seven and ten; complete understanding of volume, between ten and twelve. The fact that a child can understand one type of conservation but is unable to generalize to other types illustrates a key difference between concrete operations and formal operations. Below the age of twelve, most children have difficulty dealing with abstraction—hence the use of the term *concrete* to describe their operations, or mental acts. Because they are limited to dealing with actual experiences, they are unable to generalize or deal with hypothetical situations or weigh possibilities.

Grades 5 to 9   Around the fifth or sixth grade, children shift from the level of concrete operations to the stage of formal operations. Concrete operations require reasoning, as illustrated by the solving of conservation problems, but children's thinking at this stage is still tied to direct experience. Even though children at this age may no longer have to manipulate objects in order to understand relationships among them, their thinking is limited to actual experiences. In areas about which children have acquired no direct knowledge, they reason by analogy to something they *have* experienced.

When they reach the stage of formal operations, however, students can construct theories and make logical deductions about their consequences without having had previous direct experience with the subject. They can deal with abstractions and mentally explore similarities and differences because they have mastered reversibility and decentration. They can think their way through new problems, moving forward and backward and taking into account as many or as few qualities as seem relevant.

If you plan to teach any grade from fifth through ninth, you should keep in mind the differences between concrete and formal operations. It is likely that your students will sometimes function one way, sometimes another. Consequently, it would be well to give *all* your students plenty of opportunities to explain their thoughts, particularly with regard to abstractions, so that you can discern and take into account the level of awareness they have reached on various ideas.

When children reach the point of being able to make some consistent generalizations, they are capable of formal thought. Incomplete grasp of this kind of thinking is revealed by the way they set about solving problems. If asked to explain how to predict what will happen if objects of varying sizes and weights are placed on a balance, eleven-year-olds are likely to proceed in a disorganized manner. They may make wild guesses before they begin to experiment and may then engage in haphazard trial and error in searching for a solution. Not until they have gained sufficient experience with formal thought will they be able to plan mentally a systematic approach to solving the problem. Only after a considerable amount of experience will they be able to carry out a plan evolved entirely in their minds and accurately predict the results before they actually balance objects.

High School Grades   Some interpreters of Piaget note that a significant aspect of formal thought is that it causes the adolescent to concentrate more on possibilities than on realities (for example, see Ginsburg and Opper, 1988). (This is the ability that Erikson suggests leads to problems at the stage of identity vs. role confusion. When older adolescents can anticipate the results of a decision to prepare for a particular job and imagine what it might be like to be employed, they may feel so threatened and confused that they postpone the final choice. On the other hand, young people who try to weigh all the possibilities available may find it difficult to choose among them.)

While mastery of formal thought equips the older adolescent with impressive intellectual skills, it may contribute to role confusion. It may also lead to a tendency for the burgeoning formal thinker to become preoccupied with abstract and theoretical matters. Herbert Ginsburg and Sylvia Opper interpret some of Piaget's observations on this point in this way:

> In the intellectual sphere, the adolescent has a tendency to become involved in abstract and theoretical matters, constructing elaborate political theories or inventing complex philosophical doctrines. The adolescent may develop plans for the complete reorganization of society or indulge in metaphysical speculation. After discovering capabilities for abstract thought, he then proceeds to exercise them without restraint. Indeed, in the process of exploring these new abilities the adolescent sometimes loses touch with reality and feels that he can accomplish everything by thought alone. In the emotional sphere the adolescent now becomes capable of directing emotions at abstract ideals and not just toward people. Whereas earlier the adoles-

cent could love his mother or hate a peer, now he can love freedom or hate exploitation. The adolescent has developed a new mode of life: the possible and the ideal captivate both mind and feeling. (1988, pp. 202–203)

David Elkind (1968) suggests that unrestrained theorizing about ideals without complete understanding of realities tends to make the young adolescent a militant rebel with little patience for parents or other adults who fail to find quick solutions to personal, social, and other problems. Only when the older adolescent begins to grasp the complexities of interpersonal relationships and of social and economic problems does more tempered understanding appear. Elkind also suggests that the egocentrism of early childhood, which gives way to socialized speech and thought at the end of the elementary grades, reappears in a different form as **adolescent egocentrism.** This occurs when high school students turn their new powers of thought upon themselves and become introspective. The strong tendency to analyze self is projected upon others. This helps explain why adolescents are so self-conscious: They assume their thoughts and actions are as central to others as to themselves. The major difference between the egocentrism of childhood and of adolescence is summed up in Elkind's observation: "The child is egocentric in the sense that he is unable to take another person's point of view. The adolescent, on the other hand, takes the other person's point of view to an extreme degree" (1968, p. 153).

> **Adolescent egocentrism: one's thoughts and actions are as central to others as to oneself**

Elkind believes that adolescent egocentrism also explains why the peer group becomes such a potent force in high school. He observes:

Adolescent egocentrism . . . accounts, in part, for the power of the peer group during this period. The adolescent is so concerned with the reactions of others toward him, particularly his peers, that he is willing to do many things which are opposed to all of his previous training and to his own best interests. At the same time, this egocentric impression that he is always on stage may help to account for the many and varied adolescent attention-getting maneuvers. . . .

Toward the end of adolescence, this form of exploitative egocentrism gradually declines. The young person comes to realize that other people are much more concerned with themselves and their problems than they are with him and his problems. (1968, p. 154)

Criticisms of Piaget's Theory

Among the thousand and more articles that have been published in response to Piaget's findings are many that offer critiques of his work. Some psychologists argue that Piaget underestimated children's abilities, not only because of stringent criteria he imposed for inferring the presence of particular cognitive abilities, but also because the tasks he used were often complex and far removed from children's real-life experiences. The term *preoperational,* for instance, stresses what is

> **Piaget's theory underestimates children's abilities**

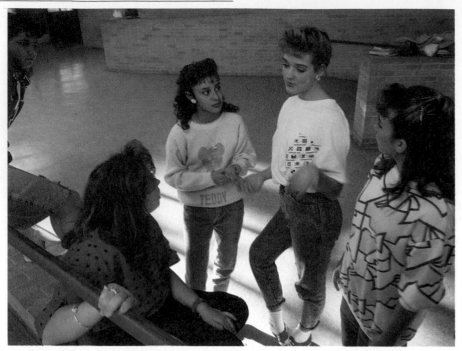

Adolescent egocentrism refers to the tendency for adolescents to be extremely concerned about the reactions of others to the point that they feel they are "always on stage." (Bob Daemmrich/The Image Works)

absent rather than what is present. Within the last decade researchers have focused more on what preoperational children *can* do. Their results (summarized by Gelman and Baillargeon, 1983) suggest that preschoolers' cognitive abilities are more advanced in some areas than Piaget's work suggested.

There is evidence that Piaget may overestimate the formal thinking capabilities of adolescents. Research summarized by Constance Kamii (1984) reveals that only 20 to 25 percent of college freshmen are able to consistently use formal operational reasoning. Epstein (1980) found that among a group of ninth-graders, 32 percent were just beginning the concrete operational stage, 43 percent were well within the concrete operational stage, 15 percent were just entering the formal operational stage, and only 9 percent were mature formal operators. Sprinthall and Sprinthall (1987) report that only 33 percent of a group of high school seniors could apply formal operational reasoning to scientific problem solving. Formal reasoning seems to be the exception, not the rule, throughout adolescence.

Finally, there is fairly widespread agreement that Piaget's case for four *distinct* cognitive stages has been weakened by empirical studies (for example, see Brainerd, 1978; Flavell, 1982; Gelman and Baillargeon, 1983). Despite these criticisms of Piaget's work, you are still likely to find that you will better understand at least some aspects of the thinking of your students if you refer to his observations when you plan lessons.

Most adolescents are not formal operational thinkers

Now that you are familiar with Piaget's theory, you can formulate specific classroom applications. You might use the suggestions offered for the grade level you expect to teach as the basis for a section in your Handbook.

SUGGESTIONS FOR TEACHING

Applying Piaget's Theory in the Classroom

Preschool and Elementary Grades*

Handbook Heading: Ways to Apply Piaget's Theory (Preschool and Elementary Grades)

1. Become thoroughly familiar with Piaget's theory so that you will be aware of how your students organize and synthesize ideas. You may gain extra insight if you analyze your own thinking, since you are likely to discover that in some situations you operate at a concrete rather than at an abstract level.

2. If possible, assess the level and the type of thinking of each child in your class. Ask individual children to perform some of Piaget's experiments and spend most of your time listening to each child explain her or his reactions.

3. Remember that learning through activity and direct experience is essential. Provide plenty of materials and opportunities for children to learn on their own.

4. Arrange situations to permit social interaction, so that children can learn from one another. Hearing others explain their views is a natural way to learn that not everyone sees things the same way. To facilitate this, placing some advanced thinkers with less mature thinkers seems preferable to homogeneous grouping.

5. Plan learning experiences to take into account the level of thinking attained by an individual or group. Encourage children to classify things on the basis of a single attribute before you expose them to problems that involve relationships among two or more attributes. Ask many questions and give your students many opportunities to explain their interpretations of experiences so you remain aware of their level of thinking.

6. Keep in mind the possibility that pupils may be influenced by egocentric speech and thought. Allow for the possibility that each child may as-

* Many of these suggestions are derived from points made in Chapter 7 of *Young Children's Thinking* (Almy, Chittenden, and Miller, 1966).

sume that everyone else has the same conception of a word he or she has. If confusion becomes apparent or if a child becomes impatient about failure to communicate, request an explanation in different terms. Or ask several children to explain their conception of an object or situation.

Secondary Grades

Handbook Heading: Ways to Apply Piaget's Theory (Preschool and Elementary Grades)

1. Become well acquainted with the nature of concrete operational thinking and formal thought so that you can recognize when your students resort to either type or to a combination of the two.

2. To become aware of the type of thinking used by individual students, ask them to explain how they arrived at solutions to problems. Do this either as part of your classroom curriculum or in response to experimental situations similar to those devised by Piaget. (Sample problems are described in the Suggestions for Further Study at the end of this chapter.)

3. Teach students how to solve problems more systematically. (Suggestions for doing this are provided in Chapters 8 and 9.)

4. Keep in mind that some high school students may be more interested in possibilities than realities. If class discussions become unrealistically theoretical and hypothetical, call attention to facts and practical difficulties. If students are contemptuous of unsuccessful attempts by adults to solve school, local, national, and international problems, point out the complexity of many situations involving conflict of interests, perhaps by summarizing arguments from both sides.

5. Allow for the possibility that younger adolescents may go through a period of egocentrism that will cause them to act as if they are always on stage and to be extremely concerned about the reactions of peers.

Piaget and Kohlberg: Moral Development

Piaget's Analysis of the Moral Judgment of the Child

Because he was intrigued by *all* aspects of children's thinking, Piaget became interested in moral development. He began his study of morality by observing how children played marbles. (He first took the trouble to learn the game himself, so that he would be able to understand the subtleties of the conception.) Piaget discovered that interpretations of rules followed by participants in marble games changed with age.

Age Changes in Interpretation of Rules   Four- to seven-year-olds just learning the game seemed to view rules as interesting examples of the social behavior of older children. They did not understand them but tried to go along with them. Seven- to ten-year-olds regarded rules as sacred pronouncements handed down by older children or adults. At about the age of eleven or twelve, children began to see rules as agreements reached by mutual consent. Piaget concluded that younger children see rules as absolute and external.

Even though children from the age of four to about ten do not question rules, they may frequently break them because they do not understand them completely. After the age of eleven or so, children become increasingly capable of grasping why rules are necessary. At that point, Piaget concluded, they tend to lose interest in adult-imposed regulations and take delight in formulating their own variations of rules to fit a particular situation. Piaget illustrates this point by describing how a group of ten- and eleven-year-old boys prepared for a snowball fight (1962, p. 50). They divided themselves into teams, elected officers, decided on rules to govern the distances from which the snowballs could be thrown, and agreed on a system of punishments for those who violated the rules. Even though they wasted a substantial amount of playtime engaging in such preliminary discussions, they seemed to thoroughly enjoy their newly discovered ability to make up rules to supplant those that had previously been imposed on them by their elders.

Reactions to Stories Involving Moral Decisions   The way children of different ages responded to rules so intrigued Piaget that he decided to use the interview method to obtain more systematic information about moral development. He made up pairs of stories and asked children of different ages to discuss them. Here is a typical pair of stories:

> There was a little boy called Julian. His father had gone out and Julian thought it would be fun to play with father's ink-pot. First he played with the pen, and then he made a little blot on the table cloth.
>   A little boy who was called Augustus once noticed that his father's ink-pot was empty. One day that his father was away he thought of filling the ink-pot so as to help his father, and so that he should find it full when he came home. But while he was opening the ink-bottle he made a big blot on the table cloth. (1948, p. 118)

After reading these stories, Piaget asked, "Are these children equally guilty? Which of the two is naughtiest, and why?" As was the case with interpretations of rules, Piaget found that younger children reacted to these stories differently from older children. (We describe these differences below.) Piaget concluded that the way six-year-olds interpreted rules and the answers they gave when confronted with the pairs of stories that their moral reasoning is quite different from that of twelve-year-olds.

Piaget refers to the moral thinking of children up to the age of ten or so as **morality of constraint,** but he also calls it *moral realism* or *heteronomous morality.* (*Heteros* is Greek for "other"; *nomos* is Greek for "law." Therefore, *heteronomous* means "subject to external rules or laws.") The thinking of children of eleven or older Piaget calls the **morality of cooperation.** The terms *autonomous morality, morality of reciprocity, moral relativism,* and *moral flexibility* are sometimes also used. After analyzing the responses of elementary school children in clinical interviews, Piaget concluded that the two basic types of moral reasoning differ in several ways. We summarize these differences in Table 2.2. To clarify and illustrate some of the differences between the moralities of constraint and cooperation summarized in the table, here are some examples and explanations of types of thinking that characterize the thinking of moral realists (that is, those who use the morality of constraint).

Moral realism: sacred rules, no exceptions, no allowance for intentions, consequences determine guilt

The Nature of the Morality of Constraint (or Moral Realism)   The younger child sees rules as *real*—ready-made and external. Because rules are imposed by outside authority, it is assumed they should always be obeyed the same way. The letter, not the spirit, of the law must be observed, and no exceptions are allowed. Reactions of younger and older children to a change in rules illustrate these characteristics of moral realism. Several elementary school children were playing baseball in a vacant lot bordered by weeds. One excellent hitter decided to get some additional batting practice by deliberately hitting several foul balls in a row. Each time a ball was hit foul, however, it took quite a bit of time to find it in the weeds. Accordingly, some of the older children proposed that anyone who hit two foul balls in a row was out. Most of the players agreed, but the youngest child in the group was so upset by this change in the official rules of baseball that he refused to play and went home in a huff. The moral realist thinks literally and in terms of blind obedience—making no allowance for motives or intentions. Furthermore, the degree of guilt is equated with the seriousness of the consequences. These characteristics of moral realism are illustrated by children's responses to the inkblot stories. Younger children interviewed by Piaget maintained that Augustus was more guilty than Julian because he had made a bigger blot. They took no account of the fact that Julian was misbehaving and that Augustus was trying to help his father.

Many aspects of these differences in the moral reasoning of younger and older children can be understood by taking into account Piaget's descriptions of cognitive development. The child of six who has not completely mastered decentration tends to think of only one thing at a time and is therefore not inclined to weigh alternatives. Before the age of seven, a child who has not made the transition from

Table 2.2 Morality of Constraint vs. Morality of Cooperation

Morality of Constraint (Typical of Six-year-olds)	Morality of Cooperation (Typical of Twelve-year-olds)
Holds single, absolute moral perspective (behavior is right or wrong)	Is aware of different viewpoints regarding rules
Believes rules are unchangeable	Believes rules are flexible
Determines extent of guilt by amount of damage	Considers the wrongdoer's intentions when evaluating guilt
Defines moral wrongness in terms of what is forbidden or punished	Defines moral wrongness in terms of violation of spirit of cooperation
(Notice that these first four differences call attention to the tendency for children below the age of ten or so to think of rules as sacred pronouncements handed down by external authority.)	
Believes punishment should stress atonement and does not need to "fit the crime"	Believes punishment should involve either restitution or suffering the same fate as one's victim
Believes peer aggression should be punished by an external authority	Believes peer aggression should be punished by retaliatory behavior on the part of the victim*
Believes children should obey because rules are established by those in authority	Believes children should obey rules because of mutual concern for rights of others
(Notice how these last three differences call attention to the tendency for children above the age of ten or so to see rules as mutual agreements among equals.)	

Moral relativism: rules are flexible, intent important in determining guilt

* Beyond the age of twelve, adolescents increasingly affirm that reciprocal reactions, or "getting back," should be a response to good behavior, not bad.

SOURCES: Freely adapted from interpretations of Piaget (1932) by Kohlberg (1969) and Lickona (1976).

egocentric to socialized speech finds it difficult to consider different points of view. And a child who has not moved from concrete operational to formal thought is unable to consider hypothetical situations and anticipate consequences. Because of the tendency to think of one thing at a time, the young child finds it difficult to comprehend situations where a rule might be revised to allow for special circumstances. The same tendency leads the younger child to reason that a big inkblot, regardless of how it is caused, is worse than a small inkblot. The younger child concentrates on obvious physical properties and does not take into account nonobservable factors, such as intentions.

Kohlberg's Description of Moral Development

Just as James Marcia elaborated Erikson's concept of identity formation, Lawrence Kohlberg has elaborated Piaget's ideas of types of moral thinking.

Kohlberg's Use of Moral Dilemmas   As a graduate student at the University of Chicago in the 1950s, Lawrence Kohlberg became fascinated by Piaget's studies of moral development. He decided to expand on Piaget's original research by making up stories involving moral dilemmas that would be more appropriate for older children. Here is the story that is most often mentioned in discussions of his work:

> In Europe a woman was near death from cancer. One drug might save her, a form of radium that a druggist in the same town had recently discovered. The druggist was charging $2,000, ten times what the drug cost him to make. The sick woman's husband, Heinz, went to everyone he knew to borrow the money, but he could only get together about half of what it cost. He told the druggist that his wife was dying and asked him to sell it cheaper or let him pay later, but the druggist said "No." The husband got desperate and broke into the man's store to steal the drug for his wife. Should the husband have done that? Why? (Kohlberg, 1969, p. 376)

Kohlberg's Six Stages of Moral Reasoning   After analyzing the responses of ten- to sixteen-year-olds to this and similar moral dilemmas, Kohlberg (1963) eventually developed a description of six stages of moral reasoning. Be forewarned, however, that Kohlberg has revised some of his original stage designations, and descriptions of the stages have been modified since he first proposed them. In different discussions of his stages, therefore, you may encounter varying descriptions. The outline presented in Table 2.3 is a composite summary of the sequence of moral development as it has been described by Kohlberg, but you should expect to find differences if you read other accounts of his theory.

The scoring system Kohlberg developed to evaluate a given response to a moral dilemma is extremely complex. Furthermore, the responses of subjects are lengthy and may feature arguments about a particular decision. To help you understand a bit more about each Kohlberg stage, simplified examples of responses to a dilemma such as that faced by Heinz are noted below. For maximum clarity, only brief typical responses to the question "Why shouldn't you steal from a store?" are mentioned.

Stage 1 Punishment-obedience orientation. "You might get caught." (The physical consequences of an action determine goodness or badness.)

Stage 2 Instrumental relativist orientation. "You shouldn't steal something from a store, and the store owner shouldn't steal things that belong to you." (Obeying laws should involve an even exchange.)

Table 2.3   Kohlberg's Stages of Moral Reasoning

Level 1 Preconventional Morality. (Typical of children up to the age of nine. Called *preconventional* because young children do not really understand the conventions or rules of a society.)

Stage 1 Punishment-Obedience Orientation. The physical consequences of an action determine goodness or badness. Those in authority have superior power and should be obeyed. Punishment should be avoided by staying out of trouble.

Stage 2 Instrumental Relativist Orientation. An action is judged to be right if it is instrumental in satisfying one's own needs or involves an even exchange. Obeying rules should bring some sort of benefit in return.

Level 2 Conventional Morality. (Typical of nine- to twenty-year-olds. Called *conventional* since most nine- to twenty-year-olds conform to the conventions of society because they *are* the rules of a society.)

Stage 3 Good Boy–Nice Girl Orientation. The right action is one that would be carried out by someone whose behavior is likely to please or impress others.

Stage 4 Law and Order Orientation. To maintain the social order, fixed rules must be established and obeyed. It is essential to respect authority.

Level 3 Postconventional Morality. (Usually reached only after the age of twenty and only by a small proportion of adults. Called *postconventional* because the moral principles that underlie the conventions of a society are understood.)

Stage 5 Social Contract Orientation. Rules needed to maintain the social order should be based, not on blind obedience to authority, but on mutual agreement. At the same time, the rights of the individual should be protected.

Stage 6 Universal Ethical Principle Orientation. Moral decisions should be made in terms of self-chosen ethical principles. Once principles are chosen, they should be applied in consistent ways.*

Preconventional morality: avoid punishment, receive benefits in return

Conventional morality: impress others, respect authority

Postconventional morality: mutual agreements, consistent principles

* In an article published in 1978, several years after he originally described the six stages, Kohlberg indicated that he had concluded that the last stage is essentially a theoretical ideal and is rarely encountered in real life.

SOURCE: Based on descriptions in Kohlberg (1969, 1976).

Stage 3 Good boy–nice girl orientation. "Your parents will be proud of you if you are honest." (The right action is one that will impress others.)

Stage 4 Law and order orientation. "It's against the law, and if we don't obey laws our whole society might fall apart." (To maintain the social order, fixed rules must be obeyed.)

Stage 5 Social contract orientation. "Under certain circumstances laws may have to be disregarded—if a person's life depends on breaking a law, for instance." (Rules should involve mutual agreements; the rights of the individual should be protected.)

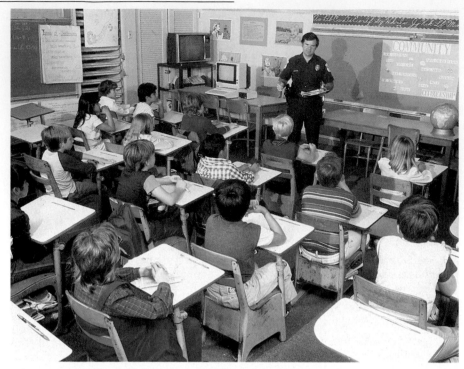

Primary grade children are at the level of preconventional morality as described by Kohlberg. They are likely to obey rules to stay out of trouble or to gain some sort of benefit in return. (Edward Slater/Southern Stock Photos)

Stage 6 Universal ethical principle orientation. "You need to weigh all the factors and then try to make the most appropriate decision in a given situation. Sometimes it would be morally wrong *not* to steal." (Moral decisions should be based on consistent applications of self-chosen ethical principles.)

Similarities and Differences Between Piaget and Kohlberg As you examined this list of stages and the examples of responses at each stage, you may have detected similarities between Piaget's and Kohlberg's descriptions of age changes in moral development. The first four of Kohlberg's stages are roughly equivalent to moral realism as described by Piaget. Kohlberg's preconventional and conventional moral thinkers and Piaget's moral realists all tend to think of rules as edicts handed down by external authority. The letter of the law is observed, and not much allowance is made for intentions or circumstances. The postconventional thinker of Kohlberg shares some similarities with the older children observed by Piaget: Rules are established by individuals who come to mutual agreement, and each moral decision is made by taking into account special circumstances.

While there are similarities in the conclusions drawn by Piaget and Kohlberg, there are also important differences. Piaget believes that moral thinking changes as children mature. He does not, however, believe that the changes are clearly related to specific ages, nor are they considered to be sequential. Piaget feels that the different types of moral thinking he describes often overlap and that a child might sometimes function as moral realist, sometimes as a more mature moral decision maker. Kohlberg (1969), by contrast, maintains that the order of the stages he has described is universal and fixed and that a person moves through the stages in sequence. Not everyone reaches the top stages, but all individuals begin at Stage 1 and work their way upward.

Another difference concerns the acceleration of moral reasoning. Piaget believes that children in the preoperational and concrete operational stages cannot be helped to understand the logic behind moral relativism until the elements of formal operational schemes have begun to form. Kohlberg, on the other hand, believes that progress through his six stages can be accelerated with the proper type of instruction.

In some respects, there are greater similarities between Piaget's description of *cognitive* development and Kohlberg's description of *moral* development than between the two outlines of moral development. Piaget describes preoperational, concrete operational, and formal operational stages. Kohlberg describes preconventional, conventional, and postconventional levels. Even though he does not stress an orderly sequence of *moral* development, Piaget does believe that children go through the stages of *cognitive* development in definite order. Piaget's formal operational stage and Kohlberg's postconventional level both stress understanding and application of abstract principles and taking into account unique circumstances in a given situation. A person cannot engage in postconventional moral reasoning, in fact, until formal thinking has been mastered.

Criticisms and Evaluations of Kohlberg's Theory

Is Kohlberg's contention that moral reasoning proceeds through a fixed universal sequence of stages accurate? Based on his analysis of research on moral development, Martin Hoffman (1980) feels that although Kohlberg's sequence of stages may not be true of every individual in every culture, it may provide a useful general description of how moral reasoning develops in American society. Carol Gilligan (1979), whose position we discuss in detail shortly, has proposed two somewhat different sequences that reflect differences in male and female socialization.

What about Kohlberg's view that moral development can be accelerated through direct instruction? Is this another "mission impossible" as some critics contend? Research on this question has produced some limited but moderately positive results. Most of these studies have used a teaching method known as *direct discussion* or *dilemma discussion.* After reading a set of moral dilemmas (like the one about Heinz and the cancer drug) and identifying those issues that could help resolve the dilemma, students, under the teacher's guidance, discuss the different ways each of them chose to resolve the dilemma. This can involve challenging one another's thinking, reexamining assumptions, building lines of argument, and responding to counterarguments.

Alan Lockwood (1979) summarized the findings of almost a dozen studies on acceleration of moral reasoning and concluded that the strongest effects (about half-a-stage increase in reasoning) occurred among individuals whose reasoning reflected Stages 2 and 3. The effect of the treatment varied considerably from one subject to another. Some individuals showed substantial increases in reasoning; others showed no change. A more recent and comprehensive review of research on this topic by Andre Schlaefli, James Rest, and Stephen Thoma (1985) came to similar conclusions. The authors found that moral education programs produce modest positive effects. They also found that the strongest effects are obtained with adult subjects.

Kohlberg's theory, like Erikson's, has been criticized for reflecting a male bias. Gilligan (1979) describes three aspects of Kohlberg's work that make it suscepti-ble to the charge of gender bias: (1) The six stages were derived from a longitu-dinal study of eighty-four boys; (2) the moral dilemmas that are used to assess level of moral development revolve around the concepts of justice, fairness, and the preservation of individual rights; and (3) these concepts are reflected most strongly in the postconventional level of morality. Gilligan argues that because females are socialized to focus more on understanding, helping, and cooperating with others than on preserving individual rights, and because this orientation is reflected most strongly in the two conventional stages, they are more likely than males to be judged deficient in moral development. As Gilligan puts it, "While Kohlberg's subject worries about people interfering with one another's rights, this woman (Gilligan's subject) worries about 'the possibility of omission, of your not helping others when you could help them' " (1979, p. 444).

Stephen Thoma (1986) offers a partial answer to Gilligan's criticism. After re-viewing over fifty studies on gender differences in moral development, he drew three conclusions. First, the effect of gender on scores from the Defining Issues Test (the DIT is a device that uses responses to moral dilemmas to determine level of moral reasoning) was very small. Less than half of 1 percent of the differences in DIT scores was due to gender differences. Second, females almost always scored higher. This slight superiority for females appeared in every age group studied (junior high, high school, college, adults). Third, differences in DIT scores were strongly associated with differences in age and level of education. That is, in-dividuals who were older and who had graduated from college were more likely to score at the postconventional level than those who were younger and who had less education. Thoma's findings suggest that females are just as capable as males of using justice and fairness concepts in their reasoning about hypothetical moral dilemmas.

But there is one aspect of Gilligan's criticism that cannot be answered by Thoma's analysis of existing research. She argues that when females are faced with their own real-life moral dilemmas (abortion, civil rights, environmental

> Moral education programs may pro-duce modest acceleration in moral development

pollution), they are more likely to favor a caring/helping/cooperation orientation than a justice/fairness/individual rights orientation. Perhaps the best approach that educators can take when they involve students in discussions of moral issues is to emphasize the utility of both orientations.

Males and females may use different approaches to resolving real-life moral dilemmas

Educational Implications of Kohlberg's Theory

In the 1970s, Kohlberg experimented with the use of discussion techniques to "teach" moral reasoning. An interesting outgrowth of that work (for example, see Blatt and Kohlberg, 1978) and his observations in 1969 of life on an Israeli kibbutz is the *just community,* an approach that brings students and teachers together to settle their own problems and make their own rules on a one-person, one-vote basis. [In addition, students and teachers discussed how to handle immoral and illegal actions (for example, the theft of stereo equipment from a camp where students had gone for an outing).] While the just community approach seems to have met with some success (for example, see Kohlberg, 1978; Power, 1981, 1985), it is useful only when a school system agrees to give students the time and power to make many of their own decisions about school rules and interpersonal relationships. It does not seem likely at the present time that many school boards would be willing to agree to those terms. Perhaps this is why the concept has been tried in only a few, relatively small alternative schools. Another problem with the just community has to do with the nature of participatory democracy. As soon as more than a few people become involved, participatory democracy becomes unwieldy. Piaget drew attention to this point when he described how a small group of ten-year-old boys spent as much time agreeing on rules to govern a snowball fight as they did actually playing. While rule making may be enjoyable when it is a novelty, those who have been involved in a participatory democracy for very long are likely to confess that they sometimes wish an external authority would simply tell them what the rules are so that they can go about their business. Furthermore, comparatively few laws or punishments in adult life are "negotiable" through group discussion. Small groups of citizens do not get together to discuss how tax laws should be established and enforced, for example, nor do they debate what should be done to those who break such laws. Most laws in our society are established by elected representatives, and they are enforced by the police and the courts.

Because of these potential weaknesses of the just community approach, teachers may find that other techniques of moral instruction based on Kohlberg's theory will be more workable. *Moral Reasoning* (1976) by Ronald Galbraith and Thomas Jones (subtitled "A Teaching Handbook for Adapting Kohlberg to the Classroom") presents several realistic moral dilemmas. In addition, teachers are advised how they might encourage students to write their own moral dilemmas. Both types of dilemmas can be used to stimulate thought and discussion. Richard Hersh, Diana Paolitto, and Joseph Reimer (1979) have developed techniques of

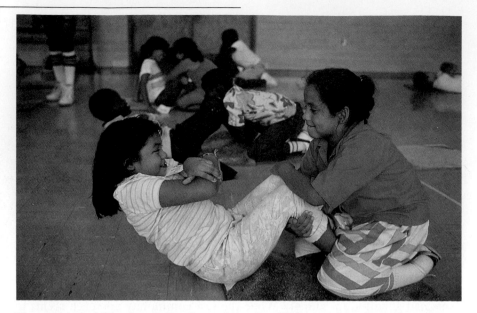

Hartshorne and May found that the tendency for children to cheat depends on the situation. A child who is a good athlete but a poor speller might be honest when taking a physical fitness test but dishonest when taking a social studies test. (Above: Bob Daemmrich/Stock, Boston. Facing page: Bob Daemmrich)

moral education based on the observations of Piaget and Kohlberg that are more elaborate and sophisticated variations of the basic approach recommended by Hugh Hartshorne and Mark May in the 1930s. Hartshorne and May (1930a, p. 413) recommended that teachers promote discussions of actual situations in detail so that children who found themselves in similar situations would recognize commonalities and be helped to choose a desirable course of action. Hersh, Paolitto, and Reimer recommend to teachers procedures for implementing what they refer to as developmental moral education. If, for some reason, these sources are not available, but you would still like to occasionally engage your students in a discussion of a moral dilemma, the daily newspaper is an excellent source of material. Biology teachers, for example, can point to stories of the conflicts produced by machines that keep comatose patients alive or by medical practices based on genetic engineering. Science teachers might bring in articles that describe the moral dilemma produced by the debate over nuclear power versus fossil fuel. Civics or government teachers could use news items that reflect the dilemma that arises when freedom of speech conflicts with the need to protect national security.

Does Moral Thinking Lead to Moral Behavior?

Piaget's description of cognitive development and Kohlberg's theory of moral development shed light on the results of an exhaustive series of studies of morality

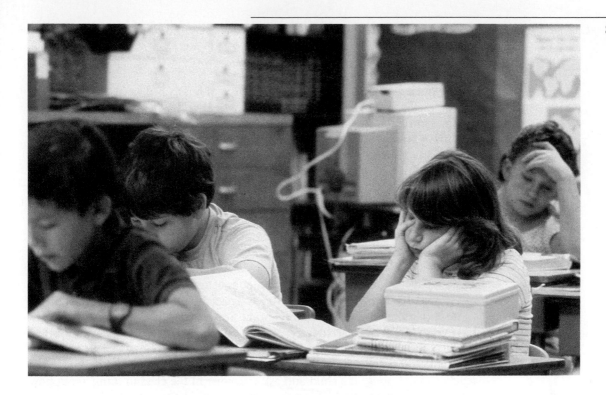

supervised by Hartshorne and May (1929, 1930a, 1930b). They observed thousands of children at different age levels reacting in situations that revealed their actual moral behavior. They also asked the children to respond to questions about hypothetical situations, to reveal how much they understood about right and wrong behavior. Elementary school children, for example, were allowed to correct their own papers or record their own scores on measures of athletic skill without being aware that accurate measures were being made independently by adult observers. The children were also asked what they *thought* was the right thing to do in similar situations. A comparison of the two sets of data made it possible to determine, among other things, if children practiced what they preached. Hartshorne and May wanted information about these two aspects of moral development to discover if the immoral behavior of young children was due to ignorance. They discovered, however, that many children who were able to describe right kinds of behavior in hypothetical situations indulged in wrong behavior in real-life situations.

One significant discovery of Hartshorne and May was that children react in specific, rather than consistent, ways to situations that call for moral judgment. Even a child who was rated as among the most honest in a group would behave in a dishonest way under certain circumstances. A boy who was an excellent student but an indifferent athlete, for example, would not cheat when asked to correct his own paper, but he *would* inflate scores on sports skills. A girl who was an excellent

Moral behavior depends on circumstances

athlete but a terrible speller would alter dozens of misspelled words on a paper but be completely accurate in recording her physical performance.

Another significant, and dismaying, discovery of Hartshorne and May was that children who went to Sunday school or who belonged to such organizations as the Boy Scouts or Girl Scouts were just as dishonest as children who were not exposed to the kind of moral instruction provided by such organizations. Hartshorne and May concluded that one explanation for the ineffectiveness of moral instruction in the 1920s was that too much stress was placed on having children memorize platitudes such as the Ten Commandments or the Boy Scout oath and law. They suggested that many children who could recite "Thou shalt not steal" or who could unhesitatingly reel off "Trustworthy, loyal, helpful, friendly, courteous, kind, obedient, cheerful, thrifty, brave, clean, and reverent" either did not understand what they were saying or saw no connection between such elegant words and actual deeds. Hartshorne and May suggested that it would be more effective to invite children to discuss real-life moral situations as they occurred. Instead of having children chant "Honesty is the best policy," for example, they urged teachers to call attention to the positive consequences of honest acts. If a pupil in a school reported that he or she has found money belonging to someone else, the teacher might praise the child and ask everyone in the class to think about how relieved the person who had lost the money would be to get it back.

After reviewing research carried out in the forty-five years since Hartshorne and May published their findings, Thomas Lickona reported that "a huge and ever-expanding body of research . . . has replicated Hartshorne and May's basic finding: Variations in the situation produce variations in moral behavior" (1976, p. 15). Lickona adds, though, that recent research also supports another of Hartshorne and May's conclusions: Some children are more "integrated" (or consistent) than others in reacting to moral situations. It would appear to be a mistake, therefore, to assume that there is *no* consistency in moral thinking and behavior. If that hypothesis were endorsed, there would be little reason to assume that a child develops any kind of personal code of ethics or that parents and teachers should try to promote the development of a strong conscience in children.

Piaget's description of cognitive development and Kohlberg's description of moral reasoning development help explain some of Hartshorne and May's conclusions. Elementary school children are in the concrete operational stage. They think in terms of actual experiences and treat situations that look different in different ways. Because many of these youngsters are also at Kohlberg's third stage (good boy–nice girl), their moral behavior is influenced by their eagerness to please or impress others. Thus, the inability of elementary grade children to comprehend and apply general principles in varied situations and their desire to do what they think will please or impress authority figures may explain, in part, the ineffectiveness of moral instruction that stresses the memorization of abstract principles.

SUGGESTIONS FOR TEACHING

Encouraging Moral Development

1. Recognize that younger children will respond to moral conflicts differently from older children.

2. Try to take the perspective of students and stimulate their perspective-taking abilities.

3. Develop an awareness of moral issues by using a variety of real and hypothetical moral dilemmas and by using daily opportunities in the classroom to heighten moral awareness. (Moral education should be an integral part of the curriculum; it should not take place during "moral education period.")

4. Create a classroom atmosphere that will enhance open discussion. (For example, arrange face-to-face groupings, be an accepting model, foster listening and communication skills, and encourage student-to-student interaction.)

Specific suggestions for supervising classroom discussions offered by Hersh, Paolitto, and Reimer (1979) include the following:

1. Highlight the moral issue to be discussed. (Describe a specific real or hypothetical moral dilemma.)

2. Ask "Why?" questions. (After asking students what they would do if they were faced with the moral dilemma under discussion, ask them to explain why they would act that way.)

3. Complicate the circumstances. (After students have responded to the original dilemma, mention a factor that might complicate matters, for example, if the dilemma involved a best friend.)

4. Use personal and naturalistic examples. (Invite students to put themselves in the position of individuals who are confronted by moral dilemmas described in newspapers or depicted on television.)

Before you use any techniques of moral education in your classes, it would be prudent to check with your principal. In some communities, parents have insisted that they, not teachers, should take the responsibility for moral instruction.

Suggestions for Further Study

Erikson's Description of Development

Erik Erikson's books are of considerable significance in speculating about development and education. In the first six chapters of *Childhood and Society* (2d ed., 1963), he describes how studying American Indians and observing patients in treatment led him to develop the Eight Ages of Man (described in Chapter 7). In the final chapters of this book, Erikson analyzes the lives of Hitler and Maxim Gorky with reference to his conception of development. *Identity: Youth and Crisis* (1968) features a revised description of the eight stages of development, with emphasis on identity and role confusion. Erikson comments on many aspects of his work in an interview with Richard Evans, published under the title *Dialogue with Erik Erikson* (1967). James Marcia reviews research on identity statuses in Chapter 5 (pp. 159–187) of the *Handbook of Adolescent Psychology* (1980), edited by Joseph Adelson.

Piaget's Theory of Cognitive Development

Jean Piaget has probably exerted more influence on theoretical discussions of development and on educational practices than any contemporary psychologist. Of his own books, you might wish to consult *The Language and Thought of the Child* (1952a), *The Origins of Intelligence in Children* (1952b), and *The Psychology of the Child* (1969), which was written in collaboration with Bärbel Inhelder. H. E. Gruber and J. J. Vonèche have edited *The Essential Piaget: An Interpretive Reference and Guide*, which Piaget describes in the foreword as "the best and most complete of all anthologies of my work." An inexpensive paperback that provides a biography of Piaget and an analysis of his work is *Piaget's Theory of Intellectual Development* (3d ed., 1938) by Herbert Ginsburg and Sylvia Opper. Other books about Piaget are *Piaget for Teachers* (1970) by Hans Furth, *Piaget's Theory of Cognitive and Affective Development* (4th ed., 1989) by Barry Wadsworth, *Understanding Piaget* (2d ed., 1980) by Mary Pulaski, and *Children and Adolescents: Interpretive Essays on Jean Piaget* (3d ed., 1981) by David Elkind.

Using Piaget's Interview Method to Assess Cognitive Development

Jean Piaget devised a series of simple experiments to gain insight into the thinking of children at different age levels. You can use similar experiments to determine the level of thinking of pupils in your classes. If you carry out some of the following experiments with at least some of your pupils, you may be surprised by the amount of insight you acquire. You are almost sure to become aware of ways in which your pupils' thinking differs from yours. In addition, you may understand why some approaches to teaching are—or are not—appropriate with some or all of your students. It would be to your advantage to try out these experiments now, instead of waiting until you actually begin to teach. You should be able to carry out all the experiments for any age level in a single interview of not more than thirty minutes if you have familiarized yourself with the materials ahead of time.

It is not necessary to have a private testing room. You can interview your subject in a hall, a playground, or a school area that is not in a main traffic zone.

After you complete your experiments, you might record your results and conclusions and compare your findings with those of fellow students who interviewed different children.

The experiments described on the following pages can be carried out with easily obtainable objects. You should be able to get most of the items in just one trip to a shopping center or a department, drug, or variety store. After you obtain these materials, read the descriptions in the equipment sections of the experiments you will be carrying out. These explain how you can convert your acquisitions into full-fledged experimental apparatus. Place cards and the like in clasp envelopes, and store all your materials in a cardboard box of appropriate size. You will then be equipped with a test kit of your own devising.

If you carry out any of these experiments, record the name, age, grade, and sex of your subject, and try to record as much as you can of what the pupil does and says.

Piaget Experiment 1—Classification of Objects   Approximate age and grade level: Five to seven years, kindergarten to second grade.

Purpose: To discover how the child classifies things. A child who does not grasp the concept of *class* will put together objects in a haphazard or unsystematic way; one who has partial understanding will group some similar objects but fail to group others. A child who understands the nature of classification will put together similar objects in a consistent way.

Equipment: Take some pieces of cardboard or some index cards, and draw six squares approximately 2 inches by 2 inches and six circles 2 inches in diameter. Cut along the lines, and then cut two of the squares along a diagonal line from one corner to the opposite (to form four triangles); then cut two of the circles in half. With paint, crayon, or colored pencil, color one of each shape in each of four colors.

Procedure: Place the pieces of cardboard in front of the child, and thoroughly mix them up so that they are in a random order. Then say: *Put together things that are alike—that are the same.*

Describe how the child proceeds (for example, confidently or tentatively) and what she or he does. When the child has finished, point to one group of pieces and ask: *How are these the same?* Record the child's answer.

Note: If you do not believe the child has used the same reasoning in making the other groupings, ask for the explanation for each of these as well. Point to another group of pieces and ask: *How are these the same?* Record the child's answer. Point to still another group of pieces and ask: *How are these the same?* Record the child's answer.

Piaget Experiment 2—Conservation of Number Approximate age and grade range: Five to seven years, kindergarten to second grade.

Purpose: To discover if the child grasps that the number of objects in a row remains the same even if the distance between them is changed. Children of four or so will be unable to decenter and are likely to say that a longer row has more blocks—even though they can count the blocks in both rows. Older children will be able to understand that the number is constant, even when the appearance of the blocks is changed.

Equipment: Twenty blocks, poker chips, or the equivalent.

Procedure: Place the blocks (or whatever) in front of the child, and space out eight of the blocks about an inch apart in a row. Place the remaining blocks in a pile close to the child. Then say: *Can you count the blocks? How many are there?* Point to the blocks you have arranged in a row. If the child can't count them accurately, give assistance. Then say: *Now take as many of these blocks as you need to make the same number.* Give assistance if necessary.

Describe how the child proceeds.

Next, take the blocks in the row nearest you, and space them about 3 inches apart. Take the leftover blocks and place in a row about 1 inch apart. Point to the longer row, and say: *Let's say these are my blocks.* Point to the short row and say: *And these are your blocks. Do I have more blocks, or do you have more blocks, or do we have the same?* Record the child's response.

Then ask: *Why do you think so?* Record the child's response.

Finally, take the blocks that were spaced 3 inches apart and move them so that they are 1 inch apart, just below the other row. Then say: *Now, do you have more blocks, or do I have more blocks, or do we have the same?*

Note the child's response and reactions (surprise, confusion, no outward appearance of being bothered).

Piaget Experiment 3—Conservation of Space Approximate age and grade range: Five to seven years, kindergarten to second grade.

Purpose: To discover how the child handles a different situation involving conservation. A child who is able to handle the problem presented in Experiment 2 may encounter difficulty when confronted with the same basic problem presented in a different form. In solving the problem in Experiment 2, the child must grasp the fact that the number of blocks stays the same even though the space between them is changed. In this experiment the child must understand that four blocks placed on pieces of paper of equal size take up the same amount of space, even though they are arranged differently.

Equipment: Eight small blocks, poker chips, or the equivalent; two pieces of paper or cardboard at last 8½ by 11 inches.

Procedure: Place the two pieces of paper in front of the child and arrange the blocks in a pile to one side. Say: *Let's pretend these are fields owned by two farmers. They are exactly the same size, and both farmers have the same amount of space for their cows to graze in. One farmer decides to build a barn* (you might say "silo" if you use poker chips) *on his field, and we will make believe this is his barn.* (Take one of the blocks and place it near one corner of one piece of paper.) *The other farmer builds a barn on her field, too.* (Put a block on the other piece of paper in the same position as that on the first.) *Do they still have the same amount of space for their cows to graze in?* Record the child's response.

Then say: *Now let's suppose that both farmers make a lot of money and build three more barns. One farmer builds his barns this way* (place three blocks right next to the block already on one sheet of paper), *the other builds her barns this way* (place three blocks several inches apart at different places on the other piece of paper). *Do they still have the same amount of space for their cows to graze in, or does one farmer have more open land than the other?* Record the child's response.

Then ask: *Why do you think so?* Record the child's response.

Finally, take the blocks that were scattered, and place them together so that both sets of blocks are arranged in exactly the same way on each piece of paper. Then ask: *Now, does each farmer have the same amount of space for cows to graze in, or does one have more open land than the other?*

Note the child's response and reactions.

Piaget Experiment 4—Conservation of Continuous Quantity Approximate age and grade range: Five to seven years, kindergarten to second grade.

Purpose: To discover if a child who can understand conservation of number can also grasp conservation of quantity. A child at the level of concrete operations will be unable to generalize from the block experiment and will solve the following problem only if she or he has had sufficient experience with liquids in glasses of different sizes.

Equipment: Two plastic or glass tumblers of the same size, one plastic or glass bowl or vase (or a tall thin tumbler).

Procedure: Fill one tumbler about two-thirds full of water; the other about one-third full. Put these down in front of the child and say: *Is there more water in this glass* (point to one) *or this one* (point to the other), *or are they are same?* Record the child's response.

Then pour water from the fuller glass into the emptier one until they are equal and ask: *What about now? Is there more water in this glass* (point to one) *or this glass* (point to the other), *or are they the same?* Record the child's response. (If the child says one has more water, invite him or her to pour liquid back and forth from one glass into the other until satisfied that they are the same.)

Next, pour water from one glass into the bowl (or vase) and ask: *Is there more water in this one* (point to the glass) *or this one* (point to the bowl or vase), *or do they contain the same amount of water?* Record the child's response.

Then ask: *Why do you think so?* Record the child's response.

Finally, pour the water from the bowl or vase back into the glass and ask: *Now is there more water in this glass* (point to one) *or this glass* (point to the other), *or are they the same?* Note the child's response and reactions.

Piaget Experiment 5—Conservation of Substance   Approximate age and grade range: Five to seven years, kindergarten to second grade.

Purpose: To discover if a child understands that the amount of a substance remains the same even though its shape is changed. Children who are unable to decenter will be unable to grasp that the amount stays constant, since they will concentrate on only one quality. Older children will be able to allow for both qualities at once. They will be able to mentally reverse the action that changed the shape of the substance, which means they are capable of dealing with *operations*. However, if you ask them to deal with an abstract (not actually present) situation of a similar type, they may experience difficulty, indicating that they are at the level of *concrete* operations.

Equipment: A small amount of plasticene or clay.

Procedure: Take a piece of plasticene or clay and divide it as equally as possible. Roll the pieces into two balls and ask the child if he or she thinks the two are the same size. If the pupil says that one is bigger than the other, remove as much as necessary from the larger ball until you get agreement that they are identical. Then take one ball, roll it into a sausage shape, and ask: *Is there more clay here* (point to ball) *or here* (point to sausage), *or do they both have the same amount of clay?* Record the child's response.

Then ask: *Why do you think so?*

Then roll the sausage shape back into a ball and ask: *Is there more clay here* (point to one ball) *or here* (point to the other ball), *or are they the same?* Note the child's response and reactions.

Next, ask the child if the two balls are equal. If she or he says they are not, add or take away clay until the child agrees that they are the same. Then say: *Suppose I put these two pieces on two scales. Would this piece be heavier, or would this piece, or would they both be the same?* Record the child's response.

Then roll one ball into a sausage shape, and ask: *What would happen if I weighed these now? Would this one* (point to ball) *or this one* (point to sausage) *be heavier, or would one be as heavy as the other?* Record the child's response.

Then ask: *Why do you think so?* Record the child's response.

Piaget Experiment 6—Analyzing Aspects of Formal Thought (Solving a Problem)   Approximate age and grade range: Twelve years and above, sixth grade and above.

Purpose: To discover how students attempt to solve a problem. Children at the level of concrete operations are able to solve problems if they have had actual experience with the kinds of objects and situations involved, but they are unable to handle new and unique situations. In addition, they are likely to approach a problem in a haphazard, unsystematic way. Students at the level of formal operations, on the other hand, can deal with combinations of ideas in a systematic way, propose and test hypotheses, and imagine what might happen in situations they have never before encountered.

Equipment: A piece of string about 6 feet long and three fishing weights, one small, one medium, and one large. (Any objects of different weights to which a string can be attached may be substituted for the fishing weights.)

Procedure: Take three pieces of string 18 inches long, and attach one of the weights to the end of each. Pick up the string with the smallest weight and start if swinging, much like a pendulum, in both these ways: by holding the string at different places and letting the weight drop (when the string is held taut) from different positions and by *pushing* the weight rather than simply letting it fall. Also, call attention to the fact that the strings are equal in length but the weights are different.

Then say: *There are four factors involved here: the length of the string, the difference in weight at the end of the string, the height from which the weight is released, and the force with which the weight is pushed. I want you to figure out which of these factors—or what combination of them—determines how fast the weight swings. Experiment with these pieces of string any way you like, and when you think you have it figured out, tell me what your solution is. Or if you can, give me your solution without actually handling the strings.*

Describe how the student proceeds.

What solution does the student offer?

Once the solution is given, ask the student to prove it to you. If you detect an oversight, demonstrate the nature of the error and observe the student's reaction. (Note: The length of the string is the major determinant of the speed of the swing.)

Piaget Experiment 7—Analyzing Aspects of Formal Thought (Tendency to Theorize)   Approximate age and grade range: Thirteen years and above, seventh grade and above.

Purpose: To gain insight into the tendency of students who have recently mastered formal thought to engage in hypothesizing, which may center more on possibilities than on realities, and to be somewhat unrestrained in dealing with abstract and theoretical matters.

Procedure: Ask students to respond to this question: *At the present time there are between six and eight million unemployed people in this country. If you had complete power to make laws and establish and finance programs in this country, how would you try to reduce unemployment? Tell me all the ideas you come up with as you think of them.* Record the student's response.

Piaget's Description of Moral Development

Piaget describes his observations on moral development in *The Moral Judgment of the Child* (1932). Thomas Lickona summarizes research investigations stimulated by Piaget's conclusions in "Research on Piaget's Theory of Moral Development" on pages 219–240 of *Moral Development and Behavior* (1976), an excellent compilation of articles on all aspects of morality, which he edited.

Kohlberg's Stages of Moral Development

If you would like to read Kohlberg's own account of the stages of moral development, examine "Moral Stages and Moralization: The Cognitive-Developmental Approach" in *Moral Development and Behavior* (1976), edited by Thomas Lickona. Kohlberg discusses "Revisions in the Theory and Practice of Moral Development" in *Moral Development: New Directions for Child Development* (no. 2, 1978), edited by W. Damon. Techniques for encouraging moral development by taking account of Kohlberg's stages are described in *Promoting Moral Growth* (1979) by Richard Hersh, Diana Paolitto, and Joseph Reimer.

Kohlberg's Just Community

To learn more about the nature of a just community and how it works in practice, read "The Just Community Approach to Moral Education in Theory and Practice" by Kohlberg and "Democratic Moral Education in the Large Public High School" by Clark Power. Both articles appear in *Moral Education: Theory and Application* (1985), edited by Marvin Berkowitz and Fritz Oser.

Hartshorne and May's Studies of Character

The series of studies on character development carried out by Hugh Hartshorne and Mark May have never been equaled in terms of ingenuity, thoroughness, or depth. Even though they were done in the 1920s, the results of these studies are still well worth examining. The authors give detailed descriptions of how they developed and administered their various measures, as well as their results and conclusions, in a three-volume series published under the general title *Studies in the Nature of Character.* Volume 1, *Studies in Deceit* (1930) gives the background of the study and then provides a description of the methods and results of the studies of honesty. Volume 2, *Studies in Service and Self-control* (1929) describes methods and conclusions regarding those types of behavior. Volume 3, *Studies in the Organization of Character* (1930), reports a follow-up study of interrelationships between the types of behavior reported in Volumes 1 and 2. (The final summary begins on page 382.)

Summary

1. Theories organize and give meaning to facts and guide research. Developmental theories describe the sequence, continuity, and interrelatedness of aspects of development.
2. Erikson's theory of personality development is based on the epigenetic prin-

ciple of biology. Just as certain parts of the fetus are formed at certain times and combine to produce a biologically whole individual at birth, certain aspects of personality develop at certain times and combine to form a psychologically whole individual.

3. Erikson's theory describes eight stages, from birth through old age. The stages that deal with the personality development of school-age children are initiative vs. guilt (four to five years), industry vs. inferiority (six to eleven years), and identity vs. role confusion (twelve to eighteen years).

4. Individuals with a strong sense of identity are comfortable with their physical self, have a sense of purpose and direction, and know they will be recognized by others. Individuals with a poorly developed sense of identity are susceptible to role confusion.

5. Establishing a strong identity and avoiding role confusion are especially difficult for today's adolescents because of changing social values.

6. One solution to the conflict over appropriate sex role behavior is psychological androgyny.

7. When faced with making an occupational choice, some adolescents declare a psychosocial moratorium, others establish a negative identity.

8. Erikson's observations about identity were extended by Marcia, who described four identity statuses: identity diffusion, moratorium, identity achievement, and foreclosure.

9. Erikson's theory has been criticized for its heavy reliance on personal experience, for its inaccuracies in terms of female personality development, and for its failure to specify how individuals move from stage to stage.

10. Piaget believes that individuals inherit two basic intellectual tendencies: organization (the tendency to combine mental processes into more general systems) and adaptation (the tendency to adjust to the environment).

11. Adaptation occurs through the processes of assimilation (fitting an experience into an existing scheme) and accommodation (changing a scheme or creating a new one to incorporate a new experience).

12. A scheme is a mental framework that guides our thoughts and actions.

13. Equilibration is the process of trying to maintain a system of schemes that allows us to adapt to the environment.

14. On the basis of his studies, Piaget concluded that schemes evolve through four stages: sensorimotor (birth to two years), preoperational (two to seven years), concrete operational (seven to twelve years), and formal operational (twelve to eighteen years).

15. During the sensorimotor stage, the infant and toddler use senses and motor skills to explore and understand the environment.

16. In the preoperational stage, the child masters symbol systems but cannot manipulate symbols logically.

17. In the concrete operational stage, the child is capable of logical thinking but only with ideas with which he or she has had firsthand experience.

18. During the formal operational stage, the individual is capable of hypothetical reasoning, dealing with abstractions and engaging in mental manipulations.

19. Systematic instruction may have modest positive effects on the rate of cognitive development as long as the schemes that will govern the next stage have already begun to develop.
20. Piaget's theory has been criticized for underestimating children's abilities, overestimating the capability of adolescents to engage in formal operational thinking, and for postulating four distinct stages.
21. Piaget identified two types of moral reasoning in children: morality of constraint (rules are inflexible and external) and morality of cooperation (rules are flexible and internal).
22. Kohlberg defined six stages in the development of moral reasoning: punishment-obedience, instrumental relativist, good boy–nice girl, law and order, social contract, and universal ethical principle.
23. Structured discussions based on moral dilemmas may have some positive effects on the rate of development of moral reasoning.
24. Studies show that children's moral behavior varies in different circumstances.

Key Terms

epigenetic principle *(43)*
identity *(46)*
role confusion *(46)*
psychological androgyny *(49)*
psychosocial moratorium *(51)*
negative identity *(51)*
identity diffusion type *(53)*
moratorium type *(53)*
identity achievement type *(53)*
foreclosure type *(53)*
organization *(59)*
adaptation *(59)*

equilibration *(59)*
scheme *(59)*
assimilation *(59)*
accommodation *(59*
conservation *(63)*
perceptual centration *(64)*
irreversibility *(64)*
egocentrism *(65)*
decentration *(68)*
adolescent egocentrism *(71)*
morality of constraint *(76)*
morality of cooperation *(76)*

Discussion Questions

1. According to Erikson, how personality develops among six- to eleven-year-old children depends on their developing a sense of industry and avoiding a sense of inferiority. Suppose you were an elementary school teacher. What kinds of things would you do to help your students feel more capable and productive? What kinds of things would you avoid doing?
2. Between the ages of twelve and eighteen, personality development revolves around establishing an identity and avoiding role confusion. American high schools often are criticized for not helping adolescents resolve this conflict. Do you agree? Why? What do you think could be done to improve matters?

3. From Piaget's point of view, why is it wrong to think of children as "small adults"?

4. In response to reports that American schoolchildren do not score as well as many European and Asian schoolchildren on standardized achievement tests, some critics of American education argue that we should begin formal schooling earlier than age five and that it should focus on mastery of basic reading and computation skills. How would Piaget respond to this proposal?

5. How would you respond to a parent (or colleague) who argued that students have better things to do in class than discuss ways of resolving moral dilemmas?

chapter 3

AGE-LEVEL CHARACTERISTICS

KEY POINTS

Preschool and Kindergarten

Large-muscle control better established than small-muscle control and eye-hand coordination

Shift from parallel to cooperative play between 2 and 5 years

Sex differences in toy preferences and play activities noticeable by kindergarten

Young children stick to own language rules

Primary Grades

Primary grade children have difficulty focusing on small print

Accident rate peaks in 3rd grade because of confidence in physical skill

Rigid interpretation of rules in elementary grades

To encourage industry, use praise, avoid criticism

Elementary Grades

Girls taller and heavier from 10 to 14 years

After growth spurt, boys have greater strength and endurance

Average age of puberty: girls, 11; boys, 14

Peer group norms for behavior begin to replace adult norms

Delinquents have few friends, are antagonistic, lack self-confidence, do poor schoolwork

Girls superior in verbal skills, math computation

Boys superior in math reasoning, spatial abilities

Sex differences in cognitive abilities getting smaller

Impulsive thinkers look at big picture, reflective thinkers concentrate on details

Junior High

Early-maturing males likely to draw favorable responses

Late-maturing boys may seek attention

Late-maturing girls likely to be popular and carefree

Discussion of controversial issues may be difficult because of strong desire to conform to peer norms

Many teen-agers experience misery or depression

Political thinking becomes more abstract, less authoritarian, more knowledgeable

High School

Contemporary adolescents expected to be interested in sex

Adolescents may feel guilty about premarital sex but are motivated to engage in such relationships

Parents influence plans, peers influence immediate status

Girls more likely than boys to experience anxiety about friendships

Girls particularly likely to experience depression because of learned helplessness

Depression may be caused by negative set, sense of loss

Depression and unstable family situation place adolescents at risk for suicide

---

The theories described in Chapter 2 call attention to stages of psychosocial, cognitive, and moral development. While these types of behavior are important, they represent only a small part of the behavioral repertoire of a child or adolescent. In order to describe many aspects of development of potential significance to teachers, it is necessary to analyze types of behavior that are not directly related to the theories already discussed or to those (learning and information processing) to be discussed in Part 3. This chapter presents such an overview of types of behavior at different age and grade levels that are not directly related to any particular theory. In selecting points for emphasis, one basic criterion was used: Does this information about development have potential significance for teachers? In order to organize the points to be discussed, the developmental span is divided into five levels, corresponding to common grade groupings in schools: preschool and kindergarten (three to six years), primary grades (1, 2, and 3; six to nine years), elementary grades (4, 5, and 6; nine to twelve years), junior high (7, 8, and 9; twelve to fifteen years), and senior high (10, 11, and 12; fifteen to eighteen years). Because the way grades are grouped varies, you may find yourself teaching in a school system where the arrangement described in this chapter may not be followed. In that case, simply refer to the appropriate age-level designations, and, if necessary, concentrate on two levels rather than one. While you should concentrate on the descriptions of characteristics of pupils of the grade and age levels you expect to teach, you should also read the rest of the chapter with care. One reason for reading about characteristics of pupils at all levels is that even though you presently anticipate that you will teach a particular grade level, you may at some point teach younger or older pupils. Another reason is that you may gain awareness of continuities of development and come to realize how some aspects of the behavior of older children were influenced by earlier experiences. Finally, even though a particular type of behavior is discussed at a level where it is considered to be of special significance, it may be important at any age level. Techniques for encouraging students to become more sensitive to the feelings of others, to note just one example, are discussed in the section on the elementary grades, but the same techniques can be used at all grade levels.

Various types of behavior at each of the five levels are discussed under these headings: physical, social, emotional, and cognitive. Following each characteristic, implications for teachers are noted. To help you establish a general conception of what children are like at each level, brief summaries of the types of behavior stressed by the theorists discussed in the preceding chapter are listed at the beginning of each section. You can get an even clearer general picture of the types of students you will teach if you carry out one or more of these simple exercises:

1. Arrange to observe in a grade you eventually hope to teach. (All contacts with schools should be made directly or indirectly through your instructor.) Observe pupils in and out of the classroom and write down what you consider to be significant types of behavior.
2. If possible, interview one or more teachers of the grade level you hope to teach. Ask them to describe what they think are the most significant pupil characteristics at that grade level.
3. If possible, interview one or more pupils of the grade level you expect to teach. Ask them what they like and dislike about school, what they worry about, and what they wish teachers would do.

Preschool and Kindergarten (three to six years)

Stage of psychosocial development: initiative vs. guilt. Pupils need opportunities for free play and experimentation, as well as experiences that give them a sense of accomplishment.

Stage of cognitive development: preoperational thought. Gradual acquisition of ability to conserve and decenter, but children not capable of operations and unable to mentally reverse actions.

Stage of moral development: morality of constraint, preconventional. Rules viewed as unchangeable edicts handed down by those in authority. Punishment-obedience orientation focuses on physical consequences rather than intentions.

General factors to keep in mind: first experiences with school routine, interactions with more than a few peers. Preparation for initial academic experiences in group settings. Important to learn to follow directions, get along with others.

Physical Characteristics

1. Preschool children are extremely active. They have good control of their bodies and enjoy activity for its own sake. Provide plenty of opportunities for the children to run, climb, and jump. Arrange these activities, as much as possible, so that they are under your control. If you follow a policy of complete freedom, you may discover that thirty improvising three- to five-year-olds can be a frightening thing. In your Handbook you might note some specific games and activities that you could use to achieve semicontrolled play.

Handbook Heading:
Active Games

2. Because of their inclination toward bursts of activity, kindergarteners need frequent rest periods. They themselves often don't recognize the need to slow down. Schedule quiet activities after strenuous ones. Have rest time. Realize that excitement may build up to a riot level if the attention of "catalytic agents" and their followers is not diverted. In your Handbook you might list some signals for calling a halt to a melee (for example, playing the opening chords of Beethoven's Fifth Symphony on the piano) or for diverting wild action into more or less controlled activity (marching around the room to a brisk rendition of "The Stars and Stripes Forever").

Handbook Heading:
Riot-Stopping Signals and Activities

3. Preschoolers' large muscles are more developed than those that control fingers and hands. Therefore, they may be quite clumsy at, or physically incapable of, such skills as tying shoes and buttoning coats. Avoid too many finicky activities, such as pasting paper chains. Provide big brushes, crayons, and tools. In your Handbook you might note other activities or items of king-size equipment that would be appropriate for the children's level of muscular development.

Handbook Heading:
Allowing for Large Muscle Control

4. Young children find it difficult to focus their eyes on small objects; therefore, their eye-hand coordination may be imperfect. If possible, minimize the necessity for the children to look at small things. (Incomplete eye development is the reason for large print in children's books.) Again, avoid too many finicky activities.

Large-muscle control better established than small-muscle control and eye-hand coordination

5. Although the children's bodies are flexible and resilient, the bones that protect the brain are still soft. Be extremely wary of blows to the head in games or fights between children. If you notice an activity involving such a blow, intervene immediately; warn the class that this is dangerous and explain why.

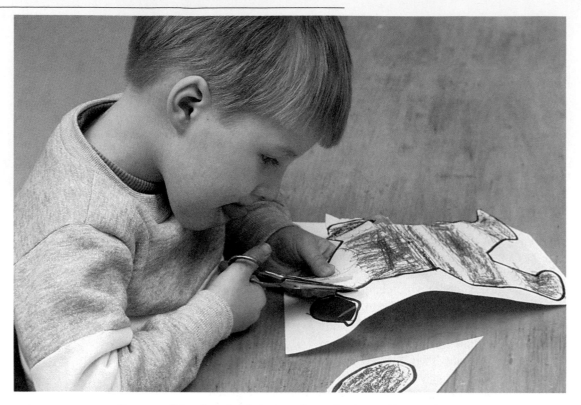

Because of the slow development of muscles controlling the fingers, young children may have difficulty handling small tools. (Miro Vintoniv/Stock, Boston)

6. Although boys are bigger, girls are ahead of boys in practically all other areas of development, especially in fine motor skills, so don't be surprised if boys are clumsier at manipulating small objects. It may be desirable to avoid boy-girl comparisons or competition involving such skills.

7. Handedness is established in most children, and 90 percent are right-handed. It is probably unwise to attempt to force a lefty to change. Being right-handed may be more convenient, but it is not that important. Trying to persuade lefties to switch may make them feel odd, guilty, nervous, and upset.

Social Characteristics

1. Most children have one or two best friends, but these friendships may change rapidly. Preschoolers tend to be quite flexible socially; they are usually willing and able to play with most of the other children in the class. Favorite friends tend to be of the same sex, but many friendships between boys and girls develop. You might make it a habit to notice whether some children seem to lack the ability or confidence to join others. In some cases a child may prefer to be a loner or an observer rather than a participant. But if you sense that a child really wants to get to

Figure 3.1   Target Diagram Showing Sociometric Choices

know others, you might provide some assistance. **Sociometric techniques** can reveal which playmates a shy child would like to get to know. To use sociometric techniques, ask each student to write down (or report orally) the name of the classmate she or he likes best. In some cases you may want to phrase the question more subtly; for example, "Write (or tell me) the name of someone you have fun with," or "Write (or tell me) the name of someone you would like to sit next to." Some advocates of sociometric techniques suggest that you request more than one choice. For most purposes, however, simply asking for the name of the best-liked classmate is probably most satisfactory, since the task of recording several choices can be complicated. Perhaps the best way to record responses is the *target diagram* (Northway, 1940) in Figure 3.1.

This diagram is largely self-explanatory. As you see, it focuses attention on the *stars* in the center and the *isolates* outside the circle. If an isolate seems content to be a loner, perhaps you should respect this preference. But when a child appears

Handbook Heading:
Using Sociometric
Techniques

eager to join others yet seems unable to take the first step, you might subtly help by pairing him or her on some activity with the classmate she or he chose when asked to name the child liked best.

If you would like more information about how to obtain, interpret, and use sociometric techniques, see *Sociometry in the Classroom* by Norman E. Gronlund (1959).

Handbook Heading:
How Much Control Is
Necessary?

2. Play groups tend to be small and not too highly organized; hence they change rapidly. You should not be concerned if children flit constantly from one activity to another. Such behavior is normal for this age group, although it may sometimes drive you wild. You might think about how much control you will want to exert over your pupils, particularly during free-play periods. At what point is insistence on silence and sedentary activities justifiable? Should you insist that pupils stick with self-selected activities for a given period of time?

3. Younger children may play beside others; older ones with others. Mildred Parten (1932) observed the free play of children in a nursery school and noted the types of social behavior they engaged in. Eventually, she was able to write quite precise descriptions of six types of behavior.

Unoccupied behavior—Children do not really play at all. They either stand around and look for a time at others or engage in aimless activities.

Solitary play—Children play alone with toys that are different from those used by other children within speaking distance of them. They make no attempt to interact with others.

Onlooker behavior—Children spend most of their time watching others. They may kibitz and make comments about the play of others, but they do not attempt to join in.

Parallel play—Children play *beside,* but not really with, other children. They use the same toys in close proximity to others but in an independent way.

Associative play—Children engage in rather disorganized play with other children. There is no assignment of activities or roles; individual children play in their own ways.

Cooperative play—Children engage in an organized form of play in which leadership and other roles are assigned. The members of the group may cooperate in creating some project, dramatize some situation, or engage in some sort of coordinated enterprise.

Handbook Heading:
Using Time Sampling to
Study Behavior

Having developed these descriptions, Parten observed a one-minute sample of the behavior of the child selected. At the end of that time, she classified the child's play into one of the six categories. She then repeated this procedure with another child, and so on. Over a period of days she accumulated a record of the type of play engaged in, consisting of twenty such samples for each child. An analysis of these records showed that two-year-olds were most likely to engage in *parallel* play (they played *beside,* but not really with, others). Older children, on the other hand, were more likely to enjoy *associative or cooperative* play (they interacted with others first in somewhat disorganized ways but eventually engaged in coordinated activities with specifically assigned roles).[1] This study calls attention to the variety of play activities common to preschool children. This knowledge may help you determine if a child *prefers* solitary play or plays alone because of shyness or lack of skills for joining in associative or cooperative play.

> **Shift from parallel to cooperative play between 2 and 5 years**

4. Quarrels are frequent, but they tend to be of short duration and quickly forgotten. When thirty children are thrown together for the first time in a restricted environment, with a limited number of objects to be shared, disputes over property rights and similar matters are inevitable. Do not be surprised if you find that the majority of quarrels and aggressive acts involve two or more boys. Research has shown that males are more likely than females to behave aggressively. The gender difference in aggression is greatest among preschoolers and least noticeable among college students (Hyde, 1986). When possible, let the children settle these differences on their own, and intervene only if a quarrel gets out of hand. If you do have to intervene, you might try one of two tactics: Suggest that one or both children engage in another equally attractive activity, or impose a turn-taking rule. (Other methods of classroom control are discussed in Chapter 13.)

5. Preschoolers enjoy dramatic play; most of the plots they invent stem from their own experiences or TV shows. Provide simple props, perhaps ones that encourage the kinds of plots you consider desirable. In your Handbook you might note some specific types of dramatic play you will want to encourage—and what you will *discourage* if you think there should be restrictions. How do you feel about war games, for example? Some people argue that games featuring aggression are desirable because they release tension. Others contend that such games predispose children to violence and tend to make them unsympathetic to suffering.

> Handbook Heading:
> Encouraging Desirable
> Forms of Dramatic Play

6. Awareness of sex roles is evident. By the time they enter kindergarten, most children have developed awareness of sex differences and of masculine and feminine roles (Wynn & Fletcher, 1987). This awareness shows up very clearly in the toys and activities that boys and girls prefer. Boys are more likely than girls to play outdoors, to engage in rough and tumble play, and to behave aggressively. Boys play with toy vehicles (cars, planes, and trucks, for example) and construction toys, and they play action games (such as football or soccer). Girls prefer art activities, doll play, and dancing (Carter, 1987). As we pointed out in Chapter 2, sex

> **Sex differences in toy preferences and play activities noticeable by kindergarten**

---

1. P. K. Smith (1978) found that contemporary preschoolers still display the same types of behavior described by Parten in the 1930s, although K. E. Barnes (1971) found that contemporary children are less socially oriented than those of the 1930s.

To encourage desirable forms of dramatic and imaginative play, provide simple props. (Mark Weinkle/Southern Light)

role differences are often reinforced by the way parents behave. Boys are encouraged to be active and independent, while girls are encouraged to be more docile and dependent. Peers may further reinforce these tendencies. A boy or girl may notice that other children are more willing to play when he or she selects a sex-appropriate toy.

Therefore, if you teach preschool children, you may have to guard against a tendency to respond too soon when little girls ask for help. If they *need* assistance, of course you should supply it, but if preschool girls can carry out tasks on their own, you should urge them to do so. You might also remind yourself that girls need to be encouraged to become more achievement oriented and boys to become more sensitive to the needs of others. Through such efforts, you may be able to help children resist some forms of sex typing and begin to acquire traits of psychological androgyny.

Emotional Characteristics

1. Kindergarten children tend to express their emotions freely and openly. Anger outbursts are frequent. It is probably desirable to let children at this age level express their feelings openly, at least within broad limits, so that they can recognize and face their emotions. In *Between Parent and Child* (1965) and *Teacher and Child* (1972), Haim Ginott offers some specific suggestions on how a parent or teacher can help children develop awareness of their feelings. His books may help you work out your own philosophy and techniques for dealing with emotional outbursts.

Suppose, for example, that a boy who was wildly waving his hand to be called on during share-and-tell time later knocks down a block tower made by a girl who monopolized sharing time with a spell-binding story of a kitten rescued by fire fighters. When you go over to break up the incipient fight, the boy angrily pushes you away. In such a situation, Ginott suggests you take the boy to a quiet corner and engage in a dialogue such as this:

You: It looks as if you are unhappy about something, Pete.

Boy: Yes, I am.

You: Are you angry about something that happened this morning?

Boy: Yes.

You: Tell me about it.

Boy: I wanted to tell the class about something at sharing time, and Mary talked for three hours, and you wouldn't let me say anything.

You: And that made you mad at Mary and at me?

Boy: Yes.

You: Well, I can understand why you are disappointed and angry. But, Mary had an exciting story to tell, and we didn't have time for anyone else to tell what they had to say. You can be the very first one to share something tomorrow morning. Now how about doing an easel painting? You always do such interesting paintings.

Ginott suggests that when children are encouraged to analyze their own behavior, they are more likely to become aware of the causes of their feelings. This awareness, in turn, may help them learn to accept and control their feelings. But because these children are likely to be in Piaget's preoperational stage of intellectual development, bear in mind that this approach may not be successful with all of them. The egocentric orientation of four- to five-year-olds makes it difficult for them to reflect on the thoughts of self or others. (This point is spelled out in the context of other stages of interpersonal reasoning in Table 3.1, page 119.)

Anger outbursts are more likely to occur when children are tired, hungry, and/ or exposed to too much adult interference. If you take such conditions into account and try to alleviate them (by providing a nap or a snack, for example), temper tantrums may be minimized. However, by the time children enter the elementary grades, they should have begun learning to control anger themselves. In your Handbook you might jot down any techniques you have observed or can think of that will help children accomplish this goal. If some of the techniques described by Ginott strike you as especially promising guidelines, note these also.

2. Jealousy among classmates is likely to be fairly common at this age, since kindergarten children have much affection for the teacher and actively seek approval. When there are thirty individuals competing for the affection and attention of just one, some jealousy is inevitable. Try to spread your attention around as equitably as possible; and when you praise particular children, do it in a private or casual way. If a child is given lavish public recognition, it is only natural for the other children to feel resentful. Think back to how you felt about teachers' pets during your own school years. If you have observed or can think of other techniques for minimizing jealousy, jot them down in your Handbook.

Cognitive Characteristics

1. Kindergarteners are quite skillful with language. Most of them like to talk, especially in front of a group. Providing a "sharing time" gives children a natural opportunity for talking, but many will need help in becoming good listeners. Some sort of rotation scheme is usually necessary to divide talking opportunities between the gabby and silent extremes. You might provide activities or experiences for less confident children to talk about, such as a field trip, a book, or a film. In your Handbook you might note some comments to use if pupils start to share the wrong thing (such as a vivid account of a fight between their parents) or if they try to "one-up" classmates (for example, "Your cat may have had five kittens, but *our* cat had a *hundred* kittens"). For titillating topics, for instance, you might say, "There are some things that are private, and it's better not to talk about them to others."

Young children stick
to own language
rules

2. Preschoolers may stick to their own rules in using language. One of the most intriguing aspects of early language development is the extent to which children stick to their own rules. This tendency is so strong that Roger Brown (1973) has concluded that efforts by parents and teachers to speed up acquisition of correct speech may not always be successful. Evidence to back up this conclusion is provided by an ingenious study by Jean Berko (1958). Berko found that if four-year-olds are shown pictures and told, for example, "Here is a goose, and here are two geese," and then asked to complete the sentence "There are two ———," most will say "gooses." Further evidence of the degree to which children stick to their own view of language is provided by this conversation (reported by Cazden, 1968), in which a mother attempts to supply subtle instruction:

Child: My teacher holded the baby rabbits and we patted them.
Mother: Did you say your teacher held the baby rabbits?

Child: Yes.

Mother: What did you say she did?

Child: She holded the baby rabbits and we patted them.

Mother: Did you say she held them tightly?

Child: No, she holded them loosely.

Given this strong tendency of children to use their own rules of grammar, you should probably limit any attempts at grammar instruction to modeling (as in the above exchange between mother and child). The possibility of getting youngsters to use adult forms of grammar would seem to be outweighed by the risk of inhibiting their spontaneous use of language. Direct and systematic instruction in grammar should be delayed until second or third grade.

3. Competence is encouraged by interaction, interest, opportunities, urging, limits, admiration, and signs of affection. Studies of young children rated as highly competent (Ainsworth and Wittig, 1972; White and Watts, 1973) lead to the conclusion that those who desire to encourage preschoolers to make the most of their abilities should follow these guidelines:

Handbook Heading: Encouraging Competence

1. Interact with the child often and in a variety of ways.
2. Show interest in what the child does and says.
3. Provide opportunities for the child to investigate and experience many things.
4. Permit and encourage the child to do many things independently.
5. Urge the child to try to achieve mature and skilled types of behavior.
6. Establish firm and consistent limits regarding unacceptable forms of behavior; explain the reasons for these as soon as the child is able to understand; listen to complaints if the child feels the restrictions are too confining; give additional reasons if the limits are still to be maintained as originally stated.
7. Show that the child's achievements are admired and appreciated.
8. Communicate love in a warm and sincere way.

Diana Baumrind's analysis (1971) of authoritative, authoritarian, and permissive child-rearing approaches shows why such techniques seem to lead to competence in children. Baumrind found that parents of competent children were **authoritative parents.** They had confidence in their abilities as parents and therefore provided a model of competence for their children to imitate. When they established limits and explained reasons for restrictions, they encouraged their children to set standards for themselves and to think about *why* certain procedures should be followed. And because the parents were warm and affectionate, their positive responses were valued by their children as rewards for mature behavior. **Authoritarian parents,** by contrast, made demands and wielded power, but their failure to take into account the child's point of view and their lack of warmth led to resentment and insecurity on the part of the child. Children of authoritarian parents may do as they are told, but they are likely to do so out of compliance or fear, not out of a desire to earn love or approval. Permissive parents, as defined by Baumrind, were disorganized, inconsistent, and lacked confidence. Their children were likely to imitate such behavior. Furthermore, such parents did not demand much of their children, nor did they discourage immature behavior.

You might refer to these observations on authoritative, authoritarian, and permissive approaches not only when you plan how to encourage competence but also when you think about the kind of classroom atmosphere you hope to establish.

Primary Grades (1, 2, and 3; six to nine years)

Stage of psychosocial development: industry versus inferiority. Important to arrange for pupils to experience a sense of industry by presenting tasks they can complete successfully. Try to minimize and correct failures to prevent development of feelings of inferiority.

Stage of cognitive development: in process of moving from preoperational to concrete operational stage. Gradual acquisition of ability to solve problems by generalizing from concrete experiences.

Stage of moral development: morality of constraint, preconventional. Rules viewed as edicts handed down by authority. Focus on physical consequences, obeying rules should bring benefit in return.

General factors to keep in mind: first experiences with school learning. Eager to learn to read and write, likely to be upset by lack of progress. Initial attitudes toward schooling are established. Initial roles in a group are formed, roles that may establish a lasting pattern (e.g., leader, follower, loner, athlete, underachiever).

Physical Characteristics

1. Primary grade children are still extremely active. Because they are frequently required to participate in sedentary pursuits, energy is often released in the form of nervous habits—for example, pencil chewing, fingernail biting, hair twirling, and general fidgeting. You will have to decide what noise and activity level

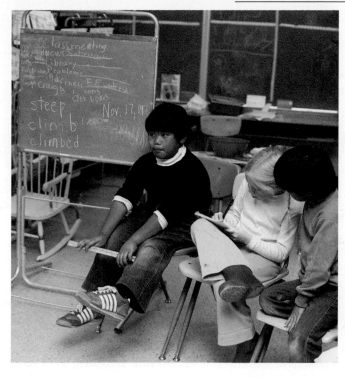

Primary grade pupils often find it difficult to sit still for extended periods of time. (Elizabeth Crews/Stock, Boston)

should prevail during work periods. A few teachers insist on absolute quiet, but such a rule can make the children work so hard at remaining quiet that they cannot devote much effort to their lessons. The majority of teachers allow a certain amount of moving about and talking. Whatever you decide, be on the alert for the point of diminishing returns—whether from too much or too little restriction.

To minimize fidgeting, avoid situations in which your pupils must stay glued to their desks for long periods. Have frequent breaks and try to work activity into the lessons themselves (for example, have children go up to the board, bring papers to your desk, move their desks into different formations). In your Handbook you might jot down other techniques for encouraging your pupils to be active while doing classwork.

Handbook Heading: Building Activity into Classwork

2. Children at these grade levels still need rest periods; they become fatigued easily as a result of physical and mental exertion. Schedule quiet activities after strenuous ones (story time after recess, for example), relaxing activities after periods of mental concentration (art after spelling or math).

3. Large-muscle control is still superior to fine coordination. Many children, especially boys, have difficulty manipulating a pencil. Try not to schedule too much writing at one time. If drill periods are too long, skill may deteriorate and the children may develop a negative attitude toward writing or toward school in general.

Primary grade chil-
dren have difficulty
focusing on small
print

4. Many primary grade pupils may have difficulty focusing on small print or objects. Quite a few children may be far-sighted because of the shallow shape of the eye. Try not to require too much reading at one stretch. Be on the alert for signs of eye fatigue (rubbing the eyes or blinking). When preparing class handouts, be sure to print in large letters or use a primary grade typewriter. Until the lens of the eye can be easily focused, young children have trouble looking back and forth from near to far objects. Another vision problem encountered by preschool and primary grade children is amblyopia, or "lazy eye." In normal vision the muscles of the two eyes work together to fuse their two images into one. Until the eye muscles become coordinated, however, children may experience double vision. In their efforts to cope with this problem, children may try to eliminate one image by closing one eye, tilting their heads, or blinking or rubbing their eyes. Treatment for amblyopia is aimed at strengthening the muscles of the weaker eye and may include covering the stronger eye with a patch, wearing glasses, eye exercises, or, in extreme cases, corrective surgery. In addition to being alert for signs of eye fatigue, therefore, you should also watch for signs of amblyopia and let the parents know if you detect one or more signs of lazy eye in any of your pupils.

Accident rate peaks
in 3rd grade because
of confidence in
physical skills

Handbook Heading:
Safe but Strenuous Games

5. At this age children tend to be extreme in their physical activities. They have excellent control of their bodies and develop considerable confidence in their skills. As a result, they often underestimate the danger involved in their more daring exploits. The accident rate is at a peak in the third grade. You might check on school procedures for handling injuries, but also try to prevent reckless play. For example, during recess encourage class participation in "wild" but essentially safe games (such as relay races involving stunts) to help the children get devil-may-care tendencies out of their systems. In your Handbook you might list other games to use for this purpose.

6. Bone growth is not yet complete; therefore bones and ligaments can't stand heavy pressure. If you notice pupils indulging in strenuous tests of strength (punching each other on the arm until one person can't retaliate, for example), you might suggest that they switch to competition involving coordinated *skills*. During team games, rotate players in especially tiring positions (for example, the pitcher in baseball).

Social Characteristics

The characteristics noted here are typical of both primary and elementary grade pupils and underlie the elementary-level characteristics described in the next section.

1. At this level children become somewhat more selective in their choice of friends. They are likely to have a more or less permanent best friend and may also

pick out a semipermanent "enemy." You might use sociograms to gain some insight into friendships and then give tentative assistance to children who have difficulty in attracting friends. Also, be on the alert for feuds, which can develop beyond good-natured quarreling.

2. Children during this age span often like organized games in small groups, but they may be overly concerned with rules or get carried away by team spirit. Keep in mind that according to Piaget, children at this age practice the morality of constraint: They find it difficult to understand how and why rules should be adjusted to special situations. When you divide a class into teams, you may be amazed at the amount of rivalry that develops (and the noise level generated). One way to reduce both the rivalry and the noise is to promote the idea that games should be fun. Another technique is to rotate team membership frequently. If you know any especially good—but not excessively competitive—team games, you might note them in your Handbook. You might also consult Student Team Learning (2nd ed., 1988) by Robert Slavin for descriptions of several team learning games that emphasize cooperation.

Rigid interpretation of rules in elementary grades

Handbook Heading:
Enjoyable Team Games

3. Quarrels are still frequent. Words are used more often than physical aggression, but many boys (in particular) may indulge in punching, wrestling, and shoving. Occasional fights are to be expected, but if certain children, especially the same pair, seem to be involved in one long battle, you should probably try to effect a truce. If you can discover the reason for the animosity, that would, of course, be so much the better.

If you have observed or can think of some effective techniques for breaking up a fight or for arranging things so that a fight can have a reasonably satisfactory (noninjurious) conclusion, you might jot them down in your Handbook.

Handbook Heading:
Handling Feuds and Fights

Emotional Characteristics

1. Primary grade pupils are sensitive to criticism and ridicule and may have difficulty adjusting to failure. They need frequent praise and recognition. Because they tend to admire or even worship their teachers, young children may be crushed by criticism. Provide positive reinforcement as frequently as possible, and reserve your negative reactions for nonacademic misbehavior. It is important to avoid sarcasm and ridicule scrupulously. Remember that this is the stage of industry versus inferiority. If you make a child feel inferior, you may prevent the development of industry.

Handbook Heading:
Avoiding Sarcasm and
Extreme Criticism

To encourage industry, use praise, avoid criticism

2. Most primary grade children are eager to please the teacher. They like to help, enjoy responsibility, and want to do well in their schoolwork. The time-honored technique for satisfying the urge to "help" is to assign jobs (eraser cleaner, wastebasket emptier, paper distributor, and the like) on a rotating basis.

Most elementary school pupils eagerly strive to obtain "helping" jobs around the classroom. Accordingly, you may wish to arrange a rotating schedule for such jobs. (The Stock Market/Palmer/Kane, 1976)

Handbook Heading:
Spreading Around
Responsibilities

In your Handbook you might note other techniques for equal distribution of helping opportunities. (Do you remember, for example, any particular responsibilities you enjoyed as a pupil?)

3. Children of this age are becoming sensitive to the feelings of others. Unfortunately, this permits them to hurt others deeply by attacking a sensitive spot without realizing how devastating their attack really is. It sometimes happens that teasing a particular child who has reacted to a gibe becomes a group pastime. Be on the alert for such situations. If you are able to make a private and personal appeal to the ringleaders, you may be able to prevent an escalation of the teasing, which may make a tremendous difference in the way the victim feels about school. (More specific comments on how to encourage sensitivity to the feelings of others will be noted in the discussion of emotional characteristics of elementary grade pupils.)

Cognitive Characteristics

1. Generally speaking, primary grade pupils are extremely eager to learn. One of the best things about teaching in the primary grades is the built-in motivation of pupils. The teacher's problem is how to make the most of it. Suggestions for doing this will be offered in Part Three.

2. They like to talk and have much more facility in speech than in writing. They are eager to recite—whether they know the right answer or not. The high school teacher may have difficulty stimulating voluntary class participation, but not the primary grade teacher. The problem here is more likely to be one of controlling participation so that children speak up only when called upon. Frequent reminders to take turns and to be good listeners are often necessary. And even if you are successful in this area, you may feel a bit unsettled to find that a pupil, after wildly waving a hand or pumping an arm to be recognized, supplies a hopelessly wrong answer. You may want to develop some phrases that gently and/or humorously indicate that an answer is erroneous or irrelevant. If you come up with some good ones, jot them down in your Handbook.

Handbook Heading: Ways to Handle Wrong Answers

3. Because of their literal interpretation of rules, primary grade children may tend to be tattletales. Sometimes telling the teacher that someone has broken a school or class rule is due to a child's level of moral development, sometimes it is due to jealousy or malice, and sometimes it is simply a way to get attention or curry favor. If a child calls your attention to the misbehavior of others and you respond by saying "Don't be a tattletale," the child may be hurt and confused. On the other hand, if you thank the child too enthusiastically and then proceed to punish the culprit, you may encourage most members of the class to begin to inform on each other. Perhaps the best policy is to tell an informant that you already are aware of the errant behavior and that you intend to do something about it. Then you might follow up by talking to the offending parties.

Elementary Grades (4, 5, and 6; nine to twelve years)

Stage of psychosocial development: industry versus inferiority. Important to keep pupils constructively busy, try to play down comparisons between best and worst learners.

Stage of cognitive development: concrete operational, beginning of formal operational. Toward the upper elementary grades some pupils may be able to deal with abstractions but most will need to generalize from concrete experiences.

Stage of moral development: transition from morality of constraint to morality of cooperation, preconventional to conventional. Shift to viewing rules as flexible mutual agreements, but "official" rules obeyed out of respect for authority or to impress others.

General factors to keep in mind: initial enthusiasm for learning may fade as the novelty wears off and as perfecting skills becomes more arduous. Differences in knowledge and skills of fastest and slowest learners become more noticeable. "Automatic" respect for teachers tends to diminish. Growth spurt and puberty lead to greater awareness of sex roles.

Physical Characteristics

Girls taller and heavier from 10 to 14 years

1. A growth spurt occurs in most girls and starts in early-maturing boys. On the average, girls between the ages of ten and fourteen are taller and heavier than boys of the same age. Because girls mature more rapidly than boys, they experience their growth spurt about two years earlier. Some girls begin their spurt as early as nine and one-half years, but the average age is ten and a half (Dusek, 1987a). In a unisex society, the fact that the average eleven-year-old female is taller and heavier than the average male of the same age might not make any difference. In the prevailing American culture, however, where differences in sex roles are often recognized (despite the feminist movement), the larger size of females between the ages of eleven and fourteen may lead to problems. In our society (and most others as well), boys want to engage in activities that permit them to demonstrate their strength and physical prowess. The epitome of "a real boy" in the elementary grades is the disheveled good athlete. (The importance of physical prowess to boys was emphasized by Paul H. Mussen and Mary Cover Jones [1957]. They found that boys who matured early and were physically advanced were more popular and better adjusted than slow-maturing, smaller and weaker boys.)

The stereotyped view of the "ideal girl" of the same age stresses "sugar and spice, and everything nice." Feminists may dismiss this as a false and treacherous caricature, but many elementary grade girls seem eager to model their behavior on such a conception of femininity. Consequently, a certain amount of anguish may be caused by the temporary sex reversal of physical superiority. The self-concept of a fifth- or sixth-grade boy who has prided himself on his virility may be rudely shattered if an early-maturing girl in his class suddenly becomes taller than he and sends him to ignominious defeat in ten consecutive games of tetherball. If the girl just described has engaged in fantasies about being demure, petite, and attractive to the opposite sex, however, the taste of victory may quickly sour in the face of guilt and confusion about her physical superiority over males.

An elementary school girl who prides herself on her athletic ability, particularly when competing with and against boys, may face an adjustment by the time she enters high school. At present there is considerable pressure to allow prepubescent females to join males in team sports, such as Little League baseball. An eleven-year-old girl athlete who is a fast maturer may be two years ahead of male teammates in physical development and, because of her advanced maturity (coupled with skill), may surpass many boys of the same age in athletic prowess. J. M. Tanner (1972, p. 5) reports that until adolescence girls are equal to boys in strength but that girls between twelve and a half and thirteen and a half, on the average, have larger muscles than boys of the same age. After the growth spurt, however, the muscles in the average boy's body are larger, as are the heart and lungs. Furthermore, the body of the mature male has a greater capacity than that of the female for carrying oxygen to the blood and for neutralizing the chemical products of muscular exercise, such as lactic acid. Thus the average male has greater strength and endurance than the average female. A girl who is the star of a Little League team is likely to discover that she cannot compete with the best male athletes in high school. This realization might lead to lowered self-esteem—unless she adjusts to the idea of being the star of all-girl athletic teams.

After growth spurt, boys have greater strength and endurance

If you notice that pupils are upset about sudden growth (or lack of it), you might try to help them accept the situation by explaining that things will eventually even out. To reduce unhappiness that arises from conflicts between physical attributes and sex roles, you might try to persuade pupils that being male or female should not in itself determine what a person does.

Handbook Heading: Helping Pupils Adjust to the Growth Spurt

2. As children approach puberty, concern and curiosity about sex are almost universal, especially among girls. The average age of puberty for girls in the United States is eleven (Dusek, 1987a); the range is from eight to eighteen years. For boys the average age of puberty is fourteen years; the range is from ten to eighteen years. Since sexual maturation involves drastic biological and psychological adjustments, children are concerned and curious. It seems obvious that accurate, unemotional answers to questions about sex are desirable. However, for your own protection, you should find out about the sex education policy at your school. Some school districts forbid discussion of sex in class even on an informal basis. If no restrictions exist but you yourself feel uncomfortable about leading such a discussion, you might make use of one of the many excellent films or pamphlets available. You might also consider asking the school nurse to lead a class discussion.

Average age of puberty: girls, 11; boys, 14

3. Fine motor coordination is quite good; therefore, the manipulation of small objects is easy and enjoyable for most children. As a result, arts and crafts and music activities are popular. Encouraging active participation in drawing, painting, model making, ceramics, and so on is an excellent way to capitalize on the newly developed manipulative skills of students in the upper elementary grades. Ideally, such activities should center on originality and creativity. Copying, assembling prefabricated kits, filling in sections on paint-by-number pictures, and similar activities are less desirable. You might encourage children to play musical instruments by holding amateur hours or concerts or by inviting individual pupils to perform during music periods. In your Handbook you might note other activities that encourage pupils to use skills in creative ways.

Handbook Heading: Encouraging Creative Expression

Social Characteristics

See the description of elementary grade social characteristics in the preceding section for characteristics that are common to both levels.

1. The peer group becomes powerful and begins to replace adults as the major source of behavior standards and recognition of achievement. During the early school years, parents and teachers set standards of conduct, and most children try to live up to them. By the end of elementary school, however, children may be more eager to impress their friends than to please the teacher. Unfortunately, some children may try to impress their classmates by defying or ignoring the teacher.

As peer groups become more important, children sometimes organize themselves into more or less exclusive, all-boy and all-girl cliques. Generally speaking, these groups operate most actively outside of school. Occasionally, a battle between two groups may lead to trench warfare in class (for example, exchanging venomous notes). If this occurs, it is sometimes effective to place members of opposing factions on cooperative committees. Such committees will need close supervision, especially during the first few days, but this stratagem may enforce a truce.

Another characteristic of group behavior at the elementary level is the tendency to devise what amount to initiation rituals (for example, demonstrations of nerve, such as shoplifting). In some cases, however, illegal activities simply stem from a desire to get back at authority for placing so many restrictions on behavior. If you encounter thefts in class or a chip-on-the-shoulder attitude, keep in mind the growing independence of children at this grade level and their need for understanding and limit setting rather than punishment.

2. Between the ages of six and twelve, the development of interpersonal reasoning leads to greater understanding of the feelings of others. Robert L. Selman (1976a, 1976b) has studied the development of **interpersonal reasoning** in children. Interpersonal reasoning is the ability to understand the relationship between motives and behavior among a group of people. The results of his research are summarized in Table 3.1. The stages outlined there reveal that during the elementary school years children gradually grasp the fact that a person's overt actions or words do not always reflect inner feelings. They also come to comprehend that a person's reaction to a distressing situation can have many facets. Toward the end of the elementary school years—and increasingly during adolescence—children become capable of taking a somewhat detached and analytical view of their own behavior as well as the behavior of others.

Not surprisingly, a child's interpersonal sensitivity and maturity seem to have an impact on relationships with others. Selman compared the responses of seven- to twelve-year-old boys who were attending schools for children with learning and

---

Peer group norms for behavior begin to replace adult norms

Table 3.1   Stages of Interpersonal Reasoning Described by Selman

Stage 0: The Egocentric Level (About ages 4 to 6)
Children do not recognize that other persons may interpret the same social event or course of action differently than they do. They do not reflect on the thoughts of self or others. They can label the overtly expressed feelings of others but do not comprehend cause-and-effect relations of social actions.

Stage 1: Social Information Role Taking (About ages 6 to 8)
Children are able to differentiate between their own interpretations of social interactions and the interpretations of others in limited ways. They cannot simultaneously think of their own view and the view of others.

Stage 2: Self-Reflective Role Taking (About ages 8 to 10)
Interpersonal relations are interpreted in relation to specific situations where each person understands the expectations of the other in that particular context. Children are not yet able to view the two perspectives at once, however.

Stage 3: Multiple Role Taking (About ages 10 to 12)
Children become capable of taking a third-person view, which permits them to understand the expectations of themselves and of others in a variety of situations as if they were spectators.

Stage 4: Social and Conventional System Taking (About ages 12 to 15+)
Each individual involved in a relationship with another understands many of the subtleties of the interactions involved. In addition, a societal perspective begins to develop. That is, actions are judged by how they might influence *all* individuals, not just those who are immediately concerned.

SOURCE: Adapted from discussions in Selman, 1976a, and Selman, 1976b

interpersonal problems with the responses of a matched group of boys attending regular schools. The boys attending special schools were below average for their age in understanding the feelings of others.

Selman believes that teachers and therapists might be able to aid children who are not as advanced in role-taking skills as their agemates by helping them become more sensitive to the feelings of others. If an eight-year-old boy is still functioning at the egocentric level, for example, he may fail to properly interpret the behavior of classmates and become a social isolate. Selman (1976a, p. 314) describes how such a boy was encouraged to think continually about the reasons behind his social actions and those of others and acquired sufficient social sensitivity to learn to get along with others.

Discussion techniques Selman recommends can be introduced in a natural, rather than a formal, way. If you see a boy react with physical or verbal abuse when jostled by a playmate, for example, you might say, "You know, people don't always intentionally bump into others. Unless you are absolutely sure that some-

Handbook Heading:
Ways to Promote Social Sensitivity

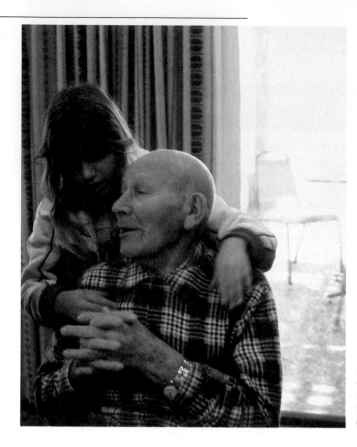

Between the ages of six and twelve children acquire greater sensitivity to the feelings of others. (Elizabeth Crews)

one has hurt you on purpose, it can be a lot pleasanter for all concerned if you don't make a big deal out of it."

A final point about fostering moral development relates to instruction or adult supervision, as contrasted with peer interactions. Piaget concluded that ten- to twelve-year-olds, who are in the process of overcoming the limitations of moral realism, seem to take delight in formulating their own rules. It appeared to Piaget that many children at this stage of moral development were so proud of their newly discovered ability to formulate rules that they preferred to ignore adult-imposed regulations and substitute their own. Accordingly, after children reach the age of ten or so, there may be value in encouraging them to participate in rule making. They are not only more likely to understand and accept rules based on mutual agreements with peers; they may also be encouraged to move from conventional to postconventional moral thinking as described by Kohlberg. (The conventional level, you may recall, stresses obedience to external authority; the postconventional level stresses formulation of rules by mutual consent.) Two qualifications to this suggestion to encourage participation should be noted, however.

First of all, most children in the upper elementary grades are still concrete thinkers and may feel obliged to make up a separate rule for every contingency. A fifth-grade teacher encountered this problem when he asked his pupils to propose class rules. Within twenty minutes over fifty rules had been proposed and when

Handbook Heading:
Encouraging Participation
in Rule Making

the teacher ran out of blackboard space, he had to call a halt. The major reason for this profusion of regulations was that a separate rule was suggested for variations of a particular type of behavior. For example, there was a rule "Don't run in the hall," followed by a rule "Don't run in the classroom," followed by a rule "Don't run on the way to the boys' room," and so on.

A second reason for exercising caution when encouraging children in the elementary grades to participate in making rules is that they may also wish to determine how rule breakers should be punished. When Piaget asked young children to propose punishments, he found that many of their choices were "astonishingly severe" (1948, p. 209). He offered this explanation for the harsh nature of child-determined punishments: "In these children's eyes, punishment consists, as a matter of course, in inflicting on the guilty party a pain that will smart enough to make them realize the gravity of their misdeed. Naturally, the fairest punishment will be the most severe" (p. 211). The same tendency for young children to propose severe punishments was observed by Urie Bronfenbrenner in Russian elementary schools. One of the techniques of character training used in the Soviet Union is to have school councils, made up of elected student representatives, determine if classmates have broken school rules and how guilty children should be punished. The punishments proposed by the children observed by Bronfenbrenner were often so severe that teachers had to intervene and suggest milder penalties (1970, pp. 66–68).

Emotional Characteristics

1. Conflict between the group code and adult rules may cause difficulty, including juvenile delinquency. John J. Conger and W. C. Miller (1966) carried out a longitudinal study of the personality characteristics of delinquent boys. They found that differences between delinquents and nondelinquents were noted as early as the primary grades. Teachers in the first three grades rated future delinquents as less considerate and fair in dealing with others, less friendly, less responsible, more impulsive, and more antagonistic to authority. Because of these tendencies, they were less well liked and accepted by their peers. They were easily distracted when engaged in schoolwork and rarely showed interest (or ability) in the subjects they studied. These general trends continued in the later elementary school years. Increasing problems with schoolwork became more apparent as the boys progressed through the grades. By the end of the ninth grade there were noticeable differences between delinquents and nondelinquents in virtually all traits measured by Conger and Miller. During the high school years delinquents were rated lower than average in self-confidence and self-respect, less cheerful and happy, less able to get along with either male or female classmates, and more eager for attention. They also were rated as more egocentric, inconsiderate, and thoughtless. They confessed that they often felt discouraged, depressed, and anxious. Finally, they seemed unable to establish close personal relationships with either peers or adults.

Delinquents have few friends, are antagonistic, lack self-confidence, do poor schoolwork

D. Magnusson, A. Duner, and G. Zetterblon (1975) reported that sixth-graders who disliked classmates, felt that they were overloaded with schoolwork, were dissatisfied with school, and had low scholastic motivation were likely to have committed delinquent acts by the ninth grade. It would seem that failure to gain satisfaction or recognition in school forced them to seek other means to impress their peers and/or try to bolster their self-esteem. Accordingly, you might do everything you can (by using techniques to be described in Chapter 12) to encourage as many students as possible to earn satisfying grades.

2. Behavior disorders are at a peak at the elementary grade level, but most children find their own ways to adapt. An extensive survey (Rosen, Bahn, and Kramer, 1964) of referrals to psychiatric clinics in all parts of the country revealed that the highest referral rates occur during the nine-to-fifteen age span, with peaks at nine and ten and at fourteen and fifteen. The referral rates and peaks varied for males and females: Boys were twice as likely as girls to receive psychiatric treatment. Peak referral years for boys were nine and fourteen; peak years for girls were ten and fifteen. The records of psychiatric clinics provide detailed data regarding behavior disorders, but such figures should be interpreted with caution because it is impossible to make allowance for selective factors of various kinds. The data on referral peaks are supported, however, by teacher evaluations made for an extensive mental health survey of Los Angeles County (1960). Ten- and eleven-year-olds were rated as emotionally disturbed more frequently than those at other age levels.

Several hypotheses have been proposed to account for the high rate of behavior disorders at the elementary grade level. E. James Anthony notes, "Among the factors responsible [for high referral rates during the age span of ten to fifteen years] have been mentioned scholastic, family, and other social pressures, psychosocial development problems, and variation in adult tolerance of behavior and therefore referral tendency" (1970, p. 681). In regard to the last point, variation in "adult tolerance," it might be reasoned that elementary school students are intellectually mature and sensitive enough to recognize conflicts and pressures but not independent enough to cope with them completely on their own. (A preschool child may be unaware of many problem situations; a high school student may take the initiative in requesting assistance from a school counselor.) Another explanation for the high referral rate between ten and fourteen years is that almost all children experience their growth spurt and many achieve sexual maturity during these years.

Cognitive Characteristics

Girls superior in verbal skills, math computation

1. There are sex differences in specific abilities and in overall academic performance. Early research on sex differences in cognitive functioning found that during the elementary school years girls, on the average, are superior in verbal fluency, spelling, reading, and mathematical computation. Boys, on the average, are superior in mathematical reasoning, in tasks involving understanding of spatial relationships, and in solving insight problems (Bee, 1978; Block, 1976; Maccoby & Jacklin, 1974).

Boys superior in math reasoning, spatial abilities

More recent research has confirmed these findings and added some interesting details to the picture. Sandra P. Marshall and Julie D. Smith (1987) examined the mathematics performance of several thousand California schoolchildren who took the *Surveys of Basic Skills* in both the third and sixth grades. Consistent with the research findings of the 1970s, they reported that girls at both grade levels significantly outscored the boys on computation problems. In addition, they found strong sex differences for certain types of errors. Boys were more likely to use the wrong rule in working a problem (for example, always subtracting the smaller number from the larger one in a subtraction problem regardless of whether the smaller number is in the minuend or the subtrahend; switching from multiplication to addition midway through a multiplication problem). Girls were more likely to make an association error (such as misinterpreting the significance and meaning of a word in a word problem).

Alan Feingold (1988) analyzed the performance of eighth- through twelfth-grade students on eight subtests of the *Differential Aptitude Test* for the years 1947, 1962, 1972, and 1980. At every grade level and year, he found that the girls outscored the boys on tests of spelling, language, and clerical speed and accuracy. The boys, on the other hand, outscored the girls on the mechanical reasoning and space relations tests. The most interesting aspect of Feingold's analysis was the discovery that sex differences in cognitive abilities are decreasing. Between 1947 and 1980, the amount by which the girls outscored the boys, and vice versa, decreased at every grade level.

Sex differences in cognitive abilities getting smaller

Females earn higher grades in school, but males are more likely to achieve at a higher level in many activities later in life. Lois Wladis Hoffman (1972) suggests that the girls' school achievements result, in part at least, from their desire to please. Boys, by contrast, appear more interested in working on tasks that interest them and less concerned about earning approval. Because of these tendencies, girls may try to earn high grades to get a positive response from parents and teachers; boys may engage in more self-motivated study. If a boy does not find a particular subject interesting, he may not make much of an effort to learn it. This, of course, will lead to poorer overall evaluations on report cards. On the other hand, a boy's tendency to study something for its own sake may pay off later in life when prolonged self-directed study is called for.

Hoffman speculates that girls may be motivated by a desire to please because they are not encouraged to strive for independence early in life. On the basis of research carried out by Howard Moss (1967), she suggests that mothers tend to think of male infants as sturdy and active and to think of female infants as delicate dolls (despite the fact that female infants are more mature and better able to cope with many forms of stress than are male infants). As a result, mothers overprotect female infants and treat them as dependent. This process continues throughout childhood (L. W. Hoffman, 1972; Fagot, 1978). Hoffman also hypothesizes that a girl may find it more difficult to develop autonomy and independence because she identifies more completely with the primary caretaker (almost always the mother) and her first teachers (almost all of whom are women) and also experiences less conflict with them. If this explanation seems plausible, you might want to try to encourage girls to be independent and to have confidence in their ability to do things on their own.

Handbook Heading:
Encouraging Girls to Be
Independent

2. Differences in cognitive style become apparent. In addition to sex differences in general and specific learning abilities, there are also differences in **cognitive style.** Cognitive styles are tendencies to respond to a variety of intellectual tasks and problems in a particular fashion. Jerome Kagan (1964a, 1964b), for instance, found that some children seem to be characteristically *impulsive* whereas others are characteristically *reflective.* He notes that impulsive children have a fast conceptual tempo; they tend to come forth with the first answer they can think of and are concerned about giving quick responses. Reflective children, on the other hand, take time before they speak; they seem to prefer to evaluate alternative answers and to give correct, rather than quick, responses. Kagan discovered that when tests of reading and of inductive reasoning were administered in the first and second grades, impulsive pupils made more errors than reflective pupils. He also found that impulsiveness is a general trait; it appears early in a person's life and is consistently revealed in a great variety of situations.

Kagan also described *analytic* and *thematic* styles of conceptualization. He reported that analytic students tend to note details when exposed to a complex stimulus. Thematic students respond to the pattern as a whole.

Tamar Zelniker and Wendell Jeffrey (1976) carried out several experiments to check on Kagan's observations. They found that reflective children perform better on tasks requiring analysis of details; impulsive children seem to do better on tasks requiring global interpretations. They concluded that impulsive children are not necessarily inferior to reflective children in problem-solving ability, as Kagan and other earlier students of cognitive style had concluded. Impulsive thinkers may do less well in many school and test situations that require analysis of details —primarily because they prefer to look at problems in a thematic or global way. The impulsive thinker is often a thematic thinker as well, possessing a fast conceptual tempo combined with a tendency to look at the big picture. Reflective thinkers are more deliberate, but their tendencies toward analytic thinking cause them to concentrate on details.

Impulsive thinkers
look at big picture,
reflective thinkers
concentrate on
details

Awareness of these varying styles of conceptualization may help you understand (in part, at any rate) the wide individual differences in the way your pupils react to different approaches to teaching. An impulsive boy, for example, may ruin class discussion by blurting out the first thing that pops into his head, upstaging the reflective types who are still in the process of formulating more searching answers. To minimize this possibility, you may want to have an infor-

Jerome Kagan found that some students are impulsive thinkers who tend to react quickly when asked a question. Other pupils are reflective thinkers who prefer to mull things over before answering. (Paul Conklin/Monkmeyer)

mal rotation scheme for recitation or sometimes require that everyone sit and think about a question for two or three minutes before answering.

Samuel Messick (1976) and Kenneth M. Goldstein and Sheldon Blackman (1978) summarize research on other cognitive styles. They note that some students more than others seem to experience things vividly and also are aware of many more aspects of a situation at a given moment. Some students are more likely than others to be distracted by conflicting ideas. Other students appear to place things in broad categories compared with classmates who classify experiences into many separate categories. Still other pupils seem to have a tendency to "level" memories by merging similar recollections, as contrasted with peers who retain distinct recollections of separate experiences. J. P. Guilford (1967) has concluded that some individuals appear to be *convergent* thinkers—they respond to what they read and observe in conventional, typical ways. Others are *divergent* thinkers—they respond in totally unexpected or idiosyncratic ways. Some pupils memorize much more easily than others; some are more capable than others of grasping ideas and evaluating their accuracy or appropriateness in a particular situation.

These differences in cognitive style first become apparent in the lower grades, but they influence students throughout their school careers. For this reason, you should expect wide variations in the way individual pupils react to learning situations. You should also not be surprised if a student does well in one kind of learning activity but poorly in another. In some cases, you will probably be well aware of the comparative strengths or weaknesses of pupils in one or more areas of cognitive functioning. Many times, however, the way cognitive styles influence pupil performance will be impossible to assess. The surest way to allow for differences in cognitive styles, therefore, is to present a variety of instructional activities so that every pupil will occasionally be asked to do schoolwork that happens to fit her or his way of thinking. (This point will be emphasized again in several later chapters. Specific suggestions for organizing learning experiences for pupils with different cognitive styles will be outlined.)

Handbook Heading:
Allowing for Differences in
Cognitive Style

Junior High (grades 7, 8, and 9; twelve to fifteen years)

Stage of psychosocial development: identity versus role confusion. Growing independence leads to initial thoughts about identity. Greater concern about appearance and sex roles than occupational choice.

Stage of cognitive development: beginning of formal operational. Increasing ability to engage in mental manipulations, test hypotheses.

Stage of moral development: transition to morality of cooperation, conventional. Increasing willingness to think of rules as flexible mutual agreements, "official" rules still likely to be obeyed out of respect for authority or to impress others.

General factors to keep in mind: growth spurt and puberty influence many aspects of behavior. Abrupt switch (for seventh-graders) from being oldest, biggest, most sophisticated pupils in elementary school to being youngest, smallest, least knowledgeable pupils in a large school. Peers begin to influence behavior more than parents. Acceptance by peers extremely important. Pupils who do poor schoolwork begin to feel bitter, resentful, and restless.

Physical Characteristics

1. Most girls complete their growth spurt at the beginning of this period. A boy's growth spurt, however, usually is not completed before the eighth or ninth grade, and it may be precipitous. Some boys add as much as 6 inches and 25 pounds in a single year. The period of accelerated growth that may begin in the late elemen-

Table 3.2   The Impact of Early and Late Maturation

	Characteristics as Adolescents	Characteristics as Adults
Early-Maturing Boys	Self-confident, high in self-esteem, likely to be chosen as leaders (But leadership tendencies more likely in lower-class than middle-class boys.)	Self-confident, responsible, cooperative, sociable. But also rigid, moralistic, humorless, conforming
Late-Maturing Boys	Energetic, bouncy, given to attention-getting behavior, not popular	Impulsive and assertive. But also insightful, perceptive, creatively playful, able to cope with new situations
Early-Maturing Girls	Not popular or likely to be leaders, indifferent in social situations, lacking in poise (But middle-class girls more confident than those from lower class.)	Self-possessed, self-directed, able to cope, likely to score high in ratings of overall psychological health
Late-Maturing Girls	Confident, outgoing, assured, popular, likely to be chosen leaders	Likely to experience difficulty adapting to stress, likely to score low in ratings of overall psychological health

SOURCES: H. E. Jones, 1946; M. C. Jones, 1957, 1965; P. II. Mussen and M. C. Jones, 1957; Peskin, 1967, 1973; Clausen, 1975; Livson and Peskin, 1980; Petersen and Taylor, 1980

tary grades involves almost all pupils in junior high. The variation between individual students is tremendous. Some early-maturing, ninth-grade girls look as if they could *almost* be the mothers of some late-maturing, seventh-grade boys.

Over a period of years, a number of investigators at the University of California examined longitudinal data to determine the impact of early and later maturation on adolescents. Then, when the subjects were in their thirties, their adult behavior and adjustment was compared to the ratings made when they were in high school. The investigations are summarized in Table 3.2.

The characteristics noted in Table 3.2 cannot be interpreted too literally for several reasons. First of all, different groups of subjects were studied, and the types of behavior various investigators found typical of early and later maturers were not always consistent. Second, as indicated by the parenthetical notes regarding leadership in early-maturing adolescent males and confidence in later-maturing adolescent girls, the impact of the timing of puberty sometimes varied depending on social class. Third, comparatively small groups of subjects were studied. Such factors as attractiveness may thus have influenced some of the characteristics (for example, popularity) studied. Finally, the subjects of these studies attended high school in the 1930s and 1940s. Changes in conceptions of sex roles and sexual behavior may have altered the significance of early and later maturation in the 1980s.

It does seem safe to conclude, however, that the behavior and development of individuals who mature substantially earlier or later than most of their peers may be influenced in significant and permanent ways. The exact nature of this influence may be difficult to predict, though, for reasons that become clear when one attempts to interpret the data in Table 3.2. After reviewing research on early and later maturation, Norman Livson had Harvey Peskin (1980) speculate that the **early-maturing boy** is likely to draw favorable responses from adults (because of his adult appearance), which promotes confidence and poise (contributing to leadership and popularity with peers). The **late-maturing boy,** by contrast, may feel inferior and attempt to compensate for his physical and social frustration by engaging in bossy and attention-getting behavior. The very success of the early-maturing boy in high school, however, may cause him to develop an inflexible conception of himself, leading to problems when he must deal with new or negative situations later in life. The need for the early-maturing boy to cope with difficult adjustment situations in high school, on the other hand, may equip him to adapt to adversity and change later in life.

Livson and Peskin observe that the late-maturing boy is psychologically and socially out of step with peers, and the same applies to the **early-maturing girl.** The **late-maturing girl,** whose growth is less abrupt and whose size and appearance are likely to reflect the petiteness featured in stereotyped views of femininity, shares many of the characteristics (poise, popularity, leadership tendencies) of the early-maturing boy. The advantages enjoyed by the late-maturing girl are not permanent, however. Livson and Peskin report that "The stress-ridden early-maturing girl in adulthood has become clearly a more coping, self-possessed, and self-directed person than the late-maturing female in the cognitive and social as well as emotional sectors. . . . It is the late-maturing female, carefree and unchallenged in adolescence, who faces adversity maladroitly in adulthood" (1980, p. 72).

If late-maturing boys in your classes appear driven to seek attention or inclined to brood about their immaturity, you might try to give them extra opportunities to gain status and self-confidence by succeeding in school work or other nonathletic activities. If you notice that early-maturing girls seem insecure, you might try to bolster their self-esteem by giving them extra attention and by recognizing their achievements.

2. Puberty is reached by practically all girls and by many boys. The sex organs (primary sexual characteristics) mature rapidly, and secondary sex characteristics appear: breast development, rounded hips, and the appearance of a waistline in girls; broadening of the shoulders and replacement of fat with muscle tissue in boys. In both sexes, pubic, axillary (armpit), facial, and body hair appear; the tex-

---

Early-maturing boys likely to draw favorable responses

Late-maturing boys may seek attention

Late-maturing girls likely to be popular and carefree

Handbook Heading: Helping Early and Late Maturers Cope

Because the growth spurt of girls occurs about two years earlier than that of boys, the average eleven- to fourteen-year-old girl is taller than the average boy of the same age. (Mel Digiacomo/The Image Bank)

ture of the skin changes (often with temporary malfunctioning of the oil-producing glands, which leads to acne), and the voice changes. All these developments have a profound impact on the appearance, biological functioning, and psychological adjustment of the young person who is reaching puberty.

The remarks made earlier about sex education in the elementary grades apply even more directly to this age group. You should check on school policy and act accordingly. Girls, particularly, need accurate information, since the changes associated with menstruation may produce fear if the process is not understood.

3. There is likely to be a certain amount of adolescent awkwardness—probably due as much to self-consciousness as to sudden growth—and a great deal of concern about appearance. Both boys and girls take pains with their grooming. In order to prevent attempts at surreptitious grooming during class, some secondary school teachers establish a class routine of completion of schoolwork two minutes before the end of a period. Those last two minutes are free for grooming or social interaction.

4. Although this age period is marked by generally good health, the diet and sleeping habits of many junior high students are poor. Because of poor diet and insufficient sleep, many junior high pupils may exhibit a certain amount of listlessness. Frequent changes of pace and breaks for relaxation may alleviate drowsiness to a certain extent.

Social Characteristics

1. The peer group becomes the general source of rules of behavior. Developing a code of behavior is a move toward adult independence and to be encouraged. In addition to forming their own rules for behavior in out-of-school situations, junior high students often are eager to participate in student government decisions. You are likely to get a favorable response if you invite the members of your class to participate in establishing class rules and routines.

Discussion of controversial issues may be difficult because of strong desire to conform to peer norms

2. The desire to conform reaches a peak during the junior high years. Adolescents find it reassuring to dress and behave like others and they are likely to alter their own opinions to coincide with those of a group. When you encourage student participation in class discussions, you may need to be alert to the tendency for students at these grade levels to be reluctant to voice "minority" opinions. If you want them to think about controversial issues, it may be preferable to invite them to write their opinions anonymously, rather than voice them in front of the rest of the class. In addition, you might use techniques of values clarification (to be discussed in Chapter 10) to encourage the formation of a set of *personal* values.

3. Students are greatly concerned about what others think of them. Both friendships and quarrels become more intense. You will have little or no control over most social interactions between students, but you may be able to function as a sympathetic listener at times. If you notice that a pupil suddenly seems depressed and preoccupied, you might ask if he or she would like to talk about whatever it is that is bothersome.

Emotional Characteristics

1. Many adolescents may go through a period of "storm and stress." Starting with G. Stanley Hall, who wrote a pioneering two-volume text on adolescence in 1904, some theorists have stressed that adolescence is a period of turmoil. Sigmund Freud came to this conclusion, and his pupil Erik Erikson described the nature of the identity *crisis* that often occurs during adolescence. Starting in the 1960s, however, a number of psychologists (notably Daniel Offer, 1969) questioned whether turmoil is inevitable during the teen years. However, Offer based his conclusions on a small number of boys carefully screened for absence of indications of behavior problems, and more comprehensive studies have been at variance with his findings. In a large-scale study of teen-agers in Great Britain, the researchers concluded that nearly half of the subjects reported "some appreciable misery or depression" and that "there can be no doubt from these findings that

Adolescents often find it reassuring to dress and behave like peers. (Frank Siteman/ Stock, Boston)

many 14–15 year olds experience quite marked feelings of affective disturbance which could well be described as 'inner turmoil' " (Rutter, Tizard, & Whitmore, 1981, p. 42). In a review of studies on adolescent turmoil, Ozzie Siegel noted that "it seems a reasonable conclusion that the adolescent process is an interruption of peaceful growth and is normatively attended by anxiety, worry, and concerns regarding self-esteem, physical appearance, and body image" (1982, p. 542). If you will think back to the outline presented at the beginning of this section on the junior high years, it will become clear that the twelve- to fifteen-year-old has a formidable number of adjustments to make all at once: identity, puberty, transition points in cognitive development. You should probably expect, therefore, to fairly frequently reach the conclusion that many students are moody, depressed, or preoccupied when they come into your classroom. As much as possible, do your best to accept such behavior rather than intensify it by unsympathetic or harsh treatment.

Many teen-agers experience misery or depression

2. Crime rates are at a peak during the adolescent years, and vandalism may be a problem in certain schools. As noted under the emotional characteristics of elementary grade pupils, differences between delinquents and nondelinquents often become apparent before children leave the sixth grade. Boys who are rated as troublesome, difficult, and aggressive often become delinquent adolescents (West and Farrington, 1973). Typically, the first illegal act is committed during the elementary school years, but both the rate and the seriousness of criminal acts increase during the secondary school years. In many communities vandalism is a serious problem; rates appear to vary from one school to another. In an analysis of twelve inner-London schools, Michael Rutter and several associates (1979) found that the amount of damage to school property was significantly less in schools that had an academic emphasis, made available incentives and rewards, arranged good conditions for students, and provided opportunities for students to participate in decision making.

Handbook Heading:
Ways to Reduce Vandalism

The causes of delinquency are complex and will often be beyond your control. It would seem, though, that you might be able to reduce tendencies toward vandalism if you emulated some of the characteristics of schools and teachers described by Rutter and his colleagues. The positive impact of favorable techniques is more likely to be felt if all teachers in a school use similar methods, but even without cooperation from others, you could do the following: Make ample use of rewards, praise, and appreciation; try to make your room as pleasant and comfortable as possible; permit your students to participate in making decisions; emphasize academic achievement; serve as a model by respecting and caring for school property and equipment and functioning as an efficient class manager.

Group management techniques will be outlined in detail in suggestions for arranging class discussions in Chapter 9 and at the beginning of Chapter 13. They include being well prepared, arranging smooth transitions from one activity to another, keeping the attention of the entire class instead of concentrating on individuals (during group activities), and showing that you are "with it" by dealing with disruptive acts quickly and efficiently.

Cognitive Characteristics

1. This is a transition period between concrete operational and formal thought. Some pupils move through the stages of cognitive development outlined by Piaget more rapidly than others. In addition, students who *sometimes* exhibit characteristics of formal thought do not *always* think that way. Accordingly, it would be wise to check on how completely junior high students grasp abstract concepts. A simple way to obtain such information is to give a brief, ungraded, anonymous quiz after introducing a topic such as "Differences Between Capitalism and Communism." If you discover that many pupils explain concepts in concrete terms, use many concrete examples in class presentations.

2. This is a transition period between the moralities of constraint and cooperation. In discussions of school or class rules, or of laws or ethics, you may discover that strong differences of opinion will be voiced. Some students may think of all rules as sacred and unchangeable; others may grasp that extenuating circumstances and intentions should be considered. Instead of introducing topics that are the equivalent of moral dilemmas by using whole-class discussion techniques, it might be preferable to begin by asking students to write personal interpretations. Then you might refer to different points of view (without identifying those who expressed them) in structuring small-group discussions. In small groups, more students can express opinions, and those who are shy about speaking in front of the entire class may be more inclined to participate. Encouraging interchange of ideas between individuals may help pupils who think almost exclusively in terms of the morality of constraint become more flexible about making moral judgments.

3. Between the ages of twelve and sixteen, political thinking becomes more abstract, liberal, and knowledgeable. Joseph Adelson (1971, 1972) used an interview approach to obtain information about the development of political thought during the adolescent years. At the start of the interviews, the subjects were requested to imagine that a thousand people ventured to an island in the Pacific for the purpose of establishing a new society. The respondents were then asked to explain how these people might establish a political order, devise a legal system, and deal with other problems of public policy.

The analysis of the interview responses showed no significant sex differences in understanding political concepts and no significant differences attributable to intelligence and social class, although brighter students were better able to deal with abstract ideas and upper-class students were less likely to be authoritarian. The most striking and consistent finding was the degree to which the political thinking of the adolescent changes in the years between twelve and sixteen. Adelson concluded that the most significant changes were (1) an increase in the ability to deal with abstractions, (2) a decline in authoritarian views, and (3) an increase in political knowledge.

Increased ability to deal with abstractions is a function of the shift from concrete to formal operational thought. When thirteen-year-olds were asked, "What is the purpose of laws?" a typical answer was "So people don't steal or kill"' (1972, p. 108). A fifteen- or sixteen-year-old, by contrast, was more likely to say, "To ensure safety and enforce the government" (p. 108). The young adolescent who thinks in concrete terms concentrates on individuals and finds it difficult to take into account society as a whole. When asked about the purpose of laws to require vaccination of children, for example, the twelve-year-old is likely to say it is to prevent sickness in the child who receives the treatment. The fifteen-year-old who has mastered aspects of formal thought is likely to take into account how it will protect the community at large. Concrete thinking causes the twelve-year-old to concentrate on the immediate present because he or she is unable to analyze the significance of past events or project ideas into the future. As Piaget noted in his discussion of moral realists, the younger child is not likely to take motives into account. When asked to explain why many prisoners are recidivists, for example, only older adolescents would mention such motives as having a grudge against society. Adelson and his colleagues found that when twelve-year-olds were asked

> Political thinking becomes more abstract, less authoritarian, more knowledgeable

how prisoners should be treated, many of them recommended that they be punished and taught a stern lesson. Adelson speculates that the tendency for younger adolescents to be punitive and authoritarian might be attributed to several factors: preoccupation with wickedness, the inability of the young adolescent to grasp the concept of rights, and the conviction that laws are immutable. By fourteen and fifteen, the adolescents interviewed by Adelson were more likely to consider circumstances and individual rights and to recommend rehabilitation rather than punishment.

If you will be teaching courses in social studies, you may find this information useful in lesson planning. It may also help you understand why students may respond to discussions of political or other abstract matters in different ways.

High School (grades 10, 11, and 12; sixteen, seventeen, and eighteen years)

Stage of psychosocial development: identity versus role confusion. Concern about sex roles and occupational choice. Different identity statuses become apparent.

Stage of cognitive development: formal thought. Increasing ability to engage in mental manipulations, understand abstractions, test hypotheses.

Stage of moral development: morality of cooperation, conventional. Increasing willingness to think of rules as mutual agreements and to allow for intentions and extenuating circumstances.

General factors to keep in mind: achievement of sexual maturity has a profound influence on many aspects of behavior. Peer group and reactions of friends extremely important. Concern about what will happen after graduation, particularly for students who do not intend to continue their education. Awareness of the significance of academic ability and importance of grades for certain career patterns. Need to make personal value decisions regarding use of drugs, premarital sex, and code of ethics.

Physical Characteristics

1. Most students reach physical maturity, and virtually all attain puberty. Although almost all girls reach their ultimate height, some boys may continue to grow even after graduation. Tremendous variation exists in height and weight and in rate of maturation. As noted earlier, late-maturing boys seem to have considerable difficulty adjusting to their slower rate of growth. There is still concern about appearance, although it may not be as strong as it was during the junior high years. Glandular changes leading to acne may be a source of worry and self-consciousness to some students. The most significant glandular change accompanying puberty is arousal of the sex drive.

2. Many adolescents experience confusion regarding sexual relationships. In a discussion of the development of sexuality in adolescence, Patricia Y. Miller and William Simon (1980) point out that puberty, a biological event, causes adolescents to function as "self-motivated sexual actors," which is a social event. They comment that in technological societies "young people are defined as sexually mature while simultaneously being defined as socially and psychologically immature" (1980, p. 383). The confusion resulting from conflicts between sexual, social, and psychological conceptions of maturity is intensified by contemporary attitudes toward sex. Compared to previous generations, "contemporary adolescents are expected to be more interested in sex, to become experienced earlier, and once experienced, to approach regular sociosexual activity with greater competence" (p. 390). They go on to observe that "the contemporary adolescent must fashion an interpersonal sexual script from materials provided by a society that is nearly obsessed with the sexual possibilities of adolescence." They add that because of the high rate of divorce and the large number of adults on the "sexual marketplace," the adolescent in contemporary America "increasingly sees the surrounding adult social world as itself more sexually active and sexually interested than it used to be" (p. 390).

Contemporary adolescents expected to be interested in sex

In addition to difficulties caused by such factors, the young person may be further confused because "the sex education of the adolescent is emphatically attached to moral education" (p. 392). Miller and Simon believe that this is the case because gender-role expectations establish attitudes toward sexual morality. (The traditional view of the "good girl," for example, is that she does not engage in premarital sex.) They note, "Many of the specific images that form the core of the individual's earliest sense of the sexual are thoroughly imbued with vague but powerful moral tones" (p. 392). Evidence to support the point that sex and morality are intertwined was supplied by R. C. Sorensen (1973). Sorensen found that 76 percent of the thirteen- to fifteen-year-old girls and 43 percent of the sixteen- to nineteen-year-old girls he interviewed reported sometimes or often feeling guilty about masturbation. The corresponding figures for males were 43 percent at thirteen to fifteen and 47 percent at sixteen to nineteen. Sorensen also asked his subjects to express their psychological reactions to their first sexual experience. Of the girls, 36 percent reported that they had felt guilty (compared with 3 percent of the boys); 31 percent of the girls said they felt embarrassed (compared with 7 percent of the boys).

Many adolescents may experience confusion about sexual relationships. They are expected to be interested in sex but at the same time attitudes toward sex are often imbued with strong moral overtones. (Lawrence Migdale/Stock, Boston)

Adolescents may feel guilty about premarital sex but are motivated to engage in such relationships

It appears, then, that quite a few adolescents and youth feel guilty about sexual activities. Even though they may endorse the traditional view that premarital sex is wrong, adolescents and youth are nevertheless motivated to engage in such relationships. As Miller and Simon observe, contemporary adolescents and youth may feel that they are *expected* to have early sexual experience and to develop a high level of competence. In addition, engaging in sexual relations may be reinforcing for reasons outlined by S. Jessor and R. Jessor (1975). They point out that adolescents and youth may be motivated to have sexual relations as early as possible for one or more of these reasons: to prove to themselves and others that they have achieved a mature status, to establish a sense of independence, to affirm sexual identity, to gain support for the belief that they are attractive to others, to reject social conventions or behave in a socially unacceptable manner (perhaps out of a desire to establish a negative identity), and to gain respect from peers.

These factors explain why premarital sex may seem appealing to adolescents and youth, even when they at least partially endorse the view that such activity is morally wrong. Jessor and Jessor found, for example, that while 60 percent of their female respondents mentioned fear of pregnancy as a reason for not engaging in premarital sex, 60 percent also mentioned fear of parental disapproval and 55 percent mentioned fear of damaging their reputation.

3. Increased sexual activity among adolescents has led to high rates of illegitimate births and sexually transmitted diseases. The percentage of young women fifteen to nineteen years of age who reported having had premarital sex increased from 30 to 50 percent between 1971 and 1979 (Zelnick and Shah, 1983). Six in ten females had intercourse for the first time—at an average age of just over sixteen—with a male they were "committed to" (engaged or going steady). Most adolescent males, by contrast, have sex for the first time with a "casual" acquaintance. Adolescents who live in a family with only one parent (usually the mother) are more likely to be sexually active than adolescents who live with both parents (B. C. Miller, Higginson, McCoy, & Olson, 1987; Newcomer and Udrey, 1987).

Less than one third of all contemporary teen-agers who engage in premarital sex make use of contraceptives. Although the proportion who reported using contraceptives increased during the 1970s, in the 1980s two out of five births to women under twenty were illegitimate. It has been estimated that if present trends continue, "it will not be long before most adolescent births occur outside of marriage" (Furstenberg, Lincoln, & Menken, 1981, p. 2). One explanation for this trend is that the age at which first intercourse takes place has become lower, and younger girls are less knowledgeable about birth control than older ones. Furthermore, half of all teen-age pregnancies occur during the first six months of sexual activity. Those who have studied teen-age sexuality (for example, Furstenberg, Lincoln, & Menken, 1981) strongly advocate that sex education courses for girls be presented in junior high school. In one survey, however, it was reported that only 7 percent of junior high schools in large school districts included discussion of birth control techniques in such courses (Sonenstein and Pitman, 1984). Despite the fact that some sexually transmitted diseases have "become epidemic" (according to a 1981 report by the U.S. Department of Health), discussion of such diseases also appears to be the exception rather than the rule in sex education courses. The rising incidence of acquired immune deficiency syndrome (AIDS), for which there is no known cure, provides another compelling reason for including broad-based sex education classes in the junior high school curriculum.

Because of the highly controversial and emotionally toned nature of opinions about birth control and abortion, even teachers who present courses on sex education must follow district guidelines. Perhaps the most significant result of teen-age sexuality for most classroom teachers, therefore, will be the likelihood of pregnant students attending class.

Social Characteristics

1. Parents are likely to influence long-range plans; peers are likely to influence immediate status. A number of studies have attempted to compare the beliefs, attitudes, and values of parents and their children and also to compare the extent to which parent-peer and peer-peer opinions agree and conflict. Studies of values (reviewed by Feather, 1980), of political thinking (reviewed by Gallatin, 1980), of moral development (reviewed by M. L. Hoffman, 1980), and of occupational choice (reviewed by D. Rogers, 1972) lead to the conclusion that high school students are probably influenced in these areas of their lives more by parents than by peers. A visit to any high school, on the other hand, will reveal that in terms of dress, hair styles, interests, social relationships, and the like, the influence of peers is extremely potent. The hypothesis that parents and peers influence different aspects of adolescent behavior has been developed by C. V. Brittain (1968), who suggests that parents have a greater impact on decisions that have implications for the future (such as choice of a career) while peers influence decisions that involve current status and identity needs (such as choice of friends). L. E. Larsen (1972) evaluated Brittain's hypothesis and concluded that the influence of parents was greatest when there was mutual affection and respect. It might be concluded, then, that parents are likely to influence the values, moral and political beliefs, and long-range plans of high school students. When adolescents seek to establish an immediate sense of identity or status, however, they are more likely to be influenced by peers.

| Parents influence plans, peers influence immediate status |

2. Girls seem to experience greater anxiety about friendships than boys. Factors that cause girls to become concerned about the reactions of others were summarized in the preceding chapter. Tendencies to become dependent on others appear to stimulate adolescent girls to seek intimacy in friendships (Coleman, 1980). Boys, on the other hand, often stress skills and interests in forming friendships, and their tendencies to be competitive and self-reliant may work against the formation of close relationships with male companions. Because they often wish to form an intimate relationship with another girl, female adolescents are more likely than boys to experience anxiety, jealousy, and conflicts regarding friendships with same-sex peers. You should not be surprised, therefore, if secondary school girls are much more preoccupied with positive and negative aspects of friendships than boys are.

| Girls more likely than boys to experience anxiety about friendships |

Emotional Characteristics

1. Toward the end of the secondary school years, girls may be more likely than boys to experience emotional disorders. The statistics on clinic referrals mentioned earlier indicated that boys were about twice as likely as girls to have adjustment problems during the peak years from nine to fifteen. Toward the end of the high school years, however, girls may display more emotional disorders of certain types (particularly depression) than boys do. Explanations of this change (summarized by Rutter, 1980, pp. 60–61) include the following: Females have a greater tendency than males to express emotional disturbance by depression, females have a disadvantaged status in American society that causes them to feel depressed, and toward the end of the adolescent years females begin to conclude that they have little control over significant aspects of their lives.

This last factor is often referred to as **learned helplessness** because it is assumed that a helpless feeling has been learned through experiences and through the reactions of others. (M. E. P. Seligman [1975] has developed a comprehensive analysis of the view that learned helplessness—in both males and females—leads to depression.) As noted earlier, several factors might predispose older high school girls to feel that they will be unable to control their future lives. Fagot (1978) found that parents reward girls for asking for help but respond negatively when they engage in physical or athletic activities. Block (1973) concluded that boys in our society are encouraged to achieve and to be competitive and girls are encouraged to give comfort to others. L. W. Hoffman (1972) reported that girls are more eager than boys to secure teacher approval and that boys are more likely to work independently. Douvan and Adelson (1966) pointed out that teen-age boys feel that their destiny is in their own hands whereas girls (of the 1960s) felt that what they would become as adults depended to a large extent on the man they would marry.

Some of these factors may be less influential today (and in the future) because of changed perceptions of sex roles. Furthermore, there is greater awareness of how some of these socializing influences shape the dependent behavior of girls. Even so, you might try to convince teen-age girls in secondary school classes that they *are* capable of controlling their own lives. A general way to do this would be to urge them to focus on academic and occupational goals that will open up a wide range of job possibilities leading to independence and a sense of self-control. To reinforce this point, try to arrange for women who have succeeded in a variety of endeavors to talk to your class. If such models are not available, draw attention to newspaper accounts of successful women. A more specific technique is to observe how individual pupils, particularly girls, respond to failure. C. S. Dweck and E. S. Bush (1976) found that when boys are told that they are failing, they tend to respond with greater effort. When girls are told that they are failing, by contrast, they tend to attribute their failure to lack of ability. Chapter 11, "Motivation," offers detailed suggestions for encouraging students to stop thinking that failure is due to lack of ability and to start thinking that it is due to lack of effort. These techniques include setting challenging but attainable goals, encouraging self-direction in learning, telling students that they *can* do better after they have performed poorly, and building up feelings of self-esteem. (All the techniques can also be used to help high school boys who suffer from depression due to learned helplessness.)

2. The most common type of emotional disorder during adolescence is depression. While females may have greater tendencies than males to feel depressed, this does not mean that such reactions occur only in high school girls. Extreme

Girls particularly likely to experience depression because of learned helplessness

Handbook Heading: Helping Girls Acquire Feelings of Self-Control feelings of depression are the most common reason for referring teen-agers of both sexes to psychiatric clinics.

Common symptoms of depression include self-depreciation, crying spells, and suicidal thoughts and attempts. Additional symptoms in adolescents below the age of seventeen are fatigue, hypochondriasis, and difficulty in concentrating (I. B. Weiner, 1980, p. 455). High school students who experience such symptoms typically try to ward off their depression by restless activity or flight to or from others. They may also engage in problem behavior or delinquent acts carried out in ways that make it clear they are appealing for help. (A depressed fifteen-year-old boy may carry out an act of vandalism, for instance, at a time when a school authority or police officer is sure to observe the incident.) Adolescents over the age of seventeen who suffer from depression are likely to show little self-confidence and to feel worthless and discouraged. To combat such feelings they may join antiestablishment groups, manifest a "what's the use of it all?" attitude, or turn to sex and drugs. When it becomes sufficiently extreme, and when unfortunate experiences accumulate, depression may lead to suicide or attempted suicide.

A. T. Beck (1970) suggests that depression consists of a *cognitive set* made up of negative views of oneself, the world, and the future. As noted above, Seligman (1975) has proposed that depression is caused by *learned helplessness,* which leads to feelings of having no control over one's life. Irving Weiner (1975) emphasizes that depression typically involves a *sense of loss* that may have many causes. Depression may stem from the abrupt end of a personal relationship through death, separation, or broken friendship. An individual may undergo a sharp drop in self-esteem as a result of failure or guilt. A person may experience a loss of bodily integrity following illness, incapacitation, or disfigurement.

Techniques for changing a negative self-concept to a positive view of self were mentioned under the preceding point. The most effective all-purpose approach to minimizing depression, though, is to help as many of your students as possible to experience success as they learn. Techniques to accomplish that goal are discussed in the next six chapters of this book.

3. If depression becomes severe, suicide may be contemplated. Suicide is now a major cause of death among adolescents and young adults. Among fifteen- to twenty-four-year-olds, approximately five thousand individuals take their own life every year. Only accidents and homicides claim more victims. The number of reported suicides in this age group has increased 200 percent in the last thirty years.

Suicide among the young seems to be associated with a variety of demographic and family variables. It occurs most frequently in the late fall and early winter and in the states of Alaska and Nevada. For every Caucasian youth who commits suicide, about ten Native American youths do so. Southern states with large

Depression may be caused by negative set, sense of loss

Handbook Heading: Helping Students Overcome Depression

Many high school students, girls in particular, experience periods of depression. An invitation to talk for just a few moments with a sympathetic teacher might conceivably divert an extremely depressed adolescent from contemplating suicide. (Mieke Maas/ The Image Bank)

black populations, on the other hand, tend to have the lowest suicide rates. Individuals who commit suicide tend to come from families that have a history of alcohol and drug abuse; such individuals have often been placed outside the family for some period of time, and they often show symptoms of delinquency, aggression, or depression.

Four times as many females as males *attempt* suicide, almost always by taking an overdose of drugs. But three times as many young males as females *succeed* in killing themselves, usually with a gun.

The single most important signal of a youth at risk for suicide is depression. Along with the common symptoms noted under point 2, other signs of depression include poor appetite, weight loss, changes in sleeping patterns, difficulty in concentrating, academic problems, and poor self-concept. These symptoms take on added significance when accompanied by parents who commit abuse, who use drugs and alcohol excessively, or who behave suicidally themselves (Strother, 1986).

Depression and unstable family situation place adolescents at risk for suicide

If you notice that a student in one of your classes seems extremely depressed, take the trouble to ask if there is anything you can do to provide support. Your interest and sympathy may prevent a suicide attempt. In addition, don't hesitate to refer a seemingly depressed student to the school guidance counselor or the school psychologist. Their training and skills make them well equipped to diagnose and treat depression.

Cognitive Characteristics

1. High school students become increasingly capable of engaging in formal thought, but they may not use this capability. As noted in the evaluation of Piaget's theory in the preceding chapter, it appears that formal thinking is not as universal or consistent as he originally thought it was. High school students are more likely than younger students to grasp relationships, mentally plan a course of action before proceeding, and test hypotheses systematically. Without supervision and guidance, however, they may not use such capabilities consistently. As a consequence, you might take advantage of opportunities to show students at these grade levels how they can function as formal thinkers. Call attention to relationships and ways previously acquired knowledge can be applied to new situations. Provide specific instruction in techniques of problem solving. (Ways you might do this will be discussed in Chapter 9.) Finally, make sure that your pupils understand abstract concepts by using the technique mentioned in the section on the junior high years: Give ungraded, anonymous quizzes to assess depth of understanding. If many pupils appear to be thinking at the concrete level, use concrete examples in your class presentations.

2. Keep in mind that novice formal thinkers may engage in unrestrained theorizing, be threatened by awareness of possibilities, and be subject to adolescent egocentrism. Suggestions for taking into account these various aspects of formal thinking were noted in Chapter 2. If students become unrealistically theoretical in class discussions, try to call attention to realities and to the complexity of most problems. If some students seem threatened by their newfound ability to imagine possibilities (in the form of future decisions and the various options that are open to young adults, for instance), urge them to concentrate on short-term goals and immediate decisions. If younger adolescents act as if they were perpetually "on stage," be tolerant of their self-consciousness. Try to avoid class activities that force pupils to recite or perform in front of classmates.

Suggestions for Further Study

Comparing Real Students with Hypothetical Students

As noted at the beginning of this chapter, it will be extremely beneficial if you are able to actually observe pupils of the grade level you expect to teach. If you do have the opportunity to observe the behavior of students in and out of the classroom, compare your impressions with the age-level characteristics described in this chapter. You might also pick out the single characteristic that impresses you the most and speculate about what you might do—if anything—to allow for it when you begin to teach.

Time Sampling

Observing social behavior can be quite fascinating. If you would like to make a systematic record of some aspect of interactions between children, time sampling is easy and enjoyable. You could begin by using Parten's classifications of the social behavior of nursery school children. (For details of her descriptions and techniques, see her article "Social Participation Among Preschool Children" *Journal of Abnormal and Social Psychology,* 1932, *27,* 243–269.) Or select some form of behavior that interests you (elementary school playground interaction and high school between-class behavior are two possibilities). To develop your own list of categories, simply observe children of the age you have selected while they engage in a particular type of behavior and write down what they do. Eventually, you should be able to describe five or so categories that cover most aspects of their behavior. At that point, pick out a pupil to observe for ten seconds. At the end of that time, put a check mark in the appropriate column opposite the pupil's name. Then select another pupil, observe him or her for ten seconds, record the behavior, and so on. If you sample behavior on several different occasions, you will have a record of the types of behavior engaged in by different pupils. Parten's technique is just one of many types of time sampling. A summary of several variations of the basic technique is presented on pages 92–104 of "Observational Child Study" by Herbert F. Wright, Chapter 3 in the *Handbook of Research Methods in Child Development* (1960), edited by Paul H. Mussen. Additional observational techniques are described by Gilbert R. Guerin and Arlee S. Maier in Chapter 4 of *Informal Assessment in Education* (1983). They describe the characteristics, strengths, and limitations of the chronolog, frequency-recording, sequence-sample, trait-sample, event-recall, and rating-scale methods of observation.

Helping Girls and Boys Resist Sex Stereotypes

There are a number of publications for persons who would like to encourage young girls to overcome, at least partially, the stereotyped view of females presented in movies, TV shows and commercials, books, and magazines. Perhaps the best-known book of this type is *Free to Be You and Me* (1974) by Marlo Thomas and several associates. A similar publication is *What I Want to Be When I Grow Up* (1975) by Carol Burnett, George Mendoza, and Sheldon Secunda.

In *We've All Got Scars* (1983), Raphaela Best, a reading specialist for an affluent school district, describes how the school's "second curriculum" (sex role socialization) and "third curriculum" (self-taught sex education) affect interpersonal relationships and classroom achievement in six-, seven-, and eight-year-old boys and girls.

In the *Sex Equity Handbook for Schools* (1982), Myra Pollock Sadker and David Miller Sadker provide an overview of those aspects of education where sex equity is most needed (for example, instructional materials and teacher-student interactions), describe strategies and lesson plans for eliminating sex bias in the classroom, and provide a directory of sources of nonsexist instructional materials and classroom strategies.

For any prospective or practicing teacher interested in learning how to reduce his or her own gender bias, as well as the gender bias of others, *Building Gender Fairness in Schools* (1988) by Beverly Stitt is a useful resource. This book is made up of two parts. Part 1 contains a collection of six readings on various aspects of gender bias (for example, "Sexism in Education," "How Fair Is Your Language?" and "Confronting Sex Bias in Instructional Materials." Part 2 contains a sequenced set of eleven instructional units, each of which presents a competency to be mastered by the preservice or in-service teacher. The competencies become increasingly complex and difficult. Unit 1, for example, attempts to develop an awareness of the effects of gender bias. The goal of Unit 5 is to identify gender-fair curriculum materials. The goal of Unit 11 is to conduct applied research to develop policies and programs to achieve gender fairness.

Becoming Aware of Differences in Cognitive Style

When you begin to teach, you may be baffled by the extent of the differences in the way your pupils respond to class activities. To gain awareness of the range of individual differences, make it a point to look for variations among students when you observe or participate in a classroom. Such awareness may prepare you for the wide range of reactions your students will display when you take over a classroom. It may also help you make plans to allow for such variations. Listed below are pairs of terms that summarize essentially opposite types of thinking, perceiving, and reacting. They are based on descriptions of cognitive styles noted in this chapter's discussion of the work of Jerome Kagan (1964), Samuel Messick (1976), and J. P. Guilford (1967). Observe students in a public school or college class, and try to pick out—for as many pairs as you can—a student who exemplifies each extreme. Then give a brief description of the behavior that led you to select that student as a model of that particular style. Finally, speculate about what, if anything, you might do to allow for such differences when you begin to teach.

Impulsive. Tendency to give first answer, to be eager to respond quickly.

Reflective. Tendency to think things over, to be deliberate and cautious in responding.

Analytic. Tendency to note details, preference for specifics.

Thematic. Tendency to respond to whole pattern, interest in "big picture."

Attentiveness to detail. Tendency to recognize and respond to many aspects of a situation.

One-track responding. Tendency to concentrate on only one aspect of a situation at a time.

Concentrated attention. Tendency to concentrate on a particular task or idea and to resist distractions or interruptions.

Distractibility. Tendency to be diverted from one task or idea when conflicting or different activities or ideas are present.

Resistance to change. Reluctance to accept unexpected or unconventional views or evidence.

Flexibility. High degree of adaptability to new, different, or unexpected points of view.

Conventionality. Tendency to seek or provide one right answer or a conventional answer.

Individuality. Tendency to respond in nonconventional, unexpected, or individual ways.

On the basis of your observation, are there any procedures or techniques you might want to try in your classes to allow for the differences you noted?

Impact of Puberty and the Growth Spurt

To appreciate the nature and magnitude of changes that take place at the time of puberty, arrange to visit a seventh-grade and a ninth-grade classroom. Observe the students not only in class but also in the halls and after school. Describe differences in physical appearance and in behavior between the seventh- and ninth-graders, paying particular attention to differences between boys and girls. You might also try to pick out the most and least mature children in a group and concentrate on their behavior in and out of the classroom. If you make an observation of this type, note your reactions and comment on the implications of differences you detect.

Early and Late Maturation

For a summary of research on early and late maturation, refer to "Perspectives on Adolescence from Longitudinal Research" by Norman Livson and Harvey Peskin in the *Handbook of Adolescent Psychology* (1980), edited by Joseph Adelson.

Biological and Physiological Aspects of Adolescence

For more complete information about biological changes at adolescence, consult *Growth at Adolescence* (2nd ed., 1962) by J. M. Tanner. Condensed versions of the material in his book can be found in Chapter 3 of *Carmichael's Manual of Child Psychology* (3rd ed., 1970), edited by Paul H. Mussen, and Chapter 1 of *Twelve to Sixteen: Early Adolescence* (1972), edited by Jerome Kagan and Robert Coles.

Advanced treatments of this topic can be found in the *Handbook of Adolescent Psychology* (1987), edited by Vincent B. Van Hasselt and Michel Hersen. In particular, consult Chapter 3, "Biological Theoretical Models of Adolescent Development," and Chapter 7, "Pubertal Processes: Their Relevance for Developmental Research."

Emotional Characteristics of Adolescense

Useful, although advanced, information about the emotional aspects of adolescence can be gleaned from several chapters of the *Handbook of Adolescent Psychology* (1987), just mentioned. Chapter 9 covers adolescent sexuality; Chapter 16 discusses depression and suicide; and Chapter 17 discusses the causes and nature of substance abuse.

Summary

1. Preschool and kindergarten children are quite active and enjoy physical activity. Incomplete muscle and motor development, though, limits what they can accomplish on tasks that require fine motor skills, eye-hand coordination, and visual focusing.
2. The social behavior of preschool and kindergarten children is marked by rapidly changing friendships and play groups, a variety of types of play, short quarrels, and a growing awareness of sex roles.
3. Kindergarteners openly display their emotions. Anger and jealousy are common.
4. Kindergarteners like to talk and are reasonably skilled at using language. Preschoolers tend to apply their own rules of grammar.
5. Primary grade children exhibit many of the same physical characteristics as preschool and kindergarten children (high activity level, incomplete muscle and motor development, frequent periods of fatigue). Most accidents occur among third-graders because they overestimate their physical skills and underestimate the dangers in their activities.
6. Friendships are made on a more selective basis by primary grade children. Quarrels occur fairly frequently and involve verbal arguments as well as punching, wrestling, and shoving.
7. Primary grade pupils are becoming more emotionally sensitive. As a result, they are more easily hurt by criticism, respond strongly to praise, and are more likely to hurt another child's feelings during a quarrel.
8. Primary grade pupils are eager to learn and like to speak up in class.
9. Elementary grade girls grow more quickly and begin puberty earlier than elementary grade boys. All children have developed sufficient fine motor coordination to enjoy arts and crafts and musical activities.
10. The social behavior of elementary grade children is increasingly influenced by peer group norms and the development of interpersonal reasoning.
11. Delinquency occurs more frequently among elementary grade children than at earlier ages. Emotional disorders reach a peak during these years.
12. Although sex differences in cognitive abilities among elementary students have decreased over the past forty years, they are still noticeable. Differences in cognitive style are also apparent.
13. In junior high, boys catch up with and begin to exceed girls in physical development. Almost all girls and many boys reach puberty. Diet and sleeping habits may change for the worse.
14. Because the peer group is the primary source for rules of acceptable behavior, conformity and concern about what peers think reaches a peak during the junior high years.
15. Anxiety, worry, and concern about self-esteem, physical appearance, and acceptance by peers are prominent emotions among many adolescents. School vandalism peaks during the junior high years.
16. Junior high school marks a transition between concrete operational and formal operational thought and between moral realism and moral relativism.

17. Physical development during the high school years is marked by physical maturity for most students and by puberty for virtually all. Sexual activity increases.
18. The long-range goals of adolescents are likely to be influenced by parents, whereas immediate status is likely to be influenced by peers.
19. Female adolescents are more likely than male adolescents to experience emotional disorders. Depression is the most common emotional disorder during adolescence. Depression coupled with an unstable family situation places adolescents at risk for suicide.
20. Cognitively, high school students become increasingly capable of formal operational thought, although they may function at the concrete operational level a good deal of the time.

Key Terms

sociometric techniques *(103)*
unoccupied behavior *(104)*
solitary play *(104)*
onlooker behavior *(104)*
parallel play *(104)*
associative play *(104)*
cooperative play *(104)*
authoritative parents *(109)*

authoritarian parents *(109)*
interpersonal reasoning *(118)*
cognitive style *(124)*
early-maturing boy *(128)*
late-maturing boy *(128)*
early-maturing girl *(128)*
late-maturing girl *(128)*
learned helplessness *(139)*

Discussion Questions

1. Given the physical, social, emotional, and cognitive characteristics of preschool and kindergarten children, what type of classroom atmosphere and instructional tactics would you use to foster learning and enjoyment of school?
2. The primary and elementary years correspond to Erikson's stage of industry versus inferiority. The implication of this stage is that educators should do whatever is necessary to encourage a sense of industry and competence in each student. On a scale of 1 to 10, where 1 is the low end of the scale, how well do you think schools accomplish this goal? What is it that schools do (or do not do) that prevented you from assigning them a 10?
3. During the junior high years the peer group becomes the general source for rules of behavior. Why? What are the advantages and disadvantages of the peer group establishing the norms for behavior?
4. Given the high rates of illegitimate births and sexually transmitted diseases among high school students, you could persuasively argue that adolescents should receive more sex education than they do. What are the advantages and disadvantages of the school providing this education, instead of the home?

chapter 4

ASSESSING PUPIL VARIABILITY

KEY POINTS

The Meaning of Variability

Intraindividual variation: differences in a person's behavior over time and situation

Interindividual variation: differences between individuals at a given point in time

Standardized Tests

Standardized tests: items presented in standard fashion, results reported with reference to standards

Standardized test scores used to direct instruction and select students for programs

Reliability: similarity between two rankings of test scores obtained from same individuals

Validity: how well a test measures what users want it to measure

Content validity: how well test items cover a type of learning

Predictive validity: how well a test score predicts later performance

Construct validity: how accurately a test measures a particular attribute

Meaningfulness of standardized test scores depends on representativeness of norm group

Achievement tests measure how much has been learned about a subject

Diagnostic tests designed to identify specific strengths and weaknesses

Aptitude tests provide estimates of potential ability

Competency tests determine if potential graduates possess basic skills

Norm-referenced scores compare one student with others

Criterion-referenced scores indicate degree of mastery of objectives

Percentile rank: percentage of scores at or below a given point

Standard deviation: degree of deviation from the mean of a distribution

Z score: how far a raw score is from the mean in standard deviation units

T score: how far a raw score is from the mean in numerical terms

Stanine score: pupil performance indicated with reference to a 9-point scale based on normal curve

The Nature and Measurement of Intelligence

First intelligence tests devised to measure probability of school success

Intelligence tests not good predictors of job success, marital happiness, life happiness

Intelligence tests attempt to measure general and specific factors

Intelligence involves more than what intelligence tests measure

Intelligence tests measure a sample of intellectual skills

IQ scores can change with experience, training

IQ test items based on knowledge and situations felt to be common to most children

Legal Challenges to Standardized Testing

In real world, test-based decisions sometimes harm children

Conflicting opinions regarding bias in intelligence tests

Overreliance on test scores can bar gifted and talented minority children from special programs

---

Sit back for a few minutes and think about some of your friends and classmates over the past twelve years. Make a list of their physical characteristics (height, weight, visual acuity, athletic skill, for example), social characteristics (outgoing, reserved, cooperative, sensitive to the needs of others, assertive), emotional characteristics (self-assured, optimistic, pessimistic, egotistical), and intellectual characteristics (methodical, creative, impulsive, good with numbers, terrible at organizing ideas). Now analyze your descriptions in terms of similarities and differences. In all likelihood, they point to many ways in which your friends and classmates have been alike, but to even more ways in which they have differed from each other. That is because although human beings share many important characteristics, they also differ from each other in significant ways (and we tend to notice the differences more readily than the similarities).

Now imagine yourself a few years from now, when your job as a teacher is to help every student learn as much as possible despite all the ways in which your students differ from one another. The variability among any group of students is one reason why teaching is both interesting and challenging. Richard Snow, who has written extensively about individual differences in education and how to deal with them, has summarized the problem as follows:

> Individual differences among students present a pervasive and profound problem to educators. At the outset of instruction in any topic, students of any age and in any culture will differ from one another in various intellectual and psychomotor abilities and skills, in both general and specialized prior knowledge, in interests and motives, and in personal styles of thought and work during learning. These differences, in turn, appear directly related to differences in the students' learning progress. (1986, p. 1029)

The significance of these observations on variability is that while it usually will be essential for you to plan lessons, assignments, and teaching techniques by taking into account *typical* characteristics, it will also be necessary for you to expect and make allowances for differences between pupils. Students vary not only in terms of all the characteristics described in Chapters 2 and 3, but also in terms of general and specific abilities to learn. The fact that some students learn more easily and successfully than others is one of the major problems you will need to deal with as a teacher.

The Meaning of Variability

Intraindividual variation: differences in a person's behavior over time and situation

When psychologists discuss variability, they often do so in terms of two broad categories. One category is called **intraindividual variation**. Since the prefix *intra* means within, the focus here is on how a given individual changes over time or acts differently in different situations. Can you recall, for example, any friends or classmates who gradually became more outgoing, or who excelled in algebra but struggled to write a coherent paragraph in English composition? A student's attention span, interest level, or motivation may change over time and tasks, because youngsters are sensitive to changes in such classroom variables as the subject matter, the pacing of instruction, the personality of the teacher, and the type of test being given. In Chapter 2 we pointed out how personality and thinking change with age and offered suggestions for teaching based on these differences. Likewise, in Chapter 3 we summarized physical, social, emotional, and intellectual changes (as well as similarities) as children progress from preschool through high school. In Chapters 7 through 11 we will mention intraindividual variability in learning and motivation.

Interindividual variation: differences between individuals at a given point in time

The second category is called **interindividual variation**. Since the prefix *inter* means between, the focus here is on differences between individuals at any given point in time. Keep in mind that some ways in which students differ from each other are more important than others. The ones you want to pay special attention to are those that relate strongly to classroom achievement. What follows is a *sam-*

Throughout their school years, students are interested in how they perform academically compared to classmates. (David S. Strickler/The Picture Cube)

ple (in alphabetical order) of points of individual difference that have, through extensive research, been related to achievement:

age	intelligence	personality
attention span	interest	prior knowledge
attitudes	learning strategies	problem solving
stage of cognitive development	learning style	self-concept
cognitive style	memory capacity	social class
ethnicity	motivation	social competence
gender	perceptual skill	values

Most of the research on interindividual variation revolves around scholastic aptitude (another term for intelligence) and achievement, because large numbers of standardized tests have been constructed to measure these variables. These tests make it possible to identify both the range of variability among a group of students and the strengths and weaknesses of each student. Ideally, schools can use this information to select and place children in instructional programs that match their characteristics or to adjust programs to better meet individual needs.

Because standardized assessment of scholastic aptitude and achievement is such a popular practice in the United States (as well as many other countries), this chapter focuses on the nature of standardized tests, how they are used to assess pupil variability, and how these test results can be employed in putting together effective instructional programs for "typical" students. The next chapter describes techniques for dealing with the range of interindividual variability—intellectual, emotional, and social—that exists in the typical classroom and may in some cases require special kinds of instruction. As we will see, and as Richard Snow (1986) has pointed out, the use of standardized tests to assess variability and guide the subsequent placement of students into different instructional programs is truly a double-edged sword: it has the potential to harm students, as well as to help them.

Standardized Tests

The Nature of Standardized Tests

Standardized tests: items presented in standard fashion, results reported with reference to standards

The kinds of assessment instruments described in this chapter are typically referred to as **standardized tests,** although the term *published tests* is sometimes used. You have almost certainly taken several of these tests during your academic career, and so you are probably familiar with their appearance and general characteristics. They are called standardized tests because they contain a standard set of items that are presented to students in uniform fashion, the answers are evaluated according to precise scoring standards, and the scores are interpreted by comparing them to the scores obtained from a norm group. They are called published tests because they are prepared, distributed, and scored by publishing companies or independent test services. The more inclusive term *published tests* has also been introduced because the scores from some types of instruments (to be described later) are interpreted with reference to predetermined criteria rather than the performance of a norm group. Standardized tests are widely used in American schools to provide information about student academic performance that cannot be obtained from teacher-made tests or grades.

Uses of Standardized Tests

The homemade tests you will devise for use in your classroom (a type we will cover in Chapter 12) will be custom designed to fit the texts and learning materials used by your students. Sometimes, however, you will want to obtain information about how well your students are performing compared with students in other classrooms.

In order to educate millions of American children who live in a complex and highly mobile society, it is essential to have them move through a reasonably standard basic curriculum. All the children who finish the sixth grade in several elementary schools in a large city, for instance, should have mastered the same basic learning tasks before they enter a common junior high or middle school. In addition, when a child moves to a different neighborhood within a city, or a different city within a state, or to a different part of the country, it is highly desirable to have some idea what the child knows about basic subjects. Standardized tests do an effective job of providing information about the mastery of general subject matter and skills.

When you read the test profiles that report how students in your classes have performed on standardized tests, you will be in a position to evaluate some of your students' strengths and weaknesses. If certain pupils are weak in particular skill areas and you want to help them overcome those weaknesses, test results *may* give you *some* insights into possible ways to provide remedial instruction. If most of your students score below average in certain segments of the curriculum, you will know that you should devote more time and effort to presenting those topics and skills to the entire class. You can and should, of course, supplement what you learn from standardized test results with your own tests and observations.

In addition to being used in planning instruction, standardized tests are used to select students for placement in certain types of school programs and for admission to college and graduate school. Tests of achievement and scholastic aptitude, for example, help schools identify and place students in classes for the mentally retarded, the learning disabled, and the gifted and talented. Your college admissions committee took the grades you earned in high school into consideration when you applied for admission, but they also asked you to take a standardized test. That test allowed them to compare you with other applicants based on an academic achievement score that was not influenced by differences in grading standards among schools.

Standardized test scores used to direct instruction and select students for programs

This brief description of standardized tests indicates that they can be used to determine student progress, identify academic strengths and weaknesses, evaluate the effectiveness of instruction, plan instructional and remedial programs, place students in specialized programs, and make comparisons of student performance independently of teacher evaluations of classroom performance.

Steps in the Development of Standardized Tests

Most standardized tests are designed to make it possible to compare the performance of a particular pupil with the performance of other pupils. (Some exceptions will be noted later.) In order to do that with any degree of confidence, it is necessary to follow a rather elaborate procedure. First, specialists with knowledge and experience in various fields of study describe what a well-informed pupil should know at a particular point in school. Next, questions designed to systematically evaluate such understanding are written by experts who specialize in test construction. The questions are arranged in a provisional form and tried out on a sample of pupils. The clarity and effectiveness of the questions is evaluated and they are then selected, revised, and arranged into subsequent forms until the test makers are satisfied that they have produced an adequate instrument. At that point the final form is given to a sample of students representative of the target population for the test. If the test is to be used to determine elementary school performance in basic skills, for instance, the final form will be given to groups of students from schools in all geographic areas and from all socioeconomic levels so that a cross section of the entire school population of the United States is represented. If the test is to be used to select students for college entrance, it will be given to seniors from a carefully selected sample of high schools in all parts of the country.

The performance of the sample of students selected to take the test in its final form is used to establish standards to be used in judging the performance of all students who eventually take the test. This process involves a number of quite sophisticated statistical procedures and requires considerable expertise. Finally, a detailed test manual is prepared explaining what the test is designed to measure, how it was standardized, how it should be administered, how scores are calculated, and what they mean. Such a test manual is considered to be essential so that those who consider using the test can make inferences about how effective it will be. It is highly unlikely that you will be asked to serve on a committee that selects standardized tests for use in your school before you have had several years of teaching experience. Even though you will not need to actually evaluate tests, though, it will be useful for you to have some knowledge about factors considered by those who are given the responsibility for selecting standardized tests.

Criteria for Evaluating Standardized Tests

Like most things, standardized tests vary in quality. To use test scores wisely, you need to be an informed consumer—to know what characteristics distinguish well-constructed from poorly constructed tests. Eight criteria are widely used to evaluate standardized tests: reliability, validity, normed excellence, examinee appropriateness, teaching feedback, usability, retest potential, and ethical propriety. Each of these criteria will be explained individually.

Reliability   A basic assumption that psychologists make about human characteristics (such as intelligence and achievement) is that they are relatively stable, at least over short periods of time. For most people this assumption seems to be true. Thus, you should be able to count on a test's results being consistent, just as you might count on a reliable worker doing a consistent job time after time. This stability in test performance is known as **reliability.** It is one of the most important characteristics of standardized tests and can be assessed in a number of ways.

To illustrate the importance of reliability, imagine that you have assigned each of your students to one of three reading groups on the basis of scores from the ABC Test of Reading Comprehension. One month later, you administer the ABC

Test again and find that many of those who scored at the top initially (and were placed in the top reading group) now score in the middle or at the bottom. Conversely, many students who initially scored low now have average or above average scores. What does that do to your confidence in making decisions based on scores from this test? If you want to be able to consistently differentiate among individuals, you need to use an instrument that performs consistently.

Psychologists who specialize in constructing standardized tests assess reliability in a variety of ways. One method is to administer the same test to the same people on two occasions and measure the extent to which the rankings change over time. This approach results in *test-retest reliability.* Another method is to administer two equivalent forms of a test to the same group of students at the same time. This approach results in *alternate form reliability.* A third approach is to administer a single test to a group of students, create two scores by dividing the test in half, and measure the extent to which the rankings change from one half to the other. This method results in *split-half reliability* and measures the internal consistency of a test.

Regardless of which method is used to assess reliability, the goal is to create two rankings of scores and to see how similar the rankings are. This degree of consistency is expressed as a correlation coefficient (abbreviated with a lower-case *r*) that ranges from zero to one. Well-constructed standardized tests should have correlation coefficients of about .95 for split-half reliability, .90 for test-retest reliability, and .85 for alternate form reliability (Kubiszyn and Borich, 1987). Bear in mind, however, that a particular test may not report all three forms of reliability and that reliabilities for subtests and for younger age groups (kindergarten through second grade) are likely to be lower than these overall figures.

Reliability: similarity between two rankings of test scores obtained from same individuals

Validity   The term **validity** is usually defined as how well a test appropriately measures what its users intend it to measure. If you are eager to find out about the reading ability of third-graders, you will want to use a test that actually measures reading ability. If you want to measure the scholastic aptitude of high school seniors, you will want to pick a test that indicates overall scholastic proficiency. These two examples illustrate two different kinds of validity. Testing experts distinguish between *content validity,* or how well the test items seem to cover a given type of learning, and *predictive validity,* or how well a test predicts later performance. If you were a third-grade teacher, you might be able to estimate the *content* validity of a test simply by examining the questions. But in order to find out about the *predictive* validity of the Scholastic Aptitude Test, for example, you would need information about the relationship between scores on that test and grade-point averages earned in college. Another way to estimate how well a test measures what its users intend to measure is to estimate its *construct validity.* Some tests purport to measure psychological *constructs* or attributes. A measure of construct validity indicates how accurately such tests actually measure particular attributes. A test of musical aptitude, for example, should differentiate be-

Validity: how well a test measures what users want it to measure

Content validity: how well test items cover a type of learning

Predictive validity: how well a test score predicts later performance

**Construct validity:
how accurately a test
measures a particular
attribute**

tween students who respond quickly to music instruction and those who do not. A test of reading comprehension should differentiate between students who understand the meaning of what they read and students who understand little of what they read.

Normed Excellence   For a test score to have any meaning, it has to be compared to some yardstick or measure of performance. Standardized tests use the performance of a norm group as the measure against which all other scores are compared. A **norm group** is a sample of individuals carefully chosen so as to reflect the larger population of students for whom the test is intended. In many cases, the larger population is all elementary school children or all high school children in the United States. The norm group must closely match the larger population it represents on such major demographic variables as age, sex, race, region of country, family income, and occupation of head of household. These variables are considered major because they are strongly associated with differences in school performance. If, for example, the U.S. Census Bureau reports that 38 percent of all Hispanic males between the ages of six and thirteen live in the southwestern region of the country, a good test constructor testing in the Southwest will try to put together a norm group that has the same percentage of six- to thirteen-year-old Hispanic males. As you might suspect, problems of score interpretation arise when the major demographic characteristics of individuals who take the test are not reflected in the norm group. Suppose you were trying to interpret the score of a fourteen-year-old black male on the EZ Test of Academic Achievement. If the oldest students in the norm group were twelve years of age and if black children were not part of the norm group, you would have no way of knowing if your student's score is below average, average, or above average, compared to the norm.

**Meaningfulness of
standardized test
scores depends on
representativeness of
norm group**

Examinee Appropriateness   Because developing a standardized test is a substantial undertaking that requires a considerable investment of money, time, and expertise, most tests of this type are designed for nationwide use. But the curriculum in school districts in different types of communities and in different sections of the country varies to a considerable extent. Therefore, it is important to estimate how appropriate a given test is for a particular group of pupils. When you are estimating the content validity of a test, you should pay attention not only to how well the questions measure what they are supposed to measure, but also to whether they are appropriate in terms of level of difficulty and in relation to the vocabulary and characteristics of your students.

Teaching Feedback   Most standardized tests are designed to be used all over the country, but generally the scores are used by particular teachers interested in individual pupils. An achievement test in reading will provide meaningful feedback only if the scores tell teachers something that can be used to improve instruction. If that is to happen, the scores should ordinarily reveal significant things about pupil performance and be reasonably easy to interpret.

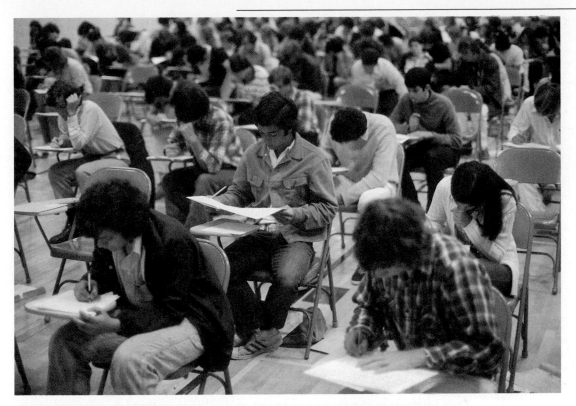

When high school seniors take exams such as the Scholastic Aptitude Test (or the equivalent) the results are reported in terms of norm-referenced scores. Each student's performance is compared to that of the sample of students who made up the standardization group when the test was devised. (Mimi Forsyth/Monkmeyer)

Usability   Most standardized tests are group tests designed to be given by one examiner to a class of students. (Some intelligence tests and a few performance tests that measure specialized aptitudes are individual tests given to one individual at a time.) As a result, the instructions and questions are typically printed in a test booklet, and the answers are recorded on a separate sheet that can be electronically processed. Sometimes special pencils must be used, and quite often students are given a specified number of minutes to work on each section. A test is usable if it provides clear instructions to the teacher (or other administrator) that can be put into practice without a great deal of difficulty or confusion and if it does not force students to waste time dealing with the mechanics of recording answers. (Perhaps you can recall taking standardized tests that were so confusing you were not sure you recorded the correct answer even when you were certain you knew it.)

Retest Potential   Quite often it is desirable to obtain before-and-after information about student performance. But if students are tested before they study a unit and then tested again after instruction has taken place, an alternate form of the first exam should be available. Simply giving the same test over again would yield misleading information because students might remember specific questions and answers. Therefore, the availability of an equivalent but different form of a standardized test may be an important consideration.

Ethical Propriety   In the 1960s, when some school districts embarked on a veritable test-giving binge, attempts were sometimes made to measure not only achievement, but various kinds of "adjustment" as well. Some of the questions used to tap personality variables asked students to consider questions viewed as potentially harmful (such as "Do you love your mother more than your father?"). As a consequence, many school boards now insist that all tests be examined to determine if they contain questions that might be classified as offensive or likely to arouse feelings of confusion or guilt.

Types of Standardized Tests

The kinds of standardized tests you took most frequently during your elementary school years and perhaps during your secondary school years were **achievement tests,** designed to assess how much you had learned—or achieved—in basic school subjects. The very first standardized test you took was probably designed to evaluate aspects of reading performance. Then, at intervals of two years or so, you probably worked your way tensely and laboriously through *achievement batteries* designed to assess your performance in reading as well as math, language, and perhaps other subjects. During your high school years, you may have taken one or more achievement batteries that evaluated more sophisticated understanding of the basic reading-writing-arithmetic skills, as well as course content in specific subjects. At some point during your elementary school years, you may have also been asked to take a **diagnostic test,** intended to reveal your strengths and weaknesses in basic subjects and perhaps also in study skills. You may also have taken a *scholastic aptitude* test, intended to assess your general aptitude as a student rather than your actual knowledge of subject-area skills and content. **Aptitude tests** are intended to reveal potential maximum performance, or how well a pupil is capable of performing. Thus, your teachers may have discovered that your general aptitude for learning was higher than your achievement and urged you to make greater use of your potential.

If one of your teachers felt that there was a substantial discrepancy between scores on scholastic aptitude and achievement tests or if you were ever considered for a special program of some sort, you may have been asked to take an *individual test of intelligence.* All the tests described up to this point have been *group* tests given to several students at the same time. Because group tests often make no provision for identifying and correcting students' misconceptions about how to respond to particular items, such tests are apt to contain some amount of what test specialists call measurement error. When more accuracy is desired, it is usually better to have a trained examiner give a test that has been designed for one pupil at a time. Many individual tests provide extensive explanations and illus-

Achievement tests measure how much has been learned about a subject

Diagnostic tests designed to identify specific strengths and weaknesses in basic learning skills

Aptitude tests provide estimates of potential ability

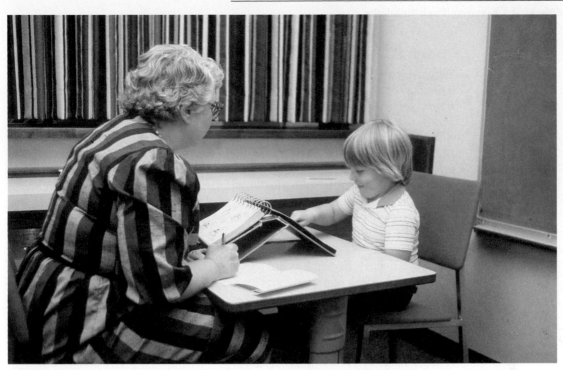

When maximum accuracy is desired—as when an estimate of intelligence is needed to determine eligibility for a special class—an individual test (such as the one shown here) is given by a trained examiner to one pupil at a time. (D. Logan/H. Armstrong Roberts)

trations of how to respond to items, allow the examiner to provide some degree of corrective feedback, and suggest ways of establishing a testing atmosphere in which the student will feel comfortable. Accordingly, the most highly regarded tests of intelligence (which will be described a bit later) are individual tests.

Depending on when and where you graduated from high school, you may have been asked to take a **competency test** a few months before the end of your senior year. Competency tests began to be used in the mid-1970s, when it was discovered that many graduates of American high schools were unable to handle basic skills. In many school districts, therefore, students were asked to prove that they were competent in reading, writing, and arithmetic before they were awarded diplomas. It is almost certain that some time during your senior year of high school you took a test required by the admissions committee of the college you hoped to attend. You probably took either the *Scholastic Aptitude Test* (SAT) or the *American College Testing Program* (ACT) exam. If you decide to continue on to graduate school, you can expect to take the *Graduate Record Exam* (GRE).

Most of the exams just described are referred to as **norm-referenced tests** since performance is evaluated with reference to norms—the performance of others—established when the final form of the test was administered to the sample of students who made up the standardization group. After taking an achievement battery in the elementary grades, for example, you were probably told that you

Competency tests determine if potential graduates possess basic skills

Norm-referenced scores compare one student with others

had performed as well on reading comprehension questions as 80 percent (or whatever) of all of the students who took the test. If you take the Graduate Record Exam, you will be told how far from the average score of 500 you are (in terms of a score to be described shortly). Thus, you will learn just where you stand in a distribution of scores arranged from lowest to highest. Recently, however, a *criterion-referenced* approach to reporting achievement scores has been developed. In scoring **criterion-referenced tests,** instead of being compared with the performance of other pupils, an individual's performance is evaluated with reference to mastery of specific objectives in various well-defined skill areas. Because of this feature, you may find criterion-referenced tests more useful than norm-referenced tests in determining who needs how much additional instruction in what areas (provided, of course, the test's objectives closely match your own). The criterion-referenced approach is intended to reduce overtones of competition and emphasize mastery of objectives at a rate commensurate with students' abilities. (An approach to evaluation that stresses mastery of objectives will be detailed in Chapter 12, on classroom measurement). A disadvantage of criterion-referenced tests is their lack of breadth; they usually cover a relatively small number of objectives. Norm-referenced achievement tests, on the other hand, usually cover a broader range of knowledge and skill.

Criterion-referenced scores indicate degree of mastery of objectives

Interpreting Standardized Test Scores

Scores on the most widely used standardized tests are typically reported on student profile forms that summarize and explain the results (see page 165 for an example of a test profile). While most profiles contain sufficient information to make it possible to interpret scores without additional background, you should know in advance about the kinds of scores you may encounter, particularly because you may be asked to explain scores to students as well as their parents. The likelihood of parents wanting information about standardized test scores increased in 1975, when Congress added a new part to the General Education Provisions Act titled Privacy Rights of Parents and Students. The Privacy Rights amendment stipulates that all educational institutions must provide "parents of students access to all official records directly related to the students and an opportunity for a hearing to challenge such records on the grounds they are inaccurate, misleading, or otherwise inappropriate" (*Federal Register,* Jan. 6, 1975, p. 1028). This law was passed primarily to reduce the possibility that damaging statements about children recorded in cumulative folders might have negative repercussions, but it may lead to requests for detailed interpretation of test scores. Thus, in addition to explaining test scores to parents during parent conferences, you may be asked to supply such explanations "on demand." You should therefore know how to interpret standardized test scores, which can sometimes be misunderstood.

Grade Equivalent Scores   The **grade equivalent score** is established by interpreting performance on tests in terms of grade levels. A student who made a grade equivalent score of 4.7 on an achievement test, for example, got the same number of items right on this test as the average fourth-grader in the standardization group achieved by the seventh month of the school year. The grade equivalent score was once widely used at the elementary level, but because it may lead to misinterpretations, it is not as popular as it once was. One problem with grade equivalent scores is the tendency to misinterpret a score above a student's actual grade level as an indication that the student is capable of consistently working at that level. This kind of assumption might lead parents to agitate for an accelerated promotion. Such scores may show that a student did somewhat better on the test than the average student a grade or two above her or him, but they do not mean that the student tested has acquired knowledge of all the skills covered in the grade that would be skipped if demands for acceleration were granted.

Percentile Ranks   Probably the most widely used score for standardized tests is the **percentile rank.** This score indicates the percentage of students who are at and below a given student's score. It provides specific information about relative position. Students earning a percentile rank of 87 did as well as or better than 87 percent of the students in the particular normative group being used. They did not get 87 percent of the questions right—unless by coincidence—and this is the point parents are most likely to misunderstand. Parents may have been brought up on the percentages grading system, in which 90 or above was A, 80 to 90 was B, and so on down the line. If you report that a son or daughter has a percentile rank of 50, some parents are horrorstruck or outraged, not understanding that the child's score on this test is average, not a failure. In such cases the best approach is to emphasize that the percentile rank tells the percentage of cases at or below the child's score. You might also talk in terms of a hypothetical group of 100; for example, a child with a percentile rank of 78 did as well as or better than 78 out of every 100 students who took the test.

> **Percentile rank:** percentage of scores at or below a given point

Although the percentile rank gives simple and direct information on relative position, it has a major disadvantage: The difference in achievement between students clustered around the middle of the distribution is often considerably less than the difference between those at the extremes. The reason is that most scores are clustered around the middle of most distributions of large groups of students. The difference in raw score (number of items answered correctly) between students at percentile ranks 50 and 51 may be one point. But the difference in raw score between the student with a percentile rank of 98 and one ranked 97 may be ten or fifteen because the best (and worst) students scatter toward the extremes. This quality of percentile ranks means that ranks on different tests cannot be averaged. To get around that difficulty, standard scores are often used.

Standard Scores   Standard scores are expressed in terms of a common unit—the **standard deviation.** This statistic indicates the degree to which scores in a group of tests (a distribution) differ from the average or mean. (The **mean** is the arithmetical average of a distribution and is calculated by adding all scores and

> **Standard deviation:** degree of deviation from the mean of a distribution

dividing the total by the number of scores.) The standard deviation is most valuable when it can be related to the normal probability curve. Figure 4.1 shows a normal probability curve indicating the percentage of cases to be found within three standard deviations above and below the mean. The **normal curve** is a mathematical concept that depicts a hypothetical bell-shaped distribution of scores. Such a perfectly symmetrical distribution rarely, if ever, occurs in real life. However, since many distributions of human characteristics and performance closely *resemble* the normal distribution, it is often assumed that such distributions are typical enough to be treated as "normal." Thus, information derived by mathematicians for the hypothetical normal distribution can be applied to the approximately normal distributions that are found when human attributes are measured. When very large numbers of pupils are asked to take tests designed by specialists who take pains to cancel out the impact of selective factors, it may be appropriate to interpret their scores on such tests with reference to the normal curve.

Z score: how far a raw score is from the mean in standard deviation units

T score: how far a raw score is from the mean in numerical terms

For purposes of discussion and for purposes of acquiring familiarity with test scores, it will be sufficient for you to know about two of the standard scores that are derived from standard deviations. One, called a **z score,** tells how far a given raw score is from the mean in standard deviation units. A z score of −1.5, for example, would mean that the pupil was one and one-half standard deviation units below the mean. Because some z scores (such as the one in the example just given) are negative and involve decimals, **T scores** are often used instead. T scores use a preselected mean (50) to get away from negative values.

Most standardized tests that use T scores offer detailed explanations of how they should be interpreted either in the test booklet or on the student profile of

Figure 4.1 The Normal Probability Curve

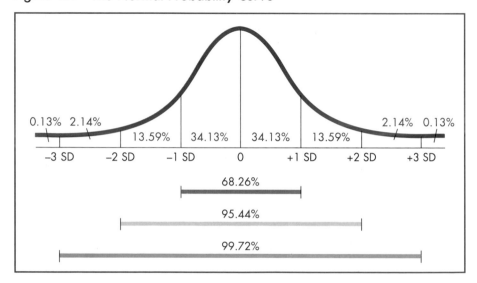

scores. Many test profiles, in fact, explain the meaning of all scores used in the form of a narrative report. (See Figure 4.4, page 165.)

To grasp the relationship between percentile ranks, z scores, and T scores, examine Figure 4.2. The diagram shows each scale marked off below a normal curve. It supplies information about the interrelationships of these various scores, provided the distribution you are working with is essentially normal. In a normal distribution, for example, a z score of +1 is the same as a T score of 60 or a percentile rank of 84; a z score of −2 is the same as a T score of 30 or a percentile rank of about 2. (In addition, notice that the distance between the percentile ranks clustered around the middle is only a small fraction of the distance between the percentile ranks that are found at the ends of the distribution.)

Stanine Scores   During World War II, air force psychologists developed a statistic called the **stanine score** (an abbreviation of "standard nine-point scale"), reflecting the fact that it is a type of standard score and divides a population into nine groups. Each stanine is one-half of a standard deviation unit, as indicated in Figure 4.3.

Stanine scores were developed for use in wartime training programs where efficiency was of paramount importance. The test specialists who devised the statistic, for instance, developed a battery of several tests that identified pilot candi-

Figure 4.2   Relationship Between z Scores, T Scores, and Percentile Ranks

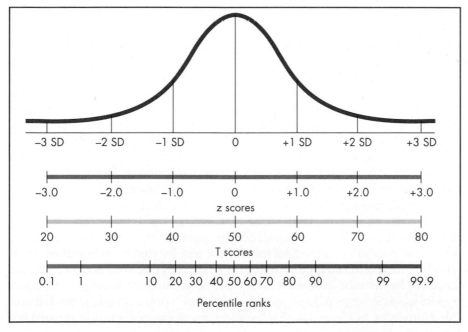

Figure 4.3   Percentage of Cases in Each Stanine (with Standard Deviation Units Indicated)

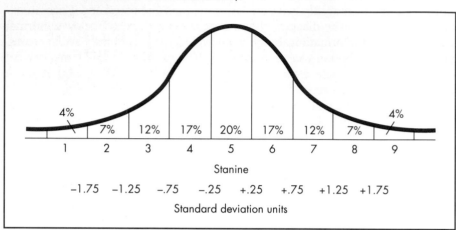

dates most likely to respond quickly and effectively to instruction. All of the candidates for pilot training who arrived at an Air Force base at a particular time would be given the battery of tests and their performance would be reported in terms of stanines. If only a few pilots were needed at that particular moment during the war, only candidates in stanines 8 and 9 might be selected for training. If more pilots were needed, those in the next highest stanines might also be admitted to the training program. When stanines were first introduced on test profiles reporting the performance of public school children on standardized tests, they were often used to group students. (Students in stanines 1, 2, and 3 would be placed in one class, those in 4, 5, and 6 in other classes, and so on.) For reasons to be described later in this chapter as well as the next, grouping has become a highly controversial issue in American schools. Consequently, stanine scores are now used to indicate relative standing. They are easier to understand than z scores or T scores since any child or parent can understand that stanines represent a 9-point scale with 1 as the lowest, 5 as average, and 9 as the highest. Furthermore, unlike percentile ranks, stanine scores can be averaged. In some cases, however, when it is desirable to have more precise information about relative standing, percentile ranks may be more useful, even though they cannot be averaged.

Percentile ranks and stanines are often used when local norms are prepared. As noted in describing how standardized tests are developed, the norms used to determine a student's level of performance are established by asking a representative sample of pupils to take the final form of the test. Inevitably, there will be differences (in texts used and time during a school year or years when certain topics are covered, for instance) between school systems. Accordingly, some test publishers report scores in terms of local, as well as national, norms. (Examine the test profile reproduced in Figure 4.4.) Each student's performance is thus compared not

Stanine score: pupil performance indicated with reference to a 9-point scale based on normal curve

Figure 4.4 Example of a Student Diagnostic Report

Based on Reading Yardsticks score report, Copyright © 1981. Reprinted with permission of the Publisher, THE RIVERSIDE PUBLISHING COMPANY, 8420 W. Bryn Mawr Avenue, Chicago IL, 60631. All rights reserved.

STUDENT DIAGNOSTIC REPORT
THE RIVERSIDE PUBLISHING COMPANY

STUDENT RECORD FOR: RITA FINNEGAN

Test: READING YARDSTICKS		
Level: 11	Date 10/81	Form 1
Sex: F	Process No. 000-1429-002	
Building KENNON MIDDLE	Grade 5	System: KENNON
Teacher: MRS. ECKLAND	Norms: FALL	

Criterion-Referenced Interpretation — Performance on Objectives

** = DID NOT REACH MASTERY LEVEL OF 60 X 60 AS SET BY SCHOOL DISTRICT

Part / Subtest / Objective	Number of Items	Number of Times Attempted	Percent Correct Student	Percent Correct Building
VOCABULARY	40	38	90	67
SYNONYMS	10	9	80	51
ANTONYMS	10	9	80	55
MULTI-MEANING WORDS	10	10	100	82
PRONOUN REFERENTS	10	10	90	80
COMPREHENSION	60	58	67	52
LITERAL READING COMPREHENSION	13	12	82	79
DETAILS	5	5	100	77
VISUALIZING	3	2	67	63
SEQUENCE	5	5	100	81
INTERPRETIVE READING COMPREHENSION	19	19	73	71
MAIN IDEA	5	5	80	76
DRAW CONCLUSIONS	5	5	60	54
CAUSE AND EFFECT	9	9	78	63
EVALUATIVE READING COMPREHENSION	14	14	**57	49
PREDICT OUTCOMES	5	5	60	52
FACT VS. OPINION	5	5	60	53
CHARACTER TRAITS	4	4	**50	51
LANGUAGE COMPREHENSION	14	13	**56	62
SIMILES AND METAPHORS	5	4	67	59
IDIOMS	3	3	**33	42
PUNCTUATION, PERIOD, QUESTION MARK	3	3	75	73
PUNCTUATION, QUOTATION MARKS	4	3	75	73
STRUCTURAL ANALYSIS	55	45	64	64
WORD PARTS	55	45	64	64
PLURALS	5	5	80	81
POSSESSIVES	5	5	80	56
SYLLABICATION; NUMBER OF SYLLABLES	10	8	60	51
SYLLABICATION; WORD DIVISION	10	8	60	78
BASE WORDS	10	8	60	65
AFFIXES, WORD MEANING	10	7	**50	53
CONTRACTIONS	5	4	80	66
STUDY SKILLS	55	49	68	66
REFERENCE MATERIAL	39	35	73	70
DICTIONARY, ALPHA ORDER, GUIDE WORDS	3	3	100	92
ALPHA ORDER, SECOND-FOURTH LETTERS	5	5	67	71
DICTIONARY: CHOOSING DEFINITIONS	5	3	60	58
PRONUNCIATION KEY	3	3	75	80
ENCYCLOPEDIA	3	3	67	62
CARD CATALOG	4	4	**50	50
PARTS OF BOOKS	4	4	75	77
CHOOSING REFERENCE SOURCES	4	4	80	78
MAPS	5	5	80	85
ORGANIZATIONAL STUDY SKILLS	16	14	63	61
TOPIC: SUBTOPICS	4	3	75	74
TOPIC: RELEVANT DETAILS	4	4	**50	80
FOLLOWING DIRECTIONS	4	3	75	69
TEST TOTAL	210	204	150	69

Norm-Referenced Interpretation

Subtest	Scores RS	LCL PR	Profile (Below Average 1 — 25 — Average 50 — 75 — Above Average 99)
VOCABULARY	36	76	/////////////////
LITERAL READING COMPREHENSION	11	60	/////////////
INTERPRETIVE READING COMPREHENSION	14	52	////////////
EVALUATIVE READING COMPREHENSION	8	53	////////////
LANGUAGE READING COMPREHENSION	8	24	//////
WORD PARTS	35	49	/////////////
REFERENCE MATERIAL STUDY SKILLS	28	50	////////////
ORGANIZATIONAL STUDY SKILLS	10	46	////////////

RITA'S ESTIMATED ITBS SCORES ARE AS FOLLOWS:

	OCTOBER 1981	MAY 1982	SEPTEMBER 1982
VOCABULARY			
GE	63	70	74
PR	76	76	76
NCE	65	65	65
SS	137	146	151
READING COMPREHENSION			
GE	51	57	61
PR	49	49	49
NCE	50	50	50
SS	124	130	136
WORK-STUDY SKILLS			
GE	52	58	62
PR	50	50	50
NCE	50	50	50
SS	124	131	137

NOTE THAT IN ADDITION TO A DESCRIPTION OF WHERE SHE IS NOW, RITA'S PROJECTED GROWTH IS REPORTED FOR THE COMING YEAR.

Narrative Interpretation

HOW WELL IS RITA DOING IN READING? TO HELP ANSWER THIS QUESTION, RITA TOOK READING YARDSTICKS IN OCTOBER 1981. HER TEST RESULTS ARE SHOWN ON THE LEFT.

LET'S GO OVER THE RESULTS FOR RITA. WE START AT THE FAR LEFT, UNDER THE SECTION HEADED "CRITERION-REFERENCED INTERPRETATION." THE FIRST SUBTEST IN READING YARDSTICKS IS VOCABULARY. UNDER VOCABULARY, FOUR OBJECTIVES ARE MEASURED. THE FIRST OBJECTIVE IS SYNONYMS. RITA ATTEMPTED 9 OF 10 TEST EXERCISES UNDER SYNONYMS. SHE GOT 8 OF THEM CORRECT. HER PERCENT CORRECT IS 80. THIS COMPARES WITH THE BUILDING PERCENT CORRECT OF 51, WHICH WAS BASED ON 247 FIFTH GRADE STUDENTS WHO TOOK THE TEST WITH RITA. RITA'S PERCENT CORRECT IN SYNONYMS IS HIGHER THAN THE BUILDING PERCENT CORRECT. THIS MEANS THAT RITA MAY BE STRONGER IN SYNONYMS THAN OTHER FIFTH GRADE STUDENTS IN THE BUILDING. USING THIS APPROACH, WE CAN LOOK AT HOW RITA DID ON EACH OF THE READING OBJECTIVES.

HOW DID RITA DO COMPARED WITH OTHER STUDENTS? WE ALREADY HAVE SOME INFORMATION, BUT THE SECTION ON THE LEFT UNDER "NORM-REFERENCED INFORMATION" GIVES MORE. FOR EXAMPLE, RITA'S PERCENTILE RANK IN VOCABULARY IS 76. THIS MEANS THAT RITA SCORED HIGHER THAN 76 PERCENT OF THE FIFTH GRADE STUDENTS IN THE BUILDING. ON THE OTHER HAND, 24 PERCENT SCORED AS WELL OR BETTER. RITA SEEMS TO BE SOMEWHAT ABOVE AVERAGE IN VOCABULARY COMPARED TO OTHER FIFTH GRADE STUDENTS. LET'S SEE HOW RITA DID ON THE OTHER SUBTESTS. RITA HAS SOMEWHAT ABOVE AVERAGE IN LITERAL READING COMPREHENSION, ABOUT AVERAGE IN INTERPRETIVE READING COMPREHENSION, ABOUT AVERAGE IN EVALUATIVE READING COMPREHENSION, SOMEWHAT BELOW AVERAGE IN LANGUAGE, ABOUT AVERAGE IN WORD PARTS, AVERAGE IN REFERENCE MATERIAL STUDY SKILLS, AND ABOUT AVERAGE IN ORGANIZATIONAL STUDY SKILLS.

LET'S LOOK AT RITA'S HIGH AND LOW POINTS IN READING FOR DIAGNOSTIC PURPOSES. WE LOOK AT EACH PAIR OF TEST SCORES, TO SEE IF THERE IS BETTER THAN A 50 PERCENT CHANCE THAT THE OBSERVED DIFFERENCES BETWEEN THEM ARE RELIABLE ONES. RITA IS HIGHER IN VOCABULARY THAN IN WORD PARTS, IN LITERAL READING COMPREHENSION THAN IN LANGUAGE, AND IN WORD PARTS THAN ORGANIZATIONAL STUDY SKILLS.

RITA'S LEVEL OF PERFORMANCE ON THE IOWA TESTS OF BASIC SKILLS (ITBS) IS ESTIMATED ON THE LEFT, FOR VOCABULARY, READING COMPREHENSION, AND WORK-STUDY SKILLS. GRADE EQUIVALENTS (GE), NATIONAL PERCENTILE RANKS (PR), AND NORMAL CURVE EQUIVALENTS (NCE) ARE ESTIMATED FOR BOTH CURRENT STATUS AND PROJECTED FOR A YEAR FROM NOW. THE PROJECTED GROWTH IS AN AVERAGE GROWTH. SOME STUDENTS WILL GROW MORE AND SOME LESS. RITA CAN BE RETESTED IN MAY 1982 OR SEPTEMBER 1982 WITH THE ITBS OR YARDSTICKS AND HER ACTUAL SCORES COULD THEN BE COMPARED WITH THE PROJECTED GROWTH SCORES.

COULD RITA BENEFIT FROM SPECIAL HELP IN READING? ALL OF THE FIFTH GRADE STUDENTS WHO WERE TESTED WITH RITA HERE COMPARED WITH ONE ANOTHER ON EACH OF THE READING SUBTESTS. STUDENTS IN THE LOWER ONE-FOURTH OF THE GROUP ON ANY SUBTEST WOULD SEEM TO BENEFIT FROM SPECIAL HELP. IN THESE TERMS, RITA NEEDS HELP IN LANGUAGE.

LEGEND: RS = Raw Score (number of test items correct); SS = Standard Score; LCL PR = Local Percentile Rank; NAT SMP PR = National Sample Percentile Rank; GE = Grade Equivalent; NCE = Normal Curve Equivalent only with the performance of the members of the standardization group, but also with the performance of all students in the same school system.

At the beginning of this chapter, we pointed out that the primary reason for administering standardized tests is to place students in instructional programs that best match their strengths and weaknesses. In instances where teachers fully understand the characteristic being measured, where reliable, valid, and well-normed tests are readily available, and where teachers know how to appropriately interpret test results, this strategy for dealing with individual differences can work quite well, particularly when it is supplemented with teacher observations and informal assessments. Effective remedial reading and math programs, for example, are based to a large extent on scores from diagnostic reading and math tests. But when the characteristic being measured and the nature of the test are poorly understood, inappropriate decisions and controversy often result. Nowhere are these negative outcomes more likely than in the assessment of intelligence. Since many instructional and placement decisions are based on intelligence test scores, it is important that you clearly understand this characteristic and how it is measured. Hence, this is the topic of the next section.

The Nature and Measurement of Intelligence

The Origin of Intelligence Testing

Our account of the origin of intelligence testing begins in the year 1904. In that year the Minister of Public Instruction for the Paris, France, school system appointed a commission of experts to study and recommend procedures for educating mentally retarded children. One member of the commission was a French psychologist and expert on individual differences by the name of Alfred Binet.

One of the commission's recommendations was that children should be admitted to a school for the mentally retarded only after being given an educational and medical examination. Since the commission's recommendation did not specify the nature and extent of the educational examination, Binet and his commission colleague Theophile Simon proposed in 1905 a thirty-item scale of intelligence that attempted to measure the same mental processes that contribute to classroom achievement (processes like memory, attention, comprehension, discrimination, and reasoning). The logic behind the Binet-Simon scale stemmed from the work of Francis Galton, one of the first individuals to analyze measurement. Galton emphasized that a test consists of the *"sinking of shafts at critical points"* (1890, p. 373). Binet and Simon tried to select sample bits of behavior (critical points) that reflected mental ability.

This first test of intelligence was normed on a group of fifty nonretarded children who ranged from three to eleven years of age. Children suspected of mental retardation were given the test and their performance was compared with children from the norm group who were of the same chronological age. Those who performed significantly below their intellectually normal agemates were judged incapable of profiting from normal classroom instruction and assigned to a school for the mentally retarded. Binet and Simon refined the 1905 scale in 1908 and 1911, the year Binet died.

The next significant development took place in 1916 when Lewis Terman of Stanford University published an extensive revision of Binet's 1911 test. This revision, which came to be known as the Stanford-Binet, proved to be extremely popular for three reasons. First, following the suggestion in 1912 of a German psychologist named William L. Stern, Terman expressed a child's level of performance as a global figure called an intelligence quotient (or IQ). Second, Terman's norm group included four hundred American children from a variety of backgrounds. They ranged from four years of age through nineteen years. Third, Terman provided clearer and more detailed instructions for administering the items than Binet had provided for the earlier versions. These additions and refinements made the Stanford-Binet a more reliable and useful instrument (Edwards, 1971; Seagoe, 1974).

We have provided this abbreviated history lesson to illustrate two important points. First, intelligence tests were originally devised to differentiate between children who could profit from normal classroom instruction and those who required special education. Thus, the items that Binet and Simon included in their scale related most closely to academic success. The Stanford-Binet has been revised several times since 1916, and many other similar tests have appeared (notably the intelligence scales devised by David Wechsler). Nevertheless, intelligence test items are still selected based on their relationship to school success. Trying to predict job success, marital bliss, happiness in life, or anything else on the basis of an IQ score is an attempt to make the test do something for which it was not designed. As some psychologists have pointed out, this type of test might better have been called a test of scholastic aptitude or school ability rather than a test of intelligence. The second point concerns Stern and Terman's use of the IQ as a quantitative summary of a child's performance. Binet, worried that educators would use a summary score as an excuse to ignore or get rid of disinterested or troublesome students, never endorsed this application. His intent "was to identify in order to help and improve, not to label in order to limit" (Gould, 1981, p. 152). A bit later we will describe the difference between an individually administered test (like the Stanford-Binet or the Wechsler tests) and a group-administered test. We will also examine the legal challenges to standardized testing practices. And we will see that Binet's concern was well-placed.

Now that you understand the context in which intelligence tests originated, we can turn to a more detailed consideration of what intelligence tests do and do not measure.

First intelligence tests devised to measure probability of school success

Intelligence tests not good predictors of job success, marital happiness, life happiness

What Intelligence Tests Measure

In 1904, the British psychologist Charles Spearman noticed that children given a battery of intellectual tests (like the memory, reasoning, and comprehension tests used by Binet and Terman) showed a strong tendency to rank consistently from test to test: Children who scored high (or average or below average) on memory tests tended to score high (or average or below average) on reasoning and comprehension tests. Our use of the words *tendency* and *tended* indicates, of course, that the rankings were not identical. Some children scored well on some tests but performed more poorly on others. Spearman explained this pattern by saying that intelligence was made up of two types of factors: a general factor (abbreviated as g) that affected performance on all intellectual tests and a set of specific factors (abbreviated as s) that affected performance only on specific intellectual tests. Spearman ascribed the tendency for score rankings to remain constant over tests to the g factor. That the rankings varied somewhat from test to test, he said, resulted from individual differences in specific factors. Not surprisingly, Spearman's explanation is called the two-factor theory of intelligence.

When you examine such contemporary intelligence tests as the Stanford-Binet, the Wechsler Intelligence Scale for Children—Revised, or the Wechsler Adult Intelligence Scale—Revised, you will notice that the items in the various subtests differ greatly from one another. They may involve mental arithmetic, explaining the meanings of words, describing how two things are alike, indicating what part is missing from a pictured object, reproducing a pictured geometric design with blocks, or tracing a path through a maze. These varied items are included because, despite their apparent differences, they relate strongly to each other and to performance in the classroom. In other words, intelligence tests still reflect Binet's original goal and Spearman's two-factor theory. In practice, the examiner can combine the scores from each subtest into a global index (the IQ score), offer a prediction about the tested individual's degree of academic success for the next year or so, and make some judgments about specific strengths and weaknesses.

Intelligence tests attempt to measure general and specific factors

Other Views of Intelligence

Intelligence involves more than what intelligence tests measure

However, as David Wechsler (1975) has persuasively pointed out, *intelligence is not simply the sum of one's tested abilities.* Wechsler defines intelligence as the global capacity of the individual to act purposefully, to think rationally, and to deal effectively with the environment. Given this definition, which is endorsed by many psychologists, an IQ score reflects just one facet of a person's global capacity—the ability to act purposefully, rationally, and effectively on academic tasks in a *classroom* environment. However, people display intelligent behavior in other settings (at work, home, and play, for example), and other characteristics contribute to intelligent behavior (such as persistence, realistic goal setting, the productive use of corrective feedback, creativity, and moral and aesthetic values). A true assessment of intelligence would take into account behavior related to these other settings and characteristics. That such an assessment would be highly subjective and take a great deal of time is one reason why current intelligence tests assess only a small sample of cognitive abilities. But if recent formulations of intelligence by psychologists Robert J. Sternberg (1988) and Howard Gardner (1983) become widely accepted, future intelligence tests may be broader in scope than those in use today. Even before such tests are devised, these theories serve a useful purpose by reminding us that intelligence is multifaceted and can be expressed in many ways.

Robert Sternberg's *triarchic theory of intelligence* has, as its name suggests, three main parts. Two of the three parts deal with thinking processes that we describe in Chapters 8 and 9 and so will not be described here. The third part, the contextual subtheory, focuses on an aspect of intelligence that has been and still is largely overlooked.

In describing the contextual subtheory, Sternberg argues that part of what makes an individual intelligent is the ability to achieve personal goals (for example, graduating from high school or college with honors, working for a particular company in a particular capacity, having a successful marriage). One way to accomplish personal goals is to understand and adapt to the values that govern behavior in a particular setting. For example, if most teachers in a particular school (or executives in a particular company) place a high value on conformity and cooperation, the person who persistently challenges authority, suggests new ideas without being asked, or operates without consulting others, will, in all likelihood, receive fewer rewards than those who are more willing to conform and cooperate and, according to Sternberg's theory, this person would be less intelligent. Where a mismatch exists and the individual cannot adapt to the values of the majority, the intelligent person will explore ways to make the values of others more consistent with his or her own values and skills. An enterprising student may try to convince his or her teacher, for example, that short-answer questions are better measures of achievement than essay questions or that effort and classroom participation should count just as much toward a grade as test scores. Finally, where all attempts at adapting or attempting to change the views of others fail, the intelligent person will seek out a setting where his or her behaviors are more consistent with those of others. Many gifted and talented students seek out private alternative schools where their particular abilities are more highly prized.

The basic point that Sternberg is making is that intelligence should be viewed as a broad characteristic of people that is evidenced not only by how well they answer a particular set of test questions but also by how well they function in different settings. The individual with average test scores who knows how to get people to do what he or she wants is, in this view, at least as intelligent as the person who scores at the 99th percentile of a science test.

Howard Gardner's conception of intelligence is, like Sternberg's, broader than currently popular conceptions. It is different from Sternberg's, however, in that it describes six separate types of intelligence. Accordingly, Gardner's work is referred to as the *theory of multiple intelligences.*

The intelligences described by Gardner are: linguistic, logical-mathematical, spatial, musical, bodily-kinesthetic, and personal (both interpersonal and intrapersonal). Since these intelligences are presumed to be independent of each other, an individual would likely show different levels of skill in each of these domains. One student may show, for example, evidence of becoming an outstanding trial lawyer, novelist, or journalist because his or her linguistic intelligence produces a facility for vividly describing, explaining, or persuading. Another student may be able to manipulate aspects of sound (like pitch, rhythm, timbre) to produce musical experiences that people find highly pleasing. The student who is adept at understanding his or her own and others' feelings and how those feelings relate to behavior would be exhibiting high intrapersonal and interpersonal intelligence. Like Sternberg's work, Gardner's theory cautions us against focusing on the results of IQ tests to the exclusion of other worthwhile behaviors.

Limitations of Intelligence Tests

So where does that leave us in terms of trying to decide what intelligence tests do and do not measure? Four points seem to be in order. First, the appraisal of intelligence is limited by the fact that it cannot be measured directly. Our efforts are confined to measuring the overt manifestations (responses to test items) of what is ultimately based on brain function and experience. Second, as our summary of historical events and analysis of Wechsler's definition make clear, the intelligence we test is a sample of intellectual capabilities that relate to classroom achievement better than they relate to anything else. That is why, as we stated earlier, many psychologists prefer the terms *test of scholastic aptitude* or *test of school ability.* Third, no intelligence test score is an "absolute" measure. Many people—parents especially—fail to grasp this fact. An IQ score is not a once-and-for-all judgment of how bright a person is. It is merely an estimate of how successful a child is in handling certain kinds of problems at a particular time on a particular test *as compared with other children of the same age.* Fourth, since IQ tests are designed to predict academic success, anything that enhances classroom performance (like a wider range of factual information or more effective learning skills) will likely have a positive effect on intelligence test performance. In other words, IQ scores are not necessarily permanent. Research on the stability of IQ scores shows that while they do not change significantly for most people, they can change dramatically for given individuals, and changes are most likely to occur among individuals who were first tested as preschoolers (Brody and Brody, 1976). This last point is often used to support early intervention programs like Head Start and Follow Through.

Intelligence tests measure a sample of intellectual skills

IQ scores can change with experience, training

These school pictures record the changes in the appearance of a boy from the early elementary grades to the end of high school. If he had been tested with an individual intelligence test on the day each of these pictures was taken, it is likely that his IQ scores would have varied by at least several points. (Courtesy of Jack and Michaela Nelson)

Given the constraints and qualifications we have just mentioned about interpreting IQ scores, you may be wondering whether the information they provide is worth knowing. While every person must decide that for herself or himself, we believe that if you are fully aware of the nature and limitations of intelligence tests, they can be an effective tool for analyzing how individuals differ. Despite their shortcomings, they provide an objective, economical, and timely assessment of an individual's current level of intellectual functioning.

We mentioned earlier that Binet had wanted intelligence tests to be used to identify and help academically weak students. That goal is best accomplished when a trained examiner administers a well-designed test to one person at a time. In this way, the examiner can present test items clearly, correct misconceptions about how to respond, help the pupil maintain a high level of motivation, and note the test taker's emotional responses and problem-solving strategies. Since at some point in your teaching career you are likely to have one or more students taking an individual intelligence test, the next section briefly describes this type of instrument. The particular test we have chosen to describe is the Wechsler Intelligence Scale for Children—Revised, because it is one of the most frequently given individual intelligence tests.

Description of an Individual Intelligence Test

The Wechsler Intelligence Scale for Children—Revised (WISC-R, 1974) is one of three individual intelligence tests devised by David Wechsler that are currently in use. The other two are the Wechsler Preschool and Primary Scale of Intelligence (1967) and the Wechsler Adult Intelligence Scale—Revised (1981).

The WISC-R can be given to children from six through sixteen years of age. It is comprised of twelve subtests equally divided between a verbal scale and a performance scale. The names of the subtests and the sequence in which they are given is as follows:

Verbal	**Performance**
1. Information	2. Picture Completion
3. Similarities	4. Picture Arrangement
5. Arithmetic	6. Block Design
7. Vocabulary	8. Object Assembly
9. Comprehension	10. Coding
11. Digit Span	12. Mazes

The WISC-R yields three summary scores: a verbal IQ, a performance IQ, and a full-scale IQ. The mean of the test is 100, and the standard deviation is 15. If you refer back to Figure 4.1 and do some arithmetic, you will realize that 99.72 percent of all IQ scores fall between 55 and 145 (these scores represent 3 standard deviations below the mean and the 3 standard deviations above the mean, respectively).

For each subtest, a precise set of directions tells the examiner where to begin, how to present the items, what type of help or correction to offer, when to stop, and how to score the responses. In addition, examiners are trained to write down spontaneous comments the child may make and to note problem-solving strategies and unusual emotional reactions. This information is then interpreted to provide a picture of the child's intellectual strengths and weaknesses and a prediction about academic performance.

The items for each subtest range from easy to difficult in order to accommodate the six-to-sixteen-year age range and the full range of intellectual ability that can be seen at any age. Item 5 on the Similarities subtest, for example, asks the child to explain how the terms apple and banana are alike. Item 14, however, asks for an explanation of how the more abstract concepts of liberty and justice are alike.

Since those who construct intelligence tests are primarily interested in a general capacity, they want to avoid, as much as possible, measuring abilities that are largely the result of a particular set of home or school experiences. If they ask questions too directly related to a specific kind of home or curriculum, they will measure only how well children have responded to these experiences. Children who have not had these experiences may then be unfairly judged as lacking in scholastic aptitude. To avoid this sort of error, test makers try to base the questions on knowledge and situations common to practically all children. The degree to which they have met this challenge—eliminating biased test items—is currently a matter of heated debate. As we will see in the next section, it is an issue that sharply divides judges, psychologists, and educators.

IQ test items based on knowledge and situations felt to be common to most children

Legal Challenges to Standardized Testing

We have tried to point out in this chapter that standardized tests in general and intelligence tests in particular are specialized instruments for assessing how and by how much individuals differ from one another. In an ideal world every standardized test would have high reliability, high validity, and excellent norms; every person who had access to students' test scores would interpret them properly; and every decision based on test scores would result in a higher quality of education for the test taker. But, as you well know, we do not live in an ideal world. In the real world some tests are poorly designed and normed, experts disagree about how reliable and valid tests need to be in order to be useful, and educational decisions based on test scores sometimes harm children. Feeling unfairly discriminated against by the testing process, some parents have brought their grievances to court. In this section we will examine three court cases to illustrate how legal rulings have affected the assessment of pupil variability.

In real world, test-based decisions sometimes harm children

In 1979 the Florida state legislature passed a law stipulating that high school seniors would have to pass a competency test before they could be granted a diploma. When it became apparent that many more black students than white students were failing the test (about 20 percent versus 2 percent, respectively) and being denied diplomas, the law was challenged in a federal court. In *Debra P. v. Turlington* (1979) the judge concluded that the testing program was unconstitutional because it perpetuated the effects of past discrimination and because it was put into effect without an adequate phase-in period. He ruled that the test could not be used for four years so that students who had been in the schools prior to desegregation would have the opportunity to graduate. He expressed the opinion, though, that the test "had adequate content and construct validity and bore rational relation to state interest." He also ruled that the "plaintiffs failed to establish that the test was racially or ethnically biased."

A very different judicial ruling on the use of standardized tests came in the case of *Larry P.* v. *Riles* (1979). Until the late 1970s, students who had obvious difficulty coping with the standard curriculum in California public schools were given individual intelligence tests. If the score they earned fell within a designated range (and was consistent with other evidence), they were placed in special classes. Certain psychologists (Mercer, 1975, among others) and many minority-group leaders objected to the use of intelligence tests for that purpose and presented their case in federal court. In general, they claimed that the tests (Stanford-Binet and the WISC-R) were biased in favor of white, middle-class culture. One basis of their argument was that black children represented 29 percent of the student population in Larry P.'s school district but comprised 66 percent of all students in classes for the educable mentally retarded. The judge in this case concluded that the standardized intelligence tests then used in California "are racially and culturally biased, have a discriminatory impact against black children, and have not been validated for the purpose of essentially permanent placement of blacks into educationally deadened, isolated, and stigmatizing classes for the so-called educable mentally retarded." He ruled that black students could not be placed in classes for the educable mentally retarded on the basis of an assessment that relied primarily on the results of an IQ test.

The third case we will consider, *PASE* v. *Hannon* (1980), contained many of the same elements as *Larry P.* v. *Riles* but produced a diametrically opposite ruling. The case was brought by Parents in Action for Special Education on behalf of "black children who have been or will be placed in special classes for the educable mentally handicapped in the Chicago school systems." Judge John Grady, who presided over the case, examined each item on the two tests (the Stanford-Binet and the WISC-R) used to identify children for special classes in Chicago. On the basis of his analysis, only eight items on the WISC-R and one on the Stanford-Binet impressed him as being biased against black children. He therefore ruled, in opposition to the decision in the *Larry P.* case, that poor performance on the "biased" items was not sufficient to result in misclassification. (This informal approach to determining item bias is not accepted by most test experts, who favor statistical analysis of responses. [See Reynolds et al., 1984, pp. 252–254, for commentary on the *Larry P.* and *PASE* cases.])

Conflicting opinions regarding bias in intelligence tests

The three cases just summarized illustrate the lack of agreement that exists among psychologists, lawyers, judges, and parents about using standardized test scores in educational decision making. It is difficult to evaluate the charge that standardized tests unfairly discriminate against certain groups. Substantial evidence has been offered to support arguments on both sides of the question. Jane

In recent years a number of critics have argued that most standardized tests are biased in favor of children from middle-class homes and biased against children from lower-class and/or minority group backgrounds. (Above: Frank Siteman/Stock, Boston; Left: Gatewood/The Image Works)

Mercer, one of the most prolific critics of tests, has repeatedly offered data (1975, 1977) to support the view that most standardized tests are so biased against minority-group children that they should be declared illegal. Arthur Jensen, on the other hand, supplies a formidable array of evidence in *Bias in Mental Testing* (1980) to substantiate the view that the most highly regarded standardized tests are not biased with respect to any native-born English-speaking minority group in this country. In his book Jensen makes a distinction between *bias* and *unfairness.* He suggests that an unbiased test may be used in an unfair manner, and a biased test may be used in a fair way. Thus he calls attention not only to what a standardized test score indicates, but to how that score is used.

On the average, American children who come from upper- and middle-class homes perform better in school and on standardized tests than children who come from lower-class or minority-group homes. (Jensen summarizes research findings in *Bias in Mental Testing.*) Some critics of tests argue that improperly used test scores perpetuate or increase such differences. Some cite the underrepresentation of minority-group students in programs for the gifted and talented as an example of how overreliance on a narrow range of test scores can harm students. Selection for gifted and talented programs is often based largely on classroom performance, standardized achievement test scores, and intelligence test scores. However, talented members of minorities often hold values about school and academic achievement that differ from the norm. Their classroom performance and test scores may suffer as a result, thereby making them ineligible for these programs (Whitmore, 1987). Consider Sioux children, for example. If they succeed in school, their Sioux peers think of them as lacking in independent thought, spontaneity, and creativity. Many Cherokee youngsters do not believe that success in school will have a positive impact on the quality of their lives on the reservation (Brantlinger and Guskin, 1985). Gifted and talented lower-class black children may not embrace such traditional middle-class values as deferring immediate gratification (as in "Study first, then go out and play"), accepting the importance of symbolic indicators of success (like grades or test scores), and focusing on the future (as in "Learning geometry and trigonometry now will help you become an engineer later") (Frasier, 1987; Stronge, Lynch, and Smith, 1987).

Defenders of standardized tests (for example, Jensen), on the other hand, maintain that tests can be used to help *reduce* differences in academic performance if they are interpreted properly. If a test accurately reveals that a pupil is below average in ability, for example, it is often wise to acknowledge that fact and arrange instructional experiences accordingly. If it is assumed that no differences in ability exist, teachers might be inclined to expose all pupils to the same sequences of educational experiences presented in the same way. In such a situation, more capable and better prepared students are likely to thrive and less capable students with inadequate backgrounds are likely to fall further and further behind. Busing, Head Start, and Follow-Through programs, continuation

Overreliance on test scores can bar gifted and talented minority children from special programs

schools, and equal opportunity and affirmative action regulations are all based on the premise that some American children are raised in learning environments that are less desirable than others and that such students need assistance if they are to compete against more favored agemates. Paradoxically, many of the same individuals who argued for programs to reduce inequalities are now arguing that tests that call attention to inequalities should be prohibited by law.

The basic issue we have discussed in this section is whether relying on standardized test scores, particularly IQ scores, helps or harms students. You should recognize that this issue cannot be resolved to everyone's satisfaction. Every psychologist, teacher, parent, lawyer, or legislator must take his or her own position on the basis of available evidence. Our view is that standardized tests can benefit students if those who use the scores fully understand both the nature of the characteristic being measured and the nature of the test.

Mid-Chapter Review

Several quite similar terms have been introduced in this chapter. To help you distinguish between them and clarify your understanding, they are summarized below.

Types of Variability

Intraindividual variation: the variability in a person's physical, social, emotional, and cognitive behavior over time and situations

Interindividual variation: the variability between different people's physical, social, emotional, and cognitive behavior at a given point in time

Criteria for Evaluating Tests

Reliability: how similar two rankings of test scores are that are obtained from the same individuals

Validity: how well a test appropriately measures what its users intend it to measure

Content validity: how well test items cover the content of a subject or type of learning

Predictive validity: how well a test score allows accurate predictions of later performance

Construct validity: how accurately a test measures a particular attribute

Types of Tests

Achievement test: indicates how much has been learned about a particular subject

Diagnostic test: Identifies specific strengths or weakness in a learning skill

Aptitude test: estimates potential (how well a pupil is capable of performing) in specific or general abilities that can be applied to various tasks

Competency test: determines if a student has achieved basic reading, writing, and mathematical competencies

Norm-referenced test: indicates how well a student has performed compared to others

Criterion-referenced test: indicates how well a student has mastered a set of objectives

Types of Scores

Raw scores: number of points earned on a test

Percentile rank: percentage of cases at or below a given raw score

Z score: how far a raw score is from the mean in standard deviation units

T score: how far a raw score is from the mean in numerical terms

Stanine score: pupil performance indicated with reference to a 9-point scale derived from the normal curve

Intelligence Testing

The first practical test of intelligence was devised by Alfred Binet in 1905 to distinguish mentally retarded from normal students.

Current intelligence tests continue to predict academic success better than outcomes like job success or marital happiness because they are based on Binet's purpose for mental testing.

Current intelligence tests are assumed to measure a general intellectual factor and specific intellectual factors.

Other views of intelligence, like those of David Wechsler, Robert Sternberg, and Howard Gardner, are broader in scope than Binet's and Spearman's views.

The question of whether intelligence tests are racially and culturally biased has been debated, with no resolution, by psychologists, lawyers, and judges.

SUGGESTIONS FOR TEACHING

Using Standardized Tests

Handbook Heading:
Using Standardized Tests

1. Before giving a standardized test, emphasize that students should do their best and give them suggestions for taking such tests.
2. Examine the test booklet and answer sheet in advance so that you are familiar with the test.
3. Do your best to minimize distractions and interruptions during the testing period.
4. Follow the instructions for administration with scrupulous care.
5. Emphasize that you cannot answer questions during the test.
6. Be cautious when interpreting scores and always give the pupil the benefit of the doubt.
7. Do your best to control the impact of negative expectations.
8. If student folders contain individual intelligence test scores, ask for an interpretation by the psychometrist who administered the test (or an equally knowledgeable person).

1. Before giving a standardized test, emphasize that students should do their best and give suggestions for taking such tests.

For maximum usefulness, scores on standardized tests should be as accurate a representation of actual ability as possible. Accordingly, the day before a standardized test is scheduled tell your students that they should do their best. Emphasize that the scores will be used to help them improve their school performance and that they should concentrate on answering questions as well as they can without feeling that they are competing against others. You may be able to partly reduce the anxiety and tension that are almost inevitable under formal testing conditions by giving some test-taking hints in advance. Norman E. Gronlund notes the following skills that might be stressed (depending on the type of test and the grade level of the student):

1. Listening to or reading directions carefully.
2. Listening to or reading test items carefully.
3. Setting a pace that will allow time to complete the test.

Handbook Heading:
Explaining Test-taking
Skills

4. Bypassing difficult items and returning to them later.
5. Making informed guesses rather than omitting items.
6. Eliminating as many alternatives as possible on multiple-choice items before guessing.
7. Following directions carefully in marking the answer sheet (e.g., darken the entire space).
8. Checking to be sure the item number and answer number match when marking an answer.
9. Checking to be sure the appropriate response was marked on the answer sheet.
10. Going back and checking the answers if time permits. (1985b, p. 332)

2. Examine the test booklet and answer sheet in advance so that you are familiar with the test.

Ideally you might take the test yourself so that you become thoroughly familiar with what your students will be doing. If there are any aspects of recording scores that are especially tricky, you might mention these when you give your test-taking skills presentation or at the time you hand out examination booklets and answer sheets.

3. Do your best to minimize distractions and interruptions during the testing period.

You probably know from personal experience how annoying and unnerving it can be to be interrupted while taking an important test. To minimize such distractions, you might put a "Testing in Progress" sign on the door, and perhaps ask that the bell system be disconnected. If not all pupils in the school take tests the same day, you might ask teachers of other classes to request their pupils to be quiet in hallways and to move away from the building during recess periods.

4. Follow instructions for administration with scrupulous care.

For maximum accuracy, standardized tests should be given in standard fashion. Therefore, you should examine the instructions for administering the test ahead of time and read specific instructions to pupils exactly as written. You should also be completely faithful to instructions for handing out materials, timing tests, and collecting answer sheets promptly.

5. Emphasize that you cannot answer questions during the test.

After reading instructions, emphasize that you will be unable to answer questions once testing has begun. Stress that any questions about how to proceed must be asked before test booklets are opened.

6. Be cautious when interpreting scores and always give the pupil the benefit of the doubt.

The profiles or reports you will receive a few weeks after a test has been administered will contain information that is potentially beneficial to you and to your pupils. If misused or misinterpreted, however, the information is potentially harmful. Misinterpretations of scores could lead to complaints by parents. As you examine scores, therefore, concentrate on ways you can make positive use of the results. Look for areas of weakness in pupil performance that need special attention. At the same time, do your best to avoid forming negative expectations. Chances are overall test scores will often reinforce your own impressions of the general abilities of pupils. You can't help forming such impressions, and they can often work to the advantage of students. If a student has had trouble with almost every assignment and classroom test you have given, it will often happen that test scores will reflect that level of performance. If such a pupil scores higher than expected, though, you might ask yourself if your expectations for that pupil have been too low and make a resolution to give extra help and encouragement, using the test scores to provide direction.

Handbook Heading:
Interpreting Test Scores

If a pupil's test scores are lower than you expected them to be, examine them to discover areas of weakness but guard against thinking "Well, I guess he had me fooled. He's not as sharp as I thought he was. Maybe I had better lower grades a notch on the next report card." There are many reasons why a student may not do well on a test (for example, anxiety, fatigue, coming down with an illness, worry about some home or school interpersonal situation), and scores may not be an accurate reflection of current capability. Thus, whenever there is a discrepancy between test scores and observed classroom performance, always assume that the more favorable impression is the one to use as an indication of general capability. Try to use indications of below-average performance in constructive ways to help students overcome inadequacies.

7. Do your best to control the impact of negative expectations.

As you peruse student test scores, do your best to resist the temptation to label or categorize pupils, particularly those who have a consistent pattern of low scores. Instead of succumbing to thoughts that such students are incapable of learning, you might make an effort to concentrate on the idea that they need extra encouragement and individualized attention. Use the information on test profiles to help them overcome their learning difficulties, not to justify fatalistically ignoring their problems. (Specific techniques for guarding against the tendency to communicate negative expectations will be described in Chapter 12, "Evaluation of Classroom Learning.")

8. If student folders contain individual intelligence test scores ask for an interpretation by the psychometrist who administered the test (or an equally knowledgeable person).

As noted in the discussion of court cases involving use of IQ scores, you should be extremely careful about how you interpret scores on tests such as the Stanford-Binet or WISC-R. Such scores are not likely to be found in the folders of more than a few of your students, but when they *are* included, ask for an interpretation by a qualified person, particularly if the parents ask for an explanation.

Suggestions for Further Study

Taking an Intelligence Test

If you wonder what it is like to take an individual test of intelligence, you might check on the possibility that a course in individual testing needs subjects for practice purposes. (In most courses of this type, each student is required to give several tests under practice conditions.) Look in a class schedule for a course in psychology or education designated Individual Testing, Practicum in Testing, or something similar. Contact the instructor and ask whether he or she wants subjects. If you do find yourself acting as a guinea pig, jot down your reactions to the test immediately after you take it. Would you feel comfortable having the score used to determine whether you would be admitted to some program or qualify for a promotion? Did the test seem to provide an adequate sample of your intelligence? Were the kinds of questions appropriate for your conception of intelligence? Write down comments on the implications of your reactions.

References for Evaluating Standardized Tests

To find out the kinds of information available for evaluating standardized tests, examine the ninth *Mental Measurements Yearbook* (1985), edited by James V. Mitchell, Jr., or one of the publications of UCLA's Center for the Study of Evaluation: *CSE Pre-School Test Evaluations, CSE Elementary School Test Evaluations,* and *CSE Secondary School Test Evaluations.*

Technical Aspects of Testing

For more information about standardized tests and scores, consult one or more of these books: *Essentials of Psychological Testing* (4th ed., 1984) by Lee J. Cronbach, *Psychological Testing* (6th ed., 1988) by Anne Anastasi, *Measurement and Evaluation in Teaching* (5th ed., 1985) by Norman Gronlund, *Essentials of Educational Measurement* (4th ed., 1986) by Robert L. Ebel and David A. Frisbie.

Summary

1. Two types of pupil variability can be observed: intraindividual and interindividual. Intraindividual variability refers to differences in an individual's behavior over time and situations. Interindividual variability refers to the differences between individuals at a given point in time.
2. Most of the research on interindividual variation revolves around scholastic aptitude, achievement, and their assessment with standardized tests.
3. Standardized tests are used primarily to direct instructional efforts and to select students for specialized programs.
4. One of the most important characteristics of a standardized test is its reliability—the similarity between two rankings of test scores obtained from the same individuals.
5. Another important characteristic of standardized test is validity. A valid test appropriately measures what its users intend it to measure.
6. A third important characteristic of a standardized test is its norm group—a sample of students specially chosen and tested so as to reflect the population of students for whom the test is intended. The norm group's performance becomes the standard against which scores are compared.
7. Standardized achievement tests measure how much has been learned about a particular subject.
8. Diagnostic tests identify specific strengths and weaknesses in basic learning skills.
9. Aptitude tests estimate students' potential in specific or general abilities that can be applied to various tasks.
10. Competency tests are given to determine if high school students have learned basic reading, writing, and mathematical skills.
11. Norm-referenced tests compare all scores to the performance of a norm group.
12. Criterion-referenced tests judge scores in terms of mastery of a set of objectives.
13. Percentile rank indicates the percentage of scores that are at or below a person's score.
14. A z-score indicates how far in standard deviation units a raw score is from the mean.
15. A T-score indicates in whole positive numbers how far a raw score is from the mean.

16. A stanine score indicates in which of nine normal-curve segments a person's performance falls.
17. One of the most widely used and poorly understood standardized tests is the intelligence or IQ test.
18. The first practical test of intelligence was devised by Alfred Binet to identify students who would be best served in a special education program.
19. Because of their focus on academic success, intelligence tests are not good predictors of anything else, such as job success, marital happiness, and life satisfaction.
20. Intelligence, broadly defined, is the global capacity of the individual to act purposefully, think rationally, and deal effectively with the environment.
21. The intelligence that we test is but a sample of intellectual skills—those that closely relate to classroom achievement.
22. As a person's intellectual skills improve with experience and/or training, the individual's IQ score may improve.
23. In the 1970s and 1980s legal questions arose over the effects of compctency tests and intelligence tests. Judges have ruled inconsistently as to whether these tests unfairly discriminate against minorities.

Key Terms

intraindividual variation *(150)*
interindividual variation *(150)*
standardized tests *(152)*
reliability *(154)*
validity *(155)*
norm group *(156)*
achievement test *(158)*
diagnostic test *(158)*
aptitude test *(158)*
competency test *(159)*

norm-referenced test *(159)*
criterion-referenced test *(160)*
grade equivalent score *(160)*
percentile rank *(161)*
standard deviation *(161)*
mean *(161)*
normal curve *(162)*
z score *(162)*
T score *(162)*
stanine score *(163)*

Discussion Questions

1. If you are like most people, you took a variety of standardized tests throughout your elementary and high school years. The results of those tests were probably used to help determine what you would be taught and how. Do you think that those tests adequately reflected what you had learned and were capable of learning and, therefore, were always used in your best interest? What can you do to increase the chances that test scores will be used to help *your* students fulfill their potential?
2. Think about norm-referenced tests and criterion-referenced tests. Which do you think you prefer? Why? Can you describe a set of circumstances when a

norm-referenced test would be clearly preferable to a criterion-referenced test and vice-versa?

3. If you had to tell parents about the results of a standardized test, which type of score could you explain most clearly: raw score, percentile rank, z score, T score, or stanine score? Which do you think would be most informative for parents? for you as a teacher? If you do not understand best the one that you think most informative, what do you intend to do about it?

4. Imagine that you are sitting in the faculty lounge listening to a colleague describe one of her students. Your colleague points out that this student has a C+ average and received an IQ score of 92 (low average) on a recently administered test. She concludes that since the student is working up to his ability level, he should not be encouraged to set higher goals since that would only lead to frustration. Your colleague then asks for your opinion. How do you respond?

chapter 5

DEALING WITH PUPIL VARIABILITY

KEY POINTS

Ability Grouping

Between-class ability grouping: classes of students with similar intelligence, achievement test scores

No support for between-class ability grouping

Joplin Plan, within-class ability grouping for math produces moderate increases in learning

Joplin Plan, within-class ability grouping may allow for better quality instruction

Ability grouping rejected in the 1960s on the grounds of discrimination

Standardized tests said to be biased against minority groups

The Project on Classification of Exceptional Children

Labels may cause stigmatization but also may lead to special education

The Education for All Handicapped Children Act (PL 94-142)

IEP must include objectives, services to be provided, criteria for determining achievement

Due process provisions intended to protect rights of pupil

Tests used to determine placement must be valid, administered in native language

Handicapped students must be educated in least restrictive environment

Mainstreaming: policy of placing handicapped pupils in regular classes

Learning disabled, speech impaired, mentally retarded, emotionally disturbed most common under PL 94-142

Speech impaired, learning disabled, visually handicapped, hard of hearing most likely to attend regular classes

Interdisciplinary assessment team determines if pupil needs special services

Classroom teacher, parents, several specialists prepare IEP

Students with Mental Retardation

Mildly retarded students may frustrate easily, lack confidence, self-esteem

Mildly retarded students tend to oversimplify, have difficulty generalizing

Give mildly retarded students specific assignments that can be completed quickly

Students with Learning Disabilities

Learning disabilities: disorders in basic processes that lead to learning problems not due to other causes

Increase in learning disabled due to faulty assessment procedures, poor-quality tests

Help learning disabled learn to reduce distractions, attend, perceive

Emotionally Disturbed Students

Emotional disturbance: poor relationships, inappropriate behavior, depression, fears

Term *behavior disorders* calls attention to behavior that needs to be changed

Pupils with behavior disorders tend to be either aggressive or withdrawn

Foster interpersonal contact among withdrawn students

Use techniques to forestall aggressive or antisocial behavior

Gifted and Talented Students

Gifted and talented students show high performance on wide range of tasks

Inconsistency often exists between definition, identification, and teaching of gifted students

Minorities underrepresented in gifted classes because of overreliance on test scores

Some rapid learners convergent, others divergent thinkers

Disadvantaged Pupils

Disadvantaged pupils often lack motivation, academic know-how

Lower-class adolescents often have low career aspirations

Teacher-directed learning stressing answers to specific questions effective with disadvantaged

With older disadvantaged, use small steps, concreteness, activity, dramatization, observation

Bilingual and Culturally Diverse Students

Multicultural education: understand, accept, reward different thinking, behavior patterns

Multicultural programs foster motivation, better understanding of others

---

If you have had the opportunity to observe or work in an elementary or secondary classroom recently, you know that today's teacher can expect to have a wide variety of students who differ in abilities, talents, and backgrounds. The reasons for such diversity include compulsory attendance laws, patterns of immigration, and laws that govern which students can and cannot be placed in special classes, not to mention normal variation in physical, social, emotional, and cognitive development. The task of guiding each member of a diverse group of students toward high levels of learning is one of teaching's major challenges. We hope to help you meet this challenge by making you aware in this chapter of different ways of dealing with pupil variability.

Historical Developments in Dealing with Variability

Prior to the turn of the century, dealing with pupil variability was an issue few educators had to face. Most communities were fairly small, and students in a given school tended to come from similar ethnic and economic backgrounds. In addition, lower-class families often viewed a child's labor as more important than a complete, formal education, and many states had not yet enacted compulsory attendance laws. As a result, many lower-class children did not attend school regularly or at all. In 1900, for example, only 8.5 percent of eligible students attended high school (Boyer, 1983), and these students were almost entirely from the upper and middle classes (Gutek, 1988). In comparison with today's schools, then, student populations were considerably less diverse.

By 1920 this picture had changed, largely because of three developments. First, by 1918 all states had passed compulsory attendance laws. Second, child labor laws had been enacted by many states, as well as by Congress in 1916, to eliminate the hiring of children and adolescents in mines and factories. Third, large numbers of immigrant children arrived in the United States from 1901 through 1920. During those years 14.5 million individuals, mostly from eastern and southern Europe, arrived on U.S. shores (Morris, 1961). The result was a vast increase in the number and diversity of children attending elementary and high school.

Educators initially dealt with this growth in pupil variability by forming age-graded classrooms. All students of a particular age were grouped together each year to master a certain portion of the school's curriculum. The assumption behind this approach was that teachers could be more effective in helping students learn when classrooms were more *homogeneous* than *heterogeneous*. Whether or not this assumption was well founded—an issue we will address shortly—it was (and still is) so widely held by educators that two additional approaches to creating even more homogeneous groups were eventually implemented—ability grouping and special class placement.

Ability grouping involved the use of standardized mental ability or achievement tests to create groups of students who were considered very similar to each other in learning ability. In a limited sense, this approach was made possible by the pioneering work of Alfred Binet and Lewis Terman. It was, however, the work of one of Terman's graduate students, Arthur Otis, and a group of Army psychologists led by Robert Yerkes that made possible the mass use of standardized tests. The U.S. entry into World War I in 1917 made it necessary to efficiently test the mental ability of large numbers of recruits to make appropriate decisions about selection, placement, and classification. Building on Otis's attempt to create a group-administered version of the Stanford-Binet, Yerkes and his colleagues produced two of the first group-administered, paper-and-pencil tests of intelligence: the Army Scale Alpha and the Army Scale Beta (a nonverbal scale for non-English-speaking and illiterate recruits). In the years after World War I, group-administered intelligence and achievement tests were quickly developed to serve the needs of business and education (Matarazzo, 1972).

The use of standardized mental ability tests for selection and placement in education received another boost from the success of testing programs in the armed forces during World War II (for example, stanines were used to select candidates for pilot training). Primary schools of the 1950s often assigned children on the basis of standardized test scores to fast, average, or slow ability groups, and they remained in those groups through the elementary grades. High schools placed students into different tracks geared toward post–high school goals like college, secretarial work, or vocational school.

For more or less normal children, age-grading and ability testing were seen as workable approaches to creating more homogeneous classes. But compulsory attendance laws also brought to school children with more severe mental and physical disabilities. These students were deemed incapable of profiting from any type of normal classroom instruction and so were assigned to special schools. Unfortunately, and as Alfred Binet feared, labeling a student as mentally retarded or physically handicapped often resulted in vastly inferior education. Early in this century, special schools served as convenient dumping grounds for all kinds of children who could not adapt to the regular classroom (Ysseldyke & Algozzine, 1990).

This chapter describes and evaluates current versions of these two approaches to dealing with pupil variability. We first look at ability grouping, which nowadays takes several forms and is still used to reduce the normal range of variability in cognitive ability and achievement that one finds in the typical classroom. We then detail the varied types and degrees of special class placement for children whose intellectual, social, emotional, or physical development falls outside (above as well as below) the range of normal variation. In discussing this approach we pay particular attention to Public Law 94-142, which was enacted to counter past excesses of special class placement and to encourage the placement of children with handicaps in regular classes to the greatest extent possible.

Ability Grouping

Types of Ability Groups

Four approaches to ability grouping are popular among educators today: *between-class ability grouping, regrouping,* the *Joplin Plan,* and *within-class grouping.* Given their widespread use, you may be able to recall a few classes in which one or another of these techniques was used. If not, you will no doubt encounter at least one of them during your first year of teaching.

Between-Class Ability Grouping   The goal of **between-class ability grouping** is that each class be made up of students who are homogeneous in standardized intelligence or achievement test scores. Three levels of classes are usually formed—high, average, and low—although some schools use four levels. Students in one ability group typically have little or no contact with students in others during the school day. While each group covers the same subjects, a higher group does so in greater depth and breadth than lower groups. At the high school level this approach is often called *tracking*. Instead of labeling the groups as having high, average, and low ability, they are usually referred to as college preparatory, business/secretarial, vocational/technical, and general. The rationale behind between-class ability grouping is that it improves the teacher's efficiency and effectiveness, since the level and pace of instruction can match the intellectual characteristics of the learners. Low achievers, for example, can have the individual attention, slow pace, repetition, and review that they require, and high achievers can be given more autonomy and more difficult tasks.

Regrouping   The groups formed under a **regrouping** plan are more flexible in assignments and are narrower in scope than between-class groups. Students of the same age, ability, and grade but from different classrooms come together for instruction in a specific subject, usually reading or mathematics. If a student begins to significantly outperform the other members of the group, a change of group assignment is easier since it involves just that particular subject. Regrouping has two major disadvantages. First, it requires a certain degree of planning and cooperation among the teachers involved. They must agree, for example, to schedule reading and arithmetic during the same periods. Second, many teachers are uncomfortable working with children who they only see once a day for an hour or so.

Joplin Plan   The **Joplin Plan** is a variation of regrouping. The main difference is that the regroupings take place *across* grade levels. All third-, fourth-, and fifth-graders, for example, whose grade-equivalent scores in reading are 4.6 (fourth grade, sixth month) would come together for reading instruction. The same would be done for mathematics. The Joplin Plan has the same advantages and disadvantages as simple regrouping.

Within-Class Ability Grouping   The most popular form of ability grouping, occurring in almost all elementary school classes, **within-class ability grouping** involves dividing a single class of students into two or three groups for reading and math instruction. Like regrouping and the Joplin Plan, it has the advantages of being flexible in group assignments and restricted to one or two subjects. In

In ability grouping, students are selected and placed in homogeneous groups with other students who are considered to have very similar learning abilities. (Allen Green/Photo Researchers)

addition, it eliminates the need for cooperative scheduling. One disadvantage of this approach is that the teacher needs to be skilled at keeping the other students in the class productively occupied while working with a particular group.

Evaluations of Ability Grouping

Because ability grouping has been practiced in one form or another for several decades and occurs in virtually all school districts, its effects have been intensively studied. Robert E. Slavin (1987) has conducted a review and analysis of ability grouping research. His main findings are as follows:

1. There is no support for between-class ability grouping. Of fourteen studies, not one demonstrated that students who were assigned to homogeneous classes outperformed students who were assigned to heterogeneous classes. Slavin also found little support for the contention that between-class ability grouping benefits high achievers.
2. Regrouping for reading or mathematics can be effective if the instructional pace and the level of the text match the student's actual achievement level

No support for between-class ability grouping

rather than the student's nominal grade level. In other words, a fifth-grader who scores at the fourth-grade level on a reading test should be reading out of a fourth-grade reading book.

3. The Joplin Plan yields moderate to strong positive effects compared with instruction in heterogeneous classes.

4. Within-class ability grouping in mathematics in grades 3 through 6 produced moderately positive results compared with instruction in heterogeneous classes. Low achievers appeared to benefit the most from this arrangement. Because within-class ability grouping for reading is an almost universal practice at every grade level, researchers have not had the opportunity to compare its effectiveness with whole-class reading instruction. Nevertheless, it would be reasonable to expect pretty much the same results for reading as were found for mathematics.

> **Joplin Plan, within-class ability grouping for math produce moderate increases in learning**

These findings clearly suggest that if ability grouping is going to be used, it should take one of two forms: within-class ability grouping for mathematics in the upper elementary grades, and the Joplin Plan. We don't know at present why these forms of ability grouping work. It is *assumed* that the increase in class homogeneity allows for more appropriate and potent forms of instruction (for example, greater flexibility in moving students into and out of a particular group, greater availability of high-achieving role models, and greater effort by the teacher to bring lower-achieving groups up to the level of higher-achieving groups). If this assumption is correct, within-class ability grouping and the Joplin Plan must be carried out in such a way that homogeneous groups are guaranteed to result. The best way to achieve similarity in cognitive ability among students is to group them on the basis of past classroom performance, standardized achievement test scores, or both. The least desirable (but frequently used) approach is to base the assignments solely on an IQ score. Because of the poor results that usually occur when IQ score determines group membership, ability grouping (particularly between-class ability grouping) and standardized testing have been strongly criticized in recent years.

> **Joplin Plan, within-class ability grouping may allow for better quality instruction**

Reactions Against Ability Grouping and Testing

> **Ability grouping rejected in the 1960s on the grounds of discrimination**

Starting in the early 1960s, critics from diverse backgrounds began to point out some of the disadvantages of ability grouping. Minority-group leaders successfully argued in the courts that such procedures constituted a form of discrimination. Under tracking arrangements, elementary school children who qualified for high-ability groups were very likely to acquire knowledge and skills that equipped them for college preparatory programs in high school. Classmates who were placed in low-ability groups, on the other hand, were likely to be treated (and come to think of themselves) as poor students. They were also exposed to a simplified curriculum. As a consequence, they had little if any chance to perform adequately in a high school college preparatory program. Many dropped out of school; those who graduated with low grade-point averages were frequently denied admission to college. Awareness of the long-term impact of ability grouping caused judges, legislators, and educators either to prohibit or to discourage attempts to divide pupils on the basis of estimates of ability.

The trend away from between-class ability grouping was one manifestation of an attempt to equalize educational opportunities. A related trend was criticism of standardized tests. During the decades when pupils were placed in tracks, in high-average-low sections, or in special classes, most decisions were based partly or entirely on scores on standardized tests. Starting in the early 1970s, individuals and advocacy groups began to criticize the use of standardized tests to differentiate between pupils. They argued that such tests discriminated against certain types of students and caused them to be labeled in prejudicial ways. Jane R. Mercer (1975), to note just one critic, called attention to the possibility that IQ tests discriminate against certain children when she investigated the backgrounds of 812 residents of Riverside, California, classified as retarded. She found that in this group there were 300 percent more Mexican-Americans and also 50 percent more blacks than their proportion in the general population, but only 60 percent as many Anglo-Americans. Furthermore, persons in the lowest socioeconomic categories were greatly overrepresented and those at the upper levels underrepresented.

Standardized tests said to be biased against minority groups

As a result of reports prepared by Mercer and others (and of lawsuits based on the evidence reported), the federal government and many states passed laws prohibiting schools from using intelligence test scores as the sole basis for classifying children as retarded. (Details of the federal law will be described in the next section.) One of the reasons for prohibiting exclusive use of certain tests was the argument that once a child was labeled as mentally retarded, teachers would expect the child to act that way. Support for this argument was supplied by research on the impact of teacher expectations. (The nature of such expectations, how they may influence pupil behavior, and ways you might try to avoid causing negative self-fulfilling-prophecy reactions in your pupils will be discussed in Chapter 12's section on "Reducing Subjectivity.")

The discussion in this chapter has so far focused on students whose intellectual, social, emotional, and physical characteristics fall within a range that is considered normal. But for reasons detailed in the next two sections, teachers are also required at times to deal with students having some degree of mental, emotional, or physical handicap.

Until recently, pupils with handicaps often were placed in special classes or schools on the assumption that they needed special forms of education provided by specially trained teachers. However, many of the criticisms and arguments marshaled against ability grouping came to be applied as well to special classes for the handicapped. As a result, influential members of Congress were persuaded in the early 1970s that it was time for the federal government to take steps to correct the perceived inequities and deficiencies in our educational system. One of the first steps taken was to authorize an investigation that came to be called the Project on Classification of Exceptional Children.

The Project on Classification of Exceptional Children

In announcing the project, the Secretary of Health, Education, and Welfare explained that it was intended to call attention to and reduce the unfortunate consequences of labeling children as retarded or emotionally disturbed. He requested that those in charge of the project review classification procedures, assess the impact of present labeling procedures on the lives of children, and make recommendations for improving practices. Nicholas Hobbs, an eminent specialist in exceptionality, was asked to supervise the efforts of close to one hundred experts from various fields, and also edited the project reports. Detailed analyses of thirty-one aspects of classification are presented in Hobbs's *Issues in the Classification of Children* (1975a). A summary and synthesis of material covered in the comprehensive report are offered in his *The Futures of Children* (1975b).

Disadvantages and Advantages of Labeling

In *The Futures of Children* Hobbs pointed out that over 7 million children under the age of nineteen had been identified as handicapped by the Bureau of Education for the Handicapped, U.S. Office of Education. He then summarized disadvantages and advantages of referring to these children as handicapped, or exceptional, and of classifying them under more specific labels, such as mentally retarded or emotionally disturbed. A paraphrased digest of some of the points made by Hobbs (1975c, pp. 3–4) in discussing labeling appears below.

Children who are labeled as handicapped or exceptional may be permanently stigmatized, rejected, and denied opportunities for full development. Yet if they are not labeled, they may fail to benefit from special programs intended to help them.

Labels may cause stigmatization but also may lead to special education

Children labeled as mentally retarded or the equivalent may be assigned to inferior educational programs in schools or placed in institutions without the benefit of legal protection extended to "normal" individuals. Yet we are able to evaluate children with reasonable accuracy and have developed educational techniques that are quite effective in helping children with low intelligence make the most of their abilities.

Large numbers of minority-group children are inaccurately classified as mentally retarded on the basis of scores earned on inappropriate tests. Yet such children often do need instruction that differs from that given to majority-group children in typical classrooms.

While *The Futures of Children* and *Issues in the Classification of Children* emphasized the disadvantages and advantages of labeling, others noted additional factors leading to inequalities in American education.

Awareness of Deficiencies in Educational Services

A group called the Children's Defense Fund, for example, sponsored a project to determine the number of American children who were *not* attending school. In the summary of the report, the authors noted:

> According to our analysis of the 1970 U.S. Bureau of Census data on non-enrollment, nearly two million children 7 to 17 years of age were not enrolled in school. Over one million were between 7 and 15 years of age. More than three quarters of a million were between the ages of 7 and 13. (Washington Research Project [1978], p.1)

Another organization, the National Advisory Committee on the Handicapped, accumulated statistics on the estimated number of handicapped children who were failing to receive special services in the public schools. They reported (1968) that in the case of some types of handicaps less than 20 percent of children in need of special services were receiving them.

The Education for All Handicapped Children Act (PL 94-142)

Growing awareness of trends such as these stimulated the Bureau of Education for the Handicapped and the National Advisory Committee on the Handicapped (as well as other groups and individuals) to persuade Congress to pass (in November 1975) Public Law 94-142, the Education for All Handicapped Children Act, intended "To assure the free, appropriate public education of all handicapped children." PL 94-142 stipulated that by 1978 all states wishing to receive federal funds would be required to put into effect the various provisions of the Act.

Provisions of Public Law 94-142

One of the key provisions of PL 94-142 is the development of an **individualized education program (IEP)** for each child identified as having a handicapping condition. The IEP must include the following:

IEP must include ob-
jectives, services to
be provided, criteria
for determining
achievement

(a) A statement of the child's present levels of educational performance;
(b) A statement of annual goals, including short-term instructional objectives;
(c) A statement of the specific special education and related services to be provided to the child, and the extent to which the child will be able to participate in regular educational programs;
(d) The projected dates for initiation of services and the anticipated duration of the services; and
(e) Appropriate objective criteria and evaluation procedures and schedules for determining, on at least an annual basis, whether short-term objectives are being achieved. (*Federal Register,* August 23, 1977, p. 42491)

The IEP is to be planned by the pupil's classroom teacher in collaboration with a person qualified in special education, one or both of the pupil's parents, the pupil (when appropriate), and other individuals at the discretion of the parents or school. (An example of an IEP is depicted on page 206.)

Due process provi-
sions intended to
protect rights of pupil

Other provisions of PL 94-142 allow for **due process**—legal procedures and safeguards intended to protect the rights of the pupil. Due process elements include the right of the parents to examine all of their child's school records, prior notice to parents of any change in identification or placement, and parental consent before a student is evaluated or placed.

A provision referred to as *protection in evaluation procedures* includes the following regulations:

Tests used to deter-
mine placement must
be valid, adminis-
tered in native
language

1. A "full and individual evaluation" of a student must be made prior to initial placement in a special educational program.
2. All tests used must have been validated for the specific purpose for which they are used.
3. Tests must be administered in the pupil's native language.
4. When tests are administered to students who have impaired sensory, manual, or speaking skills, the results must reflect aptitude or achievement rather than the impairment.
5. No single procedure is to be the sole criterion on which special education placement is determined.
6. Evaluations for placement in special classes are to be made by a multidisciplinary team, including at least one teacher or other specialist with "knowledge in the area of suspected disability."

If you teach in an area with a large concentration of students having limited English proficiency (children of Hispanic origin whose families have recently immigrated to the United States, for example), you may find long delays between referral and assessment of a child suspected of having a handicap, as well as deviations from some of the protection in evaluation procedures. The reason is a shortage of both bilingual psychologists and tests that include a representative sample of ethnic minorities in their norms. Few tests include, for instance, South American, Central American, Mexican, Cuban, or Puerto Rican children. When such tests are used to assess Spanish-speaking children, they are simply translated from English into Spanish. Because standardized tests are designed to reflect cultural experiences common to the United States, and because English words and phrases may not mean quite the same thing when translated into Spanish, these tests may not be measuring what they were developed to measure. That is, they may not be valid. The results of such assessments should therefore be interpreted very cautiously (Nuttall, 1987; Wilen & Sweeting, 1986).

Finally, the **least restrictive environment** provision of PL 94-142 stipulates that each state must establish policies and procedures to ensure that a handicapped child is placed in the most normal educational setting that his or her handicapping condition will allow.

> All handicapped students, including those in public or private institutions or other care facilities, are educated with children who are not handicapped, and that special classes, separate schooling, or other removal of handicapped children from the regular education environment occurs only when the nature or severity of the handicap is such that an education in regular classes with the use of supplementary aids and services cannot be achieved satisfactorily. (Section 612-5)

Handicapped students must be educated in least restrictive environment

The least restrictive environment provision establishes a basic policy that is often referred to as **mainstreaming,** since as many handicapped children as possible are to enter the mainstream of education by attending school in classes with nonhandicapped pupils. Thus, an evaluation is made for each pupil included under PL 94-142 to determine the feasibility of at least part-time instruction in a regular class.

Mainstreaming: policy of placing handicapped pupils in regular classes

Taking into account the various developments that led to the passage of PL 94-142, it is not difficult to understand why the law was enacted. While all the provisions are well intended, few of them are easy to put into practice. Accordingly, you will be curious about what PL 94-142 means to a regular classroom teacher.

What PL 94-142 Means to Regular Classroom Teachers

By the time you begin your teaching career, PL 94-142 will have been in effect for some time. Each state was required to have established laws and policies for implementing the various provisions by 1978. Thus, the trial and error process that inevitably follows a radical departure from previous routine will have taken place by the time you enter a classroom. The first guiding principle to follow, therefore, is *Find out what the local ground rules are.* You will probably be told during orientation meetings about the ways PL 94-142 is being put into effect in your state and local school district. But if such a presentation is not given or is incomplete, it

The least restrictive environment provision of the Education for All Handicapped Children Act (PL 94-142) has led to *mainstreaming*—the policy that handicapped children should attend regular classes to the maximum extent possible. (Blair Seitz/ Photo Researchers)

would be wise to ask about guidelines you should follow. Your second guiding principle, then, should be *When in doubt, ask.*

The degree to which you will actually be involved with PL 94-142 decisions and pupils will depend on several factors. If you teach in the primary grades of an inner-city school, for instance, you will be much more aware of PL 94-142 than if you teach advanced college-preparatory classes in a high school located in an affluent suburb. Children who come from disadvantaged minority-group backgrounds are more likely (for reasons to be described later in this chapter) to be classified as exceptional under the law than those from upper-class white backgrounds. Teachers in the lower grades are almost always the first school personnel to observe signs of exceptionality and to make initial referrals. In addition, there are more likely to be children deemed exceptional under PL 94-142 in classes where pupils are grouped primarily or exclusively by age than in classes for pupils who have undergone a process of selection (for example, college-preparatory seniors taking advanced chemistry). Because most secondary schools have vocational and college-preparatory programs, some high school teachers are more likely than others to have a larger proportion of students with low academic ability. A teacher of home economics or industrial arts, for example, may be asked to teach a disproportionate number of students who have experienced difficulties with the academic curriculum.

Another set of factors that may contribute to the degree of your involvement with exceptional children will be a result of how your local school system has chosen to resolve two somewhat conflicting demands: restrictions against ability grouping and current insistence on upholding academic standards and avoiding inflated grades. As noted in the evaluation of reactions against ability grouping, as well as in comments on the mainstreaming provisions of PL 94-142, court rulings at the state and federal levels have had a chilling effect on the use of tracking systems (particularly at the elementary grade levels) and the assignment of students to special education classes on a full-time basis (Valente, 1987). At the same time, there is a renewed emphasis on realistic grading because of evidence that contemporary American schoolchildren perform less well on achievement tests than their predecessors. (It is argued that inflated grades given by teachers of the 1970s contributed substantially to the decline in scores on achievement tests.) As a result of these two trends, you are likely to be asked to teach in a single classroom students who will vary substantially in academic ability *and* to evaluate their performance stringently. "Automatic promotion" is likely to be discouraged and various measures will be used to evaluate achievement. As a result, parents of pupils in the elementary grades (in particular) may be alarmed if they discover that their children are receiving low grades or earning low scores on achievement tests. If they are assertive—and aware of PL 94-142—they may insist that their child be considered for special educational services.

With these general considerations as background, consider some questions you may be asking yourself about the impact of PL 94-142 as you approach your first teaching job.

What Kinds of Students Are Classified as Handicapped Under PL 94-142?

According to the U.S. Department of Education, during the 1986–1987 academic year, about 4.4 million students (somewhat less than 11 percent of the total number of students) received special education services under PL 94-142.

The Department of Education recognizes eleven categories of special students. Many states use the same categories. Others use fewer, more inclusive, classification schemes. Commonly used categories are listed below, together with brief definitions of each type, but you should be prepared to find other categories and terms used in various reports, articles, and books.

Deafness. Absence of hearing in both ears. Or a hearing disability that prevents understanding of speech with or without a hearing aid.

Hardness of hearing. Significant difficulty in understanding speech, even when equipped with a hearing aid.

Blindness. Visual acuity of 20/200 or less in the better eye with correction, or visual acuity of more than 20/200 if the widest diameter of the field of vision subtends an angle no greater than 20 degrees. As you probably know, 20/20 vision means that a person with "perfect" sight can see print of a given size at 20 feet. Visual acuity of 20/200 means that the person sees at 20 feet what an individual with "perfect" vision sees at 200 feet. The field of vision aspect of blindness means that the person views things as if looking through a tunnel.

Visual impairments. Visual acuity between 20/70 and 20/200 in the better eye after correction.

Speech impairments. A disorder such as stuttering, impaired articulation, or a language or voice impairment that adversely affects educational performance.

Physical and health impairments. Conditions such as orthopedic handicaps, cerebral palsy, epilepsy, heart disease, or diabetes.

Mental retardation. Subaverage general intellectual functioning as indicated by abnormally low scores on intelligence tests as well as deficits in adaptive behavior. (Adaptive behavior is essentially how well a person functions in social environments.) (A more precise definition of mental retardation will be provided later in this chapter.)

Learning disabilities. Disorders in basic psychological processes that lead to learning problems not traceable to physical handicaps or mental retardation. (A more complete definition of learning disabilities will be presented later in this chapter.)

Emotional disturbance. Personal and social problems exhibited in an extreme degree over a period of time that adversely affect the ability to learn and get along with others. (A more complete definition of emotional disturbance will be presented later in this chapter.)

| Learning disabled, speech impaired, mentally retarded, emotionally disturbed most common under PL 94-142 |

Percentages of each type of student who received special educational services during the school year 1986–1987 are indicated in Table 5.1.

As you can see, the most common types of exceptional children receiving services were those classified as learning disabled, speech impaired, mentally retarded, and emotionally disturbed.

Which Types of Students Are Most Likely to Attend Regular Classes?   Figure 5.1 supplies information about the percentage of each type of pupil served in regular classes, separate classes, separate schools, and other educational environments.

| Speech impaired, learning disabled, visually handicapped, hard of hearing most likely to attend regular classes |

As you can see, students most likely to spend most or part of each day in a regular classroom are those classified as speech impaired, learning disabled, visually handicapped, and hard of hearing. Those least likely to attend regular classes are pupils who are emotionally disturbed, orthopedically handicapped, mentally retarded, deaf and hard of hearing, deaf-blind, and deaf.

Table 5.1   Students Receiving Special Education Services:
1986–1987

Handicapping Condition	Percentage of Total School Enrollment[1]	Percentage of Handicapped Students Served
Learning disabled	4.73	43.60
Speech impaired	2.86	25.80
Mentally retarded	1.68	15.00
Emotionally disturbed	0.95	8.70
Multihandicapped	0.22	2.20
Hard of hearing and deaf	0.14	1.50
Orthopedically handicapped	0.14	1.30
Other health impaired	0.17	1.20
Visually handicapped	0.07	0.61
Deaf-blind	0.01	0.04
Total	10.97	100.00

1. Percentages are based on handicapped children aged 3–21 as a percent of total school enrollment for preschool through twelfth grade.

SOURCE: U.S. Department of Education, "To Assure the Free, Appropriate Public Education of All Handicapped Children," *Tenth Annual Report to Congress on the Implementation of the Education of the Handicapped Children Act* (Washington, D.C.: U.S. Department of Education, 1988).

What Help Will Regular Classroom Teachers Receive from Specialists?   Depending on the size, policies, and financial resources of the school system in which you teach, you might work with one or more of the following specialists in meeting the provisions of PL 94-142:

Special education teachers, trained and certified to teach children with one or more specific handicaps, often in self-contained (separate) classrooms.

Resource room teachers, who instruct students with handicaps in special resource rooms for part of a school day.

Itinerant teachers, who travel from school to school in a district and usually provide short-term (for example, one day a week) instruction.

Consultation teachers, who consult with regular classroom teachers and offer suggestions for instructing atypical pupils.

Clinical teachers, who either provide instruction or therapy of various kinds in separate clinics or who use clinical teaching techniques. Clinical teaching techniques may center on methods derived from various forms of psychotherapy or be based on the premise that instruction should be arranged to match pupil strengths and weaknesses.

Guidance counselors, who often function as coordinators for assessment and IEP teams, supervise comprehensive testing programs, and advise students about personal, academic, or vocational problems.

Figure 5.1   Environments in Which 3- to 21-Year-Old Handicapped Children Were Served During the School Year 1986–1987

U.S. Department of Education, "To Assure the Free, Appropriate Public Education of All Handicapped Children," *Tenth Annual Report to Congress on the Implementation of the Education of the Handicapped Children Act* (Washington, D.C.: U.S. Department of Education, 1988).

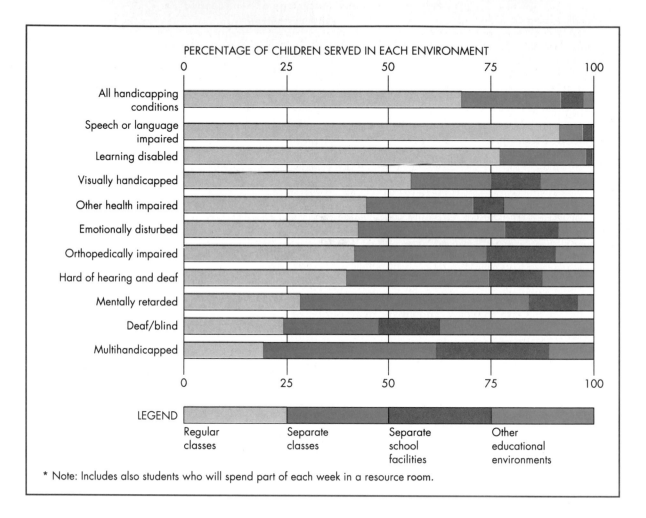

School psychologists, who administer and evaluate tests, sometimes provide psychotherapy, and consult with teachers and parents who are concerned about pupil problem behavior.

Occupational therapists, who assist handicapped students to develop self-help skills such as feeding or dressing, as well as motor and perceptual skills such as writing or distinguishing between shapes.

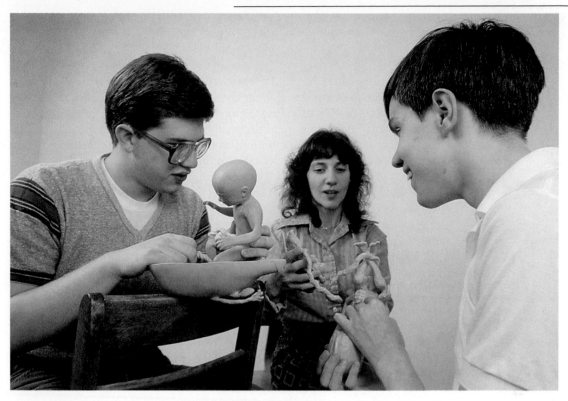

Even under PL 94-142, with its emphasis on mainstreaming, certain types of handicapped pupils (such as the blind) often spend at least part of each day in separate classes taught by specially trained teachers. (Edith G. Haun/Stock, Boston)

Physical therapists, who help handicapped pupils develop or recover physical strength and endurance.

Speech-language pathologists, who make assessments and provide therapy for pupils with speech and/or language disabilities.

Audiologists, who administer hearing tests and recommend ways pupils might correct or compensate for hearing disabilities.

What Are the Regular Classroom Teacher's Responsibilities Under PL 94-142?

Regular classroom teachers may be involved in activities required directly or indirectly by PL 94-142 in four possible ways: referral, assessment, planning of an individual education program, and implementation and evaluation of the IEP.

Referral. The first step leading to the provision of services under PL 94-142 is referral—someone comes to the conclusion that a child differs from the normal to the point that special instruction may be required. When a child is physically handicapped, the parents may explain the extent and severity of the handicap to school authorities when the child is enrolled. In some cases, a written statement from a physician or licensed eye or ear specialist may be required. For some disabilities, however, the initial referral is likely to come from a regular classroom teacher. Learning disabilities, emotional disturbance, and mild mental retardation may not become apparent until after a child has actually been exposed to normal school conditions for a period of months or years.

Once you decide that a student's behavior differs sufficiently from that of other students to raise the possibility of special services or perhaps special class placement, you will need to collect data to support your referral. In general, you should have information about the student's current educational status (this would include attendance records, scores from tests and quizzes, and evaluation of homework assignments), how the student has responded to various instructional strategies, and any information provided to you by the parents (Cartwright, Cartwright, & Ward, 1989; Kubiszyn & Borich, 1987).

Because you will be inexperienced, because referral is an important first step, and because classifying a pupil as eligible for special education under PL 94-142 is a significant (and often costly) decision, you are almost certain to be given advice and assistance about how to handle a possible referral. In any event, if a referral is seen as appropriate by the person or persons delegated to process referrals, the next step is assessment.

Assessment. The initial assessment procedures, which must be approved by parents, are usually carried out by school psychologists who are certified to administer tests. As noted earlier, typically several tests are given. For example, one group of school psychologists reported that an average of eleven tests were given before a student was classified as learning disabled (Thurlow and Ysseldyke, 1979). If the initial conclusions of the school psychologist support the teacher's perception that the student needs special services, the **interdisciplinary assessment team** required under PL 94-142 will be formed. Depending on the type of personnel available and the nature of a child's handicapping condition, an interdisciplinary team may consist of several of the following specialists: school psychologist, guidance counselor, classroom teacher, school social worker, learning disability specialist, speech therapist, physician, psychiatrist. Since a classroom teacher is sometimes asked to be a member of this team, you may serve in this capacity. In all likelihood, you will be asked to describe the referred child's intellectual, social, emotional, and physical performance. You should be prepared to provide such information as the quality of the child's homework and his or her test scores, ability to understand and use language, ability to perform various motor functions, alertness at different times of the day, and interpersonal relationships with classmates (Kubiszyn & Borich, 1987). If the team decides that the student *does* qualify for special services, the next step is preparation of the individualized education program.

Interdisciplinary assessment team determines if pupil needs special services

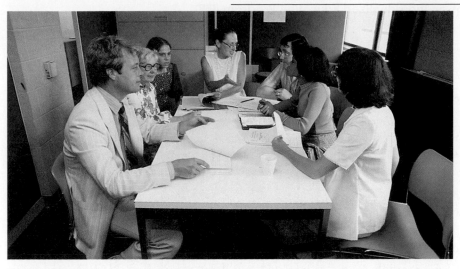

One of the provisions of PL 94-142 stipulates that an individualized education program must be prepared by specialists in the education of exceptional children, the classroom teacher, and perhaps the parents when a handicapped child is mainstreamed. (Bohdan Hrynewych/Stock, Boston)

Preparation of the IEP. At least some, if not all, of the members of the assessment team work with the teacher (and the parents) in preparing the IEP. The necessary components of an IEP were described earlier, and they are illustrated in Figure 5.2.

Implementation of the IEP. Depending on the nature and severity of the handicap, the student may spend part or all of the school day in a regular classroom or be placed in a separate class or school. If the pupil stays in a regular classroom, the teacher will be expected to put into practice the various instructional techniques listed in the IEP. One or more of the specialists listed earlier may give assistance by providing part-time instruction or treatment and/or by supplying specific advice. The classroom teacher may also be expected to determine if the listed objectives are being met and to furnish evidence of attainment. Various techniques of instruction, as well as approaches to evaluation that stress pupil mastery of individualized assignments, will be discussed in several of the chapters that follow. Specific techniques that you might use when instructing exceptional students most likely to be placed in regular classrooms, including some who qualify under the provisions of PL 94-142, will be summarized later in this chapter.

Because the IEP is planned by a multidisciplinary team, you will be given direction and support when providing regular class instruction for pupils who have a handicapping condition as defined under PL 94-142. Thus, you will not be expected to start from scratch or handle planning and instructional responsibilities entirely by yourself.

Classroom teacher, parents, several specialists prepare IEP

Figure 5.2 Example of an Individualized Education Program (IEP)

INDIVIDUAL EDUCATIONAL PLAN

DATE: 11/11/82

STUDENT: Last Name _____ First _____ Middle _____
Grade Level: 5.3 Birthdate/Age: 8-4-71

School of Attendance _____ Home School _____

School Address _____ School Telephone Number _____

Child Study Team Members

	Case Manager	LD Teacher
Name: Homeroom	Title	Parents
Name: Facilitator	Title	
Name: Speech	Title	

Summary of Assessment results

IDENTIFIED STUDENT NEEDS: Reading from last half of DISTAR II - present performance level

LONG TERM GOALS: To improve reading achievement level by at least one year's gain. To improve math achievement to grade level. To improve language skills by one year's gain.

SHORT TERM GOALS: Master grade level vocabulary and reading skills. Master math skills in basic curriculum. Master spelling words from level 3 list. Complete units 1-9 from grade level 3 curriculum.

MAINSTREAM MODIFICATIONS

Description of Services to be Provided

Type of Service	Teacher	Starting Date	Amt. of time per day	OBJECTIVES AND CRITERIA FOR ATTAINMENT
Level III	LD teacher	11-11-82	2 1/2 hrs.	Reading: will know all vocabulary through the "Honeycomb" level. Will master skills as presented through Distar II. Will know 123 sound-symbols presented in "Sound Way to Reading". Math: will pass all tests at Basic 4 level. Spelling: 5 words each week from level 3 list. Language: will complete Units 1-9 of the 4th grade language program. Will also complete supplemented units from Language Step by Step.

Mainstream Classes	Teacher	Amt. of time per day	OBJECTIVES AND CRITERIA FOR ATTAINMENT
SLD	LD	3/4 hrs.	Out of seat behavior: sit attentively and listen during mainstream class discussions. A simple management plan will be implemented if he does not meet this expectation. Mainstream modifications of Social Studies: will keep a folder in which he expresses through drawing the topics his class will cover. Modified district social studies curriculum. An oral reading/text to him, and oral questions will be asked. No formal testing will be made.

The following equipment, and other changes in personnel, transportation, curriculum, methods, and educational services will be made:
Distar II Reading Program Spelling Level 3 "Sound Way to Reading" Program Vocabulary tapes

Substantiation of least restrictive alternatives: The planning team has determined academic needs are best met with direct SLD support in reading, math, language and spelling.

ANTICIPATED LENGTH OF PLAN: 1 yr. The next periodic review will be held: May 1983
DATE/TIME/PLACE

☒ I approve this program placement and the above IEP
☐ I do not approve this placement and/or the IEP
☐ I request a conciliation conference

_____ PARENT/GUARDIAN

_____ Principal or Designee

Form 2011

White Copy - Cumulative Folder   Golden Rod - Case Manager
Pink Copy - Special Teacher   Yellow Copy - Parent

The types of atypical students you will sometimes be expected to teach in your classroom will vary. Some will be special education students who are being mainstreamed for a certain part of the school day. Others, while different from typical students in some noticeable respect, will not qualify for special education services under PL 94-142. The remainder of this chapter describes atypical pupils from both categories and techniques for teaching them. Of those students whose handicapping conditions are covered by PL 94-142, you are most likely to encounter mentally retarded, learning disabled, emotionally disturbed, and speech impaired students (as indicated earlier, in Table 5.1). Mentally retarded, learning disabled, and emotionally disturbed students often require special forms of instruction, and we will focus on these categories. In addition, although not mentioned in PL 94-142, students who are gifted and talented, disadvantaged, or bilingual and culturally diverse require special forms of instruction, as we will also discuss.

Students with Mental Retardation

The Classification of Children with Mental Retardation

As noted in Chapter 4 and at the beginning of this chapter, there has been a trend away from the rigid use of classification schemes in American education. It is sometimes essential, nevertheless, as Hobbs pointed out in *The Futures of Children,* to classify children who differ in significant ways from the norm in order to plan and finance special education for them. The need for classifying mentally retarded children has been recognized by the American Association on Mental Deficiency (AAMD), which proposed this definition: "Mental retardation refers to significantly subaverage intellectual functioning existing concurrently with defects in adaptive behavior and manifested during the developmental period" (Grossman, 1977, 1983). The AAMD applies the term **mental retardation** to individuals having IQ scores of 67 and below and classifies those with IQ scores within that range into the following categories:

Mild retardation—IQ score between 67 and 52

Moderate retardation—IQ score between 51 and 36

Severe retardation—IQ score between 35 and 20

Profound retardation—IQ score of 19 and below

Owing to both the legal challenges to IQ testing and special class placement and the trend toward mainstreaming, students classified as mildly retarded who were once separated are more likely now to be placed in regular classes. You probably will not encounter a great many mainstreamed children classified as moderately or severely retarded, because of the specialized forms of care and instruction they need. You may, however, be asked to teach for at least part of the day one or more higher-scoring mildly retarded children.

Characteristics of Children with Mild Retardation[1]

Students who have below average IQ scores follow the same general developmental pattern as their peers with higher IQ scores, but they differ in the rate and degree of development. Accordingly, pupils with low IQ scores may possess characteristics typical of pupils with average IQ scores who are younger than they are. One general characteristic of such students, therefore, is that they often appear immature compared with their agemates. Immature pupils are likely to experience frustration frequently when they find they are unable to do things their classmates can do, and many mildly retarded students tend to have a low tolerance for frustration. It helps to remember that a mildly retarded child generally needs to expend effort to cope with situations that more favored peers take in stride. Related to frustration proneness is a tendency toward self-devaluation. When students with retardation become aware that they are having difficulty doing what classmates do with ease, they are likely to doubt their own abilities and suffer from lack of confidence and low self-esteem.

| Mildly retarded students may frustrate easily, lack confidence, self-esteem

The intellectual characteristics of mildly retarded children include tendencies to oversimplify concepts, the inability to generalize, short memory and attention span, the inclination to concentrate on only one aspect of a learning situation and to ignore incidentals, and delayed language development. Several of these characteristics can be understood more completely if they are related to Piaget's description of cognitive development. The mildly retarded students in secondary schools may never move beyond the level of concrete operations. Younger children with retardation will tend to classify things in terms of a single feature. Older ones may be able to deal with concrete situations but find it difficult to grasp abstractions, generalize from one situation to another, or state and test hypotheses.

| Mildly retarded students tend to oversimplify, have difficulty generalizing

Now that you are familiar with some characteristics of mildly retarded pupils, it is time to discuss techniques of teaching. The following suggestions take into account the characteristics just described, as well as points made by Samuel Kirk and James J. Gallagher (1989, pp. 168–172) and by O. P. Kolstoe (1970, pp. 22–23).

1. Many of the points in this section are based on a discussion of characteristics of mentally retarded children in *A Curriculum Guide for Teachers of the Educable Mentally Handicapped* (undated) by Herbert Goldstein and Dorothy M. Seigle and in *Educating Exceptional Children* (6th ed., 1989) by Samuel Kirk and James J. Gallagher.

For the sake of emphasis, many of the characteristics and teaching techniques described in this section refer to children who might barely qualify for mainstreaming (as opposed to special class placement). Most of the students with retardation you are likely to have in your classes will exhibit less extreme variations of the following traits. The basic teaching techniques that are recommended, though, should be effective with all pupils who learn less rapidly than most of their classmates.

SUGGESTIONS FOR TEACHING

Instructing Mildly Retarded Students

1. As much as possible, try to avoid placing mildly retarded students in situations that are likely to lead to frustration. When, despite your efforts, such students indicate that they are close to their limit of frustration tolerance, encourage them to engage in relaxing change-of-pace pursuits or in physical activities.

2. Do everything possible to encourage a sense of self-esteem.

3. Present learning tasks that contain a small number of elements, at least some of which are familiar to the pupil.

4. Give a series of brief lessons that can be completed in short periods of time instead of comprehensive assignments that require sustained concentration and effort.

5. Build overlearning into lessons. Keep going back over material previously learned, but make drill as interesting and enjoyable as possible.

6. Try to arrange what is to be learned into a series of small steps, each of which leads to immediate feedback.

7. Devise and use record-keeping techniques that make it clear that assignments have been completed successfully and that progress is taking place.

1. As much as possible, try to avoid placing mildly retarded students in situations that are likely to lead to frustration. When, despite your efforts, such students indicate that they are close to their limit of frustration tolerance, encourage them to engage in relaxing change-of-pace pursuits or in physical activities.

Since children with retardation are more likely to experience frustration than their more capable peers, it is desirable to try to minimize the frequency of such experiences in the classroom. Probably the most effective way to do this is to give mildly retarded pupils individual assignments so that they are not placed in situations where their work is compared with that of others. No matter how hard

Handbook Heading:
Helping Mildly Retarded
Pupils Deal with
Frustration

you try, though, you will not be able to eliminate frustrating experiences, partly because you will have to schedule some all-class activities and partly because even individual assignments may be difficult for a mildly retarded child to handle. If you happen to notice that such a pupil appears to be getting more and more bothered by inability to complete a task, you might try to divert attention to a less demanding form of activity or have the pupil engage in physical exercise of some kind.

Examples

Have a primary grade pupil who is having trouble with arithmetic problems do some artwork or run to the end of the playground.

Have a secondary grade pupil who is frustrated by inability to complete an assignment take a note to the office.

2. Do everything possible to encourage a sense of self-esteem.

Handbook Heading:
Combating the Tendency
to Communicate Low
Expectations

Children with mild retardation are prone to devalue themselves because they are aware that they are less capable than their classmates at doing many things. One way to combat this tendency toward self-devaluation is to make a point of showing that you have positive feelings about less capable students. If you indicate that you have positive feelings about an individual, that person is likely to acquire similar feelings about himself or herself.

Jere Brophy and Thomas Good (1974) report that many teachers, usually without realizing it, tend to communicate low expectations to students of low ability. Following is a list of some of the ways in which teachers tend to cause mildly retarded students to think of themselves as less capable than classmates. An antidote for combating the tendency described follows each point.

Tendency: Wait less time for mildly retarded pupils to answer.

Antidote: Make it clear that you will allow plenty of time for the pupil to come up with an answer.

Tendency: Respond to a wrong answer supplied by a mildly retarded student by giving the correct answer or by calling on another student.

Antidote: Repeat the question, give a clue, ask a different question.

Tendency: Praise mildly retarded students less frequently.

Antidote: Remind yourself to give frequent personal attention to such students.

Tendency: Expect and demand less from mildly retarded students.

Antidote: Remember how the self-fulfilling prophecy may shape aspirations and esteem. Try to convey the expectation to mildly retarded pupils that they can learn.

Perhaps the best overall strategy to use in building self-esteem is to help children with retardation successfully complete learning tasks. Suggestions 3 through 7 offer ideas you might use.

3. Present learning tasks that contain a small number of elements, at least some of which are familiar to the pupil.

Since students with retardation tend to oversimplify concepts, try to provide learning tasks that contain only a few elements, at least some of which have been previously learned.

Handbook Heading:
Giving Mildly Retarded
Students Simple
Assignments

Examples

Give mildly retarded primary grade students books that tell a simple story and that contain words the pupil has recently learned.

Ask secondary school social studies students with mild retardation to prepare a report on the work of a single police officer, as opposed to preparing an analysis of law enforcement agencies (which might be an appropriate topic for the best student in the class).

4. Give a series of brief lessons that can be completed in short periods of time instead of comprehensive assignments that require sustained concentration and effort.

Students with retardation tend to have a short attention span. If they are asked to concentrate on demanding tasks that lead to a delayed payoff, they are likely to become distracted or discouraged. Therefore, it is better to give a series of short assignments that produce immediate feedback than to use any sort of contract approach or the equivalent where the student is expected to engage in self-directed effort leading to a remote goal.

Give mildly
retarded students
specific assign-
ments that can be
completed quickly

Examples

With mildly retarded elementary school pupils, make frequent use of curriculum materials that consist of a series of short, quickly graded tasks that call attention to progress.

Ask secondary school English students to read a series of short stories instead of a novel.

5. Build overlearning into lessons. Keep going back over material previously learned, but make drill as interesting and enjoyable as possible.

Mildly retarded children have a short memory span and find it difficult to place what is learned in their long-term storage system. Explanations for this include

Handbook Heading:
Using Overlearning
with Mildly Retarded
Students

their tendency to oversimplify concepts and their limited ability to generalize. A person with high intelligence is able to grasp the structure of a field of study and comprehend relationships. Both of these abilities make memorizing simpler and forgetting less likely. The child with mild retardation, by contrast, tends to learn one isolated thing at a time. This is essentially what is meant by rote memorization, and it is unfortunate that many individuals with mild retardation can learn only by repeatedly going over specific items again and again. When teaching such pupils, it is often necessary, therefore, to engage in what amounts to drill, but you might do your best to avoid making this drill seem pointless or tedious.

Examples

Have mildly retarded primary grade students form a group and practice the same ten spelling words every day for a week. Then include the same words in lists presented during following weeks. To give such sessions a bit of variety, use different games, such as spelling baseball, or have children pick out cards containing a word to be spelled.

In a secondary school home economics class, have students bake a series of cakes by following recipes that are essentially the same but produce a variety of desserts.

6. Try to arrange what is to be learned into a series of small steps, each of which leads to immediate feedback.

Students who lack confidence, tend to think of one thing at a time, are unable to generalize, and have a short memory and attention span usually respond quite positively to programmed instruction (to be described more completely in Chapter 7). Programmed instruction offers a systematic step-by-step procedure that emphasizes only one specific idea per step, or frame, and it offers immediate feedback. These characteristics fit very well with those of mildly retarded children. You might look for published programs in the subject or subjects you teach or develop your own materials, perhaps in the form of a workbook of some kind.

Examples

In the primary grades, use programmed readers and look for programs in spelling and arithmetic.

At the secondary level, distribute a list of questions on a chapter, and urge mildly retarded students to be especially conscientious in completing brief answers to one question at a time.

Children with mild retardation are more likely to respond to instruction if they are presented with simple learning tasks and provided with immediate feedback. (Jerry Howard/Positive Images)

7. Devise and use record-keeping techniques that make it clear that assignments have been completed successfully and that progress is taking place.

Handbook Heading:
Giving Mildly Retarded Students Proof of Progress

When a student experiences difficulties in learning, it is especially important to provide tangible proof of progress. When students correctly fill in blanks in a programmed workbook and discover that their answers are correct, they are encouraged to go on to the next question. You might use the same basic approach in more general ways by having students with retardation keep records of progress. (This technique might be used with *all* students in a class, not just mildly retarded ones.)

Examples

Make individual charts for primary grade pupils. As they successfully complete assignments, have them color in marked-off sections; or paste on gold stars or the equivalent; or trace the movement of animal figures, rockets, or whatever, toward a destination.

At the secondary level, make up a chart showing which scores on a series of tasks are to be recorded. Then encourage students to record each score as the work is completed.

At any grade level, use a mastery approach: Establish criteria. Present lessons. Measure achievement. Provide remedial instruction if necessary. Measure achievement again. Record successful completion of each unit and total points as they are accumulated. (Mastery learning is explained in detail in Chapter 12.)

Students with Learning Disabilities

By far the greatest number of students who qualify for special education under PL 94-142 are those classified as learning disabled. According to U.S. Department of Education figures, the number of students identified as learning disabled increased from 969,423 in 1977–1978 to 1,926,097 in 1986–1987. These figures lead to two questions: What are the characteristics of students with learning disabilities? Why have the numbers of students classified as learning disabled increased so dramatically during the last few years?

Characteristics of Students with Learning Disabilities

In the early 1960s groups of concerned parents called attention to a problem in American education: A significant number of pupils in public schools experienced difficulties in learning but were not eligible for special classes or remedial instruction programs. These children were not mentally retarded, deaf, blind, or otherwise handicapped, but they were unable to respond to aspects of the curriculum presented in regular classrooms. In 1963 parents of such children formed the Association for Children with Learning Disabilities to call attention to the scope of the problems not traceable to any specific cause. Their efforts were rewarded in 1968, when the National Advisory Committee on the Handicapped of the U.S. Office of Education developed a definition of specific **learning disabilities,** which was utilized by Congress the following year in the Learning Disability Act of

1969. That definition was revised and inserted in PL 94-142. It stresses the following basic points (Lerner, 1989):

1. The individual has a *disorder in one or more of the basic psychological processes.* (These processes refer to intrinsic prerequisite abilities such as memory, auditory perception, visual perception, and oral language.)
2. The individual has *difficulty in learning,* specifically, in the areas of speaking, listening, writing, reading (word recognition skills and comprehension), and mathematics (calculation and reasoning).
3. The problem is *not primarily due to other causes,* such as visual or hearing impairments, motor handicapped, mental retardation, emotional disturbance, or economic, environmental, or cultural disadvantage.
4. A *severe discrepancy exists between the student's apparent potential for learning and low level of achievement.* (p. 7)

> **Learning disabilities: disorders in basic processes that lead to learning problems not due to other causes**

You should be aware, however, that other definitions of learning disabilities are preferred by many specialists in the field. A widely used definition was proposed by the National Joint Committee on Learning Disabilities (NJCLD) in 1981 (Hammill, Leigh, McNutt, & Larsen, 1981). The NJCLD definition states:

Learning disabilities is a generic term that refers to a heterogeneous group of disorders manifested by significant difficulties in the acquisition and use of listening, speaking, reading, writing, reasoning, or mathematical abilities. These disorders are intrinsic to the individual and presumed to be due to central nervous system dysfunction. Even though a learning disability may occur concomitantly with other handicapping conditions (e.g., sensory impairment, mental retardation, social and emotional disturbance) or environmental influences (e.g., cultural differences, or inappropriate instruction, psycholinguistic factors), it is not the direct result of those conditions or influences.

Important concepts in the NJCLD definition (summarized by Lerner, 1989) include the following:

1. *Learning disabilities are a heterogeneous group of disorders.* (Individuals with learning disabilities exhibit many kinds of problems.)
2. *The problem is intrinsic to the individual.* (Learning disabilities are due to factors within the person rather than to external factors, such as the environment or the educational system.)
3. *The problem is thought to be related to a central nervous system dysfunction.* (There is recognition of the biological basis of the problem.)
4. *Learning disabilities may occur along with other handicapping conditions.* (There is recognition that individuals can have several problems at the same time, such as learning disabilities and emotional disorders.) (p. 8)

The complexity of the PL 94-142 and NJCLD definitions and the fact that they are somewhat different indicate that it may often be difficult to make a diagnosis. The PL 94-142 provisions stipulate, for instance, that those who make evaluations should decide whether there is a "severe discrepancy between achievement and intellectual ability" in the various areas listed. But precisely how does one determine ability levels and decide when a discrepancy is severe? Because the diagnosis of learning disabilities is complex and because once students are referred they tend to receive services under PL 94-142 (Ysseldyke, 1983), many schools have established *teacher assistance teams* (Chalfant & Pysh, 1983) to help individual classroom teachers make referral evaluations. Thus, you are not likely to have to make a decision about the presence or absence of a learning disability all by yourself.

Reasons for the Increase in Pupils Classified as Learning Disabled

When the number of students classified as learning disabled almost doubled in six years, many people wondered if this increase was due, at least in part, to mislabeling. Evidence presented by Lorrie Shepard, Mary Lee Smith, and Carol Vojir (1983) suggests that mislabeling did, and probably still does, play a significant role. These researchers randomly selected for analysis the records of 790 Colorado school children classified as learning disabled. Their findings can be summarized as follows:

1. Psychological assessments were often either incomplete or based on poor-quality tests. For example, 40 percent of the students were either missing an IQ test or an achievement test or were given achievement tests that lacked normative data (recall from Chapter 4 that normed excellence is one of the characteristics of a well-constructed standardized test).
2. The ability-achievement discrepancy that is so critical to the definition of learning disability may be as much a function of the particular tests used as a basic cognitive deficiency of the child. In 12 percent of the cases, children took two IQ tests and two math achievement tests. Only 5 percent of those who had two math scores showed significant discrepancies between IQ and both tests. In 15 percent of the cases, children took two reading achievement tests. Only 27 percent of those who had two reading scores showed significant discrepancies between IQ and both reading tests.
3. Until about fourth grade, the average learning disabled student scored at or slightly below grade level at the time of classification.
4. The researchers judged 57 percent of the children, on the basis of the information in their files, to be suffering from other problems (such as mild retarda-

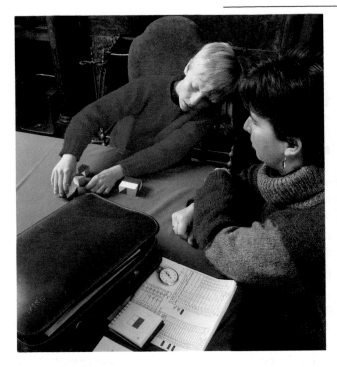

Learning disabilities often result from perceptual problems which are analyzed through use of specialized tests. Several tests are usually administered in order to identify a pupil as learning disabled under PL 94-142. (Dan McCoy/ Rainbow)

tion, emotional disturbance, hearing impairment, and minor behavioral problems). In other words, Shepard, Smith, and Vojir judged only about 43 percent of the sample to have been properly classified.

Increases in learning disabled due to faulty assessment procedures, poor-quality tests

Shepard, Smith, and Vojir offered several possible reasons for such massive mislabeling:

1. The desire to provide remedial and support services to students who would not otherwise receive them because they did not qualify for any other handicapping category under PL 94-142.
2. A lack of understanding about the definition of learning disability and its relevant diagnostic indicators.
3. Administrative pressures to find and serve all handicapped pupils in order to maintain the viability of special education programs.
4. Pressure from parents to secure remedial services for their failing children.

Note that Shepard and her colleagues found that some children labeled as learning disabled seemed to better fit the categories of mental retardation or emotional disturbance. As a potential member of an interdisciplinary assessment team, you should carefully compare the classification criteria of the two categories we have covered so far with criteria for the next category, emotional disturbance. By doing so, you may in the future be able to help others avoid this type of mislabeling.

In recent years the number of pupils classified as learning disabled has increased. This increase seems to be largely due to mislabeling, which is caused by faulty assessment procedures, poor-quality tests, and various pressures to provide remedial and support services to low-achieving students.

Emotionally Disturbed Students

Students who exhibit poor relationships with others, or engage in inappropriate behavior, or who are abnormally depressed or fearful may be classified as *emotionally disturbed* under PL 94-142. Many psychologists use the term *behavior disorder,* which calls attention to the behavior that needs to be changed, in preference to the term *emotionally disturbed.*

Pupils with behavior disorders tend to be either *aggressive* (exhibiting negative and hostile behavior), or *withdrawn* (manifesting depression and lack of confidence).

Gifted and Talented Students

Students who learn at a significantly faster rate than their peers or who possess superior talent in one or more areas also need to be taught in special ways if they are to make the most of their abilities. Unlike mentally retarded, learning disabled, and emotionally disturbed children, however, students with superior capabilities are not covered by PL 94-142. Instead, the federal government provides technical assistance to states and local school districts in establishing programs for superior students. Although most states have such programs, some experts in special education (for example, Horowitz & O'Brien, 1986) feel that they are not given the resources they need to adequately meet the needs of all gifted and talented students. The suggestions for teaching that follow a bit later reflect this situation. All of them are inexpensive to implement and require few additional personnel.

A recent definition of the term **gifted and talented** was part of a bill passed by Congress in 1988:

Gifted and talented students show high performance on wide range of tasks

The term *gifted and talented children and youth* means children and youth who give evidence of high performance capability in areas such as intellectual, creative, artistic, or leadership capacity, or in specific academic fields, and who require services or activities not ordinarily provided by the school in order to fully develop such capabilities. (Title IV–H.R. 5, 1988, pp. 227–228)

Identifying Gifted and Talented Students

The AAMD classification of mental retardation refers to specific IQ scores in establishing the upper and lower limits of various categories. It is not possible to be that specific about the test scores of atypically bright students. From the 1920s through the 1950s an IQ score of 140 was commonly accepted for classifying children as gifted. Beginning in the early 1960s, this dividing line was increasingly criticized. A number of psychologists (such as Getzels & Jackson, 1962) called attention to the fact that many children who deserved to be classified as gifted did not earn IQ scores of 140 or above, primarily because the tests used to measure IQ seemed to discriminate against divergent thinkers.

Because of these criticisms, most states have eliminated mention of a specific IQ score from their definition of gifted students. A 1985 survey (Cassidy & Johnson, 1986) found only four states that use some sort of numerical cut-off score. While this is seen as a step in the right direction, critical weaknesses in the identification of gifted and talented children remain. The main problem is a lack of correspondence between the definition of giftedness adopted by a school district, the methods used to identify gifted pupils, and the type of instruction given to them. Robert D. Hoge (1988), for example has argued that giftedness is usually defined by school boards in terms of one or more of the following characteristics: superior performance on a standardized intelligence test, superior performance on a standardized achievement test, superior performance on tests of specific aptitudes, evidence of creativity, or a high level of motivation. The actual identification of gifted children, however, is usually made on the basis of an IQ score and/or teacher nominations. To compound the problem even further, the teachers of gifted and talented pupils, working from the school district's definition, emphasize such things as independent work, the exercise of creativity, and leadership. Since, as we saw in Chapter 4, IQ tests are not designed to measure such qualities as motivation, creativity, and leadership, relying on them as the only or major index of giftedness produces at least two problems: errors of placement (and nonplacement) occur, and students are exposed to forms of instruction for which they may not be prepared.

Inconsistency often exists between definition, identification, and teaching of gifted students

The issue of nonplacement is particularly acute for certain minority-group members. As we mentioned in Chapter 4, blacks, Hispanics, and Native Americans are greatly underrepresented in gifted and talented programs. Similar observations have been made about gifted students with a learning disability (for example, Suter & Wolf, 1987). A major reason why these groups are underrepresented, to repeat the point made in Chapter 4 as well as in the preceding paragraph, is overreliance on a narrow range of standardized tests as indicators of giftedness. Other characteristics that might be taken into account in deciding on placement are creativity, wide-ranging interests, leadership, communication skill, critical thinking ability, and task persistence.

Minorities underrepresented in gifted classes because of overreliance on test scores

Several reasons may explain the stress on achievement and mental ability as indicators of giftedness at the expense of the characteristics just mentioned. One is the historical emphasis on IQ. Another is educators' unfamiliarity with ways of measuring human characteristics other than by standardized tests. A third reason is a general ignorance of characteristics that are more highly valued by the minority culture than by the majority culture. Members of many Native American tribes, for example, place as much value on a child's knowledge of tribal traditions, storytelling ability, and artistic ability as they do on problem-solving ability and scientific reasoning (Tonemah, 1987). A child's giftedness may therefore be evident in such "unmeasurable" skills. The importance of becoming more sensitive to the cultural values of ethnic and racial minorities is discussed more extensively in the last section of this chapter.

Other methods of identifying gifted and talented children (be they from a minority or from the majority) include nominations from peers, community leaders, and the students themselves (in the form of biographical statements). Checklist and rating scales exist that include such characteristics as logical reasoning skills, interpersonal communication skills, ability to improvise with commonplace materials, use of expressive speech, and use of humor. Other types of standardized tests are also relevant, such as the Torrance Tests of Creative Thinking, the Raven Standard Progressive Matrices (a nonverbal test of inductive reasoning), and the Watson-Glaser Test of Critical Thinking (Frasier, 1987; Stronge, Lynch, & Smith, 1987; Tonemah, 1987).

Characteristics of Gifted and Talented Students

After surveying a number of definitions and lists of characteristics, as well as proposals for identifying exceptionally capable children, James J. Gallagher concluded that what such individuals have in common "is the ability to absorb abstract concepts, to organize them more effectively, and to apply them more appropriately than the average youngster" (1975, p. 19). That is probably as concise and accurate a description of gifted and talented children as can be found. Perhaps the only points that need to be added to Gallagher's description are that some gifted children are ideal students and impress their teachers that way; others may be thought of as pests or perhaps classified by some teachers as below average in ability. A few differences between these two types merit mention.

Some pupils with high IQ scores respond to instruction easily, give answers that are precisely what the teachers want, and are models of good conduct. In terms of Guilford's description of intellectual operations (noted in Chapter 3), such students might be classified as extremely competent *convergent* thinkers. When teachers are asked to nominate the most capable pupils in their classes, they tend to choose children of this type. Although such individuals tend to do exceptionally well in school and in later life, they are typically not very innovative (Terman & Oden, 1959). They become successful doctors, lawyers, professors, and businesspeople, but they are not likely to make original contributions in their

When planning instructional experiences for gifted and talented students, it may help to make a distinction between *convergent* and *divergent* types. Albert Einstein, for example, was regarded as incapable of learning by most of his teachers. He may have given that impression because of his unorthodox approach to many things. This photo, for instance, shows him recording a formula at a conference of scientists. He never explained what it meant and his colleagues were unable to figure out its significance. (UPI/Bettmann Newsphotos)

fields. Other rapid learners do *not* respond to instruction in expected ways. They may act bored, often respond to questions in unorthodox or unsettling ways, and perhaps give the impression that they are uncooperative or disruptive. Many pupils of this type might be classified as brilliant *divergent* thinkers. Allowing for the possibility of unconventional types of mental superiority helps explain why Einstein and Edison (to note only two of the most frequently mentioned examples) were considered to be extremely poor learners by their teachers. The later achievements of Einstein and Edison suggest that gifted divergent learners may become highly productive and creative—provided their spark of genius is not completely squelched in school.

Some rapid learners convergent, others divergent thinkers

Accelerated Instruction: Pros and Cons

Gifted and talented students, whether convergent thinkers or divergent thinkers, constantly challenge a teacher's skill, ingenuity, and classroom resources. While trying to teach the class as a whole, the teacher is faced with the need to provide

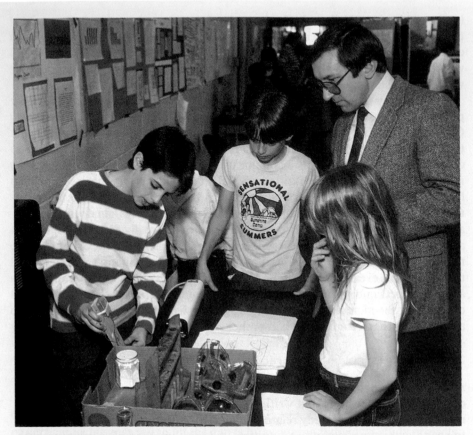

Gifted students should be encouraged and helped by their teachers to develop creative hobbies and to pursue interests in particular subjects. (Mark Antman/The Image Works)

dress or desk to be entered in the county fair. A related point is that you should help high school seniors who are talented in your field to apply for scholarships. Some schools—and teachers—place winners each year, basically because they take the trouble to assist logical candidates.

5. Check into the possibility of correspondence courses or tutoring.

In small school districts, one or two brilliant children are occasionally found to have IQ scores several dozen points higher than those of other above average pupils. One way to provide for them is tutorial instruction. In some cases, this is given by a principal or a teacher with released time. Because of the expense, the solution is more likely to be a correspondence course. A combination of these two techniques, called the Sponsor-Correspondent Plan, has met with a good deal of success. It establishes a liaison between a brilliant pupil and someone with training and experience in the area of that pupil's greatest interest. Often the person who serves as a sponsor is a retired expert in the field.

Suppose a brilliant boy in a small high school is fascinated by inorganic chemistry. Because of his intellect and his single-minded drive, he learns more about the subject than his teacher—who also teaches three other subjects—knows. The teacher asks a university or professional organization if it knows of a retired inorganic chemist who might enjoy assisting a young enthusiast. If such a person is found, the sponsor and the pupil correspond with each other and, as often as circumstances permit, have personal conferences. Highly successful experiences with this technique have been reported. If you find yourself teaching in a small school and bedeviled by an embryonic Einstein, it could be your salvation.

6. Perhaps experiment with having gifted students act as tutors.

Depending on the grade, subject, and personalities of those involved, gifted pupils might be asked to act occasionally as tutors, lab assistants, or the equivalent. Some bright students welcome such opportunities and are capable of providing instruction so that their peers do not feel self-conscious or humiliated. Others may resent being asked to spend school time helping others and/or lack skills in interpersonal relationships. If you do decide to ask a gifted student to function as a tutor, therefore, it would be wise to proceed tentatively and cautiously.

Disadvantaged Pupils

The word *disadvantaged* is used in this book to call your attention to the need for some students to receive special kinds of instruction. Some educators favor the term *culturally different,* but it seems preferable to use the term **disadvantaged pupils** to emphasize that the most significant difference between some pupils is the degree to which they have been exposed to out-of-school experiences that equip, or fail to equip, them to perform academically. Only by acknowledging the nature of the disadvantages attributable to certain types of backgrounds can teachers arrange compensatory school experiences. Since this is the case, it seems more logical to say not only that many lower-class students come from a different culture, but also that they are at a disadvantage. To make this clear, here is a review of factors that may influence the behavior of disadvantaged students. Once these factors are listed, it will be possible to derive some general guidelines for teaching such pupils.

Characteristics of Disadvantaged Pupils

1. Many low-income Americans do not receive satisfactory health care. As a consequence, the incidence of premature births and birth defects in lower-class children, as compared to the middle-class children, is greater and the infant mortality rate is higher (as consistently revealed by the National Institutes of Health statistics). Since poor children do not receive medical or dental care regularly, it is difficult to compile accurate statistics on general health. It seems reasonable to assume, however, that the infant mortality rate reflects a trend that probably continues in later years. That is to say, lower-class children probably continue to suffer from untreated illnesses at a rate that may be at least twice that of middle-class children.

The lasting impact on disadvantaged children of inadequate prenatal care, prematurity, birth complications, and treatment during the first months of postnatal existence was revealed in a study carried out by E. E. Werner, J. M. Bierman, and F. E. French (1971). These researchers studied the development of all 670 children born on the island of Kauai in 1955. Each newborn infant was rated on a scale of severity of prenatal and birth complications. Later, periodic assessments were made of physical health, intelligence, social maturity, and environmental variables. Werner and her colleagues found that most children from middle- and upper-income homes who were judged to have had a poor start because of prenatal or birth complications seemed to have overcome their early handicaps by the time they entered school. On intelligence tests, for instance, they scored only slightly below children from similar backgrounds who were judged to have had uneventful prenatal and birth experiences. Children from lower economic backgrounds who had experienced difficulties at the beginning of their lives, however, seemed to remain at a disadvantage. They scored from 19 to 37 points lower on IQ tests than children from similar backgrounds who were judged to have had normal prenatal and birth experiences. On the basis of this finding, as well as other analyses of their data, Werner and her associates concluded that the single most important variable leading to retardation or aberrations in development in disadvantaged children is the poor environment in which they mature. This conclusion is supported by other research summarized by Arnold Sameroff and Michael J. Chandler (1975, pp. 205–210).

2. Many lower-class parents use forms of child care that work against their children's success in school. Robert D. Hess and Virginia Shipman (1965) observed mother-child interactions in lower-class homes and found that the mothers often were inattentive and unresponsive to the child, used impoverished language, tended to lack self-confidence, were disorganized in the way the home was run, and functioned quite often at the preoperational stage of cognitive development. These child-care techniques are essentially the opposite of those that Diana Baumrind (1971) found were used by parents of highly competent children.

3. Disadvantaged children typically have not been exposed to a wide variety of experiences. The parents of middle-class children in America frequently function as teachers, although *tutors* would be a more appropriate word, since instruction is often given to one child at a time. Every time they talk to their children, answer questions, take them on trips, buy books or educational toys, middle-class parents provide knowledge and experiences that accumulate to make school learning familiar and easy. A child who does not receive such continuous tutoring in the home is clearly at a disadvantage when placed in competitive academic situations.

4. Disadvantaged pupils may not be strongly motivated to do well in school, and they may not be knowledgeable about techniques of becoming successful in school. Middle-class parents who have benefited in a variety of ways from education serve as effective and enthusiastic advocates of schooling. Because doing well in school paid off for them, they are eager to persuade their children to do well academically in order to achieve similar or greater benefits. They also serve as positive models. By contrast, lower-class parents who did not do well may describe school in negative terms and perhaps blame teachers for their failure in classrooms and subsequent failures later in life. If the parents were inept students, they are unable to tell their children about how to study for exams, meet requirements, select courses, or acquire the general all-around academic know-how that middle-class parents pass on to their offspring.

Disadvantaged pupils often lack motivation, academic know-how

5. Lower-class adolescents typically have low career aspirations. The impact of social class on career choice was revealed by a comprehensive study (J. K. Little, 1967) of all the graduating seniors in Wisconsin's public and private high schools. At the time of graduation, students were asked to note the occupations they hoped to enter. The choices were later compared with the jobs they actually attained. Students who were in the lower third of their graduating class in socioeconomic status had significantly lower aspirations than those in the middle and upper thirds. In addition, the later actual job attainments of the lower-class students were close to their expectations.

Lower-class adolescents often have low career aspirations

A lower-class student who has had a history of failure in school is understandably reluctant to risk further failure by working toward a remote, difficult-to-achieve vocational goal. Furthermore, parents may not offer much encouragement. R. L. Simpson (1962) found that high school students, regardless of social class, were likely to seek higher education and higher-level careers if their parents urged them to, but they were unlikely to do so if their parents were neutral or negative about preparation for a career. Lower-class parents who dropped out of school and were later unable to find satisfying jobs—or any jobs at all—are less likely to urge their children to go to college than are middle-class parents who have discovered firsthand the employment value of a college degree.

6. In addition to having a low level of aspiration and a low need for achievement, disadvantaged pupils from minority groups may also feel role confusion and have poor self-esteem. Erik Erikson has stressed that two key components of identity are being accepted by those who count and knowing where one is going. A disadvantaged adolescent who has no definite career plans after leaving school (with or without a diploma) is more likely to experience role confusion than a sense of identity achievement. If such an adolescent is unable to find a job (and the unemployment rate for minority-group youth is typically several times greater than the average rate for that age group), low self-esteem may contribute to the formation of a negative identity.

Using this list of points as a framework, it is possible to draw up a number of general guidelines for teaching disadvantaged students.

SUGGESTIONS FOR TEACHING

Instructing Disadvantaged Pupils

1. Be alert to the potential dangers of labeling. Concentrate on individuals while guarding against the impact of stereotyping.
2. When evaluating standardized test scores of any kind, keep in mind the possibility that the norms may not be appropriate for disadvantaged pupils.
3. Allow for the possibility that disadvantaged pupils may have inadequate diets and may not receive adequate medical attention.
4. Remain aware that disadvantaged pupils may not be familiar with many things you take for granted. Try to supply experiences that such students may have missed.
5. Use every possible means for motivating disadvantaged pupils to do well in school.
6. Teach study and test-taking skills and academic "tricks of the trade."
7. Give specific assignments, arrange for abundant practice, supply immediate feedback, stress overlearning.
8. In the secondary grades, introduce topics in a concrete way; then have students develop their own learning materials, make observations, engage in role playing, be active as they learn.

1. Be alert to the potential dangers of labeling. Concentrate on individuals while guarding against the impact of stereotyping.

Under certain circumstances, the potential dangers of labeling noted in the preceding chapter may lead to unfortunate consequences. The negative impact of labels can be minimized, however, if pupils are placed in categories primarily for the purpose of improving instruction or securing services. Instead of thinking that a disadvantaged student is beyond help, for example, you might ask yourself, "What kinds of disadvantages does this pupil need to overcome?" and also "What kinds of strengths does this student have?" By asking these questions, you concentrate on *individuals,* which is the surest way to avoid succumbing to the perils of stereotyping. It is reported that Samuel Johnson, the famous English literary figure, was once asked, "Are men more intelligent than women?" He replied, "Which man? Which woman?" If you think in the same way, you can avoid the error of assigning to individuals characteristics that are sometimes attributed to a group. For example, instead of searching for evidence to determine if blacks, on the average, have more or less of a certain characteristic than whites, on the average, you should simply concentrate on the unique individual characteristics of a particular black or white student.

2. When evaluating standardized test scores of any kind, keep in mind the possibility that the norms may not be appropriate for disadvantaged pupils.

PL 94-142 stipulates that disadvantaged children have the right to be evaluated with reference to appropriate norms. Some states have laws mandating that standardized tests are not to be used as the sole criterion for identifying students as mentally retarded. Such laws are ineffective, however, if individual teachers take test scores too literally. Remember the suggestions for interpreting standardized test scores noted at the end of the preceding chapter, particularly the idea that you should give the pupil the benefit of the doubt. Test scores should always be interpreted tentatively and with caution and used to help pupils overcome weakness.

3. Allow for the possibility that disadvantaged pupils may have inadequate diets and may not receive adequate medical attention.

In searching for explanations of why disadvantaged students may have learning difficulties, some of the first factors to be considered are diet and health. A pupil who is malnourished or has a debilitating illness or an undetected physical handicap of some sort (for example, nearsightedness) cannot be expected to function as an effective learner. If you suspect that a student needs medical attention, you might inquire about possible aid from governmental agencies or charitable organizations. (This is a situation in which labeling may work to the advantage of a pupil. Only after an individual has been classified as coming from a poverty-level family or the equivalent are certain kinds of aid made available.)

4. Remain aware that disadvantaged pupils may not be familiar with many things you may take for granted. Try to supply experiences that such students may have missed.

Many disadvantaged students have led extremely restricted lives. They may have had no experience with everyday objects or situations presented in books or featured in instructional materials. When teaching such pupils, it is prudent to find out what they know and do not know. If inner-city primary grade children have never taken a drive through a rural area, they may have difficulty reading a simple story about farm life. In a situation such as this, it would be beneficial to try to arrange a field trip through rural areas or at least to show a film or film strip about country life to familiarize disadvantaged children with what more favored pupils already know. Regardless of the grade level you teach, you might make it a practice to ask disadvantaged pupils if they have had any personal experience with objects and situations mentioned in books and lessons. If they have not, try to supply familiarity with such experiences in direct or pictorial form.

5. Use every possible means for motivating disadvantaged pupils to do well in school.

Perhaps the major reason disadvantaged pupils do not do well in school is not lack of ability but lack of interest in learning. A number of circumstances conspire to prevent lower-class students from acquiring a desire to do well in school: lack of encouragement from parents, the absence of models in the form of parents and siblings who have benefited from schooling, a level of aspiration set low to avoid possible failure, lack of success leading to a low need for achievement. One of the major tasks of the teacher of disadvantaged pupils is arousing and sustaining interest in learning. Techniques for doing this will be described in detail in Chapter 11.

6. Teach study and test-taking skills and academic "tricks of the trade."

Handbook Heading:
Ways to Teach Academic "Tricks of the Trade"

Regardless of their background, most students are not likely to maintain a strong desire to achieve in school unless they receive reinforcement for their efforts in the form of good grades. To earn high grades consistently, students must usually develop specialized learning skills. If the parents of a lower-class child are unable to tell their offspring about such skills, it may be necessary for you to give suggestions about how to study, what to look for on tests, how to budget time during exams, and so on.

Disadvantaged pupils may not be familiar with many things that are discussed in texts. Accordingly, it may be desirable to give them first-hand experience with things, objects, or creatures they may not have encountered in their homes or neighborhoods. (Alan Carey/The Image Works)

Examples

Give many "practice" examinations so that your pupils get plenty of experience answering questions. Such practice may make them feel less threatened when taking important exams or standardized tests.

After handing back exams, discuss why certain answers were satisfactory or unsatisfactory. Then offer specific tips for writing good answers to similar questions that might be encountered in the future. (Do this on an individual basis, if possible.)

Invite high school students who are doing well in college to return to their secondary schools and talk to seniors about study techniques that lead to success.

Ask counselors from nearby community and four-year colleges to describe the kinds of financial and tutorial aid that are available.

A number of evaluations of teaching techniques that have proven effective with disadvantaged primary grade pupils have been published (Soar, 1973; Stallings & Kaskowitz, 1974; and others). Barak Rosenshine (1976) reviewed them and offered the following conclusions regarding techniques that did and did not lead to improved performance as measured by standardized tests:

Most Productive

Pupils study texts, complete workbook exercises, or respond to direct questions asked by the teacher.

Pupils work individually at their desks completing workbook exercises at own pace but under direct supervision of the teacher.

Pupils work on specific exercises in small groups.

Teacher makes almost all decisions about what will be learned.

Teacher asks direct questions that have a specific answer.

Students asked to give many answers, required to guess if they aren't sure of the right answer, are given immediate feedback for every answer.

Least Productive

Pupils engage in self-selected learning (as in open education approaches), participate in learning games.

Pupils given free study time, allowed to socialize with classmates as they study, not provided with close supervision.

Pupils work alone (and without close teacher supervision).

Students often allowed to choose what they will learn.

Teacher asks general questions or invites pupils to comment on or suggest related ideas.

Teacher asks open-ended questions, does not require direct answers, feedback is vague or absent.

Jere E. Brophy and Carolyn M. Evertson (1976) made detailed observations of teachers who were consistently effective as instructors of disadvantaged second- and third-graders. Many of their findings corroborate the conclusions of Rosenshine. That is, the effective teachers they observed used a structured approach, made specific assignments, arranged for pupils to get plenty of practice working with basic texts and workbooks, and gave immediate feedback. Brophy and Evertson also describe some interesting subtleties in the techniques used by effective teachers of the disadvantaged. Quite often, for instance, such teachers had to "patiently and doggedly (work) to get responses" (p. 79) during class recitation periods. Upper- and middle-class pupils observed by Brophy and Evertson typically had to be kept under control during such periods. They were so eager to prove that they had come up with the right answer more quickly than classmates that they often threatened to disrupt the lesson. Lower-class pupils, by contrast, often were reluctant to answer and exhibited anxiety about being called on for fear of not being able to supply the right answer. In their efforts to overcome students' fear of failure, teachers in lower-class schools moved at a slow pace, gave extra time for pupils to think before speaking, and encouraged *any* kind of answer, even if it was wrong. If a wrong answer *was* supplied, the teacher either gave hints so that the student could correct the error or else matter-of-factly provided the correct response and went on to another question. Brophy and Evertson also stressed that it seems to be especially important for teachers of the disadvantaged to allow for closely supervised practice immediately after a new skill is demonstrated or a new idea is introduced. If disadvantaged pupils do not get off to a good start with a new skill, they are likely to practice errors during unsupervised study periods. Lack of a rich background experience and of self-confidence are likely to limit self-correcting tendencies. A related point emphasized by Brophy and Evertson is that it appears to be preferable for teachers of the disadvantaged to *overteach* and ask pupils to *overlearn* rather than the opposite.

Although all of the research findings just summarized were based on observations of primary grade pupils and teachers, the same basic techniques may be effective with disadvantaged students of any age.

Examples

Use curriculum materials that feature repeated, brief, and easily graded exercises.

Instead of having pupils study individually just before exams, have them study together in groups of two to five.

Make recitation periods as relaxed as possible. If pupils still act afraid to speak up for fear of appearing ignorant, have them write out answers, perhaps in the form of formative quizzes. Insist that they at least take a stab at answering every question and point out that a "wrong" answer often gives clues as to what is missing or misunderstood.

To encourage students to overlearn without becoming bored or turned off by repetition, first have them study material individually but under your close supervision, and then have them study together in small groups. In both types of study sessions, try to provide a series of short, interesting, varied exercises with clear terminal behavior.

If students demonstrate on a quiz that they seem to have mastered a particular unit, give them a slightly different quiz a week later to make sure the material or skill has been retained.

8. In the secondary grades, introduce topics in a concrete way; then have students develop their own learning materials, make observations, engage in role playing, and be active as they learn.

Techniques for teaching disadvantaged secondary school students have been developed and practiced by Hilda Taba and Deborah Elkins, who explain their approach in *Teaching Strategies for the Culturally Disadvantaged* (1966). The basic guidelines for instructional strategies recommended by Taba and Elkins include continual diagnosis to discover gaps in knowledge and areas in need of attention and the simultaneous pursuit of objectives in six areas: (1) knowledge, thinking, attitudes, and skills; (2) providing for heterogeneity; (3) pacing learning by providing "bite-size" chunks arranged in hierarchical fashion; (4) extensive use of dramatization, play making, and role playing; and (6) providing experiences in observing and interviewing.

> With older disadvantaged, use small steps, concreteness, activity, dramatization, observation

   The implementation of these guidelines can be illustrated by a unit called "Human Hands." The unit was introduced at a concrete level. Students were asked to trace their hands, and the tracings were used first as a basis for discussing the beauty and similarity of hands and then as a stimulus for writing on the topic "Important Things My Hands Can Do." The descriptions provided were analyzed and tallied on the board under different categories to encourage awareness of concepts. The final list of categories was reproduced and added to the written theme as the beginning of an individual notebook for each pupil. Then the teacher read a story, and students were asked to discuss how hands were used by the characters; afterward, the original categories were revised and expanded. For homework, the students were asked to observe an adult for thirty minutes and write down everything the person did with his or her hands. These reports were discussed, tallied, categorized, and added to the notebooks; then each student summed up general observations on hands in a short paragraph, which was later reproduced in a booklet and distributed to the members of the class. Next, help-wanted ads in newspapers were analyzed to illustrate how hands are used in many different occupations. Magazines were distributed, and students were asked to cut out pictures of hands; newspaper articles on hands were collected. All of these were used in group discussion and as the basis for written exercises to be added to the notebooks.

The same general techniques were used for units on "Walls in Our Life" and "Aspirations." The purpose of the latter topic was to build understanding of goals and encourage the development of realistic aspirations. It featured interviews with parents and other adults, the dramatization of original plays, and role playing (some students acted as employers; others as job seekers).

Teaching Strategies for the Culturally Disadvantaged offers detailed suggestions for setting up and carrying out social studies units for secondary school students, although the basic methods described could be adapted for use with almost any grade level or subject. It is one of the most practical how-to-do-it books on teaching secondary school students from disadvantaged backgrounds, and it is highly recommended.

Bilingual and Culturally Diverse Students

Bilingual Education

A Bilingual Education Act was added to the Elementary and Secondary Education Act of 1965 in a first attempt to meet the English-language needs of primary grade children. The original strategy was *transitional;* that is, the intention was to move students as quickly as possible into the standard school curriculum taught in English. At first, provisions in the act covered only schools that received federal funding. In 1974, however, the Supreme Court ruled (in *Lau* v. *Nichols*) that all schools must meet the needs of linguistically different children whether or not a school received federal aid. The act was amended to take into account that decision. The revised act of 1974 also stipulated that bilingual students should be helped to "progress effectively through the school system." In addition, it was mandated that parents should be involved in decisions about such programs. Finally the revised law stressed that federal funding should gradually be replaced by state and local financing. (Many states already have passed their own versions of bilingual education laws.)

The provision in the 1974 act that parents should be included in decision making, together with arguments presented by minority-group leaders and educators, led to an emerging emphasis on *maintenance* rather than transition. Instead of attempting to have bilingual children make the transition to an all-English curriculum as quickly as possible, it has been argued that they should continue to be taught in both languages so that they will at least maintain their original level of competence in the parent language. Some minority-group leaders and educators went a step further and argued that bilingual students should receive federal or state aid to continue to receive instruction in both languages through the secondary grades. Bilingual students should not just maintain their original level of

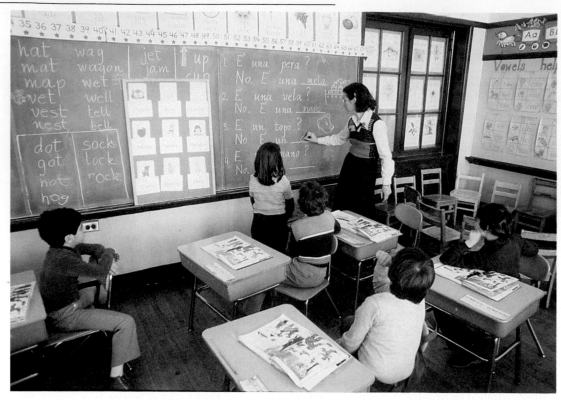

Awareness of the limitations of knowledge of just one language (as well as of the problems faced by school children reared in non-English-speaking homes) has led to expansion of bilingual education. (Bohdan Hrynewych/Stock, Boston)

competence in their native language, it is asserted, but should become increasingly proficient.

The Bilingual Education Act was amended again in 1978. At that time the stipulation that students should "progress effectively through the school system" was deleted and replaced by more specific stress on the achievement of competence in English. In addition, provisions were written to include not only children who had difficulty speaking and understanding English, but also those who needed help reading and writing English. The 1978 act also increased funding for research and teacher preparation.

In comparison to immersion (English-only) programs, how successful have bilingual education programs been in helping non-English-speaking students learn English and other subjects? After analyzing twenty-three studies, Anne C. Willig (1985) concluded that participation in bilingual education programs produced small to moderate gains on tests of reading, language skills, mathematics, and total achievement when measured by tests in English. When measured by tests administered in the student's native language, participation in bilingual education led to significantly better performance on tests of listening comprehension, reading, writing, total language, mathematics, social studies, and attitudes towards school and self.

Federal funds made available for bilingual education have been used to establish programs in seventy-four languages, but 65 percent of the money finances Spanish-English programs. Therefore, you are most likely to be asked to teach in a bilingual education program if you have a Spanish major or minor. Because of the increase in federal funding for research, as well as development of state and local regulations, it is likely that you will be supplied with guidelines and curriculum materials if you qualify to teach bilingual children. You might also anticipate teaching two languages to students in bilingual classes. The 1978 act stipulates that at least 40 percent of the pupils in any bilingual class should come from English-speaking homes. (The percentages of English-speaking and foreign-language-speaking pupils vary in different state laws.) It is assumed that such a mixture will make it possible for English-speaking children to acquire a second language at the same time that children who speak a foreign language learn English. It is also assumed that the children will "instruct" each other as they interact in class.

Multicultural Education

The Basis of Multicultural Education   Arguments for and against transition or maintenance in bilingual education programs are related to the issue of **multicultural education.** The basic assumption on which multicultural education rests is that cultural values and experiences predispose children to think and behave in particular ways. When these values and experiences are understood, accepted as worthwhile, incorporated into instructional lessons, and rewarded by the teacher, the students involved will perform better academically than they otherwise would (Gollnick & Chinn, 1986; Lynch, 1986). The performance of a Hispanic child, for example, might improve if the teacher sits close to the child, touches the child occasionally, smiles frequently, and allows the child to tutor younger students, since Hispanic cultures value these forms of encouragement (Triandis, 1986). Teachers might achieve better relationships with newly arrived Asian students by recognizing that body posture speaks as loudly as words. Tightly crossed arms and legs, for example, say "stay away," and direct eye contact is considered impolite (Yao, 1988).

The concept of multicultural education has roots in several precursors, including bilingual education programs. Until World War I, bilingual public schools were fairly common, particularly in areas with large numbers of German immigrants. After the war, however, public financing of bilingual schools was abruptly withdrawn, partly as a reaction against Germany and partly because of increasing nationalism and isolationism. American society strongly endorsed the "one country, one culture" policy favored by European nations; Americans resolved to

Multicultural education: understand, accept, reward different thinking, behavior patterns

stay out of European affairs and stressed as never before the conception of America as a melting pot. (It was expected that the immigrants who were melted down would be recast in the mold of white Anglo-Saxon Protestants, however. If they did not fit that mold, they would have problems achieving success in American society.) Foreign languages were classified as electives to be studied in a superficial way only by college preparatory students. Most pupils were given intensive instruction only in English.

American involvement in World War II and our subsequent recognition as the leader of the free world called attention to a basic disadvantage of the one-language policy that had been in effect between the wars: Very few Americans were able to communicate with non-Americans in the latter's native language. Awareness of our deficiencies as linguists led to a postwar National Defense Education Act, in which foreign-language learning was stressed as a national priority. The same awareness of our ignorance of foreign languages also contributed to passage of the Bilingual Education Act of 1965. Those who supported the act pointed out that pupils who entered school with a thorough knowledge of a tongue other than English should be encouraged to retain their proficiency, not to sacrifice it in the process of learning English. The most telling argument in favor of bilingual education, though, stressed the tremendous handicap imposed on non-English-speaking primary grade pupils who were expected to master a curriculum presented entirely in a foreign language.

Another progenitor of multicultural education was the social unrest of the 1960s and early 1970s. As an outgrowth of urban riots and the civil rights movement, minority groups argued not only for bilingual education programs in public schools, but also for ethnic studies. It might be said that many American citizens realized that they did not wish to fit the white Anglo-Saxon Protestant mold and began to express a desire to be Americans who have different characteristics. Michael Novak (1971) has referred to this movement as the "rise of the unmeltable ethnics."

For Whom Is Multicultural Education Intended?   In theory, a multicultural orientation is applicable to every student, since every student represents an identifiable cultural or ethnic group. In practice, the programs are directed primarily at members of minority groups. Some of these groups have been a part of American society for generations, while others have arrived more recently. The former category takes in Native Americans, African-Americans, and Mexican-Americans whose ancestors became citizens as a consequence of the Mexican-American War (1846–1848). The latter category includes people whose families immigrated from Puerto Rico (although since Puerto Rico is an American commonwealth, all Puerto Ricans are U.S. citizens), Cuba, Mexico, China, Japan, Korea, the Philippine Islands, Cambodia, Laos, Vietnam, Thailand, El Salvador, Nicaragua, and Guatemala (Gutek, 1988; Kellogg, 1988).

Reasons for Multicultural Education   Some people seem to believe that multicultural education programs represent a rejection of basic American values and that this opposition to traditional values is the only rationale behind such programs. We feel this belief is mistaken on both counts. We see multicultural programs as being consistent with basic American values (like tolerance of differences and equality of opportunity) and justified in several ways.

One argument in favor of multicultural programs is that they foster teaching practices that are effective in general as well as for members of a particular group. To return to the example offered earlier, expressing an interest in a child through occasional touching and smiling and allowing the child to tutor a younger student are practices likely to benefit most students, not just those of Hispanic origin.

A second argument is that multicultural programs can encourage student motivation. These programs demonstrate respect for a child's culture and teach about the contributions that the child's group has made to American society. Proponents argue that these features both personalize education and make it more meaningful (the benefits of meaningful and personalized learning are discussed in more detail in Chapters 8, 9, and 10). When children perceive disrespect for their cultural background, the result can be disastrous. Consider the following comment by a New York City student:

> I came upon a world unknown to me, a language I did not understand, and a school administration which made ugly faces at me every time I spoke Spanish. Many teachers referred to us as animals. Believe me, maintaining a half-decent image of yourself wasn't an easy thing. . . . I had enough strength of character to withstand the many school personnel who tried to destroy my motivation. But many of my classmates didn't make it. (First, 1988, p. 210)

A third argument in favor of multicultural programs is that students may profit from understanding different cultural values. For example, the respect for elders that characterizes Native American and Oriental cultures is likely to become increasingly desirable as the percentage of elderly Americans increases over the years. Similarly, learning the Native American value of living in harmony with nature may come to be essential as we run out of natural resources and attempt to alleviate environmental pollution (Triandis, 1986).

Multicultural programs foster motivation, better understanding of others

A fourth argument is that because of immigration and demographic trends, America is becoming increasingly culturally diverse. Estimates are that in the ten-year period 1981–1990, almost 9 million legal immigrants will have arrived in the United States. If this projection is accurate, it will virtually match the all-time immigration record of 1901–1910. Recent immigrants have come largely from Latin America and Asia, with most settling in the major cities of California, New York, Texas, and Florida. Immigrant mothers bore 10 percent of all babies born in the United States in 1986. Native-born women in 1986 averaged 67.5 births per

One technique for exploring cultural conflict is to have students search through newspapers and news magazines for articles that describe clashes. Ask them to try to identify the source of the conflict and how it might be positively resolved. Another technique is to involve students in games that simulate group conflict. Class members can, for example, play the role of city council members who represent the interests of diverse ethnic groups and who have been ordered by the federal government to integrate their school system (Appleton, 1983). In the suggestions for further study we will indicate where you can find and learn more about simulations of cultural conflict. The use of simulations as well as the discussion of newspaper articles will probably work best at the high school level, because adolescents are better able than younger students to understand the abstract concepts involved in these activities.

Suggestions for Further Study

Ability Grouping

Additional discussions of the merits and effects of ability grouping can be found in *Handicapping the Handicapped* (1986, pp. 16–23) by Hugh Mehan, Alma Hertweck, and J. Lee Meihls and *Classroom Composition and Pupil Achievement* (1986) by Yehezkel Dar and Nura Resh. An alternative to ability grouping, *mixed ability teaching,* is discussed by Margaret I. Reid, Louise R. Clunies-Ross, Brian Goacher, and Carol Vile in *Mixed Ability Teaching: Problems and Possibilities* (1981) and by John Evans in *Teaching in Transition: The Challenge of Mixed Ability Grouping* (1985). Legal aspects of ability grouping are discussed by Joseph Bryson and Charles Bentley in *Ability Grouping of Public School Students* (1980).

Pros and Cons of Labeling

The pros and cons of classifying children as "exceptional" or "handicapped" are analyzed at length in Volumes 1 and 2 of *Issues in the Classification of Children* (1975), edited by Nicholas Hobbs. A briefer treatment of the major points is found in *The Futures of Children* (1975) also by Hobbs.

Texts on the Education of Exceptional Children

The following books provide general coverage of the education of exceptional children: *Educating Exceptional Children* (6th ed., 1989) by Samuel A. Kirk and James J. Gallagher, *Introduction to Special Education* (2nd ed., 1990) by James E. Ysseldyke and Bob Algozzine, *Educating Special Learners* (3rd ed., 1989) by G. P. Cartwright, C. A. Cartwright, and M. E. Ward.

Books with Emphasis on Teaching Techniques

For information about teaching techniques for use with various types of exceptional pupils, consult one or more of the following: *Structured Experiences for Integration of Handicapped Children* (1983) by Karen Anderson and A. Milliren, *Educating Young Handicapped Children: A Developmental Approach* (2nd ed., 1983) edited by S. Gray Garwood, and *Teaching Students with Learning and Behavior Problems* (2nd ed., 1989) by Deborah Deutsch Smith. The Smith book is divided into three parts. Part One describes general teaching and classroom skills that all teachers of special students should possess. Part Two presents techniques for managing disruptive behavior and teaching appropriate social skills. Part Three describes techniques for improving reading, writing, mathematics, and study skills.

Teaching the Mentally Retarded

Specialized techniques for teaching the mentally retarded can be applied, in many cases, to teaching mildly retarded pupils in regular classrooms. The following books provide suggestions: *Educating Mentally Retarded Persons in the Mainstream* (1980) edited by Jay Gottlieb, *Intelligence, Mental Retardation, and the Culturally Different Child: A Practitioner's Guide* (1984) by John L. Manni and David W. Winikur.

Learning Disabilities

The following books provide information about the diagnosis and remediation of learning disabilities: *Educating the Learning Disabled* (1982) by E. Siegel and R. Gold, *Learning Disabilities* (5th ed., 1989) by Janet Lerner, *Teaching Students with Learning Problems* (2nd ed., 1985) by Cecil D. Mercer and Ann R. Mercer, and *Developmental and Academic Learning Disabilities* (1984) by S. Kirk and J. Chalfant.

Teaching Gifted and Talented Learners

These books describe various techniques to use in instructing gifted and talented learners: *Handbook of Instructional Resources and References for Teaching the Gifted* (1980) by F. Karnes and E. Collins, *Curriculum Development for the Gifted* (1982) by C. Marker, and *Teaching the Gifted Child* (3rd ed., 1988) by James Gallagher.

Inner-City Schools

Between the late 1950s and the early 1970s, several accounts of the experiences of individual teachers in inner-city schools were published. Edward R. Braithwaite described what it was like to teach in a London slum in *To Sir, with Love* (1959). Bel Kaufman's *Up the Down Staircase* (1964), a fictional narration of life in a

New York City high school, is probably the most widely read exposition of life in a big-city school. At about the time that *Up the Down Staircase* was establishing itself on the best-seller lists, three young men were either starting or finishing descriptions of their experiences in ghetto schools. Jonathan Kozol accepted a position as a substitute teacher in a Boston elementary school. He held the position for about six months before he was dismissed, at which time he expanded the notes he had taken into *Death at an Early Age* (1967). Herbert Kohl told what it was like to teach sixth grade in Harlem in *36 Children* (1967), and James Herndon commented on academic life in an Oakland junior high school in *The Way It Spozed to Be* (1968). He described further experiences with teaching in a different junior high in *How to Survive in Your Native Land* (1971). At the same time Herndon was finishing his second book, Stephen Daniels described his experiences in a Philadelphia junior high school in *How 2 Gerbils, 20 Goldfish, 200 Games, 2,000 Books and I Taught Them How to Read* (1971). Any of these books will give you awareness of what it is like to teach disadvantaged students.

Teaching Techniques Used with Disadvantaged Pupils

The books noted in the preceding paragraph might be read not only for a general impression of what it is like to teach the disadvantaged but also to gain ideas for teaching techniques. If you want to read them for this purpose, you might browse until you find a section describing teaching techniques, or you might sample sections beginning at the pages indicated in the following books:

To Sir, with Love, pages 65, 85, 98.

Up the Down Staircase, pages 63, 114, 129, 139, 142, 191, 199.

36 Children, pages 27, 34, 44, 61, 64, 114, 129, 137, 176.

The Way It Spozed to Be, pages 130, 139, 144.

How to Survive in Your Native Land, pages 24, 44, 145, 155.

How 2 Gerbils, pages 39, 48, 57, 66, 71, 73, 91, 94, 98, 112, 124, 132, 150.

Bilingual and Multicultural Education

An excellent source on bilingual and multicultural education is *Bilingual Schooling in the United States* (2nd ed., 1978) by T. Anderson and M. Boyer. Other books you might consult include *Bilingual Educational Publications in Print* (1983), *Multiethnic Education: Theory and Practice* (1983) by M. Saunders, and *Cultural Pluralism in Education* (1983) by Nicholas Appleton. Don't overlook Appendixes A and B of the Appleton book. Appendix A (pp. 248–255) describes eleven interesting classroom exercises to increase multicultural awareness and understanding. Appendix B (pp. 256–273) describes actual court cases and hypothetical dilemmas that involve cultural conflict, games that simulate group conflict, and a bibliography of sixteen simulations that includes relevant ages, time required, number of participants, and addresses of the publishers.

Summary

1. Two early attempts at dealing with pupil variability were ability grouping and special class placement. Ability grouping sorted normal students into separate classes according to mental ability test scores while special class placement was used to separate normal students from those with mental and physical disabilities.
2. The four currently popular approaches to ability grouping are between-class ability grouping, regrouping, the Joplin Plan, and within-class grouping.
3. There is no research support for between-class ability grouping and limited support for regrouping. Moderately positive results have been found for the Joplin Plan and within-class ability grouping.
4. Ability grouping, particularly between-class ability grouping, and the IQ tests used to assign students to groups have been criticized as unfairly discriminating against minority groups.
5. The Education for All Handicapped Children Act (Public Law 94-142) was enacted in 1975 to ensure that students with handicapping conditions received the same free and appropriate education as nonhandicapped students.
6. Major provisions of PL 94-142 include the development of an individualized education program, due process, protection in evaluation procedures, and the least restrictive environment (also known as mainstreaming).
7. Students who are speech impaired, learning disabled, visually handicapped, or hard of hearing are most likely to attend regular classes.
8. The regular classroom teacher's responsibilities under PL 94-142 may include participation in referral, assessment, preparation of the IEP, and implementation of the IEP.
9. Children with mild mental retardation are likely to be mainstreamed for some part of the school day and week. They are likely to have a low tolerance for frustration, lack confidence and self-esteem, oversimplify matters, and have difficulty generalizing from one situation to another.
10. Students with learning disabilities have a disorder in one or more basic psychological processes, which leads to learning problems not attributable to other causes.
11. Recent evidence suggests that many children are mislabeled as learning disabled because of inappropriate assessment procedures and poor-quality tests.
12. The true number of emotionally disturbed schoolchildren is unknown because of variation in identification procedures, vague definitions of emotional disturbance, and differences in interpretation of definitions.
13. Most classifications of disturbed behavior focus on aggressive behavior or withdrawn behavior.
14. Gifted and talented students are highly capable in performing tasks that require intellectual, creative, artistic, or leadership ability.
15. Minorities are underrepresented in gifted and talented classes because standardized test scores are emphasized at the expense of other indices such as creativity, leadership, communication skill, critical thinking ability, and persistence.

16. Disadvantaged pupils often receive irregular health care, experience child-care practices that do not effectively prepare them for school, are not exposed to a wide variety of experiences, are not motivated to do well in school, and have low career aspirations and a low need for achievement.

17. Compared to English-only programs, bilingual education programs help non-English-speaking students achieve moderate gains on tests of reading, language skills, and mathematics.

18. Multicultural education programs assume that minority students will learn more and have a stronger self-concept if teachers understand, accept, and reward the thinking and behavior patterns characteristic of the student's culture.

19. Multicultural education programs foster generally effective teaching practices, have a positive effect on student motivation, and enhance understanding of the values and customs of other cultures.

Key Terms

between-class ability grouping *(190)*
regrouping *(190)*
Joplin Plan *(190)*
within-class ability grouping *(190)*
individualized education program (IEP) *(195)*
due process *(196)*
least restrictive environment *(197)*
mainstreaming *(197)*

interdisciplinary assessment team *(204)*
mental retardation *(207)*
learning disabilities *(214)*
emotional disturbance *(222)*
behavior disorders *(222)*
gifted and talented *(230)*
horizontal enrichment *(235)*
vertical enrichment *(235)*
disadvantaged pupils *(239)*
multicultural education *(251)*

Discussion Questions

1. You yourself probably experienced ability grouping, in one form or another, at the elementary and secondary levels. Try to recall the ability grouping used in your schools. Think about whether it might have been between-class grouping, regrouping, the Joplin Plan, or within-class grouping. Could you tell which group you were in? Did you have feelings about being in that group? How did you feel about classmates who were in other groups? Do you think this practice aided or hindered your educational progress? Why? Given your own experiences as a student and what you have learned from this chapter, would you advocate or employ some form of ability grouping for your own students someday?

2. Many regular classroom teachers say that while they agree with the philosophy behind PL 94-142, they feel that their training has not adequately prepared them for meeting the needs of students with handicapping conditions.

Would you say the same thing of your teacher education program? Why? If you feel that your training is not adequately equipping you to teach mentally retarded, learning disabled, and emotionally disturbed students, what might you do to prepare yourself better?

3. Relatively little money is spent on programs for the gifted and talented compared to the amounts made available for the handicapped. Defenders of this arrangement sometimes argue that since money for educational programs is always short, and since gifted students have a built-in advantage rather than a handicap, we *should* invest most of our resources in programs and services for the handicapped. Do you agree or disagree? Explain why.

4. How have your experiences with members of ethnic or racial minority groups been similar to or different from what you have heard and read about those groups?

2

SPECIFYING WHAT IS TO BE LEARNED

Chapter 6
Devising and Using Objectives

DEVISING AND USING OBJECTIVES

KEY POINTS

Taxonomies of Objectives

Taxonomy: categories arranged in hierarchical order

Cognitive taxonomy: knowledge, comprehension, application, analysis, synthesis, evaluation

Taxonomy of affective objectives stresses attitudes and values

Psychomotor taxonomy outlines steps that lead to skilled performance

National Assessment Objectives

National Assessment provides lists of objectives, results of periodic evaluations of knowledge, attitudes, skills

Ways to State and Use Objectives

Mager: state specific objectives that identify act, define conditions, state criteria

Gronlund: state general objectives, list sample of specific learning outcomes

Mager-style objectives useful in arranging classroom exercises

Gronlund-type objectives lead to comprehensive coverage of a skill or topic

Multiple Values of Objectives

Using objectives can lead to improved planning, instruction, evaluation

Evaluations of the Effectiveness of Objectives

Objectives work best when students are aware of them

General objectives lead to more incidental learning than specific objectives

Does not seem to be essential to arrange objectives in strict hierarchical order

Most test questions stress knowledge, ignore higher levels of cognitive taxonomy

Suggestions for Teaching

Before devising objectives, examine curriculum materials, find out about tests

Check on availability of appropriate lists of objectives

Use taxonomies to make survey of what students should be able to do

Use specific learning outcome descriptions to arrange learning experiences

Occasionally invite student to participate in developing objectives

Periodically refer to taxonomies to improve instruction and evaluation

In Chapter 1, theories of instruction or models of learning were mentioned. The purpose of such theories or models is to provide a basic strategy of instruction that consists of four phases:

1. Take into account what students are like and how much they know.
2. Specify what is to be learned.
3. Provide instruction to help students achieve specified objectives by taking advantage of what has been discovered about learning, cognitive strategies, and motivation.
4. Determine if students have achieved specified objectives.

The preceding part was devoted to descriptions of what students are like and how they differ. It is now time to consider ways to specify what is to be learned.

Reasons for Thinking About Objectives

To grasp why this chapter on objectives appears before chapters on learning, motivation, and evaluation, imagine that it is your first day in your own classroom. If you plan to teach in the elementary grades, you will observe (probably with mixed feelings of excitement, curiosity, and a bit of anxiety) the arrival of the twenty-five or so children who will be spending up to five hours a day in your room for the next nine months. If you expect to teach at the secondary level, you will experience the same feelings as you observe the arrival of the first of five (typically) batches of students whose destiny has been linked to yours by a computer and/or an administrator. They will size you up probably even more keenly than you will sort out your first impressions of them. If you remember some of the things you read in Chapters 2 and 3 of this book, you will be familiar with at least some of the characteristics of the pupils who will seat themselves in front of you. If you recall

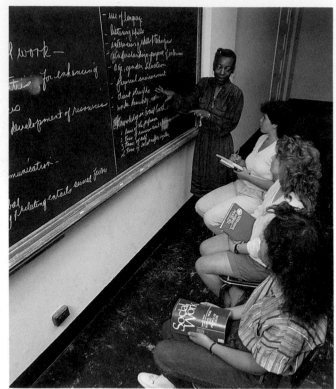

Educators who advocate use of instructional objectives point out that it makes sense to concentrate at the very beginning on what you will want your students to do at the end of a unit of study. (The Stock Market/Randy Duchaine, 1986)

the emphasis of variability stressed in Chapters 4 and 5, you may detect, even on the basis of extremely brief first impressions, noticeable differences between students. You might find yourself thinking, "I'll bet she's going to be a sharp student" or "That boy looks so scared and unhappy about being back in school I wonder if he has learning problems?"

After the bell rings and you conclude that all your charges are present, you will close the door, walk to the front of the room, and introduce yourself. You will either call roll or otherwise check that all students are present or accounted for. You will probably need to make some announcements, then you will explain classroom routine and pass out books and materials. Eventually, though the moment of truth is going to arrive—you are going to have to start teaching. When that climactic moment comes, you had better convey the impression that you know what you are doing and make clear to your students exactly what you want them to do. This chapter on objectives is intended to help you achieve both of those goals not only the first day, but every day in the classroom.

Your reactions at this point may be "Well, sure, of course I'm going to have planned what I'm going to do the first day and at least for the next few days after that." The plans you make for presenting lessons, though, are likely to be much more effective if you take into account the values of stating instructional objectives in specific terms. Furthermore, the specific objectives you devise are more likely to be effective if you start at the *end* of an instructional sequence rather than just taking a stab at formulating a beginning. To grasp that point, suppose that you follow the common practice of many teachers and prepare lesson plans by examining texts and other curriculum materials in order to devise an instructional sequence. Your first inclination is likely to be to concentrate on what is going to happen tomorrow and put off thinking about what is going to happen two weeks or a month ahead when the time comes to evaluate what students have learned. You might reason that there is no point thinking about tests until it is time to prepare tests. Quite a few teachers operate in such one-thing-at-a-time ways, and you are probably familiar with the results—disorganized lessons, lectures, and assignments, followed by exams that may not have much to do with what you think you were supposed to have learned. You can avoid falling into that common trap by concentrating at the very beginning on what you will want your students to be able to do at the end of a unit of study. If you decide in advance what you desire your students to achieve, you can prepare lessons that logically lead to a particular result and also use evaluation techniques efficiently designed to determine if achievement has occurred.

To help you grasp why and how specific objectives can be used to make teaching and testing effective, a history of various approaches to and arguments for goals and objectives will be presented as background for specific suggestions that follow.

Goals Listed by Educational Leaders

Until the 1970s (and it still occurs sometimes) most discussions of what children should learn in school took the form of lists of general goals of education. From time to time, for example, educational leaders have been invited to Washington to participate in what are referred to as White House Conferences on Education. Participants in one of these conferences convened in 1956 proposed this list of qualities they thought it would be desirable for American children to acquire as they passed through our educational system:

1. The fundamental skills of communication—reading, writing, spelling, as well as other elements of effective oral and written expression; the arithmetical and mathematical skills, including problem solving. . . .
2. Appreciation of our democratic heritage.
3. Civic rights and responsibilities and knowledge of American institutions.
4. Respect for and appreciation for human values and for the beliefs of others.
5. Ability to think and evaluate constructively and creatively.
6. Effective work habits and self-discipline.
7. Social competency as a contributing member of . . . family and community.
8. Ethical behavior based on a sense of moral and spiritual values.
9. Intellectual curiosity and eagerness for life-long learning.

10. Esthetic appreciation and self-expression in the arts.
11. Physical and mental health.
12. Wise use of time, including constructive leisure pursuits.
13. Understanding of the physical world and man's relation to it as represented through basic knowledge of the sciences.
14. An awareness of our relationship with the world community. (U.S. Committee for the White House Conference on Education, 1956)

This list clearly mentions skills, attitudes, and interests that are desirable, if not essential, for someone who hopes to live successfully and happily in America. Unfortunately, these statements do not provide very useful guidelines for teachers charged with the responsibility for achieving them. Precisely how, for example, are you supposed to instill an appreciation for our democratic heritage?

Taxonomies of Objectives

Awareness of the vagueness of such goals stimulated a group of psychologists who specialized in testing to seek a better way to describe educational objectives. They reasoned that group tests used to measure school achievement could be made more effective and accurate if they were based on a school curriculum derived from a systematic list of objectives. The fact that psychologists interested in testing took the lead in describing specific objectives is related to the point made a bit earlier that you should start at the end rather than just jumping in at the beginning. It makes more sense to decide in advance what is important enough to be tested rather than simply teaching an assortment of information and skills and then discovering in hit-or-miss fashion how much has been achieved. After experimenting with various ways to prepare lists of objectives that would be more useful to teachers than vaguely worded sets of goals, the test specialists decided to

Taxonomy: categories arranged in hierarchical order

develop taxonomies of educational objectives. A **taxonomy** is a classification scheme with categories arranged in hierarchical order. Because goals of education are extremely diverse (take another look at those listed by the White House Conference participants), the decision was made to prepare taxonomies in three *domains:* cognitive, affective, and psychomotor. The taxonomy for the **cognitive domain** stresses knowledge and intellectual skills; the taxonomy for the **affective domain** concentrates on attitudes and values; and that for the **psychomotor domain** focuses on physical abilities and skills.

Taxonomy for the Cognitive Domain

The taxonomy for the cognitive domain was prepared by Benjamin S. Bloom and several associates (1956). It consists of six hierarchically ordered levels of instructional outcomes: knowledge, comprehension, application, analysis, synthesis, evaluation. The taxonomy is described as a hierarchy because it was reasoned that comprehension relies on prior mastery of knowledge or facts, application depends on comprehension of relevant ideas, and so on through the remaining levels. An abridged outline of the taxonomy for the cognitive domain appears below.

Taxonomy of Educational Objectives: Cognitive Domain

1.00 *Knowledge.* Remembering previously learned information.
  1.10 *Knowledge of specifics.*
    1.11 *Knowledge of terminology.* What terms and symbols will your students need to know? (e.g., verbs, nouns, $+$, $-$, H_2SO_4).
    1.12 *Knowledge of specific facts.* What specific facts will your students need to know? (e.g., names of the states, chief exports of Brazil, the properties of H_2SO_4).
  1.20 *Knowledge of ways and means of dealing with specifics.*
    1.21 *Knowledge of conventions.* What sets of rules will your students need to know? (e.g., rules of etiquette, rules of punctuation).
    1.22 *Knowledge of trends and sequences.* What awareness of trends and sentences will your students need to have? (e.g., nature of evolution, changes in attitudes about the role of women in American society).
    1.23 *Knowledge of classifications and categories.* What classifications and category schemes will your students need to know? (e.g., types of literature, types of business ownership, types of government).
    1.24 *Knowledge of criteria.* What sets of criteria will your students need to be able to apply? (e.g., factors to consider in judging the nutritional value of a meal or the qualities of a work of art).
    1.25 *Knowledge of methodology.* What sorts of methodology will your students need to master? (e.g., ways to solve problems in math, how to set up an experiment in chemistry).
  1.30 *Knowledge of the universals and abstractions in a field.*
    1.31 *Knowledge of principles and generalizations.* What general principles will your students need to know? (e.g., laws of heredity, laws of motion).
    1.32 *Knowledge of theories and structure.* What general theories will your students need to know? (e.g., nature of free enterprise system, theory of evolution).

2.00 *Comprehension.* Grasping the meaning of information.
  2.10 *Translation.* Ability to put communication into another form (e.g., stating problems in own words, reading a musical score, translating words and phrases from a foreign language, interpreting a diagram, grasping the meaning of a political cartoon).
  2.20 *Interpretation.* Ability to reorder ideas and comprehend interrelation-

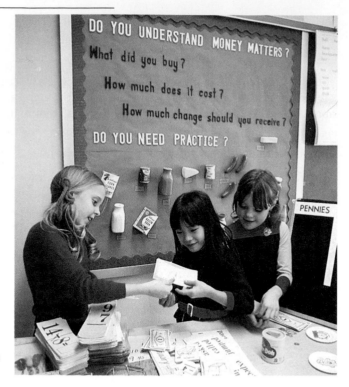

The taxonomy of objectives for the cognitive domain calls attention to the point that *knowledge* and *comprehension* must occur before *application* can take place. (David Strickler/The Picture Cube)

ships (e.g., giving own interpretation of a novel or a poem, gathering data from a variety of sources, and preparing an organized report).

2.30 *Extrapolation.* Ability to go beyond given data (e.g., theorizing about what might happen if . . . , drawing conclusions from given sets of data, predicting trends).

3.00 *Application.* Applying knowledge to actual situations (e.g., taking principles learned in math and applying them to laying out a baseball diamond, applying principles of civil liberties to current events).

4.00 *Analysis.* Breaking down objects or ideas into simpler parts and seeing how the parts relate and are organized (e.g., discussing how democracy and communism differ, detecting logical fallacies in an argument).

5.00 *Synthesis.* Rearranging component ideas into a new whole (e.g., planning a program or panel discussion, writing a comprehensive term paper).

6.00 *Evaluation.* Making judgments based on internal evidence or external criteria (e.g., evaluating a work of art, editing a term paper, detecting inconsistencies in the speech of a politician).

Taxonomy for the Affective Domain

In addition to arranging instructional experiences to help students achieve cognitive objectives, virtually all teachers are also interested in encouraging the development of attitudes and values. To clarify the nature of such objectives, a taxonomy for the affective domain was prepared (Krathwohl, Bloom, and Masia, 1964). Affective objectives are more difficult to define, evaluate, or encourage than cognitive objectives because they often are demonstrated in subtle or indirect ways. Furthermore, certain aspects of value development are sometimes considered to be more the responsibility of parents than of teachers. Finally, because values and attitudes involve a significant element of personal choice, they are often expressed more clearly out of school than in the classroom. The complete taxonomy for the affective domain stresses out-of-school values as much, if not more, than in-school values. The following abridgment concentrates on the kinds of affective objectives you are most likely to be concerned with as a teacher. You will probably recognize, though, that there may not be much you can do to substantially influence the kinds of objectives described in the higher levels of the taxonomy since they represent a crystallization of values formed by experiences over an extended period of time. (*Values clarification,* a technique for encouraging the development of a value system, will be described in Chapter 10.)

Taxonomy of affective objectives stresses attitudes and values

Taxonomy of Educational Objectives: Affective Domain

1.0 *Receiving (attending).* Willingness to receive or attend.

    1.1 *Awareness.* Being aware of distinctive features (e.g., listening attentively, concentrating on distinctive features of a complex stimulus).

    1.2 *Willingness to receive.* Showing a willingness to consider various interpretations and the opinions of others (e.g., listening to discussions of controversial issues with an open mind, respecting the rights of others).

    1.3 *Controlled or selected attention.* Actively attending to experiences or presentations of the ideas of others (e.g., willingly participating in class discussions, reading articles that present both sides of a controversial issue).

2.0 *Responding.* Active participation indicating positive response or acceptance of an idea or policy.

    2.1 *Acquiescence in responding.* Exhibiting acceptance of expectations and responsibilities (e.g., completing homework assignments, obeying school rules).

    2.2 *Willingness to respond.* Voluntarily or willingly choosing to respond (e.g., willingly participating in class discussion, voluntarily completing optional assignments).

    2.3 *Satisfaction in response.* Experiencing a sense of satisfaction or enjoyment by responding in a particular way (e.g., showing enjoyment when working on a self-selected project, enthusiastically participating in group activities).

3.0 *Valuing.* Expressing a belief or attitude about the value or worth of something.

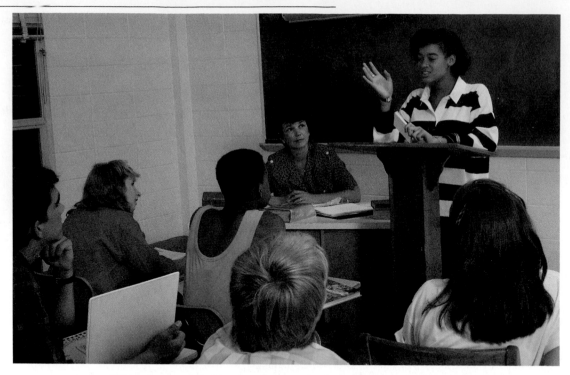

The taxonomy of objectives for the affective domain emphasizes that *receiving* (attending) and *responding* typically precede *valuing*—where a person expresses support for a particular point of view. (Billy E. Barnes/Southern Light)

3.1 *Acceptance of value.* Endorsing a basic proposition or assumption (e.g., endorsing the concept of democratic forms of government, accepting the idea that good health habits are important).

3.2 *Preference for a value.* Expressing willingness to be identified with a value (e.g., expressing support for a particular point of view, defending an opinion questioned by another student).

3.3 *Commitment.* Expressing a strongly held value or conviction (e.g., participating in a campaign to clean up the playground, volunteering to serve on a school committee formed to raise funds for starving children).

4.0 *Organization.* Organizing various values into an internalized system.

4.1 *Conceptualization of a value.* Understanding how a value relates to values already held (e.g., recognizing the need to seek a balance between economic growth and conservation of natural resources).

4.2 *Organization of a value system.* Bringing several, possibly disparate, values together into a consistent system (e.g., recognizing own abilities, limitations, and values and developing realistic aspirations).

5.0 *Characterization by a value or value complex.* The value system becomes a way of life.

5.1 *Generalized set.* Exhibiting a predisposition to act in certain ways (e.g., a person's lifestyle influences reactions to many different kinds of situations).

Taxonomy for the Psychomotor Domain

While cognitive and affective objectives are important at all grade levels, so are psychomotor objectives. Regardless of the grade level or subject you teach, at some point you are likely to want to help your students acquire physical skills of various kinds. In the primary grades, for example, you will want your pupils to learn how to print legibly. In many subjects in junior and senior high school, psychomotor skills (for example, driving a car, playing a violin, adjusting a microscope, manipulating an electric typewriter, operating a power saw, throwing a pot, swinging a golf club) may be essential. Recognition of the importance of physical skills prompted Elizabeth Simpson (1972) to prepare a taxonomy for the psychomotor domain. An abridged version of the taxonomy follows.

Psychomotor taxonomy outlines steps that lead to skilled performance

Taxonomy of Educational Objectives: Psychomotor Domain

1.0 *Perception.* Using sense organs to obtain cues needed to guide motor activity.
    1.1 *Sensory stimulation.* Interpreting a sensory stimulus (e.g., listening to the sounds made by violin strings before tuning them).
    1.2 *Cue selection.* Identifying relevant cues and associating them with appropriate behavior (e.g., recognizing sounds that indicate malfunctioning of equipment).
    1.3 *Translation.* Relating sensory cues to performing a motor act (e.g., relating musical tempo and rhythm to dance forms).

2.0 *Set.* Being ready to perform a particular action.
    2.1 *Mental set.* Being mentally ready to perform (e.g., knowing the steps to follow in order to replace a carburetor).
    2.2 *Physical set.* Being physically ready to perform in terms of body position, posture, focusing of visual and auditory attention (e.g., having instrument ready to play and watching conductor at start of a musical performance).
    2.3 *Emotional set.* Being willing and eager to perform (e.g., exhibiting eagerness to use a sewing machine to make a garment).

3.0 *Guided response.* Performing under guidance of a model.
    3.1 *Imitation.* Copying the performance of someone else (e.g., swinging a tennis racket just after observing an expert demonstrate a stroke).
    3.2 *Trial and error.* Trying various responses until the correct one is selected (e.g., experimenting with various ways to use a saw with a particular type of material).

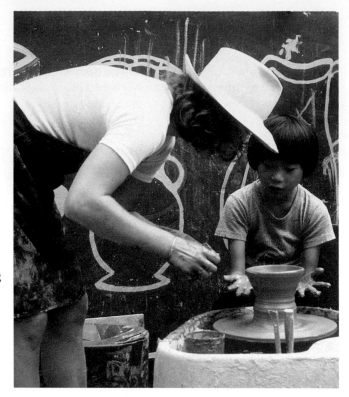

A basic instructional technique for helping students master psychomotor objectives is to demonstrate a skill and then give guidance as students try out the skill. (Ira Kirschenbaum/ Stock, Boston)

4.0 *Mechanism.* Being able to perform a task habitually with some degree of confidence and proficiency (e.g., demonstrating the ability to get first serve in service area 70 percent of the time).

5.0 *Complex or overt response.* Performing a task with a high degree of proficiency and skill (e.g., typing all kinds of business letters and forms quickly with no errors).

6.0 *Adaptation.* Using previously learned skills to perform new but related tasks (e.g., using skills developed learning how to operate an electric typewriter to operate a word processor).

7.0 *Origination.* Creating new performances after having developed skills (e.g., creating a new form of modern dance).

The hierarchically arranged lists of objectives you have just examined clearly provide more tangible descriptions of objectives than the goals listed by the participants in the White House Conference. Although they were devised to aid educators charged with developing comprehensive curricula, they can be used by classroom teachers in a variety of ways that will be described later in this chapter. Before turning to applications and uses of objectives, however, yet another approach to stating educational goals will be described. As part of a comprehensive program to assess the performance of public school students in this country, sets of objectives have been devised for basic subjects taught in American schools.

National Assessment Objectives

In the 1960s the amount of public money spent on education exceeded $30 billion per year. By 1986–1987 the amount had increased to over $160 billion (Ornstein & Levine, 1989, p. 275). When legislators, taxpayers, and educators realized how quickly educational expenditures were increasing, they quite naturally began to wonder whether the investment was paying dividends. Many individuals were convinced that education was not all that it might be, but these opinions were based on impressions. There was no trustworthy way to determine what students were actually learning—or not learning—in American schools. For this reason, the Education Commission of the States was formed in 1964 for the purpose of initiating what came to be called the **National Assessment of Educational Progress.**

The purpose of National Assessment is to provide information about the knowledge, understanding, skills, and attitudes that American children acquire in the public schools. To accomplish this, it was decided to test periodically thousands of individuals at four age levels—nine, thirteen, seventeen, and twenty-six through thirty-five—in ten learning areas: art, career and occupational development, citizenship, literature, mathematics, music, reading, science, social studies, and writing.

Groups of teachers, scholars, educators, and laymen drew up lists of educational goals and objectives for each of the ten areas. Then specialists in each subject area prepared examinations to measure how well these objectives were being achieved. Finally, a rotating schedule for administering the tests was developed, and the examinations were administered to representative samples of individuals.

The results are reported in terms of geographic region, size of community, type of community, age, sex, race, and socioeducational background. (No data on specific students, school districts, cities, or states are provided.) The information gives data on general trends (for example, big cities and small towns are low in science and writing) and specific questions (only 20 percent of the seventeen-year-olds tested knew that in human females the egg is released an average of fourteen days after menstruation begins). Figure 6.1 shows a page from a National Assessment test of ability to recognize literary works and characters.

Major objectives for several of the current measurement areas are listed here. Subobjectives for one section of each list are also supplied. These lists indicate the kinds of objectives experienced educators feel should be stressed by teachers of

Figure 6.1
Page from the
National Assessment
of Educational
Progress
"Recognizing
Literary Works and
Characters"

From the National
Assessment of Educational
Progress, a project carried out
under a grant from the
National Institute of
Education and administered
by the Education Commission
of the United States.

Exercise R308

Ages 13, 17, Adult
Objective IA

Many people or animals that we read about in books become so well-
known that we can name them just from a picture. Above is a picture
of a man who appears in a story.

What is the name of the <u>man</u> in the picture?

Write your answer on the line provided.

Sherlock Holmes
_____

	Age 13	Age 17	Adult
Acceptable responses	57.2%	78.5%	75.6%
Unacceptable responses	7.2	4.7	3.2
I don't know.	34.8	15.7	19.9
No response	.8	1.1	1.4

**National Assessment
provides lists of ob-
jectives, periodic
evaluations of knowl-
edge, attitudes, skills**

various subjects and also the kind of information supplied in National Assessment reports. If you would like more complete information about any of the lists,
including all the subobjectives for different grade levels, you can obtain booklets
from National Assessment at the address supplied at the end of this chapter. The
objectives lists are occasionally revised. Subsequent lists of objectives may thus
differ from those summarized here. You are urged to examine all the lists, even

though they do not relate to subjects you expect to teach because they illustrate different ways to describe objectives.

Citizenship and Social Studies Objectives

   I. Demonstrates skills necessary to acquire information.
  II. Demonstrates skills necessary to use information.
 III. Demonstrates an understanding of individual development and the skills necessary to communicate with others.
 IV. Demonstrates an understanding of and interest in the ways human beings organize, adapt to, and change their environments.
  V. Demonstrates an understanding of and interest in the development of the United States.
    A. Understands the principles and purposes of the United States.
    B. Understands the organization and operation of the governments in the United States.
    C. Understands political decision making in the United States.
    D. Understands the electoral process in the United States.
    E. Understands the basis and organization of the legal system in the United States.
    F. Knows rights of individuals in the United States.
    G. Recognizes civil and criminal judicial systems in the United States.
    H. Has a commitment to support justice and rights of all individuals.
    I. Understands economics in the United States.
    J. Understands major social changes that have occurred in American society.
    K. Has a commitment to participating in community service and civic improvement.

Mathematics Objectives

  I. Mathematical knowledge.
 II. Mathematical skill.
   A. How well can students perform computations, including computations with whole numbers, integers, fractions, decimals, percents, ratios, and proportions?
   B. How well can students make measurements?
   C. How well can students read graphs and tables?
   D. How well can students perform geometric manipulations like constructions and spatial visualizations?
   E. How well can students perform algebraic manipulations?
   F. How well can students estimate the answers to computations and measurements?

III. Mathematical understanding.

IV. Mathematical application.

Music Objectives

I. Perform a piece of music.

II. Read standard musical notation.

III. Listen to music with understanding.

IV. Be knowledgeable about some musical instruments, some of the terminology of music, methods of performance and forms, some of the standard literature of music, and some aspects of the history of music.

    A. Know the meanings of common musical terms used in connection with the performance of music, and identify musical instruments and performing ensembles in illustrations.

    B. Know standard pieces of music by title, or composer, or brief descriptions of the music, or of literary-pictorial materials associated with the music from its inception.

    C. Know prominent composers and performers by name and chief accomplishment.

    D. Know something of the history of music.

V. Know about the musical resources of the community and seek musical experiences by performing music.

VI. Make judgments about music, and acknowledge the value and the personal worth of music.

Reading and Literature Objectives

I. Values reading and literature.

II. Comprehends written works.

III. Responds to written works in interpretive and evaluative ways.

    A. Extends understanding of written works through interpretation.

        1. Demonstrates an awareness of the emotional impact of written works.

        2. Applies personal experiences to written works.

        3. Applies knowledge of other works or fields of study.

        4. Analyzes written works.

IV. Applies study skills in reading.

Science Objectives

I. Know the fundamental aspects of science.

II. Understand and apply the fundamental aspects of science in a wide range of problem situations.

III. Appreciate the knowledge and processes of science, the consequences and limitations of science, and the personal and social relevance of science and technology in our society.

A. Appreciate facts and simple concepts, laws (principles), and conceptual schemes. Appreciate science as a dynamic body of knowledge.
B. Appreciate inquiry skills as fundamental tools for solving problems.
C. Appreciate the scientific enterprise. Have one's value system affected by his/her understanding of the scientific enterprise. Appreciate the need for, and value of, the activities and products of science.

The White House Conference goals, the taxonomies of objectives, and the National Assessment sets of objectives illustrate quite different ways to analyze what pupils should learn in schools. All three approaches, however, call attention to these points:

1. The need to consider cognitive, affective, and psychomotor factors.
2. The need to take into account acquisition of immediate knowledge, traits, and skills, as well as the long-term impact of learning.

The White House Conference participants agreed, for example, that students should master the "fundamental skills of communication" but that they should also develop "eagerness for life-long learning." The three taxonomies stress that lower-level knowledge, habits, and skills should be acquired as background for more comprehensive and higher-level attributes such as analysis, synthesis, and evaluation; acquiring a set of values; creating something original. National Assessment sets of objectives typically include acquisition of specific information and skills, as well as applications to out-of-school situations.

Ways to State and Use Objectives

Many psychologists have offered suggestions for use of objectives, but the following discussion is limited to recommendations made by two of the most influential writers on the subject: Robert F. Mager and Norman E. Gronlund.

Mager's Recommendations for Use of Specific Objectives

With the publication of a provocative and unorthodox little treatise titled *Preparing Instructional Objectives* (1962), Mager sparked considerable interest in the use of objectives. The book opens with this statement:

Once an instructor decides he will teach his students something, several kinds of activity are necessary on his part if he is to succeed. He must first decide upon the goals he intends to reach at the end of his course or program. He must then select procedures, content, and methods that are relevant to the objectives; cause the student to interact with appropriate subject matter in accordance with principles of learning;

and, finally, measure or evaluate the student's performance according to the objectives or goals originally selected. (p. 1)

As you undoubtedly recognized, this is a description of the model of instruction that is being used as the organizational frame of reference for this book, and Mager was one of several psychologists who were given credit in Chapter 1 for suggesting the model.

Having described his model of instruction, Mager then emphasizes the importance of objectives, pointing out that "You cannot concern yourself with the problem of selecting the most efficient route to your destination (of having students exhibit knowledge or perform a skill) until you know what your destination is" (p. 1). Having described how important it is to state objectives at the beginning of a unit of study, Mager then offers these suggestions for writing **specific objectives** of instruction:

Mager: state specific objectives that identify act, define conditions, state criteria

1. Describe what you want learners to be doing when demonstrating achievement and indicate how you will know they are doing it.
2. In your description, identify and name the behavioral act that indicates achievement, define the conditions under which the behavior is to occur, state the criterion of acceptable performance.
3. Write a separate objective for each learning performance.

Here are some examples of the types of objectives Mager recommends:

Correctly solve at least seven addition problems consisting of 3 two-digit numbers within a period of three minutes.

Correctly answer at least four of the five questions on the last page of story booklet 16 in the Reading Comprehension series of booklets.

Given pictures of ten trees, correctly identify at least eight as either deciduous or evergreen.

Correctly spell at least 90 percent of the words on the list handed out last week.

Given an electric typewriter, set it up to type a business letter (according to the specifications provided on page 352 of the text) within two minutes.

(Note that the criterion of acceptable performance can be stated as a time limit, a minimum number of correct responses, or a proportion of correct responses.)

Mager's proposals were widely endorsed immediately after the publication of *Preparing Instructional Objectives,* but in time it became apparent that the very specific kinds of objectives he recommended were most useful in situations where students were asked to acquire knowledge of factual information or learn simple skills. Norman E. Gronlund concluded that a different type of objective was more appropriate for more complex and advanced kinds of learning.

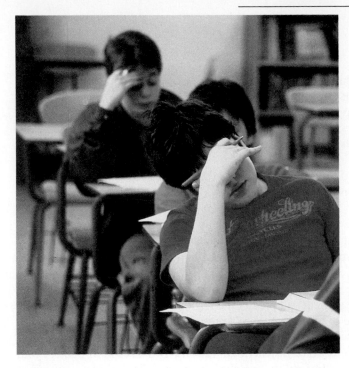

Students who have not been provided with clearly stated instructional objectives may lack motivation to learn. (Bob Daemmerich Photos)

Gronlund's Recommendations for Use of General Objectives

Gronlund (1985, 1988) has developed a two-step procedure for writing a more general type of objective. He suggests that teachers follow this procedure:

1. Examine what is to be learned with reference to lists of objectives such as those included in the three taxonomies and in National Assessment booklets. Use such lists to formulate **general objectives** of instruction that describe types of behavior students should exhibit in order to demonstrate that they have learned.
2. Under each general instructional objective, list up to five *specific learning outcomes* that begin with an *action verb* and indicate specific, observable responses. These sets of specific learning outcomes should provide a representative sample of what pupils should be able to do when they have achieved the general objective.

If you were teaching an educational psychology course and you wanted to write a Gronlund-type objective that specified understanding the four stages of Piaget's theory of cognitive development, it might look like this:

1. The student will understand the characteristics of Piaget's four stages of cognitive development.

Gronlund: state general objective, list sample of specific learning outcomes

1.1 Describes in his or her own words the type of thinking in which pupils at each stage can and cannot engage.
1.2 Predicts behaviors of pupils of different ages.
1.3 Explains why certain teaching techniques would or would not be successful with pupils of different ages.

On the other hand, if you wanted to cover the same outcome with Mager-type objectives, it might look like this:

1. Given a list of the names of each of Piaget's four stages of cognitive development, the student will, within twenty minutes, describe in his or her own words two problems that pupils at each stage should and should not be able to solve.
2. Given a videotape of kindergarten pupils presented with a conservation of volume problem, the student will predict the response of 90 percent of the pupils.
3. Given a videotape of fifth-grade pupils presented with a class inclusion problem, the student will predict the response of 90 percent of the pupils.
4. Given eight descriptions of instructional lessons, two at each of Piaget's four stages, the student will be able to explain in each case why the lesson would or would not succeed.

Gronlund recommends that you begin with general objectives for several reasons. One reason is that most learning activities are too complex to be described in terms of a specific objective for every learning outcome, as proposed by Mager. A second reason is that the types of objectives recommended by Mager may tend to cause both instructors and pupils to concentrate on memorizing facts and mastery of simple skills. As indicated in the taxonomies presented earlier, these types of behaviors are at the lowest levels of the taxonomies of objectives. A third reason is that specific objectives result in long cumbersome lists that restrict the flexibility of the teacher. Gronlund argues, for example, that the performance criteria should be kept separate from the objective in order to vary the standards as needed without having to rewrite the objective. This feature is useful if the same behavior is to be evaluated several times over the course of a unit of instruction, with successively higher levels of performance required. A fourth and final reason is that general objectives help keep you aware that the general outcome (such as comprehension, application, or analysis) is the main target of your instructional efforts and not the more specific objectives. The latter provide just a *sample* of the types of behaviors that signify the general outcome. A different sample could just as easily be used.

To illustrate differences between general objectives and specific outcomes, Gronlund has prepared lists of phrases and verbs that can be used in writing each type of objective for each of the levels of all three taxonomies of educational objectives. These lists can be found in Chapter 5 of Gronlund's *Stating Behavioral Objectives for Classroom Instruction* (3rd ed., 1985) and Appendix E of his *Measurement and Evaluation in Teaching* (5th ed., 1985). Gronlund provides a different outline of the taxonomies than that presented in this chapter. Accordingly, his basic approach to listing objectives has been adapted to fit the description of the taxonomies presented a few pages earlier. The lists in Tables 6.1, 6.2, and 6.3, therefore, are similar in general outline to those devised by Gronlund, and contain many of the same action verbs, but represent an approach to outlining objectives and outcomes with reference to the taxonomies that differ from his tables.

Table 6.1 Taxonomy for the Cognitive Domain: Objectives and Outcomes

Level of Taxonomy	General Objectives	Specific Outcome Action Verbs
Knowledge	Knows terms Knows specific facts Knows rules Knows trends and sequences Knows classifications and categories Knows criteria Knows methods and procedures Knows principles and generalizations Knows theories and structure	Defines, names, states, identifies, describes, differentiates, distinguishes
Comprehension	Translates communications Interprets relationships Extrapolates from given data	Interprets, converts, explains, predicts, generalizes, infers
Application	Applies principles	Uses, solves, constructs, prepares, demonstrates
Analysis	Analyzes organization and relationships	Discriminates, outlines, diagrams, differentiates, infers, explains
Synthesis	Produces new arrangement	Designs, organizes, rearranges, compiles, modifies, creates
Evaluation	Judges on basis of external criteria Judges on basis of evidence	Appraises, compares, contrasts, discriminates, criticizes, detects

Handbook Heading:
Using the Taxonomy of
Cognitive Objectives

Handbook Heading:
Using the Taxonomy of
Affective Objectives

	Table 6.2 Taxonomy for the Affective Domain: Objectives and Outcomes	
Level of Taxonomy	**General Objectives**	**Specific Outcome Action Verbs**
Receiving (Attending)	Shows awareness of distinctive features Shows willingness to receive Indicates attention	Describes, identifies, selects, demonstrates
Responding	Accepts need for regulations and responsibilities Chooses to respond in acceptable ways Shows satisfaction in responding	Demonstrates, tells, performs
Valuing	Endorses propositions Shows preference for values Expresses commitment to values	Explains, justifies, demonstrates, defends
Organization	Understands relationships between values Develops a value system	Explains, defends, justifies
Value Complex	Acts in ways consistent with values	Displays, practices, demonstrates

Using General Objectives and Specific Outcomes

To illustrate how you might take advantage of the information just summarized, a few examples of use of objectives and specific outcomes at different grade levels and with different subjects will be provided.

Third-Grade Mathematics   To begin, you might examine the National Assessment objectives for mathematics, noting that four basic objectives are listed: knowledge, skill, understanding, and application. Next, you might refer to the taxonomy for the cognitive domain and peruse the various descriptions under the headings of knowledge, comprehension, and application. (Since third-graders are concrete operational thinkers, you reason that analysis, synthesis, and evaluation objectives are too advanced to be appropriate.) Using the knowledge heading of

Table 6.3   Taxonomy for the Psychomotor Domain: Objectives and Outcomes

Level of Taxonomy	General Objectives	Specific Outcome Action Verbs
Perception (Attending)	Recognizes significant cues Relates cues to actions	Chooses, detects, identifies, differentiates, demonstrates
Set	Displays mental readiness to perform Displays physical readiness to perform Displays emotional readiness to perform	Begins, proceeds, starts, volunteers, shows, demonstrates
Guided Response	Imitates a response Experiments with responses	Shows, demonstrates, manipulates
Mechanism	Performs task habitually	Shows, demonstrates, manipulates
Complex Response	Performs with confidence and proficiency	Shows, demonstrates, manipulates
Adaptation	Adapts skills to fit situation	Alters, varies, revises
Organization	Creates new performance	Originates, composes, constructs, devises

Handbook Heading:
Using the Taxonomy of
Psychomotor Objectives

the taxonomy as a guide, you might ask yourself what terms, symbols, and rules your students need to know and what methods they need to know how to use. Next, you refer to Mager's suggestions for preparing objectives to see if his approach would be appropriate. You conclude that his recommendations might be very useful in arranging short classroom exercises. You devise a page of addition and subtraction problems and plan to hand them out the next day with the announcement that anyone who gets more than eight out of ten correct will earn a passing grade. You also announce that similar exercises will be handed out every day and that those who get a passing grade on four in a row will not have to complete the exercise scheduled for Friday.

Mager-style objectives useful in arranging classroom exercises

Next, you refer to the lists of objectives and outcomes derived from Gronlund's description, paying particular attention to the knowledge category of the taxonomy for the cognitive domain. You decide that "Knows methods and procedures" is especially important, so you write it down, followed by these specific outcomes (which you devise after referring to the complete list of specific outcome action verbs):

Gronlund-type objectives lead to comprehensive coverage of a skill or topic

1. Identifies plus and minus signs in problems.
2. Describes how to add and subtract numbers.
3. Demonstrates ability to add and subtract numbers.
4. Shows ability to take sets of numbers supplied and arrange them to be added or subtracted by self or others.
5. Explains how to use knowledge of addition and subtraction to handle situations outside of school (for example, deciding if enough money has been saved to buy three different objects of known value).

Sixth-Grade Music   Even though you don't know a great deal about musical performance and had only a brief unit on music in an education course, you suddenly discover that you are supposed to present a unit on musical knowledge to your sixth-grade class. You examine the National Assessment music objectives and are delighted to discover that the preliminary work has already been done for you by experts. You decide that a logical first objective is "Knows musical instruments," and you refer to the list of objectives and specific outcomes relating to knowledge in the taxonomy for the cognitive domain to devise these specific outcomes:

1. Names the instruments of an orchestra when pictures of each are displayed.
2. Identifies the instruments of an orchestra when each is played on a recording.
3. States differences between the instruments of an orchestra and of a band.
4. Differentiates between recordings played by an orchestra and a band.

Eighth-Grade Literature   You begin by examining the National Assessment objectives for reading and literature, noting the basic objectives: values, comprehends, responds, and applies. Next you examine the taxonomy for the cognitive domain as well as that for the affective domain, since both types of objectives are included in the National Assessment list. You conclude that the comprehension, application, analysis, synthesis, and evaluation levels from the cognitive domain all may be appropriate, at least to some extent. The receiving, responding, and valuing levels of the affective domain also seem worth examining. A brief look at Mager's recommendations leads you to conclude that his approach is not appropriate for your classes, so you concentrate on the lists of general objectives and specific outcomes for the levels of the taxonomies you have selected. Since *values* was the first objective listed by the National Assessment committee, you peruse the outline for the affective domain and record the general objective "Values well-written short stories." Under that statement you list these specific outcomes:

1. Selects a well-written short story from a book containing stories of varying quality.
2. Identifies well-written and poorly written short stories.
3. Explains why a short story identified as good is superior to one identified as poorly written.

If you are asked to present a unit on music to an elementary school class, you might start by referring to the list of objectives prepared by the National Assessment committee on music. (Royce L. Bair/Monkmeyer)

4. Tells classmates why a particular short story is good.
5. Justifies preference for a favorite short story.

High School Social Studies   You begin by examining the National Assessment objectives for your subject and are impressed by those listed under "Use analytic-scientific procedures effectively," particularly the sub-objective regarding detection of errors and unwarranted generalizations. You turn to the outline of the taxonomy for the cognitive domain and concentrate on the analysis, synthesis, and evaluation levels. Using the lists of objectives and outcomes as a guide, you select the general objective "Judges on basis of evidence," and list these specific outcomes:

1. Identifies limitations of evidence given in an article to justify statement.
2. Distinguishes between evidence and opinions.
3. Relates evidence to conclusions.
4. Detects conclusions based on insufficient or irrelevant evidence.
5. Explains why it is not always possible to determine the direction of cause and effect relationships.

6. Criticizes statements made by public figures that cannot be backed up by evidence.

High School Physical Education   Since you are about to introduce archery as an activity for the first time, you turn directly to the taxonomy for the psychomotor domain. You realize that most of your students have never had a bow in their hands, so you decide to concentrate on the first two levels (perception and set) the first day. You jot down the general objective "Relates cues to actions" and list these specific outcomes:

1. Detects balance point of bow.
2. Differentiates between feel of moderate and extreme string pressure.
3. Identifies correct placement of arrow in bow and above hand.
4. Chooses proper stance to achieve good balance.

Multiple Values of Objectives

The brief examples just provided give only a sketchy idea of the usefulness of objectives since they illustrate only selected aspects of a few limited teaching units. Even so, they are sufficient to reveal the potential of objectives. If you follow the procedures just illustrated in systematic and comprehensive ways as you prepare lessons, you will not only develop firsthand appreciation of the values of objectives, but you and your students will also be likely to benefit in a variety of ways. To get maximum value from objectives, it would be to your advantage to follow this procedure.

First examine the texts and curriculum materials you will be asked to use. Then, look over curriculum outlines and lesson plan instructions that may have been supplied by your supervisors. Next, note your own general ideas about what should be included in lessons and assignments. At that point, peruse appropriate National Assessment lists for your grade and subject to get some initial leads about how to state objectives. (If one or more of the brief lists presented earlier in this chapter are relevant, you might write to National Assessment headquarters and order the complete objectives booklets.) In addition, look through teachers' journals for your grade level or subject area. Quite often individuals or groups present lists of objectives they have devised through a process of trial and error. If you are unable to find lists in journals, but still desire at least some direction, write to one or more of the organizations that specialize in providing objectives for teachers. (Names and addresses are supplied in the Suggestions for Further Study.)

After you have found helpful lists of objectives and/or developed your own, systematically go through all three taxonomies of objectives and begin to develop a master set of instructional goals. Make it a point to include objectives from all three taxonomies (if appropriate) and to include at least some objectives from higher levels (depending on the stage of cognitive development of your pupils). Then refer to the suggestions offered by Mager and Gronlund and begin to experiment with various ways to actually write objectives.

Regardless of how much assistance you get from other sources, you and your students will benefit if you make an effort to devise lists of objectives that are custom-designed for use in your classroom. That statement is based on the following assumptions:

1. You are more likely to arrange learning experiences in a logical and comprehensive order if you devise sets of objectives than if you operate on a one-thing-at-a-time basis.

2. You will provide yourself with leads for developing specific classroom activities and perhaps get clues you can use in remedial instruction. The description of objectives for third-grade math, for instance, illustrates how taking the trouble to list specific outcomes not only provides ideas for class exercises, but also might give you information about sources of learning problems. Asking students to explain *how* they add and subtract, for example, might reveal reasons why some pupils are unable to solve problems consistently. The description of objectives for eighth-grade literature illustrates how an apparently elusive goal such as encouraging appreciation of good literature might be made quite tangible and attainable.

> Using objectives can lead to improved planning, instruction, evaluation

3. You will give yourself guidelines for doing an effective job of evaluation. For instance, if you ask students to *supply* answers (for example, name, define), you know in advance that you should use short answer questions or the equivalent. If you ask them to *identify* or *differentiate,* you know you can logically use multiple-choice questions. If you ask them to *perform* in some way (for example, demonstrate), you know that you should develop ways to evaluate performance. Quite often you will discover that *what* you should evaluate also has been specified by your objectives. Take the music unit for the sixth-grade class. To evaluate achievement in that unit, all you would need to do would be to follow the objectives in order. That is, first ask students to write down the various instruments of an orchestra as you hold up pictures. Then ask them to identify the instruments when you play a recording. Next, ask them to explain the difference between instruments used in an orchestra and a band. Finally, play band and orchestra recordings and ask them to differentiate between the two.

In addition to reasoning about potential values of objectives, however, you should also take into account research on their effectiveness. A brief analysis of such research will not be provided.

Evaluations of the Effectiveness of Objectives

The publication of the various taxonomies and of books by Mager, Gronlund, and others led to widespread use of objectives in American schools and colleges. To determine if objectives were as useful as enthusiasts claimed or implied they were, many psychologists compared the achievement of students who had and had not been provided with specific instructional goals. The results of such research proved to be inconclusive. In one review of over fifty studies, for example, the authors (Duchastel & Merrill, 1973) noted: "A number of studies have shown facilitative effects. However, an equal number of studies have failed to demonstrate any significant difference" (p. 54). The authors concluded that since "objectives sometimes help and are almost never harmful . . . one might as well make them available to students" (p. 63). It is probably safe to assume that the supporters of objectives were less than pleased with this conclusion.

The reason why early studies on the effectiveness of objectives produced such inconsistent results was that the researchers were not asking quite the right question. For example, four variables that work in combination with objectives are individual differences (in ability or motivation, for instance), variations in the subject matter under study, variations in the type of objective provided, and variations in the outcome that is measured (which might be recall, recognition, comprehension, or problem solving). When researchers simply ask whether students who receive objectives will learn more than students who do not, they are assuming such variables to be of little or no importance. It would be nice if the world were that simple. It is not—particularly when classroom learning is the phenomenon under study. More consistent and useful results ensued when researchers began asking more pointed questions, such as, For what type of learner will objectives work best? What types of things are learned with different types of objectives? For what types of subjects will objectives produce the best results? Later reviews (for example, Faw & Waller, 1976; Klauer, 1984; Melton, 1978) were able to draw the following conclusions:

Objectives work best when students are aware of them

1. Objectives seem to work best when students are aware of them, treat them as directions to learn specific sections of material, and feel they will aid learning.
2. Objectives seem to work best when they are clearly written and the learning task is neither too difficult nor too easy.
3. Students of average ability seem to profit more from being given objectives than do students of higher or lower ability.
4. Objectives lead to improvement in intentional learning (what is stressed as important) but to a decline in incidental (not emphasized by the teacher) learning. General objectives of the type recommended by Gronlund seem to lead to more incidental learning than specific objectives of the type recommended by Mager.

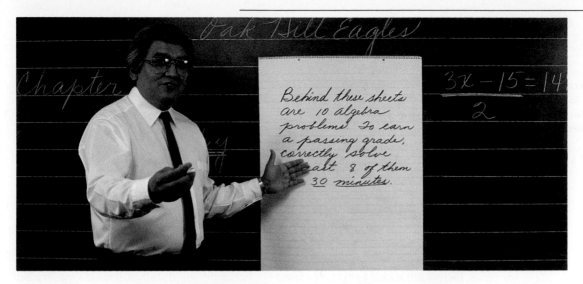

Mager recommends that teachers use objectives that identify the behavioral act that indicates achievement, define the conditions under which the behavior is to occur, and state the criterion of acceptable performance. (Bob Daemmerich Photos)

This last point might be clarified by referring to the Key Points in this book. The Key Points function as a type of instructional objective in that they call your attention to sections of the text that are considered to be particularly important and are likely to be stressed on examinations. If you were to be given an announced exam on the Key Points for this chapter and another unannounced exam immediately after on the other parts of this chapter, you would almost certainly earn a higher score on the Key Points test. Use of Key Points as objectives directs your attention to important parts of the text but also tends to cause you to pay less attention to other potentially significant sections of chapters. An antidote to this tendency was mentioned in Chapter 1: pay particular attention to the Key Points but don't skip over other parts of a chapter because you might miss information that could clarify understanding of Key Points and/or be useful to you later. Despite that suggestion, you are still virtually certain to engage in more intentional than incidental learning. If the Key Points (or some other form of objectives) were omitted, however, you might be even worse off. Realizing that you will be unable to learn everything in every chapter of this book, you might waste valuable study time procrastinating about which parts of the text you should concentrate on when preparing for exams. Furthermore, you might feel as if you had been "tricked" into doing too much incidental learning that didn't lead to a payoff. (Perhaps you have found yourself preoccupied with this bitter thought as you left an examination room: "Rats. I wasted all that time learning a lot of junk I never used answering questions.") Incidental learning is an advantage when discussing education in abstract terms. It may be an unrealistic expectation when dealing with real learning situations involving exams. It does appear (Klauer, 1984), however, that using objectives of the type recommended by Gronlund

General objectives
lead to more inciden-
tal learning than
specific objectives

leads to more incidental learning than using specific objectives such as those recommended by Mager. Thus, you may be able to encourage at least some incidental learning by first stating general objectives and then a sample of specific
outcomes.

A final observation on evaluations of the effectiveness of objectives relates to
the kinds of outcomes that are typically stressed by researchers. Most of the research investigations upon which the conclusions summarized earlier were based
concentrated on pupil achievement as the measure of the impact of objectives.
Researchers often fail to take into account less easily measured factors such as
positive pupil response to explicit directions, the teacher's feelings of confidence
and satisfaction when presenting well-organized lessons, or the ease and efficiency with which evaluations can be made. When these not-so-easy-to-prove
factors are added to evidence from the better designed studies, it seems reasonable
to say that there are definite advantages to using objectives.

A final aspect of objectives that has been studied by a number of psychologists
centers on arranging what is to be learned in strict hierarchical order. The various
taxonomies were based on the assumption that learning experiences ideally
should be systematically arranged so that lower-level skills are acquired as background for advanced skills. Evaluations of efforts to use the taxonomies to develop highly systematic hierarchies of learning experiences lead to the conclusion
(Furst, 1981) that it is rarely possible to use them exactly as published to plan a

Does not seem to be
essential to arrange
objectives in strict
hierarchical order

completely consistent overall curriculum. It appears, therefore, that while there
are some benefits to be gained by analyzing sequences of things to be learned, you
should not attempt to devise a perfectly ordered set of objectives, with each item
in a series preparing the way for the next. You are likely to find that it won't work
and may get discouraged about using objectives.

At the same time, you should habitually make it a point to analyze the kinds of
abilities represented by each of the levels in the various taxonomies, particularly
the taxonomy for the cognitive domain. Benjamin S. Bloom, organizer and driving force of the team that prepared the first taxonomy, recently made this observation about how it has been used (or not used):

Most test questions
stress knowledge, ig-
nore higher levels of
cognitive taxonomy

After the sale of over one million copies of the *Taxonomy of Educational Objec-
tives-Cognitive Domain* (Bloom, Engelhart, Furst, Hill, & Krathwohl, 1956) and
over a quarter of a century of use of this domain in preservice and in-service teacher
training, it is estimated that over 90% of test questions that U.S. public school students are *now* expected to answer deal with little more than information. Our instructional material, our classroom teaching methods, and our testing methods
rarely rise above the lowest category of the Taxonomy—knowledge. (1984, p. 13)

Handbook Heading:
Ways to Use Instructional
Objectives

Now that you are familiar with types of objectives, various recommendations
for using them, and evaluations of their effectiveness, it is time to turn to specific
applications. The following Suggestions for Teaching summarize and reinforce
points already discussed.

Mid-Chapter Review

Characteristics of Taxonomies of Objectives

Taxonomy: classification scheme of categories arranged in hierarchical order

Cognitive taxonomy: objectives stressing knowledge, comprehension, application, synthesis, evaluation

Affective taxonomy: objectives stressing attitudes and values

Psychomotor taxonomy: objectives stressing skills

Nature of National Assessment

National Assessment program involves comprehensive, periodic analyses of knowledge, attitudes, and skills

National Assessment publications provide lists of objectives and reports of results of periodic testing programs

Uses of Objectives

Objectives help teachers plan lessons so that students learn efficiently

Mager: use specific objectives by identifying behavioral act that indicates achievement, defining conditions, stating criteria

Specific objectives are useful in arranging classroom exercises but tend to discourage incidental learning

Gronlund: examine what is to be learned, state general objectives, list sample of specific learning outcomes

General objectives with specific outcomes lead to comprehensive coverage, improve planning and instruction, make evaluation simple and efficient

Arranging objectives or learning experiences in strict hierarchical order does not seem to be essential

Referring to taxonomies may be desirable when planning evaluation procedures to make sure higher-level skills are not ignored

SUGGESTIONS FOR TEACHING

Using Instructional Objectives

1. Look over texts, curriculum guides and report cards (for the elementary grades), ask about achievement and competency tests, and think about your own goals to get a general picture of what you want your students to achieve.

2. Check to see if appropriate and useful lists of objectives for your subject and grade level have been developed by others.

3. Examine the taxonomies of objectives for the three domains, and make a preliminary outline of objectives and activities.

4. Refer to Tables 6.1, 6.2, and 6.3 listing objectives and specific outcomes, and begin to write sets of objectives.
   a. Describe a general objective in brief terms.
   b. Under that general objective list from three to five specific outcomes that begin with an action verb. Try to write specific outcomes that reflect a representative sample of what a student should do when demonstrating achievement of the objective.

5. Examine your lists of objectives to determine how they might be converted into specific classroom learning exercises and/or examination questions.

6. Examine your lesson plans to determine if you should occasionally use specific objectives that include a statement of the criterion of acceptable performance.

7. Develop your own variations of types of instructional objectives described in this and other books.

8. Try to remain aware of the extent to which you direct and control learning. Whenever possible, permit and encourage students to make choices and to manage their own learning.

9. From time to time during a report period, refer to the taxonomies to check whether you have been paying adequate attention to affective and psychomotor, as well as cognitive, objectives and to the higher levels of each of the taxonomies.

1. Look over texts, curriculum guides and report cards (for the elementary grades), ask about achievement and competency tests, and think about your own goals to get a general picture of what you want your students to achieve.

At the beginning of this chapter the point was made that you will not be able to determine at the end of a report period or year whether your students have achieved specific objectives unless you describe those objectives before you start. Perhaps the most logical way to begin to formulate objectives is to institute a survey of general goals and progressively refine them until you have devised specific objectives and learning outcomes. First of all, it would be wise to find out what others have already decided you should do. Most of the texts you will be asked to use probably will have been selected by state and/or local committees. It is quite likely that you will be asked to follow curriculum guides developed for use in your school system. At the elementary level, the kinds of report cards you will be expected to fill out and/or the kinds of points you will be expected to stress in parent conferences often will indicate what your students will be expected to achieve. It would also be prudent to find out whether your students will be asked to take achievement or competency tests. At present in American education there is quite a bit of stress on measuring student competency in basic skills. Even though it is usually unwise and ineffective to try to "teach to a test," it does make sense to stress the kinds of abilities that are measured by tests used to evaluate student (and perhaps teacher) achievement. If you will be teaching high school English, for example, and you discover that students in your school will not graduate unless they pass a competency test that includes questions designed to measure their ability to write clearly and accurately, it would be sensible to treat that skill as an important objective. Finally, you might note some of your own general goals that are not directly related to texts, curriculum guides, or examinations.

Before devising objectives, examine curriculum materials, find out about tests

In developing a "starter" list of objectives, you might include items such as these:

Knows important information covered in required text.

Understands information stressed in curriculum guide.

Demonstrates proficiency in subjects listed on report card.

Demonstrates proficiency in types of skills measured by achievement and competency exams.

Applies at least some of the things learned in class to out-of-class situations.

Works diligently and cooperatively in the classroom.

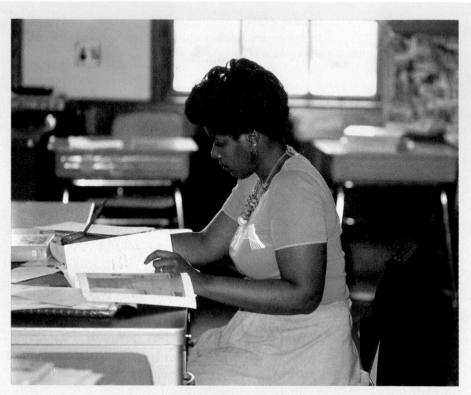

The first step in using instructional objectives is to look over texts, curriculum guides, and perhaps inquire about standardized tests your pupils will be asked to take, to get a general picture of what you want your students to achieve. (B. Cole/The Picture Cube)

Even if such a list of objectives may be a bit vague, it represents an attempt to develop a general conception of what you want your students to achieve by the last day of class.

2. Check to see if appropriate and useful lists of objectives for your subject and grade level have been developed by others.

Check on availability of appropriate lists of objectives

After you have outlined the general objectives you want your students to achieve in your particular school and classroom, it makes sense to check on the availability of objectives prepared by experienced educators. It may be well worth the trouble to obtain appropriate National Assessment booklets, for example. You should also ask experienced teachers or supervisors in your school if they know of lists of objectives that have proven to be useful. In addition, peruse recent issues of teachers' journals for articles on objectives. If you are unable to find any sets of goals that provide helpful leads, you might write to the organizations that serve as clearing houses for objectives (whose addresses are supplied in the Suggestions for Further Study).

3. Examine the taxonomies of objectives for the three domains and make a preliminary outline of objectives and activities.

The taxonomies of objectives for the cognitive, affective, and psychomotor domains can be used as all-purpose guides for translating general goals into specific objectives and classroom practices. After you have made your general survey of what you want your students to achieve, for example, you might systematically work your way through the taxonomy for the cognitive domain and jot down brief answers to the following questions:

Use taxonomies to make survey of what students should be able to do

What sorts of terms and symbols will my students need to know?

What specific facts will they need to know?

What sets of rules will they need to know?

What awareness of trends and sequences will they need to have?

What classifications and categories will they benefit from knowing?

What sets of criteria will they need to be able to apply?

What methods will they need to master?

What general principles will they benefit from knowing?

What theories will they benefit from knowing?

What sorts of translations will they need to perform?

What sorts of interpretations will they need to make?

What sorts of extrapolations will they need to make?

What sorts of applications should they be able to make?

What kinds of analyses will they need to make?

What kinds of syntheses should they be able to make?

What kinds of evaluations should they be able to make?

Handbook Heading: Using the Taxonomy of Cognitive Objectives

A similar procedure might be followed for the various categories in the affective and psychomotor domains. The purpose of carrying out this sort of survey would be to get a more complete idea of the kinds of things your students should be able to achieve by the last day of class. It will probably be impossible for you to list all items for an entire year or report period with reference to such sets of questions, but if you follow this procedure for at least the first teaching unit you expect to present, you should end up with an outline of information that can be converted into more specific objectives and learning outcomes. Then you could repeat the procedure for the next teaching unit, and so on. In preparing such lists, remember to take into account the cognitive abilities of your students so that you do not waste time speculating about higher levels of a taxonomy if these are not appropriate. If you will be teaching students in the upper elementary grades or beyond, though, pay *special* attention to the higher-level categories. Devising lists of objectives under analysis, synthesis, and evaluation categories may be more difficult than devising lists under the knowledge category, but higher-level skills are too often omitted (as noted by Bloom) when examinations are prepared. (One of the major advantages of objectives, you are reminded, is that they can be used to make evaluations more systematic and effective.)

Having written down lists of things your students should achieve, it is now time to convert them into objectives and specific learning outcomes.

4. Refer to Tables 6.1, 6.2, and 6.3 listing objectives and specific outcomes and begin to write sets of objectives.
   a. Describe a general objective in brief terms.
   b. Under that general objective, list from three to five specific outcomes that begin with an action verb. Try to write specific outcomes that reflect a representative sample of what a student should do when demonstrating achievement of the objective.

Since selected examples of objectives for different grade levels and subject areas were given earlier and since it is impossible to provide further examples for all subjects at all grades, the following examples are based on material in this chapter. The general objectives and specific outcomes are written so that they can be applied to almost any subject matter. The examples in parentheses refer to points covered in this chapter. Thus, the examples serve to review what has been covered, to permit you to test your knowledge, and to help you prepare for exams.

Examples

Knows essential terms

1. Defines essential terms (e.g., *taxonomy, cognitive, affective, psychomotor, domain, transfer*)
2. Illustrates understanding of terms when presented with sets of examples (e.g., match the terms *goals, general objectives, specific outcomes,* with an example of each)
3. Distinguishes between similar terms (e.g., explain difference between *specific objectives* and *general objectives*)
4. Discriminates between terms (e.g., note differences between *goals, objectives,* and *specific outcomes*)

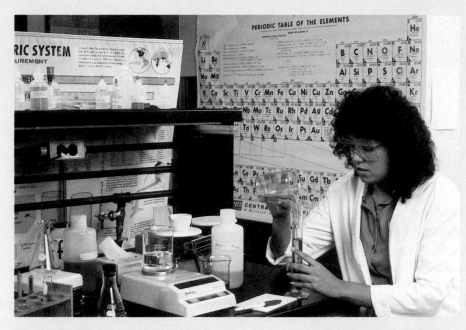

In order for students to gain maximum benefit from classification schemes such as the periodic table of the elements they need to know *terms* as well as *methods* and *procedures*. Referring to the taxonomy of objectives for the cognitive domain will help you make sure they acquire necessary background information before attempting advanced problem solving. (Bob Daemmerich/Stock, Boston)

Knows methods and procedures

1. Describes how to use knowledge of procedures (e.g., tell where to look for information about hierarchies and lists of objectives)
2. States steps to follow when using a given procedure (e.g., describe how to use Mager-style objectives and Gronlund-style objectives)
3. States procedure to follow when provided with problems (e.g., describe how to proceed when instructed to teach math in third grade, music in sixth grade, and so forth)

Interprets ideas and concepts to display comprehension

1. Interprets general ideas in specific terms (e.g., provide examples of general objectives and specific outcomes for teaching a given subject)
2. Converts suggestions described for one situation to another (e.g., take example for teaching a sixth-grade unit on music and apply it to teaching a ninth-grade unit on art appreciation)

3. Explains how to adapt given procedures to special circumstances (e.g., describe how to use Mager-style objectives when teaching typing)

Applies principles to hypothetical or actual situations

1. Uses principles to develop procedures (e.g., explain how to prepare objectives for a unit on general science)
2. Solves a problem by applying principles (e.g., develop useful objectives for a required teaching unit)
3. Demonstrates ability to apply principles (e.g., develop a set of Gronlund-style objectives for a unit you expect to teach)

Analyzes organization and relationships

1. Outlines nature of relationships in a given set of data (e.g., explain hierarchical arrangement of taxonomies)
2. Discriminates between parts of an organized whole (e.g., note differences between lower and higher levels of taxonomies)
3. Differentiates between organizational schemes (e.g., explain differences between the taxonomies for the cognitive, affective, and psychomotor domains)

Produces new arrangement

1. Compiles given ideas into a new arrangement (e.g., draw up a list of general objectives for your particular grade level and subject)
2. Combines separate sets of ideas into a new pattern (e.g., tell how you might use techniques recommended by both Mager and Gronlund in the same teaching unit)
3. Creates custom-designed approach by modifying original description (e.g., take examples given in this chapter and modify them so that they fit your own teaching situation)

Judges on basis of criteria or evidence

1. Criticizes misuse of a given technique (e.g., specify when Mager-style objectives are not appropriate)
2. Discriminates between proper and improper applications (e.g., make judgments about whether the cognitive level of students is likely to permit them to engage in analysis, synthesis, and evaluation)
3. Detects inconsistencies in applications (e.g., note when specific outcomes are not defined in terms of action verbs)

4. Evaluates criticisms (e.g., evaluate the conclusions of research on the effectiveness of use of objectives)

The sets of objectives just illustrated are arranged in a hierarchical order that parallels the arrangement of the taxonomy for the cognitive domain. While it would be important to make sure that objectives centering on knowledge were mastered first, the results of research noted earlier lead to the conclusion that it is not necessarily an advantage to arrange higher levels of the taxonomy in order. For instance, rather than try to devise a perfectly ordered step-by-step sequence, you might ask students to demonstrate their ability to analyze or evaluate before you ask them to make applications, if that seems a more logical or convenient way to proceed.

After you have prepared sets of objectives for the cognitive domain, examine the affective and psychomotor taxonomies to determine if there are attitudes and skills you will want your students to acquire along with subject matter. The first level in the taxonomy of affective objectives, for instance, is *receiving or attending,* which includes showing willingness to receive and indicating attention. Suppose you conclude that many of your pupils need to pay closer attention to class demonstrations. You might devise an objective such as this:

Handbook Heading: Using the Taxonomy of Affective Objectives

Observes attentively
1. Puts away distracting material when a demonstration is announced
2. Observes demonstration with alertness
3. Follows instructions for following up on demonstration accurately
4. Describes procedure accurately after having seen a demonstration
5. Answers questions about how to proceed after having seen a demonstration
6. Correctly carries out a procedure shown in a demonstration

Or suppose you want to try to encourage your students to develop an appreciation for the values of science. You might devise an objective such as this:

Appreciates the values of scientific methods and discoveries
1. Describes the characteristics of scientific methods
2. Distinguishes between scientific and non-scientific conclusions
3. Explains why conclusions based on scientific evidence are more trustworthy than conclusions based on hunches or opinions
4. Identifies scientific conclusions by referring to trustworthy evidence

Or suppose you would like your students to become more considerate of others. You might devise an objective similar to this one:

Appreciates the rights and feelings of others

1. Explains how one person's actions may be irritating or distracting to others
2. Invites others to indicate if certain actions are bothersome or distracting
3. Lists kinds of behavior of others that are bothersome or irritating
4. Keeps a record of own behavior that might be bothersome to others
5. Describes specific actions that might be taken to show greater consideration for others

Handbook Heading: Using the Taxonomy of Psychomotor Objectives

Suppose you notice that your students seem to be having trouble with the sequence of steps in carrying out some activity. You might devise an objective similar to this one:

Knows sequence of steps in a procedure

1. Describes correct sequence of steps
2. Explains how to carry out each step
3. Shows how to carry out each step
4. Combines all steps in correct order with confidence

Other objectives derived from the taxonomies for the affective and psychomotor domains might be written by referring to Tables 6.2 and 6.3.

5. Examine your lists of objectives to determine how they might be converted into specific classroom learning exercises and/or examination questions.

As you looked over the various examples of objectives provided earlier and in the preceding suggestions, you may have noticed that many of them give specific leads for arranging classroom learning experiences and for devising exams. The objective "Knows terms," for example, could be converted into this announcement to your students:

Use specific learning outcome descriptions to arrange learning experiences

"Here is a list of the most important terms in the next chapter of the text. As you read the chapter, write down definitions of each term. I will give you my definitions after you finish, and we can discuss differences between yours and mine. You will be asked to define five terms selected from this list on the exam scheduled for Friday."

Or "Here is a list of ten terms and twenty examples. Write down the correct term next to each example. A test item just like this one will be included on the next exam."

Or "These three terms are very similar. Read pages 75–79 of the text and carefully describe differences between the terms that are explained on those pages. You will be asked to explain these differences on the next exam, so if you aren't sure about what you have written, ask me to look over your descriptions."

These examples illustrate that when you take the trouble to describe specific learning outcomes, you not only give yourself instructions on ways to present lessons, but you also pretty much determine in advance how you will evaluate achievement.

You undoubtedly recognized as you read the suggestions just offered that the basic procedure outlined so far is based on Gronlund's recommendations for using objectives. His approach is quite versatile and has many advantages, but you should also consider other alternatives.

6. Examine your lesson plans to determine if you should occasionally use specific objectives that include a statement of the criterion of acceptable performance.

As noted in the discussion of Mager's recommendations and in the section on evaluations of objectives, too much stress on specific objectives tends to cause teachers to concentrate on knowledge and simple skills and to discourage incidental learning. Even so, there are times when you may find it desirable to describe precisely what you want your students to do and specify the criterion for acceptable performance.

Examples

In order to "pass" this unit you will need to spell correctly at least eighteen of these twenty words on the quiz to be given on Friday.

By the end of this month you should be able to type a 240-word selection in less than six minutes with no errors.

After you watch this film, you should be able to list five basic kinds of crops and give an example of each within three minutes.

In order to earn an A in this course, you will need to answer correctly at least twenty of twenty-five questions on each of five exams.

After you take notes on this lecture, you will be asked to list four types of trees and give an example of each. If you correctly supply all four types and examples, you will not have to take a quiz at the end of the period.

7. Develop your own variations of types of instructional objectives described in this and other books.

The top levels of the various taxonomies stress creating something new, or at least modifying things to fit particular situations. As a result of reading this chapter, therefore, it would be fitting for you to devise your own variations of the techniques described. Here are a few variations you might consider as examples of ways you might modify the basic suggestions that have been supplied. They all stress objectives but in different ways than those already described.

Here are some ways you might use objectives to help your pupils study texts and respond selectively to lectures and assignments:

Before distributing a new text to the class, go through it and underline all terms that some students may not understand. List and define these terms; then give an informal quiz to determine if students have learned them.

Invite students to list all terms that they are not sure about as they read or listen. Suggest that they look up such terms in a dictionary or encyclopedia. Perhaps invite discussion of different interpretations of the same terms and decide on an "official" definition that will be used in class discussion or on exams.

Go through each chapter in a text and list Key Points under major headings. If you plan to use these as the basis for exam questions, inform students of that fact.

Look over lecture notes and select the most important points. List these on the board before you begin to lecture.

Say to your students, "There may seem to be an overwhelming amount of factual information in this book. Here are the facts that I want you to concentrate on when you prepare for exams." Then hand out an organized list of these facts.

You might state objectives for a unit of study in ways such as these:

The basic goal of this unit is to help you learn to appreciate and enjoy poetry. When you have finished it you should be able to

1. distinguish between superior and inferior poetry.
2. give reasons for classifying a poem as superior or inferior.
3. explain why you like some poems better than others.
4. find books and magazines that contain poems you are likely to enjoy.

The primary objective of this unit is to help you comprehend and apply the laws of thermodynamics. To earn a passing grade on this unit you will be asked to

1. state the first and second laws of thermodynamics in the same basic terminology used in the text. (Slight alterations will be permitted, provided they do not change the meaning of the law.)
2. rewrite these laws in your own words.
3. predict what will happen in various energy-producing situations.
4. explain how any energy system works.

At the end of this unit on use of the table saw, you will be expected to

1. state five safety rules to observe every time you use the saw.
2. set up the saw for crosscutting and ripping.
3. use the dado head to cut half-lap joints, tongue-and-groove joints, and box joints.

The two examples below suggest how you can call attention to the advantages of developing knowledge of classifications and categories:

"There are so many different kinds of birds it's hard to identify them without some classification scheme. Here is a scheme devised by a famous ornithologist."

"Here are pictures of ten trees. Pick out the ones that are deciduous. Then, see if you can find other ways to call attention to similarities and differences."

The following approaches might encourage students to use criteria and external and internal standards when making judgments:

"We're going to look at some slides of different buildings. Before you see them, though, let's list some things that make a building well designed or poorly designed."

"There are usually several different brands of any food product. What are some factors to consider when making a choice?"

"We all buy clothes from time to time. Let's discuss factors you might consider before you make your next purchase."

"I'm going to project some slides of different sets of dining room furniture. I'd like you to pick out the set you like the most and describe why you like it. What features of the set make it seem more attractive to you than the other sets? Then next week we will take a field trip to a large furniture store, and you can make a detailed examination of different dining room sets and use what you learn today to select the furniture you would like best."

"I'm going to play two different recordings of the same musical composition. Listen very carefully. Choose the one you prefer and then write down why you think one is better than the other."

These ways can help you to focus on just one of the key verbs in the taxonomy for the cognitive domain and use it to develop a teaching exercise:

"Here is an excerpt from a recent speech by the President. *Translate* it into your own words."

Ask students to write their own brief summary of a chapter, their *interpretation* of a poem, or the meaning of a short story. Then arrange students in small groups to compare how they interpreted others' information.

Show a political cartoon from a newspaper and ask students to give their *interpretation* of what the artist intended to convey.

"As you read the next two chapters, I want you to draw up your own *analysis* of what is covered. Try to pick out points that are important and organize them into an outline."

"Here are copies of three different newspaper reports of the same event. I'd like you to prepare a *synthesis* of the points made and write your own composite interpretation of what occurred."

"Your political science assignment this week is to watch the presidential candidate's debate on television this Wednesday and *evaluate* the arguments of each candidate. On Thursday morning we will divide into small groups to compare our evaluations, and then we will have a class election to find out which candidate 'won.' "

8. Try to remain aware of the extent to which you direct and control learning. Whenever possible, permit and encourage students to make choices and to manage their own learning.

Occasionally invite students to participate in developing objectives

One of the potential problems of becoming involved in instructional objectives is that you might get carried away by the technique and prearrange almost all student learning. Although this may be appropriate in some courses, most of the time you will get a better response from pupils if you occasionally or frequently invite them to decide what they will study and how they will do it. If you want students to help you select and arrange instructional objectives, you might follow the ten-step sequence proposed by Leland and Mary Howe in *Personalizing Education* (1975): (1) Have students brainstorm ideas. (2) Select the best of these. (3) Prepare a flow chart. (4) Carry out a question census. (5) List resources. (6) Develop activities from the questions. (7) Analyze purposes under the headings *knowledge, cognitive skills, values.* (8) Revise the curriculum. (9) Decide how the unit will be structured, taught, and evaluated. (10) Carry out the plan. (More information about this sequence will be provided in the discussion of humanistic education to be presented in Chapter 10.)

9. From time to time during a report period, refer to the taxonomies to check whether you have been paying adequate attention to affective and psychomotor, as well as cognitive, objectives and to the higher levels of each of the taxonomies.

Periodically refer to taxonomies to improve instruction and evaluation

Since it is unlikely that you will be able to prepare a master set of objectives at the beginning of a school year or report period, you may slip into the habit of referring to these suggestions or the taxonomies at the beginning of the year and then forget about them. To avoid falling into that trap, you might make it a point periodically to reassess your approach to using objectives. The first year you teach, spending a few minutes pondering the use of objectives every Monday morning could yield substantial dividends for you and your pupils. At the beginning of each week, take the trouble to think about possible ways you might use objectives to clarify lessons, ensure coverage of higher-level cognitive and physical skills, and improve examinations.

Suggestions for Further Study

Taxonomy of Educational Objectives: Cognitive Domain

This chapter presents an abridged outline of the taxonomy developed by Benjamin S. Bloom and several associates in *Taxonomy of Educational Objectives, Handbook I: Cognitive Domain* (1956). To better understand the taxonomy and to gain insight into coordinating objectives and evaluation, examine Bloom's book—particularly Chapter 1, "The Nature and Development of the Taxonomy," and Chapter 2, "Educational Objectives and Curriculum Development." The remainder of the book consists of definitions of the general and specific classifications, followed by illustrations and exam questions.

Taxonomy of Educational Objectives: Affective Domain

To become more familiar with the possible values of the *Taxonomy of Educational Objectives: Affective Domain* (1964), refer to the complete list and explanation of objectives in the book by David B. Krathwohl, Benjamin S. Bloom, and Bertram B. Masia.

Taxonomy of Educational Objectives: Psychomotor Domain

The Psychomotor Domain (1972) by Elizabeth J. Simpson gives a complete description of the taxonomy for the psychomotor domain noted in this chapter. A different *Taxonomy of the Psychomotor Domain* (1972) has been developed by A. J. Harrow.

Mager and Gronlund on Objectives

If you would like to read Robert Mager's complete description of his recommendations for writing specific objectives, peruse his brief paperback *Preparing Instructional Objectives* (2nd ed., 1975). Norman Gronlund explains his approach to using objectives in *Stating Behavioral Objectives for Classroom Use* (2nd ed., 1978) and in *Measurement and Evaluation in Teaching* (5th ed., 1985).

Where to Seek Information About Objective-Item Pools

Collections of instructional objectives and related test items may be obtained from the following sources:

Institute for Educational Research
1400 West Maple Ave.
Downer's Grove, Illinois 60515

Instructional Objectives Exchange
Box 24095
Los Angeles, California 90024

Objectives and Items CO-OP
School of Education
University of Massachusetts
Amherst, Massachusetts 01002

Westinghouse Learning Corporation
P.O. Box 30
Iowa City, Iowa 52240

National Assessment Publications

National Assessment objectives booklets and publications that report the results of recent assessments are described in the NAEP publications catalogue, which can be obtained free of charge by writing to:

National Assessment of Educational Progress
P.O. Box 6710
Princeton, New Jersey 08541-6710

Summary

1. Early attempts at specifying the outcomes of education focused on general goals that meant different things to different people.
2. The vagueness of such goals stimulated psychologists to formulate taxonomies of specific, clearly stated objectives in each of three domains: cognitive, affective, and psychomotor.
3. The taxonomy for the cognitive domain that was prepared by Benjamin Bloom and several associates is comprised of six levels: knowledge, comprehension, application, analysis, synthesis, and evaluation.
4. The taxonomy for the affective domain that was prepared by David Krathwohl and several associates is comprised of five levels: receiving, responding, valuing, organization, and characterization by a value or value complex.
5. The taxonomy for the psychomotor domain that was prepared by Elizabeth Simpson is comprised of seven levels: perception, set, guided response, mechanism, complex or overt response, adaptation, and origination.
6. The National Assessment of Educational Progress was begun in 1964 to determine how well individuals of various ages have mastered cognitive, affective, and psychomotor objectives. These lists indicate the kinds of objectives experienced educators feel should be stressed by teachers of various subjects.
7. Robert Mager states that well-written objectives should specify what behav-

iors the learner will exhibit to indicate mastery, the conditions under which the behavior will be exhibited, and the criterion of acceptable performance.

8. Norman Gronlund believes that complex and advanced kinds of learning do not lend themselves to Mager-type objectives. Complex outcomes are so broad in scope that it is impractical to ask students to demonstrate everything they have learned. Instead, Gronlund suggests that teachers first state a general objective and then specify a sample of related specific outcomes.

9. Formulating objectives helps you plan a logical sequence of instruction, provides you with ideas for classroom activities and remedial instruction, and helps you specify tests that will determine if learning has occurred.

10. Objectives work best when students are aware of them and understand their intent, when they are clearly written, when they are provided to average students for tasks of average difficulty, and when intentional learning is measured.

11. Incidental learning occurs more often with Gronlund-type objectives than with Mager-type objectives.

12. Most teachers use test questions that measure knowledge-level objectives, largely ignoring higher-level outcomes.

Key Terms

taxonomy *(270)*
cognitive domain *(270)*
affective domain *(270)*
psychomotor domain *(270)*

National Assessment of
  Educational Progress *(277)*
specific objectives *(282)*
general objectives *(283)*

Discussion Questions

1. Based on the content of this chapter and your experiences as a student, do you agree that writing objectives and providing them to students is a worthwhile expenditure of a teacher's time and effort? If so, then what steps will you take to assure that, unlike many teachers today, you will make writing objectives a standard part of your professional behavior?

2. One criticism of writing objectives is that it limits the artistic side of teaching. That is, objectives lock teachers into a predetermined plan of instruction and eliminate the ability to pursue unplanned topics or interests. Can you respond to this criticism by recalling a teacher who provided you and your classmates with objectives but was still enthusiastic, flexible, spontaneous, and inventive?

3. Although, for the sake of clarity and simplicity, textbooks discuss objectives in terms of separate domains, many educational outcomes are in reality a combination of cognitive, affective, and psychomotor elements. Can you describe a few instructional outcomes that incorporate objectives from two or three domains (such as playing a piece of music "with feeling")?

4. As Benjamin Bloom has pointed out, over 90 percent of the test questions teachers write reflect the lowest level of the cognitive taxonomy. How can you avoid doing the same thing?

P A R T

3

Providing Instruction

313

c h a p t e r 7

BEHAVIORAL LEARNING THEORIES

KEY POINTS

Classical Conditioning

Pavlovian conditioning: reflexive response associated with new stimulus

Conditioning principles: reinforcement, extinction, generalization, discrimination

Operant Conditioning

Operant conditioning: voluntary response influenced by consequences that follow

Positive reinforcement: strengthen a desired behavior by presenting a positive stimulus after the behavior occurs

Negative reinforcement: strengthen desired behavior by removing a negative stimulus after the behavior occurs

Punishment: weaken undesired behavior by presenting a negative stimulus after the behavior occurs

Time-out: weaken undesired behavior by temporarily removing positive reinforcement

Extinction: weaken undesired behavior by ignoring it

Spontaneous recovery: extinguished behaviors may reappear simultaneously

Generalization: responding in similar ways to similar stimuli

Discrimination: responding in different ways to similar stimuli

Complex behaviors are shaped by reinforcing closer approximations to terminal behavior

Fixed interval schedules: reinforce after regular time intervals

Variable interval schedules: reinforce after random time intervals

Fixed ratio schedules: reinforce after a set number of responses

Variable ratio schedules: reinforce after a different number of responses each time

Educational Application of Operant Conditioning Principles

Programmed instruction: arrange material in small steps, reinforce correct responses

Linear programs provide one path; branching programs have multiple paths

Effectiveness of programmed instruction depends on program quality, student characteristics

Program is key to success of CAI; most programs of poor quality

CAI can supplement regular classroom instruction, especially for low achievers

Behavior modification: shape behavior by ignoring undesirable responses, reinforcing desirable responses

Premack principle: required work first, then chosen reward

Token economy is a flexible reinforcement system

Contingency contracting: reinforcement supplied after student completes mutually agreed-upon assignment

Time-out works best with disruptive, aggressive children

Corporal punishment is used in most schools

Punishment is likely to be ineffective because of temporary impact, side effects

Social Learning Theory

Observational learning occurs when one person imitates another

Processes of observational learning: attention, retention, production, motivation

Imitation is strengthened through direct reinforcement, vicarious reinforcement, self-reinforcement

Persistence, self-confidence, cognitive skills can be learned by observing models

Suggestions for Teaching

Delayed feedback may be more effective than immediate feedback

Reinforcement menu: student-selected enjoyable activities

Now that you are familiar with characteristics of students at different ages, with pupil variability, and with a variety of ways to specify what is to be learned, it is time to turn to the third phase in the model of learning. The third step in the sequence of instruction, helping students achieve specified objectives, is the aspect of the model of learning that will demand most of your attention when you begin to teach. You will improve your teaching effectiveness if you frequently think about student characteristics and prepare instructional objectives, but most of your time in the classroom will be devoted to instruction or supervision of student activities. If you will be teaching in the elementary grades, you will need to find ways to keep your students constructively occupied for up to five hours each day. If you will be teaching in the secondary grades you will need to arrange instructional activities for periods ranging from forty minutes to several hours.

The Organization of Chapters in Part Three

The various types of objectives described in the preceding chapter call attention to *what* you will be doing. The five chapters that make up this part give you scientifically based ideas about *how* you might do it. Part three consists of four chapters on learning and one on motivation. To understand why, think for a moment about what you will be doing when you begin to teach. If you obtain a position in an elementary school you will be responsible for teaching some, or perhaps all, of the following subjects: reading, writing, arithmetic, science, social studies, citizenship, arts and crafts, music, and physical education. If you are heading for a position in a secondary school you will specialize in advanced instruction of one or more of the subjects just listed or in courses in vocational education. Now, think for a moment about what you will be doing. At the elementary school level you will ask your pupils to read texts (once they *have* learned to read), complete exercises in workbooks, watch demonstrations, practice skills, participate in group work, engage in class discussions, work on individual and group projects, and prepare for and take exams. At the secondary school level you will carry out more advanced and sophisticated variations of the activities just listed. In addition, you may sometimes present lectures similar to those you are presently so familiar with in college courses. In certain cases, you may ask pupils to spend a good proportion of class time completing experiments or the equivalent (as in a chemistry course), or creating products (as in home economics, business, or shop courses).

This brief outline of what you will be doing as a teacher calls attention to the fact that you will be primarily concerned with helping students learn. That is why this part begins with four chapters on learning. You will also need to try to keep your students constructively busy for up to five hours a day. That is why this section ends with a chapter on motivation. Since learning is such a basic activity, psychologists have been interested in studying how animals and humans change their behavior as a result of experience from the time the first psychology departments were established in American and European universities. Different psychologists have approached the study of learning with different theoretical orientations, however, and they have used different methods of study. As a result, there are varied, sometimes conflicting, opinions about how teachers should arrange learning activities in classrooms. Such differences of opinion are not necessarily a disadvantage since contrasting views of learning provide a variety of ideas about ways to teach different kinds of subject matter.

The first chapter on learning, for instance, is devoted to *behavioral* learning theories. Behavioral theories were proposed by psychologists who argue that the only scientific way to study learning is to base all conclusions on observations of how overt behavior is influenced by forces in the external environment. Principles of such theories, to note just one application, can be used to make the learning of factual material extremely efficient. The second chapter on learning is

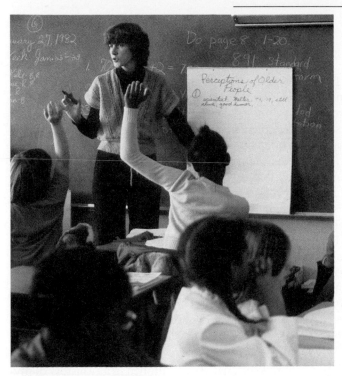

The first four chapters in this section devoted to Phase Three of the model of instruction are concerned with aspects of learning because your primary concern as a teacher will be helping students learn.
(Elizabeth Crews)

devoted to *information processing.* As the name implies, psychologists who specialize in this area of study are curious about how humans encode, store, and retrieve information. Many of the principles proposed by information processing theorists can be used to make comprehension and memorization more efficient and to help students recall and apply what they have memorized. Information processing takes a cognitive approach to learning. The third learning chapter outlines other cognitive learning theories and focuses especially on the nature of *problem solving.* While recent theorizing and research on the process of problem solving draws heavily from information processing, theories of how this process should be taught reflect widely different points of view. Some psychologists argue that students learn problem-solving skills most effectively when they have the opportunity to experiment and discover solutions to problems. Other psychologists argue that direct step-by-step instruction in the use of problem-solving skills produces better problem solvers than a discovery approach. Following the chapter on cognitive learning theories and problem solving, *humanistic* approaches to education are briefly discussed. Humanistic teaching concentrates on the affective (or emotional) side of learning. Many humanistic education techniques center on the establishment of a warm, positive classroom atmosphere; others are intended to encourage students to examine attitudes, values, and feelings.

Each of the chapters on learning includes some discussion of ways to keep students constructively occupied. But arousing and sustaining interest in learning is such a basic problem for almost all teachers that it merits extensive coverage. Accordingly, a separate chapter on *motivation* follows the four on learning.

Now that you are familiar with the organization of the chapters in part three, we are ready to examine the nature of behavioral theories of learning.

All psychologists who endorse the behavioral view share the belief that those who study learning should base their conclusions on observations of how the overt behavior of organisms is influenced by factors in the external environment. They differ, however, in how they study learning and the types of learning they analyze. You may have noticed that this chapter is titled "Behavioral Learning Theories"—in the plural. That title emphasizes that there is no single behavioral view of learning, but several different ones. Three of these theories, *classical conditioning, operant conditioning,* and *social learning,* will be summarized in this chapter. Differences between these three interpretations of the behavioral view will become clear as early experiments by leading exponents of each variation are discussed. Original experiments are described not only to give some historical perspective, but also because they illustrate basic principles in simplified form.

Classical Conditioning

The Russian scientist Ivan Pavlov is certain to be mentioned in any history of psychology, but he began his career in a different field of study. During the late 1800s and early 1900s he specialized in research on the physiology of digestion, work which earned him a Nobel Prize in 1904. As part of his research on digestion, Pavlov set out to measure the degree to which dogs salivated while eating. A dog, placed in a harness so that it could not move about, was given a measured amount of food and the resulting saliva collected by means of a surgical incision on the underside of the dog's mouth (see Figure 7.1). One day Pavlov noticed an intriguing aspect of the dog's behavior. It began to salivate at the *sight* of food or even the individual who brought it. Pavlov decided to study this phenomenon systematically. He set up a carefully controlled situation in which a bell was sounded just before the dog was presented with a small amount of food. After several pairings of bell and food, the bell alone aroused salivation. Pavlov called the food an *unconditioned stimulus* (abbreviated UCS)—because it naturally elicits salivation in hungry organisms—and the salivation an *unconditioned response* (UCR)—since it was a naturally occurring reflex. The new stimulus (the bell) he called a *conditioned stimulus* (CS) because it was a previously neutral stimulus that did not elicit salivation. The response to the bell was labeled a *conditioned response* (CR). The complete sequence of events Pavlov studied can be diagrammed this way:

Pavlovian conditioning: reflexive response associated with new stimulus

CS (bell) ⟶
UCS (food) ⟶ UCR (salivation)
UCS (food) ⟶ UCR (salivation)
CS (bell) ⟶ CR   (salivation)

In Pavlov's view, the CR was learned because of repeated *reinforcement,* which in this case means following the CS by the UCS and UCR at appropriate time in-

Figure 7.1   Pavlov's Apparatus for Studying Conditioning

tervals. If the food was not resupplied from time to time, the response would begin to disappear or *extinguish*. Pavlov also pointed out that a dog who learned to salivate to the sound of a bell would salivate to similar sounds, such as a buzzer or whistle. He called this tendency *stimulus generalization*. Such generalized responses could be overcome by supplying reinforcement after the bell was rung but never after a whistle was sounded. When this occurred, he said, *discrimination* had taken place.

The kind of learning described by Pavlov—in which a naturally occurring involuntary response becomes associated with a previously neutral stimulus—is often called **classical conditioning** because it is based on classic experiments that were excellent examples of scientific methodology. While Pavlov's experiments were ingenious and thought provoking, theorists interested in learning soon realized that classical conditioning applies only to essentially involuntary reflex actions (such as salivation or fear). Such reactions are not very common types of behavior. As a consequence, experimenters sought other ways to analyze associations between stimuli and responses. The psychologist who did this most successfully was B. F. Skinner.

> **Conditioning principles: reinforcement, extinction, generalization, discrimination**

Operant Conditioning

In a survey of psychology department heads conducted in 1967 (Myers, 1970, p. 1045), B. F. Skinner was chosen as the most influential American psychologist of the twentieth century. Skinner was accorded this honor because he put together a theory that not only successfully combines many different ideas but also serves as the basis for a variety of applications to human behavior. Skinner's theory emphasizes **operant conditioning,** a type of learning that is significantly different from that supplied by Pavlov. In operant conditioning, a voluntary response is strengthened when it is reinforced.

The Skinner Box

Most of the experiments on which principles of operant conditioning are based involved an ingenious apparatus invented by Skinner and appropriately referred to as a Skinner box. A Skinner box (see Figure 7.2) is a small enclosure that contains only a bar (or lever) and a small tray. Outside the box is a hopper holding a supply of food pellets that are dropped into the tray when the bar is pressed under certain conditions.

A hungry rat is placed in the box, and when—in the course of exploring its new environment—it approaches and then presses the bar, it is rewarded with a food pellet. Then food pellets are supplied under some conditions when the bar is pushed down (for example, when a tone is sounded) but not under others. The rat would learn this and the rate of pressing would drop noticeably when the tone was not sounded.

All the basic principles of Pavlovian conditioning are found in this experiment. The rat learned to press the bar more frequently when this behavior was *reinforced* by a food pellet. If it was not reinforced, *extinction* occurred. For a while the rat *generalized* and pushed the bar at the same rate whether a tone was sounded or not. Eventually, after selective reinforcement had been repeated often enough, it *discriminated* and pushed the bar more frequently when the tone was sounded.

The Skinner box's prominent role in operant conditioning experiments reflects Skinner's view of psychology as a natural science. One important assumption that underlies all natural sciences is that natural phenomena (like weather patterns, earthquakes, sunspots, and human behavior) may appear on the surface to be random but really operate according to set laws. That is, forces in the environment cause such events to occur. What psychology needed, in Skinner's view, was the means by which a researcher could control the environment to observe the law-bound and hence predictable influence of environmental factors on behavior. All sciences operate pretty much in this fashion. The meteorologist, for example, tries to create and control weather conditions in a laboratory to study the effects of temperature, humidity, and air flow on various weather phenomena like tornadoes and drought.

A second assumption underlying Skinner's work is that a science develops most effectively by studying some phenomenon at its most simple, fundamental level. What is learned at this level can then be used to understand more complex processes. In the case of behavior, the most fundamental elements are the stimulus situation, the response, and the consequences (positive, negative, or neutral)

Figure 7.2   A Rat in a Skinner Box

The rat's behavior is reinforced with a food pellet when it presses the bar under conditions preselected by the experimenter. The rat does not respond in a reflexive manner, as is the case with Pavlovian conditioning, but engages in self-selected behavior. In the process of exploring the Skinner box, for instance, the rat is almost certain to touch the bar. When that occurs, the experimenter supplies a food pellet and bar-pressing behavior is reinforced. Eventually, the rat may be reinforced only when a particular sequence of actions (for example, pressing the bar five times in succession) is performed. (Richard Wood/The Picture Cube)

that follow the response. The Skinner box, then, allows researchers to study, in a controlled, precise, and objective fashion, the most basic aspects of learning.

Differences Between Operant and Classical Conditioning

Although the Skinner box experiment seems similar to Pavlov's work with dogs, Skinner has pointed out important differences, notably in regard to the source of the behavior. In Pavlov's experiment the dog was essentially passive, and its response (salivation) had to be *elicited* by the experimenter. Skinner's rats *emitted* behavior in an essentially spontaneous way. And since the rats "operated" the bar, Skinner's kind of conditioning is called *operant*. (Some psychologists use the term *instrumental* since the behavior is instrumental in bringing about the reinforcement.)

Another way of comparing operant and classical conditioning is in terms of the elements of the learning process each one emphasizes. Classical conditioning repeatedly pairs two stimuli (CS followed by UCS) close together in time. This pairing leads the organism to respond to one stimulus (the CS) in the same way it naturally responds to the other stimulus (the UCS). The emphasis here is on the association that forms between an earlier occurring stimulus (often called an antecedent stimulus) and a response. For example, most young children react to sudden, loud noises by attempting to avoid or withdraw from the situations. Operant conditioning, on the other hand, emphasizes the relationship between a response and how that response is treated by the environment. The nature of the antecedent stimulus is not always taken into account. The reason for this occasional disregard is that in many everyday situations several stimuli operate simultaneously, making it difficult or impossible to know precisely what triggered a particular behavior. For example, we may eat lunch at noon because that is when we are hungry *and* because that is when we can socialize with others as we eat. In sum, classical conditioning emphasizes the relationship between antecedent stimuli and responses whereas operant conditioning emphasizes the relationship between responses and their consequences.

Basic Principles of Operant Conditioning

The basic idea behind operant conditioning is really quite simple: All behaviors are accompanied by certain consequences, and these consequences strongly influence (some might say determine) whether or not these behaviors are repeated and at what level of intensity. This section describes the nature of different types of consequences and several related principles that can be applied to aspects of human learning.

In general, the consequences that follow behavior are either positive or negative. Depending on conditions that we will discuss shortly, these consequences either increase (strengthen) or decrease (weaken) the likelihood that the preceding behavior will reoccur under the same or similar circumstances. When consequences strengthen a preceding behavior, the term *reinforcement* is used. There are positive and negative forms of reinforcement. When consequences weaken a preceding behavior, the terms *punishment* and *extinction* are used. There are two forms of punishment, type I and type II.

Positive Reinforcement   Although the term *positive reinforcement* may be unfamiliar to you, the idea behind it probably is not. If you can recall spending more time studying for a certain subject because of a compliment from the teacher or a high grade on an examination, you have experienced positive reinforcement. Specifically, **positive reinforcement** involves strengthening behavior—that is, in-

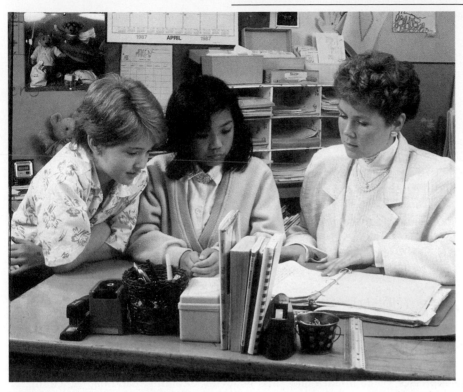

Students are likely to be eager to learn if they are presented with a series of learning tasks and supplied with evidence that they are successfully completing those tasks. Such evidence might take the form of scores on self-graded tests, a record booklet that makes it possible to chart progress, and warm praise from the teacher. (The Stock Market/Jeffry W. Myers)

creasing and maintaining the probability that a particular behavior will be repeated—by presenting a positive stimulus (for example, praise, candy, money, the opportunity for free play) immediately after the desired behavior has occurred. This positive stimulus is the *positive reinforcer.* What makes a positive reinforcer different from a reward is that the former strengthens the preceding behavior. Thus, two students who rarely study may be given the same amount of money for studying one hour every day after school. If, in the first case, there is no effect on amount of study in the future, the money is considered a reward. If in the second case, the student continues to study for an hour each day, the money is considered a positive reinforcer.

Negative Reinforcement People often confuse negative reinforcement with positive reinforcement or with punishment (a third type of consequence that we will take up next); so a careful consideration of similarities and differences is critical. The goal of positive reinforcement is to increase the strength of a desired behavior by supplying a positive stimulus. The student is motivated to learn new behaviors in order to obtain the positive reinforcer. The goal of **negative reinforcement** is the same—to *increase* the strength of a desired behavior. The

Negative reinforcement: strengthen desired behavior by removing a negative stimulus after the behavior occurs method, however, is different. Instead of supplying a positive stimulus, *an aversive (meaning unpleasant or unwanted) stimulus is removed whenever a target behavior is exhibited.* The student is now motivated to learn new behaviors so as to escape or avoid the aversive stimulus.

In laboratory studies, animals in a Skinner box have been taught to jump over a barrier, push on a panel, step on a pedal, or press a lever to escape or avoid mild does of electric shock or other intense stimulation (Keller, 1954). In everyday life, negative reinforcement occurs quite frequently. Examples include the child who picks up his clothes or toys to stop his parents' nagging, the driver who obeys speed limits to avoid getting a ticket, and the person who abuses alcohol or drugs to escape from stressful life situations (Nye, 1979). Later in the chapter we will describe how educators use negative reinforcement and we will discuss its desirability relative to positive reinforcement.

Punishment   So far, we have talked about behavioral consequences that serve to strengthen and maintain *desired* behaviors. We will now discuss three consequences that reduce the likelihood of *undesired* behaviors being repeated. The first is **punishment** (also called type I punishment). Punishment is defined by operant psychologists as the presentation of an aversive stimulus that weakens, suppresses, or eliminates undesired behavior. Scolding, paddling, ridiculing, or making a student write five hundred times "I will not chew gum in class" are all examples of punishment if, *and only if,* the student ceases the undesired behavior.

| Punishment: weaken undesired behavior by presenting a negative stimulus after the behavior occurs |

Many people confuse negative reinforcement with punishment. Both involve the use of an aversive stimulus, but the effect of the aversive stimulus on behavior is what matters. Remember that negative reinforcement strengthens a desired behavior, whereas punishment works against an undesired behavior.

Time-out   A consequence that is considered to be a different form of punishment (and so is called type II punishment) is **time-out.** Like type I punishment, time-out decreases the frequency of or eliminates undesired behavior. However, instead of presenting an aversive or negative stimulus, time-out *temporarily removes the opportunity to receive positive reinforcement.* Thus, a student who frequently disrupts classroom routine to get attention may be sent to sit in an empty room for ten minutes. Many consider time-out to be type II punishment because removal from a reinforcing environment (as well as the angry tone of voice and facial expression that normally go with it) is usually looked upon as an aversive consequence by the individual being removed. Other sorts of type II punishment include an athlete who is suspended from competition and a child who temporarily loses certain privileges.

| Time-out: weaken undesired behavior by temporarily removing positive reinforcement |

Extinction   A third consequence that weakens undesired behavior is **extinction.** Extinction occurs when a previously reinforced behavior decreases in frequency, and eventually ceases altogether, because reinforcement is withheld. Examples of

| Extinction: weaken undesired behavior by ignoring it |

Table 7.1	Conditions That Define Reinforcement, Punishment, and Extinction			
Type of Stimulus	+ Environmental Action	+ Effect on Behavior	= Result	
Positive	Present	Strengthen	Positive reinforcement	
Negative	Withdraw	Strengthen	Negative reinforcement	
Negative	Present	Weaken	Punishment I	
Positive	Withdraw	Weaken	Punishment II	
Positive	Withhold	Weaken	Extinction	

extinction include a mother ignoring a whining child, a teacher ignoring a student who spontaneously answers a question without waiting to be called on, and a counselor ignoring a client's self-deprecating remarks. As we shall see later, both extinction and time-out are most effective when combined with other consequences such as positive reinforcement.

To help yourself define and remember the distinguishing characteristics of positive reinforcement, negative reinforcement, punishment, and extinction, study Table 7.1.

Spontaneous Recovery   Extinction is sometimes a slow and difficult means of decreasing the frequency of undesired behavior when used alone, because "extinguished" behaviors occasionally reappear without having been reinforced (an occurrence known as **spontaneous recovery**). Under normal circumstances, however, the time between spontaneous recoveries lengthens and the intensity of the recurring behavior becomes progressively weaker. If the behavior undergoing extinction is not terribly disruptive, and if the teacher (or parent, counselor, or supervisor) is willing to persevere, these episodes can sometimes be tolerated on the way to more complete extinction.

Spontaneous recovery: extinguished behaviors may reappear spontaneously

Generalization   When an individual learns to make a particular response to a particular stimulus and then makes the same or a similar response in a slightly different situation, **generalization** has occurred. Pigeons in a Skinner box that have been reinforced for pecking at a red spot will also peck at other spots that differ somewhat in hue (for example, orange or yellow), shape, and size. The less similar the new stimulus is to the original, however, the weaker the response. Eventually, with increased variation, the new stimulus grows so different in appearance from the original that the response rarely occurs.

Generalization: responding in similar ways to similar stimuli

Whether or not generalization is desirable depends, of course, on the circumstances. It is highly pleasing to parents and teachers to see students who were positively reinforced for using effective study skills in history use those same skills in chemistry, social studies, algebra, and so on. On the other hand, it is disappointing to see students ignore or question a teacher's every request and direction because they have been reinforced for responding that way to their parents at home.

<table>
<tr><td>Discrimination: responding in different ways to similar stimuli</td></tr>
</table>

Discrimination   When inappropriate generalizations occur, as in the above example, they can be essentially extinguished through discrimination training. Quite simply, **discrimination** involves learning to notice the unique aspects of seemingly similar situations (for example, that teachers are not parents, although both are adults) and to respond differently to each situation. This process can be encouraged by reinforcing only the desired behaviors (for instance, attention, obedience, and cooperation) and withholding reinforcement following undesired behaviors (such as, inattention or disobedience) when they occur in the teacher's presence. In the terminology of operant conditioning, behavior comes to be controlled by discriminative stimuli. Thus, driving a car is a reasonably safe activity in our society because all drivers learn to make the same unique response to green, amber, and red traffic lights (most of the time, at any rate).

Shaping   Up to now, the descriptions and illustrations of basic operant conditioning principles have not distinguished relatively simple behaviors that people and animals enact spontaneously in final form from more complex behaviors that rarely occur spontaneously in finished form. A bit of reflection, however, should enable you to realize that many of the behaviors human beings learn (such as playing a sport or writing a term paper) are complex and are acquired gradually. The one principle that best explains how complex responses are learned is *shaping*.

Some of the experiments on shaping conducted by Skinner were carried out with pigeons placed in an apparatus similar to the original Skinner box. Instead of a bar to be pushed, the pigeon shared quarters with a disk to be pecked (since pigeons spontaneously peck a great deal). By manipulating the presentation of a positive reinforcer in specific ways, Skinner trained his pigeons to, among other things, peck out tunes on a toy xylophone and play a game similar to table tennis. The pigeon-musicians acquired their skill by pecking first one key, then two, then three, and then four in sequence. At first, pecking one key was reinforced with food. Eventually, the pigeons received food only when all four bars on the xylophone were pecked in the correct sequence. (If you would like to attempt roughly similar feats with a pet dog or cat, read Skinner's article "How to Teach Animals" in the December 1951 issue of *Scientific American,* pp. 26–29.)

The basic principle of learning in **shaping** is to reinforce actions that move progressively closer to the desired *terminal behavior* (to use Skinner's term). Actions that do not represent closer approximations of the terminal behavior are ignored. The key to success is to take one step at a time. The movements must be gradual enough so that the person or animal becomes aware that each step in the sequence is essential.

Complex behaviors are shaped by reinforcing closer approximations to terminal behavior

At least three factors can undermine the effectiveness of shaping. First, supplying too much positive reinforcement for early, crude responses may reduce the learner's willingness to attempt a more complex response. Second, expecting too much progress too soon (by making the next step in the sequence too "large") may decrease the likelihood of an appropriate response. If this results in a long period of nonreinforcement, what has been learned up to that point may be extinguished. Expecting a student to work industriously on a homework assignment for ninety minutes just after you have shaped forty-five minutes of appropriate homework behavior is probably too big a jump. If it is, the student may revert to his or her original level of performance owing to the lack of reinforcement. Third, delaying reinforcement of the terminal behavior allows time for additional, unrelated behaviors to occur. When the reinforcement eventually occurs, it may strengthen one or more of the more recent behaviors rather than the terminal behavior. For example, a teacher may shape a student to study each subject for several hours per week (a tactic that has been proved effective) but may not give weekly grades. If the student then stays up half the night cramming for the next day's midterm exam, a high grade may reinforce the cramming more than the distributed studying. The solution in this case would be to schedule more frequent exams to allow for more immediate reinforcement (Nye, 1979).

Schedules of Reinforcement   If you have been reading this section on basic principles carefully, you may have begun to wonder if the use of operant conditioning principles, particularly positive reinforcement, requires you to be present every time a desired response happens. If so, you might have some justifiable reservations about the practicality of this theory. The answer is yes, up to a point, but after that, no. As we have pointed out, when you are trying to get a new behavior established, especially if it is a complex behavior that requires shaping, learning proceeds best when every desired response is positively reinforced and every undesired response is ignored. This is known as a *continuous reinforcement* schedule.

Once the behavior has been learned, however, positive reinforcement can be employed on a noncontinuous or intermittent basis to perpetuate it. There are four basic *intermittent reinforcement* schedules: fixed interval (FI), variable interval (VI), fixed ratio (FR), and variable ratio (VR). Each schedule produces a different pattern of behavior.

The two interval schedules govern the delivery of reinforcement according to the passage of time. When that interval of time is fixed, as in a **fixed interval schedule,** a learner is reinforced for the first desired response that occurs after a

Fixed interval schedules: reinforce after regular time intervals predetermined amount of time has elapsed (for example, five minutes, one hour, or seven days). Once the response has occurred and been reinforced, the next interval begins. Any desired responses that are made during an interval are ignored. If the pattern of behavior that is usually produced by a fixed interval schedule were to be graphed on paper, it would be scallop shaped. That means the reinforced behavior occurs at a lower level during the early part of the interval and gradually rises as the time for reinforcement draws closer. Once the reinforcer is delivered, the relevant behavior declines in frequency and gradually rises toward the end of that next interval. Fixed interval schedules of reinforcement occur in education when teachers schedule exams or projects at regular intervals. The grade or score is considered to be a reinforcer. As you are certainly aware, it is not unusual to see little studying or progress occur during the early part of the interval. However, several days before an exam or due date, the pace quickens considerably.

If you would like to see a more consistent pattern of behavior, you might consider using a **variable interval schedule** of reinforcement. With this schedule, the length of time between reinforcements is essentially random but averages out to a predetermined interval. Thus, four successive reinforcements may occur at the following intervals: one week, four weeks, two weeks, five weeks. The average interval is three weeks. Teachers who give surprise quizzes or who call on students to answer oral questions on the average of once every third day are invoking a variable interval schedule.

A **fixed ratio schedule** provides reinforcement whenever a predetermined number of responses are made. A rat in a Skinner box may be reinforced with a food pellet whenever it presses a lever fifty times. A factory worker may earn twenty dollars each time he or she assembles five electronic circuit boards. A teacher may reinforce a student with praise for every ten arithmetic problems correctly completed. Fixed ratio schedules tend to produce high response rates since the faster the learner responds, the sooner the reinforcement is delivered. However, a relatively brief period of no or few responses occurs immediately after the reinforcer is delivered. The larger the ratio (meaning the number of responses required for a reinforcement), the longer the pause. If this response pattern were graphed on paper, it would look something like a set of stairs.

A **variable ratio schedule,** like a variable interval schedule, tends to eliminate these irregularities, thereby producing a more consistent response rate. This is accomplished by reinforcing after a different number of responses from one time to the next according to a predetermined average. If you decided to use a variable ratio 15 schedule, you might reinforce a desired behavior after 12, 7, 23, and 18 occurrences, respectively (that is, after the 12th, 19th, 42nd, and 60th desired behaviors). Because the occurrence of reinforcement is so unpredictable, learners tend to respond fairly rapidly for long periods of time. If you need proof, just watch people play the slot machines in Las Vegas. Variable ratio schedules also

Variable interval schedules: reinforce after random time intervals

Fixed ratio schedules: reinforce after a set number of responses

Variable ratio schedules: reinforce after a different number of responses each time

help to explain why scientists continue to work on the same problem (such as cancer research) for many years. Every once in a while (sometimes a great while) a scientist will obtain results that provide a better understanding of the nature of the problem. When that will occur is, of course, unpredictable. It may be the next experiment, but it may not occur for another thirty experiments. Out of such reinforcement schedules arise Nobel Prize winners!

Educational Applications of Operant Conditioning

By arranging conditions and supplying reinforcement according to the principles just described, Skinner succeeded in shaping the behavior of rats and pigeons in quite amazing ways, as pigeons playing ping-pong and the xylophone attest. Because he was so successful in getting animals to learn new forms of behavior, he concluded that similar techniques could be used to shape human behavior. He wrote a novel, *Walden Two* (1948), in which he described a utopian community based on principles of operant conditioning. The child-rearing specialists at Walden Two use the same methods that Skinner employed on animals to strengthen desirable traits (such as perseverance) and to eliminate undesirable traits (such as jealousy). The leader of Walden Two, who speaks for Skinner, defends this practice by arguing that highly successful and creative people get that way, not because of inherited tendencies, but because of a fortunate series of reinforcements. Instead of just hoping that such traits as perseverance and self-control will be reinforced, the scientific child rearers of Walden Two *arrange* situations to make sure that this happens. Psychologists who were impressed by Skinner's writings used techniques similar to those of the fictional child rearers of Walden Two to shape many different kinds of human behavior (see, for example, Craighead, Kazden, & Mahoney, 1981).

About the time Skinner was working on *Walden Two,* his daughter was a student in public school. When he asked her what the class had done each day and examined the books and assignments she brought home, Skinner became increasingly appalled about the kind of education his child was receiving. He concluded that traditional teaching techniques were terribly confused and inefficient and also primarily negative, in the sense that most children study to avoid negative consequences. It appeared to Skinner, for example, that his daughter studied most diligently to avoid being embarrassed or punished or to avoid a low grade. When he analyzed teacher-pupil behavior with reference to principles of operant conditioning, he was especially bothered by the fact that there was almost always a substantial interval between when pupils answered questions and when they received feedback as to whether their responses were correct or incorrect. Skinner realized that it was physically impossible for a teacher responsible for a class of

B. F. Skinner (Chris
J. Johnson/Stock,
Boston)

thirty to respond to more than a few students at a time, but he was still bothered by this situation. Finally, he noticed that lessons and workbooks were often poorly organized and did not seem to lead students to any specific goal. Skinner became convinced that if the principles of operant conditioning were systematically applied to education, all these limitations could be either reduced or eliminated.

In the intervening thirty-five years, little, according to Skinner, has changed. In an article written in 1984 titled "The Shame of American Education," Skinner makes the following assertion:

> I claim that the school system of any large American city could be so redesigned, at little or no additional cost, that students would come to school and apply themselves to their work with a minimum of punitive coercion and, with very rare exceptions, learn to read with reasonable ease, express themselves well in speech and writing, and solve a fair range of mathematical problems. (p. 984)

Skinner's claim is based on four prescriptions related to operant conditioning: (1) Be clear about what is to be taught; (2) teach first things first; (3) allow students to learn at their own rate; and (4) program the subject matter. The primary means by which this group of goals would be accomplished are programmed instruction and teaching machines (that is, computer-assisted instruction). The next sections will describe the nature of these applications and assess the extent to which they improve classroom learning. In addition, we will discuss behavior modification, a general application of operant conditioning principles.

Programmed Instruction

The key idea behind Skinner's approach to teaching is that learning should be *shaped*. Programs of stimuli and consequences should be designed to lead students step by step to a predetermined end result. In the mid-1950s Skinner turned this shaping approach into an innovation called programmed instruction.

Programmed instruction can be described as specially designed written material that presents small amounts of written information to the student in a predetermined sequence, provides prompts to draw out the desired written response, immediately reinforces correct responses, and allows the student to work through the program at his or her own pace. Programmed materials can be presented via machine or put in book form. In addition to immediate reinforcement, they incorporate such basic operant conditioning principles as shaping and extinction.

According to Skinner (1968, 1986) when programmed materials are well designed and appropriately used, they produce the following effects:

1. Reinforcement for the right answer is immediate.
2. The teacher can monitor each student's progress more closely.
3. Each student learns at his or her own rate, completing as many problems as possible within the allotted time.
4. Motivation stays high because of the high success level designed into the program.
5. Students can easily stop and begin at almost any point.
6. Learning a complex repertoire of knowledge proceeds efficiently.

Developing a Program   The first step in developing a program is to define precisely what is to be learned (the terminal behavior). Then, facts, concepts, and principles must be arranged in a sequence designed to lead the student to the desired end result. This requires first making the steps small enough so that reinforcement occurs with optimal frequency, then putting them in the proper order and arranging them so that students will be adequately prepared for each frame, or numbered problem, when they reach it.

> Programmed instruction: arrange material in small steps, reinforce correct responses

In arranging the sequence of steps, programmers may use a **linear program,** which tries to ensure that every response will be correct, since there is only one path to the terminal behavior. Or they may use a **branching program,** in which there is less concern that all responses be right. If students give a wrong answer, the program provides a branching set of questions to enable them to master the troublesome point. Another type of branching program provides students with a more complete explanation of the misunderstood material and then urges them to go back and study the original explanations more carefully.

> Linear (one-path) and branching (multiple-path) programs

Skinner prefers the linear approach, illustrated in Figure 7.3, because it requires students to supply their own responses and because it makes the most of reinforcement. Other psychologists favor branching programs, illustrated in

Figure 7.3   Section from a Linear Program

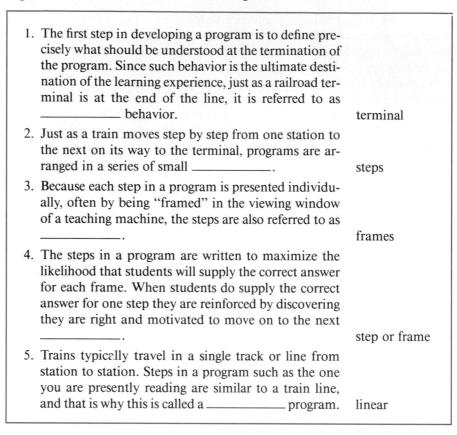

1. The first step in developing a program is to define precisely what should be understood at the termination of the program. Since such behavior is the ultimate destination of the learning experience, just as a railroad terminal is at the end of the line, it is referred to as _____ behavior.

   terminal

2. Just as a train moves step by step from one station to the next on its way to the terminal, programs are arranged in a series of small _____.

   steps

3. Because each step in a program is presented individually, often by being "framed" in the viewing window of a teaching machine, the steps are also referred to as _____.

   frames

4. The steps in a program are written to maximize the likelihood that students will supply the correct answer for each frame. When students do supply the correct answer for one step they are reinforced by discovering they are right and motivated to move on to the next _____.

   step or frame

5. Trains typically travel in a single track or line from station to station. Steps in a program such as the one you are presently reading are similar to a train line, and that is why this is called a _____ program.   linear

Figure 7.4, because students are able to advance in larger steps and because the program can "talk back" to them and thus come closer to approximating a human tutor.

In composing a program, the writer strives to progressively reduce the degree of *prompt*, or the number of *cues* necessary to elicit the correct answer. In the language of programming, the prompt is *vanished*. But in reducing cues, it is important to remember Skinner's experiments with pigeons and not go too far too fast.

Evaluations of the Effectiveness of Programmed Instruction   In the years since Skinner first proposed the use of programmed instruction, hundreds of research studies have been conducted to assess its effectiveness as a teaching tool. A general conclusion we can draw from these studies is that pupils taught with programmed materials usually score about the same or slightly higher on achievement tests as pupils instructed in nonprogrammed ways (see, for example,

Figure 7.4   Section from a Branching Program

Page 1

There are two basic types of programs, linear and branching. Linear programs are arranged so that there is only one path to the terminal behavior. Accordingly, the program writer tries to ensure that students will be able to answer every frame. One of the disadvantages of such programs is that capable students may be bored by the simplicity and repetition involved. Branching programs, on the other hand, are more like a tutor-pupil dialogue. After being supplied with background information, students are asked to choose between alternatives. If they select the correct answer, they are instructed to move on to new material. If they select the wrong answer, they are given additional information intended to clarify the point. Branching programs therefore allow greater flexibility for differences in student ability, background, and understanding.

Which of the following statements describes a *linear* program?

Some students are likely to be asked to read more frames than other students. (If you think this statement is correct, turn to page 3.)

All students follow the same path to their terminal behavior. (If you think this statement is correct, turn to page 2.)

Page 2

Right. You understand that linear programs require all students to follow the same sequence or line of frames. Go on to page 4.

Page 3

Well . . . no. Read the description of linear and branching programs on page 1 over again. This time, think of a train line that is arranged with stations on a single line or track. A linear program is like a one-track train line, which is why it is called linear. All students are asked to answer all questions. A branching program, on the other hand, provides additional information for those who don't grasp a point the first time. A student who understands a point the first time won't need to read the supplementary material and will therefore read fewer frames than one who needs more information. After you are sure you grasp this point, turn to page 4.

Jamison, Suppes, & Wells, 1974; Kulik, Cohen, & Ebeling, 1980). Kulik, Cohen, and Ebeling found that college students who learned from programmed materials scored on average at the 60th percentile on classroom exams, whereas students who learned from lecture and a standard text scored at the 50th percentile.

Effectiveness of programmed instruction depends on program quality, student characteristics

The inability of researchers to demonstrate a stronger effect for programmed instruction is likely due to two factors: the poor quality of many programs and the fact that human learners are more complex than laboratory animals. Animals learn simple tasks most effectively when they receive immediate feedback for each response, presumably because they are unable to store or process information in sophisticated ways. But human beings, who are able to memorize all kinds of information and associate past and present memories and experiences, may find that a response-feedback-response-feedback routine becomes tedious, annoying, or unnerving. A student taking a program may quickly grasp a point and be eager to learn something else, only to be asked to respond, find out if the response is correct, respond, and so on. When people are asked to deal with complex ideas, immediate feedback may interfere with their attempts to process information in personally meaningful ways. Indeed, a number of studies have revealed that students who receive immediate feedback (which is necessary for shaping animal behavior) about their performance on an exam do not score as well on a retest as students who wait at least a day before receiving feedback (Sassenrath, 1975; Surber & Anderson, 1975; Kulhavy, Yekovich, & Dyer, 1976; Kulhavy, 1977). It appears, therefore, that some of the features of programmed instruction that Skinner argued were its greatest strengths may actually be weaknesses in certain situations.

Today, programmed instruction is used more selectively, and the results appear to be more positive than they were twenty or twenty-five years ago. Kulik, Cohen, and Ebeling (1980), for instance, found that studies conducted during the 1970s were more likely to report positive results than studies conducted during the 1960s. They took this finding as evidence that programmed instruction is no longer viewed as a panacea but is now being used where it can do the most good. This reaffirms what was suggested in Chapter 1's section on "Teaching as an Art and a Science": that whenever you as a teacher apply any psychological principle in your classroom, you will need to ask, For whom is this instructional technique likely to be beneficial? With what materials? For what outcome?

Computer-Assisted Instruction

When programmed materials were first made commercially available during the mid-1950s, they were designed to be presented to students in one of two ways: in book form (as illustrated in Figures 7.2 and 7.3) or incorporated into mechanical teaching machines. The earliest teaching machines were simple mechanical devices. A program was inserted in the machine and the first statement or question was "framed" in a viewing window. (That is why the individual steps of a program are referred to as **frames**.) The student printed an answer on a designated line, then moved a knob that pulled a transparent cover over what had been written (to prevent erasing a wrong answer). At the same time, information appeared in the opening revealing whether or not the response was correct. After checking the correctness of the response, the student turned another knob, which presented the next frame, and so on. Today, mechanical teaching machines have been almost totally supplanted by the computer, particularly the microcomputer, since computers can do everything the machine could do and more. Nevertheless, we would do well to remember that a teaching machine—be it mechanical or electronic—is only as good as the instructional program that runs it (the "software" in today's computer terminology).[1] Skinner (1984) has made this point repeatedly, most recently in the following manner:

> A good program of instruction guarantees a great deal of successful action. Students do not need to have a natural interest in what they are doing, and subject matters do not need to be dressed up to attract attention. No one really cares whether Pac-Man gobbles up all those little spots on the screen. Indeed, as soon as the screen is cleared, the player covers it again with little spots to be gobbled up. What is reinforcing is successful play, and in a well-designed instructional program students gobble up their assignments. (p. 952)

With this caveat in mind, we can now turn to a consideration of the nature and effectiveness of computer-assisted instruction.

Uses of Computers   Perhaps the most general distinction that can be made about the use of computers in schools is *learning about computers* versus *learning with computers.* The first approach, used primarily at the high school level, emphasizes two things: understanding how computers work, and learning how to use the various computer languages, such as BASIC, PASCAL, and LOGO, that control its functions (for example, to teach, analyze and display data, or process words). The second approach is what we refer to as **computer-assisted instruction** (CAI), whereby students use the computer and instructional programs to master typical school subject matter, like English, science, and arithmetic. CAI is typically found at the elementary level (Hassett, 1984) and relies on one or more of the following types of programs: drill and practice, tutorial, problem solving, and dialogue.

Drill and practice programs are much like programmed texts. They usually require frequent responses, provide immediate feedback, and typically serve as a review of previously learned knowledge and skills. For example, students may work with a set of problems on arithmetic computation, a review of English vo-

---

1. In case you have never quite understood the terms *hardware* and *software* when used with reference to computers, *hardware* refers to the machine and electronic devices and *software* to the program, language, or instructions used in the machine.

cabulary, or a set of spelling exercises. Because these programs can be produced relatively easily and quickly, they dominate the marketplace. The Educational Products Information Exchange (EPIE), a nonprofit organization that classifies and evaluates computer programs, estimates that drill and practice programs comprise almost 50 percent of the educational programs that are on the market (Hassett, 1984). As we shall see shortly, drill and practice programs can be valuable adjuncts to the curriculum, particularly if they are well designed. They can also be so poorly designed as to be little more than expensive "electronic workbooks."

Tutorial programs go one step beyond drill and practice in that they attempt to teach new concepts. Tutorial programs may be written in either a linear or branching format. When a branching format is chosen, the program writer has to anticipate where incorrect responses are likely to be made and provide remedial frames. As a result, these programs are more complex, take longer to develop, and are more expensive to develop than simple linear programs (Hassett, 1984; Saracho, 1982).

Problem-solving programs might be viewed as elaborated tutorials. Not only do they teach new material but they also provide opportunities for the learner to apply what has been learned. Some of the more interesting problem-solving programs employ simulations of real-life situations. Bower and Hilgard (1981) mention one such program. As the ruler of a mythical empire, students learn the consequences of applying economic principles to the functioning of a society by manipulating the empire's various resources. For every action made by the student, the computer provides a consequence to which the student must respond.

Dialogue programs perhaps most fully exploit the capabilities of the computer. Their goal is to mimic the instructional dialogue that often occurs between student and teacher. For example, a program in reading instruction would begin with the computer examining a student's file to determine current reading level and displaying appropriate reading exercises. The student reads the material, is presented with a set of questions, and types responses on the keyboard. The computer evaluates the responses and displays the results of the evaluation. If the student's responses are correct, the computer provides more difficult passages and questions. If the responses are incorrect, less difficult exercises are presented (Saracho, 1982). Bower and Hilgard (1981) briefly describe examples of dialogue programs that teach geography, cause-and-effect relationships, diagnosing defects in electronic equipment, and diagnosing faults in arithmetic reasoning.

Program Quality   If you like to think in terms of analogies, you might consider the program to be the brain of CAI. It is the one component that allows the computer to "come to life" and fulfill its potential. It is more important than how much information the computer can store, how many disk drives it has, how many columns of characters it can display on its screen, and so on. Thus, one should pay particular attention to the quality of available programs in deciding

Some forms of computer-assisted instruction feature use of typewriter keyboards linked with television screens that present questions, record what is typed, and supply answers. (Bohdan Hrynewych/Southern Light)

which computers to buy, or whether one should be purchased at all. This is doubly important since most opinions of program quality are strongly negative (for example, Hassett, 1984; Kindel & Benoit, 1984; Walker, 1983). Consider, for example, the following statement by James Hassett (1984):

> One advantage of presenting material on a computer rather than through a textbook or an overhead projector is that a computer can ask questions as it goes along. In theory, this means that instruction can be tailored to each student's knowledge and abilities in a way that will increase motivation, attention, and learning. In practice, much of the available software is poorly developed and deadly dull. (p. 24)

Program is key to success of CAI; most programs of poor quality

Hassett (1984) also notes that out of more than seven thousand educational programs, the Educational Products Information Exchange (EPIE) judged only about 25 percent as meeting minimum technical and instructional standards. Further, only 3 to 4 percent were judged to be excellent in quality.

Why are good programs in such short supply? Largely because their development requires a set of capabilities that are difficult to find in one person or among a small group of people. In general, an educational software developer should be familiar with computer languages, learning theory, instructional techniques, and principles of instructional development. "The best teachers, as a consequence, frequently are not the best software writers, and vice versa" (Kindel & Benoit, 1984).

The importance of integrating learning principles into the design of instructional programs has been discussed by Julie Vargas (1986). She finds that poor-quality programs often overlook such basic operant conditioning principles as offering maximum opportunities for active responding, providing immediate feedback, and shaping behavior. Some drill and practice programs, for example, incorporate into their lessons a variety of attention-getting features (such as familiar tunes, trains that puff across the screen, and animal characters that gesture or make facial expressions) in an attempt to keep the student interested and motivated. The more often these features are used, the more time students spend watching them rather than practicing skills. As a result, it takes longer for students to make basic cognitive skills automatic (such as adding or multiplying numbers or recognizing and spelling words). Even worse, the student may become distracted altogether from the goal of the drill if the motivational features are too numerous and compelling. In other instances, tutorials and simulations often violate the principles of shaping. Instead of breaking a lesson into small, easy-to-handle steps, providing prompts, and requiring mastery of each step before moving on to more complex responses, they typically throw students into a situation that requires learning by trial and error.

A basic principle of instructional development that authors of poor-quality programs frequently ignore (deliberately or otherwise) is the field test. Even though a program may have been revised several times by its author and reviewed by a panel of experts, its effectiveness as instructional material is still essentially unknown. The best way to identify and eliminate problems of step size, clarity, sequencing, feedback, attention getting, motivation, and so on, is to try the program out on a representative group of students. The principle of conducting a field test strikes people as so obviously necessary that they just assume it is a standard part of instructional software development. Unfortunately, this assumption is unfounded. EPIE researchers found that creators of 50 percent of a group of 163 popular programs skipped this step (Hassett, 1984).

To help you evaluate the quality of instructional software you may one day want to use in your classroom, an eight-point checklist devised by Julie Vargas is presented in Table 7.2.

Do Computers Aid Learning?   The answer to this question, like the answer to most of the questions posed in this book, is that it depends—in this case, largely on the nature of the learner. Jamison, Suppes, and Wells (1974) reviewed and summarized about ten years of CAI research. They found that CAI had a modest beneficial effect on the achievement of elementary school children, particularly disadvantaged students, when it was used as a supplement to regular classroom instruction. Similar beneficial effects for Spanish-speaking migrant children in grades three through six were reported by Olivia Saracho (1982).

Table 7.2   Eight Points to Consider When Choosing a CAI Program

1. Does the software require a high frequency of responding (as opposed to screens of material to read)? For tutorials and drills, how many problems does a student actually do in a 10-minute session?

2. Is the responding relevant to your goals? (Do students do what they are to learn)?

3. Do students have to respond to the critical parts of the problems?

4. Is most of the screen content necessary for the response, or does the program assume that students will learn content without having to respond overtly to it?

5. Does the screen ask students to discriminate between at least two possible responses?

6. Can students see their progress as they work with the program from day to day or session to session?

7. Are students mostly successful going through the program (as opposed to becoming frustrated)? Do they enjoy using the program?

8. For series, or lessons to be used repeatedly: Does the program adjust according to the performance level or progress of the student?

SOURCE: From "Instructional Design Flaws in Computer-Assisted Instruction" by J. S. Vargas, 1986, *Phi Delta Kappan, 67*, p. 744. Copyright 1986 by Phi Delta Kappa. Adapted by permission.

In a more recent review, Kulik, Bangert, and Williams (1983) summarized the results of fifty-one studies of CAI conducted using students in grades six through twelve. They also found a moderately positive effect. Students exposed to CAI scored on average at the 63rd percentile on their exams, whereas students exposed to conventional teaching scored on average at the 50th percentile. This effect remained fairly constant across program type (whether drill and practice, tutorial, or simulation, for instance), grade level (elementary or secondary), subject matter (math, science, or whatever), and type of implementation (as a supplement or a substitute). There were hints that CAI benefited disadvantaged and low-aptitude students somewhat more than it did more favored students and that CAI resulted in better retention of information after several months. In addition, CAI students expressed very favorable attitudes toward the computer and took less time to learn a given amount of material.

> CAI can supplement regular classroom instruction, especially for low achievers

These findings suggest that CAI, when properly designed, can effectively supplement a teacher's attempts to present, explain, apply, and reinforce knowledge and skills. The relatively high degree of structure inherent in CAI seems to be particularly helpful to low-achieving students. Whether CAI ever becomes more than a moderately effective supplement to classroom instruction will depend largely on the quality of the software. While predicting future developments is a risky business, you would probably do well to expect advances in software quality to be gradual.

Behavior Modification

Behavior modification: shape behavior by ignoring undesirable responses, reinforcing desirable responses

Although used in many ways, the term **behavior modification** basically refers to the use of operant conditioning techniques to—as the phrase indicates—modify behavior. Since those who use such techniques attempt to manage behavior by making rewards contingent upon certain actions, the term *contingency management* is also sometimes used.

After Skinner and his followers had perfected techniques of operant conditioning in modifying the behavior of animals, they concluded that similar techniques could be used with humans. We will briefly discuss several techniques in this section that teachers may use to strengthen or weaken specific behaviors. Techniques applied in education to strengthen behaviors include shaping, token economies, and contingency contracts. Techniques that aim to weaken behaviors include extinction and punishment.

Shaping   An explanation of shaping was provided earlier in the chapter (pp. 326–327). You may want to take a few minutes now to review those few paragraphs. Most attempts at shaping important classroom behaviors should include at least the following steps (Walker & Shea, 1980):

1. Select the target behavior.
2. Obtain reliable baseline data (that is, determine how often the target behavior occurs in the normal course of events).
3. Select potent reinforcers.
4. Reinforce successive approximations of the target behavior each time they occur.
5. Reinforce the newly established target behavior each time it occurs.
6. Reinforce the target behavior on a variable reinforcement schedule (pp. 327–329).

To illustrate how shaping might be used, imagine that you are a third-grade teacher (or a high school teacher) with a chronic problem: One of your students rarely completes more than a small percentage of the arithmetic (or algebra) problems on the worksheets you distribute in class, even though you know the student possesses the necessary skills.

To begin, you decide that a reasonable goal would be for the student to complete at least 85 percent of the problems on a given worksheet. Next, you review the student's work for the past several weeks and determine that, on average, only 25 percent of the problems per worksheet are being completed. Your third step is to select positive reinforcers that you know or suspect will work. Reinforcers come in a variety of forms. Most elementary school teachers typically use such things as stickers, verbal praise, smiles, hugs, and special classroom privileges (for example, feed the gerbil, clean the erasers). Occasionally, a teacher might hand out small pieces of candy like M&M's. High school teachers can use letter or numerical grades, public forms of recognition (like displaying high-quality work in the classroom or awarding certificates for achievement, effort, citizenship, and the like), material incentives (such as discarded classroom materials, board games, computer games, and books, so long as school policy and your financial resources allow it), and of course, privately given verbal praise. Since some adolescents get embarrassed at being singled out for attention, display the work of or give awards to several students at the same time (Emmer, Evertson, Sanford, Clements, & Worsham, 1984).

One popular shaping technique that has stood the test of time involves having students first list favorite activities on a card. Then they are told that they will be able to indulge in one of those activities for a stated period of time after they have completed a set of instructional objectives. This technique is sometimes called the **Premack principle** after the psychologist, David Premack (1959), who first proposed it. It is also called *Grandma's rule,* since it is a variation of a technique that grandmothers have used for hundreds of years ("Finish your peas and you can have dessert").

Once you have decided on a sequence of objectives and a method of reinforcement, you arc ready to shape the target behavior. For example, you can start by reinforcing the student for completing five problems (25 percent) each day for several consecutive days. Then you reinforce the student for completing five problems and starting a sixth. Then you reinforce the student for six completed problems, and so on. Once the student consistently completes at least 85 percent of the problems, you provide reinforcement after every fifth worksheet on the average (a variable ratio schedule).

Token Economies   A second technique used to strengthen behavior in the classroom, the **token economy,** was introduced first with people who had been hospitalized for emotional disturbances and then in special education classes. A token is something that has little or no inherent value but can be uscd to "purchase" things that do have inherent value. In society, money is our most ubiquitous token. Its value lies not in what it is made of, but in what it can purchase—a car, a house, or a college education. By the same token (if you will excuse the pun), students can accumulate check marks, gold stars, or happy faces and "cash them in" at some later date for any of the reinforcers already mentioned.

One reason for the advent of the token economy approach was the limited flexibility of more commonly used reinforcers. Candies and cookies, for instance, tend to lose their reinforcing value fairly quickly when supplied continuously. It is not always convenient to award free time or the opportunity to engage in a highly

---

Premack principle: required work first, then chosen reward

Token economy is a flexible reinforcement system

preferred activity immediately after a desired response. Social rewards may or may not be sufficiently reinforcing for some individuals. Tokens, however, can always be given immediately after a desirable behavior, can be awarded according to one of the four schedules mentioned earlier, and can be redeemed for reinforcers that have high reinforcing value.

The research literature on token economies must be viewed with some caution since much of it pertains to hospitalized psychiatric patients and classrooms for disturbed, delinquent, retarded, or learning disabled children. Because these studies have shown that token economies do result in more desirable forms of behavior, it is tempting to conclude that the same effect would occur in normal classrooms. While we don't know that for sure, the few studies that have examined the effect of token economies on the classroom learning of normal students have produced positive results (for example, Ayllon & Roberts, 1974; Campbell & Willis, 1979; McLaughlin, 1981).

Contingency contracting: reinforcement supplied after student completes mutually agreed-upon assignment

Contingency Contracting   A third technique teachers use to strengthen behavior is **contingency contracting.** A contingency contract is simply a more formal method of specifying desirable behaviors and consequent reinforcement. The contract, which can be written or verbal, is an agreement worked out by two people (teacher and student, parent and child, counselor and client) in which one person (student, child, client) agrees to behave in a mutually acceptable way, and the other person (teacher, parent, counselor) agrees to provide a mutually acceptable form of reinforcement. For example, a student may contract to sit quietly and work on an arithmetic assignment for thirty minutes. When the student is done, the teacher may reinforce the child with ten minutes of free time, a token, or a small toy. Contracts can be drawn up with all members of a class individually, with selected individual class members, or with the class as a whole. As with most contracts, provisions can be made for renegotiating the terms. The technique is flexible enough to incorporate the previously discussed techniques of token economies and shaping. It is possible, for example, to draw up a contract that provides tokens for successive approximations to some target behavior.

Extinction, Time-out, and Response Cost   The primary goal of behavior modification is to strengthen desired behaviors. Toward that end, techniques such as shaping, token economies, and contingency contracts are likely to be very useful. There will be times, however, when you have to weaken or eliminate undesired behaviors because they interfere with instruction and learning. For these occasions, you might consider some form of extinction. The most straightforward approach is to simply ignore the undesired response. If a pupil bids for your attention by clowning around, for instance, you may discourage repetition of that sort of behavior by ignoring it. It is possible, however, that classmates will not ignore the behavior, but laugh at it. Such response-strengthening reactions from

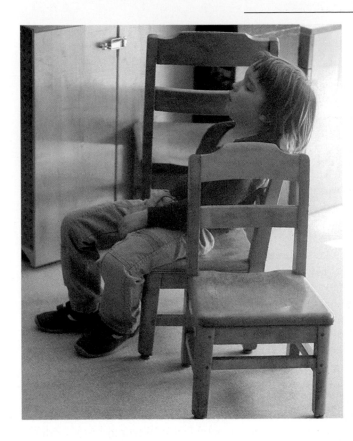

The time-out procedure recommended by behavior modification enthusiasts involves weakening an undesirable form of behavior (such as shoving on the playground) by temporarily removing positive reinforcement (by having the culprit remain in a corner of the classroom for five minutes while the rest of the class continues to enjoy another activity). (George E. Jones III/ Photo Researchers)

classmates will likely counteract your lack of reinforcement. Accordingly, you need to observe what happens when you try to extinguish behavior by not responding.

If other students are reinforcing a youngster's undesired behavior, you may want to apply the time-out procedure briefly discussed earlier (p. 324). Suppose a physically active third-grade boy seems unable to keep himself from shoving classmates during recess. If verbal requests, reminders, or warnings fail to limit shoving, the boy can be required to take a five-minute time-out period immediately after he shoves a classmate. He must sit alone in the classroom for that period of time while the rest of the class remains out on the playground. Time-out appears to be most effective when it is used with aggressive, group-oriented children who want the attention of the teacher and their peers (Walker & Shea, 1980). The rules for the procedure should be clearly explained, and after being sentenced to time-out—which should not last more than five minutes—a child should be given reinforcement for positive forms of behavior—for example, "Thank you for collecting all the playground balls so nicely, Tommy."

A third technique that is another form of type II punishment, and can be used with a token economy, is **response cost.** With this procedure, a certain amount of positive reinforcement (for example, 5 percent of previously earned tokens) is

Time-out works best with disruptive, aggressive children

withdrawn every time a child makes an undesired response. Anyone who has been caught exceeding the speed limit and been fined at least fifty dollars can probably attest to the power of response cost as a modifier of behavior.

Punishment   Punishment is one of the most popular behavior modification techniques, particularly when it takes the form of corporal punishment. It is also one of the most controversial.

The extent to which corporal punishment is used in American public schools was documented in a survey of 324 principals in 18 randomly selected states by Terry Rose (1984). Rose found that corporal punishment occurs in virtually every region of the country, in communities of every size, and at every grade level; it is administered by the majority of principals of either sex, and it is applied to male students more often than to female students.

One of the reasons that corporal punishment is controversial springs from a difference of opinion about the relationship between punishment and discipline. Many people feel that discipline—meaning the willingness to behave consistently in desired ways—is best developed through fear of punishment. The alternative point of view holds that discipline is the result of internal controls and is best learned through approaches that enhance self-esteem and encourage cooperation (Hyman & D'Alessandro, 1984).

A second source of controversy about corporal punishment is the extent and nature of the relevant research. There is a general lack of research-based evidence outside of the psychological laboratory that speaks directly to the effectiveness of punishment as a modifier of classroom behavior. What supportive evidence there is tends to come from isolated anecdotes and case histories (Rose, 1984). On the other hand, considerable laboratory evidence, collected from human and animal subjects, suggests that corporal punishment is likely to be ineffective in modifying behavior. The following reasons are typically cited.

> **Corporal punishment is used in most schools**

> **Punishment is likely to be ineffective because of temporary impact, side effects**

1. Mild punishment (which is the kind usually applied) does not permanently eliminate undesirable behaviors. At best, it suppresses them temporarily.
2. Punished behaviors may continue to occur when the punisher is not present.
3. Punishment may actually increase the strength of undesirable behavior. Many teachers assume that a public reprimand is aversive. But for some students, teacher and peer attention, regardless of the form it takes, is a positive reinforcer and thus serves to increase behaviors the teacher seeks to eliminate.
4. Punishment may produce undesirable emotional side effects. Just as a shocked rat comes to fear a Skinner box, punished children may perceive the teacher and the school as objects to fear and avoid. The result is truancy, tardiness, and high levels of anxiety, all of which impair ability to learn.
5. Punishers model a type of behavior (physical aggression) that they do not want students to exhibit.
6. To be effective, punishment must often be severe and must occur immediately

after an undesirable response. Legal and ethical restrictions do not allow severe punishment.

Should You Use Behavior Modification?   This may seem a strange question to ask given the number of pages we have just spent covering behavior modification methods. Obviously, we feel that the results of decades of research on these techniques justifies their use by teachers. Nevertheless, there are criticisms of behavior modification that are not adequately addressed by research findings and that you should carefully consider.

One criticism is that many students, including those in the primary grades, will eventually catch on to the fact that they get reinforced only when they do what the teacher wants them to do. Some may resent this and misbehave out of spite. Others may weigh the amount of effort required to earn a favorable comment or a privilege and decide the reinforcer isn't worth the trouble. Still others may develop a "What's in it for me?" attitude. That is, some students may come to think of learning as something they do only to earn an immediate reinforcer. The potential danger of using behavior modification over an extended period of time is that learning may come to an abrupt halt when no one is around to supply reinforcement. (This point is addressed by the next theory to be examined, social learning theory.)

A second major criticism is that behavior modification methods, because of their potential power, may lend themselves to inappropriate or even unethical uses. For example, teachers may shape students to be quiet and obedient because it makes their job easier, even though such behaviors do not always produce optimum conditions for learning.

In response to these criticisms, Skinner and other behavioral scientists argue that if we do not systematically use what we know about the effects of stimuli and consequences on behavior, we will leave things to chance. In an uncontrolled situation some fortunate individuals will have a favorable chain of experiences that will equip them with desirable attitudes and skills; others will suffer an unfortunate series of experiences that will lead to difficulties and disappointment. In a controlled situation it may be possible to arrange experiences so that almost everyone acquires desirable traits and abilities. What behavioral psychologists seem to be saying is that educators could be accused of being unethical for not making use of an effective learning tool. The challenge, of course, is to use it wisely.

Despite the popularity of operant conditioning among many American psychologists, a number of researchers beginning in the 1940s, were eager to study types of human behavior that could not be readily explained in terms of principles of operant conditioning. They shared the desire of Skinner and his followers to study behavior as objectively as possible, but they wanted to analyze human behavior in social settings—to see how children acquire acceptable forms of social behavior (or become socialized). Together, they contributed to the development of what came to be called social learning theory—the third and last behavioral theory to be discussed in this chapter.

Social Learning Theory (observational learning)

In essence, **social learning theory** attributes changes in behavior to observation and imitation. In one of the earliest reports of research and speculations of this type, Neal E. Miller and John Dollard introduced the key ideas reflected by the title of their book: *Social Learning and Imitation* (1941).

Miller and Dollard pointed out that it is not always essential for children to have their own spontaneous actions reinforced in order to acquire a new pattern of behavior (as Skinner was maintaining). They suggested that reinforcement and learning can occur in children when their behavior *matches* that of another person. A boy might be praised by his mother, for example, when imitating some form of desirable behavior he had seen displayed by an older brother. Albert Bandura and Richard Walters agreed with Miller and Dollard about the significance of imitation, but in *Social Learning and Personality Development* (1963) they argued that merely *observing* another person might be sufficient to lead to a learned response (which explains why social learning is also called **observational learning**). They pointed out that reinforcement is not always necessary. Eventually, Bandura emerged as the acknowledged spokesman for the social learning theory point of view, and he presented what is generally considered to be the definitive exposition of this theory in *Social Foundations of Thought and Action* (1986). According to Bandura (1986), the degree to which people observe and imitate a model's behavior can be explained in terms of four processes: attention, retention, production, and motivation.

> Observational learning occurs when one person imitates another

Processes in Observational Learning

Attention   Clearly, if learning is *observational*, paying attention to a model's behavior is a critical first step. If an individual chooses not to observe a model or observes in a half-hearted fashion, little can be expected in terms of retention, production, and motivation with regard to the modeled behavior. What factors, then, affect the willingness of a child to observe and mimic the behavior of a model? The most important factor seems to be the degree of similarity between the model and the observer. On the basis of an extensive review and analysis of previous research, Dale Schunk (1987) drew the following conclusions about the effect of observer-model similarity on observational learning:

1. When children are concerned about the appropriateness of behavior, or when they have self doubts about their capabilities, they are more likely to model a peer than an older child or adult.
2. Age similarity seems less important for the learning of skills, rules, and novel responses than competence of the model. When children question the competence of peers, they tend to model the behavior of adults.
3. Children learn academic skills from models of either sex, but they are more apt

to perform behaviors displayed by models who they believe are good examples of their sex role.

4. Children who have a negative self-concept, or who have had learning problems in the past, are more likely to imitate a peer who exhibits some initial learning difficulties and overcomes them (a coping model) than a peer who performs flawlessly (a mastery model). Improvements in self-concept and achievement are more likely to occur in response to coping models than to master models.

Retention   Once we have noticed a model's behavior with the intention of imitating it, we must encode that behavior in memory. Encoding may encompass just the observed behaviors or it may also include an explanation of why, how, and when something is done. In the case of behavior, the encoding may be visual (that is, mental pictures) and/or verbal. In the case of behavioral rules, the encoding will likely be in terms of verbal propositions. The benefit of encoding behavioral rules is the ability to generalize the response. Modeled behaviors may be unitary, terminal behaviors (for example, working on a problem until it is solved) or they may be components of a complex behavior (such as striking a golf ball with a golf club). Once the behavior has been modeled, the observer should have several opportunities to engage in overt and/or covert rehearsal.

> Processes of observational learning: attention, retention, production, motivation

Production   Bandura divides production into (a) selecting and organizing the response elements, (b) refining the response on the basis of informative feedback. The smooth operation of the production process is based on the assumption that the necessary response elements have been previously acquired (for example, gripping a golf club, addressing the ball, executing the swing, following through).

Motivation   Like Skinner, Bandura acknowledges the motivational value of reinforcement and incorporates it into his theory. Unlike Skinner, however, he thinks of reinforcement in broader terms. As a result, Bandura talks about direct reinforcement, vicarious reinforcement, and self-reinforcement.

As part of observational learning, *direct reinforcement* occurs when an individual watches a model perform, imitates that behavior, and is reinforced (or punished) by the model or some other individual. A primary grade pupil, for example, may be told by the teacher to observe how a fellow pupil cleans up his or her desk at the end of the day. If that behavior is imitated, the teacher will praise the child. **Vicarious reinforcement** refers to a situation where the observer anticipates receiving a reward for behaving in a given way, because someone else has been so rewarded. A pupil who observes that a classmate is praised by the teacher for completing an assignment promptly, may strive to work quickly and diligently on the next assignment in anticipation of receiving similar praise. **Self-reinforcement** refers to a situation where the individual strives to meet personal standards and does not depend on or care about the reactions of others. A high

> Imitation is strengthened through direct reinforcement, vicarious reinforcement, self-reinforcement

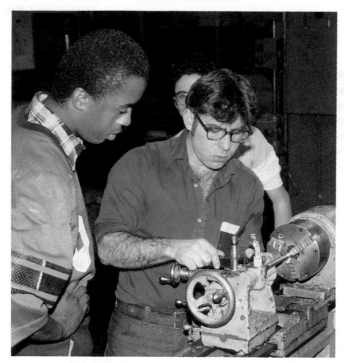

When teaching students a potentially dangerous skill, it is particularly important to remember the principles of observational learning noted by Bandura. First, make sure everyone is paying close attention as you demonstrate. Then, determine if retention has occurred by having each student give a "dry run" demonstration. Next, have students reproduce the correct procedures themselves. Finally, provide reinforcement for correct performance. (Jeff Dunn/The Picture Cube)

knocked over. Many of the subjects of his experiments may have observed Bobo dolls being hit (in television commercials, for instance) before they watched the model in the experimental situations. As Bandura himself has stressed, the behavior of models must be encoded in a person's memory before it will have an impact on behavior. When information is encoded in one's memory, though (as we shall see in the next chapter), it is typically associated with already stored information. Thus, the observation of a "new" kind of behavior is very likely to be incorporated with already stored information from observations of previous experiences of the same type. If you were asked to try to trace the source of a particular aspect of your own behavior, for instance, you might be able to report that is was probably due to imitation but be unable to specify the particular individuals or events that served as models. In most cases you might conclude that there were multiple models from whom you "abstracted" specific variations to add to previously imitated behavior.

Perhaps the safest conclusion to draw about the effectiveness of observational learning, therefore, is that it undeniably influences behavior in many ways even though it may not be possible to trace causes with precision.

Now that you are familiar with behavioral learning theories, it is time to examine Suggestions for Teaching derived from the experimental findings and principles that have just been discussed. Before examining the Suggestions, though, you may find it helpful to peruse the mid-chapter review presented below.

Mid-Chapter Review

Types of Behavioral Learning Theories

Classical conditioning (Pavlov): reflexive response associated with a new stimulus (original experiment: salivation in dogs)

Operant conditioning (Skinner): voluntary response strengthened by reinforcement (original experiment: rats in Skinner box)

Social learning theory (Bandura): ways observation and imitation of a model lead to learned behavior (original experiment: imitation of aggression by young children)

Basic Principles of Operant Conditioning

Positive reinforcement: response strengthened when followed by a positive consequence

Negative reinforcement: response strengthened when disagreeable stimulus removed

Punishment: response weakened when followed by a disagreeable stimulus

Time-out: response weakened when positive reinforcement is temporarily removed

Extinction: response weakened when it is ignored

Generalization: tendency for a conditioned response to be aroused by any stimulus similar to the original stimulus coupled with reinforcement

Discrimination: ability to distinguish between similar stimuli when one is reinforced, other is not

Shaping: movements in direction of preselected terminal behavior strengthened by reinforcement

Schedules of Reinforcement

Fixed interval: supply reinforcement after preselected intervals of time (leads to bursts of responses as end of interval approaches)

Variable interval: supply reinforcement after intervals of various lengths that correspond to a preselected average (leads to steady rate of response, limits extinction)

Fixed ratio: supply reinforcement after preselected number of responses (leads to series of rapid responses)

Variable ratio: supply reinforcement after different numbers of responses that correspond to a predetermined average (leads to high and steady rate of response, limits extinction)

Applications of Operant Conditioning

Programmed instruction: arrange material to be learned in small, sequential steps, provide feedback regarding correctness of responses

Linear program: single sequence of frames presented to all students

Branching program: main sequence of frames supplemented by shorter remedial sequences of frames to correct misunderstandings

Computer-assisted instruction: present programs through use of computers

Behavior modification: use of operant conditioning principles to shape desired classroom behaviors

Premack principle: strengthen desired behavior by using student's preferred behaviors as reinforcers

Social Learning Theory Processes

For observational learning to be effective, students should attend to significant features of the model's behavior, retain what they observe, produce the activity, experience satisfaction or reinforcement

SUGGESTIONS FOR TEACHING

Applying Behavioral Theories in the Classroom

1. Remain aware that behavior is the result of particular conditions.
2. Use reinforcement to strengthen behavior you want to encourage.
   a. When students are dealing with factual material, do your best to give feedback frequently, specifically, and quickly.
   b. When older students are dealing with complex and meaningful material, use delayed feedback.

c. Use several kinds of reinforcers so that each retains its effectiveness.

d. Enlist the aid of parents in reinforcing desirable behavior.

3. Use awareness of extinction to combat forgetting and to reduce the frequency of undesirable forms of behavior.

4. Be alert for generalization. When it occurs, use reinforcement (or lack of it) and explanations to bring about discrimination.

5. Take advantage of knowing about the impact of different reinforcement schedules to encourage persistent and permanent learning.

a. When students first attempt a new kind of learning, supply frequent reinforcement. Then supply rewards less often.

b. If you want to encourage periodic spurts of activity, use a fixed-interval schedule of reinforcement.

6. Consider using published programmed texts and microcomputer programs.

7. Use programmed approaches to teaching by describing terminal behavior, organizing what is to be learned, and providing feedback.

a. Describe the terminal behavior. That is, list exactly what you want students to learn after they have completed a given unit of study.

b. If appropriate, arrange the material to be learned into a series of steps or into an outline of points.

c. Provide feedback so that correct responses will be reinforced and students will become aware of and correct errors.

8. When students must struggle to concentrate on material that is not intrinsically interesting, use special forms of reinforcement to motivate them to persevere.

a. Select, with student assistance, a variety of reinforcers.

b. Establish, in consultation with individual students, an initial contract of work to be performed to earn a particular reward.

c. Once the initial reward is earned, establish a series of short contracts leading to frequent, immediate rewards.

9. To reduce the tendency for pupils to engage in undesirable forms of behavior, first try withholding reinforcement and calling attention to rewards that will follow completion of a task. If that does not work, consider the possibility of taking away a privilege or resorting to punishment.

10. Remember the basic processes of observational learning and make effective use of observation and imitation.

1. Remain aware that behavior is the result of particular conditions.

Skinner and his followers believe that it should be possible to specify the conditions leading to any act of behavior if observations are made systematically. That is why they argue that you have two choices: Either shape behavior systematically, or do it in a haphazard way. This argument does not take into account that in a classroom (as contrasted with a Skinner box) many causes of behavior may not be observable or traceable. Furthermore, it is clearly impossible for a classroom teacher to handle teaching routine and also minutely observe and analyze the behavior of thirty pupils. You might as well accept the fact, therefore, that quite often you are going to be a haphazard shaper of behavior. Nevertheless, there will be times when you and your pupils may benefit if you say to yourself, "Now, there *have* to be some causes for that behavior. Can I figure out what they are and do something about changing things for the better? Am I doing something that is leading to types of behavior that are making life difficult for some or all of us in the room?" When engaging in such speculations, keep in mind that reinforcement strengthens behavior. Check to see if you are inadvertently rewarding pupils for misbehavior (by calling attention to them, for example, or failing to reinforce those who engage in desirable forms of behavior).

Handbook Heading: Checking on Causes of Behavior

Examples

If you become aware that it takes a long time for your students to settle down at the beginning of a period and that you are reacting by addressing critical remarks specifically to those who dawdle the longest, ignore the dawdlers, and respond positively to those who are ready to get to work.

Assume that you give students thirty minutes to finish an assignment. To your dismay, few of them get to work until almost the end of the period, and you find that you have to do a lot of nagging to hold down gossip and horseplay. When you later analyze why this happened, you conclude that you actually encouraged the time-killing behavior because of the way you set up the lesson. The next time you give a similar assignment, tell the students that as soon as they complete it, they can have class time to work on homework, a term project, or the equivalent and that you will be available to give help or advice to those who want it.

2. Use reinforcement to strengthen behavior you want to encourage.

Four basic principles of conditioning are reinforcement, extinction, generalization, and discrimination. Awareness of each of these can be of value when you arrange learning experiences, but the most important and significant is reinforcement. Several techniques of teaching can be derived from knowledge of the impact of rewards on behavior. When you think about how and when to supply reinforcement, though, keep in mind that immediate feedback is not always desirable. When Skinner became convinced of the need for immediate feedback after each response, he had just completed his experiments with rats and pigeons and had listened to his daughter describe her experiences in elementary school. If a pigeon is to be induced to peck a disk or a third-grader is to learn to read, spell, or do math problems, immediate feedback for each response is desirable. But when older students are asked to deal with complex and meaningful material, occasional and/or delayed feedback may be preferable.

When feedback from a test is delayed by several days, for instance, learners perform better on a retest (by changing wrong answers to right ones) than when feedback is provided immediately after the first exam. This phenomenon is known as the *Delay-Retention Effect*. Presumably, wrong answers interfere with learning and recalling the correct answer provided by the immediate feedback (Surber & Anderson, 1975). Moreover, the Delay-Retention Effect is moderated by the confidence of the learner in the chosen answer. Feedback has minimal effects when learner confidence in a response is low, regardless of whether that response was right or wrong. In these cases, the learner may not sufficiently understand the question, the material, or both. Similarly, feedback has a negligible effect when confidence is high and the correct answer is chosen, since it merely confirms what the learner knows. Feedback has its greatest effect when confidence is high but the answer is incorrect. The natural response is to wonder why the answer was wrong and to use the feedback to reconcile the discrepancy (Kulhavy, 1977; Kulhavy, Yekovich, & Dyer, 1976).

As you decide how and when to supply feedback, therefore, take into account the kind of learning you are dealing with and the intellectual capacities of your students.

Delayed feedback may be more effective than immediate feedback

a. **When students are dealing with factual material, do your best to give feedback frequently, specifically, and quickly.**

Elementary grade students spend much of their time learning specific bits of information—the alphabet, how to spell *house,* the product of 6 and 6, and so on. Furthermore, they are at the concrete operations stage of cognitive development. For both these reasons, it usually makes sense to provide frequent and immediate feedback as often as possible when instructing elementary grade pupils. If a child misspells a word or supplies the wrong answer to an arithmetic problem it is important to call attention to the error as specifically and quickly as possible. When a pupil supplies a correct answer, it is just as important to reinforce the response so that it will be strengthened. Accordingly, you should strive to supply frequent, detailed, and immediate feedback when teaching most subjects to elementary school children or when teaching factual information to older students.

One of the basic principles of instruction derived from operant conditioning experiments is that teachers should provide elementary grade students with immediate reinforcement for correct responses. (Bob Daemmerich/The Image Works)

Examples

Handbook Heading:
Ways to Supply Specific
and Immediate
Feedback

After giving a problem, go over the correct answer immediately.

Have pupils team up and give each other feedback.

Have some pupils go to the board while others work at their desks.

Give a problem, and have those at their desks compare their answers to the one at the board that you identify as correct.

Meet with students in small groups so that you can give each pupil more individual feedback.

When you assign reading or give a lecture or demonstration, have a short self-corrected quiz or an informal question-and-answer session immediately afterward.

In your Handbook, you might note other techniques that you could use to supply specific and immediate reinforcement for correct responses.

b. When older students are dealing with complex and meaningful material, use delayed feedback.

The techniques listed above are intended to supply immediate feedback. Although quick knowledge of correctness is desirable in many types of learning, as noted earlier there may be advantages to supplying delayed feedback when students are dealing with meaningful material. To grasp why this may be true, think about how you feel when you are asked to answer a comprehensive essay question on an exam or to write a term paper. You are almost sure to come up with ideas over a period of time, and some of these may occur after you have handed in an assignment. Have you ever experienced the frustration of thinking of a terrific point just *after* leaving an examination room or dropping off a term paper? If so you can comprehend why immediate feedback is not always necessary or desirable. Sometimes students will think more about a subject and come up with their own "corrections" if there is an interval of time between writing an answer and receiving an evaluation of it. (Just after you finish an exam, do you examine your notes and the text to check on certain questions? If so, you are engaging in self-feedback, which might mean more to you than an answer supplied immediately by a teacher or program.) You should not feel that supplying corrections of student work several days or even weeks after it was completed will necessarily be ineffective. It may be more effective than had you responded immediately.

Examples

Hand back and discuss all exams. Even though students may have written their answers a week or more earlier, they will still be getting feedback when they look at the answer they wrote as you discuss it.

On written work, correct spelling and grammatical errors (if you can), and make brief favorable comments when a section is particularly well phrased or when an important point is emphasized. Make general favorable comments—if deserved —at the end of the paper.

Before handing back a term paper, essay exam, or the equivalent, you might ask students to jot down additional points they thought of after they completed the work. Or you might announce, "If you realized after you completed your work that you had made a mistake, make a note of it and mention how you would correct it if you were to do the assignment over again now. Then we can see if your evaluation agrees with mine." If you try out this idea, you might make some sort of allowance (perhaps in the form of some bonus points) for corrections made by students before they examine your corrections.

If you can think of other ways to supply delayed feedback, note them in your Handbook.

Handbook Heading:
Ways to Supply Delayed
Feedback

c. Use several kinds of reinforcers so that each retains its effectiveness.

In many learning situations the correct answer to a problem serves as the reinforcer. In other situations, however, the reinforcer will take the form of a comment or a smile from you, a mark or a grade or some other symbol of achievement, or the chance to engage in a desired activity. Some enthusiasts for behavior modification urge teachers to try to shape their own praising behavior by first making a record of the number of favorable comments, smiles, and so on, emitted before behavior control is instituted (called the baseline period by behavior modification specialists) and then engaging in a systematic effort to increase the frequency of each type of reinforcement.[2] It seems possible, however, that if you are too methodical about supplying reinforcement, students might think that you are insincere. If you try to increase your praising ratio from ten to twenty per period, for example, you might have to work extra hard at projecting enthusiasm and genuine appreciation. On the other hand, if you do not pay any attention to how you dispense reinforcement you may be inefficient or actually work against yourself. Perhaps the best policy is to think frequently about how and when you use different types of reinforcement but not to the point of keeping a tally of techniques.

Handbook Heading:
Ways to Supply Different
Types of Reinforcement

Examples

When a student gives a correct answer, makes a good point in class discussion, or does something helpful, say things like: "Good." "That's right." "Terrific." "Great." "Very interesting point." "I hadn't thought of that." "I really appreciated what you did." "That was a big help." (If you believe in being prepared you might list in your Handbook similar statements to use as verbal reinforcers. In addition to making such comments, smile and show that you are sincere.)

Walk over to stand near and smile encouragingly at a pupil who seems to be working industriously.

With younger pupils give a pat on the back after an especially good achievement.

Encourage students to keep a private chart of their achievements and to record their progress, perhaps with colored ink, gold stars, or the like. (Before you dismiss gold stars or the equivalent as infantile or silly, glance through several issues of a local newspaper and count the number of pictures or articles reporting awards that have been made. If the most improved junior varsity football player is given a 2-foot-high trophy, for example, why shouldn't a math student get a similar—though less impressive—symbol of achievement.)

2. If this idea sounds appealing to you, you will find instructions and sample forms to use on pages 485–590 of *Teaching: A Course in Applied Psychology* (1971) by Becker, Englemann, and Thomas.

Announce in advance how many points a particular assignment will count toward a final grade. Award bonus points for work completed ahead of time or for extra work.

d. Enlist the aid of parents in reinforcing desirable behaviors.

Although you control the classroom environment while students are in school, this accounts for only about half of their waking hours. Consequently, parents might supplement your efforts at shaping behavior. Several investigations of home-based reinforcement programs have shown improved social and academic behaviors in special education and mainstream classes from kindergarten through high school (Barth, 1979). If you have the opportunity to talk to parents in personal conferences or at PTA meetings, give them some specific instruction in ways to supply reinforcement.

3. Use awareness of extinction to reduce the frequency of undesirable forms of behavior.

When dealing with nonacademic forms of behavior, you will sometimes want to use knowledge of extinction to reduce the frequency of minor misconduct. The basic rule is to consistently ignore behavior that you would prefer to have weakened or disappear. It is not always possible or desirable to do so of course. Sometimes your lack of response will be offset by positive responses from students, and some students may get the idea that they can exhibit normally prohibited behaviors if peers who do the same receive no negative consequences.

Examples

If a student experiments with knocking his books off his desk in an effort to arouse a response, pay no attention and continue with the lesson.

If a student says something transparently provocative in class discussion, don't comment, and immediately call on someone else.

4. Be alert for generalization. When it occurs, use reinforcement (or lack of it) and explanations to bring about discrimination.

Regardless of the grade level or subject you teach, your students will tend to apply what they learn in one situation to what they perceive to be similar situations. Sometimes this is desirable. In other cases, however, it will cause problems. When you become aware that pupils are generalizing in ways that lead to errors or misconceptions, encourage them to discriminate by using selective reinforcement or by calling their attention to differences.

Examples

When a kindergartner says, "I saw two gooses," explain that even though it seems like the logical way to say it, the word for more than one goose is *geese*.

If a high school language student conjugates an irregular verb by applying rules for regular verbs, point out that the verb is irregular and should simply be memorized.

5. Take advantage of knowing about the impact of different reinforcement schedules to encourage persistent and permanent learning.
   a. When students first attempt a new kind of learning, supply frequent reinforcement. Then supply rewards less often.

Keep in mind the impact of different schedules of reinforcement by taking into account Skinner's experiments with rats and pigeons. When Skinner wanted to encourage rats and pigeons to learn bar pressing and disk pecking, he first reinforced every response. While this was the most efficient way to train the animals initially, the behavior extinguished rapidly as soon as reinforcement stopped. After the animals had learned the basic skill, they were more likely to continue to respond at a steady rate when put on a fixed ratio, variable ratio, or variable interval schedule of reinforcement. You can use the same techniques of reinforcement in your classroom.

Examples

Handbook Heading:
Ways to Use Schedules
of Reinforcement

When introducing new material, give a point for every correct response. Then specify that a point can be earned only if five questions are answered correctly.

When students first try a new skill or type of learning, praise almost any genuine attempt, even though it may be inept. Then as they become more skillful, reserve your praise only for especially good performances.

Avoid a set pattern of commenting on student work.

Make favorable remarks at unpredictable intervals.

If students in physical education catch on that the instructor walks methodically up and down checking to see if everyone is doing calisthenics, they may do their pushups (or whatever) only when they know they are being watched. To encourage steady exercise, it would be better to follow an unpredictable pattern when observing this kind of behavior.

If you can think of other ways to use fixed-ratio or variable-interval schedules of reinforcement, note them in your Handbook.

b. If you want to encourage periodic spurts of activity, use a fixed-interval schedule of reinforcement.

Occasionally, you will want to encourage students to engage in spurts of activity, since steady output might be too demanding or fatiguing. In such cases, supply reinforcement at specified periods of time.

Examples

Schedule a quiz every Wednesday.

When students are engaging in strenuous or concentrated activity, circulate and provide praise and encouragement by following a set pattern that will bring you in contact with each student at predictable intervals.

6. Consider using published programmed texts and microcomputer programs.

Over the past twenty years, hundreds of programmed texts have been published. They cover all sorts of subjects, and they vary considerably in quality. You can consult several journals to discover what is available: *The Journal of Programmed Instruction, Programmed Instruction,* and *Programmed Instructional Materials.*

You should realize, however, that even if you find a program that seems appropriate for your curriculum, that is rated as adequate, and that your school district can afford, you still face complications. It has been found, for example, that programs perfected on one group of children may not succeed with another group. This sometimes occurs because the curriculum in the standardization school was atypical in subtle ways and prepared the children for some of the questions. Children who are products of a different curriculum may be unable to answer these questions, and if they get off the track just once or twice, the entire program may be ineffective.

You may also be faced with the task of holding down competition so that pupils don't race to see who can finish first. It seems logical to assume that children who skim through a program are less likely to absorb it thoroughly than those who take their time. You may want to disguise, as much as possible, the rate at which individual students are learning.

The fact that pupils finish the program at different times—which Skinner sees as an *advantage* of machine instruction—creates still another problem. Unless you are able to assign individual students one program after another, which is unlikely, you will be faced with the task of organizing activities for an ever-increasing number of pupils. Finding ways to occupy the time of students who

The results of many operant conditioning experiments lead to the conclusion that the frequency of reinforcement is of greater significance than the amount of reinforcement. Therefore, having students work on a series of brief contracts leading to frequent payoffs provided immediately after the task is completed is preferable to having them work toward a delayed, king-size award.

Examples

Ask students to learn how to spell a list of fifty tough words by rewarding themselves after they have mastered batches of five or ten.

Have students accumulate points toward a final grade by completing an exam or project every week, instead of scheduling one or two comprehensive exams and a blockbuster term paper.

9. To reduce the tendency of pupils to engage in undesirable forms of behavior, first try withholding reinforcement and calling attention to rewards that will follow completion of a task. If that does not work, consider the possibility of taking away a privilege or resorting to punishment.

Students often engage in types of behavior that are disruptive in one way or another. Theoretically, such behavior will tend to extinguish if it is not reinforced. Therefore, as noted by Suggestion 3, your first reaction might be to ignore it. Unfortunately, however, you will not be the only reinforcing agent in the classroom. As noted earlier, you may ignore a wisecrack, but classmates sitting around the culprit may respond enthusiastically and strengthen the tendency to wisecrack. Furthermore, in some cases you simply cannot ignore behavior. If a pupil is on the verge of destroying school property or injuring a classmate, you must respond immediately.

You may need to follow a sequence something like this when confronted by undesirable but relatively minor misbehavior, such as two boys fooling around when assigned to work together on a chemistry experiment.

First, ignore the behavior.

Second, remind the class that those who finish the experiment early earn five bonus points and will be allowed to see a film.

Third, approach the boys and tell them (privately and nicely) that they are disturbing others and making life difficult for themselves because if they do not complete the experiment in the allotted time, they will have to make it up at some other time.

Fourth, resort to punishment by informing the boys (in a firm but not nasty way) that they must leave the classroom immediately and report to the vice principal to be assigned to a study hall for the rest of the class period. Tell them they will

Handbook Heading:
Ways to Use Behavior
Modification to
Maintain Control

have to complete the experiment when the rest of the class has free experiment time.

Finish by pointing out that once the work is made up, they will be all caught up and in a good position to do above average work the rest of the period.

This sequence is based on studies (for example, Hall, Axelrod, Foundopoulos, Shellman, Campbell, & Cranston, 1971) leading to the conclusion that punishment is most effective when it occurs immediately after a response, cannot be avoided, is as intense as seems necessary, and provides the individual with an alternative and desirable response.

Constructive classroom control will be discussed more completely in Chapter 13, but in this outline of applications of behavioral theory it is appropriate to call attention once again to a few undesirable by-products of punishment. Even though punishment may be effective in inhibiting student behavior, there is the risk that the individual will come to associate anxiety, shame, and anger aroused by the act with the punisher and the situation. A student may come to fear and hate a teacher, a classroom, a subject of study, or the whole idea of school, particularly if punishment is excessively harsh, protracted, or embarrassing. This may be especially true if the punishment is perceived as unfair or if there is no escape from it.

You are reminded that behavioral psychologists make a distinction between punishment and negative reinforcement. Skinner describes punishment as the use of an aversive stimulus intended to inhibit the response that preceded it. Negative reinforcement, on the other hand, is designed to strengthen an escape response. The sequence outlined above ended with punishment—the boys were required to endure the aversive consequences of being banished to a study hall. Instead of resorting to punishment in a situation, suppose you say, "If you don't stop that fooling around and finish that experiment, I'll give you both an F for this unit." That would be an application of negative reinforcement because if the boys responded as planned they would do the experiment not to gain a reward but to avoid negative consequences.

Negative reinforcement is sometimes effective, but it may be risky because it is not always possible to predict the kind of escape behavior that will be used. In this case, your intention would be that the boys would try to escape the low grade by working diligently on the experiment. If the boys resented the threat, though, or were fooling around because they did not know how to get started on the experiment, they might literally escape from the whole situation by not coming to class for several days. Consequently, it is preferable to use positive reinforcement and stress the rewards that will follow desired activities.

10. Remember the basic processes of observational learning and make effective use of observation and imitation.

368 Chapter 7 / Behavioral Learning Theories

Students learn many skills and forms of classroom behavior by observing and imitating others. You can enhance learning of skills and promote desirable kinds of behavior if you take into account the four basic processes of observational learning: attention, retention, production, motivation. If you plan to demonstrate the correct way to perform some skill or process, first make sure you have the attention of everyone in the class. (Techniques for securing attention will be discussed in the analysis of information processing in Chapter 8.) Then, after explaining what you are going to do (perhaps noting particular points students should look for), demonstrate. Immediately after you demonstrate, have all the students in the class try out the new skill to foster retention. Or, for complex skills, have them write down the steps to follow before they try the activity on their own. Finally, arrange for all the students to get feedback and experience satisfaction and/or reinforcement immediately after they imitate your behavior by proving to themselves that they can carry out the activity on their own.

Examples

Show primary grade pupils how to solve multiplication problems by first placing a large, colorful poster on a bulletin board with a diagram of the process. Explain the diagram and then demonstrate how to solve some simple problems. As soon as you finish, hand out a worksheet containing several simple problems similar to those you just demonstrated. Have students work on the problems for a specified period of time, and then secure their attention once again and demonstrate on the board the correct procedure for solving each problem. Have students correct their own papers as you demonstrate, point out that they now know how to do multiplication problems, and praise them for learning the skill so rapidly.

In a high school business class, follow a similar procedure when showing students how to set up a word processor to type a form letter. Make sure everyone is paying attention. Demonstrate the correct procedure. Have students write down the steps they should follow in order to imitate your actions. Have them study the steps before setting up their own word processor. Have them reproduce the letter. Provide reinforcement to supplement their own satisfaction in having completed the task successfully.

Select low-achieving students who have mastered a skill to demonstrate the skill to other low-achieving students.

Pair a socially competent student with a less socially competent classmate to work on a task.

A final point to remember about observational learning is that, in the lower grades in particular, you will be an admired model your students will be inclined to imitate. If you are well-organized and businesslike, but also thoughtful and considerate, your pupils may act that way themselves.

Suggestions for Further Study

B. F. Skinner on B. F. Skinner

In three highly readable volumes, B. F. Skinner describes his interests, aspirations, triumphs, and failures; the people and events that led him into psychology; and the forces that led him to devise operant conditioning. *Particulars of My Life* (1976) covers the period from early childhood through the early postcollege years. Skinner describes his ill-fated aspiration as a college student to be a writer and his eventual interest in psychology. In *The Shaping of a Behaviorist* (1979) Skinner chronicles his years as a graduate student at Harvard University, his first faculty position at the University of Minnesota, and his subsequent position as chairman of the psychology department of Indiana University. *A Matter of Consequences* (1983) picks up with Harvard's invitation to join its psychology faculty just after World War II.

B. F. Skinner and Operant Conditioning

A highly readable summary and critical analysis of Skinner's brand of operant conditioning can be found in Robert D. Nye's (1979) *What Is B. F. Skinner Really Saying?* According to Nye, "Two major thoughts accompanied the writing of this book: a growing sense of the importance of Skinner's work and the awareness that his ideas are often misjudged." Consequently, Nye attempts to provide "a clear, concise picture of what Skinner has said in various writings . . . so that individuals can decide for themselves whether or not the Skinnerian approach has value." In nine well-written chapters, Nye provides a brief biography of Skinner, describes the basic concepts of operant conditioning, analyzes the misunderstandings that have arisen about operant conditioning, and compares operant conditioning with such alternative theoretical systems as Sigmund Freud's psychoanalysis and Carl Rogers' humanism.

The Technology of Teaching

The Technology of Teaching (1968) is B. F. Skinner's most concise and application-oriented discussion of operant conditioning techniques related to pedagogy. There are several sections of this book you might want to sample. For an overview of programmed learning and teaching machines, see Chapter 3. In Chapter 5, "Why Teachers Fail," Skinner describes what he perceives to be common mistakes made by many teachers. In Chapter 8, "The Creative Student," he discusses determinism and the issue of personal freedom. If you read any of these chapters, or another of your choice, you might record your reactions to general or specific arguments in the book.

Skinner's Utopia

In *Walden Two* (1948) B. F. Skinner describes his conception of a utopia based on the application of science to human behavior. To get the full impact of the novel and of Skinner's ideas, you should read the entire book. (As a matter of fact, it may be hard to put down once you begin it.) However, if you cannot read the whole thing at this time, Chapters 12 through 17—in which the approach to child rearing and education at Walden Two is described—may be of special interest to you as a future teacher. Read from page 95 to page 148 to get a good sample of life in Skinner's utopia. Then record your reactions perhaps including an opinion as to whether you might like to join a society based on the ideas of Walden Two. You might also take a stab at sketching out a utopia of your own—perhaps you will be able to improve on Skinner's version.

Trying a Program Yourself

A good way to find out about a pedagogical technique is to try it yourself—from the student point of view. To clarify your thoughts about programmed instruction, record your reactions to any programmed books, units, or courses you have taken. If you have never been exposed to this technique, seek out a programmed unit and work through it. To find a suitable program, ask your instructor for assistance, check with classmates who have used one in the past, browse through a college bookstore, or consult with the person in charge of the curriculum and materials section of the library.

Computer-Assisted Instruction

If and when you find yourself in a position to employ computer-assisted instruction, take the time and effort to identify well-designed programs. Two publications can help you in this effort. *EPIEgram Materials* is published by the Educational Products Information Exchange, a nonprofit organization. In addition to evaluating CAI programs, this magazine critically examines textbooks, filmstrips, and programmed materials. If your library does not subscribe to *EPIEgram Materials,* you can write to the EPIE Institute, P.O. Box 839, Water Mill, NY 11976, and enter your own subscription. *Software Reports,* which is published by Trade Service Corporation, 10096 Torreyana Road, San Diego, CA 92121, provides program evaluations in twenty subject areas that cover every grade level. Each review includes a summary of the program's features, a description of the program, a graded evaluation, and comments made by the evaluator.

Behavior Modification

If the possibilities of behavior modification seem attractive, you may wish to examine issues of the journals *Behavior Modification, Behavior Research and Therapy, Child Behavior Therapy,* and the *Journal of Applied Behavior Analysis.* If you browse through the education and psychology sections of your college bookstore, you are likely to find a number of books on behavior modification. Or you might look for these titles in the library: *Classroom Management for Elementary Teachers* (1984) by Carolyn Evertson, Edmund Emmer, Barbara Clements, Julie Sanford, and Murray Worsham; *Classroom Management for Secondary Teachers*

(1984) by Edmund Emmer, Carolyn Evertson, Julie Sanford, Barbara Clements, and Murray Worsham; *Achieving Educational Excellence: Using Behavioral Strategies* (1986) by Beth Sulzer-Azaroff and G. Roy Mayer; and *Making It Till Friday: A Guide to Successful Classroom Management* (3rd ed., 1988) by James P. Long, Virginia H. Frye, and Elizabeth W. Long.

Summary

1. Behavioral theories of learning focus on how the responses that people learn to make are influenced by the stimuli that precede and/or follow the response.
2. An early behavioral theory, classical conditioning, was devised by Ivan Pavlov. This theory explains how animals and human beings learn to respond to a new, introduced stimulus in the same way they respond to some naturally occurring stimulus, such as food.
3. Four basic learning principles that derive from Pavlov's work are reinforcement, extinction, generalization, and discrimination.
4. A second behavioral theory, operant conditioning, was devised by B. F. Skinner. This theory explains how animals and people learn new behaviors as a result of the consequences that follow a response.
5. Basic learning principles that derive from Skinner's work are positive reinforcement, negative reinforcement, punishment, time-out, extinction, spontaneous recovery, generalization, and discrimination.
6. Complex behaviors can be learned by reinforcing closer approximations to the final behavior and ignoring nonapproximate behaviors, a process called shaping.
7. Once a new behavior is well established, it can be maintained at that level by supplying reinforcement on an intermittent schedule. The four basic schedules are fixed interval, variable interval, fixed ratio, and variable ratio.
8. One of the first educational applications of operant conditioning principles was programmed instruction. Programmed instruction involves presenting written material in small steps according to a predetermined sequence, prompting the correct response, and presenting positive reinforcement in the form of knowledge of results.
9. Linear programs, the type favored by Skinner, contain only one sequence of frames leading to the terminal behavior. They use extremely small steps and heavy prompting, since they make no provision for incorrect responses.
10. Branching programs use larger steps and less prompting. If an incorrect response to a frame occurs, the learner is routed through a "branch"—a remedial set of frames—before proceeding further.
11. Programmed instruction is likely to be an effective supplement to regular classroom instruction when the programs are well designed and supplied to low-achieving students.
12. A second application of operant conditioning principles is computer-

assisted instruction (CAI). CAI involves presenting programmed materials on a computer screen.

13. The main types of CAI programs are drill-and-practice, tutorial, problem solving, and dialogue.

14. The most important part of CAI is the program. Independent evaluations of CAI programs find that only 3 to 4 percent are of excellent quality.

15. Computer-assisted instruction can be an effective supplement to regular classroom instruction, particularly for low-achieving students.

16. A third application of operant conditioning principles is behavior modification. The goal of behavior modification is to help students learn desirable behaviors by ignoring or punishing undesired behaviors and reinforcing desired ones. Techniques for achieving this goal include shaping, token economies, contingency contracts, extinction, and punishment.

17. A third behavioral theory, social learning theory, was devised largely by Albert Bandura. This theory explains how individuals learn by observing a model (who may or may not be reinforced for the behavior involved) and imitating the model's behavior.

18. The processes involved in social learning (also called observational learning) are attention, retention, production, and motivation (reinforcement). The reinforcement can come from someone else (direct), from anticipating that one will be treated as the model was (vicarious), or from meeting personal standards (self-reinforcement).

19. Research suggests that many social behaviors, such as aggression, may be learned by imitation of a model. Many academic-related behaviors, such as persistence, self-confidence, and cognitive skills, can also be learned by observing and imitating a model.

Key Terms

classical conditioning *(319)*
operant conditioning *(320)*
positive reinforcement *(322)*
negative reinforcement *(323)*
punishment *(324)*
time-out *(324)*
extinction *(324)*
spontaneous recovery *(325)*
generalization *(325)*
discrimination *(326)*
shaping *(326)*
fixed interval schedule *(327)*
variable interval schedule *(328)*
fixed ratio schedule *(328)*
variable ratio schedule *(328)*

programmed instruction *(331)*
linear program *(331)*
branching program *(331)*
frames *(335)*
computer-assisted
  instruction *(335)*
behavior modification *(340)*
Premack principle *(341)*
token economy *(341)*
contingency contracting *(342)*
response cost *(343)*
social learning theory *(346)*
observational learning *(346)*
vicarious reinforcement *(347)*
self-reinforcement *(347)*

Discussion Questions

1. The theory of operant conditioning holds that we learn to respond or not respond to certain stimuli because our responses are followed by positive or negative consequences. How many of your own behaviors can you explain in this fashion? Why, for example, are you reading this book and answering these questions?

2. Many educators have a negative attitude about operant conditioning because they feel it presents a cold, dehumanizing picture of human learning. That is, because it portrays learning as governed by the consequences that follow responses, it ignores the role of such things as free will, motives, and creativity. Did you feel this way as you read through the chapter? Do you think positive attributes of operant conditioning balance out possible negative aspects of the theory?

3. Skinner has argued that society too frequently uses aversive means to shape desired behavior (particularly punishment) rather than the more effective positive reinforcement. As you think about how your behavior has been shaped by your parents, teachers, friends, supervisors at work, law enforcement officials, and so on, would you agree or disagree with Skinner's observation? Can you think of some possible reasons why we tend to use punishment more frequently than positive reinforcement?

4. Although computers and computer-assisted instruction have become widespread in public school classrooms, the number of well-designed instructional programs is disappointingly low. One way to encourage the development of better-quality programs is to be an informed consumer. How can you keep yourself, colleagues, and parents informed about instructional programs that do and do not deserve consumer support? Are there any other things you can do to encourage the development of effective programs?

5. Can you recall a teacher who you admired so much that you imitated some aspects of his or her behavior (if not immediately, then some time later)? What was it about this teacher that caused you to behave in the same way? How might you have the same effect on your students?

chapter 8

INFORMATION PROCESSING THEORY

KEY POINTS

The Information Processing View of Learning

Information processing: how humans attend to, recognize, transform, store, retrieve information

A Model of Information Processing

Sensory register: stimuli held briefly for possible processing

Recognition: noting key features and relating them to stored information

Attention: focusing on a portion of currently available information

Information in long-term memory influences what we attend to

Short-term memory: about seven bits of information held for about twenty seconds

Maintenance rehearsal: hold information for immediate use

Elaborative rehearsal: use stored information to aid learning

Organizing material reduces numbers of chunks, provides retrieval cues

Meaningfulness effective because new information is associated with stored knowledge

Long-term memory: permanent storehouse of unlimited capacity

Information in long-term memory organized as schemata

Metacognition

Metacognition: knowledge of how we think

Insight into one's learning processes improves with age

Helping Students Become Strategic Learners

Strategy: plan to achieve a long-term goal

Tactic: specific technique that helps achieve long-term goal

Rote rehearsal not a very effective memory tactic

Acronym: word made from first letters of items to be learned

Acrostic: sentence made up of words derived from first letters of items to be learned

Pegword: associate memory pegs with items to be learned

Loci method: visualize items to be learned stored in specific locations

Keyword method: visually link pronunciation of foreign word to English translation

Mnemonic devices organize, provide retrieval cues, can be acquired

Taking notes and reviewing notes aids retention and comprehension

Learning strategy components: metacognition, analyze, plan, implement, monitor, modify

Suggestions for Teaching

Unpredictable changes in environment usually command attention

Attention span can be increased with practice

Distributed practice: short study periods spaced out over time

Serial position effect: tendency to remember items at beginning and end of a long list

Concrete analogies can make abstract information meaningful

In discussing the organization of this part, we distinguished between behavioral and cognitive theories. We noted that behavioral theories, especially operant conditioning, emphasize the role of external factors in learning. Behavioral psychologists focus on the nature of a stimulus to which a student is exposed, the response that the student makes, and the consequences that follow the response. They see no reason to speculate about what takes place in the student's mind before and after a response. The extensive Suggestions for Teaching presented at the end of the chapter on behavioral learning theories serve as evidence that conclusions and principles based on analyses of external stimuli, observable responses, and observable consequences can be of considerable value to teachers.

Cognitive psychologists, however, are convinced that it is possible to study nonobservable behavior, such as thought processes, in a scientific manner. Some cognitive psychologists focus on meaningful learning and problem solving; their work is discussed in the next chapter. Many cognitive psychologists are especially interested in an area of study known as **information processing theory**, which seeks to understand how people acquire new information, how they store information and recalled it from memory, and how what they already know guides and determines what and how they will learn.

Bits and pieces of information processing theory and research first trickled into the psychological literature during the mid-1950s. That trickle soon became a flood. Today, information processing theory is a major force in the psychology of learning and can be of great value to teachers in enhancing student learning. Given the prominence of this view of learning, it will be useful to spend a little time tracing its roots.

The Origins of Information Processing Theory

Whenever a particular point of view attains rapid prominence in a field of study, it is usually due, at least in part, to a growing disenchantment with the current view of things. In psychology during the 1950s and 1960s, this current view seemed taken up with studying the conditions under which rats learned to run mazes or people learned lists of nonsense syllables (a consonant-vowel-consonant arrangement of three letters). Many psychologists came to believe that such an approach would not help explain how people learn to perform more complex tasks. At least three factors contributed to this disenchantment.

The first was the experience of many psychologists who were asked during World War II to help train large numbers of individuals in the use, maintenance, and repair of complex equipment and weapons. As psychologists studied how an aircraft pilot divided his attention among a plane's controls, instructions from a radio, detecting blips on a radar screen, interpreting various instrument readings, and deciding when to fire on an enemy, they began to think of human beings as complex information transmitters, receivers, and decision makers (Miller, 1983).

A second factor was the influence of communications research on psychologists during and after World War II. Engineers working on communication systems (telephone, telegraph, radio) were interested in such things as how many messages could pass through a system in a given period, whether two messages could be communicated simultaneously with no loss of information, and how stimuli could be converted from one form into another. Psychologists began to use these concepts as metaphors for human thought (Miller, 1983; Siegler, 1983).

The third factor behind the rise of information processing theory was the development of computers and the field of computer science. The operation of computers suggested to psychologists that a human being might also be seen as a symbol-manipulating system. The main parts of the system are the memory stores where information is held and the processes that govern how information is coded, stored, retrieved, and manipulated (Miller, 1983).

In sum, information processing theory became a popular approach to the study of learning because the concepts and questions it adopted from other fields provided psychologists with a framework for investigating the role of a variable that behaviorism had ignored—the nature of the learner. Instead of being viewed as relatively passive organisms that respond in fairly predictable ways to environmental stimuli, learners were now seen as highly active interpreters and manipulators of environmental stimuli. The stage was set for psychology to study learning from a broader and more complicated perspective—namely, as an *interaction* between the learner and the environment.

The Information Processing View of Learning

Information processing theory rests on a set of assumptions of which three are worth noting. First, information is processed in steps or stages. The major steps typically include attending to a stimulus, recognizing it, transforming it into some type of mental representation, comparing it with information already stored in memory, assigning meaning to it, and acting on it in some fashion (Miller, 1983). At an early processing stage, human beings encode information (represent it in thought) in somewhat superficial ways (as when they represent sights and sounds as sights and sounds) and at later stages in more meaningful ways (as when they grasp the gist of an idea or its relationship to other ideas). Second, there are limits on how much information can be processed at each stage. Although the absolute amount of information human beings can learn appears to be limitless, it must be acquired gradually. Third, the human information processing system is interactive. Information already stored in memory influences and is influenced by perception and attention. We see what our prior experiences direct us to see and, in turn, what we see affects what we know.

> Information processing: how humans attend to, recognize, transform, store, retrieve information

Thus, according to the information processing view, learning results from an interaction between an environmental stimulus (the *information* that is to be learned) and a learner (the one who *processes*, or transforms, the information). What an information processing psychologist wants to know, for instance, is what goes on in a student's mind as a teacher demonstrates how to calculate the area of a triangle or while the student reads twenty pages of a social studies text or responds to test questions.

To deal effectively with such questions we must specify more clearly what we mean by the terms *learner* and *environmental stimulus*. One useful approach has been suggested by John Bransford (1979). He describes four general factors that interact with each other to affect the learning process. The first two concern the learner; the last two concern the task environment.

1. The first factor, *learner characteristics*, pertains to the broad, fairly stable attributes that a learner brings to a task—attributes like prior knowledge, attitudes, motives, and cognitive style. Some students may know quite a bit about a sub-

ject being studied while others may know very little. Some may show a strong interest in a topic while others would rather study something else. Some may approach tasks impulsively and superficially while others may tackle the same tasks in a deliberate, analytical style.

2. The second factor, *learner activities*, concerns the kind of mental operations learners employ when presented with a task. Students may underline key points while they read, take notes during a lecture, rehearse information, or generate visual images of things they want to remember. Which of these activities students engage in, and to what extent, depends largely on the last two factors.

3. Factor three involves the *nature of the learning material*. The vast majority of classroom materials that students learn from are written and linguistic in nature. Written materials may be long or short, filled with concrete ideas or abstract ones, and organized logically or illogically, just to name a few possibilities.

4. The fourth factor, *nature of the criterion*, deals with the manner in which the learner is expected to demonstrate his or her competence. Typically, students take written exams, although they may also be asked to give an oral presentation (for example, to make a speech or participate in a debate) or to produce a complex motor response (such as typing fifty words per minute). An exam can ask students to recall or recognize information, to apply knowledge, or to demonstrate any of several other forms of knowledge. Each outcome places different demands on a learner.

When learning is viewed this way, as an interaction among the above four factors, we are less apt to classify students with such simplistic and useless labels as "lazy" or "slow." Some students may not perform well because they lack or have an inadequate understanding of prerequisite knowledge. Other students may lack useful study skills. Still others may perform very well on tests that measure verbatim knowledge but poorly on tests that require analysis and synthesis of different ideas.

The first two factors—learner characteristics and learner activities—tend to be the focal point of information processing theory and research. Unlike operant conditioning theory or social learning theory, information processing is not associated with a particular individual or a single theoretical formulation. Rather, it encompasses a large number of research studies in such areas as perception, attention, memory, comprehension, and problem solving.

A great many studies have looked at the various information processing decisions that different types of learners make when confronted with a learning task. As you read this book, for example, numerous other stimuli may compete for your attention. Will you close the book because someone just turned on the television, or because you feel drowsy, or because you were just invited out for pizza? Assuming you decide to read, do you underline key points, take notes, organize your notes into a topical outline, think of analogies for abstract ideas, or imagine yourself applying educational psychology principles in your own classroom?

We believe that this is one chapter you ought to read very carefully, because the information processing decisions you make affect when you learn, how much you learn, how well you learn—indeed, whether you learn at all. To give you an appreciation of the information processing approach to learning and how it can help teachers and students do their jobs, the next section describes several basic cognitive processes and their role in how people store and retrieve information. The section following that describes research on selected learning tactics and discusses the nature of strategic learning.

A Model of Information Processing

A popular approach to summarizing and illustrating ways that we process information is to construct diagrams called *flow charts.* Figure 8.1 presents a simplified version of a flow chart, derived from the work of several theorists (for example, Atkinson & Shiffrin, 1968; Norman & Rumelhart, 1970). The various boxes in Figure 8.1 depict what are often referred to as memory stores and control processes.

The information processing model of learning identifies three *memory stores,* called the sensory register (SR), short-term memory (STM), and long-term memory (LTM). Each store varies as to how much information it can hold and for how long. (Our use of the term *memory stores* is not meant to suggest specific locations in the brain where information is held; it is a metaphorical device for classifying different memory phenomena.)

The *control processes* govern the manner in which information is encoded and its flow between memory stores. These processes include *recognition, attention, maintenance rehearsal,* and *elaborative rehearsal* (also called *elaborative encoding*). As described below, each control process is associated primarily with a particular memory store. The control processes play a key role in the information processing system for two reasons. First, they determine the quantity and quality of information that the learner stores in and retrieves from memory. Second, though, it is the learner who decides whether, when, and how to employ them. That they are under our direct, conscious control will take on added importance when we discuss educational applications a bit later. Before we get to applications, however, we need to make you more familiar with the three memory stores and the control processes specifically associated with each of them.

The Sensory Register and Its Control Processes

The Sensory Register   A description of how human learners process information typically begins with environmental stimuli. Our sense receptors are con-

Figure 8.1   An Information Processing Model of Learning

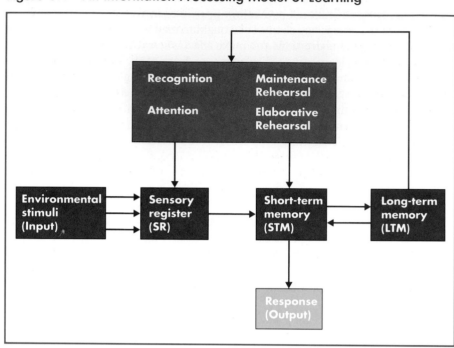

stantly stimulated by visual, auditory, tactile, olfactory, and gustatory stimuli. These experiences are initially recorded in the **sensory register** (SR), the first memory store. It is called the sensory register because the information it stores is thought to be encoded in the same form in which it is originally perceived. The purpose of the SR is to hold information just long enough (about one to three seconds) for us to decide if we want to attend to it further. Information not selectively attended to and recognized decays or disappears from the system. At the moment you are reading these words, for example, you are being exposed to the appearance of letters printed on paper, to sounds in the place where you are reading, and to many other stimuli. The sensory register might be compared to an unending series of instant-camera snapshots or videotape segments, each lasting from one to three seconds before fading away. If you recognize and attend to one of the snapshots, though, it will be "processed" and transferred to short-term memory.

The Nature of Recognition   **Recognition** involves noting key features of a stimulus and relating them to already stored information. The process of recognition is interactive in that it depends partly on information extracted from the stimulus itself and partly on information stored in long-term memory. The ability to recognize a dog, for example, involves noticing those physical features of the animal that give it "dogness" (for example, height, length, number of feet, type of coat) and combining the results of that analysis with relevant information from LTM (such as that dogs are household pets, are walked on a leash by their owner, are used to guard property). To the degree that an object's defining features are ambiguous (as when observing a dog from a great distance) or a learner lacks relevant prior knowledge (as many culturally disadvantaged students do), recognition and more meaningful processing will suffer. Recognition of words and sentences during reading, for example, can be aided by such factors as clear printing, knowledge of spelling patterns, knowledge of letter sounds, and the frequency with which words appear in natural language. The important point to remember is that recognition and meaningful processing of information is most effective when we make use of all available sources of information (Klatzky, 1980, p. 64).

One implication of this work to be discussed in more detail in this and other chapters is that, according to the information processing view, primary and elementary grade students need more structured learning tasks than junior high or high school students. Because of their limited store of knowledge in long-term memory and narrow ability to logically relate what they do know to the task at hand, younger students should be provided with clear, complete, explicit directions and learning materials (see, for example, Doyle, 1983).

The Impact of Attention   The environment usually provides us with more information than we can deal with at one time. From the multitude of sights, sounds, smells, and other stimuli impinging on us at a given moment, only a fraction are noticed and recorded in the sensory register. At this point, yet another reduction typically occurs. We may process only one-third of the already selected information recorded in the SR. We continually focus on one thing at the expense of something else. This selective focusing on a portion of the information currently stored in the sensory register is what we call **attention**.

Attention: focusing on a portion of currently available information

As with any human characteristic, there are individual differences in attention. Some people can concentrate on a task while they are surrounded by a variety of sights and sounds. Others need to isolate themselves in a private study area. Still others have difficulty attending under any conditions. What explains these differences? Again, information from long-term memory plays an influential role. According to Neisser (1976), "perceivers pick up only what they have schemata for, and willy-nilly ignore the rest" (p. 79). In other words, we choose what we will see (or hear) by *anticipating* the information it will provide. Students daydream, doodle, and write letters rather than listen to a lecture because they anticipate hearing little of value. Moreover, these anticipatory schemata are likely to have long-lasting effects. If someone asked you now to read a book about English grammar, you might recall having been bored by diagramming sentences and memorizing grammatical rules in elementary school. If that were the case, you might not read the grammar text very carefully. A basic challenge for teachers is to convince stu-

Information in long-term memory influences what we attend to

By using characters such as Big Bird, the creators of "Sesame Street" have demonstrated the attention-getting effectiveness of novel and bizarre stimuli. (© 1990 Children's Television Workshop. Big Bird © 1990 Muppets, Inc.)

dents that a learning task will be useful, enjoyable, informative, and meaningful. Later in this chapter we present some ideas as to how this might be accomplished.

Short-Term Memory and Its Control Processes

Short-Term Memory   Once information has been attended to, it is transferred to **short-term memory** (STM), the second memory store. Short-term memory can hold about seven unrelated bits of information for approximately twenty seconds. While this brief time span may seem surprising, it can be easily demonstrated. Imagine that you look up and dial an unfamiliar phone number, and you receive a busy signal. If you are then distracted by something or someone else for fifteen to twenty seconds, chances are you will forget the number. Short-term memory is often referred to as "working memory," since it holds information we are currently aware of at any given moment.

The following analogy also may help you grasp the nature of short-term memory. Visualize your STM as a filing cabinet with a capacity of seven pictures that will hold their image for about twenty seconds. As new items are placed in the file,

Short-term memory: about seven bits of information held for about twenty seconds they are either incorporated into one of the existing pictures, or they push out one that was previously encoded.

Rehearsal   A severe limitation of short-term memory, as you can see, is how quickly information disappears or is forgotten in the absence of further processing. This problem can be dealt with through *rehearsal*. Most people think of rehearsal as repeating something to oneself over and over either silently or out loud. The usual purpose for such behavior is to memorize information for later use, although occasionally we simply want to hold information in short-term memory for immediate use (for example, to redial a phone number after getting a busy signal). Rehearsal can serve both purposes, but not in the same way. Consequently, cognitive psychologists have found it necessary and useful to distinguish between two types of rehearsal: maintenance and elaborative.

Maintenance rehearsal (also called *rote rehearsal* or *repetition*) has a mechanical quality. Its only purpose is to use mental and verbal repetition to hold information in short-term memory for some immediate purpose. While this is a useful and often used capability (as in the telephone example), it has no effect on long-term memory storage.

Elaborative rehearsal (also called *elaborative encoding*), on the other hand, consciously relates new information to knowledge already stored in long-term memory. In this way it facilitates both the transfer of information to long-term memory and its maintenance in short-term memory. For example, if you wanted to learn the lines for a part in a play, you might try to relate the dialogue and behavior of your character to similar personal experiences you remember. As you strive to memorize the lines and actions, your mental "elaborations" will help you store your part in long-term memory so that you can retrieve it later. Elaborative rehearsal, whereby information from long-term memory is used in learning new information, is the rule rather than the exception. Mature learners don't often employ maintenance rehearsal by itself. The decision to use one or the other, however, depends on the demands you expect the environment to make on you. If you will need to remember things for future use, use elaborative rehearsal; if you want to keep something in consciousness just for the moment, use rote rehearsal.

When discussing rehearsal processes, it is important to keep in mind that younger children may not behave in the same way as more mature learners. Kindergarten pupils rarely engage in spontaneous rehearsal. By the age of seven, however, children do typically use simple rehearsal strategies. When presented with a list of items, the average seven-year-old rehearses each word by itself, several times. From the age of ten, rehearsal becomes more like that of an adult. Several items may be grouped together and rehearsed as a set.

So far, we have explained the effect of elaborative rehearsal in terms of relating new information to information already stored in long-term memory. That's fine as a very general explanation. To be more precise, we need to point out that elab-

> **Maintenance rehearsal:** hold information for immediate use

> **Elaborative rehearsal:** use stored information to aid learning

orative rehearsal is based on *organization* (as in the above example where several items are grouped together on some basis and rehearsed as a set) and *meaningfulness* (as in the earlier example where lines in a play are related to similar personal experiences).

Organization   Quite often the information we want to learn is complex and interrelated. We can simplify the task by organizing several separate chunks of information into a few "clumps" of information, particularly when each part of a clump helps us remember other parts. The value of organizing material was illustrated by an experiment (Bower, Clark, Lesgold, & Winzenz, 1969) in which two groups of subjects were asked to learn a list of words, but under different conditions. One group was given the entire list in a random order for four trials. The second group was given the list arranged under different headings (see Figure 8.2). The subjects in this group were urged to concentrate on learning items listed under the headings designated Level 1 and Level 2 during trial one, Levels 1, 2, and 3 during trial two, Levels 1, 2, 3, and 4 during trials three and four. After trial four the second group recalled almost twice as many words as the first. The organized material was much easier to learn not only because there were fewer chunks to memorize, but also because each item in a group served as a cue for the other items. When you decide to store pertinent material from this chapter in your long-term memory in preparation for an exam, you will find the job much easier if you organize what you are studying. To learn the various parts of the information processing model under discussion, for instance, you might group the ideas being described under the various headings used in this chapter (as we do in the *Study Guide*).

Organizing material reduces numbers of chunks, provides recall cues

Meaningfulness   In a review of research on meaningful learning, Ronald E. Johnson (1975) concludes that "meaningfulness is potentially the most powerful variable for explaining the learning of complex verbal discourse" (pp. 425–426). In defining meaningfulness, Johnson notes: "Learning may be said to be meaningful to the extent that the new learning task can be related to the existing cognitive structure of the learner, i.e., the residual of his earlier learnings" (p. 427). This observation stresses the point that memories are more likely to be retained in long-term storage if they can be related to what is familiar—or already remembered. Another way of stressing the same idea is to say that a new idea associated with an old one is likely to be remembered. Johnson emphasizes that the degree of meaningfulness depends on the "associational background of the learner" (p. 427). The use of the word *associational* calls attention to the significance of connecting what is to be learned with what the learner already knows. In making associations, it is desirable to relate ideas to a variety of other ideas and experiences by noting points of similarity, since superficial similarities are not likely to lead to encoding. The questions that we pose to you at the end of each chapter, for example, are designed to foster meaningful encoding by getting you to relate text information with relevant prior experience.

Meaningfulness effective because new information is associated with stored knowledge

Figure 8.2   Superordinate-Subordinate Arrangement of Words

From G.H. Bower, M.C. Clark, A.M. Lesgold, and D. Winzenz, "Hierarchical Retrieval Schemes in Recall of Categorized Word Lists," *Journal of Verbal Learning and Verbal Behavior*, 1969, 8, 323–343. Copyright 1969 by Academic Press. Reproduced by permission of the publisher and the authors.

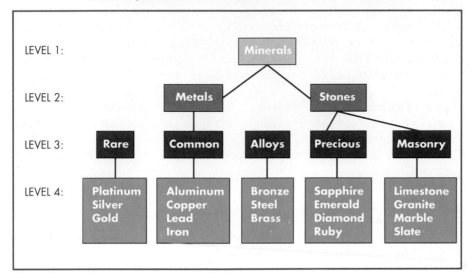

Long-Term Memory

So far, we have discussed two memory stores—the sensory register and short-term memory. We have also referred, in a general way, to **long-term memory** (LTM). This third memory store is perhaps the most interesting. On the basis of neurological, experimental, and clinical evidence, most cognitive psychologists believe that the storage capacity of long-term memory is unlimited and contains a permanent record of everything an individual has learned, although some doubt exists about the latter point (for example, Loftus & Loftus, 1980).

The neurological evidence comes from the work of Wilder Penfield (1969), a Canadian neurosurgeon who operated on over one thousand patients who experienced epileptic seizures. To determine the source of the seizures, Penfield electrically stimulated various parts of the brain's surface. During this procedure many patients reported vivid images of long-dormant events from their past. It was as if a neurological videotape had been turned on.

The experimental evidence, while less dramatic, is just as interesting. In a typical memory study (such as Tulving & Pearlstone, 1966), subjects receive a list of nouns to learn. After giving subjects ample opportunity to recall as many of the words as possible, the researchers provide retrieval cues, for instance, category labels such as "clothing," "food," or "animals." In many cases, cued subjects quickly recall additional items. Experiments on how well people recognize previously seen pictures have produced some startling findings. Thirty-six hours

Long-term memory: permanent storehouse of unlimited capacity

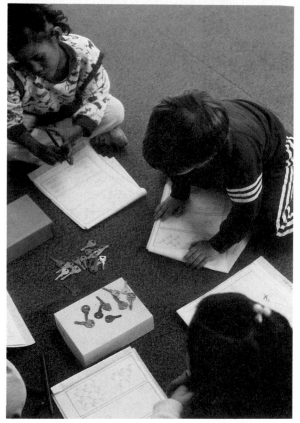

Long-term memory storage
and meaningfulness can be
enhanced by relating what
is to be learned to what is
familiar to the student.
(Above: Bob Daemmerich/
The Image Works; below:
Lew Merrim/Monkmeyer)

after viewing over 2,500 pictures the average number of correct identifications made by a group of college students was about 2,250 or 90 percent (Standing, Conezio, & Haber, 1970). In fact, it has been estimated that if one million pictures could be shown, recognition memory would be 90 percent or better (Standing, 1973).

Finally, psychiatrists and psychotherapists have reported many case histories of individuals who have been helped to recall seemingly forgotten events through hypnosis and other techniques (Erdelyi & Goldberg, 1979).

How Information Is Organized in Long-Term Memory   As we have seen, long-term memory plays an influential role throughout the information processing system. The interests, attitudes, skills, and knowledge of the world that reside there influence what we perceive, how we interpret our perceptions, and whether we process information for short-term or long-term storage. In most instances, retrieving information from long-term memory is extremely rapid and accurate, like finding a book in a well-run library. Consequently, we can conclude that information in long-term memory must be organized. The nature of this organization is a key area in the study of memory. The insights it provides help illuminate the encoding and retrieval processes associated with long-term memory.

Many cognitive psychologists believe that our store of knowledge in long-term memory is organized in terms of **schemata** (which is plural for *schema* and is related in meaning to Piaget's *scheme*). Richard C. Anderson (1984) defines a schema as an abstract structure of information. It is abstract because it summarizes information about many different cases or examples of something, and it is structured because it represents how its own informational components are interrelated. Schemata give us expectations about objects and events (dogs bark, birds fly, students listen to their teachers and study industriously). When our schemata are well-formed and a specific event is consistent with our expectation, comprehension occurs. When schemata are poorly structured or absent, learning is slow and uncertain. The following example should make this notion of schemata more understandable. For most everyone raised in the United States, the word *classroom* typically calls to mind a scene that includes certain people (teacher, students), objects (desks, chalkboard, books, pencils), rules (attend to the teacher's instructions, stay in the classroom unless given permission to leave), and events (reading, listening, writing, talking, drawing). This is a generalized representation, and some classrooms may contain more or less of the above characteristics. However, as long as students and teachers share the same basic classroom schema, each will generally know what to expect and how to behave in any given classroom. It is when people do not possess an appropriate schema that comprehension, memory, and behavior problems arise.

This notion was first investigated during the early 1930s by Sir Frederick Bartlett (1932), an English psychologist. In one experiment, Bartlett had subjects read and recall a brief story entitled "The War of the Ghosts" that was based on North

Information in long-term memory organized as schemata

American Indian folklore. Since Bartlett's subjects had little knowledge of Indian culture, they had difficulty accurately recalling the story, omitting certain details and distorting others. The distortions were particularly interesting because they reflected an attempt to interpret the story in terms of the logic and beliefs of Western culture. The conclusion that Bartlett drew from this and similar studies was that remembering is not simply a matter of retrieving a true-to-life record of information. People often remember their *interpretations* or *constructions* of something read, seen, or heard. In addition, when they experience crucial gaps in memory, people tend to fill in these blanks with logical reconstructions of what they think must have been. People then report these reconstructions as memories of actual events (di Sibio, 1982).

For those who would argue that Bartlett's findings were simply the result of an atypical reading passage, similar ones have been reported more recently with other kinds of reading materials. Mary di Sibio (1982) cites one study in which some subjects read the sentence "The secretary circled the dates," whereas others read "The proofreader circled the dates." Those who read the first sentence were more likely to recall it when given the word *calendar* as a cue than when given the word *manuscript*; the reverse was true for those who read the second sentence. The explanation for this effect is that in the process of comprehending the sentence information, subjects make inferences about its meaning and store that in memory as well. These inferences are presumably based on some prior knowledge of how things happen in the world, namely that secretaries circle dates on a calendar while proofreaders circle dates on a manuscript. Thus, retrieval is most effective when cues match particular stored inferences.

Another study cited by di Sibio (1982) illustrates how prior knowledge may come into play during recall and lead subjects to guess at what they learned based on their schema. The typical result when this happens is distorted recall. In this study, two groups of college subjects read the same biographical passage. One group was told that the passage was about a fictitious dictator named Gerald Martin. The other group was told that the passage was about Adolph Hitler. Subjects were tested either five minutes after reading or after one week. They were asked to distinguish sentences taken from the passage ("old" sentences) from sentences which never actually appeared but were consistent with the topic ("new" sentences). Subjects in both groups could accurately distinguish "old" from "new" sentences after the five-minute delay. After one week, however, subjects who read the Adolph Hitler passage were far more likely to mistakenly recognize a new sentence such as "He hated the Jews particularly and so persecuted them."

These experiments vividly demonstrate the importance of providing students with relevant background knowledge and helping them use it to understand and accurately remember new information. Sometimes it is better to back up and build a solid basis for subsequent learning than to spend all of your teaching time on the materials to be learned.

The discussion up to this point has focused on a general explanation of how people attend to, encode, store, and retrieve information. In a word, we have described some of the major aspects of *thinking*. During the last twenty years, researchers have inquired into how much knowledge individuals have about their own thought processes and what significance this knowledge has for learning. The term that was coined to refer to how much we know of our own thought processes is *metacognition*. As we will see, it plays a very important role in learning.

Metacognition

The Nature and Importance of Metacognition

The notion of metacognition was proposed by developmental psychologist John Flavell (1976) to explain why children of different ages deal with learning tasks in different ways. For example, when seven-year-olds are taught how to use both a less effective technique (simple repetition) to remember pairs of nouns and a more effective technique (imaging the members of each pair doing something together), most of them will use the less effective technique when given a new set of pairs to learn. Most ten-year-olds, however, will opt to use the more effective method (Kail, 1984). The explanation for this finding is that the seven-year-old has not had enough learning experiences to recognize that some problem-solving methods are better than others. To the younger child, one means is as good as another. This lack of metacognitive knowledge makes true strategic learning impossible for young children.

One way to grasp the essence of metacognition is to contrast it with cognition. The term *cognition* is used to describe the ways in which information is processed, that is, the ways it is attended to, recognized, encoded, stored in memory for various lengths of time, retrieved from storage, and used for one purpose or another. **Metacognition** refers to our knowledge about those operations and how they might best be used to achieve a learning goal. As Flavell has put it,

> I am engaging in metacognition . . . if I notice that I am having more trouble learning A than B; if it strikes me that I should double-check C before accepting it as a fact; if it occurs to me that I had better scrutinize each and every alternative in any multiple-choice type task situation before deciding which is the best one; if I become aware that I am not sure what the experimenter really wants me to do; if I sense that I had better make a note of D because I may forget it; if I think to ask someone about E to see if I have it right. Such examples could be multiplied endlessly. (1976, p. 232.)

Metacognition is obviously a very broad concept. It covers everything an individual can know that relates to how information is processed. Recent research indicates significant differences in what younger and older children know about metacognition. What follows is a discussion of some of these differences.

Metacognition: knowledge of how we think

Age Trends in Metacognition

Two recent reviews of research on metacognition (Duell, 1986; Kail, 1984) reviewed studies of ways students of different ages use memorization techniques and how well they understand what they are doing. They came to the following conclusions:

1. In terms of diagnosing task difficulty, most six-year-olds know that more familiar items are easier to remember than less familiar items and that a small set of items is easier to recall than a large set of items. What does not develop until a child is about nine years of age, however, is awareness that the amount of information one can recall immediately after studying it is limited. Consequently, children through the third grade usually overestimate how much they can store in and retrieve from short-term memory.

2. Similar findings have been obtained for reading tasks. Most second-graders know that interest, familiarity, and story length influence comprehension and recall. However, they are relatively unaware of the effect of how ideas are sequenced, of the introductory and summary qualities of first and last paragraphs, and of the relationship between reading goals and tactics. Sixth-graders, by contrast, are much more aware of the effects of these variables on comprehension and recall. Partly because of these differences in metacognitive knowledge, young children tend to treat reading as a task of decoding symbols rather than of constructing and comprehending meaning. Recent research has clearly shown that children's metacognitive awareness about reading is positively related to performance on a variety of reading tasks.

3. Most children know very little about the role their own capabilities play in learning. For example, not until about nine years of age do most children realize that the amount of information they can recall immediately after studying is limited. Consequently, children through the third grade usually overestimate how much they can store in and retrieve from short-term memory. One likely reason for this developmental difference is that younger children base their prediction on irrelevant personal characteristics (such as "I just think I'm pretty smart"), whereas older children focus more on relevant task characteristics.

4. There are clear developmental differences in how well students understand the need to tailor learning tactics to task demands. For example, four- and six-year-old children in one study cited by Kail did not alter how much time they spent studying a set of pictures when they were told that a recognition test would follow either three minutes later, one day later, or one week later. Eight-year-olds did use that information to allocate less or more study time to the task. In another study, children of various ages were trained to use interactive visual imagery to learn a

list of concrete noun pairs. When given a similar task and left on their own, most of those below ten years of age reverted to the less effective technique of rote rehearsal.

5. In terms of monitoring the progress of learning, most children younger than seven or eight are not very proficient at determining when they know something well enough to pass a memory test. Also, most first-graders typically don't know what they don't know. When given multiple opportunities to study and recall a lengthy set of pictures, six-year-olds chose to study pictures they had previously seen and recalled as well as ones they hadn't. Thus, they wasted time studying things they already knew. Third-graders, by contrast, focused on previously un- seen pictures.

The general conclusion that emerges from these findings is that the youngest school-age children have only limited knowledge of how their cognitive processes work and when to use them. Consequently, primary grade children do no system- atically analyze learning tasks, formulate plans for learning, use appropriate tech- niques of enhancing memory and comprehension, or monitor their progress, because they do not (some would say cannot) understand the benefits of doing these things. As children develop and gain more experience with increasingly complex academic tasks, they acquire a greater awareness of metacognitive knowledge and its relationship to classroom learning. In this process, teachers can assist their students and guide them toward maximum use of their metacognitive knowledge. To help you understand how, the next section discusses learning tac- tics and strategies.

Insight into one's learning processes improves with age

Helping Students Become Strategic Learners

With some effort and planning, the teacher can make logically organized and rel- evant lessons. However, this is only half the battle, since students must then at- tend to the information, encode it into long-term memory, and retrieve it when needed. Getting students to use the attention, encoding, and retrieval processes discussed in the previous section is not always easy. The sad fact is that most chil- dren and adults are inefficient learners (as evidenced, for example, by Annis & Annis, 1979; Bjork, 1979; Brown, Campione, & Day, 1981; Covington, 1985; Simpson, 1984). Their attempts at encoding rarely go beyond rote rehearsal (for example, rereading a textbook chapter), simple organizational schemes (outlin- ing), and various cuing devices (underlining or highlighting). When the nature of the learning task changes, few students think about changing their encoding tech- niques accordingly.

One reason for this state of affairs is that students are rarely taught how to make the most of their cognitive capabilities. This is surprising, not to mention disappointing, since it is widely recognized that the amount of independent learning expected of students increases consistently from elementary school through high school and into college. Perhaps we rely too much on subject matter instruction (such as lecturing or computer-assisted instruction) at the expense of teaching students *how* to learn (Rohwer, 1984). The rest of this chapter will try to convince you that it need not be this way, at least for your students. The rise of information processing theory has led researchers to study how cognitive processes can be taught to and used by students as learning tactics and strategies.

The Nature of Learning Tactics and Strategies

The distinction between tactics and strategy, while relatively new to the psychology of learning, has been part military training for thousands of years. In a military context, *strategy* refers to the accomplishment of general, long-term objectives by *planning* a course of action and placing forces in the most advantageous position *prior to* actual engagement with the enemy. *Tactics*, on the other hand, refers to the accomplishment of specific and more immediate objectives by *arranging* and *directing* forces *in action*.

A **learning strategy**, then, can be described as a general *plan* someone formulates for determining how best to achieve an overall academic goal *before* dealing with the learning task itself. A **learning tactic** is a specific *technique* one uses in the service of the strategy *while* confronted with the task. Perhaps the most important thing to understand about these two concepts is that tactics must be chosen so as to be consistent with the goals of a strategy. If you had to recall verbatim the preamble to the U.S. Constitution, for example, would you use a learning tactic that would help you understand the gist of each stanza or one that would allow for accurate and complete recall? It is surprising how often students fail to consider this point.

Strategy: plan to achieve a long-term goal

Tactic: specific technique that helps achieve long-term goal

Using Learning Tactics Effectively

A fairly lengthy list of learning tactics could be generated by looking through several how-to-study books (for example, Morgan, 1979; Maddox, 1983; Pauk, 1984) and how-to-remember books (for example, Kellett, 1980; Lorayne & Lucas, 1974). Your list would likely reflect influences of both recent information processing theory (for instance, visual imagery and organization) and more traditional methods (such as rote rehearsal, notetaking, and outlining). While many of these tactics are potentially useful, the how-to books in which they are discussed usually do not tell you how to use them as part of a broad strategy. Thus, you may not realize at first that not all tactics are equally suited to the same purpose.

One approach that you might find useful is to place tactics in one of two categories based on each tactic's intended primary purpose. One category, called *memory-directed tactics*, contains techniques that help produce accurate storage and retrieval of information. Examples of memory-directed tactics include simple rehearsal and any of several types of mnemonic devices (which we will explain shortly). The second category, called *comprehension-directed tactics*, contains techniques that aid in understanding the meaning of ideas and their interrelationships. Examples of this category include notetaking and certain forms of question asking (Levin, 1982).

There are numerous learning tactics, and we cannot discuss them all because of space limitations. Instead, we have chosen to briefly discuss a few that are either very popular with students or have been shown to be reasonably effective. The first two, rehearsal and mnemonic devices, are memory-directed tactics. Both can take several forms and are used by students of almost every age. The last two, notetaking and questioning, are comprehension-directed tactics and are used frequently by students from the upper elementary grades through college.

Rehearsal   The simplest form of rehearsal involves repeating the name of a single piece of information (for example, the date of a historic event or the capital of a state) several times either silently or out loud, and then doing the same thing with the next item to be remembered. It is not a particularly effective tactic for accurate long-term storage and retrieval because it does not produce distinct encoding or good retrieval cues (although, as discussed earlier, it is a useful tactic for short-term memory purposes). However, rote rehearsal is one of the earliest tactics to appear and is used by most everyone on occasion. According to research reviewed by Robert Kail (1984), most five- and six-year-olds do not rehearse at all. Seven-year-olds sometimes use the simplest form of rehearsal. By eight years of age, instead of rehearsing single pieces of information one at a time, youngsters start to rehearse several items together as a set. A slightly more advanced version, called *cumulative rehearsal*, involves rehearsing a small set of items for several repetitions, dropping the item at the top of the list and adding a new one, giving the set several repetitions, dropping the item at the head of the set and adding a new one, rehearsing the set, and so on. By early adolescence, rehearsal reflects the learner's growing awareness of the organizational properties of information. When given a list of randomly arranged words from familiar categories, thirteen-year-olds will group items by category to form rehearsal sets. This version of rehearsal is likely to be the most effective because of the implicit association between the category members and the more general category label. If, at the time of recall, the learner is given the category label or can generate it spontaneously, the probability of accurately recalling the category members increases significantly.

> Rote rehearsal not a very effective memory tactic

Mnemonic Devices   A **mnemonic device** is a memory-directed tactic that helps a learner transform or organize information to enhance its retrievability. Such devices can be used to learn and remember individual items of information (a name, a fact, a date), sets of information (a list of names, a list of vocabulary definitions, a sequence of events), and ideas expressed in text. They range from simple, easy-to-learn techniques to somewhat complex systems that require a fair amount of practice. Since they incorporate visual and verbal forms of elaborative encoding, their effectiveness is due to the same factors that make imagery and category clustering successful—organization and meaningfulness.

Although one is known to have originated over 2000 years ago, mnemonics were rarely made the object of scientific study until the 1960s (see Yates, 1966, for a detailed discussion of the history of mnemonics). Since that time, however, they have been frequently and intensively studied by researchers. In recent years, there have been several reviews of mnemonics research (for example, Bellezza, 1981; Higbee, 1979; Pressley, Levin, & Delaney, 1982; Snowman, 1986). In the next few pages, we briefly discuss six mnemonic devices: rhymes, acronyms, acrostics, pegwords, the loci method, and the keyword method.

Rhymes, acronyms, and acrostics. Most students learn a few time-honored *rhyme* mnemonics during their elementary school years. The spelling rule "*i* before *e* except after *c*" and the calendar rule "thirty days hath September, April, June, and November" are but two examples.

Acronym: word made from first letters of items to be learned

A second class of mnemonic is the *acronym* or first-letter mnemonic. With this technique, you take the first letter from each of a set of items to be learned and make up a word (it doesn't have to be a real word). For example, the first letter from each of the Great Lakes—Huron, Ontario, Michigan, Erie, Superior—form the word *HOMES*. In this case, you can add imagery by visualizing five homes on the shore of a lake. Another often cited example is the acronym *ROYGBIV* (pronounced *roy-gee-biv*), which stands for the spectrum of visible light—red, orange, yellow, green, blue, indigo, violet. Surveys of mnemonic use among college students have found the acronym technique to be very well known and widely used. It appears to be most effective for recalling a short set of items, particularly abstract items, in serial order. It is hard to say just how useful the acronym can be, since researchers rarely train subjects long enough to allow them to become highly proficient in its use.

Acrostic: sentence made up of words derived from first letters of items to be learned

If an acronym is not feasible, you can construct an *acrostic*, or sentence mnemonic. Simply make up a sentence such that each word begins with the first letter of each item to be learned. Thus, *ROYGBIV* becomes "Richard of York Gave Battle in Vain." To learn and remember the nine planets, the sentence "Men Very Easily Make Jugs Serve Useful New Purposes" works quite well. A variation of the acrostic is to embed information to be learned in a meaningful sentence. For instance, when trying to decide whether the port or starboard side of a ship is left or right, just remember one of the following sentences: "The ship *left port*" or "The *star boarder* is always *right*." The acrostic is most useful for recalling abstract items of information. It can be used by students of all ages but seems to be most effective for those who might otherwise rely on rote rehearsal, such as pri-

Students who study a foreign language can make good use of many mnemonic devices, particularly the keyword method. (Terry McCoy/The Picture Cube)

mary grade children, low-ability children, or children from lower socioeconomic classes.

The pegword. This mnemonic is particularly useful for learning lists of items. As the name implies, the idea is to link up or associate the list items with memory pegs. The pegs, previously learned associations based on rhyme, are one-bun, two-shoe, three-tree, four-door, five-hive, six-sticks, seven-heaven, eight-gate, nine-line, ten-hen. Once the pegs have been learned, you make up an interacting image consisting of the first list item and the first peg. If the first item on your errand list is to buy house paint, you might imagine a bun floating in a can of paint. If your next errand is to buy roses at the florist, think of a bouquet of red roses growing out of a shoe. Two advantages of the pegword mnemonic are that a list can be accessed at any point by remembering the relevant number rhyme and recall may proceed just as easily forward or backward. Because this technique incorporates visual imagery, it is most effective with concrete items. It has been proved effective with children, military personnel, and graduate students for a variety of recall measures. It can be used to learn most anything that can be arranged in lists (including the ten commandments, according to one study).

The loci method. The oldest known mnemonic, the method of loci (pronounced *low-sigh* and meaning "places"), is also one of the most popular. The loci method is similar to the pegword mnemonic in that the loci, or places, serve as memory pegs. Commonly used loci are rooms in a house, buildings on a campus, or stores on a street. In practice, the first task is to form a set of memory locations that

Pegword: associate memory pegs with items to be learned

Loci method: visualize items to be learned stored in specific locations

constitute a natural series, are numbered, are highly familiar, and can be easily imagined. Second, images of the things you want to remember (for example, objects, events, or ideas) should be generated and placed in each location as you mentally walk from one location to another. Within each location there should be particular pieces of furniture (chair, table, piano) or architectural features (fireplace, mantel, archway, lobby) on, in, or under which one or more images can be placed. Finally, when you want to recall, simply retrace your steps through each location, retrieve each image from where it was originally placed, and decode each image into a written or spoken message. The loci method is an effective memory-directed tactic for children, college students, and the elderly. When combined with an outlining tactic, it can be used to recall ideas from prose. It is effective for both free recall and serial recall.

The keyword method. The last mnemonic to be discussed is also the newest to be devised. Called the *keyword method*, it first appeared in 1975 as a means for learning foreign language vocabulary (Atkinson, 1975; Atkinson & Raugh, 1975; Raugh & Atkinson, 1975). The technique is fairly simple and involves two steps. First, isolate some part of the foreign word that, when spoken, sounds like a real English word. This is the keyword. Second, form an interacting visual image between the keyword and the English translation of the foreign word. Thus, the foreign word becomes associated to the keyword by an acoustic link and the keyword becomes associated to the English translation by an imagery link. As an example, take the Spanish word *pato* (pronounced *pot-o*), which means "duck" in English. The keyword in this case is *pot*. The next step, generating a visual image combining pot and duck, can be satisfied by imagining a duck with a pot over its head, as in Figure 8.3. The keyword mnemonic has proved effective in one form or another with preschoolers, elementary school children, adolescents, and college students. For children who cannot spontaneously generate visual images (preschool through fourth grade), two variations have been devised. In one, children are given the keyword and a picture that incorporates the keyword and the English translation. The other variation uses sentences instead of pictures. The sentence variation can also be used to remember abstract material. The keyword is a very flexible mnemonic. Besides foreign language vocabulary, it also facilitates the recall of cities and their products, states and their capitals, medical definitions, and famous people's accomplishments.

Keyword method: visually link pronunciation of foreign word to English translation

Why mnemonic devices are effective. Mnemonic devices work so well because they enhance the encodability and retrievability of information. First, they provide a context (such as acronyms, sentences, mental walks) in which apparently unrelated items can be organized. Second, the meaningfulness of material to be learned is enhanced through associations with more familiar, meaningful information (for example, memory pegs or loci). Third, they provide distinctive retrieval cues that must be encoded with the material to be learned. Fourth, they force the learner to be an active participant in the learning process (Morris, 1977).

Mnemonic devices organize, provide retrieval cues, can be acquired

Figure 8.3   Illustration of the Keyword Method

From R. C. Atkinson, "Mnemonotechnics in Second-Language Learning," *American Psychologist*, 1975, *30*(8) 821–828. Copyright 1975 by the American Psychological Association. Reproduced by permission of the publisher.

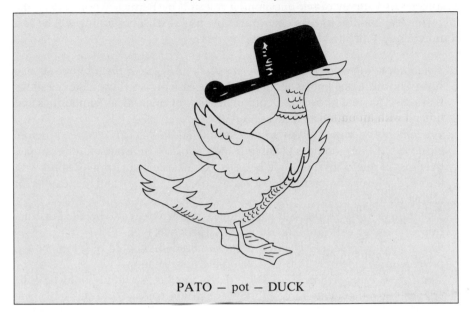

PATO – pot – DUCK

In summary, teaching students how to use mnemonic devices has two major benefits. First, it points out to students that the ability to learn and remember large amounts of information is an acquired capability. Too many people mistakenly assume that an effective memory is innate and requires high intelligence. Second, mnemonic devices are interesting, easy to learn, and productive. As such, they can motivate students in general and low-achieving students in particular.

Self-questioning   Since students are expected to demonstrate much of what they know by answering written test questions, self-questioning can be a valuable learning tactic. The key to using questions profitably is to recognize that different types of questions make different cognitive demands. Some questions require little more than verbatim recall or recognition of simple facts and details. If an exam is to stress factual recall, then it may be helpful to generate such questions while studying. Other questions, however, assess comprehension, application, or synthesis of main ideas, or other high-level information. Since many teachers favor higher-level test questions, we will focus on self-questioning as an aid to comprehension.

Much of the research on self-questioning addresses two basic questions: Can students as young as fourth grade be trained to write comprehension questions about the content of a reading passage? And does writing such questions lead to better comprehension of the passage in comparison to students who do not write questions? The answer to both questions is, yes—if certain conditions are present. According to a survey of self-questioning research by Bernice Wong (1985), the following five conditions help determine how useful self-questioning will be as a comprehension-directed learning tactic.

1. *The amount of prior knowledge the questioner has about the topic of the passage*: The more one knows about a topic, the easier it is to formulate questions that reflect factual knowledge, comprehension of main ideas, similarities and differences among different ideas, and so on.
2. *The amount of metacognitive knowledge the questioner has compiled*: Before effective self-questioning is possible, a student has to be aware of, for example, the types of questions that could be asked (for example, questions dealing with knowledge level, comprehension level, or application level) and the reasons for asking them.
3. *The clarity of instructions*: Students should be given clear and detailed instructions in how to write good questions of a particular type.
4. *The amount of practice allowed the student*: Students should be given enough practice in writing questions to develop high proficiency.
5. *The length of each practice session*: Each practice session should be long enough for all students to comfortably read the passage and think of good questions. Giving students twenty minutes to read a 1,400-word passage and write six comprehension questions is likely to produce poorly framed questions.

Notetaking   When you take notes on the contents of a reading passage or a lecture, depending on your objectives, your notes may be lengthy or brief, a verbatim reproduction of the text, or a paraphrase. The information you write down may be limited strictly to the passage content, or it may be integrated with relevant prior knowledge. And you may plan to use your notes to enhance accurate recall or to help with comprehension (Cook & Mayer, 1983).

As a learning tactic, notetaking comes with good news and bad. The good news is that notetaking can benefit a student in two ways. First, the process of taking notes while listening to a lecture or reading a text leads to better retention and comprehension of the noted information than just listening or reading does. Second, reviewing notes produces additional chances to recall and comprehend the noted material. The bad news is that we know very little at the present time about the specific conditions that make notetaking an effective tactic. As a result, we have no definitive answers to questions like the following: Should notes be extensive or brief? Does it make any difference whether notes are verbatim statements or paraphrases? Should a notetaker concentrate on recording facts and details, or should more general ideas be the focus? Should notes be reorganized (in outline form, for example) and then used as a basis for review, or should they be left in

> Taking notes and reviewing notes aids retention and comprehension

their original form? Is it best to review notes shortly after they have been taken or just before an exam? How long should a review session be? Is notetaking likely to be a useful tactic for every student?

The main reason why we have no definitive answers to these and other questions is a shortage of relevant research. For the time being, the best we can say is that the process of taking and reviewing notes is likely to benefit most students and should be encouraged (Kiewra, 1985, 1988).

One conclusion we would like you to draw from this section is that learning tactics should not be taught as isolated techniques, particularly to high school students. If they are taught that way, most students probably will not keep using them for very long, nor will they recognize that as the situation changes, so should the tactic. Therefore, as implied at the start of this section, students should be taught how to use tactics as part of a broader learning strategy.

Using Learning Strategies Effectively

The Components of a Learning Strategy   As noted, a learning strategy is a plan for accomplishing a learning goal. It consists of six components: metacognition, analysis, planning, implementation of the plan, monitoring progress, and modification. To give you a better idea of how to formulate a learning strategy of your own, here is a detailed description of each of these components (Snowman, 1986, 1987):

> Learning strategy components: meta-cognition, analyze, plan, implement, monitor, modify

1. *Metacognition:* In the absence of some minimal awareness of how we think and how our thought processes affect our academic performance, a strategic approach to learning is simply not possible. We need to know, at the very least, that effective learning requires an analysis of the learning situation, formulation of a learning plan, skillful implementation of appropriate tactics, periodic monitoring of our progress, and modification of things that go wrong. In addition, we need to know why each of the above steps is necessary, when each step should be carried out, and how well prepared we are to perform each step. Without this knowledge, students who are taught one or more of the learning tactics mentioned earlier do not keep up their use for very long, nor do they apply the tactics to relevant tasks.

2. *Analysis:* Any workable plan must be based on relevant information. By using the four learning factors that were described in the beginning of the chapter (p. 377–378), the strategic learner can generate this information by playing the role of an investigative journalist and asking questions that pertain to what, when, where, why, who, and how. In this way the learner can identify important aspects of the material to be learned (what, when, where), understand the nature of the criterion (why), recognize relevant personal learner characteristics (who), and identify potentially useful learning activities or tactics (how).

3. *Planning*: Assuming that satisfactory answers can be gained from the preceding analysis, the strategic learner would formulate a learning plan by hypothesizing something like the following: "I know something about the material to be learned (I have to read and comprehend five chapters of my music appreciation text within the next three weeks), the nature of the criterion (I will have to compare and contrast the musical structure of symphonies that were written by Beethoven, Schubert, and Brahms), my strengths and weaknesses as a learner (I am good at tasks that involve the identification of similarities and differences, but I have difficulty concentrating for long periods of time), and the nature of various learning activities (skimming is a good way to get a general sense of the structure of a chapter; mnemonic devices make memorizing important details easier and more reliable; notetaking and self-questioning are more effective ways to enhance comprehension than simple rereading). Based on this knowledge, I should divide each chapter into several smaller units that will take no longer than thirty minutes to read, take notes as I read, answer self-generated compare-and-contrast questions, use the loci mnemonic to memorize details, and repeat this sequence several times over the course of each week."

4. *Implementation of the plan*: Once the learner has formulated a plan, each of its elements must be implemented—*skillfully*. A careful analysis and a well-conceived plan will not work if tactics are carried out badly. Of course, a poorly executed plan may not be entirely attributable to a learner's tactical skill deficiencies. Part of the problem may be a general lack of knowledge about what conditions make for effective use of tactics (as is the case with notetaking).

5. *Monitoring progress*: Once the learning process is underway, the strategic learner assesses how well the chosen tactics are working. Possible monitoring techniques include writing out a summary, giving an oral presentation, working practice problems, and answering questions.

6. *Modification*: If the monitoring assessment is positive, the learner may decide no changes are needed. If, however, attempts to memorize or understand the learning material seem to be producing unsatisfactory results, the learner will need to re-evaluate and modify the analysis. This, in turn, will cause changes in the plan and the implementation.

This learning strategy model is obviously complex and requires a certain level of intellectual maturity. Thus, you may be tempted to conclude that while *you* could do it, learning to be strategic is beyond the reach of most elementary grade students. As we are about to show, however, recent research suggests that under the right circumstances, youngsters can learn and productively use many of these strategic components.

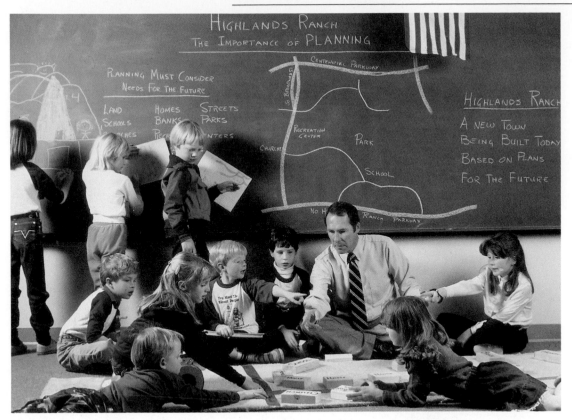

Students can formulate strategic learning plans that identify and analyze the important aspects of a task. Then, they can tailor these plans to their own strengths and weaknesses as learners. (The Stock Market/Brownie Harris)

Research on Learning Strategy Training An ambitious project to teach third- and fifth-grade children how, when, and why to use various elements of a reading comprehension strategy was evaluated on two occasions by Scott Paris and his associates (Paris, Cross, & Lipson, 1984; Paris & Oka, 1986). Over the course of an academic year, several hundred third- and fifth-grade children participated either in a supplemental reading comprehension training program called Informed Strategies for Learning (ISL) or in a control condition.

The basic purposes of the ISL program were to increase the students' metacognitive awareness of reading strategies, convince them that reading strategies are useful skills, and teach them how to use strategic skills to improve reading comprehension. The entire package of instructional materials included four main units, with each unit containing five modules. The goal of the units was, respectively, (a) planning and preparing to read, (b) identifying meaning, (c) reasoning about text content, and (d) monitoring comprehension. Each of the modules within a unit dealt with a particular aspect of that unit's goal. To make the point of each module clear, a concrete metaphor was developed and presented as a bulletin board display. For example, the module on task evaluation used the metaphor "Be a Reading Detective" to point out the importance of analyzing such comprehension clues as passage topic, length, and difficulty. Each module was presented over three lessons and included the following activities: Introduce the metaphor; describe the strategic skill; explain and demonstrate how to use the skill; provide opportunities to practice using the skill; provide corrective feedback; initiate discussions of thoughts and feelings about how, when, and why to use the skill; and encourage independent use of the skill.

The major findings from this program are mostly positive:

1. As measured by a twenty-item test, ISL children showed a much greater awareness than control group children of why one should use strategic reading skills, when such skills should be used, how to use them, and what benefits to expect from them.
2. Fifth-grade ISL children showed more metacognitive awareness than third-grade ISL children.
3. Third-grade and fifth-grade ISL children scored higher on two different measures of reading comprehension than third-grade and fifth-grade control group children.
4. Children's comprehension strategies, metacognitive knowledge, and motivation were all significantly related to achievement.
5. ISL did not improve self-perception about reading or perceived self-competence.

Another study of strategy training aimed at improving reading comprehension is the *reciprocal teaching* (RT) program of Annemarie Palincsar and Ann Brown (1984). The title of this program indicates that the students learn certain comprehension skills by demonstrating them to each other. Palincsar and Brown trained a small group of seventh-graders whose reading comprehension scores were at least two years below grade level to use the techniques of summarizing, self-questioning, clarifying, and predicting to improve their reading comprehension. These four methods were chosen because they can be used by students to improve *and* monitor comprehension.

During the early training sessions the teacher explained and demonstrated the four methods while reading various passages. The students were then given gradually increasing responsibility for demonstrating these techniques to their peers, with the teacher supplying prompts and corrective feedback as needed. Eventually, each student was expected to offer a good summary of a passage, pose questions about important ideas, clarify ambiguous words or phrases, and predict upcoming events, all to be done with little or no intervention by the teacher.

This program was evaluated in terms of two general questions. First, did the RT students improve in their ability to summarize, question, clarify, and predict? The answer to this question was yes. Early in the program students produced overly detailed summaries and many unclear questions. In later sessions concise summaries and questions dealing explicitly with main ideas were the rule. For example, questions on main ideas increased from 54 percent to 70 percent. In addition, the questions were increasingly stated in paraphrase form rather than as verbatim statements from the passage.

The second question was did the RT students improve their reading comprehension scores? Again the answer was yes. By the end of the study, RT-trained students were scoring as well as a group of average readers on tests of comprehension (about 75 percent correct for both groups) and much better than a group that was taught how to locate information that might show up in a test question (75 percent correct versus 45 percent correct). Most impressively, these levels of performance held up for at least eight weeks after the study ended (no measures were taken after that point) and generalized to tests of social studies and science (20 percent correct prior to training versus 60 percent correct after training).

The message of strategy-training programs like Informed Strategies for Learning and reciprocal teaching is that knowledge of the learning process and the conditions that affect it should be as much a part of the curriculum as learning to read, write, and compute. Proponents have argued persuasively that mastery of traditional basic skills is influenced by the nontraditional but more basic skills of strategic reasoning (see, for example, Bracey, 1983). Consequently, children should be made aware gradually of the general relationship between cognitive means and academic ends, the potential range of application of various learning tactics, how to determine if learning is proceeding as planned, and what to do if it is not.

Mid-Chapter Review

The Nature of Information Processing Theory

Information processing theory: study of the ways people acquire, store, recall, and use information

A Model of Information Processing

A popular model of information processing visualizes three memory stores and a set of processes that determine whether and how stimuli undergo further processing:

Sensory register (SR): first memory store; hold stimuli briefly (about one to three seconds) in original form for possible future processing

Recognition: noting key features of a stimulus and relating them to already stored information

Attention: selective focusing on a portion of the information currently stored in the sensory register

Short-term memory (STM): second memory store, also called working memory; holds about seven bits of information for about twenty seconds (or longer if maintenance rehearsal is used)

Maintenance rehearsal: using mental and verbal repetition to hold information in STM for immediate use

Elaborative rehearsal: encoding new information in long-term memory by consciously relating it to already stored knowledge

Organization: grouping what is to be learned into fewer chunks in ways that provide retrieval cues

Meaningfulness: relating a new learning task to existing cognitive structure (previously learned information)

Long-term memory (LTM): third memory store; permanent storehouse of information, which is thought to have an essentially unlimited capacity

Schema: abstract representations of ideas and experiences that are stored in LTM and make comprehension possible

Metacognition

Metacognition: knowledge of how we process information under a variety of conditions and with what effects

Helping Students Become Strategic Learners

Learning strategy: a plan for accomplishing a general learning goal, consisting of six elements: metacognition, analysis, planning, implementation of plan, monitoring of progress, and if necessary, modification

Learning tactic: a specific technique, consistent with a person's overall learning strategy, that is used in mastering a learning task

Memory-directed tactics: tactics (such as rehearsal and mnemonic devices) whose primary purpose is to insure accurate storage and retrieval of information

Comprehension-directed tactics: tactics (such as notetaking and self-questioning) whose primary purpose is to insure comprehension of ideas and their interrelationships

Mnemonic devices: memory-directed tactics that transform or organize information, thereby making it more retrievable; popular types include rhymes, acronyms, acrostics, pegword, the loci method, and the keyword method

SUGGESTIONS FOR TEACHING

Helping Your Students Become Efficient Information Processors

1. Develop and use a variety of techniques to attract and hold attention, and give your students opportunities to practice and refine their skills in maintaining attention.
   a. Be aware of what will capture your students' attention.
   b. To maintain attention, emphasize the possible utility of learning new ideas.
   c. Teach students how to increase their span of attention.
2. Point out and encourage students to recognize that certain bits of information are important and can be related to what is already known.
3. Use appropriate rehearsal techniques, including stress on meaning and chunking.
4. Organize what you ask your pupils to learn and urge older students to organize material on their own.
5. As much as possible, stress meaningfulness.
6. Demonstrate a variety of learning tactics and allow students to practice them.
   a. Teach students how to use various forms of rehearsal and mnemonic devices.
   b. Teach students how to formulate comprehension questions.
   c. Teach students how to take notes.
7. Encourage students to think about the various conditions that affect how they learn and remember.
8. Each time you prepare an assignment, think about learning strategies you and your students might use.

1. Develop and use a variety of techniques to attract and hold attention, and give your students opportunities to practice and refine their skills in maintaining attention.
   a. Be aware of what will capture your students' attention.

You can help your students learn more effectively if you keep in mind how the sensory register works. As the first memory store in the information processing

Handbook Heading:
Techniques for
Capturing Attention

**Unpredictable
changes in envi-
ronment usually
command attention**

system, the SR holds sensory information (sights, sounds, smells, and the like) just long enough for the learner to attend selectively to whatever will receive additional encoding. Attention to first impressions is influenced by characteristics of the information itself and by the learner's related past experiences. Learners are more likely to attend to things they expect to find interesting or meaningful.

Almost all students at one time or another have difficulty concentrating on a task. Remember that human beings are sensitive to abrupt, sudden changes in their environment. Thus, anything that stands out, breaks a rhythm, or is unpredictable is almost certain to command a student's attention.

Examples

Print key words or ideas in extra-large letters on the board.

Use colored chalk to emphasize important points written on the board.

Give students colored marking pens and urge them to underline key words or phrases in any learning materials that will not need to be used later by other students.

When you come to a particularly important part of a lesson, say "Now really concentrate on this. It's especially important." Then present the idea with intensity and emphasis.

When lecturing about or discussing a particular historical figure, dress and act the part (if you are uninhibited and/or a former member of a dramatic club).

Start off a lesson with unexpected remarks, such as "Imagine that you have just inherited a million dollars and . . ."

b. **To maintain attention, emphasize the possible utility of learning new ideas.**

Handbook Heading:
Techniques for
Maintaining Attention

While it is possible to overdo attempts at making the curriculum relevant, it never hurts to think of possible ways of relating school learning to the present and future lives of students. When students realize that the basic purpose of school is to help them adapt to their environment, they are more apt to pay close attention to what it is you are trying to do.

Example

Teach basic skills, such as arithmetic computation, arithmetic reasoning, spelling, writing, and reading, as part of class projects that relate to students' natural interests (for example, keeping records of money for newspaper deliveries; measuring rainfall, temperature, and wind speed; writing letters to local television stations to express opinions on or request information about television shows).

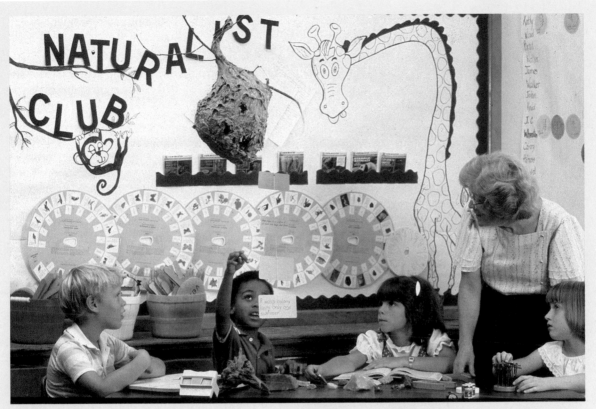

To call attention to information or procedures, it is often a good idea to use bizarre, novel, colorful, or appealing posters and displays. (The Stock Market/Wayne Eastep, 1987)

c. Teach students how to increase their span of attention.

Remember that attending is a skill that many students have not had an opportunity to refine. Give your students plenty of opportunities to practice and improve their ability to maintain attention.

Examples

Institute games that depend on maintaining attention, such as "Simon Says," keeping track of an object hidden under one of several boxes (the old shell game), or determining whether two pictures are identical or different. At first, positively reinforce students for all correct responses. Then reinforce only for improvements in performance. Remind students that their success is a direct result of how well they attend.

> Attention span can be increased with practice

> Handbook Heading: Techniques for Increasing Attention Span

Read a short magazine or newspaper story and ask students to report who, what, where, when, and why.

Whisper a message to one student and have her or him repeat it to another, who in turn, repeats it to another, and so on down the line. The last child to hear the message then repeats it aloud and compares it with the original message you whispered.

2. Point out and encourage students to recognize that certain bits of information are important and can be related to what is already known.

Attention is one control process for the sensory register; the other is recognition. Sometimes the two processes can be used together to induce students to focus on important parts of material to be learned. Sometimes you can urge your students to recognize key features or familiar relationships on their own.

Examples

When teaching letter or object recognition to primary graders, have them trace the letter or object with their index finger while saying the name of each item aloud.

When teaching word recognition, display words in bright colors and in different-sized letters.

Have students practice grouping numbers, letters, or classroom items according to some shared feature, such as odd numbers, multiples of five, letters with circles, or things made of wood.

Say, "This math problem is very similar to one you solved last week. Does anyone recognize something familiar about this problem?"

Say, "In this chapter the same basic point is made in several different ways. As you read, try to recognize and write down as many variations on that basic theme as you can."

3. Use appropriate rehearsal techniques, including stress on meaning and use of chunking.

One of the basic ways that information is encoded in long-term memory is through elaborative rehearsal. Only rarely do we learn something at first glance. Most of the time we have to elaboratively rehearse something several times in order to remember it. Without knowledge of learning strategies, or in the absence of proper guidance by a teacher, however, many students resort to "thoughtless" rehearsal. They simply repeat words over and over again without

To help students encode information, show them how to recognize similarities. One way to do this is to call attention to ways chunks of information (such as parts of the human body) can be grouped according to some shared feature. (David S. Strickler/ Monkmeyer)

attempting to search for meaning or relate what they are saying to what they already know. A story is told of an elementary school boy who persisted in saying, "I have went." After correcting him a dozen times, his teacher finally exploded and sentenced him to write "I have gone" a hundred times after school. As the student reached the ninetieth repetition late that afternoon, the teacher left the room on an errand. When she returned, she discovered that the hapless pupil had finished his task and departed. On the board were a hundred progressively sloppier "I have gone's," together with this note: "Dear teacher, I have wrote 'I have gone' a hundred times and I have went home."

The moral of this tale is, of course, that repetition does little good unless students are helped to *understand* their errors. This story also points up the futility of requiring an excessive number of repetitions. It is usually more effective to ask error makers to do something the correct way a few times and *think about it* than to force them to do it a hundred times, which will be so tedious and distasteful that they will almost certainly think about something else. For example, it is much better for a girl who can't remember how to spell *principal* to write the word five times and make use of a mnemonic device by thinking to herself, "The principal is a pal," than to write it a hundred times and think that her teacher is a louse.

The power of chunking information into meaningful units was demonstrated in a study conducted with a single college student of average memory ability and intelligence (Ericson, Chase, & Faloon, 1980). Over twenty months he was able to improve his memory for digits from seven to almost eighty. Being a track and field buff, he categorized three- and four-digit groups as running times for imaginary races. Thus, 3492 became "3 minutes and 49.2 seconds, near world record time." Number groups that could not be encoded by running times were encoded as ages. These two chunking techniques accounted for almost 90 percent of his associations.

Handbook Heading:
Ways to Use Chunking to
Facilitate Learning

The main purpose of chunking is to enhance learning by breaking tasks into small, easy-to-manage pieces. To a large degree, students can learn to do this for themselves if you show them how chunking works. In addition, you can help by not requiring students to learn more than they can reasonably handle at one time. If you have a list of fifty spelling words to be learned, it is far better to present ten words a day, five days in a row, during short study periods than to give all fifty at once. This method of presentation is called **distributed practice**. In distributed practice, it is usually necessary to divide the material into small parts, which—because of the serial-position effect—seems to be the best way for students to learn and retain unrelated material (for example, spelling words). The **serial position effect** refers to people's tendency to learn and remember the words at the beginning and end of a list more easily than those in the middle. When you use short lists, you in effect eliminate the hard-to-memorize middle ground.

Distributed practice: short study periods at frequent intervals

Serial position effect: tendency to remember items at beginning and end of a list

Distributed practice may not be desirable for all learning tasks, however. If you ask pupils to learn roles in a play, short rehearsals might not be effective, because students may have a difficult time grasping the entire plot. If you allow enough rehearsal time to run through a whole act, on the other hand, your students will be able to relate one speech to another and comprehend the overall structure of the play. When students learn by way of a few rather long study periods, spaced infrequently, psychologists call it **massed practice**.

You might also tell your students about the relative merits of distributed versus massed practice. Robert Bjork (1979) has pointed out that most students not only are unaware of the benefits of distributed study periods, but go to considerable lengths to block or mass the study time devoted to a particular subject.

The above suggestions about teaching chunking are likely to be most effective with children who are around ten years of age. Between the ages of five and seven, children rarely engage in spontaneous rehearsal. Between seven and ten, rehearsal strategies are very primitive, with each term rehearsed separately. Finally, around ten years of age, items may be grouped together and rehearsed as a set, making chunking possible.

4. Organize what you ask your pupils to learn and urge older students to organize material on their own.

Simply grouping items is appropriate when dealing with "illogical" information such as the order of the letters of the alphabet or telephone numbers. But most information you will ask your students to learn will make sense in one way or another. At least some items in most sets of information will be related to other items, and it will be desirable to call attention to interrelationships. The experiment described earlier in which one group of students was given a single long list of items to learn, another group the same items presented in logically ordered groups, illustrates the value of organization. By placing related items in groups, you reduce the number of chunks to be learned and also make it possible for students to benefit from cues supplied by the interrelationships between items in any given set. By placing items in logical order, you help students grasp how information at the beginning of a chapter or lesson makes it easier to learn information that is presented later.

Handbook Heading:
Organizing Information
into Related Categories

Examples

If students are to learn how to identify trees, birds, rocks, or the equivalent, groups items that are related (for example, deciduous and evergreen trees). Call attention to distinctive features and organizational schemes that have been developed.

Print an outline of a chapter on the board, or give students a duplicated outline, and have them record notes under the various headings.

Whenever you give a lecture or demonstration, print an outline on the board. Call attention to the sequence of topics and call attention to how various points emerge from or are related to other points.

5. As much as possible, stress meaningfulness.

Much of the information you will ask students to learn will be logical and meaningful. Even students at the college level, however, often treat information that makes sense as if it were nonsensical. Instead of using what they already know to encode new information, many students resort to rote memorization, which is

Handbook Heading:
Ways to Stress
Meaningfulness

not only tedious but also ineffective. So when you present material to be learned, emphasize the logic behind it and urge students to look for meaning on their own.

Concrete analogies offer one effective way to add meaning to material. Consider someone who has no knowledge of basic physics but is trying to understand a passage about the flow of electricity through metal. For this person, statements about crystalline lattice arrays, free-floating electrons, and the effects of impurities will mean very little. However, such abstract ideas can be explained in more familiar terms—the molecular structure of a metal bar can be compared to a tinker toy arrangement, for example, or the effect of impurities to placing a book in the middle of a row of falling dominoes. Such analogies increase recall and comprehension (Royer & Cable, 1975, 1976).

Concrete analogies can make abstract information meaningful

Examples

Give students opportunities to express ideas in their own words and to relate new knowledge to previous learning.

When you explain or demonstrate, express complex and abstract ideas several different ways. Be sure to provide plenty of examples.

Construct essay tests and homework assignments that emphasize comprehension and application. Give credit for thoughtful answers even though they do not exactly match the answer you would have given.

For topics that are somewhat controversial (for example, nuclear energy, genetic engineering, pesticide use) require students to present both pro and con arguments.

6. Demonstrate a variety of learning tactics and allow students to practice them.
   a. Teach students how to use various forms of rehearsal and mnemonic devices.

Handbook Heading: Ways to Teach Memory Tactics

At least two reasons recommend the teaching of rehearsal. One is that maintenance rehearsal is a useful tactic for keeping a relatively small amount of information active in short-term memory. Second, it is one of a few tactics that young children can learn to use. If you do decide to teach rehearsal, we have three suggestions. First, remind young children that rehearsal is something that learners consciously decide to do when they want to remember things. Second, remind students to rehearse no more than seven items (or chunks) at a time. Third, teach upper elementary grade students the more advanced forms of rehearsal (such as cumulative rehearsal and rehearsing sets of items that form homogeneous categories).

Upper elementary grade students (fourth, fifth, and sixth graders) can be taught advanced forms of maintenance rehearsal, such as cumulative rehearsal, and forms of elaborative rehearsal, such as rehearsing sets of items that form homogeneous categories. As with younger students, provide several opportunities each week to practice these skills.

As you prepare class presentations, or encounter bits of information that students seem to have difficulty learning, ask yourself if a mnemonic device would be useful. You might prepare a list of the devices discussed earlier and refer to it often. Part of the value of mnemonic devices is that they make learning easier. They are also fun to make up and use. Moreover, rhymes, acronyms, and acrostics can be constructed rather quickly. You might consider setting aside about thirty minutes two or three times a week to teach mnemonics. First, explain how rhyme, acronym, and acrostic mnemonics work, and then provide an example. For younger children use short, simple rhymes like "Columbus crossed the ocean blue in fourteen hundred ninety-two." For older students, the rhymes may be longer and more complex. The following rhyme is often used as a way to remember the value of pi from one to twenty decimal places:

> Pie.
> I wish I could reproduce pi.
> Eureka cried the great inventor,
> Christmas pudding Christmas pie
> Is the problem's very center.

If you count the number of letters in each word you come up with the answer—3.14159265358979323846.

Acrostics can be used to remember particularly difficult spelling words. The word *arithmetic* can be spelled by taking the first letter from each word of the following sentence: A Rat in the House May Eat the Ice Cream.

Once students understand how the mnemonic is supposed to work, have them construct mnemonics to learn various facts and concepts. You might offer a prize for the most ingenious mnemonic.

The pegword and loci mnemonics are particularly suited for learning long lists of items in serial order. For both, the first step involves learning a set of memory pegs. Because the pegs rhyme with the ordinal position they represent (for example, one-bun, two-shoe), they are fairly easy to learn. Familiar places are used as the pegs for the loci method and therefore will vary from person to person. As with rhymes, acronyms, and acrostics, explain how the pegword and loci mnemonics work and provide a demonstration. Once students have memorized the pegs or locations, allow them to practice with short lists of concrete nouns, abstract nouns, and mixed lists. Gradually lengthen the lists to ten, fifteen, and twenty or more items and introduce material from the curriculum. This may include the names of elements that make up the periodic table from lightest to heaviest, the names of bones in the human body, the names of various traffic signs, and the like. When the class exhibits skill in memorizing lists of items, you might encourage them to list ideas from a reading passage or speech and learn them with either mnemonic.

The keyword method should be used whenever pairs of items have to be learned. Learning a foreign language vocabulary, abstract or technical terminology, the accomplishments of people, and states and their capitals are tasks ideally suited to the keyword mnemonic. Because the keyword technique uses imagery, one of the first things you will have to do is explain what an image is and provide students with sufficient practice in generating images. Then, help students generate appropriate keywords. Keywords are known words that sound like or are some part of the word to be learned. Adapting the keyword method to learning two-part facts, like states and their capitals, is a little different in that it involves generating two keywords (for example, Levin, Shriberg, Miller, McCormick, & Levin, 1980). To learn the association Maryland-Annapolis, for instance, the student would need a keyword for Maryland, such as *marry*, and a keyword for Annapolis, such as *apple*. The two keywords are then embedded in an interacting visual image. Imagine, if you will, two apples being married. For Springfield, Illinois, imagine a field of springs making a lot of noise.

*Handbook Heading:
Ways to Teach
Comprehension Tactics*

b. Teach students how to formulate comprehension questions.

We concluded earlier that self-questioning could be an effective comprehension tactic if students were trained to write good comprehension questions and given opportunities to practice the technique. We suggest you try the following instructional sequence:

1. Discuss the purpose of student-generated questions.
2. Point out the differences between knowledge-level questions and comprehension-level questions. An excellent discussion of this distinction can be found in the *Taxonomy of Educational Objectives, Handbook I: Cognitive Domain* (Bloom and others, 1956).
3. Provide students with a sample paragraph and several comprehension questions. Again, good examples of comprehension questions and guidelines for writing your own can be found in the *Taxonomy*.
4. Hand out paragraphs from which students can practice constructing questions.
5. Provide corrective feedback.

6. Give students short passages from which to practice.
7. Provide corrective feedback (Andre & Anderson, 1978–79).

c. Teach students how to take notes.

Despite the limitations of research on notetaking, mentioned earlier, three suggestions should lead to more effective notetaking. First, provide students with clear, detailed objectives for every reading assignment. The objectives should indicate what parts of the assignment to focus on and how that material should be processed (whether memorized verbatim, reorganized and paraphrased, or integrated with earlier reading assignments). Second, inform students that notetaking is an effective comprehension tactic when used appropriately. Think, for example, about a reading passage that is long and for which test items will demand analysis and synthesis of broad concepts (as in "Compare and contrast the economic, social, and political causes of World War I with those of World War II"). Tell students to concentrate on identifying main ideas and supporting details, paraphrase this information, and record similarities and differences. Third, provide students with practice and corrective feedback in answering questions that are similar to those on the criterion test.

7. Encourage students to think about the various conditions that affect *how* they learn and remember.

Although awareness of the factors that affect comprehension and recall develops with age and experience, classroom performance may be improved by helping students to understand the role of different variables in learning. One approach is to use the tetrahedral model of learning as a guide. In this way, you can attempt to increase awareness of how personal characteristics, learning tactics, learning materials, and criterial tasks like tests, projects, and performances affect classroom learning.

The very youngest students (through third grade) should be told periodically that such cognitive behaviors as describing, recalling, guessing, and understanding mean different things, produce different results, and vary in how well they fit a task's demands.

For older elementary students, explain the learning process more simply, focusing on the circumstances in which different learning tactics are likely to be useful. Then, have students keep a diary or log in which they note when they use learning tactics, which ones, and with what success. Look for cases where good performance corresponds to frequent reported use of tactics and positively reinforce those individuals. Encourage greater use of tactics among students whose performance and reported use of them is below average.

While this same technique can be used with high school and college students, they should also be made aware of the other elements that make up strategic learning. Discuss the meaning of and necessity for analyzing a learning task, developing a learning plan, using appropriate tactics, monitoring the effectiveness of the plan, and implementing whatever corrective measures might be called for.

8. Each time you prepare an assignment, think about learning strategies you and your students might use.

Handbook Heading:
Ways to Teach Learning
Strategies

As noted in the discussion of age trends in metacognition, virtually all elementary school pupils and many high school students will not be able to devise and use their own coordinated set of learning strategies. Accordingly, you should devise such strategies for them, explain how the strategies work, and urge them to use these techniques on their own. With high school students, you might consider giving a "How to Study" lecture at the beginning of a report period to provide your students with general information about learning strategies. Even if you do give such an orientation, though, it would still be wise to give specific instructions as each assignment is made. In devising learning strategies, follow the procedure that was described earlier in this chapter: analyze, plan, implement, monitor, modify. When you analyze, though, take into account not only the material to be learned and the nature of the tests you will give, but also the cognitive characteristics of the learners.

Examples

To help elementary school pupils prepare for a spelling test to be administered on a district-wide basis, begin by analyzing the nature of the task and the cognitive abilities of your pupils. Select mnemonic devices likely to lead to effective encoding. Divide the words students will be tested on into short lists. Schedule several brief study sessions each day, and follow each session with a nonmemorization activity. Have students pair off and test each other. Use flash cards, and encourage your students to make and use their own. Occasionally, have some students go to the board and write out words you dictate at a rapid pace. Give frequent practice quizzes. Have each pupil prepare a list of "Words I Know" and "Words I Don't Know." For words they don't know, suggest new mnemonic devices and arrange for plenty of rehearsal.

In a secondary grade class, analyze each text chapter and decide what kind of exam you intend to use to evaluate your students' understanding. Perhaps draw up a list of key points, print these on the board, and announce that they will be emphasized on exam questions. Explain what kinds of test questions you intend to ask and give some suggestions on the best ways to study in order to be able to answer such questions. Announce the date of the exam well in advance. Schedule supervised study sessions during class periods. Give your students specific suggestions about learning strategies that they might use during each study session. At least a week or so before the exam give a practice quiz featuring questions similar to those that will be on the exam, and have students note points they know and don't know. Tell them to concentrate on material that is incompletely learned and recommend trouble-shooting learning strategies. Give a follow-up quiz and repeat the monitor-modify procedure.

Suggestions for Further Study

The Nature of Information Processing Theory

For more on how information processing theory relates to teaching and learning, read Chapter 1 of *Cognitive Classroom Learning* (1986), edited by Gary D. Phye and Thomas Andre. Titled "Cognition, Learning, and Education," the chapter compares information processing with behavioral learning theory, describes the nature of memory stores and control processes, and discusses the value of an information processing perspective for educational practice.

Another source of information is Chapter 2 of *The Cognitive Psychology of Learning* (1985) by Ellen D. Gagne. This chapter, in addition to describing the characteristics of memory stores and control processes, covers the research methods that are used by information processing psychologists, how cognitive theories are developed, and how teachers can use an information processing perspective in planning instruction.

Memory Structures and Processes

Henry C. Ellis and R. Reed Hunt provide detailed analyses of the sensory register, recognition, attention, short-term memory, elaborative rehearsal, long-term memory, and retrieval in the fourth edition of *Fundamentals of Human Memory and Cognition* (1989).

Mark Grabe describes how knowledge of attentional processes can enhance instructional practices in Chapter 3 of *Cognitive Classroom Learning* (1986). Raymond W. Kulhavy, Neil H. Schwartz, and Sarah Peterson do the same for encoding processes in Chapter 5 of the same book.

Metacognition

Orpha K. Duell provides a summary of research on metacognition in Chapter 8 of Phye and Andre's *Cognitive Classroom Learning* (1986). Bonnie B. Armbruster, Catharine H. Echols, and Ann L. Brown discuss metacognition's role in reading in volume 84 of *The Volta Review* (1982).

Learning Tactics and Strategies

One of the most popular (and useful) memory improvement books available is *The Memory Book* (1974) by Harry Lorayne and Jerry Lucas. In Chapter 2 of their book, Lorayne and Lucas explain why and how you should think up ridiculous associations; in Chapter 4 they offer suggestions for using substitute words. Techniques for learning foreign and English vocabulary are explained in Chapter 7; ways to remember names and faces are described in Chapter 8.

In *Practical Aspects of Memory* (1978), edited by Michael Gruneberg, Peter Morris, and Robert Sykes, you will find nineteen articles dealing with memory in everyday life and memory aids. Among others, there are articles on minimizing absent-mindedness, the effect of humor on memory, remembering medical information, and the history of mnemonics.

Michele Slung presents over 150 mnemonic devices (mostly rhymes, acronyms, and acrostics) organized by subject matter (for example, history, music, plants and animals, anatomy) in *The Absent-Minded Professor's Memory Book* (1985).

In Part C of *Teaching Reading, Writing, and Study Strategies* (3rd ed., 1983), H. Alan Robinson describes patterns of writing (text structures) and associated comprehension tactics for four major content areas: science, social studies, English, and mathematics.

Individual Differences in Memory

One of the most striking accounts of supernormal memory is provided by Alexander Luria in *The Mind of a Mnemonist: A Little Book About a Vast Memory* (1968). Luria describes his experiments and experiences over a period of almost thirty years with the man he refers to as S. What made S. remarkable was his apparent photographic memory, allowing him to recall nonsense material he had not seen for fifteen years. Additional articles about people with unusually proficient memory capability can be found in *Memory Observed* (1982), edited by Ulric Neisser.

Robert Kail describes memory differences among normal children, as well as differences between normal and retarded children, in *The Development of Memory in Children* (1984). In addition, there is a brief discussion of the idiot savant phenomenon—an individual who is below average on all measures of ability except one, in which he or she far surpasses almost all other individuals. Kail discusses one individual whose knowledge of the calendar was essentially perfect between the years 1 and 40400 despite having an IQ score in the 60–70 range.

Mnemonic instruction with various special education populations is discussed by James E. Turnure and John F. Lane (Chapter 15) and by Margo A. Mastropieri, Thomas E. Scruggs, and Joel R. Levin (Chapter 16) in *Imagery and Related Mnemonic Processes* (1987), edited by Mark A. McDaniel and Michael Pressley.

Summary

1. Information processing theory attempts to explain how individuals acquire, store, recall, and use information.

2. Information processing theory arose in part because psychologists were dissatisfied with behavioral learning theory's omission of the mental activities of the learner.
3. From an information processing perspective, learning can be seen as an interaction among characteristics of the learner, mental activities in which the learner engages, the nature of the learning material, and the nature of the criterion.
4. A popular model of information processing is comprised of three memory stores and a set of control processes that determine the flow of information from one memory store to another. The memory stores are the sensory register, short-term memory, and long-term memory. The control processes are recognition, attention, maintenance rehearsal, elaborative rehearsal, and retrieval.
5. The sensory register holds information in its original form for two or three seconds, during which time we may recognize and attend to it further.
6. Recognition involves noticing key features of a stimulus and integrating those features with relevant information from long-term memory.
7. Attention is a selective focusing on a portion of the information in the sensory register. Information from long-term memory influences what we focus on.
8. Short-term memory holds about seven bits of information for about twenty seconds (in the absence of rehearsal). It is often called working memory because it contains information we are conscious of.
9. Information can be held in short-term memory indefinitely through the use of maintenance rehearsal, which is rote repetition of information.
10. Information is transferred from short-term memory to long-term memory by linking the new information to related information in long-term memory. This process is called elaborative rehearsal.
11. Elaborative rehearsal is based partly on organization. This involves grouping together, or chunking, items of information that share some important characteristic.
12. Elaborative rehearsal is also based on meaningfulness. Meaningfulness exists when new information can be related to the current cognitive structures (schemata) of the learner.
13. Long-term memory is thought to be an unlimited storehouse of information from which nothing is ever lost.
14. Many psychologists believe the information in long-term memory is organized in the form of schemata. A schema has been defined as a generalized abstract structure of information. When schemata are absent or crudely formed, learning and recall problems occur.
15. Metacognition refers to any knowledge an individual has about how we think and the circumstances that affect thinking.
16. Metacognitive knowledge increases gradually with experience. This helps explain why junior high and high school students are more flexible and effective learners than primary grade students.
17. A learning strategy is a general plan that specifies the resources one will use and how one will use them to achieve a learning goal.

18. A learning tactic is a specific technique used to help achieve an academic goal when confronted with a task.
19. Learning tactics can be classified as memory directed or comprehension directed. The former are used when accurate storage and retrieval of information is important. The latter are used when comprehension of ideas is important.
20. Two types of memory-directed tactics are rehearsal and mnemonic devices. Since most forms of rehearsal involve little or no encoding of information, they are not very effective memory tactics. Because mnemonic devices organize information and provide built-in retrieval cues, they are effective memory tactics.
21. Popular mnemonic devices include rhymes, acronyms, acrostics, the pegword method, the loci method, and the keyword method.
22. Two effective comprehension tactics are self-questioning and notetaking.
23. The components of a learning strategy are metacognition, analysis, planning, implementation, monitoring, and modifying.

Key Terms

information processing
  theory *(375)*
sensory register *(380)*
recognition *(380)*
attention *(381)*
short-term memory *(382)*
maintenance rehearsal *(383)*
elaborative rehearsal *(383)*
long-term memory *(385)*

schemata *(387)*
metacognition *(389)*
learning strategy *(392)*
learning tactic *(392)*
mnemonic device *(393)*
distributed practice *(410)*
serial position effect *(410)*
massed practice *(410)*

Discussion Questions

1. Can you think of any personal, everyday experiences that illustrate the nature of one or more of the three memory stores? Have you recently, for instance, retrieved a long-dormant memory because of a chance encounter with an associated word, sound, or smell?
2. Information processing psychologists have expressed disappointment that the results of their research on memory stores and processes, learning tactics, and learning strategies have not been widely implemented by teachers. Is this complaint consistent with your experience? Can you recall any instances when you were taught how to use a variety of learning tactics to formulate different strategies? How about out of school? Did you acquire any such skills without the help of a classroom teacher?
3. Many teachers have said that they would like to teach their students more about the nature and use of learning processes, but that they don't have time

because of the amount of subject material they must cover. What can you do as a teacher to avoid this pitfall?

4. A major problem in training students to use learning strategies and tactics is getting the youngsters to spend the time and effort required to master these skills. Suppose some students expressed their disinterest, saying their own methods would be just as effective (although you know full well they would not be). How would you convince them otherwise?

chapter 9

COGNITIVE LEARNING THEORIES AND PROBLEM SOLVING

KEY POINTS

The Nature of Meaningful Learning

Bruner: students should learn structure of a field of study

Spiral curriculum: reteach same idea in more complex form over time

Discover how ideas relate to each other and to existing knowledge

MACOS techniques: contrast, guessing, participation, awareness

Discovery method not appropriate for primary grade pupils

Discovery method may produce frustration

Meaningful reception learning: integrate new ideas into existing knowledge schemes

When relationships are ignored, reception learning can be nonmeaningful

Meaningful learning depends on nature of task, learner's set

Advance organizer helps relate new ideas to existing schemes

The Nature of Problem Solving

Well-structured problems: clearly stated, known solution procedures, known evaluation standards

Ill-structured problems: vaguely stated, unclear solution procedures, vague evaluation standards

Issues: ill-structured problems that arouse strong feelings

Problem finding depends on curiosity, dissatisfaction with status quo

Problem framing depends on subject matter knowledge, familiarity with problem types

Studying worked examples is an effective solution strategy

Solve simpler version of problem first, then transfer process to harder problem

Break complex problems into manageable parts

Work backwards when goal is clear but beginning state is not

Analogous problems must be very similar to target problem

Evaluate solutions to well-structured problems by estimating or checking

Intellectual skill: using rules to solve problems

Intellectual skills composed of rules, concepts, discriminations, associations

When you begin to teach, you may devote a substantial amount of class time to having pupils learn information discovered by others. But acquiring a storehouse of facts, concepts, and principles is only part of what constitutes an appropriate education. Students must also learn how to *use* what they know to accomplish whatever goals they set for themselves. In other words, students need to learn how to be effective problem solvers. One justification for teaching problem-solving skills *in addition* to assuring mastery of factual information is that life in the United States (and other technologically oriented countries) is marked by speedy change. New products, services, and social conventions are rapidly introduced and integrated into our life styles. Microcomputers, videocassette recorders, microwave ovens, anticancer drugs, in vitro fertilization, just to name a few, are relatively recent innovations that significantly affect the lives of many people.

Change, particularly rapid change, can be viewed as a mixed blessing. On the one hand, new products and services such as those mentioned can make life more convenient, efficient, and enjoyable. On the other hand, they can make life more complicated and problematic. Factory automation, for example, promises increased efficiency and productivity (which contributes to our standard of living), but it also threatens the job security of thousands of workers. Advances in medical care promise healthier and longer lives, but they introduce a host of moral, ethical, legal, and economic problems.

The educational implication that flows from these observations is clear: If we are to benefit from our ability to produce rapid and sometimes dramatic change, our schools need to invest more time, money, and effort in teaching students how to be effective problem solvers. As Lauren Resnick, a past president of the American Educational Research Association, has argued,

> We need to identify and closely examine the aspects of education that are most likely to produce ability to adapt in the face of transitions and breakdowns. Rather than training people for particular jobs—a task better left to revised forms of on-the-job training—school should focus its efforts on preparing people to be good *adaptive learners,* so that they can perform effectively when situations are unpredictable and task demands change. (1987, p. 18)

Resnick's argument, which echoes many others, is not without some justification. According to estimates made by the Carnegie Foundation, big business spends up to $100 billion a year on corporate classrooms that try to develop the thinking skills corporate management feels the schools have failed to teach (Ruggiero, 1988).

Good problem solvers share two general characteristics: a well-organized, meaningful fund of knowledge and a systematic set of problem-solving skills. Historically, cognitive learning theories have been particularly useful sources of ideas for imparting both. In this chapter, then, we examine the issue of meaningful learning as expressed by two influential cognitive psychologists, Jerome S. Bruner and David P. Ausubel, and then we go on to describe the nature of the problem-solving process and what you can do to help your students become better problem solvers. We conclude by describing the circumstances under which learned capabilities are applied to new tasks, a process known as transfer of learning.

The Nature of Meaningful Learning

For as long as there have been schools, educators have wrestled with the questions "What should students learn?" and "How should they learn it?" The debates that have occurred both in the past and today over these two questions are usually not framed in either/or terms. Most people agree that learning should in some degree take in problem-solving skills, creativity, basic intellectual skills (like reading, writing, and computation), and knowledge of basic subject matter (like history, geography, or science), and that students should both pursue their own natural interests and self-discovery of facts and problem-solving procedures and memorize a predetermined body of knowledge. Whatever differences exist among theorists are in emphasis. The emphasis favored by psychologist Jerome Bruner is twofold: Students should understand the structure of a body of knowledge rather than

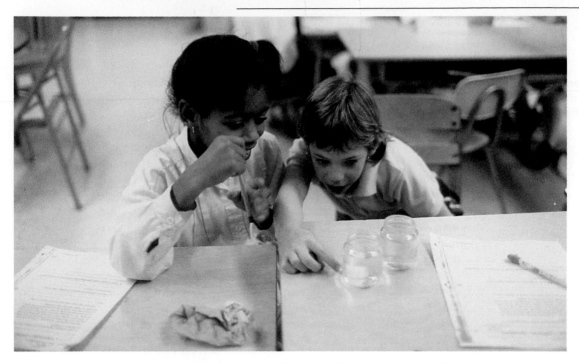

The essence of the approach to teaching advocated by Bruner is that students should be encouraged to make their own discoveries. (Elizabeth Crews)

memorize names, dates, places, rules, formulas, and so on, as isolated fragments; and they should learn how to discover what they need to know.

Bruner: The Importance of Structure and Discovery

Bruner's interest in meaningful learning and the discovery approach began with his studies on perception (1951) and thinking (Bruner, Goodnow, & Austin, 1956). His interest in finding ways to apply to education what he had discovered about these two areas drew impetus from his directorship of the Woods Hole Conference on Education. This conference was called in 1959 to find ways to improve science education in the public schools (at the time Russia had recently demonstrated its superiority in space technology). In *The Process of Education* (1960), Bruner summarized his perception of the main points brought out in the conference. This book, now viewed as a classic statement on education, triggered an interest in school learning in general, which Bruner discussed in *Toward a Theory of Instruction* (1966) and *The Relevance of Education* (1971).

Structure One of the major points emphasized in *The Process of Education* is that teaching should assist students in grasping the structure of a field of study.

Bruner: students should learn structure of a field of study

Understanding the **structure** of a subject means understanding its basic or fundamental ideas and how they relate to each other. Ideas that are truly fundamental share a number of characteristics: They can be simply represented as a diagram, picture, verbal statement, or formula (as in Einstein's formula for relativity, $E = mc^2$); they can be represented in more than one sensory modality; and they are applicable to a wide range of new problems. The operant conditioning principle of reinforcement is an example of a fundamental idea. It is simple to understand and to state; it can be stated as a simple verbal proposition or illustrated on film; and it helps explain the learning of habits, verbal skills, attitudes, motor skills, and behavior in home, work, play, and school settings. Good versus evil is another fundamental idea that appears repeatedly in varied forms in religion, literature, art, and philosophy. Bruner suggests that when students are helped to grasp the structure of a field of study, they are more likely to remember what they learn, comprehend principles that can be applied in a variety of situations, and be prepared for mastering more complex knowledge. As we will see a bit later in this chapter, understanding structure is critical to effective problem solving and transfer of learning.

Spiral Curriculum   Closely related to the issue of understanding structure is the question of when children are old enough to grasp the meaning of fundamental ideas. Bruner's response, detailed in *The Relevance of Education,* is that if you take into account the nature of children's thought, then "any subject can be taught to any child in some honest form . . ." (1971, p. 52). Since this statement has been widely quoted, and often misunderstood, a little elaboration is in order. Like Piaget, Bruner believed that children of different ages represent the world to themselves in fundamentally different ways. Toddlers and preschoolers think of the world primarily in terms of the actions that can be performed on it. Bruner calls this the *enactive* mode of representation. During much of childhood ideas are represented primarily in terms of pictures or images. This form of representation is called *iconic.* Finally, in late childhood and early adolescence ideas tend to be represented in terms of verbal propositions, mathematical formulas, logical symbols, and the like (although the enactive and iconic modes are equally available). Not surprisingly, Bruner terms this form of representation *symbolic.* Bruner argues that even young children can grasp the essence of basic ideas—albeit in a simplified, intuitive fashion—provided the presentation is geared to the child's

Spiral curriculum: reteach same idea in more complex form over time

predominant mode of representation. In later years, as thinking becomes more mature, these same ideas can be reintroduced with more complexity. Bruner refers to this practice of introducing something early in simple form and then again later in more complex form as the **spiral curriculum.**

Discovery Learning   Another point stressed by Bruner is that too much school learning takes the form of step-by-step study of verbal or numerical statements or formulas that the students can reproduce on cue but is unable to use outside the classroom. When students are presented with programmed materials, Bruner argues, they become too dependent on others. Furthermore, they are likely to think of learning as something done only to earn a reward.

Instead of using techniques that feature preselected and prearranged materials, Bruner believes, teachers should confront children with problems and help them seek solutions either independently or by engaging in group discussion. True learning, says Bruner, involves "figuring out how to use what you already know in order to go beyond what you already think" (1983, p. 183). Like Piaget, Bruner argues that conceptions that children arrive at on their own are usually more meaningful than those proposed by others, and that students do not need to be rewarded when they seek to make sense of things that puzzle them. Bruner maintains, in addition, that when children are given a substantial amount of practice in finding their own solutions to problems, they not only develop problem-solving skills but also acquire confidence in their own learning abilities as well as a propensity to function later in life as problem solvers. They learn *how* to learn *as* they learn.

This approach to education has come to be called **discovery learning** (or *discovery teaching* if you prefer to look at it from the instructor's point of view). Like the idea mentioned earlier that any subject can be taught to any child, Bruner's position on discovery learning is often misunderstood. He does not suggest that students should discover every fact or principle or formula they may need to know. Discovery is simply too inefficient a process to be used that widely, and learning from others can be as meaningful as personal discovery. Rather, Bruner argues that certain types of outcomes—understanding the ways in which ideas connect with one another, the possibility of solving problems on our own, and how what we already know is relevant to what we are trying to learn—are the essence of education and can best be achieved through personal discovery.

> Discover how ideas relate to each other and to existing knowledge

As an example of this discovery approach, Bruner describes an incident in which a student is asked to explain the purpose of a compass (the instrument used to draw perfect circles). When the student refers to it as a steadying tool, the other children in the class quickly think of other devices that serve the same purpose, like a camera tripod or a cane. Another example is Bruner's approach to teaching geography in the elementary grades. Instead of having a group of fifth-graders memorize a set of geography facts, he gave them blank outline maps that showed the location of rivers, lakes, mountains, valleys, plains, and so on. Their task was to figure out where the major cities, railways, and highways might be located. The students were not permitted to consult books or other maps; they had to figure out locations on their own by drawing on their prior knowledge and reasoning ability.

Man: A Course of Study   To illustrate how teachers could use discovery forms of instruction, Bruner supervised the development of a comprehensive set of materials for teaching social studies in the elementary grades. The program was titled

Man: A Course of Study, and it is often referred to as the MACOS curriculum. Here is Bruner's brief description of MACOS: "The content of the course is man: his nature as a species, the forces that shaped and continue to shape his humanity. Three questions recur throughout: What is human about human beings? How did they get that way? How can they be made more so?" (1966, p. 74).

In seeking answers to these questions, pupils study subjects considered to be significant in human social behavior: social organization, the management of prolonged childhood, parenthood, group relationships, and the concept of culture. Techniques used in presenting the MACOS curriculum include the following:

MACOS techniques: contrast, guessing, participation, awareness

1. *Emphasizing contrast* (for example, contrasting human beings with animals, the modern human being with the prehistoric, the adult with the child)
2. *Stimulating informed guessing* (for example, asking students to hypothesize how Eskimos decide which breathing holes to stalk in hunting seals and then showing a film to illustrate how they actually *do* decide)
3. *Encouraging participation* (for example, arranging for pupils to function as anthropologists by making observations, collecting data, and formulating and testing hypotheses)
4. *Arousing awareness* (for example, having students analyze how they are attempting to solve problems)

Bruner's approach to teaching—implicit in this description of a unit on human beings—is summarized in the following statement:

> To instruct someone in [a] discipline is not a matter of getting him to commit results to mind. Rather, it is to teach him to participate in the process that makes possible the establishment of knowledge. We teach a subject not to produce little living libraries on the subject, but rather to get a student to think mathematically for himself, to consider matters as an historian does, to take part in the process of knowledge-getting. Knowing is a process, not a product. (1966, p. 72)

Now that you have been acquainted with arguments in favor of the discovery approach and a description of teaching techniques advocated by enthusiasts, you may gain some perspective by considering four criticisms of such forms of instruction.

Evaluations of the Discovery Approach   For students to discover the value of relating new knowledge to existing knowledge and of becoming more independent problem solvers, at least two conditions must be present: Students must possess a well-organized body of relevant knowledge that can be retrieved from memory when necessary, and they must feel sufficiently confident about their learning skills to engage in independent forms of problem solving. Because of these conditions, critics have argued that discovery methods should be used sparingly and with more teacher guidance than usual with primary grade and low-achieving students. Primary grade pupils are expected to master basic facts and skills, and they are either preoperational or budding concrete operational thinkers. They (and older low achievers) seem to want, need, and benefit from learning situations where the teacher presents a series of brief assignments, supplying instruction and immediate feedback (Brophy & Evertson, 1976; Bennett, Jordan, Long, & Wade, 1976; Cantor, Dunlap, & Rettie, 1982). Because of the second condition, the need for confidence, discovery methods should be deemphasized for students of all ages until they have been taught basic problem-solving processes (which are described later in this chapter).

Even for a teacher who is quite effective and competent in using the discovery method, occasional failure is inevitable simply because not all discovery sessions are likely to be productive. The most ardent believers admit that discovery is often inefficient and that learning frequently proceeds fitfully. There may be many instances where having an enthusiastic person tell others what he or she has learned is just as effective, if not more so, than letting students discover the same thing.

A third criticism is that students may become frustrated with discovery methods. One potential source of frustration arises when teachers refuse to tell what they obviously know, especially when a project or discussion has been disorganized and unproductive. Another possible source of frustration is that the brightest students will tend to monopolize the discoveries. This situation could create jealousy, resentment, or feelings of inferiority in students who never come up with a discovery of their own.

A final criticism is that when group discussion is used to foster discovery, only one person can speak at a time. Techniques such as dividing the class into groups can be used to distribute recitation opportunities, but one pupil in each group will still inevitably function as a lecturer, and the rest of the group will be forced, at least temporarily, into the role of listeners. As listeners, they may be less involved —and less enlightened—than they would be if they were, say, working on a computer, especially if the speaker is inarticulate and long-winded or given to prefacing every phrase with "I mean . . . you know."

Our purpose in presenting these criticisms is not to discourage you from using a discovery approach but to encourage you to think about the circumstances in which it is likely to be most effective. After students have mastered a unit on some subject, for instance, you might arrange for individuals or the class to explore ideas in class discussions or in the form of group or individual projects. At the secondary level, you may want to focus on the use of discussion techniques, because they provide a change of pace from structured learning experiences and because discussion is an effective technique for helping students discover how ideas relate to each other and to what they already know. The Suggestions for Teaching that follow provide some guidelines you might find helpful if and when you decide to use classroom discussion as part of a discovery approach.

Discovery method not appropriate for primary grade pupils

Discovery method may produce frustration

SUGGESTIONS FOR TEACHING

Using the Discovery Approach in the Classroom

1. If you intend to use any kind of discovery approach, first establish a relaxed atmosphere.

2. Arrange the learning situation so that discovery is likely to take place.
   a. Ask students to discuss familiar topics or those that are matters of opinion.
   b. Provide necessary background information by asking all students to read all or part of a book, take notes on a lecture, or view a film.

3. Structure discussions by posing a specific question, by presenting a provocative issue, or by asking students to choose topics or subtopics.
   a. In some cases, encourage students to arrive at conclusions already reached by others.
   b. In other cases, present a controversial topic for which there is no single answer.
   c. If the subject is complex, ask the class to suggest subtopics.

4. If time is limited and if only one topic is covered, ask students to form a circle and have an all-class discussion.
   a. Ask questions that stimulate students to apply, analyze, synthesize, or evaluate.
   b. Allow sufficient time for initial responses, and then probe for further information (if appropriate).
   c. When selecting students to recite, use techniques likely to sustain steady but nonthreatening attention. At the same time, guard against the temptation to call primarily on bright, articulate, assertive pupils.

5. If abundant time is available and if a controversial or subdivided topic is to be discussed, divide the class into groups of five or so, and arrange for all members in each group to have eye contact with every other group member.
   a. Have students choose to be members of a group, or divide the class by rows or by a counting-off procedure.
   b. Ask the students to move chairs or desks to form circles in different parts of the room.

6. Consider appointing or having the group elect a moderator and a recorder.

7. Consider asking all pupils to spend three minutes or so individually writing out their initial reactions to the discussion topic before they begin to share ideas.

8. As the groups engage in discussion, observe benignly but silently. Intervene only if it seems necessary to keep the discussion proceeding in a constructive manner.

   a. If the group has strayed from the topic, if one individual is dominating the discussion, or if the group is pressuring one individual to alter an opinion, use subtle remarks to try to correct the situation.

   b. In most cases, avoid answering questions or participating actively in the discussion.

9. Ask the group to share conclusions after they have had ample time to discuss the topic.

   a. Allow time at the end of the period for a spokesperson from each group to report on conclusions on specific points. Perhaps list these on the board and invite comments from the class.

   b. Consider asking each group to write a brief outline of their conclusions or to prepare a project or demonstration and combine these into a notebook or culminating event.

10. Give students opportunities to make individual or small-group discoveries in the form of projects or term papers.

1. If you intend to use any kind of discovery approach, first establish a relaxed atmosphere.

For the discovery method to work properly, pupils must feel free to express ideas without fear of ridicule or failure. When you want to use this approach, therefore, you should do your best to convince your students that they are free to play with ideas. Regardless of how pointless or silly some contributions may seem, you should avoid ridiculing those who make them. And if one or more students laugh at or belittle something that is said by a classmate, do your best to gloss over the incident by noting that the idea is worth exploring or by saying something like, "Remember, they laughed at Columbus, too. We can't come up with new ideas if we aren't willing to go out on a limb a bit."

2. Arrange the learning situation so that discovery is likely to take place.

This is the crux of the discovery approach. The basic idea is to *arrange* things so that insight will take place. In some cases, you may present a topic that is a mat-

Handbook Heading:
Ways to Arrange for
Discovery to Take Place

When using discussion techniques of instruction it is important to establish a relaxed, non-threatening classroom atmosphere. (Susan Lapides)

ter of opinion or one that all students are sure to know something about. In other cases, you structure the discussion by exposing all participants to the same background information.

a. Ask students to discuss familiar topics or those that are matters of opinion.

Examples

"What are some of the techniques that advertising agencies use in television commercials to try to persuade us to buy certain products?"

"What do you think is the best book you ever read, and why do you think so?"

b. Provide necessary background information by asking all students to read all or part of a book, take notes on a lecture, or view a film.

Examples

After the class has read *Great Expectations* say, "What do you think Dickens was trying to convey when he wrote this novel? Was he just trying to tell a good story, or was he also trying to get us to think about certain kinds of relationships between people?"

"After I explain some of the principles of electrical currents, I'm going to ask you to suggest rules for connecting batteries in series and in parallel. Then, we'll see how well your rules work."

"This film shows how beavers live. After it's over, we'll discuss ways that beaver behavior is similar to human behavior."

3. Structure discussions by posing a specific question, by presenting a provocative issue, or by asking students to choose topics or subtopics.

As the examples just noted indicate, it is important to structure a discovery session by giving students something reasonably specific to discuss. Otherwise, they may simply engage in a disorganized and desultory bull session. If you are going to function as a teacher, you should organize experiences so that more learning takes place under your direction than would occur if you left children entirely to themselves. You might supply direction in the following ways.

a. In some cases, encourage students to arrive at conclusions already reached by others.

Bruner's MACOS materials illustrate this approach. Thousands of books provide detailed answers to the questions "What is human about human beings? How did they get that way? How can they be made more so?" But Bruner believes that answers mean more when they are arrived at by the individual, not supplied ready-made by others. As you look over lesson plans, therefore, you might try to select some questions for students to answer by engaging in discussion, rather than by reading or listening to what others have already discovered. In searching for such topics, you might take into account the techniques described by Bruner. Here is a list of those techniques, together with an example of each one. In your Handbook you might describe similar applications that you could use when you begin to teach. Keep in mind that gaining insight depends on appropriate previous experience.

Emphasize contrast. In a sixth-grade social studies unit say, "When you watch this film on Mexico, look for customs and ways of living that differ from ours. Then we'll talk about what these differences are and also try to figure out why they may have developed."

Stimulate informed guessing. In a junior high unit on natural science you might say, "Suppose we wanted to figure out some kind of system to classify trees so that we could later find information about particular types. What would be the best way to do it?" After students have developed their own classification scheme, show them schemes developed by specialists.

Encourage participation. In a high school political science class, illustrate the jury system by staging a mock trial.

Stimulate awareness. In a high school English class, ask the students to discuss how the author developed the plot.

b. In other cases, present a controversial topic for which there is no single answer.

Discussions might center on provocative issues about which there are differences of opinion. One caution here is to avoid topics (such as premarital sex or legalized abortion) that parents may not want discussed in school, either because they are convinced it is their prerogative to discuss them with their children or because they feel that students may be pressured to endorse your opinion because you assign grades. You should not avoid controversy, but neither should you go out of your way to agitate pupils and their parents.

Another caution is to avoid selecting issues that provoke more than they instruct. You may be tempted to present a highly controversial topic and then congratulate yourself at the end of the period if most students engaged in heated discussion. But if they simply argued vociferously about something that had nothing to do with the subject you are assigned to teach, you could not honestly claim to have arranged an instructive exchange of ideas. A final caution relates to a characteristic of formal thought described in Chapter 2: There may be a tendency for secondary school students to engage in unrestrained theorizing when they first experience the thrill of being able to deal with hypotheses and possibilities. It may be necessary to remind some students to take into account realities when they discuss controversial issues involving tangled background circumstances or conflicts of interest.

Examples

In a junior high school science class, ask students to list arguments for and against attempting to alter the genetic code of human beings.

In a high school political science class, ask students to list arguments for and against democratic forms of government.

c. If the subject is complex, ask the class to suggest subtopics.

In some cases, you may wish to ask the class to discuss a topic that has many facets. When dealing with such material, you might first ask students to list subtopics. Use this information to divide the class into groups, and have each group prepare a report of some kind.

In *Personalizing Education* (1975) Leland W. and Mary M. Howe describe a ten-step procedure to follow if you would like to have students participate in developing a teaching unit. They also supply an example of a student-developed elementary school unit on crime and law enforcement. The steps in the procedure are

1. Have students brainstorm (call out as many ideas as possible in a short period of time) about topics of interest, and list these on the board.
2. Ask students to develop a set of criteria for selecting a topic from the list of brainstormed ideas.
3. Help the class prepare a *flow chart* by breaking the main topic down into subtopics.
4. Carry out a *question census;* that is, have the students list all the questions they think are important or valuable in studying subtopics.
5. Ask students to list resources they might consult. These might be listed under the following headings: reading, audiovisuals, field trips, people, manipulative devices.
6. Have students pair off and develop activities from one or two of the questions.
7. Analyze the purposes of the unit by having students list objectives under three headings: knowledge, cognitive skills, values.
8. Examine the curriculum plan, and revise it to make it better organized and to eliminate overlap.
9. Invite students to help you decide how the unit should be structured and taught, and what requirements should be established, and how the unit should be evaluated.
10. Carry out the final plan.

4. If time is limited and if only one topic is to be covered, ask students to form a circle and have an all-class discussion.

You may sometimes wish to have the entire class discuss a topic. Such discussions are most likely to be successful if all students have eye contact with each other. The simplest way to achieve this is to ask all students to form a circle. Next invite responses to the question you have posed. As students make remarks, serve more as a moderator than as a leader. Try to keep the discussion on the topic, but avoid directing it toward a specific predetermined end result. If one or more students tend to dominate the discussion, say something like,

Handbook Heading:
Ways to Supervise
Discovery Sessions

"Maria and Jack have given us their ideas. Now I'd like to hear from the rest of you." If an aggressive student attacks or belittles something said by a classmate, say something like, "It's good to *believe* in a point of view, but let's be friendly as we listen to other opinions. This is supposed to be a discussion, not an argument or a debate."

In some instances, whole-class discussions work beautifully. A contribution by one student will spark a related one by another, and almost everyone will follow what is said with interest. On other occasions, however, the outcome can be deadly, disorganized, or both. Sometimes the first thing said by the first student will annihilate the topic and the discussion. (An opinionated young man may say, for example, "There's absolutely no point in talking about that question. We can't change anything, so why waste time talking about it?") At other times, your bright and enthusiastic question, "Well, what do you think about that?" will be followed by complete silence, which in turn will be followed by nervous shuffling, much gazing out the window, and the like. (Just in case that happens, you should always have some sort of back-up activity planned for discussion periods.) Factors that lead to successful or unsuccessful discussions are often idiosyncratic, but there are certain procedures you might follow to increase the likelihood of success.

a. Ask questions that stimulate students to apply, analyze, synthesize, and evaluate.

When you first structure a discussion session, as well as when it is under way, take care to ask questions likely to arouse thoughtful responses. If you ask students to supply information (for example, "When did the Civil War begin?"), the first correct response will lead to closure. You may end up asking a series of questions leading to brief answers—the equivalent of a program or a fill-in exam. M. D. Gall (1970) reviewed dozens of studies of classroom recitation sessions and found consistent evidence that up to 80 percent of all questions asked by teachers stressed facts and knowledge. In some situations, such as review sessions before an exam, asking a series of questions that test knowledge is logical and desirable. But when one intends to encourage pupils to make their own discoveries or to develop skills as deductive thinkers, it is preferable to ask questions likely to tap higher levels of thinking.

Examples

"You just learned how to calculate the area of a circle. Think of as many different ways as you can of how you might be able to use that bit of knowledge if you were a do-it-yourself home owner." (Application)

"What are possible reasons the Civil War took place when it did? Try to think of

as many different possible causes as you can, and I'll list them on the board."
(Analysis)

"Last month we read a novel by Dickens; this month we read a play by Shake-speare. What are some similarities in the way each author developed the plot of the story?" (Synthesis)

"We just read five short poems by Emily Dickenson. I'd like you to tell me which one you like the best and then explain why you preferred it to the others. What qualities did your favorite poem have that the others did not have, at least to the same extent?" (Evaluation)

> b. Allow sufficient time for initial responses, and then probe for further information (if appropriate).

Mary Budd Rowe (1974) found that many teachers fail to allow enough time for pupils to respond to questions. She discovered that quite often instructors would wait only one second before repeating the question or calling on another student. When teachers were advised to wait at least three seconds after asking a question, student responses increased in frequency, length, and complexity. Furthermore, students seemed to be more confident (as reflected by the way they spoke and the kinds of statements they made), and more members of the class were inclined to participate.

One possible explanation for improved student recitation when teachers wait longer for a response is that reflective thinkers have an opportunity to figure out what they want to say. But even impulsive thinkers probably welcome a few more seconds of thinking time. It seems logical to expect that snap answers would be more superficial than answers supplied after even a few seconds of reflection.

In addition to giving students ample time to make an initial response, you should also encourage them to pursue an idea. If it seems appropriate, probe for further information or clarification of a point by asking pupils who give brief or incomplete answers to explain how or why they arrived at a conclusion or to supply additional comments.

Examples

"Well, Margie, I'm sure a gardener might sometimes need to figure the area of a circle, but can you give a more specific example? If you can't think of one right away, put up your hand as soon as you can describe a specific situation where it would help to know the area of circular patch of lawn or soil."

"Yes, John, it seems certain that differences of opinion about slavery had a lot to do with the Civil War. Let's pursue that a bit further. What were some of the economic and agricultural differences between the North and South that influenced feelings about slavery?"

Good expository teaching encourages interactive learning in which students participate in the learning process. (Susan Van Etten/The Picture Cube)

Meaningful reception learning: integrate new ideas into existing knowledge schemes

When relationships are ignored, reception learning can be nonmeaningful

This ease of assimilation is the goal of Ausubel's expository teaching, and he called that goal **meaningful reception learning** (that is, the integration of new ideas into existing knowledge schemes). Not all reception learning is meaningful. Rote, or nonmeaningful, learning occurs when students are presented with a mass of information for which few relationships are provided. In the study of history, for example, students often memorize the dates of certain events (like the American Civil War), what happened during those events (battles between opposing armies, for example), and the roles of major figures (such as Abraham Lincoln, Jefferson Davis, Ulysses S. Grant, and Robert E. Lee). Ausubel maintains that while such material has meaningful components, it will not be learned as a meaningful whole so long as it remains unconnected to related knowledge schemes the student already possesses. Hence, the components are memorized in more or less verbatim fashion and tend to be quickly forgotten. A reading passage or lecture that is designed to produce meaningful reception learning, on the other hand, would explain how these events were related to political, social, and economic factors as well as to something the student may already know (like the circumstances surrounding a different Civil War or a disagreement among family members).

Having made a distinction between meaningful learning and rote learning and between reception learning and discovery learning, Ausubel points out some false beliefs regarding each type of learning. He notes that, contrary to arguments offered by some theorists, reception learning is not invariably rote learning and discovery learning is not necessarily meaningful. It is possible—and definitely desirable—for a student working through a program or studying a chapter in a text to search for meaning. In some forms of discovery learning, on the other hand, particularly where students are given a series of similar problems to solve in quick succession, they may unthinkingly apply a formula as they search for solutions.

Whether a student engages in meaningful rather than rote learning, Ausubel suggests, is a function of two factors: the nature of the learning task and the learner's intention, or learning set. A poorly written program *or* repetitive discovery projects may almost force a student to resort to rote memorization or unthinking application of a formula. Many students may use a rote memorization approach to try to learn logically organized programs or solve excellent discovery problems simply because they approach the task with the attitude that memorization is the only way to learn.

To understand why students adopt a rote or meaningful learning set, you will need to be aware of what students already know about a topic. This argument of Ausubel is similar to the information processing principle that any individual's perception of a stimulus will be a function of background experiences. It is also similar to Piaget's observation that every child's cognitive structure is unique. All of these views emphasize that teachers need to try to take into account a particular learner's thinking processes at a particular time and in a particular situation.

To help students adopt a meaningful rather than a rote learning set, Ausubel recommends that teachers use **advance organizers.** As the name suggests, advance organizers are introductory materials that provide an organizing structure to help students relate new information to existing knowledge schemes. Because no two students are likely to have identical cognitive structures, Ausubel maintains that advance organizers need to be more abstract, more general, and more inclusive than the material to be learned. Advance organizers usually are relatively brief passages written in familiar terms, although schematic diagrams and illustrations can also be used. Studies of advance organizers show that they have their strongest positive effects on measures of comprehension and problem solving rather than on measures of retention (Mayer, 1979).

Every theory has its potential limitations, and Ausubel's is no exception. The main weakness of meaningful reception learning is that the learner is largely responsible for establishing a meaningful learning set. Thus, it is possible for students to believe they have achieved a genuine understanding of something when in fact they have attained only a vague and superficial level of understanding. Students need to recognize those occasions when they do not understand the structure of a subject and be willing to do something about it. Students who have been trained to think strategically, as described in Chapter 8, are least likely to mistake superficial or rote learning for meaningful learning.

In summary, both Bruner and Ausubel agree that schools should promote meaningful learning. Bruner believes there is a legitimate place for good-quality texts and lectures just as Ausubel sees value in learning through discovery. The

> Meaningful learning depends on nature of task, learner's set

> Advance organizer helps relate new ideas to existing schemes

major difference between them and their advocates centers on how much in-school time students should devote to acquiring information created by others versus how much time they should devote to gaining experience solving problems. Bruner argues that children who gain considerable experience solving problems in school will be better equipped to solve problems outside of the classroom. Ausubel (and Skinner) argue that teachers are better off spending class time presenting subject matter as efficiently as possible. If problem-solving skills are deemed important, they should be taught systematically.

Regardless of which approach you favor, you will probably want to spend some time teaching your students how to be good problem solvers. Consequently, this chapter next turns to a discussion of the nature of problem solving.

As with most of the topics covered in this book, an extensive amount of theorizing and research on problem solving has been conducted over the years. We will focus our discussion on the types of problems that students are typically required to deal with, the cognitive processes that play a central role in problem solving, and various approaches to teaching problem solving in the classroom. We will conclude the chapter with an examination of the factors that govern whether students will, through transfer of learning, use what they have learned after they leave your classroom.

The Nature of Problem Solving

Let's begin by asking what we mean by the terms "problem" and "problem solving." According to Ellen Gagné, "a problem is said to exist when one has a goal and has not yet identified a means for reaching that goal" (1985, p. 138). **Problem solving,** then, is the identification and application of knowledge and skills that results in goal attainment. Gagné's definition encompasses a wide range of problem types, but there are three types that students frequently encounter both in school and out.

Three Common Types of Problems

Well-structured problems: clearly stated, known solution procedures, known evaluation standards

The first category is the well-structured problems of mathematics and science—the type of problem that students from kindergarten through junior high are typically required to solve. **Well-structured problems** are clearly formulated, can be solved by recalling and applying a specific procedure (called an *algorithm*), and result in a solution that can be evaluated against a well-known, agreed upon standard (Frederiksen, 1984). Examples of well-structured problems are

$$5 + 8 = \underline{\quad}, 732 - 485 = \underline{\quad}, \text{ and } 8 + 3x = 40 - 5x$$

The second category is the ill-structured problems often encountered in everyday life and in disciplines like economics or psychology. **Ill-structured problems** are more complex, provide few cues pointing to solution procedures, and have less definite criteria for determining when the problem has been solved (Frederiksen, 1984). Examples of ill-structured problems are how to identify and reward good teachers, how to improve access for physically handicapped persons to public buildings and facilities, and how to increase voter turnout for primary and general elections.

Ill-structured problems: vaguely stated, unclear solution procedures, vague evaluation standards

The third category includes problems that are also ill structured but differ from the examples just mentioned in two respects. First, these problems tend to divide people into opposing camps because of the emotions they arouse. Second, the primary goal, at least initially, is not to determine a course of action but to identify the most reasonable position. These problems are often referred to as **issues** (Ruggiero, 1988). Examples of issues are capital punishment, gun control, and nondemoninational prayer in classrooms. Beginning with the freshman year in high school, students usually receive more opportunities to deal with ill-structured problems and issues.

Issues: ill-structured problems that arouse strong feelings

Helping Students Become Good Problem Solvers

Despite the differences that exist among well-structured problems, ill-structured problems, and issues, recent theory and research suggest that good problem solvers employ the same general approach when solving one or another of these problem types (for example, Bransford & Stein, 1984; E. Gagné, 1985; Gick, 1986; Krulik & Rudnick, 1988; Nickerson, Perkins, & Smith, 1985; Ruggiero, 1988). When used to solve ill-structured problems or to analyze issues, this approach consists of five steps or processes (although the solution of well-structured problems may call for the implementation of only steps 2, 4, and 5):

1. Realize that a problem exists.
2. Understand the nature of the problem.
3. Compile relevant information.
4. Formulate and carry out a solution.
5. Evaluate the solution.

We will discuss each of these steps in the next few pages, along with some specific techniques that you can use to help your students become good problem solvers.

Step 1: Realize That a Problem Exists   Most people assume that if a problem is worth solving they won't have to seek it out—it will make itself known. Like most assumptions, this one is only partly true. Well-structured problems are often thrust upon us by teachers, in the form of in-class exercises or homework, or by supervisors at work. Ill-structured problems and issues, on the other hand, often remain "hidden" from most people. It is a characteristic of good problem solvers that they are more sensitive to the existence of problems than most of their peers.

Problem finding de-
pends on curiosity,
dissatisfaction with
status quo

The keys to problem recognition, or *problem finding* as it is sometimes called, are curiosity and dissatisfaction. You need to question why a rule, procedure, or product is the way it is, or to feel frustrated or irritated because something does not work as well as it might. The organization Mothers Against Drunk Driving, for example, was begun by a woman who, because her daughter was killed in a traffic accident by a drunk driver, was dissatisfied with current, ineffective laws. This organization has been instrumental in getting state legislatures to pass laws against drunk driving that mandate more severe penalties. As another example, John Bransford and Barry Stein (1984) mention a business that, by taking a critical look at its record-keeping procedure, was able to eliminate the generation of 120 tons of paper per year.

Problem finding does not come readily to most people, possibly because schools emphasize solving well-structured problems and possibly because most people have a natural tendency to assume that things work as well as they can. Like any cognitive process, however, problem recognition can improve with instruction and practice. Students can be sensitized in a number of ways to the absence or flaws and shortcomings of products, procedures, rules, or whatever. We will make some specific suggestions about improving problem recognition and the other problem-solving processes a bit later in the Suggestions for Teaching.

Step 2: Understand the Nature of the Problem   The second step in the problem-solving process is perhaps the most critical. The problem solver has to construct an *optimal* representation or understanding of the nature of a problem or issue. The preceding sentence stresses the word *optimal* for two reasons. First, most problems can be expressed in a number of ways. Written problems, for example, can be recast as pictures, equations, graphs, charts, or diagrams. Second, because the way we represent the problem determines the amount and type of solution-relevant information we recall from long-term memory, some representations are better than others. For obvious reasons, problem-solving researchers often refer to this process as **problem representation** or **problem framing**.

Problem framing
depends on subject
matter knowledge,
familiarity with prob-
lem types

To achieve an optimal understanding of a problem, an individual needs two things: a high degree of knowledge of the subject matter (facts, concepts, and principles) on which the problem is based, and familiarity with that particular type of problem. This background will allow the person to recognize important elements (words, phrases, and numbers) in the problem statement and patterns of relationships among the problem elements. This recognition, in turn, will activate one or more solution-relevant schemes from long-term memory. It is just this level of knowledge of subject matter and problem types that distinguishes the high-quality problem representations of the expert problem solver from the low-quality representations of the novice. Experts typically represent problems in terms of one or more basic patterns or underlying principles, whereas novices focus on limited or superficial surface features of problems.

To give you a clearer idea of the nature and power of an optimal problem representation, consider the following situation. When novices are given a set of phys-

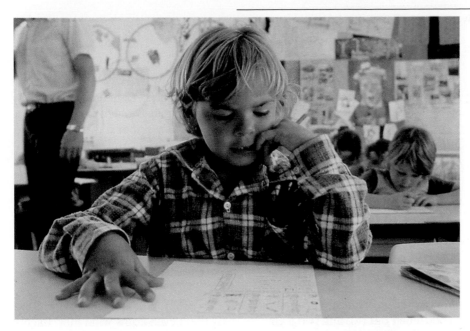

The most critical step in problem solving is determining and understanding the nature of the problem; some students need assistance with this task. (Ulrike Welsch/Photo Researchers)

ics problems to solve, they sort them into categories on the basis of some noticeable feature. For example, they group together all problems that involve the use of an inclined plane, or all the ones that involve the use of pulleys, or all those that involve friction; and then they search their memory for previously learned information. The drawback to this approach is that while two or three problems may involve the use of an inclined plane, their solutions may depend on the application of different laws of physics. Experts, on the other hand, draw on their extensive and well-organized knowledge base to represent groups of problems according to a common underlying principle such as conservation of energy or Newton's third law (Frederiksen, 1984; Gick, 1986).

As another example, compare the problem-framing abilities of chess masters and novices. Have you ever watched a chess expert play a dozen or more opponents simultaneously? The expert moves from board to board, often spending no more than ten to fifteen seconds studying the arrangement of the pieces before making a move. The opponent meanwhile has at least a couple of minutes to ponder his or her next move. The expert usually wins all the games. After watching such a demonstration you might be tempted to conclude that such a person is a genius or has a superior memory. The truth of the matter is the typical chess expert has the same memory capacity as the rest of us. What the master excels at is pattern recognition. Based upon years of playing and thinking about the game of chess, world-class players have learned to represent the array of pieces on a chess board in terms of chunks (clusters of pieces) and how those chunks are located relative to one another. It is the ability to recognize chunks and patterns among them and to know the strategic implications of each pattern at any point in a game that largely accounts for this expertise. It has been estimated that world-class chess masters can recognize at least 25,000 chunks (Frederiksen, 1984).

We have tried to show you in this section that an important aspect of the problem-solving process is the ability to activate relevant schemes (organized collections of facts, concepts, principles, and procedures) from long-term memory when they are needed. The more relevant and powerful the activated scheme, the more likely an effective problem solution will be achieved. As many observers of education have pointed out, acquiring this ability is often easier said than done. John Bransford has argued that standard educational practices produce knowledge that is *inert*. That is, it can be accessed only under conditions that closely mimic the original learning context (Bransford, Sherwood, Vye, & Reiser, 1986). Richard Feynman, a Nobel Prize–winning physicist, made the same observation in describing how his classmates at the Massachusetts Institute of Technology failed to recognize the application of a previously learned mathematical formula: "They didn't put two and two together. They didn't even know what they 'knew.' I don't know what's the matter with people: they don't learn by understanding; they learn by some other way—by rote, or something. Their knowledge is so fragile!" (1985, p. 36).

To overcome this limitation of inert and fragile knowledge, teachers need to present subject matter in a highly organized fashion, and students need to learn more about the various conditions under which their knowledge applies. We have tried to achieve the same goals with our Suggestions for Teaching and Handbook Headings. An interesting and useful approach to teaching students the knowledge and skills that underlie problem solving is the learning hierarchy of Robert Gagné. We will describe Gagné's ideas in a later section.

Step 3: Compile Relevant Information   For well-structured problems that are relatively simple and familiar (like arithmetic drill problems), this step in the problem-solving process occurs simultaneously with problem representation. As we define the problem, we very quickly and easily recall from long-term memory all the information that is needed to achieve a solution. As problems and issues become more complex, however, we run into two difficulties: the amount of information relevant to the solution becomes too great to keep track of mentally, and there is an increasing chance that we may not possess all the relevant information. As a result, we are forced to compile what we know in the form of lists, tables, pictures, graphs, and diagrams, and so on, and to seek additional information from other sources.

The key to using yourself as an information source is the ability to accurately retrieve from long-term memory information that will aid in the solution of the problem. We need to think back over what we have learned in other somewhat similar situations, make a list of some other form of representation of those ideas, and make a judgment as to how helpful that knowledge might be. Techniques for insuring accurate and reliable recall were discussed in Chapter 8.

Allow students ample time to gather information and share insights as they work toward a solution of a problem. (Elizabeth Crews/The Image Works)

In addition to relying on our own knowledge and experience to solve problems, we can also draw on the knowledge and experience of friends, colleagues, and experts. According to Vincent Ruggiero, "Investigating other people's views calls for little talking and a lot of careful listening. We do well, in such cases, to ask questions rather than make statements" (1988, p. 39). The main purpose of soliciting the views of others about solutions to problems and positions on issues is to identify the reasons and evidence those people offer in support of their positions. This skill of asking questions and analyzing responses is quite useful in debates and classroom discussions of controversial issues.

Step 4: Formulate and Carry Out a Solution   When you feel you understand the nature of a problem or issue and possess sufficient relevant information, you are ready to attempt a solution. The first step is to consider which of several alternative approaches is likely to be most effective. The literature on problem solving mentions quite a few solution strategies. We will discuss five that we think are particularly useful.

Study worked examples. This approach may strike you as so obvious that it hardly merits attention. It is worth mentioning for two reasons. First, obvious solution strategies are the ones that are most often overlooked. Second, it is a very effective solution strategy. Mary Gick (1986) cites almost a dozen studies that

Studying worked examples is an effective solution strategy

showed improvements in solving a variety of problems as a result of studying similar problems whose solutions were worked out. The beneficial effect is thought to be due to the learner acquiring a general problem schema.

Work on a simpler version of the problem. This is another common and very effective approach. Geometry offers a particularly clear example of working on a simpler problem. If you are having difficulty solving a problem of solid geometry (which involves three dimensions), work out a similar problem in plane geometry (two dimensions) and then apply the solution to the three-dimensional example (Nickerson, Perkins, & Smith, 1985; Polya, 1957). Architects and engineers employ this approach when they construct scaled-down models of bridges, buildings, experimental aircraft, and the like. Scientists do the same thing when they create laboratory simulations of real-world phenomena.

> **Solve simpler version of problem first, then transfer process to harder problem**

Break the problem into parts. The key to this approach is to make sure you break the problem into manageable parts. Whether or not you can do this will depend largely on how much subject matter knowledge you have. The more you know about the domain from which the problem comes, the easier it is to know where to break a problem into logical, easy-to-handle parts.

> **Break complex problems into manageable parts**

At least two benefits result from breaking a problem in parts: Doing so reduces the amount of information you have to keep in short-term memory to a manageable level, and the method used to solve one part of the problem can often be used to solve another part. Bransford & Stein (1984) use the following example to illustrate how this approach works.

Problem: What day follows the day before yesterday if two days from now will be Sunday?

1. What is today if two days from now will be Sunday? (Friday)
2. If today is Friday, what is the day before yesterday? (Wednesday)
3. What day follows Wednesday? (Thursday)

Work backward. This is a particularly good solution strategy to use whenever the goal is clear but the beginning state is not. Bransford and Stein (1984) offer the following example. Suppose you arranged to meet someone at a restaurant across town at noon. When should you leave your office to be sure of arriving on time? By working backward from your destination and arrival time (it takes about ten minutes to find a parking spot and walk to the restaurant; it takes about thirty minutes to drive to the area where you would park; it takes about five minutes to walk from your office to your car) you would more quickly and easily determine when to leave your office (about 11:15) than if you had worked the problem forward.

> **Work backward when goal is clear but beginning state is not**

Solve an analogous problem. If you are having difficulty solving a current problem, possibly because your knowledge of the subject matter is incomplete, it may be useful to think of a similar problem in a subject in which you are more knowledgeable. Solve the analogous problem, and then use the same method to solve the current problem. In essence, this is a way of making the unfamiliar familiar.

Although solving analogous problems is a very powerful solution strategy, it is also difficult to employ, especially for novices. In our earlier discussion of understanding the problem, we made the point that novices represent problems on the basis of superficial features while experts operate from knowledge of underlying concepts and principles. The same is true of using analogies. Novices are more likely than experts to use superficial analogies (Gick, 1986).

A potential way around this problem is to provide students with good analogies. This approach does work, but in a limited way. For students to recognize the usefulness of the analogy, it must mimic the target problem in both structure and surface details. The evidence for this conclusion comes largely from a series of studies by Mary Gick and Keith Holyoak (for example, Gick & Holyoak, 1980, 1983; Holyoak & Koh, 1987).

Analogous problems must be very similar to target problem

In the initial experiments college students read a story about a general who wanted to capture a fortress. If the general used his entire army, the attack would succeed. However, many of the surrounding villages would be destroyed during the attack because of mines planted along the roads leading to the fortress. This outcome was unacceptable. The general's solution was to divide his army into smaller groups that could slip through the minefields, send each group along a different road, and have them converge on the fortress at the same time. The students were then given a second story to read that concluded with a problem for them to solve. The second story was about a patient with an inoperable stomach tumor. The patient's doctor could destroy the tumor with a beam of high intensity x rays, but healthy surrounding tissue would be destroyed in the process. Although a beam of lower intensity would not damage healthy tissue, neither would it destroy the tumor. The problem posed to the students was how to use radiation to destroy the tumor without destroying the healthy tissue at the same time. Only 30 percent of the students realized that just as the general solved his problem by dividing his forces and having them converge on the fortress simultaneously, the doctor could destroy the tumor by using several beams of low-intensity radiation aimed from different directions.

In the later study (Holyoak & Koh, 1987) students first read a story about a physics lab that used an expensive light bulb. The filament, which was in a permanently sealed bulb, was broken. It could be repaired with a high-intensity laser beam. This solution was unacceptable, however, because a high-intensity beam would also shatter the glass. The problem was solved by using several lower-intensity beams aimed at the filament. As before, students then read the inoperable tumor story. Because the details of the light bulb and tumor stories were very similar, the outcome in this case was dramatically different. Almost 70 percent of these students were able to solve the tumor problem. This figure was increased to 75 percent by suggesting to the subjects that the first story could help them solve the problem in the second story.

Step 5: Evaluate the Solution   The last step in the problem-solving process is to evaluate the adequacy of the solution. For relatively simple well-structured problems where the emphasis is on producing a correct response, two levels of evaluation are available to the problem solver. The first is to ask whether, given the problem statement, the answer makes sense. For example, if the problem says $75 \times 5 = ?$ and the response is 80, a little voice inside the problem solver's head should say that the answer cannot possibly be right. This signal should prompt a re-evaluation of how the problem was represented and the solution procedure that was used (for example, "I misread the times sign as a plus sign and added when I should have multiplied"). The second level of evaluation is to use an alternative algorithm (a fixed procedure used to solve a problem) to check the accuracy of the solution. This is necessary because making an error in carrying out an algorithm can produce an incorrect response that is "in the ballpark." For example, a common error in multiple-column subtraction problems is to subtract the smaller number from the larger number regardless of whether the small number is in the minuend (top row) or the subtrahend (bottom row) (Mayer, 1984), as in

| Evaluate solutions to well-structured problems by estimating or checking |

$$\begin{array}{r} 522 \\ -\,418 \\ \hline 116 \end{array}$$

Since this answer is off by only 12 units, it "looks right." The flaw can be discovered, however, by adding the answer to the subtrahend to produce the minuend.

The evaluation of solutions to ill-structured problems is likely to be more complicated and time consuming for at least two reasons. First, the evaluation should occur both before and after the solution is implemented. While many flaws and commissions can be identified and corrected beforehand, some will slip through. There is much to be learned by observing the effects of our solutions. Second, because these problems are complex, often involving a dozen or more variables, some sort of systematic framework should guide the evaluation. Vincent Ruggiero suggests a four-step procedure (1988, pp. 44–46). The first step is to ask and answer a set of basic questions. Imagine, for example, that you have proposed a classroom incentive system (a token economy perhaps) to enhance student motivation. You might ask the following questions:

How exactly is it to be done, step by step?

By whom is it to be done?

When is it to be done (according to what timetable)?

Where is it to be done?

Who will finance it?

What tools or materials, if any, are to be used?

From what source will they be obtained?

How and by whom will they be transported?

Where will they be stored?

What special conditions, if any, will be required for the solution to be carried out?

The second step is to identify imperfections and complications. Is this idea, for example, safe, convenient, efficient, economical, compatible with existing policies and practices? The third step is to anticipate possible negative reactions from other people (like parents and your building principal). The last step is to devise improvements.

Over the past several pages we have described a model of the problem-solving process that can be applied to different types of problems. A critical step in this process, and the one that clearly separates novices from experts, is the construction of an optimal representation of the problem. As we pointed out earlier, it is the expert's access to a deep and well-organized reservoir of relevant prior knowledge that is largely responsible for his or her ability to formulate high-quality problem representations. The work of Robert M. Gagné, which we will discuss next, provides some useful insights into how you can help students learn basic knowledge and skill in an organized fashion.

Gagné's Approach to Problem Solving

According to Robert M. Gagné, "problem solving may be viewed as a process by which the learner discovers a combination of previously learned rules and plans their application so as to achieve a solution for a novel problem situation" (1985, p. 178). For this process to occur efficiently, students will need to master two general kinds of capabilities: intellectual skills and cognitive strategies.

An **intellectual skill** is an ability we possess to use rules to solve problems. In the course of your education, for example, you probably learned the punctuation rule "a question mark always follows an interrogative statement," and the mathematical rule "the product of two negative numbers is a positive number." The major value of acquiring intellectual skills is that they make it possible to solve many different kinds of problems without further assistance. Once you learned and understood the rule about question marks, for instance, you no longer had to ask the teacher or thumb through a reference book for guidance. Because of the autonomy that intellectual skills provide, Robert Gagné sees them as "in many ways the most important types of capability learned by human beings and the essence of what is meant by 'being educated' " (1985, p. 49). Cognitive strategies (which were discussed in Chapter 8) are mental skills that guide, control, regulate, and modify how we attend to, encode, store, and retrieve information. With these strategies, individuals can use previously learned rules to solve problems they have never before encountered. As Gagné puts it, "cognitive strategies are ways of 'using one's head' " (1985, p. 139).

Gagné suggests that any intellectual skill is composed of rules, concepts, discriminations, and basic associations (factual information). Because these compo-

> Intellectual skill: using rules to solve problems

Intellectual skills composed of rules, concepts, discriminations, associations

nents are arranged hierarchically (as shown in Figure 9.1), Gagné argues they must be learned in a fixed sequence. To formulate and use a complex rule, for example, a student must have previously learned the subordinate simple rules. To learn a simple rule, the student must have previously learned the underlying concepts. To learn concepts, the student must have previously learned the discriminations necessary to place objects, events, or ideas in different categories. Finally, the ability to make discriminations depends on the student having at some point in the past learned basic stimulus-response associations. Organizing the components of an intellectual skill in this fashion results in a **learning hierarchy.**

To put Gagné's ideas into practice, you begin with the final objective (for example, the application of a complex rule to the solution of a problem) and ask yourself the following question: "What does the learner need to know or be able to do to achieve this objective?" The answer to that question should identify the subordinate rules that make up the complex rule. Then ask yourself the same question about the subordinate rules. This should identify the concepts. Asking the question a third time leads to the identification of relevant discriminations. When you reach the level of your students' knowledge and skills, the analysis stops and instructional objectives can be prepared (by following suggestions offered in Chapter 6).

Figure 9.1   Gagné's Intellectual Skill Hierarchy

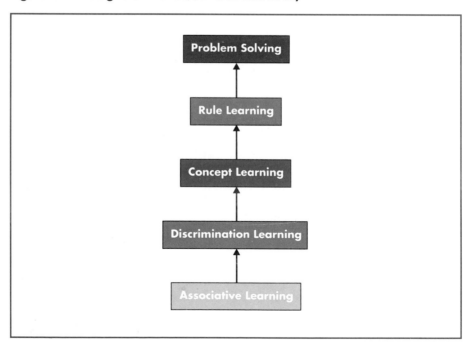

While learning associations, discriminations, concepts, and rules may be important outcomes in their own right, Gagné values them more for the contributions they make to an individual's problem-solving ability. Being able to use intellectual skills in this way has immediate and long-term benefits. The immediate benefit is an increased likelihood of solving a particular problem. The long-term benefit is that the student learns a higher-order rule (a rule about how to combine rules), which makes solving similar problems easier. This ability to take a skill learned in one situation and use it to master a similar task in another situation is known as transfer of learning and will be discussed in detail in the last section of this chapter.

Gagné describes an experiment by Maier (1930) that illustrates how students can be guided to use previously learned rules to solve a problem. College students were provided with string, poles of different length, clamps, pieces of chalk, a table, and a chair, and were told to construct two pendulums so that each would make a chalk mark at the designated point on the floor when swung over it. (The solution to the problem is illustrated in Figure 9.2). Of fifteen students who re-

Figure 9.2   The Maier Pendulum Problem

From R. Gagné, *Conditions of Learning,* Fourth Edition, p. 182. Copyright 1985 by Holt, Rinehart Winston. Reprinted by permission of the publisher and the author.

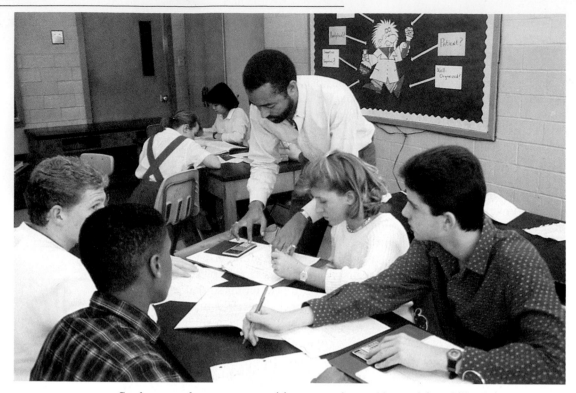

Students need many opportunities to practice problem-solving skills. (Susan Van Etten/The Picture Cube)

ceived only the statement of the problem, none achieved a solution. A second group of eighteen students was given the problem statement and then told how to make a plumb line by using a clamp, a pencil, and string; how to suspend a pendulum; how to make a long pole out of two short ones by using a clamp; and how to hold up a projector screen by wedging two poles against it. One student out of the eighteen (5.5 percent) solved the pendulum problem with these additional instructions. A third group of ten students was given the problem statement, the additional instructions, and was also told that achieving a solution was largely a matter of combining ideas and hanging the pendulum from the ceiling. Four out of ten students (40 percent) solved the problem with this information.

This discussion of problem solving has made clear that learning to solve problems means learning to find problems, represent them, draw on prior knowledge, formulate solutions, and evaluate solutions. In addition, students need opportunities to apply these processes to well-structured problems, ill-structured problems, and the analysis of issues. The Suggestions for Teaching section that follows contains guidelines and examples that will help you improve the problem-solving skills of your students.

Mid-Chapter Review

The Nature of Meaningful Learning

Jerome Bruner urged teachers to stress the structure of a field of study (how fundamental ideas relate to each other) because of the positive effect a grasp of structure has on understanding and problem solving.

Because children represent knowledge in fundamentally different ways (enactive, iconic, and symbolic modes) as they progress from childhood through adolescence, Bruner suggested the use of a spiral curriculum to foster meaningful learning. This type of curriculum reintroduces concepts in increasingly complex form as students move through the enactive, iconic, and symbolic modes of thought.

Bruner urged teachers to encourage students to discover how ideas relate to each other and to what they already know, since this is a very meaningful form of learning.

Discovery techniques devised by Bruner include emphasizing contrast, stimulating informed guessing, encouraging participation, and arousing awareness.

David Ausubel urged teachers to promote meaningful reception learning by lectures, handouts, textbooks, and the like, that students can easily relate to their existing knowledge schemes.

To help students relate new ideas to what they already know, Ausubel suggests that teachers provide advance organizers.

Problem Solving

Students should learn how to solve three general types of problems: well structured (such as mathematics and science), ill-structured (such as politics, economics, and psychology), and issues (problems that tend to divide people into opposing camps because of the strong emotions they produce).

A general model of problem solving has five steps: realize that a problem exists; understand the nature of the problem; compile relevant information; formulate and carry out a solution; evaluate the solution.

Robert Gagné believes that to become a good problem solver, students need to learn intellectual skills. An intellectual skill is an ability to use rules to solve problems.

Intellectual skills can be broken down into a hierarchy of four levels: rules, concepts, discriminations, and associations.

SUGGESTIONS FOR TEACHING

Teaching Problem-Solving Techniques

1. Develop a problem-solving orientation in students.
2. Teach students how to identify problems.
3. Teach students how to represent problems.
4. Teach students how to compile relevant information.
5. Teach several methods for formulating problem solutions.
6. Teach students the skills of evaluation.

1. Develop a problem-solving orientation in students.

Academic work (of which problem solving is a part) is often characterized as being a solitary, effortful, and "cold" activity. These characteristics are hardly likely to excite large numbers of people. Yet that is precisely where instruction in problem-solving techniques must start if it is to be successful. You must convince students that becoming skilled problem solvers is worth the time, the effort, the confusion, and the frustration that they will inevitably experience.

Contemporary students are seen as being poor problem solvers for one or more of the following reasons: Years of watching television have conditioned students to be passive observers with short attention spans; since the problem-solving process is rarely taught in schools or required at home, students rarely get rewarded for their problem-solving efforts; many students have come to believe that all opinions and sources of knowledge are equally valid; and many students accord feelings the same status as factual evidence or reasoned conclusions.

To help students develop a positive attitude toward learning and using problem-solving skills, Vincent Ruggiero (1988) suggests teachers develop and reinforce the following dispositions in students:

Interest in the source of their own attitudes, beliefs, and values

Curiosity about their mental processes

Confidence in their ability

> **Students are poor problem solvers because of too much TV, lack of reinforcement, lack of critical attitude**

Willingness to make mistakes

Sensitivity to problems and issues

Positive attitude toward novelty

Interest in widening their experience

Respect for and willingness to use intuition when appropriate

Desire to reason well and base judgments on evidence

Willingness to subject ideas to scrutiny

Willingness to entertain opposing views

Curiosity about relationships among ideas

Passion for truth

Healthy attitude toward argumentation

2. Teach students how to identify problems.

As we pointed out earlier, identification is an often overlooked part of the problem-solving process. Since the notion of finding problems is likely to strike students as an unusual activity, you may want to introduce this skill in gradual steps. One way to start is to have students list different ways in which problems can be identified. Typical responses are to scan newspaper and magazine articles, observe customer and employee behavior in a store, observe traffic patterns in the local area, and interview local residents, including, for instance, teachers, business owners, police, clergy, or government officials. A next step is to have students carry out their suggested activities in order to gain an understanding of the status quo and to find out how people identify problems. They may learn, for example, that a principal periodically has lunch with a teacher in order to learn of conditions that decrease the teacher's effectiveness. Finally, have students suggest improvements that could help solve problems they have identified.

3. Teach students how to represent problems.

The ability to construct a good representation of a problem is based on a command of the subject matter surrounding the problem and familiarity with the particular type of problem. As the work of Jerome Bruner, David Ausubel, and Robert Gagné points out, students need to acquire a genuine understanding of many of the associations, discriminations, concepts, and rules of a discipline before they can effectively solve problems in that subject-matter area. Too often, pupils are taught to state principles on cue, but they reveal by further responses

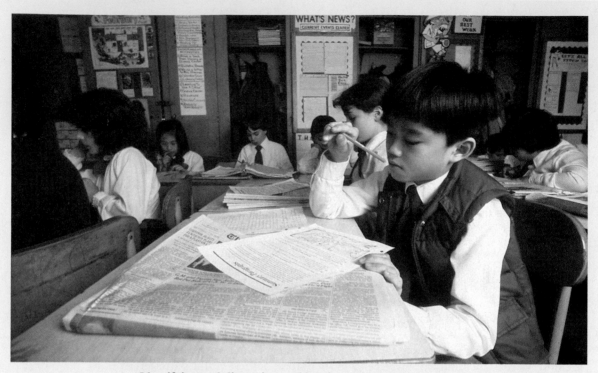

Identifying and discussing problem issues in the news gives students meaningful opportunities to put their problem-solving skills to work. (The Stock Market/Maggie Steber, 1984)

that they do not understand what they are saying. The classic illustration of this all too common trap was given by William James in his *Talks to Teachers:*

> A friend of mine, visiting a school, was asked to examine a young class in geography. Glancing at the book, she said: "Suppose you should dig a hole in the ground, hundreds of feet deep, how should you find it at the bottom—warmer or colder than on top?" None of the class replying, the teacher said: "I'm sure they know, but I think you don't ask the question quite rightly. Let me try." So, taking the book, she asked: "In what condition is the interior of the globe?" and received the immediate answer from half the class at once: "The interior of the globe is in a condition of igneous fusion." (1899, p. 150)

Comprehension of subject matter critical to problem solving

If these students had genuinely understood concepts and principles regarding the composition of the earth, instead of having simply memorized meaningless phrases, they would have been able to answer the original question.

   Different problem types lend themselves to particular forms of representation. Verbal reasoning problems that are based on relationships among categories, for example, can usually be represented by a set of intersecting circles known as a Venn diagram.

Example Problem

The government wants to contact all druggists, all gun store owners, and all parents in a town. Based on the following statistics, how many people must be contacted?

Druggists..   10
Gun store owners..   5
Parents... 3,000
Druggists who own gun stores..................................   0
Druggists who are parents.....................................   7
Gun store owners who are parents..............................   3

Solution Using Venn Diagram

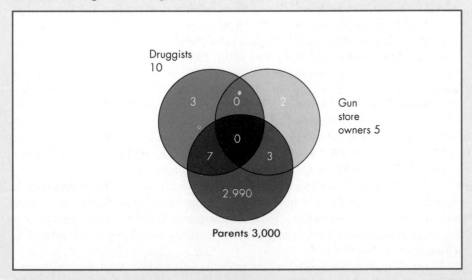

The total number that must be contacted is 2990 + 7 + 3 + 3 + 2 = 3,005 (adapted from Whimbley & Lochhead, 1966, p. 102).

Verbal reasoning problems that describe transactions can take the form of a flow diagram.

Example Problem

Sally loaned $7.00 to Betty. But Sally borrowed $15.00 from Estella and $32.00 from Joan. Moreover, Joan owes $3.00 to Estella and $7.00 to Betty. One day the women got together at Betty's house to straighten out their accounts. Which woman left with $18.00 more than she came with?

Solution Using Flow Diagram

From the diagram, it is clear that Estella left with $18.00 more than she came with (adapted from Whimbley & Lochhead, 1986, p. 126).

4. Teach students how to compile relevant information.

Good problem solvers start with themselves when compiling information to solve a problem or evidence to support a position on an issue. They recognize the importance of recalling earlier learned information (metacognitive knowledge) and are adept at doing so (cognitive skill). Poor problem solvers, by contrast, lack metacognitive knowledge, cognitive skills, or both. If their deficiency is metacognitive, they make little or no effort to recall solution-relevant memories, even when the information was recently learned, because they do not understand the importance of searching long-term memory for potentially useful knowledge. Even if a student poor in problem solving recognizes the value of searching long-term memory for relevant information, he or she may still be handicapped because of inadequate encoding and retrieval skills.

To minimize any metacognitive deficiency, make sure your instruction in problem-solving methods emphasizes the importance of retrieving and using previously learned knowledge. To minimize retrieval problems, make sure *you* recall and implement the Suggestions for Teaching we offered in the preceding chapter.

If a student does not possess all the relevant information needed to work out a solution or to analyze an issue, you will have to guide him or her toward individuals and sources that can help. In referring students to individuals, it is best to select people who are judged to be reasonably knowledgeable about the subject, are careful thinkers, and are willing to share their ideas (Ruggiero, 1988). As an example, consider the issue of whether certain books (like the novels *Catcher in the Rye* by J. D. Salinger and *Tom Sawyer* by Mark Twain) should be banned from a school's reading list. In interviewing an interested person, students might ask questions like the following, because they allow some insight into the individual's reasoning process and the evidence used to support his or her position:

What general effects do you think characters in novels who rebel against adult authority have on a reader's behavior?

Are certain groups of people, such as junior high and high school students, likely to be influenced by the motives and actions of such characters? Why do you think so?

Does a ban on certain books violate the author's right to free speech?

Does a book ban violate the principle of academic freedom? Why?

Is it the proper role of a school board to prevent or discourage students from exposure to certain ideas during school hours?

If a reasonably informed person is not available, recognized authorities can often be interviewed by phone. If a student chooses this tactic, Ruggiero suggests calling or writing in advance for an appointment, preparing questions in advance, and asking permission to tape-record the interview.

Obviously, in addition to or in lieu of personal interviews, students can find substantial information in a good library. For example, you can steer them toward books by recognized authorities, research findings, court cases, and interviews with prominent individuals in periodicals.

5. Teach several methods for formulating problem solutions.

Earlier we mentioned five methods for formulating a problem solution: study worked examples, work on a simpler version, break the problem into parts, work backward, and solve an analogous problem. Because of space limitations, we cannot present examples of each method. However, at the end of the chapter under Suggestions for Further Study we recommend several recently published books on problem solving that, taken together, provide numerous examples of each method. We also present the following example of a worked problem that breaks the problem into parts and incorporates working backward.

Example Problem

Paul owns 4 more than one-half as many books as Pete; Paul owns 32 books. How many books does Pete own?

Solution

Step 1. A diagram should be used to clarify the relationship between Paul's books and Pete's books. Starting with Pete's books, we take one-half of them.

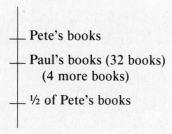

Pete's books

½ of Pete's books

If we now add 4 books, we have Paul's books (which the problem says is 32 books).

Pete's books

Paul's books (32 books)
     (4 more books)

½ of Pete's books

Step 2. To solve the problem, work backward. The diagram shows that if 4 books are taken from Paul he will have exactly one-half as many as Pete.

Paul's books − 4 = ½ of Pete's books
32 − 4 = 28 = ½ of Pete's books

Step 3. One half the number of books owned by Pete is 28. So Pete owns twice this number.

Pete's books = 2 × 28 = 56

(adapted from Whimbey & Lochhead, 1986, p. 272)

6. Teach students the skills of evaluation.

Solutions to well-structured problems are usually evaluated by applying an estimating or checking routine. Such procedures can be found in any good mathematics text. How to evaluate solutions to ill-structured problems and analyses of issues, however, is more complex and is less frequently taught. Ruggiero (1988) lists the following twelve habits and skills as contributing to the ability to evaluate complex solutions and positions:

1. Open-mindedness about opposing points of view.
2. Selecting proper criteria of evaluation. Violations of this skill abound. A

current example is the use of standardized achievement test scores to evaluate the quality of classroom instruction.

3. Understanding the essence of an argument. To foster this skill, Ruggiero recommends that students be taught how to write a *precis,* which is a concise summary of the original passage.
4. Evaluating the reliability of sources.
5. Proper interpretation of factual data (for example, recognizing that an increase in a state's income tax rate from 4 to 6 percent is not an increase of 2 percent but of 50 percent).
6. Testing the credibility of hypotheses. On the basis of existing data, hypotheses can range from highly improbable to highly probable.
7. Making important distinctions (for instance, between preference and judgment, emotion and content, appearance and reality).
8. Recognizing unstated assumptions (for example, that because two events occur close together in time, one causes the other; that what is clear to us will be clear to others; that if the majority believes something, it must be true).
9. Detecting fallacies (for instance, stereotyping, faulty analogies, straw-man arguments, or overgeneralizing).
10. Evaluating arguments.
11. Making sound judgments.
12. Recognizing when evidence is insufficient.

Teaching for Transfer

Throughout Chapters 7, 8, and 9, we have indicated that classroom instruction should be arranged in such a way that students independently apply the knowledge and problem-solving skills they learn in school to similar but new situations. This capability is typically valued very highly by educators. Referred to as **transfer of learning,** it is the essence of being an autonomous learner and problem solver. In this section, we will examine the nature of transfer and discuss ways in which you can help to bring it about.

The Nature and Significance of Transfer of Learning

On the opening pages of his widely acclaimed book titled *The Process of Education* (1960) Jerome Bruner made the following observations about transfer:

"Learning should not only take us somewhere; it should allow us later to go further more easily . . . it should serve us in the future."

One way that learning may have future value "is through its specific applicability to tasks that are highly similar to those we originally learned."

A second way learning can serve us in the future "consists of learning not a skill, but a general idea, which can then be used as a basis for recognizing subsequent problems as special cases of the idea originally mastered."

The second type of transfer is "dependent on the mastery of the structure of the subject matter," but it also involves "the development of an attitude toward learning and inquiry, toward guessing and hunches, toward the possibility of solving problems on one's own."

An important ingredient of this attitude is "a sense of excitement about discovery of regularities of previously unrecognized relations and similarities between ideas, with a resulting sense of self-confidence in one's abilities."

In the years since Bruner made these statements, psychologists have identified more specific types of transfer than the two basic categories he described. Even so, his remarks supply a basic outline of the essence of transfer.

First of all, consider his point that "learning should allow us later to go further more easily . . . it should serve us in the future." Too often, students operate on the assumption (sometimes generated by the teacher) that the only reason for learning what they are required to learn in certain classrooms is to pass exams and earn a grade. Upon finishing a test or receiving a grade, the student forgets what was learned. Occasionally the student not only forgets but also deliberately *avoids* having anything to do with what was studied because the learning experience seemed pointless and disagreeable. In such cases, learning obviously does not allow students to go on more easily.

Second, Bruner's distinction between the transfer of skills and the transfer of ideas and attitudes calls attention to the most common types of transfer. Primary grade pupils, for instance, learn the basic skills of reading, writing, and arithmetic. Those skills serve the student in all later grades and outside of the classroom as well. Upper elementary grade pupils increase their abilities to use the basic skills, and also make initial explorations of the sciences, social studies, and the arts. Greater proficiency in using the three R's plus the background they acquire in basic subjects will equip them for later advanced study, although many elementary school students may not appreciate that fact and will resist learning certain topics.

The range and degree of transfer at the high school level is strongly influenced by the subject matter. Courses like typing and auto shop are clearly designed to equip students with specific skills that they can use either in a particular occupation or to perform necessary tasks themselves. There is generally little confusion or doubt about the future value of such courses. Sequenced courses (such as math 1, 2, and 3) are specifically designed to prepare students to take advanced high school and college courses. When a course is part of a sequence, most students have at least a vague idea that what they are learning will be useful later on. In

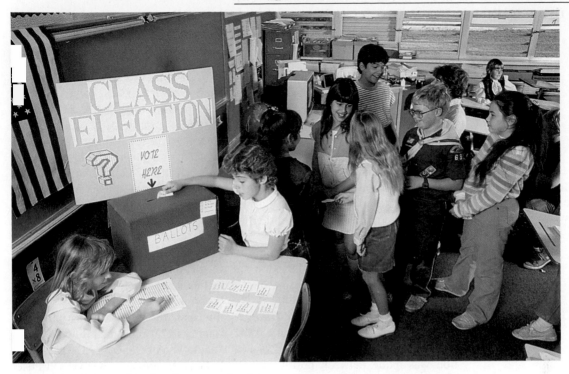

Ideally, what is learned in the classroom should serve the learner in the future.
(Edward Slater/Southern Stock Photos)

many high school and college courses, though, the transfer value of what is studied may not be clearly apparent. A high school teacher of English literature, for example, might do everything possible to persuade students that they may later experience a sense of excitement about discovery when they read literature on their own and perceive previously unrecognized relations and similarities between ideas. The teacher might wonder, though, on the basis of student response, whether such transfer will be experienced by more than a fraction of those in any class. In such cases, perhaps the teacher's only consolation is to think, "Well, at least some of them found out that they *don't* respond positively to literature."

The nature of **transfer** has been a topic of investigation among psychologists since psychology's beginnings about one hundred years ago. Consequently, most notions of transfer reflect a behavioral perspective, although a cognitive view of transfer has been proposed in recent years. In this section, we will examine transfer from both behavioral and cognitive perspectives, point out strengths and weaknesses of each perspective, and discuss how both approaches can be used to facilitate later learning.

The Behavioral View of Transfer

The Theory of Identical Elements During the early 1900s, it was common practice for high schools and colleges to require that students take such subjects as Latin, Greek, and geometry. Because they were considered difficult topics to learn, mastery of them was expected to improve a student's ability to memorize, think, and reason. These enhanced abilities were then expected to facilitate the learning of less difficult subjects. The rationale behind this practice was that the human mind could be exercised, much as any muscle in the body could be exercised, and made stronger. A strong mind, then, would learn things that a weak mind would not. This practice, known as the *doctrine of formal discipline,* constituted an early explanation of transfer. In 1901, Edward L. Thorndike and Robert S. Woodworth proposed an alternative explanation of how transfer occurs. They argued that the degree to which knowledge and skills acquired in learning one task can help someone learn another task depends on how similar the two tasks are (assuming the learner recognizes the similarities). The greater the degree of similarity between the tasks' stimulus and response elements (as in riding a bicycle and riding a motorcycle, for example), the greater the amount of transfer. This idea became known as the **theory of identical elements.**

> Behavioral view of transfer based on degree of similarity between two tasks

Positive, Negative, and Zero Transfer   In time, though, other psychologists (among them, Osgood, 1949; Ellis, 1965; Gagné, 1977) identified different types of transfer and the conditions under which each type prevailed. A useful distinction was made between positive transfer, negative transfer, and zero transfer (Ellis, 1978; Wingfield, 1979).

The discussion up to this point has been alluding to **positive transfer,** defined as a situation in which prior learning aids subsequent learning. According to Thorndike's analysis, positive transfer occurs when a new learning task calls for essentially the same response that was made to a similar, earlier learned task. The accomplished accordion player, for instance, probably will become a proficient pianist faster than someone who knows how to play the drums or someone who plays no musical instrument at all. The person who is fluent in French is likely to have an easier time learning Spanish than someone who speaks no foreign language.

> Positive transfer: previous learning makes later learning easier

Negative transfer is defined as a situation in which prior learning interferes with subsequent learning. It occurs when two tasks are highly similar but require different responses. A tennis player learning how to play racquetball, for example, may encounter problems at first because of a tendency to swing the racquetball racket as if it were a tennis racket. Primary grade children often experience negative transfer when they encounter words that are spelled alike but pronounced differently (as in "I will *read* this story, but I *read* that story last week").

> Negative transfer: previous learning interferes with later learning

Zero transfer is defined as a situation where prior learning has no effect on new learning. It can be expected when two tasks have different stimuli and different responses. Learning to conjugate Latin verbs, for one example, is not likely to have any effect on learning how to find the area of a rectangle.

Specific and General Transfer   The preceding description of positive transfer, while useful, is somewhat limiting because it is unclear whether the transfer from one task to another is due to specific similarities or to general or nonspecific similarities. Psychologists (as described by Ellis, 1978, pp. 249–250) decide whether transfer is due to specific or general factors by setting up learning tasks such as the following for three different but equivalent groups of learners:

	Initial Task	Transfer Task
Group 1	Learn French	Learn Spanish
Group 2	Learn Chinese	Learn Spanish
Group 3		Learn Spanish

If on a Spanish test, Group 1 scores higher than Group 2, the difference is attributed to **specific transfer** of similarities between French and Spanish (such as vocabulary, verb conjugations, and sentence structure). On the other hand, if Groups 1 and 2 score the same, but both outscore Group 3, the difference is attributed to nonspecific or **general transfer** of similarities between the two tasks, since Chinese shares no apparent specific characteristics with French or Spanish. In this case, it is possible that learners use cognitive strategies—such as imagery, verbal elaboration, and mnemonic devices—when learning a foreign language and that these transfer to the learning of other foreign languages. Such nonspecific transfer effects have also been demonstrated for other classroom tasks, like problem solving and prose learning (Ellis, 1978; Royer, 1979).

> Specific transfer due to specific similarities between two tasks

> General transfer due to use of same cognitive strategies

Vertical and Lateral Transfer A distinction between vertical and lateral transfer was first made by Robert Gagné (1965) in connection with early descriptions of his intellectual skill hierarchy. **Vertical transfer** occurs when a previously learned capability contributes directly to the acquisition of a more complex capability. For example, being able to discriminate between different types of triangles makes it easier to form the concepts equilateral triangle, right triangle, and so on, than if such discriminations had not been previously learned. **Lateral transfer** occurs when a previously learned capability is used to solve a problem similar to those encountered during initial learning but having a different context. A child who uses arithmetic skills acquired in elementary grade classrooms to figure out how much material and money is needed to build a dog house exhibits lateral transfer. Using previously learned rules and procedures for conducting chemistry experiments to conduct physics or psychology experiments is another example of lateral transfer. Lateral transfer, obviously, is essentially the same as general transfer. Both involve the use of cognitive strategies.

> Vertical transfer: previously learned capability aids learning of more complex capability in same area

> Lateral transfer: previously learned capability aids problem solving in different area

Strengths and Weaknesses of the Behavioral View The main strength of the theory of identical elements is its specification of the environmental conditions under which the various kinds of transfer occur, particularly specific and vertical transfer. If a teacher can identify the extent to which two tasks share defining features, devise ways to help students recognize these similarities, and arrange the components of intellectual skills hierarchically, a fairly accurate prediction can be

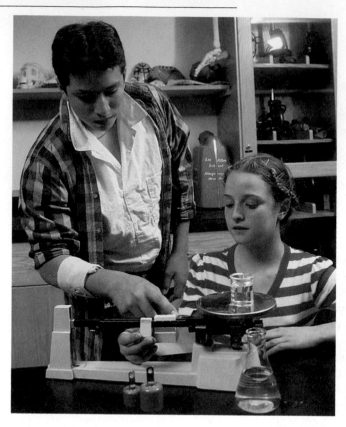

Students demonstrate lateral transfer of capabilities when they apply skills acquired in biology lab to procedures for conducting experiments in other science classes, such as chemistry and physics. (Steve Young/Lightwave)

made about how much transfer is likely to occur from one task to another. However, this approach to transfer has at least two weaknesses. First, it does not explain how students notice task similarities, retrieve relevant knowledge from memory, and apply this knowledge to aid later learning. Knowing how students think when transfer tasks are encountered would allow the teacher to specify instructional lessons more precisely when transfer is an objective. Second, specific and vertical transfer can be predicted much better than general and lateral transfer because these situations typically involve tasks where the stimulus elements are clear and easy to recognize, as with foreign languages, mathematical skills, and motor skills. But, transfer does occur between situations where the similarities are not all that obvious (for example, between in-school and out-of-school tasks). Again, the theory of identical elements provides little, if any, insight into how this transfer occurs (Royer, 1979). Recent advances in cognitive theory and research, however, have provided some possible answers to these mysteries.

The Cognitive View of Transfer

The Role of Comprehension and Memory   The cognitive view of transfer (detailed, for example, by Royer, 1979) is based on the information processing theory presented in Chapter 8. Just to refresh your memory, much of that theory is based on the assumption that we store and retrieve information in memory in a highly systematic fashion. The storage and retrieval processes are strongly influenced by comprehension, which we described as a learner's ability to relate previously acquired knowledge to new information. Previously acquired knowledge is felt to exist in memory as schemata. Schemata were described as mental models or blueprints for representing relationships among objects and events, from which numerous other examples could be derived (like variations on a theme). Yet another way to think of a schema is as a structure with a series of "slots" waiting to be filled by incoming information. It was pointed out in Chapter 8 that a hypothetical schema for the concept "classroom" would likely include slots for certain people (like teachers and students), objects (desks, chalkboard, books, pencils), and events (reading, listening, writing, talking, drawing). Since this is an idealized representation, actual classrooms may contain fewer or greater numbers of these characteristics in varying proportions. Even so, with this schema you could walk into most any classroom and readily understand what was going on, why it was going on, and what to expect. When new information does not match one of the slots in the schema, learning becomes difficult and the probability of recalling that information decreases. In this view, transfer of learning "involves the activation of a previously acquired schema when one encounters a new learning situation. Given that the activated schema is appropriate for the task, learning could occur much more readily than it would in the case where an appropriate schema was not available" (Royer, 1979, p. 65).

Cognitive view of transfer based on recall of appropriate schema

Strengths and Weaknesses of the Cognitive View   In its present form, the cognitive approach to transfer does a better job than the behavioral view of explaining nonspecific lateral transfer—that is, how knowledge learned in one context is applied to learning or problem solving in other contexts. The major limitation of the cognitive approach is that the model of memory constituting its base is still somewhat speculative and subject to change. Consequently, it is not yet possible to accurately predict how well an individual will transfer knowledge learned in school to any number of real-life situations. It is highly likely, though, that as we gain more knowledge about the workings of memory under various conditions, this limitation will diminish (Royer, 1979).

Suggestions for Further Study

Bruner on Education

Toward a Theory of Instruction (1966) is Jerome Bruner's most concise and application-oriented book on teaching. Chapter 1, "Patterns of Growth," and Chapter 3, "Notes on a Theory of Instruction," provide general descriptions of Bruner's view on teaching and learning. Chapter 4 describes how the MACOS materials were used to structure a discovery approach.

Bruner on Bruner

To learn more about Bruner, his ideas, and the circumstances that led him to study such topics as perception, concept formation, problem solving, cognitive development, and discovery learning, read *In Search of Mind: Essays in Autobiography* (1983).

Ausubel's Meaningful Reception Learning

David P. Ausubel provides detailed explanations of meaningful reception learning in *The Psychology of Meaningful Verbal Learning* (1963), *School Learning: An Introduction to Educational Psychology* (1969, Chapter 3), and *Educational Psychology: A Cognitive View* (2nd ed., 1978, Chapters 2 and 4).

Problem-Solving Processes

In *Teaching Thinking Across the Curriculum* (1988), Vincent Ryan Ruggiero describes a model for solving problems and analyzing issues, discusses teaching objectives and methods, identifies obstacles to students' cognitive development, details assignments that can be used in a variety of courses, demonstrates how instructors can design additional course-specific thinking assignments, and offers guidelines for developing a thinking skills program. Many of the same topics are covered by Barry K. Beyer in *Practical Strategies for the Teaching of Thinking* (1988).

Diane F. Halpern describes several aspects of thinking and problem solving in *Thought and Knowledge: An Introduction to Critical Thinking* (1984). Chapter 3, for example, describes the development of various reasoning skills (such as syllogistic, linear, and if-then) as well as reasoning in everyday contexts. Chapter 5 explains and illustrates with concrete examples how understanding probability helps us avoid fallacies in reasoning. Chapter 6 details the development of problem-solving skills. The last chapter, 11, explains how to reason clearly about advertising claims, research findings, legal testimony, medical decisions, legislative proposals, games of chance, and food labels. Each chapter contains a set of exercises that you can do to improve your own thinking skills and that you can adopt for use in your own classroom.

In Chapters 1, 2, and 3 of *Problem Solving: A Handbook for Elementary School Teachers* (1988), S. Krulik and J. A. Rudnick discuss the nature of problem solving, describe the nature and use of heuristics (general approaches to problem solving), and provide seventeen steps that teachers should follow when teaching problem solving. The remainder of the book provides a collection of strategy games (such as tic-tac-toe variations, blocking-strategy games, capture-strategy games), a collection of 178 nonroutine problems, a bibliography of problem-solving resources, ditto masters for selected problems, and ditto masters for strategy-game boards. Many of these games are simple enough for second- and third-graders.

Transfer of Learning

Several aspects of transfer, including transfer of motor skills, transfer of cognitive strategies, and transfer in real-life settings are discussed by different authors in *Transfer of Learning: Contemporary Research and Applications* (1987), edited by Stephen M. Cormier and Joseph D. Hagman.

Summary

1. Jerome Bruner believes that meaningful learning occurs when students grasp the structure of a field of study (the nature of fundamental ideas and how they relate to each other) and when they discover these relationships themselves.

2. Bruner believes that fundamental ideas can be understood by children of any school age, provided the ideas are presented in a manner that is consistent with the child's current mode of mental representation (enactive, iconic, or symbolic). As children progress from one mode to the next, the same ideas can be presented a second or third time with increasing complexity and completeness, a technique referred to as the spiral curriculum.

3. *Man: A Course of Study* (MACOS) is a social studies unit that illustrates Bruner's ideas about structure and discovery.

4. David Ausubel believes that meaningful learning occurs when students receive information organized so that it can be easily related to their current knowledge schemes. Students also need to adopt a meaningful learning set.

5. To help students adopt a meaningful learning set, Ausubel suggests that teachers construct and provide advance organizers. An advance organizer is introductory material that is more abstract, more general, and more inclusive than the material that is to be learned. It is intended to provide an organizing structure that helps students relate new ideas to existing knowledge schemes.

6. The types of problems that students most often come into contact with are well structured, ill structured, and issues. Well-structured problems are clearly stated and can be solved by applying previously learned procedures, and their solutions can be accurately evaluated. Ill-structured problems are often vaguely stated; they cannot always be solved by applying previously learned procedures, and their solutions cannot always be evaluated against clear and widely accepted criteria. Issues are like ill-structured problems, but with two differences—they arouse strong emotions that tend to divide people into opposing camps and they require that one determine the most reasonable position to take before working out a solution.

7. A general problem-solving model is comprised of five steps: realize that a problem exists, understand the nature of the problem, compile relevant information, formulate and carry out a solution, evaluate the solution.

8. The keys to realizing that a problem exists are to be curious about why things are the way they are and to be dissatisfied with the status quo.

9. Understanding the nature of a problem, also known as problem representation or problem framing, requires a high level of knowledge about the sub-

ject matter surrounding the problem and familiarity with the particular type of problem.

10. Relevant information can be compiled by searching long-term memory, retrieving solution-relevant information, and representing that information as lists, tables, pictures, graphs, diagrams, and so on. In addition, friends, colleagues, and experts can be tapped for information.

11. Solutions can be formulated by studying worked examples, working on a simpler version of the problem, breaking the problem into parts, working backward, or solving an analogous problem.

12. Solutions for well-structured problems can be evaluated by estimating or checking. Solutions for ill-structured problems can be evaluated by answering a set of basic questions that deal with who, what, where, when, why, and how; by identifying imperfections and complications; by anticipating possible negative reactions; and by devising improvements.

13. Robert Gagné believes that problem-solving ability is determined largely by intellectual skills and cognitive strategies. Intellectual skills are capabilities for using rules to solve problems and can be decomposed into a learning hierarchy of rules, concepts, discriminations, and associations.

14. Transfer of learning occurs when the learning of new information or skills is influenced by previously learned information or skills.

15. The behavioral view of transfer is based on Edward Thorndike and Robert Woodworth's theory of identical elements. This theory holds that transfer of learning is a function of how many elements two tasks have in common. The greater the similarity, the greater the degree of transfer.

16. Positive transfer occurs when a new learning task is similar to a previously learned task and calls for a similar response. Negative transfer occurs when a new learning task is similar to a previously learned task but calls for a different response. Zero transfer occurs when previously learned information or skills are so dissimilar to new information or skills that they have no effect on how quickly the latter will be learned.

17. Positive transfer that is due to identifiable similarities between an earlier learned task and a current one is referred to as specific transfer. Positive transfer that is due to the formulation, use, and carryover of cognitive strategies from one task to another is referred to as general transfer.

18. Vertical transfer occurs when a previously learned ability aids in learning a more complex ability in the same subject area. Lateral transfer occurs when information or skills that have been acquired in one setting (like school) are used to aid learning in another setting (like work).

19. The cognitive view of transfer attempts to explain how people recall relevant previously learned schemes that they can apply to learning new tasks.

Key Terms

structure *(426)*
spiral curriculum *(426)*
discovery learning *(427)*

meaningful reception
 learning *(444)*
advance organizers *(445)*

problem solving *(446)*
well-structured problems *(446)*
ill-structured problems *(446)*
issues *(447)*
problem representation/
  framing *(448)*
intellectual skill *(455)*
learning hierarchy *(456)*
transfer of learning *(467)*
transfer *(469)*

theory of identical
  elements *(470)*
positive transfer *(470)*
negative transfer *(470)*
zero transfer *(470)*
specific transfer *(471)*
general transfer *(471)*
vertical transfer *(471)*
lateral transfer *(471)*

Discussion Questions

1. To foster meaningful learning (and guide students away from rote learning), Jerome Bruner has argued, teachers should help students discover how the basic ideas of a subject relate to each other and to what students already know. Can you recall a class where the instructor made use of discovery techniques? What did the instructor do? How did you react? Was the learning outcome as meaningful as Bruner suggests? How could you tell? How might you use similar techniques?

2. David Ausubel has argued that to steer students toward meaningful learning, teachers should provide information that has been organized so that it can be easily related to students' existing knowledge schemes. Can you recall one or more instances when a lecture or text was organized this way? How did you react? Was the learning outcome as meaningful as Ausubel suggests? How could you tell? How might you use similar techniques?

3. An important part of Ausubel's theory of meaningful reception learning is the establishment of a meaningful learning set. What should you do to establish such a set in yourself? How can you help your students do the same?

4. Critics of American education argue that contemporary students are poor problem solvers because they receive little systematic instruction in problem-solving processes. How would you rate the quantity and quality of the instruction you received in problem solving? In terms of the five steps discussed in this chapter, which ones were you taught? What can you do to insure that your students become good problem solvers?

5. Many psychologists believe that the best way to determine if something has been meaningfully learned is to see if the individual uses it to make future learning and problem solving easier (positive transfer of learning). Can you describe some personal instances of negative transfer? Can you explain these personal examples in terms of the behavioral and cognitive views of transfer presented in this chapter?

6. Educational psychologists who have studied transfer have said to teachers that if they want transfer, they should teach for transfer. What do you think this statement means?

chapter 10

HUMANISTIC APPROACHES TO EDUCATION

KEY POINTS

Arguments Proposed by "Elder Statesmen" of Humanistic Psychology

Maslow: teachers should help and let children grow and learn

Rogers: teachers should be trusting, sincere, prize students and empathize with them

Combs: teachers should be sensitive, trusting, confident, versatile

Arguments Proposed by Other Humanistic Psychologists

Humanistic education proposed as antidote to technological approaches

Confluent education: flowing together of affective and cognitive elements

Teacher effectiveness training stresses importance of favorable teacher-student relationship

Solve classroom difficulties by determining who owns the problem

I-messages tell how you feel about a situation, not student characteristics

Learning depends on how students perceive themselves

Invitational learning: communicate to students that they are responsible, able, and valuable

Humanistic Techniques Developed by Educators

Encourage pupils to identify by using role playing, simulation games

Values clarification: encourage students to choose, prize, and act on beliefs

Humanistic educators argued that traditional grades should be abolished

An Evaluation of Humanistic Education

Humanistic education emerged as a reaction against prevailing approaches

Enthusiasm for humanistic education waned as times changed, student achievement declined

Humanistic education made up of loosely related assumptions and techniques

When appropriate, stress affective along with cognitive learning

Preferable to be a helpful teacher rather than a friend

Values clarification not likely to change
students' habits or lives

Suggestions for Teaching

Cardinal principle of humanistic education:
give pupils choices

Cardinal principle of communication: talk to
situation, not personality

Encourage value development by taking
advantage of object lessons

At the beginning of Chapter 7, we presented a brief preview of these chapters on learning, pointing out that three interpretations of learning would be discussed: behavioral theories, information processing theory and other cognitive theories, and humanistic approaches to education. These different approaches to learning derive from differences in basic assumptions, approaches to research, and interpretations of data. Behavioral theories, as you are aware, are based on observations of ways overt behavior is influenced by forces in the external environment. Information processing and other cognitive theories, by contrast, are based on speculations about what goes on in the minds of students when they encode, store, and retrieve information, and solve problems. Humanistic educators are interested in how the affective (emotional and interpersonal) aspects of behavior influence learning.

One reason for studying learning from different perspectives is that as a teacher you will be interested in helping your students achieve diverse objectives in the cognitive, affective, and psychomotor domains, and to do so, you will want to use a variety of instructional techniques. Quite often you will ask your students to study individually as they read text and complete specific assignments. At other times you will want them to engage in class discussion or prepare group or individual projects. You will want to help them improve their efficiency as information processors. Finally, you will want them to respond to you and to schooling in positive ways and develop positive feelings about themselves as individuals and students.

In sum, classroom learning is too complex a behavior to be fully understood from one point of view. It should be obvious by now that such concepts as reinforcement, feedback, shaping, modeling, encoding, retrieval from memory, analyzing, and planning complement each other even though they represent different perspectives. This chapter should be seen in the same light. Establishing an atmosphere that invites meaningful learning, cognitive growth, and a positive attitude toward self and others is as relevant to behavioral theory as it is to information processing and other cognitive theories.

Factors Leading to Enthusiasm for Humanistic Approaches

To place the peak of popularity of the humanistic approaches to be described in this chapter in chronological perspective, it is necessary to begin by considering reasons for the rise and partial decline of enthusiasm for programmed forms of instruction. After World War II, there was a wave of national confidence and pride in the accomplishments of American technology. It was reasoned that techniques that had worked so well in our triumphant war effort should be applied to education. During this era of buoyant optimism about the potentialities of technology, step-by-step approaches to teaching recommended by Skinner and others were enthusiastically endorsed and widely applied. As noted in the critique of behavioral theories in Chapter 7, though, programmed and behavior modification approaches probably were used too extensively, and often in situations where they were not completely appropriate. As a result, a certain amount of disenchantment with technological education began to develop. The social and political changes of the 1960s hastened and intensified this process. During that decade, ghetto riots and civil rights demonstrations occurred, we became enmeshed in Vietnam, and campus disruption started to escalate. Critics began to point out that preoccupation with efficiency and productivity had caused Americans to lose sight of the human side of life. Distrust of those in authority, including teachers who exerted control over learning, increased.

When a society is perceived as troubled and unstable, there is often a tendency to look for symptoms, as well as causes, in the educational system. In any event, toward the end of the 1960s, a number of influential books were written outlining in considerable detail what was wrong with American schools. These various critiques of education were influenced by (and manifestations of) disappointment with and loss of confidence in many aspects of our society. As a result of the antiauthority political climate of the country and the widespread criticisms of controlled forms of education, open and discovery techniques of instruction advocated by Piaget and Bruner gained preference over teacher-directed variations of programmed instruction. Around the time teaching approaches derived from cognitive theory were increasing in popularity, a related concept of learning emerged. A number of psychologists and educators agreed with the basic principle of cognitive theory that teachers should arrange the learning environment to permit students to make their own discoveries. These theorists proposed, however, that education should also involve awareness of emotions and feelings. Advocates of the affective position argued that both behaviorists and cognitive theorists tended to dehumanize education in the sense that neither programmed learning nor the discovery approach took into account how students feel about

Enthusiasts for humanistic education argue that behavioral and cognitive psychologists have completely ignored the importance of emotions and feelings in school situations. (Ellis Herwig/The Picture Cube)

themselves or about learning, teachers, and schooling. To correct this omission, it was argued, teachers should be made aware of the *human* side of learning. That is why this point of view is called the *humanistic* approach to education. You should take note, though, that the term **humanistic education** is used to refer to a wide variety of ideas and techniques. Different individuals use the term in different ways, they advocate humanizing education for different reasons, and they recommend use of a disparate assortment of teaching techniques. Therefore, to introduce the discussion of this approach, a brief outline of the professional development and basic observations of three "elder statesmen" of humanistic psychology will be presented. Then other conceptions of humanistic education will be outlined.

The three individuals who have had noteworthy impact on the emergence of humanistic psychology are Abraham H. Maslow, Carl R. Rogers, and Arthur Combs.

Arguments Proposed by "Elder Statesmen" of Humanistic Psychology

Maslow: Let Children Grow

Maslow earned his Ph.D. in a psychology department that supported the behaviorist position. After he graduated, however, he came into contact with Gestalt psychologists, prepared for a career as a psychoanalyst, and became interested in anthropology. As a result of these various influences, he came to the conclusion that American psychologists who endorsed the behaviorist position had become so preoccupied with overt behavior and objectivity that they were ignoring some of the most important aspects of human existence. At the same time, Maslow became convinced that a strict Freudian view of behavior, which led to the conclusion that human beings desperately strive to maintain control of themselves, also had limitations, primarily because much of it was based on the behavior of neurotic individuals. When he observed the behavior of especially well-adjusted persons—or *self-actualizers,* as he called them—he concluded that healthy children *seek* fulfilling experiences. As an alternative to the behavioristic and psychoanalytic interpretations of behavior, Maslow proposed *third force* psychology.

In Chapter 15 of *Toward a Psychology of Being* (2nd ed., 1968), Maslow describes forty-three basic propositions that summarize his views. Some of the most significant of these propositions are: Each individual is born with an essential inner nature. This inner nature is shaped by experiences and by unconscious thoughts and feelings but it is not *dominated* by such forces. Individuals control much of their own behavior. Children should be allowed to make many choices about their own development. Parents and teachers play a significant role in preparing children to make wise choices by satisfying their physiological, safety, love, belonging, and esteem needs, but they should do this by helping and letting children grow, not by attempting to shape or control the way they grow. (A more detailed outline of Maslow's view is presented in Chapter 11 in the discussion of motivation.)

Maslow: teachers should help and let children grow and learn

Rogers: Learner-centered Education

Carl R. Rogers had experiences quite similar to those of Maslow, and he came to similar conclusions. Rogers began his career as a psychotherapist who used psychoanalytic techniques. Eventually, he reached a conclusion identical to Maslow's: The psychoanalytic view sometimes made troubled human beings appear to be helpless individuals who needed the more or less constant help of psychotherapists to cope with their problems. Over a period of years, Rogers developed a new approach to psychotherapy. He called it *client-centered* (or *nondirective*) therapy, to stress the fact that the client, rather than the therapist, should be the central figure. (Or, as the term *nondirective* indicates, the therapist was not to tell the patient what was wrong and what should be done about it.) This view of therapy is a departure from psychoanalysis, where the analyst is the central figure who makes interpretations and offers prescriptions. It is also based on rejection of the strict behaviorist view, since it is assumed that the client will learn how to control his or her own behavior (and not merely be shaped by experiences).

As he practiced client-centered therapy, or the *person-centered* approach, as he eventually called it, Rogers came to the conclusion that he was most successful when he established certain conditions (1967, pp. 53–54). He did not attempt to

Carl R. Rogers
(Douglas A. Land)

put up a false front of any kind. He established a warm, positive, acceptant attitude toward his clients, and he was able to empathize with clients and sense their thoughts and feelings. Rogers concluded that these conditions set the stage for successful experiences with therapy because clients became more self-accepting and aware of themselves. Once individuals acquired these qualities, they were inclined and equipped to solve personal problems without seeking the aid of a therapist.

In addition to functioning as a therapist, Rogers also served as a professor. As he analyzed his experiences as an instructor, he concluded that the person-centered approach to therapy could be applied just as successfully to teaching. He thus proposed the idea of **learner-centered education**—that teachers try to establish the same conditions as person-centered therapists. Rogers sums up the qualities of a teacher who wants to use a learner-centered approach in this way:

> Perhaps the most basic of these essential attitudes is realness or genuineness. When the facilitator is a real person, being what she is, entering into the relationship with the learner without presenting a front or façade, she is much more likely to be effective. . . . She can be enthusiastic, can be bored, can be interested in students, can be angry, can be sensitive and sympathetic. Because she accepts these feelings as her own, she has no need to impose them on her students.
>
> There is another attitude that stands out in those who are successful in facilitating learning. . . . I think of it as prizing the learner, prizing her feelings, her opinions, her person. . . . It is an acceptance of this other individual as a separate person, having worth in her own right.

Rogers: teachers should be trusting, sincere, prize students and empathize with them

A further element that establishes a climate for self-initiated, experiential learning is empathic understanding. When the teacher has the ability to understand the student's reactions from the inside, has a sensitive awareness of the way the process of education and learning seems *to the student*, then again the likelihood of significant learning is increased. (1983, pp. 121–125)

Rogers argues (1980, pp. 273–278) that the results of learner-centered teaching are similar to those of person-centered therapy: Students become capable of educating themselves without the aid of teachers.

Combs: The Teacher as Facilitator

Arthur Combs became an enthusiastic advocate of the humanistic view after having experiences similar to those of Maslow and Rogers. He, too, became disenchanted with behaviorism and psychoanalysis and sought an alternative. While Maslow based his conception of third force psychology on the study of motivation and Rogers based his view on his experiences as a psychotherapist, Combs used the cognitive view as a starting point for his speculations. He began with the assumption that "all behavior of a person is the direct result of his field of perceptions at the moment of his behaving" (1965, p. 12). From this assumption it follows that a teacher should try to understand any learning situation by speculating about how things seem from the students' point of view. This assumption also leads to the conclusion that to help students learn it is necessary to induce them to modify their beliefs and perceptions so that they will see things differently and behave differently. Some aspects of Combs's analysis of learning are similar to those of Bruner and other cognitive psychologists, but Combs placed less emphasis on cognitive aspects of learning and more on the personal perceptions of the learner.

Combs believed that how a person perceives herself or himself is of paramount importance and that a basic purpose of teaching is to help each student develop a positive self-concept. He observed, "The task of the teacher is not one of prescribing, making, molding, forcing, coercing, coaxing, or cajoling; it is one of ministering to a process already in being. The role required of the teacher is that of facilitator, encourager, helper, assister, colleague, and friend of his students" (1965, p. 16). Combs elaborated on these points by listing six characteristics of good teachers: (1) They are well informed about their subject; (2) they are sensitive to the feelings of students and colleagues; (3) they believe that students can learn; (4) they have a positive self-concept; (5) they believe in helping all students do their best; and (6) they use many different methods of instruction (1965, pp. 20–23).

In collaboration with three colleagues, Combs (1974) later reaffirmed his belief in a humanistic approach to teaching and described how he developed a program to encourage the development of teachers with the characteristics just listed. He

Combs: teachers should be sensitive, trusting, confident, versatile also offered evidence (pp. 175–181) to support the conclusion that teachers can be helped to increase their sensitivity to students' needs, develop self-confidence, and establish a positive classroom atmosphere.

Taken together, the observations of Maslow, Rogers, and Combs lead to a conception of education stressing that teachers should trust pupils enough to permit them to make many choices about their own learning. At the same time, teachers should be sensitive to the social and emotional needs of students, empathize with them, and respond positively to them. Finally, teachers should be sincere, willing to show that they also have needs, and experience positive feelings about themselves and what they are doing.

Maslow, Rogers, and Combs were the acknowledged leaders of the humanistic movement in American psychology, but several lesser-known colleagues also advocated humanistic education.

Arguments Proposed by Other Humanistic Psychologists

Patterson: Humanistic Education as an Antidote

In *Humanistic Education* (1973), C. H. Patterson maintained that the crisis in American education perceived by Silberman and others was due to too much stress on technological approaches to teaching. He urged teachers to use more human ways to facilitate subject-matter learning and also to pay more attention to affective aspects of learning. He offered early and recent examples of humanistic education, outlined what he considered to be necessary changes in educational practices, and described the characteristics of humanistic teachers and the techniques they used (characteristics and techniques similar to those advocated by Rogers and Combs).

> Humanistic education proposed as antidote to technological approaches

Brown: Confluent Education

In *Human Teaching for Human Learning* (1971), George Isaac Brown described **confluent education,** a flowing together of affective and cognitive elements in individual and group learning. He observed, "It should be apparent that there is no intellectual learning without some sort of feeling, and there are no feelings without the mind's being somehow involved" (p. 4). He described some basic affective techniques (for example, having individuals explore each other's faces with their hands or forming groups without speaking to each other), and outlined some classroom applications. A unit in ninth-grade social studies, for instance, was introduced with lectures by the instructor on theories of the nature of humankind. Then, students were asked to try to discover things about themselves by examining their thoughts, perceptions, and aspirations. Finally, they were asked to relate

> Confluent education: flowing together of affective and cognitive elements

what they had discovered about themselves to what others had discoverd about the nature of human beings in general. Toward the end of the book, Brown warned readers to proceed with caution, but also urged teachers to try to avoid presenting affective learning as if it were isolated from the regular curriculum.

Gordon: Teacher Effectiveness Training (T.E.T.)

Thomas Gordon, who had studied with Carl Rogers, applied what he had learned about person-centered therapy to parent-child relationships in *Parent Effectiveness Training* (1970). The success of that book prompted him to write *Teacher Effectiveness Training* (1974), in which he stressed the importance of a favorable teacher-student relationship. He noted:

Teacher effectiveness training stresses importance of favorable teacher-student relationship

> The relationship between a teacher and a student is good when it has (1) Openness or Transparency, so each is able to risk directness and honesty with the other; (2) Caring, when each knows that he is valued by the other; (3) Interdependence (as opposed to dependency) of one on the other; (4) Separateness, to allow each to grow and to develop his uniqueness, creativity, and individuality; (5) Mutual Needs Meeting, so that neither's needs are met at the expense of the other's needs. (p. 24)

The basic technique Gordon recommends that teachers use is to discover who "owns" a problem. Gordon illustrates what he means by problem ownership by a rectangular diagram. A line across the top depicts an area indicating that a *student* owns a problem. A line across the bottom marks off a section representing that the *teacher* owns a problem. In between the two lines is the *teaching-learning no-problem* area, which ideally should be much larger than the other two areas. If the teacher is eager to instruct, well informed and prepared and if students are cooperative and willing to learn, there is no problem. If the teacher is not prepared, or dislikes teaching, or is preoccupied with personal difficulties, she or he owns the problem and needs to seek a solution. If students are addicted to doodling instead of paying attention or are afraid that they will not earn high enough grades to please their parents or have similar preoccupations, *they* own the problem. Gordon maintains that too often teachers use ineffective techniques, such as direct or indirect forms of blaming, when dealing with student-owned problems. Instead, teachers should indicate to students that they accept them as they are, by using techniques similar to those devised by Rogers for person-centered therapists. (These techniques, which are based on a basic *accept-reflect-clarify* strategy, are described in detail in *Teacher Effectiveness Training*.)

Solve classroom difficulties by determining who owns the problem

Gordon also recommends the use of **I-messages,** which convey how the teacher feels about a *situation*, not how she or he feels about students. If you find yourself getting angry because a class does not pay attention to a carefully planned presentation, for instance, Gordon suggests that you say, "I'm frustrated and disappointed because I worked for three hours last night getting this demonstration

I-messages tell how you feel about a situation, not student characteristics

ready, and most of you are reading the school newspaper." Such a message describes how you feel, and is to be preferred to a message that criticizes student behavior, such as "You are acting like a bunch of spoiled brats who don't respond to anything other than violent action scenes in TV programs." Gordon argues that I-messages are more effective than you-messages because they make students realize you are a real person and at the same time prevent you from attacking them personally. To be effective, I-messages should tell students in tangible and concrete ways what is creating the problem for the teacher and also make them aware of the teacher's feelings.

In *Teacher and Child* (1972) Haim Ginott offers similar, but independently developed, presentation of many of the same techniques as those recommended by Gordon.

Purkey: Inviting School Success

William W. Purkey first called attention to the significance of the relationship between a student's self-concept and school achievement in a book of that title (1970) and later stressed the importance of students' positive self-perceptions in *Inviting School Success* (1978). Along with the other psychologists noted in this section, Purkey was bothered by what he called the *factory school* atmosphere engendered by too much stress on technological approaches to teaching. He was also impressed by research on the impact of teacher expectations (which was summarized in the discussion of pupil variability in Chapter 4). He concluded that the way students respond in school depends to a significant extent on how they perceive themselves and that the way teachers react (or fail or react) influences student self-perceptions. (Erik Erikson, you may recall from Chapter 2, stresses that pupils should experience a sense of industry rather than inferiority.) To encourage students to experience feelings of positive self-worth, Purkey recommended that instructors develop and use skills of **invitational learning**.

> **Learning depends on how students perceive themselves**

Purkey defines an invitation as "a summary description of messages—verbal and nonverbal, formal and informal—continuously transmitted to students with the intention of informing them that they are responsible, able, and valuable" (p. 3). He outlines seven skills of invitational teachers:

> **Invitational learning: communicate to students that they are responsible, able, and valuable**

1. Reaching each student (e.g., learning names, having one-to-one contact)
2. Listening with care (e.g., picking up subtle cues)
3. Being real with students (e.g., providing only realistic praise)
4. Being real with oneself (e.g., honestly appraising your own feelings and disappointments)
5. Inviting good discipline (e.g., showing students you respect them)
6. Handling rejection (e.g., not taking lack of student response in personal ways)
7. Inviting oneself (e.g., thinking positively about oneself)

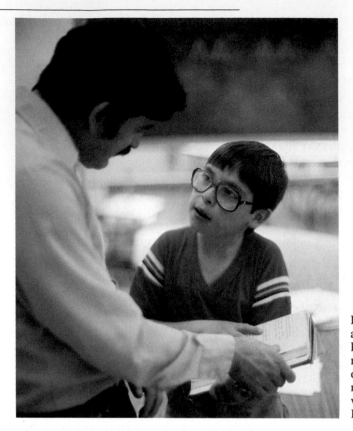

Invitational learning as described by Purkey involves communicating to students that they are responsible, able, and valuable. (Mimi Forsyth/Monkmeyer)

Purkey suggests that four student self-concept factors are likely to lead to school success: *relating* (to others), *asserting* (or experiencing a sense of self-control), *investing* (encouraging students to get involved with learning and with classmates), and *coping* (how well students meet school expectations). In the final chapter of *Inviting School Success*, Purkey suggests that teachers try to establish an atmosphere of warmth and a cooperative spirit and to convey positive expectations. Throughout the book, Purkey mentions anecdotes revealing how a single instance of personal interest, encouragement, or trust on the part of a teacher was reported to have changed a pupil's entire attitude toward self and toward school.

Taken together, the observations of Patterson, Brown, Gordon, and Purkey supplement the views of Maslow, Rogers, and Combs in calling attention to the importance of feelings, teacher-pupil relationships, and the desirability of having students develop positive feelings about themselves as they are given freedom to direct at least part of their own learning. Since this book is about ways to apply psychology to teaching, the discussion of humanistic approaches presented so far has stressed the observations of psychologists. Brief mention should also be made, though, of popular humanistic techniques developed by educators.

Humanistic Techniques Developed by Educators

A Sampling of Humanistic Education Techniques

The *Humanistic Education Sourcebook* (1975), edited by Donald A. Read and Sidney B. Simon, serves as a comprehensive source of ideas for teachers who would like to put humanistic education into practice. Some of the techniques described in the *Sourcebook* involve *sensitivity training* and *encounter groups*. These techniques are essentially group therapy sessions, and they are intended to encourage participants to explore their emotions and feelings in highly personal ways. Other techniques are intended to encourage students to identify with others, empathize with them, and engage in vicarious experiences. Techniques of this type include role playing, psychodrama, sociodrama, and simulation games. Students may be asked to assume the roles of historical figures or act out situations (such as a teacher catching a student cheating), and then reverse the roles. Or members of a group may be assigned roles and asked to follow detailed instructions for simulating a situation such as that involving world leaders at an arms control conference.

Encourage pupils to identify by using role playing, simulation games

Values Clarification

Some of the most explicit instructions available to those who would like to use humanistic techniques of teaching are to be found in books on **values clarification.** This term, which is sometimes capitalized and sometimes abbreviated V.C., was originally applied to techniques proposed by Louis Raths for helping children become more aware of their values. The first book on the subject, *Values and Teaching* (1966) by Raths, Merrill Harmin, and Sidney B. Simon, described the basic strategies of values clarification. The authors proposed that students are likely to develop a set of values that will help them make confident and consistent choices and decisions if they engage in the following activities:

Choose their beliefs and behaviors by first considering and then selecting from alternatives.

Prize their beliefs and behaviors by cherishing and publicly affirming them.

Act on their beliefs repeatedly and consistently.

Values clarification: encourage students to choose, prize, and act on beliefs

Seventy-nine strategies for helping students engage in such activities are described in *Values Clarification: A Handbook of Practical Strategies for Teachers and Students* (1972) by Sidney B. Simon, Leland W. Howe, and Howard Kirschenbaum. Students are asked to choose their beliefs freely and from carefully considered alternatives—for example, in strategy 5, "Either-Or Forced Choice" (pp. 94–97). The teacher institutes this strategy by asking students, "Which do you identify with more, a Volkswagen or a Cadillac?" Pupils indicate their preference by walking to one side of the room or the opposite; they then team up with a classmate who made the same choice and explain the reasons for the choice. Students are encouraged to cherish and publicly affirm their beliefs by engaging in activities such as that presented in strategy 12, "Public Interview" (pp. 139–162). In this strategy, a student volunteers to be interviewed by the rest of the class and publicly affirms and explains her or his stand on various issues. Pupils are urged to act repeatedly and consistently on their beliefs when the teacher uses strategies such as number 42, "Letters to the Editor" (pp. 262–263), and asks each student in the class to write at least one letter to the editor of a newspaper or magazine. Copies of the letter and clippings from the paper or magazine (if available) are posted on a bulletin board, and at the end of the month pupils read their letters to the rest of the class and explain their reasons for speaking out on the issue they had selected.

Besides proposing that teachers use techniques such as those just summarized, humanistic educators also recommended a change in grading practices. Even though grading policies are not methods of instruction, they merit mention here because they were an integral part of the humanistic education movement.

Emphasis on Pass/Fail Grading

Many humanistic educators (for example, Kirschenbaum, Simon, and Napier, 1971) argued that traditional grading practices should be abolished because they interfered with achievement of basic goals of that form of instruction. Humanistic education emphasized the development of positive feelings about self and others; stress on subject matter was to be replaced by stress on understanding of feelings and teachers were to function as facilitators or friends. Traditional grading practices interfered with the achievement of those goals, it was argued, because students who received low grades were told, in effect, that they were inferior and incapable of learning. When students were graded "on the curve," critics pointed out, they were forced to compete against each other and to view classmates as "enemies." Teachers who assigned marks on exams, papers, and report cards were forced to function as authorities and judges rather than facilitators and friends. For these and similar reasons, when humanistic education was at a peak of popularity during the early 1970s, the traditional letter-grade system was replaced in many schools, colleges, and universities by pass/fail or credit/no credit grading. When traditional grades *were* assigned, there was a tendency to relax standards and record many A's and B's on report cards.

Now that you are familiar with the nature of humanistic education, we are in a position to evaluate its effectiveness and current status.

Humanistic educators argued that traditional grades should be abolished

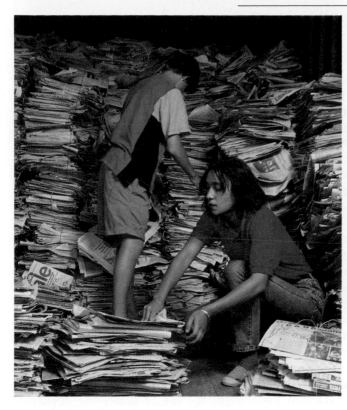

Values clarification strategies are intended to encourage individuals to choose, prize, and act on their beliefs. If pupils indicate during class discussions that they believe in conserving natural resources and maintaining an attractive environment, they are urged to do something about it—such as collecting newspapers that can be recycled. (Mark Antman/The Image Works)

An Evaluation of Humanistic Education

In order to evaluate humanistic education and speculate about how you might make constructive use of selected techniques in your classroom, it is necessary to take into account when and why it emerged and what it involves.

Humanistic Education in Different Social and Political Climates

Humanistic education emerged as a recognizable force in the late 1960s and reached a peak of popularity in the early 1970s. As noted at the start of this chapter, during that period of American history there was widespread dissatisfaction with our society and our schools. Riots and demonstrations in ghettos and on campuses were the most tangible signs of anger, disappointment, and frustration, but many Americans experienced the feeling that something was wrong with our society and that change was essential. Books attacking traditional forms of education became popular and led to interest in finding new approaches to schooling. Some parents were so convinced that public schools caused more harm than good that they formed so-called "free schools," in which pupils and teachers were

Humanistic education emerged as a reaction against prevailing approaches treated as equals and students were allowed to decide what, when, and where they would study. Thus, the time was ripe for radical changes in educational techniques, and the advocates of humanistic education were so enthusiastic about that form of education that they won a substantial number of converts.

The first point to recognize in evaluating humanistic education is to note that times have changed. Within quite a short time after pupils, parents, and teachers embraced humanistic education with gusto, the social and political climate stabilized and became more conservative. Furthermore, starting in the mid-1970s, the reports of low achievement test scores, which contributed to the loss of enthusiasm for open education and for the discovery approach, had an even more damaging impact on humanistic education approaches. Just a few years after Silberman and others had maintained that a "crisis" existed in American education that could only be alleviated by moving away from teacher-controlled instruction, other critics asserted that a new "crisis" was at hand and it could be alleviated only by a "back to basics" movement.

It is possible, however, to value and apply a mix of humanistic and information processing and other cognitive instructional methods to address both affective and cognitive goals. Bruce Hall, Melvin Villern, and W. Wade Burley (1986) found that beginning teachers who endorse humanistic outcomes in education (such as social and emotional development and clarification of social values) also endorse such teacher-directed practices as the use of behavioral objectives, higher-order questions, and advance organizers. Thus, teachers who adopt or agree with a humanistic orientation do not necessarily oppose the recent emphasis on academic excellence. In fact, they probably believe that a humanistic orientation is more likely than a nonhumanistic orientation to produce high levels of classroom achievement.

> **Enthusiasm for humanistic education waned as times changed, student achievement declined**

Analyzing Separate Aspects of Humanistic Education

A second point to note about humanistic education is the one stressed at the beginning of this chapter: The term refers to a variety of assumptions and techniques. Some theorists stress basic assumptions about children, teachers, and the learning situation. Others describe attitudes of students and teachers or stress the significance of interpersonal relationships. Still others advocate the use of specific instructional techniques. Here is a summary of points emphasized by the various advocates of humanistic education mentioned in this chapter.

> **Humanistic education made up of loosely related assumptions and techniques**

1. Assumptions about pupils and the basic nature of education.
   Maslow and Rogers: Teachers should trust children and let them make many of their own decisions, instruction should be learner-centered.

2. Characteristics of effective teachers.
   Rogers: Teachers should be trusting, sincere, prize students, and empathize with them.
   Combs: Teachers should be sensitive, trusting, confident, and versatile.
3. Affective factors should be explored as much as the cognitive side of subject matter.
   Brown: Confluent education should cause cognitive and affective elements of a learning situation to flow together.
4. Relationships between pupils and their teachers have an important impact on learning.
   Gordon: Teachers should try to establish positive relationships with pupils, determine who owns problems, use I-messages.
5. How students feel about themselves influences the way they learn.
   Purkey: Teachers should use invitational learning techniques by communicating to students that they are responsible, able, and valuable. Teachers should do everything possible to encourage students to develop positive feelings about themselves.
6. Teachers should use techniques to encourage pupils to explore their feelings and emotions.
   Suggested techniques: Sensitivity training, encounter groups
7. Teachers should use techniques for encouraging students to identify with others, empathize with them, and relate their feelings to the feelings of others.
   Suggested techniques: role playing, psychodrama, sociodrama, simulation games
8. Teachers should use techniques to help students become more aware of and act on their attitudes and values.
   Suggested techniques: values clarification strategies
9. Traditional grading practices should be replaced by pass/fail or credit/no credit evaluation procedures.

Are these techniques effective? After reviewing several dozen studies, John Swisher, Judith Vickery, and Peggy Nadenichek (1983) concluded that humanistic instructional techniques (for example, values clarification, role playing, and interpersonal relations training) were much more likely to produce positive outcomes than negative outcomes. Most of the studies reviewed reported gains for classroom management (reductions in problem behaviors and tardiness, increases in attendance), achievement, attitudes toward school, self-esteem, creativity, communication skills, and social awareness (an important outcome given the current emphasis on multicultural programs).

Despite the positive findings, there are good reasons for keeping some cautions in mind when implementing certain humanistic techniques. We discuss several of these next.

Evaluations of the Current Appropriateness of Humanistic Techniques

1. The assumptions that teachers should trust pupils and permit them to make many of their own decisions and that instruction should center on the learner

For reasons noted at the beginning of this section these assumptions should probably be treated as appropriate only in qualified ways today. You might ask students to help you as much as possible in determining instructional objectives, and you might invite them sometimes to use the contract approach or complete self-selected individual or group projects. Given the prevailing educational climate in this country, however, you should probably expect to make most of the decisions about what your students will learn and how they will learn it (or to implement decisions made by others, such as school boards and state education agencies). At the same time, you should remember that teacher expectations often influence pupil behavior. Thus, you should try to communicate the feeling that you trust pupils, in the sense that you believe they are capable of learning.

2. The assumptions that teachers should show they are sincere, demonstrate sensitivity to the needs and feelings of pupils, and exhibit confidence and versatility

All these characteristics obviously are desirable. There are a number of techniques you can use (such as I-messages) to demonstrate that you are genuine and sincere. You can also make an effort to try to see things from a student's point of view. If you make careful plans to use a variety of techniques and follow the suggestions for developing a personal handbook and making an effort to become a better teacher (as described in the last chapter of this book), you should function as a versatile and confident teacher.

3. The assumption that affective factors should be explored as much as the cognitive side of subject matter

It may be unwise to stress the affective side of learning in the mid-1990s to the same extent that Brown recommended twenty years ago. It should be possible, though, to avoid making the presentation of subject matter too objective and sterile. When you think about how to structure class discussions or give individual or group assignments, you might look for ways to get students personally involved by considering affective, as well as cognitive, aspects of learning.

When appropriate, stress affective along with cognitive learning

4. The assumption that relationships between pupils and their teachers have an important impact on learning

Behavioral theorists tend to concentrate on the most efficient ways to arrange learning situations; cognitive theorists are interested in ways students perceive relationships. Humanistic psychologists perform a valuable service when they call attention to the fact that *how* teachers present subject matter and interact with

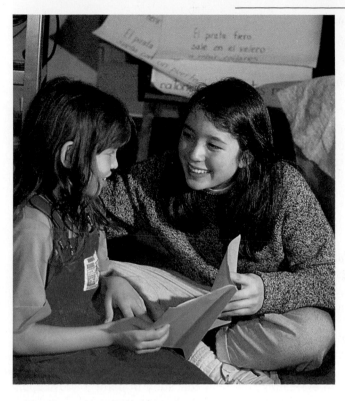

Some humanistic educators maintain that teachers should do everything possible to encourage students to develop positive feelings about themselves. (Susan Lapides)

their students is often significant. You probably know from your own experience that you are more likely to respond to a teacher who makes an effort to establish a relaxed, positive classroom atmosphere and to treat you as an individual than to one who simply handles teaching chores in an impersonal way. There are many things you can do to establish positive relationships with your students, and you can handle classroom problems with a minimum of ill feeling if you take the trouble to think about problem ownership and use I-messages.

At the same time, you should probably think of yourself as a teacher rather than a friend. Those who have tried to teach by building an extremely close personal relationship with all pupils in a class have been unable to continue that kind of education for more than a year or two. Herbert Kohl, for example, described in *36 Children* (1967) how he used a highly personal, humanistic approach to teaching in an inner-city elementary school. After two years of that kind of instruction, he felt obliged to move to Spain to recuperate. George Dennison, who described how he developed a humanistic school in *The Lives of Children* (1969), noted at the end of the book that the school closed its doors after two years. He explained, "It was not merely lack of money that closed the school. We ourselves were not strongly enough motivated to make the sacrifices that would have been necessary to sustain it" (p. 273). He then notes that he returned to a full-time career as a writer after the school closed. You should also remember that, unlike humanistic educators of the 1970s, you will almost certainly be expected to assign letter grades.

Preferable to be a helpful teacher rather than a friend

5. The assumption that how students feel about themselves influences the way they learn

In *Inviting School Success*, Purkey summarizes research that supports this point, but you may be able to endorse it simply by examining your own reactions to teachers and schooling. Students are more likely to put out in a classroom if they feel their teachers like them, have faith in them, and believe they can learn. Thus, you should do everything possible to encourage your pupils to develop positive feelings about themselves as persons and learners.

6. The assumptions that teachers should encourage pupils to explore their feelings and emotions

Of all the assumptions listed here, this one is probably most difficult to defend today. It would almost certainly be a mistake for you to devote in-class time to sensitivity training or encounter group sessions or to use psychodrama techniques in contemporary American classrooms.

7. The assumption that teachers should use techniques to encourage students to identify with others, empathize with them, and relate their feelings to the feelings of others

The remarks made in evaluating confluent education in point 3 above apply here as well. When aimed at increasing interest and involvement in subject matter, occasional use of role playing and simulation games can be effective. However, using such techniques only to make students aware of feelings, emotions, and interrelationships—independently of presenting subject matter—might lead to problems with parents and administrators.

8. The assumption that teachers should make frequent use of values clarification strategies

When values clarification strategies were first developed, lavish claims for the technique were made. In *Personalizing Education* (1975), for example, Leland and Mary Howe asserted that "if our values are clear, consistent, and soundly chosen, we tend to live our lives in meaningful and satisfying ways" (p. 17). Although they used the phrase "soundly chosen," the Howes joined with other values clarification enthusiasts in stressing that "Values Clarification is not an attempt to teach students 'right' and 'wrong' values. Rather, it is an approach designed to help students prize and act upon their own freely chosen values. Thus, V.C. is concerned with the process by which students arrive at their values, rather than the content of these values" (p. 19). There is no reason to assume, however, that students will automatically make sound choices when they engage in values clarification sessions. It is quite possible that when students are encouraged to develop clear and consistent values, they will choose those that focus on material possessions, power, self-indulgence, and the like. Considering the nature of high-pressure advertising in America and the kinds of individuals who achieve noto-

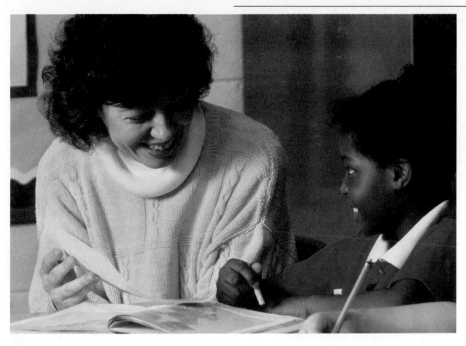

Humanistic educators call attention to the importance of positive teacher-pupil relationships in the classroom. (The Stock Market/Charles Gupton, 1988)

riety in our society, it would be surprising if such values were not favored by many young people. Simply because a person's values are made more consistent as a consequence of values clarification sessions, therefore, does not guarantee that the individual will live in a "meaningful and satisfying way." The opposite could be just as likely.

Furthermore, if Piaget's description of cognitive development is taken into account, there is reason to doubt that very many pupils will actually develop a consistent value system through values clarification exercises. Many values clarification strategies are designed to be used with elementary school children who are at the concrete operations stage of cognitive development and unable to grasp abstract concepts or generalize. To cite just one example, when they are asked to indicate if they prefer ice cream, Jell-O, or pie for dessert (a question featured in a values clarification strategy intended to give children practice in choosing among alternatives), young children will probably react in a quite literal way. They will think about their favorite dessert but not about the principle of choosing among alternatives. There is no reason to believe that when they are faced with a choice involving values they will see any connection between picking a dessert and making a moral or ethical decision.

The same tendency to respond in literal ways is likely to be characteristic of many secondary school students as well, since the transition to formal thought is a gradual process. But even high school students who are capable of dealing with abstractions and hypothetical situations may not develop a realistic or workable

Values clarification not likely to change students' habits or lives

set of values because novice formal thinkers tend to overlook realities. Secondary school students are also eager to impress others. If a high school girl volunteers to be interviewed by the class, for instance, she may supply glib and idealistic answers and be so preoccupied with making a good impression on classmates that there will be no carry-over to behavior outside of class. Simply because students can talk about positive values in discussing hypothetical situations does not mean that they will necessarily act that way when the chips are down. Because of factors such as these, it is unrealistic to expect that use of values clarification strategies will equip students with a value system that will lead to a "meaningful and satisfying life."

If you plan to use group discussion techniques fairly frequently, though, you may wish to examine books on values clarification and select strategies (keeping in mind the reservations just noted) that permit you to cover subject matter and clarify values at the same time. (Books you might consult will be noted in the Suggestions for Teaching and the Suggestions for Further Study that follow.)

9. The assumption that traditional grading practices should be replaced by pass/ fail or credit/no credit evaluation procedures

For reasons stated earlier, you will almost certainly be expected to assign (and defend) letter grades that reflect mastery of specific instructional objectives.

Mid-Chapter Review

Views of the "Elder Statesmen" of Humanistic Psychology

Humanistic psychology emerged when a number of theorists found that they were dissatisfied with behavioral and psychoanalytic interpretations of behavior, particularly the hypothesis stressed by Skinner and Freud that humans have little control over their own behavior. This hypothesis led to the assumption that it was essential for parents and teachers to shape behavior and control learning. An alternative view stressing that humans do control much of their own behavior, and that parents and teachers should allow freedom for children to explore and develop, was proposed by three eminent psychologists:

Abraham Maslow urged parents and teachers to trust children and let and help them grow.

Carl Rogers recommended that teachers be trusting and sincere, prize students, and empathize with them.

Arthur Combs maintained that teachers should be sensitive, trusting, confident, and versatile.

Proposals Made by Other Humanistic Psychologists and Educators

Psychologists who were bothered by the impersonal nature of technological and cognitive approaches to instruction proposed a variety of humanistic instructional techniques:

George Brown urged teachers to practice **confluent education,** where cognitive and affective elements would flow together.

Thomas Gordon stressed that teachers should become effective in developing positive relationships with students. He urged teachers to think about **problem ownership** and to use **I-messages.**

William Purkey stressed that learning depends on how pupils perceive themselves and urged teachers to encourage **invitational learning** by communicating to students that they are responsible, able, and valuable.

Educators joined with psychologists in urging teachers to use humanistic approaches to instruction. Some recommended use of role playing and simulation games, others advocated **values clarification** where students were encouraged to choose, prize, and act on their beliefs. Still others argued that grades should be abolished, since low grades cause students to feel inferior and incapable of learning.

Evaluating Humanistic Education

Humanistic education is difficult to evaluate because it is made up of loosely related assumptions and techniques. To understand why certain concepts and techniques were recommended, it should be noted that the humanistic movement emerged as a reaction against prevailing approaches. Enthusiasm for humanistic education peaked during a period of recent American history when there was widespread dissatisfaction with many aspects of our society as well as distrust of authority. Support for humanistic education declined when the social and political climate changed and as evidence accumulated revealing that American students exposed to student-centered instruction scored low on achievement tests.

Assumptions and techniques of humanistic education that still merit consideration, even with present emphasis on subject-matter mastery, include:

Stress on affective as well as cognitive learning

Teacher sensitivity to student feelings and needs

Inviting students to think about values and attitudes

SUGGESTIONS FOR TEACHING

Using Humanistic Techniques in the Classroom

1. Try to remain aware of the extent to which you direct and control learning. Whenever possible, permit and encourage students to make choices and to manage their own learning.

2. Establish a warm, positive, acceptant atmosphere. Do your best to communicate the feeling that you believe all the students in the class can learn and that you want them to learn.

3. When it seems appropriate, function as a facilitator, encourager, helper, and assister. Before attempting to function as a colleague or friend, think about possible complications.

4. If you feel comfortable doing it, occasionally show that you are a "real person" by telling students how you feel. When you express anger, however, comment on the situation, not on the personality traits of your students.

5. Do your best to help your students develop positive feelings about themselves. Empathize with them, and show you are sensitive to their needs and feelings.

6. If appropriate, ask students to participate in role playing or simulation games.

7. If appropriate (and acceptable), make judicious use of values clarification strategies.

8. Do your best to provide learning experiences that will lead to the development of the habits and attitudes you want to foster.

9. Make use of object lessons. When illustrative incidents occur, take advantage of them.

10. Set a good example.

1. Try to remain aware of the extent to which you direct and control learning. Whenever possible, permit and encourage students to make choices and to manage their own learning.

Humanistic psychology developed as a reaction against strict behavioristic and psychoanalytic interpretations of behavior. Maslow, Rogers, and Combs ask educators to avoid the pitfalls of assuming that children are entirely shaped by experiences or that they need to be protected and guarded at all times. The cardinal principle of humanistic education is to give students opportunities to make choices and manage their own learning. It is neither logical nor possible, however, to give students complete freedom of choice. Immature children cannot anticipate what they will need to know in order to live in a technological society and cannot be expected to supervise or sustain all their own learning experiences. Furthermore, parents, school boards, and school administrators expect teachers to earn their salaries and produce tangible results. Even so, you should be able to offer your students many opportunities to participate in decisions about what will be studied, how it will be studied, and how classroom order will be maintained. As you plan lessons, you might ask yourself, "Am I setting up a controlled situation here because it is in the best interests of the students, or am I doing it because it's easier, because I like to feel that I'm indispensable, or because it gives me a sense of power?" If you are willing, you can find many ways to give students opportunities to make choices as they learn.

Cardinal principle of humanistic education: give pupils choices

Handbook Heading: Ways to Give Pupils Choices

Examples

Ask the class to select topics to be covered (as noted in the suggestions for arranging group discussions presented in the preceding chapter).

Permit individual students to choose topics to be studied, perhaps by selecting from a suggested list or by proposing subjects on their own.

Arrange an open classroom situation so that students can engage in self-selected study of subjects of interest.

Invite students to participate in making decisions about class rules.

A number of strategies for providing opportunities for students to participate in decisions about what will be studied are described in *Personalizing Education* by Howe and Howe (1975). They describe a ten-step procedure outlined in Chapter 8 (pages 366–367) which involves preparation of a flow chart detailing steps to be followed.

Other ways to permit students a degree of choice, particularly when a prescribed curriculum must be covered, are described in Chapter 14 of *Personalizing Education*. One of these is the Student Self-Paced Style. In this approach, students are asked to study a prescribed topic, but they determine how fast, where, when, and with whom they will study. The Howes suggest that students

Handbook Heading:
Using Self-Paced and
Self-Selected Styles

correct their own work. For details of the Self-Paced Style, see pages 465–468 of *Personalizing Education*.

An approach that gives students a bit more control over their own learning is called the Student Self-Selected Learning Style. It is similar to the Self-Paced Style, except for the first step: Instead of being given assigned work, students choose their own topics. One way to facilitate this approach is to prepare a large number of activity cards that give suggestions for studying different topics. The Howes suggest that these include the following information: the name of the activity, the purpose, materials needed to complete the activity, steps to be followed, evaluation criteria to be used, and suggestions for follow-up activities. Many teachers' journals supply information that might be used in preparing such cards, or you might team up with other teachers and develop a combined set that could be reproduced. Another obvious way to accumulate such cards is to ask students to develop their own and then save the best ones each year.

Still another variation of self-directed learning consists of the *contract approach* which was described in Chapter 6 ("Devising and Using Objectives").

2. Establish a warm, positive, acceptant atmosphere. Do your best to communicate the feeling that you believe all the students in the class can learn and that you want them to learn.

These points are related to J. M. Stephens's distinction between the teacher-practitioner and the teacher-theorist that was mentioned in Chapter 1. In their eagerness to persuade teachers to be efficient and objective, some advocates of the behaviorist view ignore the impact of the teacher's attitude. Humanistic psychologists join with Stephens in calling attention to the extent to which *how* you teach will influence the response of your students. At times you will want to be efficient and objective, but because successful learning experiences seem to depend to a significant extent on interpersonal relationships, you should not attempt to play the role of an impersonal authority or leader. You are more likely to get a positive response from your students if you exude warmth, enthusiasm, and high expectations. Remember the nature of the self-fulfilling prophecy, and communicate, as best you can, the attitude that every student in the class is capable of learning.

Examples

Learn pupils' names as fast as you can, and take an interest in them as individuals.

Try to show that you are intrigued, fascinated, excited, and enthusiastic about the things you present to the class.

Urge all students to do their best, and avoid forcing students to compete for a limited number of high grades. (Detailed instructions for doing this will be presented in the learning for mastery section of Chapter 12.)

Show that you are pleased (but not surprised) when students do well; don't act as if it bothers you to give high grades.

3. When it seems appropriate, function as a facilitator, encourager, and helper. Before attempting to function as a colleague or friend, think about possible complications.

Even if you trust children and are convinced that they are often self-motivated, there are certain to be times when they will need and probably welcome prescriptions. There are also bound to be times when they will need to be coaxed or cajoled into completing even self-selected assignments. On the whole, however, you will probably get a better response from your pupils if they see you as a facilitator, encourager, and helper. This view of education is very similar to that proposed by advocates of the discovery approach, who stress that teachers should arrange lessons to permit students to gain insight. Even though you sometimes prescribe, you can dispel an impression that you are a dictator or a manipulator by explaining why you are asking your pupils to learn certain things and by inviting students to help plan classroom activities. Before you make an effort to become a close friend to all your students, consider some of the problems likely to arise when you are required to assign grades, when you try to prevent jealousy or divide your in-class and at-home time between 30 to 150 "best friends," and when you must drop one crop of "friends" in favor of a new crop each report period or year. Teachers who take a genuine interest in their pupils and show that they like them almost invariably get a better response than those who are cold and aloof, but it is usually not advisable to replace the teacher-pupil relationship with a friend-to-friend relationship.

4. If you feel comfortable doing it, occasionally show that you are a "real person" by telling students how you feel. When you express anger, however, comment on the situation, not on the personality traits of your students.

Many advocates of humanistic education believe that students are more likely to examine their emotions if they observe a teacher doing the same. In addition, it is reasoned, students may become more sensitive to ways their behavior may hurt others. Accordingly, they recommend that you not hesitate to show when you are pleased, angry, afraid, disappointed, and the like.

One of the first psychologists to propose this policy was Haim Ginott. In *Teacher and Child* (1972), he reasons that because of the realities of teaching, it is inevitable that teachers will become frustrated and angry. When this happens, the teacher is urged to be authentic and genuine (or, as Rogers puts it, a "real person"). Ginott observes, "An enlightened teacher is not afraid of his anger, because he has learned to express it without doing damage. He has mastered the secret of expressing anger without insult" (p. 85). The "secret" is summed up by the cardinal principle of communication: "Talk to the situation, not to the personality and character" (p. 84). Ginott illustrates the secret and the principle by contrasting the response of two teachers who become angry when two boys throw pieces of bread at each other. The first attacks the boys' personalities by saying, "You two slobs! Clean it up now! You are not fit to live in a pigsty. I want to talk to your parents about your disgusting behavior!" (p. 87). The second expresses anger over the situation by saying, "I get angry when I see bread made into bullets. Bread is not for throwing. This room needs immediate cleaning" (p. 87). (As you can see, Ginott's "secret" is the same as Gordon's I-message technique.)

> Cardinal principle of communication: talk to situation, not personality

The degree to which you use this technique will be a function of your personality, the age of the pupils you teach, perhaps the subject you teach, and many other factors. But if you occasionally reveal your feelings, you may gain release of frustrations, show your students how they might do the same in similar situations, and make them more aware of how their actions may be unfair or damaging to others. If you have a very low level of frustration tolerance and reveal your feelings too often, however, your students may think of you not as a "real person" but as a chronic complainer or perhaps as someone with paranoid delusions of persecution. Whenever you do express anger, try to remember Ginott's cardinal principle and vent your hostility by using I-messages to comment on the situation, not on the personalities of your students.

5. **Do your best to help your students develop positive feelings about themselves. Empathize with them and show you are sensitive to their needs and feelings.**

Just as your ability to express your feelings by talking to the situation rather than the character of the student is partly a function of your personality, so is your ability to empathize with your students. A study by Sharon Morgan (1984) found that high-empathy teachers of emotionally disturbed children were only moderately sensitive to their own needs and feelings, had moderate feelings of self-worth, and were not fearful of spontaneously expressing their feelings. They depended on others for emotional support and were sensitive to the approval and disapproval of others. This seemed to heighten their awareness of the psychological needs of others. Even if you do not possess these characteristics, you can always try to see things from the student's point of view. Reflect on how you felt when you were a student, particularly when you felt insecure, ignorant, and frightened. Remain alert for things that you say or do that might embarrass, threaten, or belittle your students.

If you suspect that some of your students do not think highly of themselves, you might experiment with techniques for helping them develop positive self-concepts. Methods for doing this are described by John T. Canfield and Harold C. Wells in *100 Ways to Enhance Self-Concept in the Classroom* (1976) and in several strategies outlined in *Personalizing Education* (pp. 81–105) by Howe and Howe. One technique is to ask members of small groups to describe a successful accomplishment they achieved before they were ten years old. Another is to ask students to list things they are proud of. Still another is to ask members of a small group to "bombard" a selected classmate with all the strengths they see in her or him. In *Values Clarification*, Simon, Howe, and Kirschenbaum suggest (strategy 11) that students "whip around" the classroom telling what they are proud of, and in strategy 62 they provide words and music so this can be done in the form of a song.

Handbook Heading: Ways To Help Students Develop Positive Feelings About Themselves

While techniques intended to help pupils develop positive feelings about themselves often produce tangible results, you should also keep in mind Erikson's observations on industry versus inferiority. Perhaps the best way to make children and adolescents feel good about themselves is to help them master required subject matter and function as successful students. You might try to achieve that goal by using a variety of teaching techniques (so that you please some of your pupils some of the time), by using motivational techniques described in Chapter 11, and by using the mastery approach described in Chapter 12.

6. If appropriate, ask students to participate in role playing, or simulation games.

Some learning situations can be made more meaningful if students are encouraged to act out, identify with, or become involved in an activity. One way to do this is by asking students to engage in role playing.

Examples

Have elementary students act out the roles of George Washington, Abigail Adams, Benjamin Franklin, and so on when they study the Revolutionary War period of American history.

Have junior high school students assume the roles of members of Congress debating some current issue.

In a high school business class, have students make believe they are job seekers and employers interviewing applicants for a position.

For more complete information on this technique see *Role Playing Methods in the Classroom* (1966) by Mark Chesler and Robert Fox.

Simulation games feature the same basic techniques as role playing but present students with more structured and elaborate situations. A number of such games are available from publishers. One game of this type is "Generation Gap." Four to ten junior or senior high school students spend fifty minutes or so discussing interactions and conflicts between parents and an adolescent son or daughter. "Ghetto," as the name implies, stimulates students to spend two to four hours becoming involved in the problems of inner-city life. "The College Game" helps high school seniors prepare for college. During a period of ninety minutes, they learn about course requirements, schedules, study habits and demands, and typical problems of first-year students. (Simulation games tend to be expensive. Accordingly, you might check your school district curriculum library to discover what is available or what might be obtained.)

7. If appropriate (and acceptable), make judicious use of values clarification strategies.

The critique of humanistic education presented earlier in this chapter raised questions about the extent to which values clarification achieves the goals claimed by its proponents. Even though there are reasons to doubt that participating in values clarification sessions will cause children to develop a consistent set of values that will make their lives more meaningful and satisfying, the technique does possess advantages. For one thing, many of the strategies are provocative and interesting, and most students seem to enjoy them. For another, children may gain important insights as they carry out some of the activities. These insights may not merge into a coherent value system or be applied consistently when out-of- school values decisions are made, but they may occasionally influence behavior. Therefore, if you will be teaching in the elementary grades, you may wish to schedule values clarification sessions. At the secondary level, you might endeavor to work values clarification into lesson plans for courses in social studies, history, science, or home economics.

Keep in mind, though, that values clarification is essentially a form of moral education. Thus, the same caution noted after the discussion of the theorizing of Piaget and Kohlberg in Chapter 2 is repeated: Before using any values clarification strategies, check with your principal. You may be teaching in a school district where parents and/or school board members have expressed the view that the proper place for moral and values education is the home, not the school.

If you browse through books on values clarification to select your own strategies to supplement these examples, keep in mind Piaget's observations on cognitive development. Remember that elementary grade pupils are concrete

Handbook Heading:
Ways To Set Up Values
Clarification Sessions

thinkers and that secondary school students are prone to engage in unrestrained theorizing. For younger pupils, look for strategies that ask them to deal with familiar, concrete situations. For older students, avoid strategies that center on extreme hypothetical situations or issues that are remote from their daily lives. Quite a few values clarification strategies appear to have been devised by individuals who were eager to be imaginative and clever. Asking secondary school students to engage in debates about fanciful situations that are totally implausible or to offer solutions to global problems may be a way to use up thirty minutes of class time, but it is not likely to have any impact on their behavior.

To limit the possibility that values clarification will be thought of primarily as game time, several enthusiasts for the technique recommend that strategies become an integral part of the curriculum. Therefore, if you are impressed with values clarification, you might look for ways to work such strategies into lesson plans. Two excellent sources to consult for ideas about how to do this are *Readings in Values Clarification* (1973), edited by Kirschenbaum and Simon, and *Clarifying Values Through Subject Matter* (1972) by Harmin, Kirschenbaum, and Simon. Separate chapters in each of these volumes offer suggestions for working values clarification into the curriculum when teaching English, history, science, math, home economics, language, health education, and other subjects. The basic procedure recommended is to analyze a unit or course by listing points to be covered under three headings: facts, concepts, and values. If you are teaching a required unit on the Constitution, for example, Kirschenbaum and Simon suggest you include under the *facts* category the list of the first ten amendments and why they were called the Bill of Rights. Under *concepts*, you might outline a discovery session topic that would call attention to social injustices the Bill of Rights was intended to correct. Under *values*, you might insert a values clarification strategy that would ask students to form small groups and discuss the rights and guarantees they have in their families. (For additional examples of facts, concepts, and values to be taught in such a unit, see pages 114–116 of *Readings in Values Clarification*.)

8. Do your best to provide learning experiences that will lead to the development of the habits and attitudes you want to foster.

Refer to the taxonomy of affective objectives (pages 273–275) and prepare a list of value and attitude goals. Then think about how you might encourage such attitudes by using techniques other than values clarification strategies.

Examples

A kindergarten teacher tried to encourage perseverance by having her pupils begin the year with short-term projects and toward the end of the year undertake more ambitious tasks.

If you want to encourage students to be sensitive to the skills of artists, novelists, or composers, point out subtle details and particularly effective sections of their works.

To make students aware of the joys of good design, encourage them to look for everyday objects that are not only useful but attractive as well.

In your Handbook you might note some specific techniques for encouraging the development of the habits, attitudes, and values you listed earlier. (If you decide, for example, that you would like to encourage awareness of the importance of keeping informed, *how* might you do this?)

Encourage value development by taking advantage of object lessons

9. Make use of object lessons. When illustrative incidents occur, take advantage of them.

In attempting to inculcate attitudes and values, you may find that it is sometimes more effective to use natural situations than to devise formal presentations.

Examples

If a national or international figure demonstrates his or her commitment to a value system (for example, a government official resigns from an influential and high-paying position to protest an unfair decision), invite the class to discuss the event.

If someone in the class does something especially thoughtful for a classmate (for example, sends a get-well card), ask the class to consider how pleased the recipient must have felt.

Use current events to illustrate the nature of certain kinds of behavior (for example, discuss the causes of riots or point out the importance of being informed about propositions on ballots).

10. Set a good example.

Some advocates of values clarification contend that systematic efforts to build attitudes are more likely to be effective than modeling because there is no way to determine which models will be imitated. While there may be a degree of validity to this argument, the fact remains that children acquire many types of behavior by imitating others and you will be one of the adult models they will have extended contact with. Therefore, the example you set may have an impact on your students, and you should make an effort to serve as a good model.

Use of values clarification strategies may encourage pupils to acquire desirable attitudes but positive values also are strengthened when students observe and imitate admirable models. (Spencer Grant/The Picture Cube)

Examples

If you want your students to become sensitive to the feelings of others, show that you are sensitive to their feelings.

If you want your pupils to be tolerant of different opinions, show that you are willing to accept differences of opinion yourself.

If you want children to be trustworthy and considerate, show that you are trustworthy and considerate in your dealings with them.

If you would like your students to get assignments in on time, be prompt in evaluating and returning their work.

Suggestions for Further Study

Maslow on Humanistic Education

If you would like to sample Abraham H. Maslow's observations on humanistic education, perhaps the best single book to read is *The Farther Reaches of Human Nature* (1971). In Part 4 of this book, you will find three articles on education, although articles in other sections may also be of interest to a future teacher. Two other books by Maslow that sum up his final observations on humanistic psychology are *Religions, Values, and Peak Experiences* (1970) and *New Knowledge in Human Values* (1970).

Rogers on Humanistic Education

Carl Rogers developed the technique of person-centered therapy over thirty years ago and has since applied the same basic idea of growth of the self to other aspects of living, including education. For a concise description of Rogers's philosophy, look for the essay "Learning to Be Free" in *Person to Person: The Problem of Being Human* (1967) by Rogers and Barry Stevens. The latter volume includes three more essays by Rogers, as well as related discussions by others who share his philosophy. In *Freedom to Learn for the 80s* (1983), Rogers presents his view of teaching, presents descriptions of actual classroom applications at the elementary, secondary, and college levels, and summarizes research on humanistic approaches to education. Rogers comments on "The Process of Education and Its Future" in Part 3 of *A Way of Being* (1980), published when he was seventy-eight. Howard Kirschenbaum describes Rogers' life and work in *On Becoming Carl Rogers* (1979).

Combs on Humanistic Education

Arthur Combs presented his views on humanistic education in *The Professional Education of Teachers* (1965), in a second edition of that book written in collaboration with Robert A. Blume, Arthur J. Newman, and Hannelore L. Wass, published in 1974, and in *Helping Relationships: Basic Concepts for the Helping Professions* (2nd ed., 1978), written with D. L. Avila and William W. Purkey. Combs presents arguments that humanistic education is still worth providing—even at a time when there is stress on subject-matter mastery—in articles in the February 1981 issue of *Phi Delta Kappan* and the April 1982 issue of *Educational Leadership*.

Texts on Humanistic Education

Humanistic Education (1973) by C. H. Patterson and *Behavior Dynamics in Teaching, Learning, and Growth* (1975) by Don E. Hamachek are texts in educational psychology written from a humanistic point of view.

A Sampling of Books on Humanistic Education Techniques

Teacher Effectiveness Training (1974) by Thomas Gordon explains the rationale and use of problem ownership techniques and I-messages. *Teacher and Child* (1972) by Haim Ginott provides a different analysis of essentially the same techniques. William W. Purkey and J. M. Novak describe "A Self-Concept Approach to Teaching and Learning" in *Inviting School Success* (2nd ed., 1984).

Surveys of Humanistic Education

If you would like to sample a variety of descriptions and interpretations of humanistic education, examine *Readings in Values Clarification* (1973), edited by Howard Kirschenbaum and Sidney B. Simon, or *Humanistic Education Sourcebook* (1975), edited by Donald A. Read and Sidney B. Simon.

Values Clarification

For more information on values clarification and detailed instructions for putting values clarification strategies into practice, refer to *Values and Teaching* (1966) by Louis E. Raths, Merrill Harmin, and Sidney B. Simon; *Values Clarification: A Handbook of Practical Strategies for Teachers* (1972) by Sidney B. Simon, Leland W. Howe, and Howard Kirschenbaum; or *Personalizing Education: Values Clarification and Beyond* (1975) by Leland W. Howe and Mary Martha Howe.

Summary

1. Humanistic approaches to education were extremely popular in the 1970s because of disenchantment with operant conditioning and its classroom applications and with social and political conditions in the United States.
2. Humanistic approaches to education emphasize that learning is strongly influenced by how students feel about themselves, the subjects they study, their teacher, and the process of schooling.
3. Based on his belief that healthy individuals seek fulfilling experiences, Abraham Maslow proposed that parents and teachers should let children grow intellectually, socially, and emotionally by satisfying their basic needs and allowing them to make choices about their own development.
4. Based on his experiences with client-centered therapy, Carl Rogers proposed that teachers be more learner-centered. This involves establishing a trusting, acceptant environment in which the teacher is genuine and empathizes with the student's point of view.

5. Arthur Combs proposed that teachers should try to understand learning tasks from the student's point of view and help each student develop a positive self-concept.
6. C. H. Patterson criticized the emphasis on technological approaches to teaching.
7. George Isaac Brown proposed that teachers practice confluent education, which he described as a flowing together of affective and cognitive elements in individual and group learning.
8. Thomas Gordon suggested that teachers use two humanistic techniques: determining who "owns" a problem and I-messages. The point of both techniques is to indicate awareness and acceptance of feelings.
9. William Purkey suggested that teachers use the technique of invitational learning to encourage feelings of self-worth in students.
10. Classroom techniques suggested by humanistic educators include role playing, simulation games, values clarification, and pass/fail grading.
11. Values clarification exercises are intended to help students develop a set of personal values in order to give them a basis for making confident and consistent choices and decisions. The three steps in these exercises are to choose beliefs and behaviors, prize beliefs and behaviors, and act on beliefs.
12. Humanistic approaches to education are less popular now than they were in the 1970s because of a more stable sociopolitical climate and concern over declining achievement test scores. Nevertheless, research findings suggest that humanistic techniques lead to improvement in achievement, classroom behavior, self-esteem, attitudes toward school, and interpersonal relationships.

Key Terms

humanistic education *(481)*
learner-centered education *(483)*
confluent education *(485)*
I-messages *(486)*
invitational learning *(487)*
values clarification *(489)*

Discussion Questions

1. Humanistic approaches to education are based partly on the assumption that students can be trusted to want to learn and become competent, productive members of society. Can you accept such an assumption? Why?
2. Can you recall any teachers who practiced the humanistic techniques sug-

gested by Maslow, Rogers, Combs, and others? Did you like these teachers? Did you feel as if you learned as much from them as from other teachers? Would you model yourself after such teachers?

3. In response to humanistic techniques like values clarification, some parents have said that the schools should stick to teaching cognitive knowledge and skills and leave values instruction to parents. How would you respond to a parent who made this argument to you?

chapter 11

MOTIVATION

KEY POINTS

The Behavioral View

Behavioral view of motivation: reinforce desired behavior

Social learning view of motivation: identification and imitation

Praise and rewards are extrinsic forms of motivation

Excessive use of rewards may lead to resentment, limit transfer, cause dependency

Intrinsic motivation undermined by rewarding performance, ignoring quality

Intrinsic motivation enhanced when reward given according to predetermined standard

Give rewards sparingly, especially on tasks of natural interest

The Cognitive View

Cognitive view of motivation: arouse disequilibrium

Cognitive theory emphasizes intrinsic motivation

Often difficult to arouse a cognitive disequilibrium

The Humanistic View

Deficiency needs: physiological, safety, belongingness and love, esteem

Growth needs: self-actualization, knowing and understanding, aesthetic

Growth-motivated person seeks pleasurable tension, is self-directed

Teachers in a key position to satisfy deficiency needs

When deficiency needs are not satisfied, person likely to make bad choices

Encourage growth choices by enhancing attractions, minimizing dangers

Achievement Motivation Theory

Need for achievement encouraged by successful experiences

Fear of success may be influenced by a variety of factors

Low achievers attribute failure to lack of ability, success to luck

High achievers attribute failure to lack of effort, success to effort, ability

The Impact of Classroom Atmosphere and of the Teacher

Cooperative reward structures promote motivation, learning

Competitive reward structures often discourage motivation

Individual reward structures best suited to learning knowledge, simple skills

Teacher attitudes derive from ability-evaluative, moral responsibility, or task mastery value systems

Enhancing Motivation for Classroom Learning

Optimal motivation likely when students have skills, value them

Suggestions for Teaching

Students respond to activity, investigation, adventure, social interaction, usefulness

Praise may influence pupil attitudes regarding ability to learn

Blame may induce panic, particularly when no help is offered

Sense of personal agency may be most important determinant of motivation

---

The last four chapters told you about the various techniques you can use to accomplish Part Three in the model of learning: help students achieve objectives. In the introduction to the first chapter in this section (Chapter 7, "Behavioral Learning Theories"), the point was made that if you will be teaching in the elementary grades, you will need to find ways to keep your pupils occupied for five hours each day. If you will be teaching in the secondary grades, you will need to arrange instructional activities for periods ranging from forty minutes to several hours. Regardless of the grade or subject you teach, you will be concerned about keeping your students constructively busy.

Many techniques for achieving that goal have already been discussed. Providing your students with instructional objectives (as described in Chapter 6) gives them specific goals to shoot for. Many aspects of behavioral learning theories and information processing and other cognitive theories also suggest how you can arrange learning activities to keep students occupied. When you present students with programmed materials, or ask them to discuss a provocative topic, or urge them to use information processing techniques to acquire specific bits of information, you are stimulating them to achieve objectives. Even so, most teachers discover, sooner or later, that they must frequently look for new and better ways to arouse and sustain interest in learning. That is why Part Three concludes with this chapter on motivation. By contrasting forms of motivation that are stated or implied by various kinds of learning theorists, each of the views already discussed will become clearer.

This chapter might have been called "Motivation to Learn" since that is the specific type of motivation that will be discussed. If you have already taken an introductory psychology course, you know that motivation is a broad topic that covers the arousal, selection, direction, and continuation of all types of behavior. Sometimes teachers complain to each other that a particular pupil or an entire class is "unmotivated." Strictly speaking, that is not an accurate statement. What they really mean is that students are not motivated to behave in the way the teacher would like them to behave. The primary emphasis in this chapter will be on how you might motivate your students to achieve instructional objectives, but you will also be asked to speculate about why pupils are sometimes motivated to avoid learning or to engage in nonlearning activities.

The Complex Nature of Motivation

Motivation is a difficult subject to analyze because so many different factors influence the inclination to learn. To appreciate this point, examine the following dichotomies. Under headings that describe particular factors are two descriptions that summarize situations, students, or teachers that might be placed at either end of a continuum. The descriptions refer to extreme opposites; there would ordinarily be many gradations in between.

The Nature of the Learning Task

Self-selected subject that has substantial built-in appeal.	Required subject with little intrinsic interest or appeal.
Subject that can be learned through often enjoyable group interaction.	Subject that must be learned through individual and often tedious effort.
Field trip to an ice cream plant.	Study period devoted to preparation for an exam on multiplication tables.
Dull subject that is presented in an interesting way.	Interesting subject that is presented in a dull way.

Characteristics of Individual Pupils

Pupil with many abilities and aptitudes.	Pupil with extremely limited abilities and aptitudes.
Pupil who has always earned high grades.	Pupil who has never earned a high grade.
Parents of student benefited from doing well in school and urge the pupil to do the same.	Parents of student had unrewarding experiences in school and are negative about education.
Student expects to benefit in a variety of ways from high grades.	Student is convinced that earning high grades will have no payoff value.

Student has had positive, rewarding experiences with a particular subject.

Student has had negative, embarrassing experiences with a particular subject.

Student admires adults and friends who are interested in a particular subject.

Student associates a particular subject with individuals who are feared or disliked.

Healthy, happy student.

Sickly, malnourished, unhappy student.

Pupil who feels physically comfortable and psychologically at case in the classroom.

Pupil who feel physically uncomfortable, is anxious and insecure in the classroom.

Pupil with strong feelings of self-esteem.

Pupil with strong feelings of self-doubt.

Confident, successful pupil who attributes failures to lack of effort and reacts to failure by resolving to try harder.

Insecure, unsuccessful pupil who attributes failure to lack of ability and is convinced that failure will be inevitable if the same task is attempted again.

Pupil with a strong desire to achieve who regularly sets and meets goals.

Pupil with little desire to achieve who either fails to set goals or daydreams about achieving impossible goals.

Pupil with parents who encourage but do not overemphasize academic achievement.

Pupil who resents parental pressure regarding academic achievement because of the feeling that he or she is working for *them.*

Pupil who welcomes competition because of the expectation of being a winner.

Pupil who dreads competition because of the expectation of being a loser.

Pupil who welcomes competition and feels that the rewards of being a winner are more important than relations with envious peers.

Pupil who avoids competition because of a feeling that being a winner will lead to problems with friends who may be less capable.

High school student who is a foreclosure or identity achievement type who has clear academic goals.

High school student who is a moratorium or identity diffusion type who has no clear academic goals.

Classroom Atmosphere

Classroom atmosphere is relaxed. There is emphasis on individual improvement. Those who fail on a first try are encouraged (and helped) to overcome limitations.

Classroom atmosphere is tense. There is emphasis on competition and public comparisons. Those who fail are penalized and often humiliated.

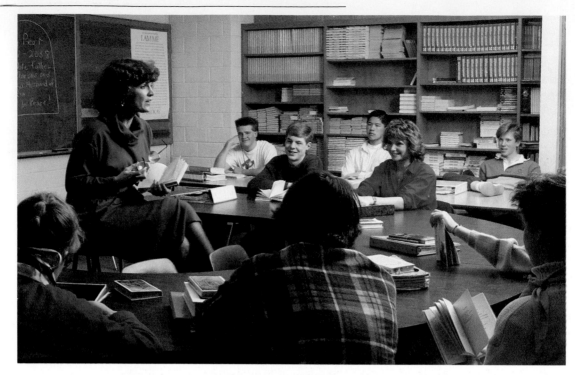

Pupils are more likely to be motivated to learn when a teacher is pleasant, sympathetic, understanding, and well organized. (Jeffry W. Myers/Stock, Boston)

The Personality and Approach of the Teacher

Teacher is enthusiastic, pleasant, sympathetic, and understanding.	Teacher obviously dislikes subject (and teaching), is ill tempered and vindictive.
Teacher takes personal responsibility for what happens in classroom. When students experience difficulties, teacher seeks ways to help them learn.	Teacher thinks of teaching as "just a job." When students experience difficulties, teacher assumes that they lack ability and that nothing can be done to alter the situation.
Teacher plans ahead, is well organized, has ability to keep things going smoothly.	Teacher does little planning, is disorganized, flits from one activity to another.

Many factors determine whether the students in your classes will be motivated or not motivated to learn. You should not be surprised to discover that no single theoretical interpretation of motivation explains all aspects of student interest or disinterest. Different theoretical interpretations do shed light, though, on particular reasons why some students in a given learning situation are more likely to want to learn than others. Furthermore, each theoretical interpretation can serve as the basis for developing techniques for motivating students in the classroom. Several theoretical interpretations of motivation—some of which are derived from the discussions of learning presented earlier—will now be summarized.

The Behavioral View

Behavioral Interpretations of Motivation

Chapter 7 outlined the behavioral view of learning. The experiments of B. F. Skinner call attention to the significance of reinforcement. After demonstrating that organisms tend to repeat actions that are reinforced and that behavior can be shaped by reinforcement, Skinner developed the technique of programmed instruction to make it possible for students to be reinforced for every correct response. Supplying the correct answer and being informed that it *is* the correct answer motivates the student to go on to the next frame, and as the student works through the program, the desired terminal behavior is progressively shaped.

Behavioral view of motivation: reinforce desired behavior

Following Skinner's lead, many behavioral learning theorists perfected techniques of behavior modification. Students are motivated to complete a task by being promised a reward of some kind. Many times the reward takes the form of praise or a grade. Sometimes it is a token that can be traded in for some desired object; at other times the reward may be the privilege of engaging in a self-selected activity.

Behavioral interpretations of learning help to reveal why some pupils react favorably to particular subjects and dislike others. Some students may enter a required math class, for instance, with a feeling of delight, while others feel that they have been sentenced to prison. Skinner suggests that such differences can be traced to past experiences. He would argue that the student who loves math has been shaped to respond that way by a series of positive experiences with math. The math hater, on the other hand, may have suffered a series of negative experiences.

Social learning theorists, such as Albert Bandura, call attention to the importance of observation and imitation. A student who identifies with and admires a teacher of a particular subject may work hard partly to please the admired individual and partly to try to become like that individual. A student who observes an older brother or sister reaping benefits from earning high grades may strive to do the same. A pupil who notices that a classmate receives praise from the teacher after acting in a certain way may decide to imitate such behavior to win similar rewards.

Social learning view of motivation: identification and imitation

Behavioral learning theory, therefore, can be used to explain the following aspects of motivation:

Why students may work on assignments that they would prefer not to do

Why students may persevere as they work toward a remote goal

Why some students will like a particular subject while others will hate it

Why a student may want to please certain teachers but not others

Why a student may want to be like an acquaintance who does well in a particular subject or in school in general

Limitations of the Behavioral View

While you may often want—or need—to use techniques of motivation based on behavioral learning principles, you should recognize certain disadvantages that come from overuse or misuse or such techniques. When pupils study in order to receive praise from a teacher, earn a high grade, or enjoy the privilege of doing something different, they experience **extrinsic motivation.** That is, the learner is seeking to earn something not related to the activity. Under ideal circumstances students should feel **intrinsic motivation:** They should study a subject for its own sake. Because of the influence of various factors, though, such learning may be the exception rather than the rule.

This point will become clear if a few motivational aspects of the behavior of individuals in and out of school are contrasted. Students are motivated to learn by being awarded grades; individuals outside of school are motivated to engage in many activities because they hope to win certificates, badges, medals, public recognition, prizes, or admiration from others. Students are motivated to learn when they realize that grades in different courses can be "traded in" for a diploma that serves as an admission ticket to further education or job opportunities; individuals outside of school may compete for prizes that have a high payoff value. (An ice skater who wins a gold medal in the Olympics, to mention just one example, can "trade in" that medal for a high-paying job in an ice show and a lucrative contract to make television commercials.) Students may be persuaded to work at not-so-enjoyable learning tasks by being promised the chance to engage in a favorite activity when they finish the job; many adults work at jobs they do not enjoy so that they can earn enough money to engage in leisure-time activities that they *do* enjoy.

Even though you may often need to try to induce students to learn by offering rewards of different kinds, you should keep in mind that such an approach involves at least three potential dangers. First, students may feel that they are being manipulated and resent the fact that they must exert themselves in order to win your approval or gain a reward. Second, learning may be seen as a temporary means to an end. As soon as an exam is written or a course completed, the extrinsic goal has been achieved and the student will tend to forget what was learned and perhaps even avoid the subject in the future. In such cases, little or no transfer will take place because the student is unlikely to receive any permanent benefit from learning and will be disinterested in seeking ways to apply what has been learned. Third, students may become too dependent on teachers.

> **Praise and rewards are extrinsic forms of motivation**

> **Excessive use of rewards may lead to resentment, limit transfer, cause dependency**

These dangers have been discussed and clarified by researchers. Mark Morgan (1984), for example, has analyzed the circumstances under which external rewards undermine or enhance intrinsic motivation for school-type tasks. One of the most important circumstances concerns the perceived relationship between performance and reward. If students conclude, for example, that they will be rewarded simply for engaging in an activity and that quality of performance will be ignored, they are likely to show a decrease in intrinsic motivation for the task. The same effect is likely to occur when students receive greater or lesser amounts of a reward depending on rate of performance (such as number of problems completed on a worksheet or number of books read within a given period). On the other hand, in two instances external rewards can enhance intrinsic motivation. First, when rewards are given according to some predetermined standard of excellence, when the task is moderately challenging, and when the reward is relatively large, intrinsic interest in the task is likely to increase. Second, intrinsic motivation can be enhanced when the task is moderately challenging and the size of the reward is consistent with the individual's perceived level of skill. If a student wins first prize in a science fair, for example, and believes that her project was truly superior to those of the other participants, a large reward may cause the student to maintain a strong interest in science.

> **Intrinsic motivation undermined by rewarding performance, ignoring quality**

> **Intrinsic motivation enhanced when reward given according to predetermined standard**

Why do external rewards undermine intrinsic motivation when they are given just for performing a task? Morgan suggests two possibilities. One is that human beings have an innate drive to be competent (an idea we discuss in the next section), and rewards that are given irrespective of quality of performance say nothing about an individual's level of competence on moderately difficult tasks. The second possibility is that beginning in early childhood we learn to equate the promise of a reward with the performance of an unpleasant activity. Students may therefore come to believe that "if somebody promises me a reward to do something, it will probably be unpleasant." Furthermore, the type of reward seems to make no difference. Tangible rewards (such as toys and candy) and social rewards (such as praise and honors) can be equally effective in undermining or enhancing intrinsic motivation. These results strongly suggest that teachers should avoid the indiscriminate use of rewards for influencing classroom behavior, particularly when an activity seems to be naturally interesting to students. Instead, rewards should be used to provide students with information about their level of competence on tasks they have not yet mastered.

> **Give rewards sparingly, especially on tasks of natural interest**

The Cognitive View

The cognitive view stresses that human behavior is influenced by the way individuals perceive things. At any given moment, people are subjected to many forces that pull and push them in different directions. The direction that behavior takes

> **Cognitive view of motivation: arouse disequilibrium**

is explained by assuming that individuals experience some sort of disequilibrium, which they feel impelled to overcome.

Cognitive Interpretations of Motivation

The techniques recommended by Bruner for structuring discovery sessions are intended to cause students to want to find out more about some topic or revise their perceptions. The question that is posed causes pupils to recognize gaps in their thinking, which they are eager to clarify or fill.

This view is related to Piaget's principles of equilibration, assimilation, and accommodation. Piaget proposes that children possess an inherent desire to maintain a sense of organization and balance in their conception of the world (equilibration). A sense of equilibration may be experienced if a child assimilates a new experience by relating it to an existing scheme, or the child may accommodate by modifying an existing scheme.

Similar explanations have been offered by other psychologists. R. W. White (1959), for instance, prefers the words *competence* or *efficacy* to equilibration. White analyzed dozens of theories and hundreds of studies of motivation, some of which attempted to trace all urges to learn to biological needs. He concluded that many types of human behavior are not traceable to physiological drives, since individuals engage in activities when all their physical needs are satisfied. Many of the things people do are motivated by curiosity, an urge to explore, or simply an impulse to try something for the fun of it.

Cognitive theory often highlights intrinsic motivation. Students who are intrinsically motivated value learning for its own sake. They try to get the intended benefit from every school task, regardless of expected outcome (for example, getting a reward), task characteristics (for example, an interesting subject), or their emotional state (for example, anxiety or fear of failure). They tend to exhibit a relaxed, persistent, task-involved state in order to increase their understanding of a topic or their level of cognitive skill (Brophy, 1983a). The advantage of such learning is that it is likely to transfer in specific and general ways. What has been learned may have been selected because it represented a problem of personal concern, so the learner is likely to benefit from and remember it. And because the learner has successfully used self-discovery techniques that can be applied to other problems, an all-purpose technique has been acquired or strengthened.

Cognitive theory, then, sheds light on the following aspects of classroom motivation:

Why it is not always necessary to offer rewards for learning

Why students may respond (or fail to respond) to class discussions or assignments that will have no impact on a grade

Why students may continue to seek an answer to a problem even though they have failed to experience reinforcement in early stages of exploration and inquiry

> Cognitive theory emphasizes intrinsic motivation

Why students will respond positively to one learning situation (because they experience a cognitive disequilibrium), but not respond to another

Why solving one problem may equip and stimulate a student to try to solve other problems

Limitations of the Cognitive View

While cognitive theory appears promising as a means for motivating pupils, it has a major (and often fatal) limitation: It is not always easy or even possible to induce students to experience a cognitive disequilibrium sufficient to stimulate them to seek answers. This is particularly true if an answer can be found only after comparatively dull and unrewarding information and skills are mastered. (How many elementary school pupils, for example, might be expected to experience a self-impelled urge to learn English grammar or to acquire skill in mathematics?) You are likely to gain some firsthand experience with the difficulty of arousing cognitive disequilibrium the first time you ask students to respond to what you hope will be a provocative question for class discussion. Some pupils may experience a feeling of intellectual curiosity and be eager to clarify their thinking, but others may stare out the window or do homework for another class.

Often difficult to arouse a cognitive disequilibrium

The Humanistic View

In Chapter 10, Abraham H. Maslow's views on humanistic education were briefly summarized. While Maslow expressed varied opinions on education, his primary interest was motivation.

Maslow's Theory of Growth Motivation

A Hierarchy of Needs   Maslow described sixteen propositions, discussed in Chapter 3 of *Motivation and Personality* (1970), that he believed would have to be incorporated into any sound theory of motivation. He eventually proposed a theory of *growth motivation* (or *need gratification*) to meet them. Maslow refers to need gratification as "the most important single principle underlying all development," adding that "the single, holistic principle that binds together the multiplicity of human motives is the tendency for a new and higher need to emerge as the lower need fulfills itself by being sufficiently gratified" (1968, p. 55). He elaborated on this basic principle by proposing a hierarchy of needs. **Deficiency needs** include *physiological* at the bottom, followed in ascending order by *safety, belongingness* and *love,* and *esteem.* The need for **self-actualization** (a need to fully develop one's potential talents and capabilities), the desires to *know* and to *understand,* and *aesthetic* needs are referred to as **growth** needs. Figure 11.1

Deficiency needs: physiological, safety, belongingness and love, esteem

Figure 11.1   Maslow's Hierarchy of Needs

From "A Theory of Human Motivation," *Psychological Review,* vol. 50 (1943), pp. 370–396. Copyright 1943 by the American Psychological Association.

presents Maslow's list of needs (which are described in Chapter 4 of *Motivation and Personality*) arranged in a literal hierarchical form.

In Maslow's theory of motivation, when individuals have satisfied their lower, or deficiency, needs (physiological, safety, belongingness and love, esteem), they will feel motivated to satisfy higher growth (or *being*) needs (self-actualization, knowing and understanding, aesthetic)—not because of a deficit but because of a *desire* to gratify the higher needs.

Differences Between Deficiency and Growth Needs   In Chapter 3 of *Toward a Psychology of Being,* Maslow lists and explains twelve ways in which deficiency needs differ from growth needs. The differences of greatest significance to teachers are summarized below:

1. Individuals act to get *rid* of deficiency needs (for example, hunger); they *seek* the pleasure of growth needs.
2. Deficiency motivation leads to reduction of disagreeable tension and restoration of equilibrium; growth motives maintain a pleasurable form of tension.
3. The satisfying and deficiency needs leads to a sense of relief and satiation; the satisfying of growth needs leads to pleasure and a desire for further fulfillment.
4. The fact that deficiency needs can be satisfied only by other people leads to dependence on the environment and a tendency to be other-directed (for example, the person seeks the approval of others); growth needs are satisfied more autonomously and tend to make one self-directed.

Margin notes:

Growth needs: self-actualization, knowing and understanding, aesthetic

Growth-motivated person seeks pleasurable tension, is self-directed

5. Deficiency-motivated individuals must depend on others for help when they encounter difficulties; growth-motivated individuals are more able to help themselves.

Implications of Maslow's Theory

The implications of Maslow's theory of motivation for teaching are provocative. One down-to-earth implication is that a teacher should do everything possible to see that the lower-level needs of students are satisfied, so that they are more likely to function at the higher levels. Students are more likely to be primed to seek satisfaction of the need to understand and know in your classes if they are physically comfortable, feel safe and relaxed, have a sense of belonging, and experience self-esteem. Since the satisfying of deficiency needs involves dependence on others and since teachers have the primary responsibility for what takes place in the classroom, it is worth emphasizing again that you will play an important role in the need gratification of your students. The more effective you are in assisting them to satisfy their deficiency needs, the more likely they are to experience growth motivation.

Teachers in a key position to satisfy deficiency needs

Even though you do your best to satisfy the lower-level needs in this hierarchy, you are most unlikely to establish a situation in which all of your students always function at the highest levels. A girl who feels that her parents do not love her or that her peers do not accept her may not respond to your efforts. And if her needs for love, belonging, and esteem are not satisfied, she is less likely to be in the mood to learn. Only under close to ideal circumstances do the higher needs emerge; only when the higher needs come into play is a person likely to choose wisely when given the opportunity. Maslow emphasizes this point by making a distinction between *bad choosers* and *good choosers.* When some people are allowed freedom to choose, they seem consistently to make wise choices. Most people, however, frequently make self-destructive choices. An insecure student, for example, may choose to attend a particular college more on the basis of how close it is to home than on the quality of its academic programs. Maslow explains such apparent contradictions in this way:

When deficiency needs are not satisfied, person likely to make bad choices

> Every human being has [two] sets of forces within him. One set clings to safety and defensiveness out of fear, tending to regress backward, hanging on to the past, *afraid* to grow . . . , *afraid* to take chances, *afraid* to jeopardize what he already has, *afraid* of independence, freedom and separateness. The other set of forces impels him forward toward wholeness of Self and uniqueness of Self, toward full functioning of all his capacities, toward confidence in the face of the external world at the same time that he can accept his deepest, real, unconscious Self. (1968, pp. 45–46)

Growth, as Maslow sees it, is the result of a never-ending series of situations offering a free choice between the attractions and dangers of safety and those of growth. If a person is functioning at the level of growth needs, the choice will ordinarily be a progressive one. However, Maslow adds:

> In this process, the environment (parents, therapists, teachers) is important in various ways, even though the ultimate choice must be made by the child:
> a. It can gratify his basic needs for safety, belongingness, love and respect, so that he can feel unthreatened, autonomous, interested and spontaneous and thus dare to choose the unknown.
> b. It can help by making the growth choice positively attractive and less dangerous, and by making the regressive choice less attractive and more costly. (1968, pp. 58–59)

The first point emphasizes the suggestion made earlier that you should do everything possible to gratify deficiency needs to encourage growth. The second point can be clarified by a simple diagram Maslow uses to illustrate a situation involving choice (1968, p. 47):

Enhance the dangers   Enhance the attractions
Safety ◄——— person ———► Growth
Minimize the attractions   Minimize the dangers

Encourage growth choices by enhancing attractions, minimizing dangers

This diagram emphasizes that if you set up learning situations that impress students as dangerous, threatening, or of little value, they are likely to play it safe, make little effort to respond, or even try to avoid learning. On the other hand, if you make learning appear appealing, minimize pressure, and reduce possibilities for failure or embarrassment, your students are likely to be willing, if not eager, to do an assigned task.

Maslow's theory can be used to explain or illuminate the following aspects of motivation:

Why pupils who feel uncomfortable because of hunger, ill health, or irritating physical conditions may not be interested in learning

Why pupils are more likely to be eager to learn in a relaxed, secure, inviting classroom than in a threatening, tense atmosphere

Why pupils who feel they are loved, accepted, and admired are more likely to be interested in learning than those who feel rejected, ignored, or mistreated

Why some pupils make wise choices when given opportunities to direct their own learning while others make self-destructive choices

Why some pupils may have a stronger desire to know and understand than others

Limitations of Maslow's Theory

While Maslow's speculations are thought-provoking, they are also sometimes frustrating. You may conclude, for instance, that awareness of his hierarchy of

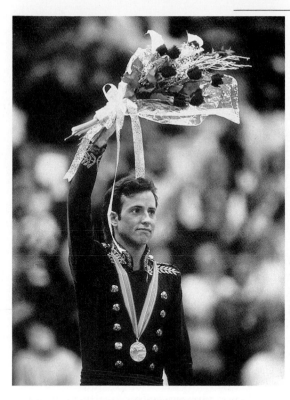

Grades earned in school are similar in many ways to medals awarded at the Olympics—both are token rewards that may later be "traded in" for a variety of material advantages and rewards. (Allsport USA/Steve Powell 1988)

needs will make it possible for you to do an excellent job of motivating your pupils, only to discover that you don't know exactly how to apply what you have learned. Quite often, for example, you may not be able to determine precisely which of a pupil's needs are unsatisfied. Even if you *are* quite sure that a pupil lacks interest in learning because he or she feels unloved or insecure, you may not (as mentioned earlier) be able to do much about it.

Then again, there will be times when you can be quite instrumental in helping satisfy certain deficiency needs. The development of self-esteem, for example, is closely tied to successful classroom achievement for almost all students. Although you may not be able to feed students when they are hungry or protect them from physical danger, you can always take steps to help them learn more effectively. To make that task easier, the next section describes an interesting and useful approach to motivation that revolves around the need to achieve.

Achievement Motivation Theory

The Need for Achievement

John W. Atkinson (1964) has developed a theory of motivation that combines the conception of *achievement motivation* proposed by David McClelland (1961) with ideas about level of aspiration. McClelland believes that in the course of development, human beings acquire a *need for achievement*, and he has conducted

Need for achieve-
ment encouraged by
successful experi-
ences

research to demonstrate the degree to which this need varies among individuals. Atkinson hypothesizes that differences in the strength of the need for achievement can be explained by postulating a contrasting need to avoid failure. Some people, he suggests, are success oriented; others have a high degree of anxiety about failure. Through experimentation, Atkinson and Litwin (1960) showed that success-oriented individuals are likely to set personal goals of intermediate difficulty (that is, they have a 50–50 chance of success), whereas anxiety-ridden persons set goals that are either very high or very low. (If anxiety-ridden individuals fail on the hard task, no one can blame them; and they are almost sure to succeed on the easy task.) Atkinson believes that the tendency to achieve success is influenced by the probability of success and the attractiveness of achieving it. A strong need to avoid failure is likely to develop in people who experience repeated failure and set goals beyond what they think they can accomplish.

The similarity of Atkinson's conception to Maslow's theory of motivation is apparent. Both emphasize that the fear of failure must be taken into account in arranging learning experiences. The same point has been stressed by William Glasser in *Schools Without Failure* (1969) and *The Identity Society* (1972). Glasser argues that for people to succeed at life in general, they must first experi-

David McClelland and J. W. Atkinson explain differences in the need for achievement by proposing that pupils who work diligently to earn high grades have had successful experiences reaching specific goals they have set for themselves. Those who lack the need for achievement have had experiences with failure, or have not set realistic goals, or both. (Left: Mark Antman/The Image Works; Right: Billy E. Barnes/The Southern Light)

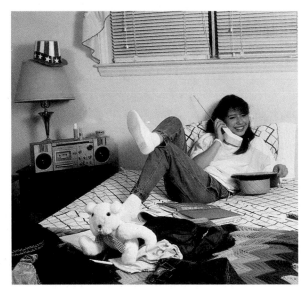

ence success in one important aspect of their lives. For most children, that one important part should be school. But the traditional approach to education, which emphasizes comparative grading, allows only a minority of students to feel successful. Most students feel that they are failures, which depresses their motivation to achieve in other areas of their lives.

One of the most intriguing aspects of differences in need for achievement is that some individuals seem to "fear" success and others seem to be motivated to avoid it.

Fear and Avoidance of Success

Reading reports of research inspired by the work of McClelland and Atkinson, Matina S. Horner became intrigued by the finding that the need for achievement in males seemed to be more fully developed than in females. She decided to make this the subject of her Ph.D. dissertation (1968) and, using a technique derived from studies by Atkinson, asked 178 university students to write a four-minute story from this cue: "At the end of first-term finals Anne finds herself at the top of her medical school class." When she analyzed the stories, Horner found three recurrent themes: (1) fear that Anne would lose friends; (2) guilt about success; and (3) unwillingness to come to grips with the question of Anne's success (in some stories, the cue was more or less ignored). She concluded that all three of these themes reflected a general *fear of success* and discovered that 65.5 percent of the stories written by women could be classified under this heading, contrasted with only 9 percent of those written by men.

As a second part of her study, she placed men and women in competitive and noncompetitive situations. She found that women who wrote fear-of-success stories performed much better when working alone than when competing against others. She reasoned that fear of success motivates many women to avoid achievement, particularly in competitive situations.

Reports of Horner's study (1970) attracted attention, and a number of articles in newspapers and magazines led readers to believe that there is a well-established tendency for almost all women to fear success. Because of the publicity and the topicality of the concept, over sixty studies derived from or similar to Horner's original research were carried out in the next three years. David Tresemer (1974, 1977) reviewed these and also analyzed the techniques used by Horner. He concluded that fear-of-success stories may be influenced by a variety of factors, including the type of cues supplied. For example, when a woman in a story is described as the best *psychology* student rather than as the best medical student, Tresemer reports, males write more fear-of-success stories than females.

Fear of success may be influenced by a variety of factors

While some students may avoid success because they fear they will jeopardize their relationships with peers, others may have a weak need for achievement because of conflicts with parents. Irving B. Weiner (1980) proposes that many adolescents who seek counseling because of academic performance problems express resentment about parental demands, which they cannot or prefer not to meet. If the resentment is strong enough, the high school student may retaliate by deliberately earning low grades (perhaps as a means for establishing a negative identity).

Explanations of Success and Failure: Attribution Theory

Some interesting aspects of success and failure are revealed when students are asked to explain why they did or did not do well on some task. The four reasons most commonly given stress ability, effort, task difficulty, and luck. To explain a low score on a math test, for example, different students might make the following statements:

"I just have a poor head for numbers." (Lack of ability)

"I didn't really study for the exam." (Lack of effort)

"That test was the toughest I've ever taken." (Task difficulty)

"I guessed wrong about which sections of the book to study." (Luck)

(Because pupils *attribute* success or failure to the factors just listed, research of this type contributes to what is referred to as **attribution theory.**)

Low achievers attribute failure to lack of ability, success to luck

Students with long histories of academic failure and a weak need for achievement typically attribute their success to easy questions or luck and their failures to lack of ability. Ability is a stable attribution (that is, people expect its effect on achievement to be pretty much the same from one task to another), while task difficulty and luck are both external attributions (in other words, people feel they have little control over their occurrence). Research has shown that stable attributions, particularly ability, lead to expectations of future success or failure while internal (under personal control) attributions lead to pride in achievement and reward attractiveness following success or to shame following failure (Nicholls, 1979; B. Weiner, 1979). Because low-achieving students attribute failure to low ability, future failure is seen as more likely than future success. In addition, ascribing success to factors beyond one's control diminishes the possibility of taking pride in achievement and placing a high value on rewards. Consequently, satisfactory achievement and reward may have little effect on the failure-avoiding strategies that poor students have developed over the years.

High achievers attribute failure to lack of effort, success to effort, ability

Success-oriented students (high need achievers), on the other hand, typically attribute success to ability and effort, and failure to insufficient effort. Consequently, failure does not diminish expectancy of success, feelings of competence, or reward attractiveness for these students. They simply resolve to work harder in the future.

It may be, then, that rewards will not motivate low need achievers to work harder so long as they attribute success to factors that are unstable and beyond their control. Such successes are seen as "flukes," which are unlikely to occur again and do little to instill a sense of pride and accomplishment. By contrast, because high need achievers expect to succeed and feel they are largely in control of their success, occasional failures do not greatly diminish their motivation for future learning.

This analysis suggests that programs designed to enhance motivation and achievement may need to include ways of altering perceived causes of performance. Quite often it is necessary for teachers to try to alter a poor student's self-concept, which may be a substantial undertaking requiring a concerted, coordinated effort. (An outline of procedures you might follow will be presented later in this chapter.)

Implications of Analyses of Achievement Motivation Theory

These various analyses of aspiration level and achievement help explain the following aspects of motivation:

Why some pupils will have a higher level of aspiration than others

Why pupils with a low level of aspiration may fail to experience success because they set unrealistic goals

Why some pupils may almost seem to avoid success

Why high-achieving pupils may resolve to try harder after a failure experience

Why low-achieving pupils may not really be encouraged by successful experiences

Limitations of Achievement Motivation and Attribution Theories

Perhaps the major limitation in speculating about aspirations, a need for achievement, fear of success, and reactions to success and failure is that such forms of behavior are often difficult to observe or analyze. Another problem may be lack of consistency. In controlled situations, it may be possible to trace how and why students set goals. But in typical classroom settings, students may not have any clear idea about their level of aspiration, unless the teacher specifically asks them to set a particular standard for themselves. Furthermore, a pupil's level of aspiration may be bumped up or down by more or less chance circumstances. A student might do well on a first exam in a course, for example, because the teacher gave in-class time for study and happened to offer advice at a crucial point during the study period. The high score on that test might inspire the student to work for an A in that class. But if the second exam happened to be scheduled the day after the student had been ill, or if the teacher inadvertently snubbed him or her in class, the student might not prepare and could end up with a D grade. Poor performance on the second exam might then cause the student to forget about the A and concentrate instead on obtaining a C– with the least amount of effort.

It also seems likely that the aspiration level will vary with different subjects and courses. Tresemer found, for instance, that responses to fear-of-success stories depended on the kind of activity described. Thus, a girl might fear success in a "masculine" subject, such as physics, but not worry about being better than a boyfriend in a "neutral" subject, such as psychology, or a "feminine" subject, such as English. In addition, a high school student's level of aspiration or need for achievement is often intertwined in reciprocal fashion with feelings about identity. A foreclosure type who endorses parental attitudes regarding goals and values may have a very clear picture of what needs to be accomplished in school and may be motivated to achieve those goals. By contrast, moratorium or identity diffusion types, who may be in conflict with parents, uncertain about what to do after graduation, and/or confused about sex roles, may drift aimlessly through high school. Finally, students may find that they seem to have an affinity for certain subjects because of aptitudes, abilities, and past experiences. Other subjects may seem extraordinarily difficult to the same students because of lack of aptitude or absence of previous experience.

The Impact of Classroom Atmosphere and of the Teacher

As noted at various points in this discussion, the atmosphere of the classroom and the attitude and personality of the teacher can affect a student's motivation. These two topics will now be explored more systematically—before the implications for teachers of research and speculations about motivation are examined.

Classroom Atmosphere

Maslow's hierarchy of needs and his diagram illustrating the clash between safety and growth in situations involving choice call attention to the significance of classroom atmosphere. If students feel frightened, insecure, or rejected, they will find it difficult to concentrate on learning. If they feel that they will be penalized for failure or that there is little likelihood of success, they are more likely to make safety rather than growth choices. The impact on student behavior of different types of learning situations has been clarified by research on classroom reward structures.

Types of Classroom Reward Structures   According to James W. Michaels (1977), there are four basic classroom reward structures. Under the first structure, *individual competition*, only a small number of individuals can obtain the greatest rewards and only at the expense of other class members. One example of individual competition is the familiar "grading on a curve," which predetermines the percentage of A, B, C, D, and F grades. That is, regardless of the actual distribution of test scores, only a small percentage of the students in a class will receive A's. Under the second structure, *group competition,* groups of students cooperate among themselves in order to compete with other groups for the available rewards. Competition in this reward structure is defined as a situation where the actions of some students are seen as blocking the goal attainment of one or more other students.

Some researchers have argued that competitive reward structures lead students to focus on ability as the primary basis for motivation. This orientation is reflected in the question, "Am I smart enough to accomplish this task?" When ability is the basis for motivation, competing successfully in the classroom may be seen as relevant to self-esteem (since nobody loves a loser), difficult to accomplish (since only a few can succeed), and uncertain (success depends on how everyone else does). These perceptions may cause some students to avoid challenging subjects or tasks and give up in the face of difficulty (Ames & Ames, 1984; Dweck, 1986).

The third structure, *group reward,* is a true cooperative situation. Rewards are distributed solely on the basis of the quality of the group's performance. An individual can obtain a reward (such as a high grade or a feeling of satisfaction for a job well done) only if the other group members can obtain the same reward. Also, all groups may receive the same rewards, provided they meet the teacher's criteria for mastery. In this case, cooperation is defined as a situation where the actions of others are seen as promoting goal attainment. Cooperative structures lead students to focus on effort and cooperation as the primary basis of motivation. This orientation is reflected in the statement, "We can do this if we try hard and work together." In a cooperative atmosphere, students are motivated out of a sense of obligation—one ought to try, contribute, and help satisfy group norms (Ames & Ames, 1984). William Glasser, whose ideas we mentioned earlier, is a fan of cooperative learning. He points out that student motivation and performance tend to be highest for such activities as band, drama club, athletics, the school newspaper, and the yearbook, all of which require a team effort (Gough, 1987).

The fourth classroom reward structure is termed *individual reward.* In this situation, the accomplishments of and rewards received by one individual are completely independent of the accomplishments and rewards of other individuals. Thirty students working by themselves at computer terminals are functioning in an individual reward structure. According to Carole and Russell Ames (1984), individual structures lead students to focus on task effort as the primary basis for motivation (as in, "I can do this if I try"). Whether or not a student perceives a task as difficult depends on how successful he or she has been with that type of task in the past. The obvious question at this point is what is the relationship between these reward structures and motivation and achievement?

Reward Structures and Motivation   Two of the leading writers on reward structures, David W. Johnson and Roger T. Johnson (1974, 1987a, 1987b) conclude that cooperative, competitive, and individualistic goal structures produce marked differences in student motivation and achievement.

Students who learn cooperatively expect to succeed at classroom tasks, show a high degree of commitment to learning, are curious about a variety of subjects, are highly persistent, and demonstrate a high degree of intrinsic motivation for learning. (This statement echoes Morgan's conclusion that extrinsic rewards enhance intrinsic motivation when they tell us we are competent at something.) In comparison to competitive and individualistic arrangements, cooperative learning produces higher levels of achievement, particularly for tasks that involve some sort of problem-solving activity, self-esteem, and liking of classmates (Ames & Ames, 1984; Johnson & Johnson, 1987a; Slavin, 1980). This last outcome should be of particular interest to those of you who expect to teach in areas that are marked by cultural diversity.

Johnson and Johnson (1987a) suggest several reasons for the effectiveness of cooperative learning:

1. The discussion process promotes the discovery and development of higher-quality learning strategies.
2. The conflict among ideas, opinions, and conclusions of group members that is an inevitable part of the discussion process produces repetition, explanation, and integration of information, thereby enhancing retention and comprehension.
3. Group members provide valuable feedback, support, and encouragement of each other's efforts.

Students who learn under a competitive reward structure have a low expectation for classroom success, show a low degree of commitment to learning, are not curious about most subjects, do not persist at tasks for very long, and are more extrinsically than intrinsically motivated. Competition, as defined above, produces these negative motivational outcomes because it consistently produces the same "winners" and "losers." That is, those students with high levels of ability and prerequisite knowledge will almost always get the lion's share of classroom rewards, whereas their less fortunate peers will almost always reap failure, frustration, and a weak sense of self-esteem. As predicted by Maslow and Atkinson, students who experience chronic failure typically do whatever is necessary to avoid failure. Avoidance techniques may involve nonparticipation, low levels of effort, or very high or very low levels of aspiration.

Ames and Ames (1984) have pointed out some additional negative aspects of competitive reward structures. They found that children reward themselves only if they win a competition. The quality of the child's past performances on similar tasks tends to be seen as irrelevant. Furthermore, children who win in competitive

Cooperative reward structures promote motivation, learning

Competitive reward structures often discourage motivation

Competitive reward structures may inspire a small number of pupils to push themselves to their limits, but cooperative reward structures are more likely to motivate
almost all students in a class to study and develop positive attitudes toward learning.
(Charles Gupton/Stock, Boston)

situations tend to reward themselves more for winning than they reward others
for winning, because of differences in attribution (for example, "My success was
due to ability, but yours was due to luck.").

Although competitive reward structures should be avoided during the initial
phases of learning, since they emphasize pre-existing differences among students,
competition can be used in the classroom when all students have the ability to
compete effectively. Thus, contests that center on the review of previously mastered knowledge (such as spelling words or definitions of terms) or similar levels
of athletic skill can be highly motivating and enjoyable.

Disagreement exists about the effect of individual reward structures on motivation and achievement. Johnson and Johnson (1987a) feel that when children
are rewarded for their own efforts while working alone, they are likely to develop
low expectations for success, a low commitment to learning, low persistence, and
an extrinsic orientation to learning. Ames and Ames (1984), on the other hand,
feel that individual reward structures may produce the greatest amount of intrinsic motivation and achievement. They found that children who performed academic tasks under an individual structure reported more effort-related,

self-instructional, and self-monitoring types of thoughts than did children under a competitive structure (for example, "I will work carefully"; "I will take my time"; "I will make a plan"). These statements reflect metacognitive awareness and strategic behavior. Recall from Chapters 8 and 9 the importance of metacognition and strategic skills to learning, remembering, problem solving, and transfer. We will have more to say shortly on the relationship between information processing skills and motivation. Individual reward structures seem to be best suited to tasks that involve acquiring knowledge and simple skills.

> **Individual reward structures best suited to learning knowledge, simple skills**

On the basis of the above discussion, you may have begun to form a preference for a particular reward structure. That's fine so long as you realize two things: All of the reward structures have a legitimate place in the classroom, and other factors also influence motivation. The attitude and personality of the teacher, which we discuss next, is one such factor.

Teacher Attitude and Personality

To realize how much a teacher's attitude and personality may influence student motivation, examine some of your own experiences with different teachers. If you admired or had a crush on an elementary school teacher, for example, you probably were eager to earn that teacher's approval by performing well in class. If you disliked or feared a teacher in the elementary grades, you may have lost all interest in learning and simply endured school until the end of the year. If an elementary grade teacher obviously liked some subjects much better than others, you probably reacted in similar fashion. If you felt that a teacher was merely putting in time in the classroom, you likely did the same. In high school you may have chosen your college major because you admired the teacher of a particular subject. You may also have made a firm resolution never to take another course in a particular subject because you associated it with a disagreeable instructor. Some teachers probably made it clear that they disliked assigning high grades, while other teachers may have seemed genuinely pleased when they could legitimately award A's.

> **Teacher attitudes derive from ability-evaluative, moral responsibility, or task mastery value systems**

That these differences in teacher attitude and personality exist is undeniable. From where, however, do they originate? According to Carole and Russell Ames (1984), they originate largely from value systems that parallel the competitive, cooperative, and individualistic reward structures just discussed. These value systems, or systems of teacher motivation, are referred to as ability-evaluative, moral responsibility, and task mastery.

An ability-evaluative system, like competition, is based on winners and losers (good teachers and bad teachers). Thus, classroom conditions are arranged to maximize the appearance of high teaching ability and minimize the appearance of low teaching ability. This may take the form of unrealistically high student-performance standards and very tight control of the classroom. Under an ability-evaluative system, teachers attempt to maintain a sense of self-worth and competence by blaming students for failure and crediting themselves for success.

A moral responsibility motivational system is like a cooperative reward structure in that it revolves around such values as cooperation, dependability, and duty. The dominant question becomes "How can I help this student?" On the positive side, this orientation leads to a persistent teacher helping role. On the negative side, it could foster student dependency or teacher burnout. When teachers are motivated by a sense of moral responsibility, they tend to blame themselves for student failure and credit the student for success.

A task mastery motivational system is most like an individual reward structure. The focus is on identifying important learning tasks and determining how they can best be accomplished by students. Thus, teacher self-worth is more closely associated with student accomplishment than with the teacher's desire to appear able or responsible. Under this system, teacher ability and effort are seen as important determinants of student accomplishment.

Enhancing Motivation for Classroom Learning

Most of the conceptions of motivation that have been discussed up to this point can be classified as *expectancy* or *performance* oriented because they describe what people expect to get for putting out a certain amount of effort. For example, operant conditioning and social learning theory suggest that people will work to achieve a goal if they expect to receive an appropriate reward. Likewise, humanistic theory holds that people will strive toward self-actualization if they expect their deficiency needs to be met. Achievement motivation theory holds that the level of excellence people work to attain depends on how they balance their level of aspiration against their fear of failure or fear of success. Attribution theory holds that the performance level people expect to attain depends on the perceived underlying causes of success and failure. According to an analysis by Jere Brophy (1983a), these approaches, while useful, are not likely by themselves to optimize student motivation because of the special nature of classrooms and academic work. Consequently, they need to be supplemented with a "motivation to learn" theory that focuses on the *value* of learning for its own sake.

Brophy argues that classroom work has three characteristics that set it apart from other endeavors. First, it is primarily cognitive. Most academic tasks require such cognitive processes as attention, encoding, retrieval, organizing, and problem solving. Second, it is compulsory. Students rarely get to choose from among a set of tasks or to choose whether they will or will not perform a particular task. Third, it is more or less publicly evaluated. It is very hard to hide the results of an exam, a book report, or a laboratory experiment from peers or parents.

Brophy discusses two implications that follow from his analysis. One is that the usual finding from achievement motivation research that most students prefer situations in which there is about a 50-percent chance of success is not likely to apply to the classroom. Given the above three characteristics of classroom tasks, most students would probably prefer easier tasks and a higher chance of success. Brophy cites supportive research showing that student motivation is enhanced when classroom success is the result of reasonable effort but is reduced when success results only from sustained effort. In addition, we know from Chapter 7 that learning occurs most smoothly and consistently when it is achieved through small, easy-to-master steps.

The second implication of Brophy's work is that performance levels are likely to be highest when motivation is optimal—relaxed but learning oriented—rather than when motivation is very high and intense. Again, given that classroom tasks are cognitive, compulsory, and publicly evaluated, motivation is likely to be optimal when students know they have the skills to master a task and value those skills. Very high motivation spurred by strong emotional arousal may well reduce performance. Thus, success experiences, effort attributions, achievement motives, or reward structures, by themselves, will not stimulate the best motivation for classroom learning. Students must also possess a sense of control over learning processes and a sense that classroom tasks provide valuable opportunities to use and refine those processes. The cognitive skills that are necessary to master most tasks and that contribute to this sense of control are the ones that were discussed in Chapter 8—metacognitive knowledge, strategic skills, and tactical skills.

> **Optimal motivation likely when students have skills, value them**

In discussing how to produce an optimal level of motivation for classroom learning, Brophy makes several general suggestions that draw from most of the motivation theories discussed in this chapter. To begin, the teacher needs to eliminate such impediments to motivation as negative attitudes, anxiety, and fear of failure. This can be done by using programmed materials to guarantee continuous progress and success, training students to set challenging but achievable goals, and training them to attribute failure to lack of effort rather than ability. Each of these approaches should have some positive effects, particularly if the task difficulty is appropriate for the student. If the task is too difficult, it may not be possible to set reasonable goals or to attribute failure to lack of effort rather than ability. This is not necessarily a trivial point; research has shown that many teachers give assignments that are too difficult for some students.

The next step is to produce positive motivation. Brophy offers several suggestions. First, make sure that the magnitude of a reward matches the quality of the work (this is the same point that Mark Morgan made earlier). Second, stimulate students to value a task because the knowledge or skills that it teaches will be valuable in the future. You might mention, for example, that people who are knowledgeable and capable often are good problem solvers, are asked by others to help solve problems, hold positions of responsibility, and are quite satisfied with their position in life. This technique should be handled with care, though, because it can easily end up motivating out of fear and anxiety ("How are you going to get a job if you can't read or do math"? "You don't want people to think you are ignorant, do you?"). Third, help students to become more aware and appreciative of the knowledge and skills that they develop and to take pride in how they apply what they have learned. One way to further this goal is to provide students with clearly articulated objectives, so they will accurately recognize the level of skill or knowledge they have attained. Thus informed, they can gauge their progress toward higher, more distant goals. Fourth, stimulate students to value and enjoy the actual process of working on academic tasks. Presumably, as students gain better control over the processes of learning, they will find academic tasks more meaningful and intrinsically motivating.

In conclusion, Brophy points out that teachers need to do much work in this area. In one study of how elementary grade teachers presented tasks, it was found that only 28 percent of the teachers introduced tasks in a way that could be described as potentially fostering intrinsic motivation (as, for instance, when the teacher states that students are expected to enjoy the task and do well on it). One type of introduction in the intrinsic motivation category, called "self-actualization" (as when the teacher suggests that new knowledge or skill will bring pleasure or personal satisfaction) was never used by the teachers studied.

Now that you are familiar with interpretations of motivation, it is time to consider how the information and speculations just summarized can be converted into classroom practice. Two lists provide some structure for the following discussion. They highlight, on the left, reasons why students may lack motivation to learn and, on the right, how you might try to change or minimize those reasons. These lists not only serve as an outline of what follows, they may also function as a trouble-shooting checklist to which you might refer when you are baffled by lack of student interest in learning.

Why Student May Be Unmotivated	Some Things You Might Do About It
Subject is boring.	Try to make subject as interesting as possible, supply incentives to learn.
Subject is presented in a boring way.	Make a systematic effort to arouse and sustain interest.
Effort must be expended before mastery or enjoyment occurs.	Explain about delayed payoff, use behavior modification techniques to encourage perseverance, provide short-term goals.
Pupil would rather not exert self.	Specify objectives, rewards, try to make lack of effort seem unappealing.

Pupil doesn't know what to do.	State specific instructional objectives, explain how these can be met, what the rewards will be.
High school pupil has identity problems, lacks clear goals.	Urge pupil to select short-term goals, think about long-term goals.
Pupil lacks aptitude or ability.	Give less capable pupils individual help, more time to complete tasks, try different kinds of instruction.
Parents of pupil are neutral or negative about schooling.	Emphasize that learning can be enjoyable, that doing well in school opens up opportunities.
Pupil comes from a disadvantaged background, has limited experiences.	Check on range of experiences, supply necessary background information.
Pupil has had negative experiences in school or with a particular subject.	Make experiences in your classroom as positive as possible, make sure reinforcement occurs frequently.
Pupil associates subject with a disliked individual.	Try to be a sympathetic, responsive person so that pupil will build up positive associations.
Pupil dislikes subject because of envy or jealousy of those who do well at it.	Play down comparisons between pupils, urge self-improvement.
Pupil feels tired, hungry, uncomfortable.	Try to allow for or alleviate discomfort.
Pupil feels insecure, anxious, scared.	Make your classroom physically and psychologically safe.
Pupil experiences little sense of acceptance, belonging, esteem.	Show pupil that you respond positively, that pupil is worthy of esteem.
Pupil has never earned high grades, has been "punished" by low grades.	Avoid public comparisons, stress self-competition and individual improvement.
Pupil has low level of aspiration.	Urge pupil to set and achieve realistic goals.
Pupil has weak need for achievement.	Try to strengthen pupil's self-confidence, stress values of achievement.
Pupil is afraid to try because of fear of failure.	Arrange a series of attainable goals, help pupil achieve them.
Pupil assumes failure is due to lack of ability and that there is no point in trying.	Try to strengthen pupil's self-concept, set up a series of short-term goals, help pupil succeed after initial failure.

Pupil learns only when required or cajoled to learn.

Invite pupil to participate in selecting goals, deciding how they will be met; encourage pupil to be self-directed.

Pupil resents learning only what others say must be learned.

Invite pupil to participate in selecting instructional objectives.

Mid-Chapter Review

Views of motivation have been stated or implied by theorists who favor each of the views of learning described in Chapters 7, 8, and 9.

The Behavioral View of Motivation

Behavioral theorists stress that individuals are motivated when their behavior is reinforced. Social learning theorists emphasize the impact of identification and imitation, pointing out that observing someone else benefiting from a certain type of behavior may motivate a person to do the same. Behavioral theorists urge teachers to reinforce students with praise and rewards of various kinds when correct or desired responses occur. Reinforcement practices can be effective, but they are *extrinsic* forms of motivation, inclining students to view learning as a means to an end—earning a reward. Excessive use of rewards may lead to resentment, limited transfer, dependence on teachers, and undermining of intrinsic motivation.

The Cognitive View of Motivation

Cognitive theorists stress that individuals are motivated when they experience a *cognitive disequilibrium,* or a desire to find the solution to a problem. Arranging for pupils to experience a personal desire to find information or solutions is an *intrinsic* form of motivation in which learning occurs for its own sake. Unfortunately, it is often difficult to arouse a cognitive disequilibrium in all, or even most, students.

The Humanistic View of Motivation

The humanistic psychologist Abraham Maslow proposed that human needs are arranged in hierarchical order. *Deficiency needs* (physiological, safety, belongingness and love, and esteem) must usually be satisfied before *growth needs* (self-actualization, knowing and understanding, aesthetic) exert an influence. When the deficiency needs have been satisfied, the growth-motivated person seeks pleasurable tension and engages in self-directed learning. Teachers are in a key position to satisfy the deficiency needs and they should remain aware that when the lower needs are not satisfied, students are likely to make either *safety* (nonproductive) choices or bad choices when they make decisions. Teachers can encourage pupils to make *growth* rather than safety choices by enhancing the attractiveness of learning situations likely to be beneficial and by minimizing the dangers of possible failure.

Achievement Motivation Theory

Maslow's distinction between safety and growth choices is similar to the concept of *level of aspiration,* which stresses that people tend to want to succeed at the highest possible level while at the same time avoiding the possibility of failure. When students *are* successful, they tend to set realistic goals for themselves, and successful experiences strengthen a *need for achievement.* It has been found, though, that some individuals (particularly females in certain situations) may experience a *fear of success,* in the sense that they worry that being successful may interfere with positive relationships with others.

Studies that led to the formulation of *attribution theory* revealed that low achievers tend to attribute failure to do well in school to lack of ability and therefore assume that there is no point in making greater efforts to succeed. When low achievers *are* successful, they tend to attribute it to luck. High achievers, on the other hand, attribute failure to lack of effort and assume they can succeed if they try harder.

The Impact of Classroom Atmosphere and of the Teacher

Classroom situations where students are forced to compete against each other tend to discourage all but the very best students from trying. Cooperative reward situations, where students work independently or cooperatively in noncompetitive ways to improve their mastery of subject matter, tend to promote motivation to learn in almost all students.

Enhancing Motivation for Classroom Learning

Because classroom learning tasks are cognitive, compulsory, and publicly evaluated, Jere Brophy argues that student motivation is at an optimal level when task difficulty is moderate (with a better than 50-percent chance of success), when students know they have the skills to master a task, and when they value those skills. To produce optimal levels of motivation, teachers need to help students eliminate negative attitudes, anxiety, and fear of failure and to value the processes and products of learning.

SUGGESTIONS FOR TEACHING

Motivating Students to Learn

1. Try to make every subject interesting. Make study as active, investigative, "adventurous," social, and useful as possible.

2. Use behavior modification techniques to help students exert themselves and work toward remote goals.

3. Make sure that pupils know what they are to do, how to proceed, how they will know they have achieved goals.

4. Take into account individual differences in ability, background, and attitudes toward school and specific subjects.

5. Do everything possible to satisfy the deficiency needs—physiological, safety, belongingness, and esteem.
   a. Allow for the physical condition of your pupils and the classroom.
   b. Make your room physically and psychologically safe.
   c. Show your students that you take an interest in them and that they belong in your classroom.
   d. Arrange learning experiences so that all students can gain at least a degree of esteem.

6. Enhance the attractions and minimize the dangers of growth choices.

7. Direct learning experiences toward feelings of success in an effort to encourage a realistic level of aspiration, an orientation toward achievement, and a positive self-concept.
   a. Make use of objectives that are challenging but attainable.
   b. Provide knowledge of results by emphasizing the positive.
   c. Permit and encourage students to direct their own learning.

8. For students who need it, try to encourage the development of need achievement, self-confidence, and self-direction.
   a. Use achievement motivation training techniques.
   b. Encourage a sense of personal agency or self-efficacy.

1. Try to make every subject interesting. Make study as active, investigative, "adventurous," social, and useful as possible.

Some subjects seem dull and boring to almost everyone; other subjects seem to have built-in appeal. If you don't plan motivational strategies, though, you

Snack time in the kindergarten takes into account the importance of satisfying physi-ological needs. (Mimi Forsyth/Monkmeyer)

Establish a classroom atmosphere in which students know what to expect and can relax about routines. Do everything you can to make your room a place that is psychologically safe. Be alert to things you do that are unnecessarily threaten-ing. Try to see things from your students' point of view in an effort to detect anx-iety-producing situations.

As much as possible, establish classroom routines in which students can take the initiative. Don't require recitation; wait for students to volunteer. Don't force students to participate in new activities; let them try such activities when they feel ready.

A humiliating or embarrassing experience may generalize so that a student comes to hate or fear everything connected with a classroom. If a student should have such an experience, go out of your way to make him or her feel comfortable and secure. Try to arrange for the pupil to have a strong, positive experience in class to displace negative associations and build up positive ones.

Students are likely to be inclined to learn if you are enthusiastic, establish a positive atmosphere, and convey the impression that you take an interest in them and that they belong in your classroom. (Lew Merrim/Monkmeyer)

c. Show your students that you take an interest in them and that they belong in your classroom.

Examples

Learn and use names as fast as you can.

Follow the open school practice of keeping detailed records for individual pupils and refer to accomplishments specifically.

Whenever possible, schedule individual tutorial or interview sessions so that you can interact with all students on a one-to-one basis. If a student is absent because of an extended illness, send a get-well card signed by the entire class.

To encourage class spirit, have group planning sessions or have "sharing," that is, invite students to talk about interesting experiences or make announcements about after-school activities.

d. Arrange learning experiences so that all students can gain at least a degree of esteem.

Examples

Play down comparisons; encourage cooperation and self-competition. (Evaluation techniques that encourage self-competition will be provided in the next chapter in an analysis of mastery learning.)

Permit students to work toward individual goals.

Allow students who possess culture-specific talents (such as storytelling, singing, dancing, or weaving) opportunities to demonstrate and teach them to others.

Give individual assistance to students who are experiencing problems.

(Further suggestions for satisfying esteem needs will be presented with subsequent points.)

6. Enhance the attractions and minimize the dangers of growth choices.

When you first begin to teach, you might keep a copy of Maslow's diagram of a choice situation in your top desk drawer. Refer to it when the need arises and ask yourself, "Am I setting things up to encourage effort, or am I encouraging the student *not* to try?" If you establish situations that cause pressure, tension, or anxiety, your students will choose safety and do their best to remain uninvolved. But if you minimize risks and make learning seem exciting and worthwhile, even the less secure students may feel impelled to join in.

Examples

Don't penalize guessing on exams.

Don't impose restrictions or conditions on assignments if they will act as dampers—for example, "You must hand in all papers typed, with no erasures or strikeovers." Some pupils may not even start a report under such conditions.

Avoid "do or die" situations, such as single exams or projects.

To encourage free participation, make it clear that you will not grade students on recitation.

Point out and demonstrate the values of learning and the limitations and disadvantages ("dangers") of not learning. For example, point out that knowing how to multiply and divide is necessary for personal bookkeeping and also that errors will lead to difficulties—perhaps making it necessary for someone else to do the work for you.

Remain aware of the disadvantages of inappropriate or excessive competition. If competition becomes excessive in a school situation, students may think of learning only as a means to an end (being better than others); they may be more interested in their relative position in a class than in their actual performance. Only a few students will be able to experience success, and the tendency to make safety rather than growth choices will be increased.

To avoid these disadvantages, encourage students to compete against themselves. Try to give each pupil some experience with success by arranging situations in which all students have a fairly equal chance in a variety of activities, and make use of group competitive situations that stress fun rather than winning.

Handbook Heading:
Ways To Encourage
Self-Competition

Examples

Have pupils set their own goals, and keep private progress charts.

Follow the open education technique of keeping a separate folder for each student rather than a grade book that indicates only relative performance.

Give recognition for such virtues as punctuality and dependability.

Give recognition for skill in arts and crafts and in music.

Use games such as "Spelling Baseball." Divide the class into two approximately equal teams. Each time a pupil spells a word correctly, award her or his team a base. Four bases, and the team has a run. Each misspelled word is an out. No team members are eliminated, and the pressure is reduced considerably. If some unfortunate makes too many outs, throw an easy word the next time that person is at bat. In order to avoid overidentification with a particular team, use different players for each game. (If permanent teams are set up or if you overemphasize the competitive nature of the game by offering a prize, the technique may backfire.)

7. Direct learning experiences toward feelings of success in an effort to encourage a realistic level of aspiration, an orientation toward achievement, and a positive self-concept.

McClelland's theory of achievement motivation and Atkinson's development of it further emphasize how some people are success oriented and others anxiety ridden. Glasser maintains that in order for individuals to succeed at life in general, they must first experience success in one important part of their lives—particularly in school. All these theorists emphasize the vital importance of success.

Students who experience early failure in any learning experience will either lose interest or actively avoid further learning, which could bring more failure. Consequently, it is vital to try to arrange learning experiences so that students will experience success. In order to feel successful, an individual must first establish goals that are neither so low as to be unfulfilling nor so high as to be impossible and then must know that the goals have been achieved. This is a two-step process: establishing goals and receiving knowledge of results.

a. Make use of objectives that are challenging but attainable.

The first step in the three-stage teaching strategy being stressed in this book is to state the desired terminal behavior. Those who favor programmed instruction advocate the use of objectives stated in behavioral terms, primarily to make instruction more efficient, but they also suggest that objectives be used to arouse, sustain, and direct student interest. When objectives are used for purposes of motivation, however, it is especially important to invite students to participate in their selection. You are likely to get a better reaction if, instead of simply stating objectives yourself, you invite your students to participate in selecting them —or at least to think along with you as you explain why the objectives are worthwhile. This will tend to shift the emphasis from extrinsic to intrinsic motivation.

Handbook Heading:
Ways To Encourage
Students To Set Their
Own Objectives

In developing objectives to serve a motivating function, you may want to use the techniques recommended by Mager to help shift the emphasis from teacher direction to student choice. Having a self-selected objective to shoot for is one of the best ways to arouse and sustain interest. You might assist your students in stating objectives in terms of a time limit, a minimum number of correct responses, the proportion of correct responses, or a sample of actions.

Examples

"How many minutes do you think you will need to outline this chapter? When you finish, we'll see that film I told you about."

"George, you got six out of ten on this spelling quiz. How many do you want to try for on the retest?"

"After reading this article on the laws of motion, see if you can state them in your own words and give two everyday examples of each."

The form of these examples implies that you are inviting students to participate in the development of their own objectives. Although this is a desirable policy to follow, sticking to it may not always be possible or appropriate. In many situations you may find it necessary to set goals yourself.

Regardless of the approach you take when you set goals for your students, keep in mind the importance of success as a basis for the development of a realistic level of aspiration and an orientation toward achievement. Don't set impossibly high standards, and try to avoid situations in which only a minority of students can succeed.

Examples

Use techniques of open education: Let students choose activities on their own; encourage students to learn from each other; use tests not to compare students, but to diagnose weaknesses and to set the stage for remedial instruction. Provide as much individualized instruction as possible.

Use the mastery approach (to be explained in detail in the next chapter): State objectives, and arrange learning materials to help students achieve them; use tests to determine if the goals have been met; provide remedial instruction for those who need it; and let students take tests as many times as they need to in order to achieve the established standard of performance.

b. Provide knowledge of results by emphasizing the positive.

In order to experience success (as a basis for establishing a realistic level of aspiration), your students must receive detailed information about their performance. In a programmed approach, feedback will be supplied automatically when students respond to a question in a program or compare their performance to criteria included in a set of instructional objectives. Knowledge of results may be vague or even absent if you attempt to arouse a cognitive disequilibrium, since there may not be any definite answer to a discussion topic. In discovery sessions —and in many other classroom situations—knowledge of performance may be supplied primarily by comments you make. If you make observations on recitation, ask questions in a discussion or on an exam, or provide comments on papers of various kinds, the kind of feedback you provide may make the difference between feelings of success or of failure. As a consequence, you should do your best to comment favorably on successful performance and avoid calling attention to failure, particularly the kind that is already apparent.

Some advocates of behavior modification suggest that teachers make broad use of praise as a reinforcer—to the point of suggesting that you shape your own behavior to increase your productivity as a praiser. Jere Brophy (1981), however, suggests that classroom teachers rarely use praise as an effective or desirable

Handbook Heading:
Ways to Supply Positive
Feedback

form of reinforcement. Behavioral theorists (O'Leary and O'Leary, 1977) have proposed that in order for praise to shape behavior, it should be provided only after performance of designated activities, it should be specific, and it should be sincere and credible. In reviewing records of actual teacher behavior in classroom situations, Brophy concluded that few teachers use praise in such ways. Most of the teachers who were observed used praise infrequently (less than 6 percent of the time), they did not wait until specified behavior had occurred before offering praise, and the favorable comments they made were more often general than specific. Accordingly, Brophy suggests that praise typically does not take the form of reinforcement; instead, it is likely to be a spontaneous reaction to student behavior. Quite often a teacher's behavior concerning praise is shaped by students rather than the reverse. Certain students *ask* for praise and reinforce the teacher by reacting positively when they receive it. Brophy found that in other cases students who aroused negative feelings in teachers for one reason or another received the most praise in classrooms. Apparently such pupils elicited praise from a teacher partly because they gave the impression of needing motivation and reassurance and partly because the teacher seemed to feel guilty about reacting negatively.

Brophy suggests that teachers tend to use praise in the following ways:

As a spontaneous expression of surprise or admiration ("Why, John! This report is really excellent!")

As compensation for criticism or vindication of a prediction ("After your last report, John, I said I knew you could do better. Well, you *have* done better. This is really excellent.")

As an attempt to impress all members of a class ("I like the way John just put his books away so promptly.")

As a transition ritual to verify that an assignment has been completed ("Yes, John, that's very good. You can work on your project now.")

As a consolation prize or to encourage students who are less capable than others ("Well, John, you kept at it and you got it finished. Good for you!")

Many of these uses of praise do not serve to reinforce student behavior in specific ways. Quite often, though, various forms of praise may influence a student's self-concept and attitude toward learning. In discussing the need for achievement and the concepts of attribution theory, earlier portions of this chapter acquainted you with differences in student reactions to failure. High achievers tend to attribute failure to lack of effort and resolve to try harder. Low achievers often attribute failure to lack of ability and assume nothing can be done about it. Brophy suggests that teachers may shape such reactions by the ways they supply praise (and criticism). C. Dweck and several associates (1978), for instance, found that teachers tended to praise boys for successful performance, but they tended to praise girls for neatness, following instructions, and the like. The same teachers tended to *criticize* girls for unacceptable performance, but they criticized boys for sloppy writing, not responding to instructions, and the like. It appeared that such differential treatment caused boys to be reinforced by praise for good work but to discount criticism because it was directed to unimportant secondary matters. Girls, on the other hand, were not likely to be influenced by praise for such inconsequential things as neatness, but they *were* often discouraged by criticism. Negative comments about performance seemed to cause girls to assume that they lacked the ability to do well academically.

Praise may influence pupil attitudes regarding ability to learn

In an effort to help teachers become aware of some of the unexpected aspects of praise, Brophy drew up the guidelines for effective praise listed in Table 11.1. He also urges teachers to supplement verbal praise in the following ways:

Write specific favorable comments on students' work, taking into account individual expectations regarding performance.

Help students set appropriate goals, evaluate their own performance, and reinforce themselves for good work.

Encourage students to attribute outcomes to their own efforts and abilities rather than to external causes that are beyond their control.

(The last two points are discussed in detail in other sections of these Suggestions for Teaching.)

While you should think about ways to use praise effectively, you should also be aware of the negative impact of blame. If you are disappointed with a class or with a particular student, or if you feel tired and frustrated because things aren't going well, you may find yourself reacting with negative comments. If this occurs, ponder the possible consequences. An extremely negative reaction to an error may induce panic, making it impossible for the pupil to think enough to replace the wrong response with the right one. When you praise a pupil for a correct response, realize that you are saying in effect, "That's right; do it again." When you reprimand a pupil for a wrong response, you are saying, "That's wrong; stop it." But if you don't help pupils find the right response or if you frighten them so that they are unable to think, they are forced to choose between doing nothing at all and repeating the original response.

Blame may induce panic, particularly when no help is offered

If pupils are told when they do something wrong but not when they do something right, they never have the chance to experience success. Continual failure leads to fear and depression; it also often leads to attempts to escape. It is natural to avoid attempting something if failure is inevitable. Sometimes students prac-

Table 11.1 Guidelines for Effective Praise

Effective Praise	Ineffective Praise
1. Is delivered contingently	1. Is delivered randomly or unsystematically
2. Specifies the particulars of the accomplishment	2. Is restricted to global positive reactions
3. Shows spontaneity, variety, and other signs of credibility; suggests clear attention to the student's accomplishment	3. Shows a bland uniformity, which suggests a conditioned response made with minimal attention
4. Rewards attainment of specified performance criteria (which can include effort criteria, however)	4. Rewards mere participation, without consideration of performance processes or outcomes
5. Provides information to students about their competence or the value of their accomplishments	5. Provides no information at all or gives students information about their status
6. Orients students toward better appreciation of their own task-related behavior and thinking about problem solving	6. Orients students toward comparing themselves with others and thinking about competing
7. Uses students' own prior accomplishments as the context for describing present accomplishments	7. Uses the accomplishments of peers as the context for describing students' present accomplishments
8. Is given in recognition of noteworthy effort or success at difficult (for *this* student) tasks	8. Is given without regard to the effort expended or the meaning of the accomplishment (for *this* student)
9. Attributes success to effort and ability, implying that similar successes can be expected in the future	9. Attributes success to ability alone or to external factors such as luck or easy task
10. Fosters endogenous attributions (students believe that they expend effort on the task because they enjoy the task and/or want to develop task-revelant skills)	10. Fosters exogenous attributions (students believe that they expend effort on the task for external reasons—to please the teacher, win a competition or reward, etc.)

Table 11.1 Guidelines for Effective Praise cont.	
Effective Praise	**Ineffective Praise**
11. Focuses students' attention on their own task-revelant behavior	11. Focuses students' attention on the teacher as an external authority figure who is manipulating them
12. Fosters appreciation of and desirable attributions about task-revelant behavior after the process is completed	12. Intrudes into the ongoing process, distracting attention from task-revelant behavior

SOURCE: Jere Brophy, "Teacher Praise: A Functional Analysis." *Review of Educational Research,* 51, No. 1 (1981), 5–32. Copyright © 1981. American Educational Research Association, Washington, D.C.

tice avoidance by lowering their level of aspiration. Sometimes physical escape in the form of sickness or truancy is the result. Perhaps the most dangerous escape is withdrawal into the world of fantasy.

Since the student gains nothing from failure, why do so many teachers use sarcasm, ridicule, and punishment? Probably because the teachers gain something from the experience; berating pupils and watching them squirm provide a sense of satisfaction and power, especially to weak and insecure people. Teachers have been known to burst into a teachers' room to brag about how they just routed a student or a class. Such demonstrations of power are tempting, and you might well watch your initial reactions as you assume control of a class.

c. Permit and encourage students to direct their own learning.

This suggestion has been made by both humanistic and behavioral psychologists. Many humanistic educators argue that when students are permitted to direct their own learning, teachers have fewer problems with motivation. To back up this argument, they (see, for instance, G. I. Brown, 1971) usually describe anecdotal reports written by teachers who used learner-centered approaches and were amazed by the enthusiasm of their students. It is true that when an individual or a group selects a topic of great intrinsic interest, and when the pieces in the puzzle fall together nicely, a great deal of enthusiasm is often generated. Unfortunately, such experiences tend to be rare. When some students are invited to direct their own learning, they become even more bored than when listening to a

Although it is desirable to encourage students to engage enthusiastically in class discussion, the topic should be chosen because it is likely to contribute to understanding, not simply because it is provocative. (Bob Daemmerich Photos)

teacher. Others may select a topic that seems appealing at first glance but that turns out on closer examination to be dull and unappealing. Furthermore, when students are first invited to work on topics of their own choice, the suggestion may be seen as a refreshing change. If the technique is used repeatedly, however, students may yearn for a teacher-directed session just for the sake of novelty.

Still another factor is that enthusiasm per se may not be a valid criterion for measuring success. Herbert Thelen's (1960) description of student-directed projects illustrates this point. The first project was a unit in the second grade called "How Do Different People Live?" The second was a television series produced by a high school class on the history of a community. The second-grade children, perhaps under the influence of a Walt Disney "True Life Adventure," chose to study *prairie dogs,* despite the efforts of the teacher to convert them to the Algonquin Indians (about whom she had a great deal of information from previous years). The dismay of the teacher turned to delight as the children not only came through with a smashing dramatic production about prairie dogs but also learned a great deal about how animals *and* people live. The TV series, on the other hand, generated much enthusiasm but no learning of subject matter. The students gained a lot of experience in taking photographs and lettering signs and solving lighting problems, but the production "incidentals" prevented them from thinking or learning about history. (This brings up an interesting question: If you endorse the argument made by some humanists [such as Combs, 1965] that how students *feel* about learning is more important than *what* they learn, what do you do when you have a bunch of committees working happily away on projects that have nothing to do with the curriculum? Is it better to have a class cheerfully laboring on incidentals or somewhat less enthusiastically engaged with genuine subject matter? This same point was raised earlier in the discussion of Cullum's technique for teaching math. Is it better to have students concentrate on learning to solve math problems or spend considerable class time building a replica of King Tut's Tomb and crawling inside it with flashlights?)

At least part of the time, though, you might experiment with student-selected learning activities. An excellent source to consult when deciding how to arrange such activities is *Personalizing Education: Values Clarification and Beyond* (1975) by Leland W. Howe and Mary Martha Howe. In Part 3, "Personalizing the Curriculum," the Howes describe how you might encourage students to participate in selecting instructional objectives and be efficient self-directed learners. These techniques were noted in Chapter 10. After selecting a topic, students compile a flow chart, which lists anything related to the main topic that can be studied. Then the participants carry out a question census by listing all the questions they think would be important or useful in studying the topic. The next step is to identify available resources that can be used in seeking answers to these questions. The final stage of the process is to have students find answers to the questions and present a written or oral report. (For details and examples, see pp. 364–395 of *Personalizing Education.*)

Handbook Heading: Ways To Permit Students To Direct Their Own Learning

To encourage individual pupils to direct their own learning, you might follow suggestions offered by Raymond J. Wlodkowski (1978) for drawing up a personal contract. He recommends that such a contract should contain these four elements:

1. What the student will learn
2. How the student can demonstrate that she or he *has* learned
3. The degree of proficiency to be demonstrated
4. How the student will proceed

Wlodkowski offers this example (p. 57) of a contract that illustrates the four elements:

Date _____

1. Within the next two weeks I will learn to multiply correctly single-digit numbers ranging between 5 and 9—e.g., 5×6, 6×7, 7×8, 8×9, 9×5.
2. When I feel prepared, I will ask to take a mastery test containing 50 problems from this range of multiplication facts.
3. I will complete this contract when I can finish the mastery test with no more than three errors.
4. My preparation and study will involve choosing work from the workbook activities, number games, and filmstrip materials.

Signed _____

(You will recognize that this learning contract fits Mager's recommendations: first identify and describe the terminal behavior, then define the conditions under which the behavior is to occur, and finally decide on the criterion for acceptable performance.)

8. For students who need it, try to encourage the development of need achievement, self-confidence, and self-direction.

Despite your efforts to provide appropriate incentives, gratify deficiency needs, enhance the attractions of growth choices, and arrange learning experiences to produce a realistic level of aspiration and a feeling of success, some of your students will still lack confidence in their ability to learn. In such cases, you may try to help students acquire a general motive to achieve.

a. Use achievement motivation training techniques.

McClelland (1965) has demonstrated that it is possible for groups of individuals, in intensive training sessions of one to three weeks, to develop a need to achieve that will be reflected in accomplishments far beyond their previous efforts. Although McClelland's technique would be difficult to use in a school setting, some of the practices he follows might be adapted for small-group or individual sessions with students who appear to lack motivation to succeed. McClelland tries to make individuals feel that they can develop a motive to achieve, shows them how the motive will be beneficial, makes acquisition of the motive appear to be an improvement in their self-image, encourages the achievement of concrete goals, keeps records of progress, and establishes an atmosphere of warm and honest support.

David A. Kolb (1965) based an Achievement Motivation Training Program on the work of McClelland, Atkinson, and others. As with McClelland's program, intensive training sessions were provided (as part of a summer school program). In the opening session, the participants (underachieving high school boys) were given information intended to make training effective. They were acquainted with characteristics McClelland has found typical of high achievers: personal responsibility for actions, willingness to take moderate risks, and the desire for knowledge of results of actions. In subsequent sessions, the boys competed in miniature racing-car contests, took various tests, and played the roles of businessmen. In all these activities, they were urged to analyze their reactions and to constantly think about how they could improve their need for achievement. After the training had been completed, its effectiveness was revealed by higher grades.

Like McClelland's program, Kolb's procedures would be difficult to follow in a regular school setting, but it would be possible to encourage students to emulate the qualities of high achievers by taking personal responsibility for attempting work (perhaps in the form of a contract), being willing to shoot for goals beyond those considered safe, and being eager to receive detailed knowledge of results. A. S. Alschuler (1969) used essentially this approach by organizing learning tasks as self-competitive games in which the student was responsible for setting personal goals and was graded on her or his own terms. A related technique described by Nicholls (1979) is to allow students opportunities to schedule their own classroom learning. For example, students can be given responsibility for deciding when to work on a particular assignment and for how long. This gives them the feeling they are working on a task because they want to, not because someone told them to. According to Nicholls, researchers have found greater continuing interest in learning tasks under self-evaluation and greater frequencies of assignment completion when opportunities for self-scheduling were increased.

Another technique for helping students to become better achievers was developed by J. S. Sorensen, E. A. Schwenn, and J. Barry (1970). They devised a checklist for self-ratings by elementary grade students on *prosocial behaviors* (see Figure 11.2). Students rated themselves and then participated in individual and small-group conferences with their teacher. During the conferences, each category on the list was defined by recalling or identifying instances of the behavior described. Then each child was asked to select one or more types of behavior in which to improve and to check his or her present rating and desired rating. At the next conference, children rated themselves to determine if improvement had been achieved. The teacher supplied reinforcement in the form of

Figure 11.2   Check List of Prosocial Behaviors

Name ——————— Sex ——— Age ——— Date ————————

Directions

Put an X under column 1 if you almost always have to be told to do the job.

Put an X under column 2 if you usually have to be told to do the job.

Put an X under column 3 if you sometimes do the job yourself and sometimes have to be told to do the job.

Put an X under column 4 if you usually do the job yourself.

Put an X under column 5 if you almost always do the job yourself.

	1	2	3	4	5
1. I listen to the teacher.					
2. I begin schoolwork right away.					
3. I correct mistakes.					
4. I work until the job is finished.					
5. I work when the teacher has left the room.					
6. If I make mistakes, I still keep working.					
7. I work on learning activities in free time.					
8. I get to class on time.					
9. I do extra schoolwork.					
10. I do my share in class projects.					
11. I read during free time.					
12. I ask questions about schoolwork.					
13. I have pencil, paper, and books ready when they are needed.					
14. I move quietly to and from my classes.					

	1	2	3	4	5
15. I listen to the ideas of others.					
16. I help my classmates.					
17. I pick up when the work is finished.					
18. I take care of my clothing, books, and other things.					
19. I take care of the school's books, desks, and other things.					
20. I follow directions.					

praise for all improvement, kept a conference record to make note of progress and problems, and asked the pupils to describe reasons why working toward improvement would benefit them. Teacher ratings of student behavior after the program had been completed indicated that most students had made significant improvement in the types of behavior listed.

Sorensen, Schwenn, and Herbert J. Klausmeier (1969) used a similar approach to encourage elementary pupils to read more. Many books were made available in the classroom. Forms for reporting titles of books read were provided. Conferences with the teacher were arranged. At the conferences, teachers were urged to keep in mind four motivational procedures:

Modeling: doing such things as telling the child that he (the adult) reads frequently and likes to read; being engaged in reading when the child comes in for the conference and starting to read a book as the child leaves the conference. . . .

Reinforcement: smiling, nodding affirmatively, saying "good," "fine," etc., when the student shows that he has independently read a book or pages in a book. The adult also reinforces positive attitude statements about reading either made spontaneously by the child or in response to questions.

Feedback: informing the child of progress by telling him how many books or pages in a book he has completed. Feedback was also given on any improvement in word recognition or comprehension skills.

Goal setting: helping the child select the next book of an appropriate difficulty level and length. The reading of the book or books then becomes the child's goal for the next conference. (1969, p. 351)

The reading frequency and achievement of almost all students increased as a result of this program, and even control pupils not included in the experiment showed improvement, indicating that the interest in reading became contagious.

If you despair at the lack of confidence, interest, or motivation of your students, you might encourage the development of the motivation to achieve by using variations of the techniques just discussed. With modifications, they could be used with all grade levels and with all types of students.

b. Encourage a sense of personal agency or self-efficacy.

Many of the suggestions just offered have stressed that students should frequently experience reinforcement or rewards for their achievements. Prior achievement affects motivation by providing students with information about the effectiveness of their problem-solving skills. According to Albert Bandura (1977), this contributes to a sense of *self-efficacy,* or the conviction that one can successfully do what is necessary to produce a particular outcome. This sense of what can and cannot be done partly determines "how much effort people will expend and how long they will persist in the face of obstacles and aversive experiences" (Bandurs, 1977, p. 194). Thus, previous success contributes to a sense of personal efficacy, which enhances motivation, which contributes to current achievement.

In many respects, self-efficacy is similar to the more familiar notion of self-concept. The relationship between self-concept, motivation, and achievement has long been an integral part of humanistic and open education programs. However, unlike Bandura, humanistic and open education theorists largely ignore the role of prior achievement and focus instead on directly enhancing self-concept as a means of increasing motivation and current achievement. There are at least two reasons behind such an approach. First, in an environment of trust and respect for the innate goodness of students, satisfactory achievements are supposed to occur more or less automatically. Second, there is evidence (see, for example, Bachman, O'Malley, and Johnston, 1978) that there is a positive and moderately strong relationship between self-concept and achievement.

We are left, then, with an interesting and important question. Should teachers design their instruction to try to *directly* enhance self-concept, or, following Bandura, should they emphasize mastery of basic academic skills? A clear answer to this question would have important implications for the enhancement of motivation.

After reviewing dozens of research studies at the preschool, primary, junior high school, and high school levels, Scheirer and Kraut (1979) concluded that "motivation for academic learning comes from the reinforcements of one's social environment for specific learned skills . . . [and that] self-concept change is likely to be an outcome of increased achievement with accompanying social approval" (p. 144). This conclusion suggests that most of the time you should think about ways to directly increase achievement (you can refer to suggestions offered in the earlier chapters on learning and in this chapter on motivation). In some cases, however, you may have to try to help particular students acquire greater confidence and self-esteem. You may also want to encourage all your students to gain experience with self-motivation and self-direction. Such forms of motivation seem most likely to develop when a student feels that he or she is the agent in control of personal behavior. J. W. Thomas suggests that "the extent to which students see themselves as a cause of their own behavior may be the single most important determinant of continued motivation" (1980, p. 231). (You may recall from the description of emotional characteristics of adolescents in Chapter 3 that the feeling of having no control over one's own behavior is referred to as *learned helplessness* and that it often contributes to a sense of depression. The techniques to be described next, therefore, can be used not only to build a desire to learn, but also to help a student overcome depression. Quite often, of course, the two conditions—lack of interest in learning and depression —will be related and exert a reciprocal influence on each other.)

> Sense of personal agency may be most important determinant of motivation

According to Bandura (1977), an individual's sense of efficacy or personal agency is shaped by four interrelated sources of information: *performance accomplishments, vicarious experience, verbal persuasion,* and *emotional arousal.* Performance accomplishments contribute to self-efficacy and motivation to learn because students acquire, either through teacher instruction or on their own, general and specific problem-solving skills. As a result, expectancy of future success is increased. Vicarious experience, if you recall the discussion in Chapter 7, is another term for modeling. Bandura believes that observing other people experience success, particularly if the models are a diverse group, can increase one's sense of efficacy. Imagine watching several friends who, you thought, had no mechanical aptitude learn how to tune a car's engine or fix an electrical appliance. You might think to yourself, "If *they* can learn to do these things, then I certainly can too." Through verbal persuasion, teachers may attempt to convince students that they can successfully deal with tasks that they perceive as overly difficult or beyond their ability. Lastly, one's sense of competence is affected by how much arousal or anxiety is generated by a learning task. Students are more likely to expect success when they are relaxed and confident. It is important to keep in mind that these four factors are interrelated.Taking steps to increase performance accomplishments, for instance, may involve modeling, verbal persuasion, and emotional arousal. Techniques for encouraging a sense of agency that involve some or all of the sources of information noted by Bandura will now be described.

You may recall from earlier in this chapter that low-achieving students tend to assume that their failures are due to lack of ability and that their successes are due to luck. Because they assume that ability is a more or less fixed trait, such students tend to attribute their failures to a factor that cannot be changed. Several psychologists have studied ways to persuade low-achieving students to attribute their failures to lack of effort—which *can* be increased—rather than to lack of ability. H. Heckhausen (1975), for instance, told fifth-graders who blamed their failures on lack of ability that they could improve exam and homework scores by trying harder. After four months of such feedback, they scored lower on a test of anxiety, higher on ability tests that emphasized speed, and were more apt to cite lack of effort than lack of ability as a reason for failure in comparison to a similar group that received no such feedback.

The greatest gains in achievement motivation and classroom learning seem to occur when teachers are shown how to develop student behaviors associated with the need to achieve, when classroom environments are more cooperative and learner directed than competitive and teacher directed, and when students are informed of the reasons behind the training and classroom restructuring (Thomas, 1980).

Techniques of this type are illustrated by a study conducted by Alschuler (1969). He wanted to see by how much the typing speed of one tenth-grade business education class could be improved over the typing speed of a similar class. To start, the teacher and students in the experimental group jointly decided what levels of performance would earn different letter grades. Each student was then required to set short-term and long-term goals, keep daily records of gains in typing speed, and specify the length and difficulty level of his or her typing test. Toward the end of the term, the performance of one class no longer overlapped the performance of the other. In other words, the slowest student in the experimental group outperformed the fastest student in the control group. The average increase in typing speed for the experimental group was 54 percent.

A comprehensive attempt at increasing achievement motivation has been reported by Richand de Charms (1976) in *Enhancing Motivation: Change in the Classroom.* The project involved training a large group of sixth- and seventh-grade teachers in the use of various motivation-enhancing techniques and behaviors. At the heart of the training was a set of teaching units developed by de Charms and his coworkers to emphasize four basic aspects of motivation: self-concept, achievement motivation, realistic goal setting, and personal causation. To give you some idea of the nature of the program, the materials and procedures developed for the sixth-graders are briefly described below.

The self-concept unit, called "The Real Me," was intended to help the students gain a clearer picture of themselves and their problems and see how the training would help them learn. One exercise for this unit involved a daily dis-

Handbook Heading:
Encouraging a Need for
Achievement

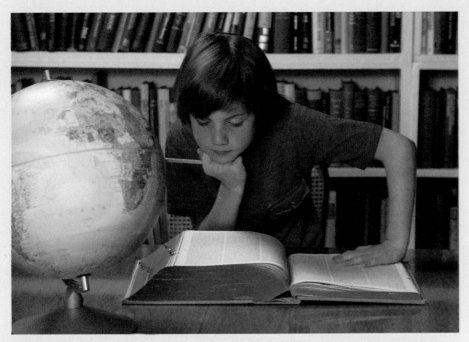

One way to analyze attitudes is to observe approach tendencies. If a student concentrates on studying a particular subject in the library for hours at a time, day after day, it is reasonable to assume that there is a tendency for that person to be eager to approach that subject. (Edward Lettau/Peter Arnold, Inc.)

cussion of a thought for the week. Some of these were "If I had three wishes," "My greatest success," "Why try?" "Failure teaches lessons, too," and "The kind of person I want to be."

The achievement motivation unit, entitled "My Stories of Success and Achievement," was designed to elicit various achievement themes. For example, at the beginning of a week the children were told to think about a story they would write on Friday in which a hero or heroine tries to do something better than it has been done before and publicly expresses the desire to succeed.

The third unit, "The Spelling Game," was designed to foster more appropriate levels of aspiration. Instead of arranging a list of easy, moderately difficult, and difficult words in random order and forcing students to spell whatever word was next on the list, students could choose what *for them* were easy, moderately difficult, and difficult words. These were determined from previous spelling tests.

The fourth unit, called "The Origin Manual," was designed to help students understand their goals and how to achieve them. Each student was given a booklet of twenty-five exercises to be completed over a five-week period. The point of the exercises was to highlight the differences between two types of people—*Origins* and *Pawns*. An Origin is, for the most part, intrinsically motivated, has a strong sense of personal agency, and is inclined to seek satisfaction of growth needs. A Pawn is extrinsically motivated, has a weak sense of personal agency, and is more concerned with the satisfaction of deficiency needs. The exercises involved identification and practice of Origin behavior, discussions of the benefits of Origin behavior, reading accounts of real-life Origin behavior (for example, stories of successful athletes), treating others as Origins, and the like.

The effectiveness of the training program was assessed by looking at achievement test scores, school attendance, and grades. Achievement growth was measured by comparing the scores of trained and untrained students on the Iowa Test of Basic Skills against the school district norm. The trained classes scored closer to the norm for their age group, while the control classes dropped further behind. Five years later, a follow-up study (cited by Thomas, 1980) found that significantly more trained boys graduated from high school than did untrained boys. Similar effects were noted for attendance. Trained students had higher attendance records and were late for school or class less frequently. Finally, trained sixth-graders had higher grades in verbal and arithmetic skills than their untrained peers.

Suggestions for Further Study

Surveys of Motivational Theories

If you would like additional information on one or more of the approaches to motivation mentioned in this chapter, a good place to start is a basic survey text. In *Human Motivation* (1985), David McClelland discusses the origin of motives, how they are learned, and on what they are based. Examined in detail are the achievement motive, the power motive, the affiliative motives, and the avoidance motives. Another text with the title *Human Motivation* (1980), by Bernard Weiner, surveys several theories of motivation, with an emphasis on attribution theory. *Motivation* (2nd ed., 1986), by Herbert L. Petri, in addition to providing basic coverage of biological, behavioral, and cognitive approaches to motivation, includes an interesting chapter (14) on work motivation.

Maslow's Theory of Motivation

If you would like to read Abraham Maslow's own account of his theory of motivation, examine *Motivation and Personality* (2nd ed., 1970) or *Toward a Psychology of Being* (2nd ed., 1968). The final chapter of the latter book describes forty-three basic propositions of growth psychology and summarizes many of the points made in both volumes.

Achievement Motivation and Attribution Theory

J. W. Atkinson presents his views on achievement motivation in *Personality, Motivation, and Achievement* (1978), written with J. O. Raynor. *Motivation and Achievement* (1974), edited by Atkinson and Raynor, is a collection of articles by various authors. Another such collection is *Achievement and Achievement Motives* (1983), edited by Janet T. Spence. This latter volume contains chapters that look at achieving styles in men and women, achievement of children from one-parent households, and achievement of Afro-American children. Bernard Weiner provides an in-depth analysis of attribution theory in *An Attributional Theory of Motivation and Emotion* (1986).

Motivational Techniques

If you would like more information and ideas on classroom applications, peruse *Motivation and Teaching: A Practical Guide* (1978) by Raymond J. Wlodkowski and *Student Team Learning* (2nd ed., 1988), by Robert E. Slavin.

Summary

1. Motivation is the willingness to expend a certain amount of effort to achieve a particular goal. Motivation to master classroom tasks is affected by the nature of the learning task, the characteristics of the student, the classroom atmosphere, and the personality and approach of the teacher.
2. The behavioral view of motivation is based on the desire of individuals to attain a positive reinforcer (in the case of operant conditioning theory) or to imitate an admired individual (in the case of social learning theory). This view emphasizes extrinsic motivation.
3. When reinforcement is used excessively by teachers, some students may resent the teacher for being manipulative, learning may occur only when reinforcement is provided, some students may become dependent on the teacher, and intrinsic motivation for a task may be discouraged.
4. The cognitive view of motivation holds that people are inherently driven to overcome gaps or inconsistencies between what they know and what they experience. This view emphasizes intrinsic motivation.
5. One limitation of the cognitive view is that it may not always be possible to induce a sense of disequilibrium in students.
6. The humanistic view of motivation, particularly Abraham Maslow's, is based on satisfying a hierarchical sequence of deficiency needs (physiological, safety, belongingness and love, esteem) so that the individual can satisfy his or her growth needs (self-actualization, knowledge and understanding, aesthetic).

7. A limitation of the humanistic view is that it may not always be possible to identify a student's unmet deficiency needs or to satisfy them once they are identified.

8. The theory of achievement motivation posits that individuals are motivated by a need to achieve. Individuals with a high need to achieve aspire to goals of intermediate difficulty in order to balance success and failure. Individuals with a low need to achieve aspire either to very easy goals or to very difficult goals because they are motivated primarily by a fear of failure.

9. Some individuals, instead of being motivated by fear of failure, are motivated primarily by fear of success.

10. Research on the explanations people gave for their success and failure found marked differences between high achievers and low achievers. High achievers attribute success to ability and effort and failure to insufficient effort. Low achievers attribute success to luck or task difficulty and failure to lack of ability.

11. A limitation of the achievement motivation and attribution approaches to motivation is that they are difficult to observe and analyze.

12. The type of classroom reward structure that a teacher selects can encourage or discourage motivation. Four basic reward structures are individual competition, group competition, group reward (cooperation), and individual reward. For most classroom tasks competitive reward structures discourage motivation and achievement, while cooperative and individual reward structures enhance motivation and achievement.

13. Teacher attitudes also influence student motivation. Some teachers are more concerned with giving the appearance of being a good teacher than with helping students. Other teachers are motivated out of a sense of moral responsibility to help students learn. Finally, some teachers see improving student learning as a task they can master through ability and effort.

14. Because classroom learning is cognitive, compulsory, and publicly evaluated, motivation for learning is likely to be optimal when students know they possess learning skills and when they value those skills.

Key Terms

extrinsic motivation (520)

intrinsic motivation (520)

deficiency needs (523)

self actualization (523)

growth needs (523)

attribution theory (530)

Discussion Questions

1. At the beginning of this chapter, we drew a distinction between extrinsic motivation (doing something solely to obtain a reward offered by someone else) and intrinsic motivation (doing something solely because it brings pleasure or satisfaction). What percentage of your behavior do you think stems from intrinsic motivation? From extrinsic motivation? Do you think

it is possible to change this ratio? How? Are any of your ideas applicable to the classroom?

2. Maslow states that for individuals to be motivated to satisfy growth needs (like knowledge and understanding), the deficiency needs have to be satisfied first. Has this been the case in your own experience? If not, how was it different?

3. A limitation of Maslow's theory is that you may not always know when a student's deficiency needs are going unmet. How can you minimize the likelihood that you will be unaware of any student's deficiency needs?

4. High need achievers usually attribute success to effort and ability and failure to lack of effort. If you think of yourself as fitting this pattern, how did you get this way? Is there anything from your own experiences that you can use to help students develop this attributional pattern?

5. Have you ever experienced a competitive reward structure in school? Were your reactions to it positive or negative? Why? Would you use it in your own classroom? For what purpose and under what circumstances?

6. Have you ever experienced a cooperative reward structure in school? Were your reactions to it positive or negative? Why? Would you use it in your own classroom? For what purpose and under what circumstances?

4

EVALUATING PERFORMANCE

Chapter 12
Measurement and Evaluation of Classroom Learning

MEASUREMENT AND EVALUATION OF CLASSROOM LEARNING

KEY POINTS

The Nature of Measurement and Evaluation

Measurement: assigning numbers to things according to rules to create a ranking

Evaluation: making judgments about the value of a measure

Types of Measures

Performance tests measure skills under realistic conditions

Performance tests can measure underlying skills or learned product

Written tests measure degree of knowledge

Reducing Subjectivity

Pygmalion effect: impact of teacher expectations leads to self-fulfilling prophecy

Limited effect of teacher expectancy on IQ scores

Strong effect of teacher expectancy on achievement, participation

Teachers respond favorably to females, compliance, neatness, achievement, attractiveness

Suggestions for Teaching

Necessary to obtain a representative sample of behavior when testing

Table of specifications helps assure an adequate sample of content, behavior

Listing objectives and outcomes simplifies test preparation

Formative evaluation: monitor progress, plan remedial instruction

Summative evaluation: measure achievement, assign grades

Younger pupils need more structure, repetition, feedback

Use many formative tests with elementary school pupils

Short-answer items easy to write but measure lower levels of learning

Multiple-choice items measure different levels of learning but are hard to write

Interpretive items measure reasoning but take time to construct

Essay items measure complex learning but are hard to grade consistently

Rating scales and checklists make evaluations of performance more systematic

Item analysis tells about difficulty, discriminability of multiple-choice items

Norm-Referenced Grading

Norm-referenced grading: compare one student to others

Norm-referenced grading based on absence of external criteria

Mean influenced by extreme scores

Median: middle score, not influenced by extreme scores

Criterion-Referenced Grading

Criterion-referenced grading: compare individual performance to stated criteria

Criterion-referenced grades provide information about strengths and weaknesses

Expectations of a normal distribution lead to low aspirations

Mastery approach: give pupils multiple opportunities to master goals at own pace

Mastery learning has several potential limitations

Mastery learning does not eliminate competition and comparisons

---

Chapters 2 to 5 of this book acquainted you with information relating to phase one of a theory of instruction or model of learning: taking into account what students are like and allowing for individual differences in characteristics and abilities. Chapter 6 was devoted to phase two: specifying what is to be learned in the form of appropriate types of instructional objectives. Chapters 7 to 11 summarized information intended to assist you to achieve phase three: helping students master instructional objectives by applying what psychologists have discovered about learning, cognitive strategies, and motivation. In this chapter, the fourth and final phase in the model of learning outlined in this book will be analyzed: determining if students have achieved instructional objectives by measuring and evaluating performance.

The Nature of Measurement and Evaluation

Measuring and evaluating student performance is something that every teacher has to do, usually quite frequently. In one study (Hiatt, 1979) it was found that 22 percent of a typical elementary school teacher's morning was taken up with activities in this category. Such activities range from listening to oral reading to administering written tests. Yet despite the amount of time spent measuring and evaluating student performance, it is a task that most teachers dislike. One likely reason is that many teachers feel they don't understand the measurement process very well. Another possibility is that the role of evaluator is seen as being inconsistent with the role of teacher (or helper). A basic goal of this chapter, then, is to help you understand the nature of classroom measurement and evaluation and how it can be used to reinforce rather than work against your role as teacher. Toward that end, we begin by defining what we mean by the terms measurement and evaluation.

> **Measurement: assigning numbers to things according to rules to create a ranking**

Measurement is the assignment of numbers to certain attributes of objects, events, or people according to a rule-governed system. For our purposes, we will limit the discussion to attributes of people. The rules that are used to assign the numbers will ordinarily create a ranking that reflects how much of the attribute different people possess (Hills, 1981). Thus, we can measure someone's level of typing proficiency by counting the number of words the person accurately types per minute, or someone's level of mathematical reasoning by counting the number of problems correctly solved.

> **Evaluation: making judgments about the value of a measure**

Evaluation involves using a rule-governed system to make judgments about the value or worth of a set of measures (Hills, 1981). What does it mean, for example, to say that a student answered 80 out of 100 earth science questions correctly? Depending on the rules that are used, it may mean that the student has learned that body of knowledge exceedingly well and is ready to progress to the next unit of instruction or that the student has significant knowledge gaps and requires additional instruction.

Measurement and evaluation are often thought of as rather mechanical procedures that teachers go through to determine how much of something has been learned. Consequently, they are usually seen as being largely, if not totally, unrelated to individual differences, learning, motivation, or instruction. In the next section we will point out the narrowness of that view by describing how measurement and evaluation relate to all of those areas.

Various Aspects of Evaluation

Although techniques of classroom measurement and evaluation are the focus of this chapter, aspects and ramifications of assessing student performance already have been mentioned in many of the preceding chapters. In the discussion of pupil variability in Chapter 4, the importance of evaluation was repeatedly stressed. In order to determine if pupils are progressing through the curriculum satisfactorily, various measures of achievement are used. One of the provisions of Individualized Educational Programs prepared for pupils classified as handicapped under PL 94–142 (which were discussed in Chapter 5) requires that "appropriate objective criteria and evaluation procedures and schedules [be used to determine] whether short-term objectives are being achieved." In order to determine if a pupil qualifies as learning disabled under PL 94–142, it is necessary to demonstrate that there is a discrepancy between ability and achievement.

In the discussion of instructional objectives in Chapter 6, various ways to state objectives so that they specify how evaluation will take place were mentioned. In his suggestions for writing instructional objectives, Robert Mager (1975) urges you to describe the conditions under which learning behavior is to occur and to define the criterion of acceptable performance. In his description of objectives, Norman Gronlund (1978) recommends describing specific learning outcomes in terms of action verbs that describe types of behavior demonstrating that students have achieved objectives.

In Chapter 7 the behavioral view of learning stressed the significance of positive feedback in the form of reinforcement. Skinner and his followers urge teachers to use programmed techniques to provide immediate reinforcement for every correct response that leads to terminal behavior. Branching programs, in particular, call attention to the need to evaluate readiness to move on to the next step in a learning sequence. It is often important to determine if essential information has been acquired before asking pupils to grapple with advanced learning. Behavior modification enthusiasts recommend that teachers praise students when they supply correct answers or behave in desired ways and arrange for pupils to choose a reward when they have successfully completed a learning task.

Whenever students attempt to retrieve information they have encoded in their long-term memory (as described in Chapter 8), it might be said that they are evaluating how well they have learned. Furthermore, mnemonic devices and meta-cognition strategies are often used when students (and/or teachers) evaluate initial learning attempts and discover that significant gaps or misinterpretations in understanding exist.

In Chapter 9 the desirability of determining what students already know was mentioned. Before asking students to engage in discovery learning or problem solving, it is wise to find out how much background information they possess. And while the results of some discovery learning techniques take the form of personal insight, quite often teachers must supply feedback either to guide pupils on the path to discovery or to assure them that their conclusions are correct.

Chapter 10 discussed the proposal by some humanistic educators that traditional grades be abolished. The procedures they offered as alternatives proved to be unsatisfactory, but humanistic critics of comparative grading practices did call attention to the desirability of seeking ways to encourage students to work toward mastery of objectives rather than having to compete against one another.

The preceding chapter pointed out that grades are one of the most common motivating devices used in schools. Furthermore, success (in the form of satisfactory marks and grades) leads to a realistic level of aspiration and fosters development of a need for achievement. In addition, depending on previous experiences, students differ in their reactions to failure. Students with a history of achievement (reflected by high grades) typically resolve to try harder when they receive a low grade; those with a history of failure assume that they lack ability and that there is no point in trying to improve. Finally, evidence was reviewed supporting the conclusion that cooperative or individualized learning situations are generally preferable to competitive situations. If only a few students can earn high grades by "defeating" classmates, the many "losers" will have little incentive to learn and may feel inferior or inadequate.

This brief review calls attention to varied facets of evaluation. Quite often your intention may be to use evaluation primarily for pedagogical purposes. You may supply information about the correctness or incorrectness of responses, for instance, or assign a grade when instructional objectives have been achieved. But almost any time you evaluate learning, you will also be influencing how students perceive themselves. Thus your evaluations of pupils will not only contribute in direct ways to how effectively they learn; such evaluations will also influence how students think of themselves and may contribute in significant ways to the direction of their lives. While this chapter will emphasize how you might evaluate learning as constructively as possible, it will also discuss the impact of grades on pupil behavior and perceptions.

Types of Measures

Just as measurement can play several roles in the classroom, teachers have several ways to measure what students have learned. Which type of measure you choose will depend, of course, on the objectives you have stated. For purposes of this discussion, objectives can be classified in terms of two broad categories: *knowing how to do something* (for example, tie a square knot, dance the waltz, operate a microscope) and *knowing about something* (for example, that knots are used to secure objects, dance is a form of social expression, microscopes are used to study things too small to be seen by the naked eye). Measures that attempt to assess how well somebody can do something are often referred to as *performance* tests. Measures that attempt to assess the range and accuracy of someone's knowledge are usually called *written* tests.

The Nature of Performance Tests

Performance tests attempt to measure how well people perform a particular skill or a set of skills under more or less realistic conditions. Deciding how realistic the conditions should be depends on such factors as time, cost, availability of equipment, and the nature of the skill being measured. Imagine, for example, that you are a third-grade teacher and one of your objectives is that students will be able to determine how much change they should receive after making a purchase in a store. If this is a relatively minor objective, or if you do not have a lot of props available, you might simply demonstrate the situation with actual money and ask the students to judge whether the amount of change received was correct. If, on the other hand, you consider this to be a major objective and you have the props available, you might set up a mock store and have each student make a purchase using real money (Gronlund, 1988).

Performance tests measure skills under realistic conditions

Performance tests may focus on a process (that is, the underlying skills that go into a performance), a product (an observable outcome like a speech or a painting), or both. The measurement of process will often be emphasized for tasks that involve psychomotor skills. For example, a speech teacher may be more interested (at least initially) in assessing how well students use gestures, pauses, and changes in voice pitch and volume than in the content of their speeches (Hills, 1981). It is also possible to assess the processes underlying cognitive tasks. You may be just as interested in knowing which learning tactics students use to prepare for an exam and how well they use them as in how much of the information they understand. At other times, the product will be more important than the process, perhaps because a variety of processes results in an equally good product. The quality of a drawing or the solution to a problem may be more important than the processes used to generate the end product.

Performance tests can measure underlying skills or learned product

Types of Performance Tests

Based on how closely each simulates real life, Norman Gronlund (1988) discusses four types of performance tests: paper-and-pencil performance, identification tests, simulated performance, and work sample.

Paper-and-Pencil Performance   These tests emphasize the application of knowledge or skill. In many instances, students are asked to construct something, such as a product map, a graph, a diagram, a short story, or a lesson plan. In other cases, paper-and-pencil performance tests are used to measure whether students are ready for a "hands-on" experience. For example, students may be asked to name and describe, from photographs or drawings, the functions of various switches, dials, and control mechanisms on a complex piece of electronic equipment before they are taught how to use it.

Identification Tests   These tests, which range from simple to complex, ask students to identify or describe things. For instance, anatomy students may be asked to identify the internal organs of an animal. Chemistry students might be asked to identify an unknown substance. Medical students may be asked to name and

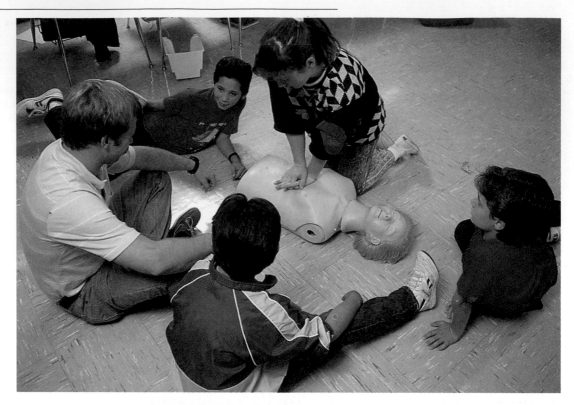

Performance tests assess how well students complete a task under realistic conditions. (Larry Kolvoord/The Image Works)

describe the functions of surgical instruments. Automotive students may be asked to listen to a malfunctioning engine, identify the probable cause, and describe the best procedure for correcting it. Like the paper-and-pencil performance test, the identification test is often used to judge whether students are ready for a more true-to-life performance.

Simulated Performance   The emphasis in simulated performance is to reproduce exactly, under controlled conditions, the response that should be made under real-life conditions. Simulations can be used in virtually any area. Examples are seen in law (mock trials), teacher education (microteaching), counselor education (microcounseling), pilot training (cockpit simulators), emergency medical services (dummy patients, mock catastrophes), and national defense (war games).

Work Sample   The work sample usually reflects the highest degree of realism. Students perform a representative sample of behaviors for a particular task under realistic conditions. Two examples of the work sample are a driving test and student teaching.

Gronlund (1988) lists four steps in constructing a performance test: (1) Specify the outcomes to be measured; (2) select an appropriate degree of realism; (3) prepare instructions that clearly specify the test situation; and (4) prepare the observational form to be used in evaluating performance. Three main types of observational forms are used to measure performance: the product scale, the checklist, and the rating scale. Detailed discussions of how to construct scales and checklists can be found in Gronlund (1981) or Ahmann and Glock (1981).

The Nature of Written Tests

As indicated at the beginning of this section, written tests attempt to measure how much people know about something. Since students learn mostly verbalized knowledge, such as facts, concepts, and principles, most of the tests they take are written.

Written tests measure degree of knowledge

In general, a written test is a set of written questions or statements to which the student must supply a written response. In the case of objective items (so-called because the subjectivity that enters into scoring is minimal), the response is very brief and unambiguous. The most popular objective test items are multiple-choice, true-false, matching, and interpretive items. In the case of created-response items, the response is longer and potentially more ambiguous. Hence, these items allow for more subjectivity in scoring. The length of the created response may range from a word or two for short-answer items to several pages for essay items. Since most of your objectives as a teacher will revolve around how much students know about something, much of this chapter will deal with written tests. You should recognize, however, that many of the issues raised (such as the next one on reducing subjectivity) pertain equally to performance tests.

Reducing Subjectivity

The foregoing reference to subjectivity calls attention to a problem you will have to deal with when you make judgments about others. It is likely that you have had at least some experiences where you felt that a teacher was less than objective, if not downright prejudiced. If you become aware of some of the factors that influence one person's perceptions of others, you may be able to reduce subjectivity to a minimum in your own evaluations. Many of these factors are reflected in a phenomenon that has been intensively studied and is known variously as the *Pygmalion effect,* the *self-fulfilling prophecy,* and the *teacher expectancy effect.*

Awareness of the Impact of Teacher Expectations

In 1968 Robert Rosenthal and Lenore Jacobson published *Pygmalion in the Classroom,* in which they reported results of a study on the impact of teacher expectations. Rosenthal and Jacobson administered a little-known group test of intelligence (Flangan's Test of General Ability) to children in grades 1 through 6 in a single San Francisco public school. The teachers of these children were not told the true name or nature of this test. Instead, they were told that the children had taken the "Harvard Test of Inflected Acquisition" and that, on the basis of the test results, certain pupils in each class were "likely to show unusual intellectual gains in the year ahead." In reality, however, there was no difference between the test performances of these "superior" pupils, who had been selected at random, and those of the other "average" children. At the end of the school year the same children took the Test of General Ability a second time.

Rosenthal and Jacobson reported in *Pygmalion in the Classroom* that the students who were labeled potential achievers showed significant gains in IQ and that the reason for these gains was that their teachers expected more of them. The authors referred to this phenomenon as the **Pygmalion effect,** because they felt that teacher expectations had influenced the students to become intelligent in the same way that the expectations of the mythical Greek sculptor Pygmalion caused a statue he had carved to come to life. Another term frequently used for this phenomenon is **self-fulfilling prophecy,** because a prophecy about behavior is often fulfilled. If teachers communicate the "prophecy" that certain students will behave intelligently, those students may behave in the expected manner.

When *Pygmalion in the Classroom* was first published, it attracted considerable attention. A number of writers on education proposed that it provided the key to revolutionizing the education of disadvantaged students. It was argued that the inadequate school performance of many students from poor backgrounds was due to low expectations on the part of teachers. If the teachers would simply communicate high expectations, it was reasoned, student performance would improve dramatically. Unfortunately, initial enthusiasm about the potency of the Pygmalion effect was soon replaced by doubts and qualifications. Some argued, for example, that Rosenthal and Jacobson's results did not strongly support their conclusions. Although the children in grades 1 and 2 who were identified as "intellectual bloomers" did score significantly higher than their "average" classmates on the IQ test at the end of the year, no such effect was found for the pupils in grades 3 through 6. Others pointed out that just because positive expectations led to higher scores, it could not be assumed that negative expectations would cause low scores (Wineburg, 1987).

In the years following the publication *Pygmalion in the Classroom,* hundreds of similar studies were carried out. Some attempted to replicate Rosenthal and Jacobson's findings, while others investigated the effects of teacher expectancy on other outcomes, like classroom achievement and participation. Periodically, the results of these studies were reviewed and summarized (for example, by Braun, 1976; Brophy, 1983b; Brophy & Good, 1974; Cooper, 1979; Raudenbush, 1984; Rosenthal, 1985). One review found that the effect of teacher expectancy on IQ scores was essentially limited to first- and second-grade students, was moderate in strength at those grade levels, and occurred only when it was induced within the

Pygmalion effect: impact of teacher expectations leads to self-fulfilling prophecy

Limited Effect of teacher expectancy on IQ scores

The heroine of G. B. Shaw's *Pygmalion*, the cockney flower girl Eliza Doolittle (Audrey Hepburn in the movie version of *My Fair Lady*) makes a grand entrance at a ball. The self-fulfilling prophecy is sometimes called the Pygmalion effect. As Eliza explains to her admirer Colonel Pickering, "The difference between a lady and a flower girl is the way she is treated, I shall always be a flower girl to Professor Higgins because he always treats me as a flower girl, and always will; but I know I can be a lady to you, because you treat me as a lady, and always will." (Movie Still Archives)

first two weeks of the school year (Raudenbush, 1984). Apparently, once teachers have had an opportunity to observe and interact with their own students, they view these experiences as more credible and informative than the results of a mental ability test. Reviews that have looked at the effect of teacher expectancy on classroom achievement and participation have generally found sizable positive *and* negative effects (for example, Braun, 1976; Brophy, 1983b; Cooper, 1979; Rosenthal, 1985). In addition, it appears that teacher expectations are more likely to maintain already existing tendencies than to drastically alter well-established behaviors. If a pupil has consistently earned low scores and grades, for example, teachers may reinforce those tendencies by treating the child as inept (Cooper, 1979).

In addition to documenting the existence of teacher expectancy effects and the conditions under which they occur, researchers have sought to identify the factors

Strong effect of teacher expectancy on achievement, participation

that might create high or low teacher expectations. Here is a list of some important factors taken from reviews by Braun (1976) and Brophy and Good (1974):

Attractive children are often perceived by teachers to be brighter, more capable, and more social than unattractive children.

Teachers tend to approve of girls' behavior more frequently than they approve of boys' behavior.

Female teachers tend to perceive the behavior of girls as closer to the behavior of "ideal students" than do male teachers.

Middle-class pupils are expected (by college students in education classes) to receive higher grades than lower-class students.

Teachers are more influenced by negative information about pupils (for example, low test scores) than they are by neutral or positive information.

Teachers appear to spend more time and to interact more frequently with high achievers than with low achievers.

High-achieving pupils receive more praise than low-achieving ones.

> **Teachers respond favorably to females, compliance, neatness, achievement, attractiveness**

It is important to bear in mind that these factors (plus others such as ethnic background, knowledge of siblings, and impressions of parents) usually operate *in concert* to produce an expectancy. A teacher may be influenced not just by a single test score, but by a test score, plus appearance, plus grades assigned by other teachers, and so forth. The task of objectively evaluating your students may be harder than you now realize. To help you minimize negative expectancies, we offer the following guidelines:

> Handbook Heading: Ways To Minimize Subjectivity

1. Try to control the influence of such factors as name, ethnic background, sex, physical characteristics, knowledge of siblings or parents, grades, and test scores. If you think you can be honest with yourself, you might attempt to describe your prejudices so that you will be in a position to try to guard against them. (Do you tend to be annoyed when you read descriptions of the exploits of members of a particular religious or ethnic group, for example?) Try to think of a pupil independently of her or his siblings and parents.

2. Make a well-planned effort to be fair and consistent in the way you interact with pupils. Perhaps keep a Question and Recitation Record to ensure that you call on all pupils in class about the same number of times. Strive to be consistently positive and enthusiastic when asking questions or responding to answers. (Don't hesitate or introduce vocal inflections when calling on less capable pupils. Such public signs of hesitation or lack of confidence may be communicated to the pupil and to classmates.) Refer to Table 11.1, page 564, to make your praise effective.

3. Perhaps keep a Positive Reinforcement Record in an effort to say favorable

things about the work of all pupils. If, after keeping such a record for two weeks, you discover that you have not said a single positive thing to one or more students, make it a point to praise those pupils at least as regularly as others.

4. If you become aware of pupil's previous low grades or are presented with low test scores, give individuals identified as poor learners the benefit of the doubt. Use the information to try to help low-scoring pupils improve their classroom performance (by using techniques to be discussed later in this chapter), and keep in mind that many factors (such as anxiety or misunderstanding instructions) may artificially lower test scores.

5. Strive to reduce the impact of distorted perceptions and negative expectations by taking advantage of the characteristics of tests.

SUGGESTIONS FOR TEACHING

Effective Techniques of Evaluation

1. As early as possible in a report period, decide when and how often to give tests and other assignments that will count toward a grade.
   a. Consider distributing a course outline on the first day of class.
   b. Announce tests and other assignments well in advance. Give a detailed description of what will be covered, how it will be evaluated, and how much it will count toward a final grade.
   c. Be considerate in scheduling.

2. Prepare a content outline and/or table of specifications of the objectives to be covered on each exam or otherwise take care to obtain a systematic sample.

3. Consider the purpose of each test or measurement exercise. Take into account the developmental characteristics of the pupils in your classes and the nature of the curriculum for your grade level.

4. Decide on the type of test items to use and write sufficient items to provide an adequate sample, measuring understanding at several levels of the taxonomies of educational objectives (if appropriate), and allowing for differences in cognitive styles.

5. Make up and use a detailed key.
   a. Evaluate each answer by comparing it to the key.
   b. Be willing and prepared to defend the evaluations you make.

6. During and after the grading process, analyze questions and answers in order to improve future exams.

1. As early as possible in a report period, decide when and how often to give tests and other assignments that will count toward a grade.
   a. Consider distributing a course outline on the first day of class.

In the opening pages of Chapter 6, "Devising and Using Objectives," you were urged to start at the end of an instructional sequence rather than just taking a stab at making a beginning. That is, you were asked to think about what you wanted your students to be able to do by the last day of class. You were also urged to write objectives that would specify or indicate how achievement would be evaluated. If you follow the suggestions for formulating objectives presented in that chapter, you should be able to develop a reasonably complete master plan that will permit you to devise a course outline even though you have only limited experience with teaching and/or a text or unit of study. If you announce at the beginning of a report period when you intend to give exams or set due dates for assignments, you not only give students a clear idea of what they will be expected to do, but you also give yourself guidelines for arranging lesson plans and devising, administering, and scoring tests. (If you will be teaching elementary grade students, it will be better to announce for a week at a time, rather than provide a long-range schedule.)

Handbook Heading:
Outlining Units of Study

b. Announce tests and other assignments well in advance. Give a detailed description of what will be covered, how it will be evaluated, and how much it will count toward a final grade.

If you are coy, absent-minded, or vague about tests and assignments, you may discourage careful study. Consider these two announcements and imagine how you might react to each. "We'll have an exam in a week or so, it, uh, will cover, uh, everything we've discussed so far." "We'll have an exam next Wednesday; it will be on the material covered in class starting with the topic of _____ and on pages 216 through 275 of the text. There will be five short-essay questions and a fifteen-item matching question based on the mimeographed outline of Key Points that I handed out." Which set of goals would look more attainable to you? Which would be more likely to motivate you to actually prepare for the exam? Suppose the first teacher then gave you a fifty-item true-false test on a twenty-five page section of the text (out of 400 pages covered so far), whereas the second gave you exactly the kind of test described. How would you feel about each class the next time an exam was scheduled? What would be your attitude toward doing a conscientious job of studying for each class?

For the most part, it seems preferable to announce tests well in advance. Pop quizzes tend to increase anxiety and tension and to force students to cram on isolated sections of a book on a day-by-day and catch-as-catch-can basis. Simple homework assignments or the equivalent are more likely to encourage more careful and consistent study than pop quizzes. When tests are announced, it is comforting to students to know exactly what material they will be held responsible for, what kinds of questions will be asked, and how much it will count toward the final grade.

If you assign term papers or other written work, list your criteria for grading the papers (for example, how much emphasis will be placed on style, spelling and punctuation, research, individuality of expression). In laboratory courses most students prefer a list of experiments or projects and some description of how they will be evaluated (for example, ten experiments in chemistry, fifteen drawings in drafting, five paintings in art, judged according to posted criteria).

c. Be considerate in scheduling

You may reduce antagonism toward tests if you are thoughtful about scheduling them—or about scheduling deadlines for other assignments. In the upper grades you might consider such occasions as a big game, a dance, or elections. You might allow students to vote on two or three dates you have selected for exams or deadlines so that the majority can pick a day when they will not be loaded down with other assignments.

Handbook Heading: Being Considerate in Scheduling

2. Prepare a content outline and/or a table of specifications of the objectives to be covered on each exam or otherwise take care to obtain a systematic sample.

If you have drawn up lesson plans, listed instructional objectives, or otherwise described the terminal behavior you are aiming for, you already have such an outline. If you have not done this by the time the first test is due, you are likely to make a resolution to be more conscientious next time. The more precisely and completely goals are described at the beginning of a unit, the easier and more efficient evaluation (and teaching) will be. Using a clear outline will help assure an adequate sample of the most significant kinds of behavior.

When the time comes to assess the abilities of your pupils, you can't possibly observe and evaluate all relevant behavior. You can't listen to more than a few pages of reading by each first-grader, for example, or ask high school seniors to answer questions on everything discussed in several chapters of a text. Because of the limitations imposed by large numbers of students and small amounts of time, your evaluation will have to be based on a *sample* of behavior—a three- or four-minute reading performance and questions covering points made in only a few sections of text material assigned for an exam. It is therefore important to try to obtain a representative, accurate sample.

Necessary to obtain a representative sample of behavior when testing

Psychologists who have studied measurement and evaluation often recommend that as teachers prepare exams they use a *table of specifications* to note the types and numbers of test items to be included so as to insure thorough and systematic coverage. The exact form that such a table will take depends on the subject or topic, the grade level, and the kinds of instructional objectives you have written. If you have prepared objectives such as those recommended by Robert Mager, you will already have a specific description of how you intend to measure achievement. For instance, if you have told your students that they will be given a collection of twenty rock specimens and that they must correctly identify and label at least fifteen of them to earn a passing grade, no further planning is necessary. If you use Mager-type objectives, your table of specifications might consist of the various sets of objectives that you plan to use during a unit or a course.

If you have written objectives such as those recommended by Norman Gronlund, the kinds of specific outcomes you have noted not only provide a sample of achievement behaviors, but they also give you clear guidelines for preparing exams. Here, for example, is the objective noted in Chapter 6 that might be used in teaching third-grade math.

Knows methods and procedures for adding and subtracting:

1. Identifies plus and minus signs in problems.
2. Describes how to add and subtract numbers.
3. Demonstrates ability to add and subtract numbers.
4. Shows ability to take sets of numbers supplied and arrange them to be added or subtracted by self or others.
5. Explains how to use knowledge of addition and subtraction to handle situations outside of schools.

To evaluate achievement of this objective you could do the following:

1. Make up a simple exercise to determine if all students consistently identify plus and minus signs.
2. Ask students to add and subtract sets of numbers and then explain how they did it.
3. Give students pages of addition and subtraction problems, first as exercises and then as an exam.
4. Give students several sets of numbers (for example, 104, 26; 14, 19, 21) and instruct them to arrange the first set so that they subtract the smaller number from the larger, arrange the second set to be added.
5. Ask students to describe an out-of-school situation they are likely to encounter in the near future where it would be essential to know how to add or subtract.

Or take the objective illustration for sixth-grade music.

Knows musical instruments:

1. Names the instruments of an orchestra when pictures of each are displayed.
2. Identifies the instruments of an orchestra when each is played on a recording.
3. States differences between the instruments of an orchestra and of a band.
4. Differentiates between recordings played by an orchestra and a band.

You might hand out the following statement on the day you announce that the class will learn about musical instruments: "By the time we finish this unit, you should be able to (1) name the instruments of an orchestra when pictures of each are displayed; (2) identify the instruments...," and so on for the other specific outcomes. Then, at the end of the unit, you could measure achievement by holding up pictures of instruments and asking students to write down their names, having them identify the instruments of the orchestra when played on a recording, and so on.

Or take the objective offered as an illustration for use in high school social studies.

Judges on basis of evidence:

1. Distinguishes between evidence and opinions.
2. Relates evidence to conclusions.
3. Detects conclusions based on insufficient or irrelevant evidence.
4. Explains why it is not always possible to determine the direction of cause and effect relationships.
5. Criticizes statements made by public figures that cannot be backed up by evidence.

To test achievement of the first specific learning outcome, you could prepare a list of ten statements and ask students to identify each with an O (for Opinion) or an E (for Evidence). To test the second, you could make up a statement and write a series of multiple-choice questions asking students to relate evidence to conclusions. To test the last, you could reproduce part of a recent speech by a public figure and ask students to note statements that cannot be backed up by evidence.

If you were not completely convinced after reading about Gronlund-type objectives in Chapter 6 that they were worth the trouble, perhaps you are convinced now. Lists of specific outcomes not only give you and your students steps to follow in working toward achievement; they also make it extremely easy to prepare appropriate evaluation procedures and instruments.

In addition to following Gronlund's suggestions for writing objectives and specific learning outcomes, you might also make use of the related approach to stating objectives that features listing what students should be able to do at the end of a unit. Here are two examples of this approach that were given in Chapter 6.

To earn a passing grade on this unit you will be asked to:

1. State the first and second laws of thermodynamics in the same basic terminology used in the text. (Slight alterations will be permitted, provided they do not change the meaning of the law.)
2. Rewrite these laws in your own words.
3. Predict what will happen in various energy-producing situations.
4. Explain how any energy system works.

At the end of this unit on use of the table saw you will be expected to:

1. State five safety rules to observe every time you use the saw.
2. Set up the saw for crosscutting and ripping.
3. Use the dado head to cut half-lap joints, tongue-and-groove joints, and box joints.

If you list objectives in this form, you will have written quite specific instructions to yourself (and to your students) about how you should measure understanding. In this instance, you might use a table of specifications to make sure that you have prepared a set of objectives for all important topics in a unit. You can also use your table to ensure that you will use a variety of test questions.

If you have invited students to participate in drawing up objectives, you should consult that list when the time comes to measure understanding. Your table of specifications in this case might stress types of questions to be written.

If you have selected and listed Key Points for a unit or chapter in a text, your evaluation task is quite clear: Write at least one question for each point. The table of specifications in this case might be used to make sure you measure understanding at different levels of the taxonomy of objectives for the cognitive domain.

Regardless of the kinds of objectives or unit outlines you have developed, you might draw up a table of specifications by first listing along the left-hand margin of a piece of lined paper the important topics that have been covered. Then insert appropriate headings from the taxonomy of objectives for the cognitive domain (or for the affective or psychomotor domains, if appropriate) across the top of the page. An example of such a table of specifications for the information discussed so far in this chapter is provided in Figure 12.1.

Table of specifications helps assure an adequate sample of content, behavior

Handbook Heading: Using a Table of Specifications

Figure 12.1   Example of a Table of Specifications for Material Covered So Far in This Chapter

Topic	Objectives					
	Knows	Comprehends	Applies	Analyzes	Synthesizes	Evaluates
Factors that lead to distorted perceptions						
Impact of teacher expectations						
Implications of research on expectations						
Characteristics of tests						

Test specialists often recommend that you insert in the boxes of a table of specifications the percentage of test items that you intend to write for each topic and each type of objective. This practice forces you to think about both the number and relative importance of your objectives before you start teaching or writing test items. Thus, if some objectives are more important to you than others, you will have a way of insuring that these are tested more thoroughly. On the other hand, if a test is going to be brief and emphasize all objectives more or less equally, you may put a check mark in each box *as* you write questions. If you discover that you are overloading some boxes and that others are empty, you can take steps to remedy the situation. (For reasons to be discussed shortly, you may not list all of the categories in the taxonomy for all subjects or at all grade levels. Tables of specifications that you draw up for your own use, therefore, may contain fewer headings across the top of the page than the table illustrated in Figure 12.1.)

Simply writing "knows," "applies," "analyzes," and so forth across the top of your table may not supply as much direction as you would like. Accordingly, you may find it helpful to refer to the tables of objectives and outcomes for the three taxonomies included in Chapter 6 (Tables 6.1, 6.2, and 6.3, pages 285–287). If you will take the trouble to flip back and examine those tables before reading further, you will realize that they provide a concise outline of all the basic objectives of each of the taxonomies, as well as specific outcome verbs you can use

Listing objectives and outcomes simplifies test preparation

when writing test questions or planning forms of evaluation. The same information for the cognitive taxonomy (derived once again from material discussed and summarized by Gronlund in *Stating Objectives for Classroom Instruction*, 3rd ed., 1985a) is provided in different form below. (You might find it very useful to make copies of Tables 6.1, 6.2, and 6.3, as well as the previous page, and have them on your desk every time you map out general evaluation strategies or write test questions.)

Knowledge Knows common terms, facts, rules, trends, classifications, criteria methods, procedures, principles, theories. (Ask students to *define, describe, identify, label, list, match, name, outline, reproduce, select, state.*)

Comprehension Comprehends facts and principles, interprets verbal or graphic material, translates from one form to another, estimates or predicts what might happen. (Ask students to *explain, generalize, give examples, state in their own words, paraphrase, rewrite, infer, predict.*)

Application Applies concepts and principles to new situations, applies laws and theories to practical situations, solves problems, constructs charts and graphs, demonstrates methods or procedures. (Ask students to *use, solve, prepare, draw, produce, construct, design, show, demonstrate.*)

Analysis Analyzes organization, identifies component parts. (Ask students to *organize, identify, subdivide, separate, differentiate, distinguish, illustrate, outline, select.*)

Synthesis Puts together separate ideas to form something new, relates one set of conclusions to another, formulates a new pattern. (Ask students to *organize, combine, compile, rearrange, plan, reconstruct, rewrite, summarize.*)

Evaluation Evaluates quality or value with reference to self-chosen or supplied criteria, makes judgments of adequacy or consistency. (Ask students to *arrange in order, compare, appraise, contrast, criticize, justify.*)

The primary reason for using various types of instructional objectives to plan evaluation, for drawing up a table of specifications, or for referring to the lists just provided, is to make your evaluations of student understanding and abilities comprehensive and systematic. Without some sort of rationale, you might make the same mistake (as described in the opening pages of Chapter 1) that the senior author of this book made when he started to teach. You might simply make up questions on material that strikes you as testable. You also might fall into the extremely common trap of writing questions that test only knowledge. You may recall the statement made by Benjamin S. Bloom quoted in Chapter 6: "It is estimated that over 90 percent of test questions that U.S. Public school students are *now* expected to answer deal with little more than information"

(1984, p. 13). Bloom stressed the word "now" to emphasize that even though over one million copies of the taxonomy for the cognitive domain have been sold, very few teachers seem to be using them.

If you take the trouble to be systematic about selecting and writing questions, you are much more likely to develop exams that are reliable and valid than if you simply dash off an assortment of test items. *Reliability,* as noted in Chapter 4, refers to the consistency of measurements and is concerned with questions such as these: If you gave the same exam a second time, would students earn essentially the same scores? If you prepare alternate-form exams on the same material, would students earn essentially the same scores on both exams? If you scored a short-answer or essay exam one night, would you end up with the same number of total points if you graded it two nights later? *Validity* refers to the extent to which a test measures what it is supposed to measure. If you want to find out if your students understand a chapter in a text, your test should give you an accurate indication that students who earn high scores understand the material better than students who end up with low scores. (The type of validity just described, you may recall, is called *content* validity, since it is concerned with how well a test measures to content of a subject of study. *Predictive* validity tells how well a test predicts future performance. You were probably asked to take the Scholastic Aptitude Test or the equivalent when you applied for admission to college because the admissions committee wanted to predict how well you would do. *Construct* validity indicates how well a test measures a particular construct or attribute. A test of musical aptitude, for example, should differentiate between students who respond quickly to instruction in music and those who do not.)

Test specialists who prepare standardized tests use a variety of statistical techniques to estimate reliability and validity and typically supply data permitting potential users to evaluate how well the test measures up in terms of consistency and accuracy. You will not have the time to use such techniques with your home-made exams, but as you prepare tests, you might attempt to assure a satisfactory degree of reliability and validity by making up a sufficient number and variety of well-written questions on all aspects of a topic. Thus, perhaps the best way to endeavor to prepare reliable and valid exams is to do a conscientious job of following the suggestions in this chapter.

3. Consider the purpose of each test or measurement exercise. Take into account the developmental characteristics of the pupils in your classes and the nature of the curriculum for your grade level.

As you prepare your table of specifications, or otherwise plan a systematic testing procedure, think about the purpose of each evaluation exercise. Do you want to make an estimate of how much students understand or to place students at

Formative evaluation: monitor progress, plan remedial instruction

Summative evaluation: measure achievement, assign grades

different levels (beginners, intermediate, advanced)? Do you want to monitor progress or plan remedial instruction (often called **formative evaluation** since the intention is to facilitate or form learning)? Do you want to try to identify sources of learning difficulties (referred to as *diagnostic* evaluation)? Do you want to discover how well instructional objectives have been met and/or determine a grade to be recorded on a report card (often called **summative evaluation**, since it sums up performance)? Do you want to combine several of these purposes? Depending on the purpose or purposes of a test, the form and content may vary. You should take this into account early in the testing sequence.

In addition to considering different uses of tests and other forms of evaluation when you plan evaluation strategies, you should also think about the developmental characteristics of the students you plan to teach and the nature of the curriculum at your grade level. As noted in the discussion of Piaget's theory in Chapter 2, there are significant differences between preoperational, concrete operational, and formal thinkers. Furthermore, because primary grade children are asked to master a curriculum that is substantially different from the curriculum upper elementary and secondary school pupils are expected to learn, different forms of evaluation should be used at each level.

Primary grade children are asked to concentrate on learning basic skills, and their progress—or lack of it—will often be apparent even if they are not asked to take tests. A second-grader who can read only a few words, for instance, will reveal that inability each time he or she is asked to read. Upper elementary grade pupils are asked to improve and perfect their mastery of skills in reading, writing, and arithmetic and also to study topics in the sciences, social studies, and other subjects. Success in dealing with many subjects, learning materials, and tests often depends on skill in reading. A fifth-grader who is a slow reader, for instance, might not be able to get through an assigned chapter or answer all the questions on a multiple-choice test in the allotted time. Because performance in several subjects must be reported, many separate evaluations must be made. In all of the elementary grades, there is usually stress on helping as many students as possible master the curriculum. Thus tests may be used as much to diagnose weaknesses and chart improvement as to establish grades.

At the secondary level, students begin to move toward either a vocational or a college preparatory curriculum and to choose electives. Because courses in many subjects are often arranged in sequence, and because the process of identifying students most likely to go on to college begins at this time, comparisons of students become more systematic and direct. It is often desirable (or necessary) to discover if a student who takes Math I, for instance, is ready to go on to Math II. Colleges and universities may request that high schools establish particular grading standards in order to facilitate the selection of candidates who apply for admission. If a school does not maintain sufficiently high standards, graduates

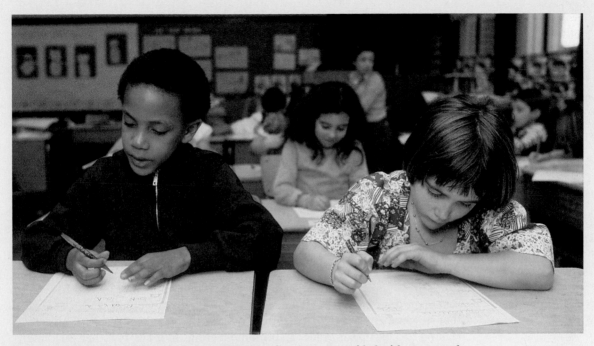

There is some evidence that elementary school pupils who are provided with structured assignments score higher on standardized tests than those who attend classes that feature considerable self-direction. (H. Armstrong Roberts)

may encounter problems when they apply for admission to certain institutions of higher learning.

Two studies of the effectiveness of second- through fourth-grade teachers call attention to significant differences between younger and older pupils that should be considered when planning evaluation strategies.

Jere E. Brophy and Carolyn M. Evertson (1976) identified several second- and third-grade teachers who consistently seemed to do an especially effective job in the classroom. After observing the techniques used by these teachers and the impact they had on their pupils, Brophy and Evertson observed.

Younger and less cognitively developed children seem to require more teacher structuring, smaller and more redundant steps in the learning process, more op-portunities to practice and get corrective feedback, more attention to basic skills and factual knowledge, and the like. As they get older and/or more cognitively de-veloped, they can begin to benefit increasingly from more indirect teaching, more verbal teaching, more opportunities for choice of assignments and independent

Younger pupils need more structure, repe-tition, feedback

work, more opportunities for group work and other student-to-student interaction, more challenging and faster paced instructional sequences, and the like (p. 140.)

The kinds of evaluation you might use if you teach in the first few grades, therefore, should be substantially different from those you might use at higher grade levels. Some primary graders will be preoperational thinkers and others will be embryonic concrete thinkers; all of them will benefit if they develop a sense of industry. Such children should have abundant opportunities to try out skills and receive immediate feedback. Instead of using weekly quizzes, it would be preferable to have these students work on exercises daily. You can then supply feedback and also provide tangible evidence of progress. (Many texts and instructional materials designed for use in the early grades are accompanied by ready-made exercises of this type.)

Use many formative tests with elementary school pupils

Upper elementary school pupils, most of whom will be concrete thinkers, might be given frequent formative examinations stressing knowledge and direct applications that can be derived from material recently presented in class. If you present a rule such as *"i* before *e* except after *c,"* for instance, you might feature words that contain the letters *i* and *e* after *c* and after other letters. Instead of basing grades on a few summative tests, you might schedule frequent exams so that students can accumulate points as they work toward instructional objectives leading to a particular grade. To promote feelings of industry rather than inferiority, students who experience difficulties might be given remedial instruction and repeated opportunities to meet specific standards. (A comprehensive method for doing this will be described at the end of this chapter.)

After you have determined the purpose of a test, drawn up your table of specifications (or selected Key Points), and considered such factors as level of cognitive development and the curriculum, you will be faced with the task of deciding what kinds of test items to use. (If you have developed lists of specific learning outcomes, you will already know which types of items to write.)

4. Decide on the type of test items to use and write sufficient items to provide an adequate sample, measuring understanding at several levels of the taxonomies of educational objectives (if appropriate), and allowing for differences in cognitive style.

Before beginning the actual composition of a test, you might first see if the publisher of the text you are using supplies examination questions. If test questions or evaluation exercises *are* available, you can use them exactly as provided or modify or supplement them with additional items of your own, so long as two conditions are met: The items should reflect your course objectives, and they should be well written. Since it is almost certain that you will need to write at least some of your own test questions, brief descriptions of different types of items will be presented in the next few pages. Each of the following sections describes the nature, advantages, and disadvantages of a particular type of question. Some guidelines for writing each type of item are also included.[1]

Handbook Heading:
Guidelines for Writing Test
Questions

Short-Answer and Completion Items

Description: The student is asked to supply a brief answer consisting of a name, word, phrase, or symbol.

Example of a short-answer item: Robert Rosenthal did research on the impact of expectations. As a synonym for the term *self-fulfilling prophecy* he uses what term? *(Pygmalion effect)*

Example of a completion item: Robert Rosenthal did research on the impact of expectations. As a synonym for the term *self-fulfilling prophecy* he prefers the term *(Pygmalion effect).*

Advantages: Easy to write. Can be written on the board or printed or typed on a single ditto master. Require pupil to *supply* the answer, not simply recognize it. Guessing and bluffing not likely to be too successful. Can ask many questions in a short period of time, get an extensive sample.

Disadvantages: Restricted to measuring simple learning at lower levels of taxonomy of objectives for the cognitive domain. Unexpected (but plausible) answers may be difficult to prevent or score. If you teach more than one section of a course, students in one class will be able to tell friends in other classes many of the questions, which may mean that you will have to make up a different test for each class.

Short-answer
items easy to
write but measure
lower levels of
learning

Guidelines:
1. Write the question so that the answer is brief and definite.
2. Guard against lifting phrases directly from the text.
3. Use direct questions as much as possible rather than incomplete statements (to facilitate grading and to reduce ambiguity).
4. If completion items are used, put blanks in a column on the right side of the paper. Or, if you print the questions on the board, have students list answers on a separate sheet of paper.

True-False or Alternative Response Items

Description: The student is asked to identify the correctness of definitions, statements, facts, or principles or to distinguish between fact and opinion.

---

1. The general form and much of the content of the following sections are derived from material in Chapters 6 through 9 of *Measurement and Evaluation in Teaching* (5th ed., 1985) by Norman E. Gronlund.

Examples: If the following statement is true, circle the T. If it is false, circle the F.

(T)　F　The tendency for one characteristic to influence all impressions is called the halo effect.

If the following statement is a fact, circle the F. If it is an opinion, circle the O.

(F)　O　A table of specifications is used to plan tests.

F　(O)　Behavioral learning theory is more valuable to teachers than cognitive theory.

If the answer to the following question is yes, circle the Y. If it is no, circle the N.

(Y)　N　Does *Pygmalion effect* mean the same as *self-fulfilling prophecy?*

Y　(N)　Has Rosenthal's research on the impact of expectations been supported consistently by research by other psychologists?

Advantages: It is possible to ask many questions in a short period of time. Answers are very easy to score. They can be an effective way to measure understanding of facts versus opinions.

Disadvantages: Restricted to measuring simple learning, usually at lowest levels of the taxonomy for the cognitive domain. Difficult to write items that can be reduced to absolute terms on other than trivial material. May penalize divergent thinkers. Permit and encourage guessing to the point that some students may spend more time trying to figure out a pattern than analyzing questions. To offset the impact of guessing, need a very large number of items.

Guidelines:

1. Avoid broad general statements or statements that stress trivia.

2. Avoid use of long, complex sentences; restrict statement to a single idea.

3. Write about an equal number of true and false statements, with both types of statements being approximately equal length.

4. Try to avoid using words such as "always," "never," "sometimes," and the like.

5. Write as many items as you think pupils can answer in allotted test time.

Matching Questions

Description: Pupil is asked to identify pairs of items to be associated.

Example: In the blank space next to each concept listed in the left-hand column, write the number next to the name of the appropriate individual listed in the right-hand column. A name may be used more than once.

_____ equilibration	1. Bandura
_____ operant conditioning	2. Erikson
	3. Gronlund
_____ growth needs	4. Mager
_____ identity vs. role confusion	5. Maslow
	6. Piaget
_____ anticipatory control	7. Sears
_____ assimilation	8. Skinner

Advantages: Compact form, can cover much material in a small amount of space. Can print test on board, have students record answers on a slip of paper. Very easy to score. Can measure ability to distinguish between similar events or place them in order (if question is arranged to stress order).

Disadvantages: Restricted to measuring factual information at lowest levels of taxonomy of objectives for the cognitive domain. Difficult to find homogeneous material or to avoid irrelevant clues. Easy for students in one class to tell friends in other classes what to study. May be simple for students to copy answers from others' papers.

Guidelines:
1. Try to stress items that are related in some way or which are of the same type. Don't just throw together an assortment of miscellaneous information.
2. Include an unequal number of premises and responses, tell students if a response can be used more than once. Do not list more than ten premises per question.
3. Keep the descriptions brief, place short responses in the right-hand column.
4. Arrange responses in a logical order (alphabetically, chronologically.)
5. Do not have a matching question continue on a second page.

Multiple-Choice Items

Description: A statement (the *stem*) is followed by several alternative statements. One of these is the answer; the others are *distracters*. The form may involve a direct question or an incomplete statement, or it may ask for the best answer. Instructions at the top of the first page of the test booklet indicate how answers should be recorded.

Examples:
Which of the following is a definition of *projection?*
1. Tendency for expectations to influence perceptions

2. Tendency to ignore evidence that is inconsistent
3. Tendency for one characteristic to influence all impressions
4. Tendency to see own undesirable traits in others

Projection is said to occur when
1. expectations influence perceptions.
2. one characteristic of a person influences all impressions of that person.
3. inconsistent evidence is ignored.
4. someone sees his or her own undesirable traits in others.

Which of the following is the clearest and most accurate definition of projection?
1. Tendency for expectations to influence perceptions
2. Tendency to ignore evidence that is inconsistent with beliefs
3. Tendency for one characteristic to influence all impressions
4. Tendency to see own undesirable traits in others

Advantages: Can measure many types of understanding, including those at the middle and sometimes upper levels of the taxonomy for the cognitive domain. Can ask many questions in a class period, get an excellent sample. Possible to reduce ambiguity often found in short-answer and true-false items. Very easy to grade, particularly when special answer sheets are used. Opportunity for guessing is reduced. Difficult for students in one class to pass on items to friends in other classes so an exam can be used several times. Give students experience with types of items that are commonly featured on standardized tests (such as those used in making decisions about college admission).

| Multiple-choice items measure different levels of learning but are hard to write |

Disadvantages: Difficult and time-consuming to write items that measure more than knowledge. Under pressure to get a test ready, there may be a tendency to write knowledge items. Students are asked to *recognize* correctness or incorrectness, not to supply information on their own. Often difficult to write a sufficient number of plausible distracters. Requires substantial time to type ditto masters, run off copies, collate, staple, number copies. May favor convergent thinkers, penalize divergent thinkers. Difficult to supply feedback for each question, which will tend to cause students to concentrate only on the score earned, not on which answers were correct and incorrect.

Guidelines:
1. Try to make the stem meaningful by itself and have it present a definite problem, without irrelevant material.
2. Try to avoid stems stated in negative terms (sometimes this is unavoidable).
3. Make sure all alternatives are grammatically consistent with the stem.

4. Try to insure that the answer is clearly more correct that the distracters, but try to make the distracters plausible.

5. Arrange the alternatives in alphabetical order (to avoid establishing a pattern).

6. Use phrases such as "all of the above" or "none of the above" sparingly or not at all.

7. Make a deliberate effort to stress translation, interpretation, application, analysis, and evaluation when you write questions. Guard against writing too many knowlege questions. You might be tempted, for instance, to supply a definition in the stem and list four terms under it. Such a question merely asks the student to supply a label. A better way to write the question would be to put a *term* in the stem followed by four definitions. This format asks the student to think about what the term means (which is more useful than attaching a label). Better yet, ask students to *translate* the text definition of a term by selecting the best alternative description from four variations (perhaps expressed in slang terms). Students might be asked to *interpret* the term by choosing the best illustration of it from four supplied. They might be asked to *apply* it by selecting the best description of uses from four supplied. They might be asked to *evaluate* it by picking out a strength or weakness from four descriptive statements.

Interpretive Items

Description: A series of objective questions is based on a descriptive paragraph, a graph, diagram, map, cartoon, or illustration.

Example: The graph on the next page indicates the percentage of teachers who reported (in a survey conducted by the National Education Association in 1970) using various types of grading procedures.

The statements that follow refer to the data recorded in the graph. Read each statement and mark your answer according to the following key:

Circle T if the graph data are sufficient to make the statement *true*.
Circle F if the data are sufficient to make the statement *false*.
Circle I if the graph data are *insufficient* to determine whether the statement is true or false.

T   F   (I)   Number grades were assigned by a greater number of elementary than secondary teachers.

(T) F I About six-tenths of all elementary teachers reported grades in conferences.

T F (I) Elementary grade teachers prefer letter grades to conferences or pass-fail grading procedures.

T (F) I Less than one-tenth of the secondary teachers surveyed reported grades in parent conferences.

(T) F I Four times as many secondary teachers assigned letter grades as participated in parent conferences.

Advantages: Measure student ability to interpret written or pictorial materials —an important form of cognitive behavior. Can measure complex learning, but in a more structured form than on an essay test. All students are supplied with identical data, which means that reasoning rather than memorization is stressed.

Disadvantages: Difficult and time-consuming to construct. Items based on written material favor good readers, penalize poor readers. Measure only the ability to solve problems that are presented in structured form. Pupils asked only to recognize correct answers, not to apply problem-solving skills on their own.

Guidelines:
1. Base questions on material that is new to pupils.
2. Write questions that are at an appropriate reading level.
3. Write questions that require analysis and interpretation of the material, not merely recognition of factual material.

Interpretive items measure reasoning but take time to construct

4. Make the number of questions roughly proportional to the length of the material.
5. If the material permits, revise it as the questions are written (to make the questions less ambiguous or more challenging).
6. To simplify preparation of exams, write or draw the material on which the questions are based on the board, or project transparencies, or use an opaque projector.

Essay Items

Description: The student is asked to recall, organize, and integrate what is known about some topic.

Example: Compare behavioral learning theory and cognitive theory in terms of basic assumptions, typical research findings, and pedagogical applications.

Advantages: Can measure complex learning, particularly the abilities to analyze, synthesize, and evaluate. Student is asked to recall, select, and apply (not just recognize) what has been learned. Students gain experience in expressing their thoughts in writing, which is a skill required in many occupations. Because students reveal the train of their thoughts in written form, it may be possible for the teacher to trace errors in understanding or reasoning. Questions can be written on the board, no need to prepare examination booklets.

Disadvantages: May be tempted to make up questions on the spur of the moment, not take into account instructional objectives in a systematic way. Extremely difficult, time-consuming, and tedious to grade. Extremely difficult to grade consistently. (The same teacher may give a substantially different grade if the papers are reread a few weeks later. Different instructors may give the same paper grades from A to D.) Because students can write on only a few topics in a typical class period, get a very limited sample. Evaluator may be influenced by such factors as handwriting and spelling. If teacher does not take the trouble to avoid looking at the name of the student, may evaluate personalities rather than answers. Temptation to reward "pets" with high grades, give low grades to students who antagonize or have registered dislike.

Essay items measure complex learning but are hard to grade consistenly

Guidelines:
1. Resist the temptation to dash off questions on the spur of the moment. Take time to devise questions that are related to instructional objectives.
2. Phrase the questions so that pupils have a clear idea what you want them to write about.
3. Tell students how many points each question will count, inform them that they will not be graded on spelling or grammar.

4. Immediately after you compose a question, write out your own answer. Use that answer to clarify the question and to grade papers. If possible and appropriate, indicate in your answer how many points you intend to award for each major idea correctly analyzed by students.

5. Have students write their names on the back of the last page of the exam so that you will be unaware of their identity as you grade papers. If you recognize handwriting, do your best to react to the answer, not the student.

6. Consider asking pupils to write essay-type analyses in the form of term papers rather than under examination conditions.

Short-Essay Items

Description: Student is asked to recall, supply, apply, or explain information about a specific point or points.

Example: Describe and explain the values of three characteristics of tests.

Advantages: Student is asked to recall (not merely recognize), apply, explain, or analyze what has been learned, a more practical and realistic kind of behavior than responding to cues supplied by others (as in objective items). Student gains experience in expressing ideas in writing, but there is emphasis on conveying meaning succinctly. Test preparation chores are not extreme—three or four questions might be arranged on a page with room for answers; or questions can be written on the board. Answers can be graded by assigning points depending on quality of answers or by grading answers plus or minus. Students reveal how much they understand, guessing and bluffing are reduced to a minimum since they either know the answer or don't know it. As the teacher reads papers, he or she acquires information that can be used to plan remedial instruction. It is possible to go over every question in class when exams are handed back.

Disadvantages: Take longer to score than objective tests. Scoring may not be consistent from one paper to another. Teacher may be influenced by such factors as handwriting and spelling. Teacher may be tempted to make up tests on the spur of the moment. Students in one class can tell friends in other classes what is on exams, which may make it necessary to devise a different exam for each class. Provide a less complete sample than objective tests.

Guidelines:

1. Resist the temptation to make up tests on spur of the moment. Try to choose a good sample of items derived from instructional objectives.

2. Immediately after you write an item, write out an acceptable answer. Use your answer to clarify the question and to grade answers.

3. Indicate the number of points each answer will count toward the total score.

4. As much as possible, ask students to translate, interpret, apply, analyze, and evaluate what they have learned. Try to stress types of learning at the higher levels of the taxonomy for the cognitive domain.

5. Have students write their names on the back of the last page of the exam.

As you think about which types of questions to use in a particular situation, consider the pupil characteristics and curriculum differences noted earlier. In the primary grades, you may not use any tests in the strict sense. Instead you might ask your pupils to demonstrate skills, complete exercises (some of which may be similar to completion tests), and solve simple problems (often on work sheets). In the elementary grades you may need to use or make up dozens of measurement instruments since so many subjects must be graded. Accordingly, it may be necessary to make extensive use of completion, short-answer, and short-essay items that can be printed on the board or on a ditto master. If you find it impossible or impractical to make up a table of specifications for each exam, at least refer to instructional objectives or a list of key points as you write questions. At the secondary level you might do your best to develop some sort of table of specifications for exams, not only to assure measurement of objectives at various levels of the taxonomy, but also to remind yourself to use different types of items.

Using different types of test items allows you to balance their advantages and disadvantages. If you teach older students, some questions are more appropriate than others for testing understanding at various levels of the taxonomy for the cognitive domain. In addition, you should try to allow for differences in cognitive style. As noted in Chapter 3, reflective thinkers perform better on tasks requiring analysis of details whereas impulsive thinkers perform better on tasks requiring synthesis and evaluation. Some children memorize much more easily than others, whereas some are better able to concentrate on several factors at once (which would be an advantage when pondering matching or multiple-choice questions). Some pupils are convergent thinkers and tend to give conventional answers, but others are divergent thinkers and tend to respond to questions in idiosyncratic ways (which might lead to problems with objective test items). If you use different types of questions on the same or different tests, you may give all pupils a chance to deal with at least some problems that "fit" their cognitive style.

In certain elementary grade subjects and in skill or laboratory subjects at the secondary level, the types of questions just described may not be appropriate. At the primary grade level, for instance, you may be required to assign a report grade in oral reading. In a high school home economics class, you may grade pupils on how well they produce a garment or a soufflé. In a woodshop class, you may base a grade on how well students construct a piece of furniture. You may grade students in a music class on instrumental or vocal performance and those

Handbook Heading:
Using Different Types of
Test Items

Rating scales and checklists make evaluations of performance more systematic

in a science class on how successfully they use laboratory equipment to carry out experiments. In such cases you can make evaluations more systematic and accurate by using *rating scales* and *checklists* and by attempting to equate (or at least take into account) the difficulty level of the performance to be rated.

To evaluate oral reading in the second grade, for instance, you might have pupils individually come to a quiet corner of the room and read the same passage. (If you simply went through a book, asking each pupil who came to you to read the next passage, some pupils would end up with much more difficult passages than others.) As they read, you might rate them on a five-point scale on such factors as pronunciation, clarity, fluency, absence of hesitation, and the like. Perhaps the best way to devise such rating scales is to listen to some sample readings of different material. As you listen, select aspects of the performance that strike you as important and ratable. Try to pick out types of behavior that can be described in specific terms and then write a description of each facet that you intend to rate.

To evaluate a product such as a garment or piece of furniture, you might use a checklist that you devised and handed out at the beginning of a course. Such a checklist should state the number of possible points that will be awarded for various aspects of the project, for example, accuracy of measurements and preparation of component parts, neatness of assembly, quality of finishing touches, final appearance, and so forth. To evaluate a performance, you might use the same approach, announcing beforehand how heavily you intend to weigh various aspects of execution. In music, for instance, you might note possible points to be awarded for tone, execution, accuracy, and interpretation. For both project and performance tasks, you might multiply the final score by a difficulty factor. (You have probably seen television coverage of Olympics events in which divers and gymnasts have their performance ratings multiplied by such a difficulty factor.)

Whenever you make ratings, you should try to allow for the sequencing of good and poor students. Any pupil who performs after the best student in a class is going to look poor by comparison. Anyone who follows the worst performer is going to look good. When making ratings you will need to try to avoid a tendency to rate all pupils at about the same level. Some raters start out with high ratings and then find they are unable to distinguish between good and excellent performers because the rating limit has been reached. Others tend to rate everyone average.

If you will be teaching secondary school subjects that will involve evaluation of projects or performance, you might jot down in your Handbook techniques used by your teachers. Note excellent evaluative approaches that you felt were fair and accurate as well as techniques to avoid at all costs.

Handbook Heading: Techniques for Evaluating Skills and Projects

5. Make up and use a detailed key.
   a. Evaluate each answer by comparing it to the key.

One of the most valuable characteristics of a test is that it permits comparison of the permanently recorded answers of all pupils to a fixed set of criteria. A complete key not only reduces subjectivity, it can also save you much time and trouble when you are grading papers and/or defending your evaluation of questions.

For short-answer, true-false, matching, or multiple-choice questions, you should devise your key as you write and assemble the items. With planning and ingenuity, you can prepare a key that will greatly simplify grading. Arrange the test items (or a separate answer sheet) so that answers will be recorded in an orderly fashion (in a column on one side of the page, for example). Then, cut a manila folder in half (or take a piece of heavy paper of the same general consistency) and prepare a template. First, take a piece of transparent paper and draw a circle or rectangle around the answer spaces. With carbon paper transfer these outlines to the heavier paper and punch or cut out openings. Print the word, phrase, or number of the answer next to each space. When the time comes to grade papers, place your template over each answer sheet and draw a red line through incorrect responses. All that remains is to tally the number of correct responses and record it on the answer sheet next to the pupil's name.

Preparing a key for essay or short-essay exams can be simplified if you follow the guidelines noted earlier in the analyses of these items. Perhaps the most important point to remember is to prepare answers *as* you write the questions. If you ask students to write answers to a small number of comprehensive essay questions, you are likely to maximize the consistency of your grading by grading all answers to the first question at one sitting, then grading all answers to the second question, and so on. If a test consists of eight or ten short-essay items (which can usually be answered in a half hour or so), it would require too much paper shuffling to follow such a procedure. One way to speed up the grading of short-essay exams (so that you can evaluate up to thirty tests in a single session of forty minutes or so) is to use plus-or-minus grading. If you use a point scale to grade short-essay answers, you will spend an agonizing amount of time deciding just how much a given answer is worth. With practice, you should be able to write short-essay questions and answers (on your key) that can be graded plus or minus. To develop skill in writing such questions, make up a few formative quizzes that will not count toward a grade. Experiment with phrasing questions that require students to reveal that they either know or don't know the answer. Prepare your key as you write the questions. When the time comes to grade papers, simply make a yes or no decision about the correctness of each answer. With a felt-tip pen make a bold check over each satisfactory answer on an exam, and simply tally the number of checks when you have read all the answers. (Counting up to eight or ten is obviously a lot quicker and easier than adding together various numbers of points for eight or ten answers.) Once you have developed skill in writing and evaluating short-essay questions that can be graded plus or minus, prepare and use summative exams. If you decide to use this type of

Handbook Heading:
Preparing a Detailed Key

The onerous chore of grading papers can be speeded up and simplified if plus-minus grading is used. (Susan Lapides)

exam, guard against the temptation to write items that measure only knowledge. Use a table of specifications or otherwise take steps to write at least some questions that measure skills at the higher levels of the taxonomy for the cognitive domain.

b. Be willing and prepared to defend the evaluations you make.

You will probably get few complaints if you have a detailed key and, when exams are returned, explain to the class how each answer was graded. To a direct challenge about a specific answer to an essay or short-essay question, you might respond by showing complainers an answer that received full credit and invite them to compare it with their own.

A major disadvantage of multiple-choice items is that it is very difficult to go over a multiple-choice test in class. At least one student may have selected each of the wrong alternatives and will want to explain why, while the other members of the class doze or fume as they wait to give *their* explanations—or make out a list of right answers to pass on to someone in another section. Going over a fifty-item test may take hours. It may take hours with just one student, particularly if he or she is a divergent thinker or argumentative. Because of such factors, instructors often simply report or post scores on multiple-choice exams and make no offer to discuss individual questions with students. The unfortunate result of such a policy is that it encourages students to think only about a score,

When returning exams to students, be prepared to explain how each answer was graded. Distributing feedback booklets to students is a good way to encourage them to think about the information covered in the test, instead of concentrating only on their scores. (Susan Lapides)

not about what they have learned (or failed to learn). Students also reason that as soon as a test is completed, the purpose for learning what was covered on the exam has been served, and information might as well be forgotten.

Perhaps the best way to encourage students to think about what has been covered in multiple-choice questions, instead of concentrating only on the score, is to prepare a *feedback booklet.* As you write each multiple-choice question, also write a brief explanation why you feel the answer is correct and why the distracters are incorrect. If you follow this policy (which takes less time than you might expect), you can often improve the questions as you write your defense of the answer. If you go a step further (to be described in the next point), you can obtain information to use in improving questions after they have been answered. This is a good policy to follow with any exam, multiple-choice or otherwise.

6. During and after the grading process, analyze questions and answers in order to improve future exams.

If you prepare sufficient copies of feedback booklets for multiple-choice exams, you can supply them to all pupils when you hand back scored answer sheets (and copies of the question booklets). After students have checked their papers and identified and examined questions that were marked wrong, invite them to select up to three questions that they wish to challenge. Even after they read your explanation in the feedback booklet, many students are likely to feel that they selected a different answer than you did for logical and defensible reasons. Permit them to write out a description of the reasoning behind their choices. If an explanation seems plausible, give credit for the answer. If several students chose the same questions for comment, you have evidence that the item needs to be revised.

If you follow the procedure of supplying feedback booklets, it is almost essential to prepare at least two forms of every exam. After writing the questions, arrange them into two tests. Have perhaps half of the questions the same, half unique to each exam. (If you have enough questions, you might prepare three forms.) If you teach multiple sections, give the first form to period 1, the next form to period 2, and thereafter use the forms in random order. This procedure will reduce the possibility that some students in later classes will have advance information about most of the questions on the test. (Having two or more forms also equips you to use a mastery approach, which will be described at the end of this chapter.)

If you find that you do not have time to prepare feedback booklets, you might invite students to select three answers to defend *as* they record their choices when taking multiple-choice exams. This will supply you with information about ambiguous questions even though it will not provide feedback to students. Allowing students to defend their answers to some or all of the items in other types of tests may also provide you with useful information about how well the items were written. If you discover, for example, that students supply a variety of wrong answers to a short-answer or completion item, you may conclude that the question was too ambiguous as written. (It's also possible that the information reflected in the item was not directly related to your objectives or was poorly taught.) As you read answers to essay and short-essay questions, you will often get quite direct insight into the word or phrase in a question that led students astray.

Turning back to multiple-choice questions, you may also want to use simple versions of item analysis techniques that measurement specialists use to analyze and improve this type of item. These techniques will allow you to estimate the difficulty level and discriminating power of each item. To do so, try the following steps suggested by Norman Gronlund (1988):

1. Rank the test papers from highest score to lowest score.
2. Select approximately the top one-third and call this the upper group. Select approximately the bottom one-third and call this the lower group. Set the middle group of papers aside.
3. For each item, record the number of students in the upper group and in the lower group who selected the correct answer and each distracter, as follows:

Handbook Heading: Analyzing Test Items

Item analysis tells about difficulty, discriminability of multiple-choice items

Item 1. Alternatives	A	B*	C	D	E
Upper Group	0	6	3	1	0
Lower Group	3	2	2	3	0

* = correct answer

4. Estimate item difficulty by calculating the percentage of students who answered the item correctly. The difficulty index for the above item is 40 percent (8/20 x 100). Note that the smaller the percentage the more difficult the item.
5. Estimate item discriminating power by subtracting the number in the lower group who answered the item correctly from the number in the upper group, and divide by one-half of the total number of students included in the item analysis. For the above example, the discrimination index is .40 (6 - 2 ÷ 10). When the index is positive, as it is here, it indicates that more students in the upper group than in the lower group answered the item correctly. A negative value indicates just the opposite.

As you can see, this type of item analysis is not difficult to do, nor is it likely to be very time consuming. In addition, it has several benefits that we will mention shortly. It is important to remember, though, that the benefits of item analysis can quickly be lost if you ignore certain limitations. One is that you will be working with relatively small numbers of students. Therefore, the results of item analysis are likely to vary as you go from class to class or from test to test with the same class. Because of this variation, you should retain items that a measurement specialist would discard or revise. In general, you should retain multiple-choice items whose difficulty index lies between 50 and 90 percent and whose discrimination index is positive (Gronlund, 1988; Hills, 1981). Another limitation is that you may have objectives that everyone must master. If you do an effective job of teaching these objectives, the corresponding test items are likely to be answered correctly by nearly every student. These items should be retained rather than revised to meet some arbitrary criteria of difficulty and discrimination.

If you keep these cautions in mind, item analysis can help you accomplish several useful measurement goals. First, it provides a vehicle for discussing the test. Easy items can be discussed briefly, difficult items (those around the 50 percent level) can be explained more fully, and defective items can be discarded rather than defended as fair. Second, item analysis reveals common errors and misconceptions and can thus serve as a basis for reteaching and restudy. Third, item analysis helps you improve your test-writing skills and assign grades in a fair and meaningful fashion (Gronlund, 1988).

Mid-Chapter Review

Nature of Measurement and Evaluation

Whenever we assign numbers to certain attributes of people (like typing ability or mathematical reasoning skills) according to a set of rules that allows us to rank people by how much of the attribute they possess, we are practicing measurement. Whenever we make judgments about the value or worth of the things we measure, we are practicing evaluation.

Types of Measures

The types of measures that most teachers use are performance tests and written tests. Performance tests are used to measure how well students perform a particular skill under somewhat realistic conditions. Depending on the teacher's objectives, they may be used to assess the adequacy of the underlying skills that go into a performance, the performance itself, or both.

Written tests are used to measure how much students know about some topic. Written test items are classified as objective or created-response depending on the type of response they require of the test taker and the resulting degree of subjectivity that enters into their scoring. Objective items include multiple-choice, true-false, matching, and interpretive. Created-response items include short-answer and essay.

Reducing Subjectivity

Pygmalion in the Classroom by Robert Rosenthal and Lenore Jacobson brought to light problems that subjectivity can create in measurement and evaluation of pupil performance. Rosenthal and Jacobson claimed that leading teachers to expect that certain pupils had untapped academic ability caused the teachers to treat those students differently, thereby causing their IQ scores to increase. Rosenthal and Jacobson called this phenomenon the *Pygmalion effect;* it is also known as the *self-fulfilling prophecy* and the *teacher expectancy effect.* While subsequent research demonstrated very modest and limited teacher expectancy effects on IQ scores, it did show much stronger and wider effects, both positive and negative, on classroom achievement and participation. Some of the factors that contribute to a teacher expectancy effect are gender, compliance, neatness, achievement, and attractiveness.

Effective Measurement and Evaluation Techniques

You can insure effective measurement and evaluation practice by adhering to the following six steps:

1. As early as possible, decide when and how often to give tests and other assignments.

2. Prepare a table of specifications to insure that you test all important subjects and outcomes.

3. Decide whether you want to test for the purpose of planning remedial instruction—a practice called *formative evaluation*—and/or for the purpose of determining how much was learned—a practice known as *summative evaluation.*

4. Decide whether you want to use objective items or created-response items, and which particular types.

5. Make up an answer key.

6. Analyze questions and answers to improve the quality of future exams.

Norm-Referenced Grading

The issue of grading is much discussed. One approach involves comparisons among students. Such forms of evaluation are called *norm-referenced* since students are identified as average (or normal), above average, or below average. An alternative approach is called *criterion-referenced* because performance is interpreted in terms of defined criteria. (As you may recall, these concepts were initially discussed in Chapter 4.) The remaining pages of this chapter discuss ways of using these two approaches.

The Nature of Norm-Referenced Grading

Under a norm-referenced system, grades are determined by comparing each student's level of performance to the "normal" or average level of other, similar students. The comparison may be to all other members of the student's class that year or it may be to the average performance of several classes stretching back over several years. It is probably better for teachers to use a broad base of typical student performance made up of several classes as grounds for comparison than to rely on the current class of students. Doing so avoids two severe distorting effects that can occur: When a single class contains many weak students, those with more well-developed abilities will more easily obtain the highest grades; if the class has many capable students, the weaker students are virtually predestined to receive low or failing grades (Hopkins & Antes, 1985; Kubiszyn & Borich, 1987).

> Norm-referenced grading: compare one student to others

A norm-referenced approach assumes that classroom achievement will naturally vary among a group of heterogeneous students because of differences in such characteristics as prior knowledge, learning skills, motivation, and aptitude. Thus, a typical norm-referenced test will reflect the assumed differences in amount of learned material, producing a distribution of scores that ranges from low to high, has few tied scores, has only a few very low scores, and has only a few very high scores.

Norm-referenced grading based on absence of external criteria

The rationale for the use of norm-referenced grading typically given by its proponents is that there are no good external criteria that can be used as a standard for evaluating and grading student performance. That is , there is no good way to externally determine how much learning is too little, just enough, or more than enough for some subject. Thus, if there is no amount of knowledge or set of behaviors that must be mastered by all students, then grades may be awarded on the basis of relative performance among a group of students (Hopkins & Antes, 1985).

One last point that should be mentioned is that grading on a norm-referenced basis does not necessarily mean that each class will have a normal distribution of grades or that anyone will automatically fail. It is possible, for example, for equal numbers of students to receive A's, B's, and C's. A norm-referenced approach simply means that the grading symbols used indicate one student's level of achievement relative to other students.

With these points in mind, let's turn now to a discussion of the mechanics of norm-referenced grading.

Depicting a Distribution of Scores

If you plan to establish grades by comparing one student to others in a class, it will obviously be essential for you to determine how test scores and other measures of student performance are distributed.

There are several ways to depict a distribution of scores. Perhaps the simplest is to take a sheet of lined paper and list the scores consecutively from lowest to highest. Then place a tally for each pupil beside the appropriate score (see Figure 12.2). If you are reasonably careful to put the tallies about the same distance from the margin, you will end up with a frequency distribution indicating how the scores are arranged. Just looking at the distribution will provide a good deal of information, but your interpretation of the relative values of the scores will be substantially clarified if you calculate the average score (the **mean**) or the middle score (the **median**). (In most school systems, a *C* grade reflects average performance.) Since the mean and median supply information about the central part of a distribution, they are called *measures of central tendency.*

Calculating a Measure of Central Tendency

The Mean   The mean is the arithmetical average compiled by adding up all the test scores and dividing the total by the number of scores. If you have between 30 and 150 pupils listed and an exam (or series of exams) with quite a few points, you are in for a good deal of figuring. It's difficult to do a sum like that in your head, and even if you use a small electronic calculator, the chore may take quite a bit of time. To simplify the job, you might follow the procedures shown in Figure 12.2. Multiply each score by the frequency of that score, add the resulting product, and then divide by the number of scores.

The mean is often computed by psychologists and test specialists because it is the first step in calculating a standard deviation (explained in Chapter 4). Although a researcher or person developing a standardized test may be interested in interpreting scores with reference to a normal curve (which can be done once standard scores are calculated), most classroom teachers do not share that interest because they hardly ever deal with groups of pupils who are distributed normally. In most classes, there are likely to be "abnormal" numbers of high or low students. Such abnormalities tend to distort the mean as a measure of central tendency because it is influenced by extreme scores. Therefore, you may find that it is preferable to calculate the median rather than the mean. The median has the advantage of being immune to the influence of extreme scores.

Mean influenced by extreme scores

The Median   The median is the middle score of distribution, and it can be figured simply by counting tallies. To find the median of the distribution depicted in Figure 12.2, first take the number of scores (33), add 1, and divide by 2. (The reason you add 1 is to find the middle score.) Thirty-four divided by 2 is 17, which means that the seventeenth tally from either the top or the bottom is the middle score in the distribution. If you count the tallies from either end of Figure 12.2, you will hit the score of 35, which is the approximate median for the distribution.[2]

Median: middle score, not influenced by extreme scores

With an odd number of scores, as in the distribution in Figure 12.2, you will always land on the same score when you count from top or bottom. With an even number of scores, you will end up halfway between two tallies that may be opposite different scores, for adding 1 to an even number of scores and dividing by 2 will always yield a 0.5 value. A simple way to allow for this is to circle both tallies that straddle the actual median. (To illustrate, add one more tally to the distribution in Figure 12.2 opposite 44 and then calculate the median. You should arrive at a median of 35.5.)

Converting Scores into Letter Grades

What you eventually do with your distribution of scores and your measure of central tendency depends on several factors. In some schools, particularly large ones where several teachers teach the same grade or offer the same course, you may be asked to follow guidelines that establish limits for different grades. You may be told to assign no more than 10 or 15 percent A's, for instance. If that is the case, you will have to comply with those guidelines. If you are *not* required to adhere to a strictly defined set of standards, perhaps the most desirable way to assign

2. A rather elaborate formula that takes into account the way scores are grouped is sometimes used to calculate the median when great precision is desired. The *exact* median of the distribution shown in Figure 12.2 is 35.375. For the purpose of assigning grades by using the approach described in this chapter, the "counting tallies" median of 35 is perfectly adequate and much, much easier to determine.

Figure 12.2   Frequency Distribution of Scores and Computation of the Mean

		Number of tallies (f)	Number of tallies times score (fX)
47	/	1	47
46	//	2	92
45	/	1	45
44			
43	/	1	43
42	/	1	42
41	//	2	82
40	/	1	40
39	//	2	78
38	/	1	38
37	//	2	74
36	//	2	72
35	////	4	140
34	///	3	102
33	//	2	66
32	//	2	64
31			
30	/	1	30
29	/	1	29
28	/	1	28
27	/	1	27
26			
25	/	1	25 $\frac{1188}{33} = 36$
24	/	1	24
		N=33	Total = 1188

Formula: Mean (M) = $\dfrac{\text{Sum total of scores } (\Sigma fX)}{\text{Number of scores (N)}}$

grades in a norm-referenced approach is to refer to the mean or median to establish the C range and then look for gaps and clusters in final distributions of total points. The advantage of this approach is that it allows *some* flexibility. It may sometimes happen that you will have an abnormally high or low proportion of excellent (or poor) students in a given class. You can allow for such situations more effectively if you look for clusters of total scores than if you drew the line that separates A students from B students at some predetermined point (under the score of the fifth student from the top, for example).

To gain some experience in using a flexible norm-referenced approach, imagine that you are either a fourth-grade teacher or a tenth-grade instructor of five sections of social studies.

If you expect to teach in the elementary grades, assume that you will be asked to assign grades of A, B, C, D, or F for *achievement* and O (Outstanding), S (Satisfactory), or N (Needs improvement) for *effort* in the following subject areas: reading, English, spelling, mathematics, social studies, science, health, music, art, and physical education. Assume that standard texts are used for reading, English, mathematics, social studies, science, and health, and that the publisher of each book has supplied examination materials, in the form of completion and short-answer questions. Assume further than you will make up your own short-answer exams and also assign projects of various kinds. Finally, assume that the first of four progress reports is to be presented to the parents in a personal conference; the other three reports are to be recorded on report cards.

You undoubtedly realize at this point that if you hope to assign grades fairly, objectively, and in a manner you can explain and defend to students and parents, you will need to be well organized. You should record some indication of pupil performance in each subject fairly regularly. Otherwise, the day and night (and perhaps early morning) before report cards are due, you will find yourself desperately trying to pull grades out of thin air. Therefore, before the school year starts, it would be wise to take a stab at drawing up a tentative master plan for evaluating each subject on the report card you will be expected to use. (Once you gain some experience, your master plan will be less tentative.)

Figure 12.3 represents a hypothetical page from a fourth-grade teacher's grade book (the same teacher who must record grades on the card described earlier). Assume that the information provided is to be used in assigning the first-period grade in social studies. The first two columns contain scores earned by pupils on twenty-item completion tests supplied by the publisher of the text. (Each item was worth one point.) The third column indicates the score on a ten-item short-answer test you prepared covering material shown in films and analyzed in class. (Each item was graded on a 3-point scale for a total of 30 points.) The fourth column records the score received for an individual project (15 points possible). The "total points" and "grade" columns are left blank in Figure 12.3 so that you can gain some experience computing totals and measures of central tendency and so that you can assign grades using norm-referenced procedures.

Figure 12.3   Page from a Fourth-Grade Teacher's Grade Book: Scores to Be Used to Determine Grade in Social Studies

	1st Exam (30 pts.)	2nd Exam (30pts.)	3rd Exam (60 pts.)	Term Project (30 pts.)	Total Points	Grade
Adams, Ann	28	26	56	26		
Baker, Charles	24	23	46	23		
Cohen, Matthew	22	20	42	22		
Davis, Rebecca	22	23	47	22		
Evans, Deborah	27	28	58	28		
Ford, Harold	14	13	30	20		
Grayson, Lee	21	22	44	22		
Hood, Barbara	25	24	51	26		
Ingalls, Robert	17	16	35	21		
Jones, Thomas	18	18	36	22		
Kim, David	29	30	58	29		
Lapine, Craig	25	26	56	27		
Moore, James	20	21	40	21		
Nguyen, Tuan	22	24	50	23		
Orton, John	19	18	37	21		
Peck, Nancy	25	24	49	24		
Quist, Ann	25	26	53	27		
Richards, Mary	21	23	44	25		
Santos, Maria	16	16	32	20		
Thomas, Eric	22	24	48	23		
Wong, Yuen	24	25	51	26		
Vernon, James	19	17	39	21		
Zacharias, Saul	20	22	44	22		

Total the scores earned by the students listed in Figure 12.3, make a frequency distribution of the total points, compute the mean and median of the distribution, and assign a grade to each pupil. (In the absence of information about personal characteristics and learning habits of the pupils listed, you cannot grade "effort," but you might think about how you would attempt to measure this quality.) After you have computed your totals, calculated measures of central tendency, and assigned grades, compare them to those arrived at by classmates. If you detect discrepancies between totals, means, medians, or grades, explain the procedures you followed to fellow students and invite them to do the same.

If you will be teaching one of the secondary grades, examine Figure 12.4. It presents a page from the grade book of the tenth-grade social studies teacher mentioned earlier. Assume that the students whose names and grades are recorded make up a section that has not been grouped in any way: that is, pupils were assigned in a random manner. The first two columns contain scores earned on thirty-item multiple-choice exams. (Each question was worth one point.) The third column indicates the score on an end-of-report-period exam made up of a variety of questions adding up to a total of 60 points. In the fourth column is the numerical score assigned to a term paper or individual study project.

The total point and grade columns in Figure 12.4 are left blank, so that you can gain some direct experience computing totals and measures of central tendency and determining grades. If you expect to teach at the secondary grade level, you are urged to total the scores for the students listed in Figure 12.4, make a frequency distribution of the totals, compute the mean and median of the distribution, and assign a grade to each pupil. Then compare your totals, your measures of central tendency, and your grades with those of classmates. If there are discrepancies, explain the procedures you followed, and invite classmates to do the same.

Whether or not you actually attempted to convert the scores in Figures 12.3 and 12.4 into grades, you probably appreciate the advantage in norm-referenced approaches of working with a spaced-out distribution of total scores. When you must divide pupils into four or five categories, it will be less agonizing for you—and for students who fall just below a cut-off point—if scores are spaced out with gaps between clusters of scores. Sometimes, as you will discover after you have prepared a few distributions, scores group themselves beautifully. You may get a small cluster of tallies at the top, followed by a gap of five or more points, followed by a somewhat larger cluster of tallies, followed by a gap, and so on down the line. At other times, scores will be spaced out at maddeningly even or perversely spaced intervals. When that happens, you may despair about where to draw lines between letter grades. In such situations, you might consider using one or more of the following strategies:

1. Draw the line separating grade levels *before* you know which tallies stand for which students. If you fail to follow this practice, you may be tempted to permit a

Figure 12.4   Page from a Secondary School Teacher's Grade Book

	1st Exam (20 pts.)	2nd Exam (20 pts.)	3rd Exam (30 pts.)	Project (15 pts.)	Total Points	Grade
Adams, Ann	15	16	20	10		
Baker, Charles	16	14	23	12		
Cohen, Matthew	18	18	26	14		
Davis, Rebecca	18	19	28	15		
Evans, Deborah	13	15	14	11		
Ford, Harold	9	10	14	5		
Grayson, Lee	16	14	21	11		
Hood, Barbara	14	14	21	10		
Ingalls, Robert	19	18	27	14		
Jones, Thomas	11	11	19	8		
Kim, David	18	17	26	13		
Lapine, Craig	15	15	18	9		
Moore, James	14	16	21	10		
Nguyen, Tuan	16	14	22	13		
Orton, John	17	16	23	12		
Peck, Nancy	15	15	22	9		
Quist, Ann	14	14	21	10		
Richards, Mary	15	15	22	11		
Santos, Maria	16	17	24	12		
Thomas, Eric	12	13	18	9		
Wong, Yuen	17	17	25	12		
Vernon, Joan	13	14	20	9		
Zacharias, Saul	15	16	22	13		

dividing line to sag under the tally representing a pupil you like or to hop over the tally representing a pupil you dislike.

2. After you draw dividing lines—and discover the identity of students who are just below each line—examine the pattern of scores earned by those students on various tests and assignments. If a pupil just below a line had a disastrous experience with an early test but showed steady improvement therafter, you might legitimately assign that pupil a higher grade. (If you follow this procedure, you should make an effort to keep your personal feelings about the student under control.)

3. To students who are up to five points or so below a dividing line, extend an invitation to write an extra report or take an additional test on topics that the student has not yet fully learned. If the report meets stipulated standards, award extra points and assign a higher grade. (To save trouble, point out that simply writing the paper does not guarantee a higher grade. The paper must meet the standards that have been agreed on.)

Perhaps the best way to minimize the need to resort to such strategies is to base grades on total scores that cover as wide a range as possible. The examples provided in Figure 12.3 and 12.4 were deliberately kept within a restricted range to reduce the amount of computation required. With *your* classes it would be better to base final grades on several tests and projects. (Even if the class range extends over 200 to 300 or more points, though, you may still discover that tallies will sometimes fall one or two points apart just where you feel obliged to draw a dividing line.)

When the time comes to figure total scores, consider this factor. The extent to which any test, paper, or project will influence a point total depends on the way the scores on each measure are distributed. If the scores on one exam are spaced out over a range of 40 to 98 points, for instance, and the scores on another supposedly equivalent exam are clustered together between 85 and 99 points, it is obvious that the score on the first exam will have a greater influence on point totals. For many students, performance on that single exam might account for the difference between one letter grade and another. There are statistical procedures to weight components so that they all contribute equally to total scores, but they tend to require a great deal of computation. Accordingly, you may wish to consider these nonstatistical methods to limit the tendency for one score to have a disproportionate impact on point totals: Try to make up exams of equivalent difficulty. Set scoring standards so that the mean and range are about the same on all measures. If scores on one exam tend to be much more widely spaced than scores on other exams, consider disregarding the wide-range exam when the time comes to figure final grades. (If you *want* a comprehensive final exam to count more than other tests, though, you may wish to have it call attention to differences between students to a greater extent than midterm exams. According to one procedure for estimating the relative impact on point totals of the various scores recorded in Figure 12.4, the third exam would determine approximately 42 percent of a student's final grade, the first and second exams would count 22 percent each, the project would count 14 percent. If the third exam was a comprehensive final, it might be desirable to have it count for almost twice as much as a midterm exam.)

By now you may have concluded that norm-referenced approaches to grading have a number of disadvantages. Even so, this approach is practiced in many schools and you may be required to use it. There is another method of evaluation, however, that allows you to meet school district requirements for assigning grades while at the same time shifting emphasis from competition against others to self-competition. The method that will now be described is a criterion-referenced approach that also incorporates features that permit students to benefit from mistakes and to improve their level of understanding and performance. Furthermore, it establishes an individual (and sometimes a cooperative) reward structure, which fosters motivation to learn to a greater extent than competitive reward structures found in most norm-referenced approaches.

Criterion-Referenced Grading

The Nature of Criterion-Referenced Grading

Criterion-referenced grading: compare individual performance to stated criteria

Under a criterion-referenced system, grades are determined by comparing the extent to which each student has attained a defined standard (or criterion) of achievement or performance. Whether the rest of the students in the class are successful or unsuccessful in meeting the criterion is irrelevant. Thus, any distribution of grades is possible. Every student may get an A or an F, or no student may receive these grades. For reasons we will discuss shortly, very low or failing grades tend to occur less frequently under a criterion-referenced system.

A common version of criterion-referenced grading assigns letter grades on the basis of the percentage of test items answered correctly. For example, you may decide to award an A to anyone who correctly answers at least 85 percent of a set of test questions, a B to anyone who correctly answers 75 to 84 percent, and so on down to the lowest grade. To use this type of grading system fairly, which means specifying realistic criterion levels, you will need to have some prior knowledge of the levels at which students typically perform. You will, then, be using normative information to establish absolute or fixed standards of performance. But while norm-referenced and criterion-referenced grading systems both spring from a normative data base (that is, comparisons among students), the former system uses those comparisons to directly determine grades, whereas the latter uses the same comparisons to establish criteria, and how well the student masters the criteria determines the grade.

Criterion-referenced grading systems (and criterion-referenced tests) have become increasingly popular in recent years primarily because of three factors.

First, educators and parents complained that norm-referenced tests and grading systems provided too little specific information about student strengths and weaknesses. Second, educators have come to believe that clearly stated, specific objectives constitute performance standards, or criteria, that are best assessed with criterion-referenced measures. Third, and perhaps most important, contemporary theories of school learning claim that most, if not all, students can master most school objectives under the right circumstances. If this assertion is even close to being true, then norm-referenced grading procedures, which depend on variability in performance, will lose much of their appeal. This third notion underlies what is often referred to as *mastery learning* and stems in large part from the work of John B. Carroll (1963) and Benjamin Bloom (1968, 1976).

Criterion-referenced grading: compare individual performance to stated criteria

A Mastery Approach to Learning and Instruction

John B. Carroll (1963) supplied the impetus for the emergence of **mastery learning.** He proposed that the focus of instruction should be the *time* required for different students to learn a given amount of material. He suggested that teachers should allow more time and provide more and better instruction for students who learn less easily and less rapidly than their peers.

Benjamin Bloom (1968) used the Carroll model as the basis for a statement in favor of mastery learning. The traditional approach, he argued, promotes the concept that if a normal distribution of students (with respect to aptitude for a subject) is exposed to a standard curriculum, achievement after instruction will be normally distributed. This approach, Bloom maintains, causes both teachers and students to expect that only a third of all students will adequately learn what is being taught, and this expectation leads to a disastrous self-fulfilling prophecy.

Expectations of a normal distribution leads to low aspirations

> This set of expectations, which fixes the academic goals of teachers and students, is the most wasteful and destructive aspect of the present educational system. It reduces the aspirations of both teachers and students; it reduces motivation for learning in students; and it systematically destroys the ego and self-concept of a sizeable group of students who are legally required to attend school for 10 to 12 years under conditions which are frustrating and humiliating year after year (1968, p. 1).

Here is the alternative Bloom suggests:

> Most students (perhaps over 90 percent) can master what we have to teach them, and it is the task of instruction to find the means which will enable our students to master the subject under consideration. Our basic task is to determine what we mean by mastery of the subject and to search for the methods and materials which will enable the largest proportion of our students to attain such mastery (1968, p. 1).

The widespread and effective use of mastery learning was stimulated by the formulation of desirable ways to devise instructional objectives (the work of

Mager and Gronlund, for example), comprehensive descriptions of the hierarchical nature of learning (such as the various taxonomies of educational objectives), and complete instructional systems (such as Individually Prescribed Instruction and computer-assisted instruction).

Ingredients of a Successful Mastery Approach   Carroll observed that "teaching ought to be a simple matter if it is viewed as a process concerned with the management of learning" (1971, p. 29). He suggested that the teacher's function is to follow this procedure:

Mastery approach: give pupils multiple opportunities to master goals at own pace

Specify what is to be learned.

Motivate pupils to learn it.

Provide instructional materials [to foster learning].

[Present] materials at a rate appropriate for different pupils.

Monitor students' progress.

Diagnose difficulties and provide remediation.

Give praise and encouragement for good performance.

Give review and practice.

Maintain a high rate of learning over a period of time (1971, pp. 29–30).

The following suggestions, which can be adapted for use at any grade level and in any subject area, are based on Carroll's outline:

Handbook Heading: Making the Most of Mastery Learning

1. Go through a unit of study, a chapter of a text, or an outline of a lecture and pick out what you consider to be the most important points—that is, those points you wish to stress because they are most likely to have later value or are basic to later learning.

2. List these points in the form of a goal card, instructional objectives (as described by Mager or Gronlund), key points, or the equivalent. If appropriate, arrange the objectives in some sort of organized framework, perhaps with reference to the relevant taxonomy of educational objectives.

3. Distribute the list of objectives at the beginning of a unit. Tell your students that they should concentrate on learning those points and that they will be tested on them.

4. Consider making up a study guide in which you provide specific questions relating to the objectives and a format that students can use to organize their notes.

5. Use a variety of instructional methods and materials to explain and illustrate objectives-related ideas.

6. Make up exam questions based on the objectives and the study guide questions. Try to write several questions for each objective.

7. Arrange these questions into at least two (preferably three) alternate exams for each unit of study.

8. Make up tentative criteria for grade levels for each exam and for the entire unit or report period (for example, A—not more than one question missed on any exam; B—not more than two questions missed on any exam; C—not more than four questions missed on any exam).

9. Test students either when they come to you and indicate they are ready or when you feel they have all had ample opportunity to learn the material. Announce all exam dates in advance, and remind students that the questions will be based only on the objectives you have mentioned. Indicate the criteria for different grade levels, and emphasize that any student who fails to meet a desired criterion on the first try will have a chance to take an alternate form of the exam.

10. Grade and return the exams as promptly as possible; go over questions briefly in class (particularly those that caused problems for more than a few students); and offer to go over exams individually with students. Allow for individual interpretations, and give credit for answers you judge to be logical and plausible, even if they differ from the answer you expected.

11. Schedule make-up exams and make yourself available for consultation and tutoring the day before. (While you are giving make-up exams, you can administer the original exam to students who were absent.)

12. If the students improve their score on the second exam but still fall below the desired criterion, consider a safety valve option: Invite them to provide you with a completed study guide (or the equivalent) when they take an exam the second time, or give them an open-book exam on the objectives they missed to see whether they can explain them in terms other than those of a written examination. If a student fulfills either of these options satisfactorily, give credit for one extra answer on the second exam.

13. To supplement exams, assign book reports, oral reports, papers, or some other kind of individual work that will provide maximum opportunity for student choice. Establish and explain the criteria you will use to evaluate these assignments, but stress that you want to encourage freedom of choice and expression. (Some students will thrive on free choice, but others are likely to feel threatened by open-ended assignments. To allow for such differences, provide specific directions for those who need them and general hints or a simple request that "original" projects be cleared in advance for the more independent thinkers.) Grade all reports Pass or Do Over, and supply constructive criticism on those you consider unsatisfactory. Announce that all Do Over papers can be reworked and resubmitted within a certain period of time. Have the reports count toward the final grade; for example, three reports for an A, two for a B, one for a C. (The student should also pass each exam at the designated level.) You might also invite pupils to prepare extra papers to earn bonus points to be added to exam totals.

This basic technique will permit you to work within a traditional A to F framework, but in such a way that you should be able, without lowering standards, to increase the proportion of students who do acceptable work. It will also permit you to make the most of the procedures suggested by Carroll, and to use an individual reward structure.

Focus on Stating Objectives   One of the advantages of a criterion-referenced approach to grading is that it focuses attention on instructional objectives. Even if you try to be conscientious about drawing up a table of specifications when preparing exams in a norm-referenced approach, you may still fail to measure objectives in a systematic or comprehensive way. With a mastery approach, however, you are following the recommendations made by those who urge use of instructional objectives. Mager offered these guidelines:

Identify and describe the terminal behavior.

Define the important conditions under which the behavior is to occur.

Define the criterion of acceptable performance.

This is exactly the procedure you will follow if you use a mastery approach. Stating objectives in precise terms and focusing on specific terminal behavior at a specified level of performance also permits you to treat instruction as if it were a branching program. Some students may achieve unit objectives on their first try and go on to the next unit. Students who have problems reaching the desired criterion level on their first effort are given additional instruction and another opportunity to show that they can perform at an acceptable level. This approach is more likely to lead to understanding and to encourage transfer than any approach that permits only one try and reports results only in terms of relative position.

Criteria for Different Letter Grades   One of the most crucial decisions in a mastery approach centers on the criteria you establish for different grade levels. If you hope to defend grades to parents, fellow teachers, and administrators, you should do everything possible to make sure that an A in your class is equivalent to an A in your colleagues' classes. James H. Block (1971) has reported that the proportion of A grades in mastery classes is typically higher than in traditional classes, not because of low standards but because more students are motivated to do A and B work. Therefore, you should be well prepared to defend your grades by retaining copies of exams and the keys used to evaluate them and by explaining the criteria for different grade levels. As Tom Kubiszyn and Gary Borich have pointed out, "it is a curious fact of life that everyone presses for excellence in education, but many balk at marking systems that make attainment of excellence within everyone's reach" (1987, p. 142).

In establishing criteria, refer to the discussion on instructional objectives in Chapter 6, particularly the observations of Mager (p. 281) and Gronlund (p. 283).

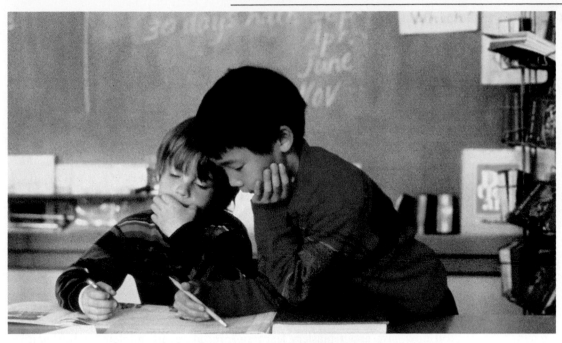

One of the advantages of mastery learning is that students may help each other learn because they are not competing against each other to earn high grades. (Elizabeth Crews/The Image Works)

You might set up standards for an exam in terms of the percentage of correct answers, the number of correct answers provided within a given time limit, or a sample of applications. An approach that has worked well in practice is to make up ten-question exams, grade each answer plus or minus, and use these standards: zero or one wrong—A, two wrong—B, three wrong—C, four wrong—D.

As noted earlier, plus or minus grading has definite advantages. It not only provides a definite number of correct and incorrect answer, but it also simplifies and speeds up grading. If you make up exams with an equivalent number of questions but evaluate each on a 5-point scale, you will be forced to read each answer with great care and then make a studied judgment of its relative value. If you use a plus or minus approach, you simplify both the judging and totaling of the final score. In many cases, you will find that the answer is obviously right or wrong and that you can evaluate it in a matter of seconds. You can read more carefully answers that are marginal, and if you eventually do mark them minus, you can do so knowing that the student will have another chance. And it is obviously much simpler to count the number of wrong answers than to add up ten scores ranging in value from 1 to 5. With practice, you may find grading exams so quick that you will be able to provide feedback the next day.

Limitations of Mastery Learning

On the basis of the evidence presented so far, you might be tempted to conclude that mastery learning is the ideal way to teach and to learn. While such optimism is understandable, it would also be somewhat premature and misplaced. The history of education is filled with innovative ideas (programmed instruction, discovery learning, and computer-assisted instruction, among others) that promised to maximize each student's achievements only to fall short of that goal. Given the complexity of school learning and the strong differences among students, it would have been truly amazing if any of these ideas had fully lived up to its promise. However, many of these same practices have made positive contributions to the improvement of learning. So it is with mastery learning. On the one hand, the research findings demonstrate that students taught under mastery conditions often learn more than students taught under nonmastery conditions (for example, Slavim, 1987; Block, Efthim & Burns, 1989). On the other hand, mastery learning is not without its problems, any one of which may limit its effectiveness. Some of these problems are inherent in the technique and probably cannot be totally eliminated. The remaining problems are often the result of misconceptions as to what mastery learning can and cannot accomplish or abuses of the technique due to an inadequate understanding of how it should be practiced. Taking the knowledge you now have about mastery learning (procedures for implementation and research findings) and considering the following problems, you will be able to make an informed decision as to whether or not to try it in your own classroom.

Some of the following criticisms of mastery learning are derived from points made by D.J. Mueller (1973) and W. F. Cox and T. G. Dunn (1979).

Mastery learning has several potential limitations

1. Mastery learning requires careful planning, preparation of several sets of evaluation materials, and extensive monitoring of student progress. Accordingly, it requires more teacher time and effort than conventional instruction.
2. The standard for mastery may be difficult to establish or defend.
3. Students may practice the "principle of least effort" by not studying for first exams on the assumption that they will pick up test-taking hints when they examine questions. As a result, the teacher will have to administer and score several exams.
4. Since some students inevitably achieve mastery faster than others, it is necessary to devise alternative assignments for those who have passed tests at an acceptable level on the first try.

All of these limitations can be overcome, however, with effort and ingenuity.

Being Realistic About Mastery Learning   Although this discussion of mastery learning has been intended to make you enthusiastic about the approach, you should be aware that it is not a panacea. For one thing, some students will disappoint, if not infuriate, you by the lengths they will go to in trying to beat the system—even after you have done everything in your power to make the system fair, just, and sensible.

Under a mastery approach, you are most likely to be able to improve the learning, attitudes, and self-concept of the typical C student. Those who have previously felt incapable of competing for high grades might give it a try in a mastery scheme. and many who try are likely to learn more and earn higher grades than they ever have under norm-referenced educational practices. Students who find it difficult to learn, however, may feel even more inadequate under a mastery approach than under a traditional approach. When every opportunity to learn is provided and slow students are still unable to respond and do as well as their classmates, it is more difficult for them to blame the system.

Mastery learning reduces competition and comparisons, but it does not eliminate them. Students who learn easily will meet the criterion for an A with little effort; they are likely to go through the required sequence so rapidly that they have considerable time for independent study. Those who learn slowly will engage in a constant battle to keep up with the required work. Because fortunate students learn faster and can engage in more self-selected study, they will probably get further and further ahead of their less capable classmates. Despite suggestions that prestige colleges ought to practice open admissions, it is most unlikely that they will do so. Furthermore, the number of jobs at the top of a scale based on interest, pay, and influence will always be limited. A mastery approach cannot by itself alter the fact that students who learn easily and rapidly are still likely to be rewarded by admission to the best colleges and to get the best jobs. Even so, you may discover that a mastery approach is well worth the extra time, effort, and trouble it requires. A greater proportion of your students will probably learn more, enjoy school more, develop better attitudes toward learning, and feel more confident and proud of themselves than they would under comparative-grading techniques. Just don't expect miracles, and be prepared for the fact that some of your students—no matter how hard they try or how much assistance you give them—will still be unable to do as well as most of their classmates in the time available.

Mastery learning does not eliminate competition and comparisons

Converting Scores into Letter Grades

To gain some direct experience with differences between norm-referenced and criterion-referenced grading, assume once again that you either teach fourth grade or instruct five sections of tenth-grade social studies. This time, however, assume that you have decided to use a mastery approach. Figure 12.5 depicts one way a teacher at *any* grade level might record grades when using mastery learning.

The first difference you will notice between the grade book page depicted in Figure 12.5 and the pages shown in Figures 12.3 and 12.4 is that there are two columns under each exam heading. The page has room for two scores because a mastery approach urges pupils to find out what errors they made on the first try on an exam, ask for clarification, study further (with or without teacher assistance), and take an alternate form of the exam in an effort to improve their score.

Figure 12.5   Page from a Teacher's Grade Book: Mastery Approach Featuring Point Grading

	1st Exam		2nd Exam		3rd Exam		Exam Total Points	Projects			Grade
	1st Try	2nd Try	1st Try	2nd Try	1st Try	2nd Try		1	2	3	
Adams, Ann	16	18	17	18	18			P	P	P	
Baker, Charles	13	14	14		10	14		P			
Cohen, Matthew	14	16	15	16	17			P	P		
Davis, Rebecca	19		19		20			P	P	P	
Evans, Deborah	16	18	17	18	16	18		P	P	P	
Ford, Harold	15	16	17		15			P	P		
Grayson, Lee	10	13	12	14	12	15		P			
Hood, Barbara	16		17		15			P	P		
Ingalls, Robert	16	18	16		15			P	P		
Jones, Thomas	11	14	12	16	15			P			
Kim, David	18		19		19			P	P	P	
Lapine, Craig	14	16	18		16			P	P		
Moore, James	17		17		17			P	P		
Nguyen, Tuan	17	18	19		16	17		P	P	P	
Orton, John	10	10	11		9						
Peck, Nancy	14		15		14			P			
Quist, Ann	16	18	17	18	18			P	P	P	
Richards, Mary	16		17		15			P	P		
Santos, Maria	13		15		14			P			
Thomas, Eric	15	16	15	17	15			P	P		
Wong, Yuen	14		15		16			P			
Vernon, Joan	11	14	13	14	12	14		P			
Zacharias, Saul	16	18	17		16	19		P	P	P	

The obvious advantage of this policy is that students who do less well than they had hoped on a first exam will feel motivated to try harder—instead of giving up, which is a common response when an exam is given only once.

Another difference between the grade records shown in Figures 12.3 and 12.4 and the one in Figure 12.5 is that the mastery plan record sheet shows space for grades on three projects, not just one. One reason for assigning more projects is that you can collect a more representative sample of students' knowledge and skills. (A multiple-project policy can also be used in a norm-referenced approach, but it is illustrated in this chapter only in the mastery approach.)

You can figure grades using data presented in Figure 12.5 by assuming that the following information was distributed to students on the first day of the report period.

Instructions for Determining Your Grade in Social Studies

Your grade in social studies this report period will be based on scores on three exams (worth 20 points each) and satisfactory completion of up to three projects.

Here are the standards for different grades:

A—Average of 18 or more on three exams, plus three projects at Pass level

B—Average of 16 or 17 on three exams, plus two projects at Pass level

C—Average of 14 or 15 on three exams, plus one project at Pass level

D—Average of 10 to 13 on three exams

F—Average of 9 or less on three exams

Another way to figure your grade is to add together points as you take exams. This may be the best procedure to follow as we get close to the end of the report period. Use this description of standards as a guide:

A—At least 54 points, plus three projects at the Pass level

B—48 to 53 points, plus two projects at Pass level

C—42 to 47 points, plus one project at Pass level

D—30 to 41 points

F—29 points or less

If you are not satisfied with the score you earn on any exam, you may take a different exam on the same material in an effort to improve your score. (Some of the questions on the alternate exam will be the same as those on the original exam; some will be different.) Projects will be graded P (Pass) or DO (Do Over). If you receive a DO on a project, you may work to improve it and hand it in again. You may also submit an *extra* project, which may earn up to 3 points of bonus credit (and can help if your exam scores fall just below a cut-off point). As you take each exam and receive a Pass for each project, record your progress on this chart.

First Exam		Second Exam		Third Exam		Project 1	Project 2	Project 3	Extra Project	Grade
1st Try	2nd Try	1st Try	2nd Try	1st Try	2nd Try					

Figure 12.6   Page from a Teacher's Grade Book: Mastery Approach Featuring + or − Grading

	1st Exam		2nd Exam		3rd Exam		Projects			Grade
	1st Try	2nd Try	1st Try	2nd Try	1st Try	2nd Try	1	2	3	
Adams, Ann	2	1	1		1		P	P	P	
Baker, Charles	4	3	4	3	5	3	P			
Cohen, Matthew	3		3		4	3	P			
Davis, Rebecca	2		2		2		P	P		
Evans, Deborah	3		4	3	3		P			
Ford, Harold	6	3	4	3	4	3	P			
Grayson, Lee	2	1	2	1	1		P	P	P	
Hood, Barbara	1		0		1		P	P	P	
Ingalls, Robert	3	2	2		3	2	P	P		
Jones, Thomas	5	4	4		4					
Kim, David	0		1		0		P	P	P	
Lapine, Craig	4	3	3		3		P			
Moore, James	3	2	2		2		P	P		
Nguyen, Tuan	3	2	3	2	3	2	P	P		
Orton, John	3	2	2		2		P	P		
Peck, Nancy	2	1	2	1	1		P	P		
Quist, Ann	3	2	4	2	2		P	P		
Richards, Mary	2	1	2	1	1		P	P	P	
Santos, Maria	4	2	3	2	3	2	P	P		
Thomas, Eric	2	1	1		1		P	P	P	
Wong, Yuen	4	3	3		3		P			
Vernon, Joan	5	3	4	3	4	3	P			
Zacharias, Saul	3	1	2	1	3	1	P	P	P	

Instructions for Determining Your Grade in Social Studies

Your grade in social studies this report period will be based on scores on three exams and successful completion of up to three projects. The exams will consist of ten questions each, and your answers will be graded plus or minus. The projects will be graded P (Pass) or DO (Do Over). Here are the standards for different grades:

A—Miss not more than one question on any exam, three projects at Pass level

B—Miss not more than two questions on any exam, two projects at Pass level

C—Miss not more than three questions on any exam, one project at Pass level

D—Miss four questions on any exam

F—Miss five or more questions on all three exams

If you are not satisfied with the grade you earn on any exam, you may take a different form of the exam to try and improve your score. (Some of the questions on the alternate form of the exam will be the same as those on the original exam; some will be different.) You may hand in an extra project, which may earn up to two bonus points (and can help if you fall just below the cutoff point on one or two exams).

If you eventually attempt a mastery approach using techniques similar to those just described, keep in mind the following procedures:

Try to set aside a specified period one day each week for exams. When deciding how many exams to give, be sure to allow at least two days for each exam. If possible, also schedule at least one make-up exam day.

Grade and return papers and exams as soon as possible so that students will know whether or not to study for a second try. If you use a point-per-exam approach, it is preferable to make up multiple-choice exams that can be graded as quickly as students finish them. If you prefer short-essay questions, try using plus or minus grading. It is considerably simpler and faster than point grading.

On second-exam days allow students who were satisfied with grades earned on the first try to work on projects or to engage in individualized study.

Start using grade standards that reflect the traditional pattern of 90 percent and above for an A, 80 to 89 percent for a B, and so forth. If it turns out that less than 10 percent of your pupils are earning A's after the first exam, it is possible that these standards are too high and should be lowered. Before drawing that conclusion, however, realize that there are several possible causes of poor test performance and low test grades, and that the other possibilities should be examined before you alter grading practices. You may find, for example, that several test items were vaguely worded, that some items did not adequately reflect course objectives, that the students did not prepare properly for the test, that they did not understand the material, or that you did not allow sufficient time for them to master the material. If you find that one or more of these factors could be responsible for lower than expected grades, apply corrective action and observe the effect on another exam before lowering your standards.

Try following either the first set of instructions to figure the grade for each pupil listed in Figure 12.5 or the second set of instructions to figure the grade for each pupil in Figure 12.6. When you have finished, compare the time and effort mastery grades take to the time and effort you spend calculating norm-referenced grades. In addition, compare your mastery grades with those assigned by classmates to identify any arithmetic errors that might have been made. Finally, speculate about how students would respond to a mastery approach as compared to norm-referenced grading techniques.

Suggestions for Further Study
Suggestions for Writing Test Items

For specific suggestions on ways to write different types of items for paper-and-pencil tests of knowledge and on how to construct and use rating scales and checklists to measure products, performances, and procedures, consult one or more of the following books: *Measurement and Evaluation in Teaching* (5th ed., 1985) by Norman E. Gronlund, *How to Construct Achievement Tests* (4th ed., 1988) by Norman E. Gronlund, *Educational Testing and Measurement* (2nd ed., 1987) by Tom Kubisyzn and Gary Borich, *Classroom Testing: Construction* (2nd ed., 1989) by Charles D. Hopkins and Richard L. Antes, *Educational Measurement and Testing* (1985) by William Wiersma and Stephen G. Jurs.

Writing Higher-Level Questions

As Benjamin Bloom and others have pointed out, teachers have a disappointing tendency to write test items that reflect the lowest level of the taxonomy—knowledge. To avoid this failing, carefully read Part II (pp. 62–200) of *Taxonomy of Educational Objectives, Handbook I: Cognitive Domain* (1956), edited by Benjamin Bloom. Each level of the taxonomy is clearly explained and is followed by several pages of illustrative test items.

Making Up Sample Test Items

A good way to become aware of the difficulties and complexities of evaluation (as well as to understand different types of tests) is to devise some test questions. Compose several kinds of questions based on a chapter or two from this text or from a text in a subject you hope to teach. Refer to the guidelines in this chapter for writing different types of questions (and/or consult one of the books mentioned above). Be sure to make up your key as you write the questions. Then ask one or two classmates to take your test. Request that they not only record their answers but also add any critical remarks about the strengths and weaknesses of specific items. Summarize the answers and criticisms, and draw up a list of guidelines to follow when you construct classroom examinations.

Analyzing Test Items

Norman Gronlund briefly discusses item analysis procedures for norm-referenced and criterion-referenced tests in Chapter 7 of *Constructing Achievement Tests* (4th ed., 1988). For norm-referenced multiple-choice tests, these include procedures for assessing the difficulty of each item, the discriminating power of each item, and the effectiveness of each alternative answer. For criterion-referenced tests, they include a measure for assessing the effects of instruction. More detailed discussions of item-analysis procedures can be found in Chapter 8 of *Educational Testing and Measurement* (2nd ed., 1987) by Tom Kubiszyn and Gary Borich and Chapter 13 of *Essentials of Educational Measurement* (4th ed., 1986) by Robert L. Ebel and David A. Frisbie.

Mastery Learning

If you would like to read comprehensive analyses of mastery learning, look for one of these books: *Human Characteristics and School Learning* (1976) by Benjamin S. Bloom, *All Our Children Learning* (1981) by Benjamin S. Bloom, *Improving Student Achievement Through Mastery Learning Programs* (1985) edited by Daniel H. Levine, and *Building Effective Mastery Learning Schools* (1989) by James H. Block, Helen E. Efthim, and Robert B. Burns.

Summary

1. Measurement involves ranking individuals according to how much of a particular characteristic they possess. Evaluation involves making judgments about the value or worth of a set of measures.
2. Performance tests are used to measure how well people perform a particular skill or produce a particular product under somewhat realistic conditions. The main types of performance tests are paper-and-pencil, identification, simulation, and work sample.
3. Written tests are used to measure how much knowledge people have about some topic. Test items can be classified as objective (multiple-choice, true-false, matching, interpretive) or created-response (short-answer, essay).
4. The teacher expectancy effect, also known as self-fulfilling prophecy or the Pygmalion effect, occurs when teachers communicate a particular expectation about how a student will perform and the student's behavior changes so as to be consistent with the expectation.

5. Although the effect of teacher expectancy on IQ scores originally reported by Rosenthal and Jacobson has never been fully replicated, research has demonstrated that teacher expectancy strongly affects classroom achievement and participation in both positive and negative ways.

6. Factors that seem to play a strong role in producing a teacher expectancy effect include a student's gender, compliance, neatness, achievement, and attractiveness.

7. To be sure that the number of various types of items on a test is consistent with your instructional objectives, prepare a table of specifications.

8. To determine how well students are learning and whether any sort of remedial instruction is needed, use formative evaluation. To determine how much of a topic has been learned so that you can assign grades, use summative evaluation.

9. Checklists and rating scales are often used to measure the performance of a skill.

10. Item analysis procedures exist to determine the difficulty and discriminability of multiple-choice items.

11. When grades are determined according to a norm-referenced system, each student's level of performance is compared to the performance of a group of similar students. Grading is competitive. A norm-referenced scheme is used by those who feel that external criteria for determining the adequacy of performance are unavailable.

12. In a criterion–referenced grading system, each student's level of performance is compared to a predetermined standard.

13. Related to criterion-referenced measurement and evaluation is the concept of mastery learning. As proposed by John Carroll and Benjamin Bloom, mastery learning holds that student achievement is largely a function of the amount of time a student is allotted for learning.

Key Terms

measurement *(584)*
evaluation *(584)*
self-fulfilling prophecy *(590)*
table of specifications *(596)*
formative evaluation *(602)*

summative evaluation *(602)*
mean *(622)*
median *(622)*
mastery learning *(631)*

Discussion Questions

1. Because students in American schools feel considerable pressure to obtain high grades, a significant number of them feel driven to cheat. Knowing that you will almost certainly have to give tests and assign grades on one basis or another, what might you do to reduce your students' tendency to cheat?

2. Over the last ten to twelve years you have probably taken hundreds of classroom tests. What types of tests best reflected what you learned? Why?

3. A norm-referenced approach to grading is often called grading on the curve. Have you ever taken a class where grades were determined in this fashion? Did you feel as if your grade accurately reflected how much you had learned? If not, explain why the grade was too low or too high.
4. Proponents of mastery learning argue that most students can master most subjects if they receive good-quality instruction and are allowed sufficient time to learn the material. On the basis of your own experience, would you agree with this assumption? Why?

5

Maintaining an Effective Learning Environment

CLASSROOM MANAGEMENT

KEY POINTS

Analyzing Your Techniques of Classroom Management

Ripple effect: group response to a reprimand directed at an individual

Teachers who show they are with it head off discipline problems

Being able to handle overlapping activities helps classroom control

Teachers who continually interrupt activities have discipline problems

Keeping entire class involved and alert minimizes misbehavior

Identify misbehavers, firmly specify constructive behavior

Well-managed classroom: students complete clear assignments in busy but pleasant atmosphere

Effective teachers plan how to handle classroom routines

During first weeks, have students complete clear assignments under your direction

Suggestions for Teaching

Establish and call attention to class rules the first day

Establish a businesslike but supportive classroom atmosphere

Violence in American Schools

Violence most likely in inner-city junior high schools with weak administrators

Analyzing Reasons for Violence

Male aggressiveness due to hormonal and cultural factors

Junior high-age boys with low grades may feel trapped

Misbehavior of high school students may reveal lack of positive identity

Violence least likely when students invited to participate in making decisions

Reducing School Violence

School violence can be reduced by improving student achievement levels

Violence less likely when students invited to participate in making decisions

Suggestions for Teaching

Be prompt, consistent, and reasonable when dealing with misbehavior

First ignore misbehavior, then stress rewards; use punishment as a last resort

Influence Techniques

Use supportive reactions to help students develop self-control

Give criticism privately, then offer encouragement

I-Messages and the No-Lose Method

I-message: tell how you feel about an unacceptable situation

No-lose method: come to mutual agreement about a solution to a problem

---

The discussion of classroom evaluation you just read completes the four-phase cycle of the model of learning that was outlined in Chapter 1. Part One asked you to take into account what students are like by becoming familiar with typical characteristics of pupils at different age levels, as well as with pupil variability. Part Two acquainted you with a variety of ways to state and use instructional objectives. Part Three described methods for arranging instructional experiences by taking into account the research and speculations of behavioral, cognitive, and humanistic psychologists. In addition, it discussed ways to motivate students by considering each of those views. Part Four outlined techniques for determining if students *have* learned and gave special emphasis to evaluating the mastery of objectives.

You are now equipped with information you can use to take into account pupil characteristics and make allowances for pupil variability. You can refer to the taxonomies, suggestions, and examples in Chapter 6 to make constructive use of instructional objectives. By drawing on the information provided in Part Three, you can prepare systematic sequences of learning experiences, arrange for students to make at least some of their own discoveries, and encourage awareness of the affective side of learning, as well as sensitivity to interpersonal relationships. You are familiar with various views of motivation and with dozens of specific motivational techniques. The chapter you just finished acquainted you with ways to make efficient use of appropriate forms of evaluation to determine if your students have achieved objectives. Information in each of the chapters you have read so far, therefore, can help you build your skills as a teacher, but your effectiveness in the classroom is likely to be enhanced if you think about ways to *orchestrate* what you have learned and combine techniques in coordinated ways. The first part of this chapter describes guidelines you might follow in order to establish and maintain an effective learning environment in which you make coordinated use of techniques described in earlier chapters.

Even though you do an excellent job of "getting it all together," however, certain factors and conditions will be beyond your control. Inevitably, some students will fail to respond to your efforts as positively as others. In addition to individual differences in responsiveness to you and to schooling, there are certain general characteristics or tendencies typical of pupils at different ages (and at all ages) that may lead to perennial kinds of classroom problems. Accordingly, you will occasionally need to deal with disruptive behavior. The second part of this chapter outlines some of the reasons why pupils may engage in disruptive behavior and concludes with an outline of several dozen techniques you might use to handle such types of behavior. You should be able to prevent many problems, though, or at least nip them in the bud, by being prepared. That is why this chapter begins with a discussion of classroom management techniques.

Analyzing Your Techniques of Classroom Management

Kounin's Observations on Group Management

Interest in the significance of classroom management was kindled when Jacob S. Kounin wrote a book titled *Discipline and Group Management in the Classroom* (1970). Kounin noted that he first became interested in group management when he reprimanded a college student for blatantly reading a newspaper in class. Kounin was struck by the extent to which the entire class responded to a reprimand directed at only one person, and he subsequently dubbed this the **ripple effect**. Chances are you can recall a situation where you were diligently working away in a classroom when the teacher suddenly became quite angry at a classmate who was disruptive. If, despite the fact that your behavior was blameless, you felt a bit tense after the incident and endeavored to give the impression that you were a paragon of student virtue, you have had personal experience with the ripple effect.

Once his interest in classroom behavior was aroused, Kounin supervised a series of observational and experimental studies of student reactions to techniques of teacher control. In analyzing the results of these various studies, he came to the conclusion that the following classroom management techniques appear to be most effective.

> **Ripple effect: group response to a reprimand directed at an individual**

1. *Show your students you are "with it."* Kounin coined the term **withitness** to emphasize that teachers who prove to their students that they know what is going on in a classroom usually have fewer disciplinary problems than teachers who appear to be unaware of incipient disruptions. An expert at classroom management will nip trouble in the bud by commenting on potentially disruptive behavior before it gains momentum. An ineffective teacher may not notice such behavior until it begins to spread and then perhaps hopes that it will simply go away. At first glance, Kounin's suggestions that you show that you are with it might seem to be in conflict with the learning theorists' prediction that nonreinforced behavior will disappear. If the teacher's reaction is the only source of reinforcement in a classroom, ignoring behavior may cause it to disappear. In many cases, however, a misbehaving pupil gets reinforced by the reactions of classmates. Therefore, ignoring behavior is much less likely to lead to extinction of a response in a classroom than in controlled experimental situations.

Teachers who show they are with it head off discipline problems

2. *Learn to cope with overlapping situations.* When he analyzed videotapes of actual classroom interactions, Kounin found that some teachers seem to have one-track minds. They are inclined to deal with only one thing at a time, and this way of proceeding causes frequent interruptions in classroom routine. One primary grade teacher observed by Kounin, for example, was working with a reading group when she noticed two boys on the other side of the room poking each other. She abruptly got up, walked over to the boys, berated them at length, and then returned to the reading group. By the time she returned, however, the children in the reading group had become bored, listless, and were tempted to engage in mischief of their own.

Kounin concluded that withitness and skill in handling overlapping activities seemed to be related. An expert classroom manager who is talking to children in a reading group, for example, might notice two boys at the far side of the room who are beginning to scuffle with each other. Such a teacher might in midsentence tell the boys to stop and make the point so adroitly that the attention of the children in the reading group does not waver. You might carry out a self-analysis of how you handle overlapping situations when you first begin to teach. If you find that you tend to focus on only one thing at a time, you might make an effort to develop skills in coping with two or more situations simultaneously.

Being able to handle overlapping activities helps classroom control

Handbook Heading: Learning To Deal with Overlapping Situations

3. *Strive to maintain smoothness and momentum in class activities.* This point is related to the previous one. Kounin found that some teachers cause problems for themselves because they constantly interrupt activities without thinking about what they are doing. Some teachers whose activities were recorded on videotape failed to maintain the thrust of a lesson because they seemed unaware of the rhythm of student behavior (that is, they did not take into account the degree of student inattention and restlessness; instead they moved ahead in an almost mechanical way). Others flip-flopped from one activity to another. Still others

Jacob Kounin found that teachers who were "with it" and maintained smoothness and momentum in class activities had few discipline problems. (Milton Feinberg/The Picture Cube)

would interrupt one activity (for example, a reading lesson) to comment on an unrelated aspect of classroom functioning ("Someone left a lunch bag on the floor"). There were also some who wasted time dwelling on a trivial incident (making a big fuss because a boy lost his pencil). And a few teachers delivered individual, instead of group, instructions ("All right, Charlie, you go to the board. Fine, now, Rebecca, you go to the board"). All these types of teacher behavior tend to interfere with the flow of learning activities. Each time pupils are interrupted they may be distracted and find it difficult to pick up the thread of a lesson. They may also be tempted to engage in mischievous activities. Kounin found greater pupil work involvement and less deviant behavior when teachers maintained momentum and smoothness instead of interrupting activities in the ways just described.

Teachers who continually interrupt activities have discipline problems

Handbook Heading: Learning How To Maintain Momentum

You might carry out a movement analysis of your teaching from time to time. Think about how you handle a class for a period or a day, and see if you can recall incidents of this sort: Your request for a change in activity seemed too abrupt. You needlessly flip-flopped back and forth between activities. You interrupted a lesson to comment on an unrelated situation that happened to come to your attention. You made a mountain out of a molehill. You gave instructions to individual pupils when it would have been simpler to address several at once. To counteract such tendencies, you might endeavor to maintain a smooth flow of activities the following class periods and days. If you succeed in doing so, it may become habitual.

4. *Try to keep the whole class involved, even when you are dealing with individual pupils.* Kounin found that some well-meaning teachers had fallen into a pattern of calling on students in a predictable order and in such a way that the rest of the class served as a passive audience. Unless you stop to think about what you are doing during group recitation periods, you might easily fall into the same trap. If you do, the "audience" is almost certain to become bored and may be tempted to engage in troublemaking activities just to keep occupied. Some teachers, for example, call on pupils to recite by going around a circle, or going up and down rows, or by following alphabetical order. Others call on a child first and then ask a question. Still others ask one child to recite at length (read an entire page, for example). All these techniques tend to spotlight one child in predictable order and cause the rest of the class to tune out until their turn comes. You are more likely to maintain interest and limit mischief caused by boredom if you use techniques such as the following:

a. Ask a question, and after pausing a few seconds to let everyone think about it, pick out someone to answer it. With subsequent questions, call on students in an unpredictable order so that no one knows when she or he will be asked to recite. (If you feel that some students in a class are very apprehensive about being called on, even under relaxing circumstances, you can either ask them extremely easy questions or avoid calling on them at all.)

b. If you single out one child to go to the board to do a problem, ask all other students to do the same problem at their desks and then choose one or two at random to compare their work with the answers on the board.

c. When dealing with lengthy or complex material, call on several students in quick succession (and in unpredictable order), and ask each to handle one section. In a primary grade reading group, for example, have one child read a sentence, then pick someone at the other side of the group to read the next sentence, and so on.

d. Use props in the form of flash cards, mimeographed sheets, or workbook pages to induce all students to respond to questions simultaneously. Then ask students to compare answers. (One ingenious elementary school teacher observed by Kounin had each pupil print the ten digits on cards that could be inserted in a slotted piece of cardboard. She would ask a question, such as "How much is 8 and 4?" pause a moment while the students arranged their answers in the slots, then say, "All show!")

> Keeping entire class involved and alert minimizes misbehavior
>
> Handbook Heading: Ways To Keep the Whole Class Involved

All these techniques are likely to be effective because they encourage participation by all students, introduce an element of suspense, and hold all students accountable for what is going on.

5. *Introduce variety, and be enthusiastic, particularly with younger pupils.* As Kounin and his associates viewed videotapes of different teachers, they concluded that some instructors seem to get much more in a rut than others. At one end of the scale are teachers who follow the same procedure day after day, respond with the same, almost reflexive comments ("That's fine."), labor a point, or continue a lesson so that it becomes almost unbearably tedious—perhaps out of lethargy or reluctance to think of something else for the class to do. At the other end of the scale are teachers who constantly seek to introduce variety, go out of their way to respond with enthusiasm and interest, and move quickly to new activities when they sense that students either have mastered or are satiated by a particular lesson. Apparently because of methodological complexities, Kounin failed to find statistical evidence that students responded differently to teachers at either end of such a scale. It seems logical to assume, however, that students would be more inclined to sleep, daydream, or get into mischief if they are exposed to dull, routine activities. Kounin pointed out, though, that variety may be most appropriate in elementary school classrooms because older students may be interested in thoroughly analyzing complex ideas and may be bothered if they are interrupted too frequently.

6. *Be aware of the ripple effect. When criticizing student behavior, be clear, firm, focus on behavior rather than personalities, and try to avoid anger outbursts.* If you take into account the suggestions just made, you may be able to reduce the amount of student misbehavior in your classes. Even so, some behavior problems are certain to occur. When you deal with these, you can benefit from Kounin's research on the ripple effect. On the basis of observations, questionnaires, and experimental evidence, he concluded that "innocent" pupils in a class are more likely to be positively impressed by the way the teacher handles a misbehavior if the following conditions exist:

a. The teacher identifies the misbehaver and states what the unacceptable behavior is. ("George! Don't flip that filmstrip at Henry.")

Identify misbehavers, firmly specify constructive behavior

b. A suggestion is made specifying more constructive behavior. ("Please put the filmstrip back in the storage box.")

c. A reason is given explaining why the deviant behavior should cease. ("If the filmstrip gets broken or dirty, no one else will be able to use it and we'll have to try to get a new one.")

d. The teacher is firm and authoritative and conveys a no-nonsense attitude.

e. The teacher does not resort to anger, humiliation, or extreme punishment. Kounin concluded that extreme reactions did not seem to make children behave better. Instead, anger and severe reprimands upset them and made them feel tense and nervous.

f. The teacher focuses on behavior, not on personality. This is the same point Thomas Gordon emphasizes in *Teacher Effectiveness Training* (1974) and that Haim Ginott stresses in *Teacher and Child* (1972). Gordon and Ginott urge

Student misbehavior can be minimized by providing changes of pace and introducing variety. (Richard Hutchings/Photo Researchers)

teachers to address the situation, not the child's character and personality. Kounin expresses the same point in different words: He concluded that students responded more favorably to teachers who mentioned "task attributes rather than personal attributes" (p. 52). In a situation where one pupil pushes another, for example, it is better to say, "Don't push because you may hurt someone," than to say "You are being thoughtless and rude and making all of us dislike you." (Further comments on techniques recommended by Ginott and Gordon will be provided later.)

University of Texas Studies of Group Management

Stimulated by Kounin's observations, members of the Research and Development Center for Teacher Education at the University of Texas at Austin instituted a series of studies on classroom management. The basic procedure followed in most studies was to first identify very effective and less effective teachers by using a variety of criteria (often stressing pupil achievement), ratings, and observations. Then classroom management techniques used by very effective teachers were analyzed in detail. In some studies (for example, Brophy, 1979; Good, 1982), basic characteristics of well-managed classrooms were described. They can be summarized as follows:

1. Students know what they are expected to do and generally experience the feeling that they are successful doing it.
2. Students are kept busy engaging in teacher-led instructional activities.
3. There is little wasted time, confusion, or disruption.
4. A no-nonsense, work-oriented tone prevails, but at the same time there is a relaxed and pleasant atmosphere.

These conclusions can be related to information presented earlier. The first point stresses that students know what they are to do and generally feel successful doing it. This conclusion might be interpreted as supporting the use of instructional objectives stated so that students know when they have achieved them. It might also be interpreted as supporting the use of mastery learning evaluation procedures. The next three points stress student productivity under teacher guidance and a no-nonsense, work-oriented atmosphere. These outcomes are more likely when teachers use procedures recommended by behavioral theorists than when they use forms of instruction advocated by cognitive and humanistic psychologists. It might be argued that such a conclusion could have been predicted, since student achievement was an important factor considered in selecting teachers classified as effective. Even so, because of current stress on student achievement, it would appear that teachers who make frequent use of preplanned instructional activities are more likely to be perceived as effective managers than teachers who use discovery approaches much of the time. Student-directed forms of learning not only tend to be less efficient than teacher-directed activities, they also increase possibilities for goofing off, mischief, or disruptive behavior. Elementary school boys working on a programmed workbook in math are less likely to get into mischief, for example, than the same boys working as a self-directed group arranging a bulletin board in the hallway outside the classroom.

Another set of studies carried out by the Texas researchers led to two recent books on group management, one for elementary school teachers (Evertson et al., 1984) and the other for secondary teachers (Emmer et al., 1984). You may wish to examine the appropriate book for your grade level (complete titles and names of authors are given in the Suggestions for Further Study), but here is a summary of basic keys to management success stressed in both volumes.

1. On the very first day with a new class, very effective teachers clearly demonstrate that they have thought about classroom procedures ahead of time. They have planned first-day activities that make it possible for classroom routine to be handled with a minimum of confusion. They also make sure students understand why the procedures are necessary and how they are to be followed.

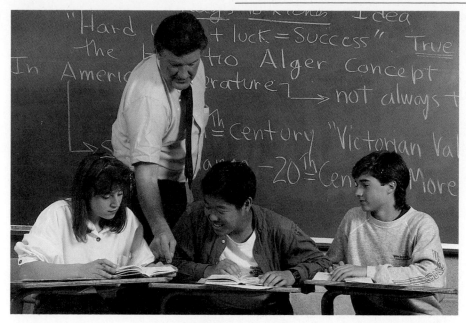

Clear communication of expectations and goals, paired with frequent feedback, leads to good classroom management. (Richard Hutchings/Photo Researchers)

2. A short list of basic classroom rules is posted and/or announced, and students are told about penalties they will incur in the event of misbehavior.
3. During the first weeks with a new group of pupils, the teacher has students engage in whole-group activities under his or her direction. Such activities are selected to make students feel comfortable and successful in their new classroom.
4. After the initial shakedown period is over, effective teachers maintain control by using the sorts of techniques described by Kounin: They show they are with it, cope with overlapping situations, maintain smoothness and momentum, and don't ignore the rest of the class when dealing with individual pupils.
5. Effective teachers give clear directions, hold students accountable for completing assignments, and give frequent feedback.

During first weeks, have students complete clear assignments under your direction

This list of factors calls attention to the importance of being thoroughly prepared the first days you meet with a new class. You should not only have thought about how you are going to handle classroom routine; you should also have planned learning activities likely to make students feel comfortable and successful. You should make sure students know about classroom rules and procedures. You should give students clear assignments, convey the message that they will be responsible for completing them, and provide positive feedback so that they are aware they have completed work successfully.

The observations of Kounin and the conclusions of the researchers at Texas can be converted into the following Suggestions for Teaching.

SUGGESTIONS FOR TEACHING

Techniques of Classroom Management

1. Show you are confident and prepared the first day of class.
2. Think ahead about how you plan to handle classroom routine and explain basic procedures the first few minutes of the first day.
3. Establish and call attention to class rules.
4. Begin classwork the first day with an instructional activity that is clearly stated and can be completed quickly and successfully.
5. During the first weeks with a new group of students, have them spend most of their time engaging in whole-class activities under your direction.
6. Give clear instructions, hold students accountable for carrying them out, and provide frequent feedback.
7. Continually demonstrate that you are competent, well prepared, and in charge.
8. Be professional but pleasant, and try to establish a businesslike but supportive classroom atmosphere.

1. Show you are confident and prepared the first day of class.

The first few minutes with any class are often crucial. Your pupils will be sizing you up, especially if they know you are a new teacher. If you act scared and unsure of yourself, you will probably be in for trouble. Even after you have had years of experience, you may find that confronting a roomful of strange pupils for the first time is a bit intimidating. You will be the center of attention and may experience the equivalent of stage fright. To switch the focus of attention and to begin to identify your pupils as individuals rather than as a threatening audience, you might consider using this strategy. Hand out 4-by-6 inch cards as soon as everyone is seated and ask your students to write down their full name, the name they prefer to be called, what their hobbies and favorite activities are, and a description of the most interesting experience they ever had. (For primary grade pupils who are unable to write, substitute brief oral introductions.) As they write, you will be in a position to make a leisurely scrutiny of your pupils as individuals. Recognizing that you are dealing with individuals should reduce the tendency to feel threatened by a group. Perhaps you have read about singers who pick out a single, sympathetic member of the audience and sing directly to her or him. The sea of faces as a whole is frightening. The face of the individual is not. Even if you are not bothered by being the center of attention, you might still consider using this card technique to obtain information you can use to learn names rapidly and to individualize instruction. (More on this later.)

Whatever you do the first few minutes, it is important to give the impression that you know exactly what you are doing. The best way to pull that off is to be thoroughly prepared.

2. Think ahead about how you plan to handle classroom routine and explain basic procedures the first few minutes of the first day.

The Texas researchers found that very effective teachers demonstrated from the first moment with a new group of students that they knew how to handle the details of their job. They also conveyed the impression that they expected cooperation. In order to demonstrate that you are a confident, competent instructor, you should plan exactly how you will handle classroom routines. You will pick up at least some ideas about the details of classroom management during student teaching experiences, but it might be worth asking a friendly experienced teacher in your school for advice about tried and true procedures that have worked in that particular school. (You might also read one of the books on classroom management recommended at the end of this chapter.) You should try to anticipate how you will handle such details as taking attendance, assigning desks, handing out books and materials, what policy you intend to establish for permitting students to go to the restroom during class, and so forth. If you don't plan ahead, you will have to come up with an improvised policy on the spur of the moment, and that policy might turn out to be highly inefficient or in conflict with school regulations.

Handbook Heading: Planning How To Handle Routines

3. Establish and call attention to class rules.

Very effective teachers observed by the Texas researchers explained class rules the first day. Some teachers list standard procedures on a chart or bulletin board; others simply state them the first day of class. Either technique saves time and trouble later because all you have to do is refer to the rule when a transgression occurs. The alternative is to interrupt the lesson and disturb the whole class while you make a hurried, unplanned effort to deal with a surprise attack. Your spur-of-the-moment reaction may turn out to be clumsy and ineffective.

When you introduce rules the first day, take a positive, nonthreatening approach. If you spit rules out as if they were a series of ultimatums, the students may feel you have a chip on your shoulder, which the unwritten code of the

Establish and call attention to class rules the first day

classroom obligates them to try to knock off. One way to demonstrate your good faith is to invite the class to suggest necessary regulations and why they should be established. Whatever your approach, encourage understanding of the reasons for the rules. You can make regulations seem desirable rather than restrictive if you discuss why they are needed. Reasonable rules are much more likely to be remembered and honored than pronouncements that seem to be the whims of a tyrant.

Examples

"During class discussion, please don't speak out unless you raise your hand and are recognized. I want to be able to hear what each person has to say, and I won't be able to do that if more than one person is talking."

"During work periods, I don't mind if you talk a bit to your neighbors. But if you do it too much and disturb others, I'll have to ask you to stop."

"If you come in late, go to your desk by walking along the side and back of the room. It's disturbing—and not very polite—to walk between people who are interacting with each other."

4. Begin classwork the first day with an instructional activity that is clearly stated and can be completed quickly and successfully.

When selecting the very first assignment to give to a new class, refer to the suggestions for preparing instructional objectives proposed by Mager and Gronlund, and arrange a short assignment that can be successfully completed before the end of the period. Clearly specify what is to be done, and perhaps state the conditions and criteria for determining successful completion. In addition, mention an activity (such as examining the assigned text) that students should engage in after they have completed the assignment. In the elementary grades, you might give a short assignment that helps students review material covered in the preceding grade. At the secondary level, pick out an initial assignment that is short, interesting, and does not depend on technical knowledge.

Examples

"Your teacher from last year told me that most of you were able to spell all of the words on the list I am going to read. Let's see if you can still spell those words. If you have trouble with certain ones, we can work together to come up with reminders that will help you remember the correct spelling."

"The first chapter in our natural science text for this fall is about birds. I want you to read the first ten pages and make a list of five types of birds that are described and prepare your own set of notes about how to recognize them. At 10:30 I am going to hold up pictures of ten birds, and I want you to see if you can correctly identify at least five of them."

In a junior high school English literature class, ask students to read an interesting short story and then write a brief synopsis of the plot.

In a high school history class, ask students to write a brief description of a movie they have seen that depicted historical events. Then ask them to indicate whether they felt the film interpretation was accurate.

5. During the first weeks with a new group of students, have them spend most of their time engaging in whole-class activities under your direction.

The very effective teachers observed by the Texas researchers followed the strategy just described, which makes sense when you stop to think about it. You can't expect students to adjust to the routine of a new teacher and classroom in just a few days. Accordingly, it would be wise to make sure students have settled down before asking them to engage in relatively unstructured activities like discovery learning. Furthermore, group discussions or group projects usually work out more successfully when the participants have a degree of familiarity with each other and a particular set of background factors (such as a chapter in a text). Thus, as you plan activities during the first weeks with a new class, prepare instructional objectives that ask students to complete assignments under your direction. Postpone using techniques recommended by cognitive and humanistic psychologists until later in a report period.

6. Give clear instructions, hold students accountable for carrying them out, and provide frequent feedback.

All three goals can be achieved by making systematic use of instructional objectives as described in Chapter 6 and by putting into practice the model of instruction described in this book.

7. Continually demonstrate that you are competent, well prepared, and in charge.

As students work at achieving instructional objectives, participate in group discussions, or engage in any other kind of learning activity, show that you are a competent classroom manager. Arrange periods so that there will be a well-organized transition from one activity to the next, maintain smoothness and momentum, and don't waste time. Use a variety of teaching approaches so that you please some of your students some of the time, and use techniques recommended by behavioral, cognitive, and humanistic psychologists. Show you are with it by being alert for signs of mischief or disruptive behavior and handling such incidents quickly and confidently by using techniques to be described later in this chapter and in the "Becoming a Better Teacher" section of the next chapter.

8. Be professional but pleasant, and try to establish a businesslike but supportive classroom atmosphere.

Establish a businesslike but supportive classroom atmosphere

If you establish classroom routines in a competent fashion and keep your students busy working to achieve clearly stated instructional objectives, you should be able to establish a no-nonsense, productive atmosphere. At the same time, you should strive to make your room an inviting and pleasant place to be. Keep in mind the observations of humanistic psychologists regarding the importance of taking into account feelings and interpersonal relationships. Put yourself in the place of students thrust into a strange classroom with an unfamiliar instructor. Try to identify with your students so that you can appreciate how they feel if they do or say something embarrassing, or have difficulty with classwork.

One of the best ways to get students to respond positively to you and make them feel welcome in your classroom is to learn their names as quickly as possible (even if you have five sections of secondary school students to teach). To accomplish that feat, refer to the cards mentioned in point 1 above. Use the information students have provided, perhaps supplemented by your own notes or sketches about distinctive physical and facial features, to establish associations between names and faces. Before and after every class period the first few days, flip through your pile of cards, try to picture the appearance of the student, and practice using their names. Refer to the description of mnemonic devices in the chapter on information processing. Once you have learned a pupil's name, use it as often as possible to maintain the memory trace. Greet pupils by name as they come in the door, use their names when asking them to recite or carry out some task, speak to them personally when you hand back assignments.

Another way to make students feel at home in your classroom is to try to establish a feeling of class spirit. One way to do this is to have a brief *sharing* period—similar to the sharing time you may remember from your kindergarten days—at the beginning of each period. Invite students to describe recent interesting experiences they have had or give announcements about extracurricular activities. If a member of the class is injured in an accident or suffers a lengthy illness, buy a get-well card and have every member of the class sign it before sending it off.

If you follow these procedures, you should be able to establish a well-managed classroom. As noted at the beginning of this chapter, however, for reasons that often will be beyond your control, you are likely to encounter occasional inci-

Students seem to respond more positively to schooling when they are treated as individuals, when their feelings and opinions are taken into account, and when they are invited to participate in making decisions. (Robert Capece/Monkmeyer)

dents of misbehavior. Thus, even though you do everything possible to prevent problems from developing, you are still likely to have to deal with disruptive behavior. Therefore, the extent of disciplinary problems, some of the factors that lead to misbehavior, and techniques for handling disruptive behavior are topics that merit attention.

Violence in American Schools

The Safe School Report

Chances are, you have read reports about the extent of violence in American schools and are understandably concerned about how dangerous teaching has become. At first glance, some of the statistics that have been reported are alarming, but closer scrutiny reveals that certain teachers are much more likely to be exposed to violence than the majority. During the "violent years" of recent American history (toward the end of the Vietnam war), physical attacks on students and teachers in public schools reached a peak. The situation became so alarming that the U.S. Department of Health, Education, and Welfare was instructed to carry out an extensive survey and prepare a report titled *Violent Schools—Safe Schools, The Safe School Study Report to the Congress* (1978). The report revealed that violence in American schools had reached a peak between 1965 and 1975 but was declining. Subsequent reports (summarized by Baker, 1985, and Bauer, 1985) lead to the conclusion that the decline has been so moderate that a definite problem still exists for teachers in certain types of school situations.

Among significant points noted in the *Safe School Study Report* were the following:

Factors associated with high levels of school violence included location of a school in a high crime area, large schools and classes, high proportion of male students, lack of firmness on the part of administrators, and perception of students that they had little control over what happened to them.

Violence most likely in inner-city junior high schools with weak administrators

Most acts of violence took place in secondary schools, but attacks on pupils and teachers were about twice as frequent in *junior* high as in senior high schools.

The highest risk areas in schools are stairways, hallways, cafeterias, and locker rooms. In all these places students are thrown together under crowded conditions. The safest places in schools were classrooms.

Administrators, teachers, and students all recommended firm discipline and supervision as the best single means for reducing violence. The authors of the report recommended greater "personalization" of schooling.

The description of factors associated with violence leads to the conclusion that while attacks on students and teachers are fairly frequent in certain schools, you are not likely to need to be concerned about your physical safety in your own classroom. Perhaps the most significant information in the report relates to implications for establishing control: Firm discipline and supervision were recommended by all respondents, students were likely to engage in violent acts when they felt they had no control over what happened to them, and greater "personalization" of education was recommended as a preventative.

Analyzing Reasons for Violence

The *Safe School Study Report* noted that the level of violence was highest in secondary schools with a high proportion of male students. One of the clear-cut sex differences that has been repeatedly supported by consistent evidence (reviewed by Parke and Slaby, 1983) is that males are more aggressive than females. It is impossible to trace the causes of this difference precisely, but it seems likely that it is due to hormonal as well as cultural factors. *Hormone* in the Greek means "to arouse" or "to urge on," which reflects the fact that these substances are released in the bloodstream and arouse reactions in various parts of the body. The male sex hormone androgen arouses high energy and activity levels. Because of long-established cultural expectancies, males in our society are encouraged to assert themselves in physical ways. As a result, tendencies toward high energy and activity levels aroused by male sex hormones may be expressed in the form of aggressiveness against others.

There is also evidence, as noted in the discussion of age-level characteristics in Chapter 3, that young girls in our society are encouraged to be dependent and to be eager to please adults, while young boys are encouraged to assert their independence (Block, 1973; Fagot, 1978). Furthermore, it appears that boys are more likely than girls to be reinforced for assertive and illegal forms of behavior. Martin Gold and Richard Petronio (1980, p. 524) speculate that delinquency in our society seems to have a masculine character. They suggest that the range of delinquent behavior that will be admired by peers is narrower for females than for males and that boys are more likely to achieve recognition by engaging in illegal acts. The same reasoning may well apply to disruptive behavior in the classroom. A boy who sasses the teacher or shoves another boy in a skirmish in the cafeteria is probably more likely to draw a favorable response from peers than a girl who exhibits the same behavior. Thus, there are a variety of factors that predispose boys to express frustration and hostility in physical and assertive ways.

Boys also seem more likely than girls to experience feelings of frustration and hostility in school. For a variety of reasons (more rapid maturity, desire to please adults, superiority in verbal skills) girls earn higher grades, on the average, than boys do. A low grade almost inevitably arouses feelings of resentment and anger. Any kind of negative evaluation is a very direct threat to a student's self-esteem. A junior or senior high school boy who has received an unbroken succession of low grades and is unlikely to graduate may experience extreme frustration and anger. Even poor students are likely to be aware that their chances of getting a decent job are severely limited by the absence of a high school diploma. At the same time, high school students who have never developed successful study habits and who are saddled with a low grade-point average may feel that it is impossible to do anything about the situation—unless there is a continuation school or the equivalent to attend. Older high school boys who do not have opportunities to attend special schools can escape further humiliation by dropping out of school; junior high school boys cannot legally resort to the same solution, which may partially explain why violent acts are twice a frequent in junior as in senior high schools.

Other explanations of disruptive classroom behavior are supplied by Erikson's observations on identity. A teen-ager who has failed to make a clear occupational

Male aggressiveness due to hormonal and cultural factors

Junior high-age boys with low grades may feel trapped

choice, who is confused about sex roles, or who does not experience acceptance "by those who count" may decide to establish a negative identity. Instead of striving to behave in ways that parents and teachers respond to in positive ways, negative identity teen-agers may deliberately engage in opposite forms of behavior. James Marcia's identity status concept (1967, 1980) may also help you understand why certain pupils cause problems in class. Foreclosure types who have accepted parental values may well be model students. Moratorium types, who are experiencing identity crises of different kinds, may feel impelled to release frustration and anger. But even pupils who are not experiencing identity problems, either because they are too young to be concerned or because they have resolved identity conflicts, may misbehave because they need to release frustration and tension.

| Misbehavior of high school students may reveal lack of positive identity |

So far, we have mentioned the role of hormonal, academic, cultural, and personality factors in school violence. Each of these explanations places the responsibility for violent behavior largely or entirely on the individual. Other explanations focus instead on schools that are poorly designed and that do not meet the needs of their students. Violent behavior, in this view, is seen as a natural (although unacceptable) response to schools that are too large, impersonal, and competitive; that do not enforce rules fairly or consistently; that use punitive ways of resolving conflict; and that impose an unimaginative, nonmeaningful curriculum on students (Zwier & Vaughan, 1984).

Evidence in support of the argument that the characteristics and climate of a school can lead to violence was mentioned in an earlier chapter. In the discussion of age-level characteristics at the high school level presented in Chapter 3, mention was made of negative reactions (such as vandalism) to schooling. Michael Rutter and several associates (1979) made a comprehensive study of twelve inner-city London schools. They found that the amount of misbehavior and damage to school property was significantly less in schools that had an academic emphasis, made available incentives and rewards, arranged good conditions for students, and provided opportunities for students to participate in decision making. The impact of school atmosphere was demonstrated by the fact that students who moved from "bad" elementary schools (characterized by considerable misbehavior) to secondary schools that fit the description just given exhibited a significant decrease in disruptive and destructive behavior.

Similar observations on the characteristics of schools that have low levels of violence were stressed by Eugene Howard, an authority on school climate and discipline, who wrote:

> Schools with positive climates are characterized by people-centered belief and value systems, procedures, rules, regulations, and policies. People care, respect, and trust one another, and the school, as an institution, cares, respects, and trusts people. In such a school, people feel a high sense of pride and ownership which comes from each individual having a role in making the school a better place (1981).

Reducing School Violence

Classroom Tactics

The recommendations for improvement noted in the *Safe School Study Report,* the results of the Rutter study, and the conclusions reached by Howard suggest that academic achievement and school atmosphere can play a significant role in school violence. To foster respectable levels of achievement by as many students as possible, teachers can make effective use of carefully selected objectives, help students establish at least short-term goals, use efficient instructional techniques (such as those advocated by behavioral theorists), teach students how to use learning strategies, and implement a mastery approach. If you show that students who do not do well on the first try at an assignment will receive your help and encouragement to improve their performance, you may be able to convert at least some resentment into a desire to achieve.

School violence can be reduced by improving student achievement levels

At the same time, it appears that students should be invited to participate in making at least some decisions about what is to be studied and about school and classroom rules. Discovery techniques and the contract approach, for example, permit some self-direction by students. Such tactics may reduce students' feelings that schooling is impersonal and that they have no control over what happens to them. As humanistic psychologists have argued, students seem to respond more positively to schooling when they are treated as individuals, when their feelings and opinions are taken into account, and when they are invited to participate in making decisions about how the school and the classroom function.

Programs to Reduce Violence and Improve Discipline

Evidence from various sources (summarized by Baker, 1985, and Bauer, 1985) that violent and disruptive acts are still common in many American schools prompted President Reagan to direct the Department of Justice and the Department of Education, in partnership with Pepperdine University, to form the National School Safety Center. (The center began operations in June 1984.) The same day he signed the directive, the president issued this statement: "I urge all federal, state, and local officials to assist this Center in addressing the needs of our nation's schools in the areas of school safety and restoration of discipline." As this message implies, the purpose of the center is to coordinate efforts to reduce violence and improve discipline in American schools, and several states and many school districts have initiated programs to make schools safer places for students and teachers.

One such program is the Just Community at the Birch Meadow Elementary School in Reading, Massachusetts (Murphy, 1988). You may recall reading about the Just Community concept at the end of Chapter 2 as an extension of Lawrence

An excellent way to limit pupil misbehavior due to boredom or tension is to provide occasional relaxing interludes. (Bob Daemmerich/The Image Works)

Kohlberg's work on moral reasoning. The goal of the Just Community at Birch Meadow was to help students take responsibility for reducing undesirable behaviors (such as petty bickering among students, the development of cliques, and graffiti on restroom walls) and promoting more desirable actions (such as cooperative learning, cleanup activities, and organizing fund raising events).

Implementation of the Just Community concept involves two types of activities: circle meetings and student councils. Circle meetings are held in each classroom. The first meeting occurs on the first day of the school year and is devoted to establishing classroom rules and punishments. Subsequent meetings can be called at any time to deal with such issues as unfair treatment of some students by others (or by the teacher), classroom safety, and revisions of classroom rules. There were two student councils at Birch Meadow, one for grades K through 3 and one for grades 4 and 5. Each class selects a representative to serve on the council. The councils meet separately with the principal in alternating weeks to decide on ways to make the atmosphere of the school more enjoyable. For example, the primary council (K through 3) conducted a playground cleanup campaign and the intermediate council raised money to purchase an American flag for the school auditorium. (For descriptions of other programs, see Nicholson et al., 1985.)

Even if you use the management techniques described earlier in this chapter, and attempt to allow for misbehavior by using techniques such as those just described, you are still likely to be faced with occasional incidents of disruption

Violence less likely when students invited to participate in making decisions

and/or defiance. Some general guidelines you might consider when you find it necessary to resort to disciplinary techniques appear in the Suggestions for Teaching that follow the Mid-Chapter Review.

Mid-Chapter Review

Techniques of Classroom Management

Interest in classroom management was stimulated in the early 1970s by the writings of Jacob Kounin. On the basis of observations and experiments, Kounin concluded that teachers who maintained effective control of student behavior possessed one or more of the following skills: (1) withitness, (2) ability to handle overlapping situations, (3) ability to maintain smoothness and momentum when teaching a lesson, (4) ability to keep the whole class involved in a lesson, (5) use of various materials and methods with an air of enthusiasm, and (6) ability to capitalize on the ripple effect by identifying the misbehaver and firmly specifying a more constructive behavior.

More recent studies at the University of Texas found that in well-managed classrooms, students have a clear idea of what they are expected to accomplish, are kept busy in a work-oriented but relaxed and pleasant atmosphere, and feel successful in carrying out their assigned tasks. These findings suggest that teachers should have a plan for handling classroom routine, should specify rules for classroom behavior, should provide understandable lessons that can be completed quickly and successfully, and should establish a businesslike but supportive classroom atmosphere.

Violence in American Schools

Because of increased reports of violence in American schools during the early and mid-1970s, the U.S. Government conducted its own study of the problem and issued its findings in 1978 in the *Safe School Study Report*. School violence was found to be most likely to occur in: (1) large schools that have a high proportion of males and that are not firmly run by administrators, (2) schools in which students feel they have little say or control over what happens to them, (3) junior high and high schools, (4) stairways, hallways, cafeterias, and locker rooms.

The causes of school violence have been attributed to physiological factors (such as high levels of the male hormone androgen), cultural factors (such as reinforcing males to be competitive and aggressive), academic factors (such as the generally lower grades achieved by boys), personality factors (such as the frustration that accompanies identity formation), and school climate factors (such as large, impersonal schools that emphasize punitive ways of resolving conflicts).

Reducing School Violence

Following the finding that school violence can be partly attributed to low levels of academic achievement, teachers may be able to help reduce school violence by providing students with clear objectives, using instructional techniques derived from operant conditioning, teaching students how to use learning strategies, and using a mastery approach.

Because school violence also seems to be associated with large, impersonal schools where students feel they have no control over what happens to them, students should be given some opportunity to determine rules for behavior and punishments for infractions of rules. One schoolwide program for achieving such a goal is the Just Community.

SUGGESTIONS FOR TEACHING

Handling Problem Behavior

1. Have a variety of influence techniques planned in advance.
2. Be prompt, consistent, and reasonable.
3. Avoid threats.
4. Whenever you have to deal harshly with a student, make an effort to re-establish rapport.
5. Consider making occasional use of behavior modification techniques.
6. When you have control, ease up—some.

1. Have a variety of influence techniques planned in advance.

You may save yourself a great deal of trouble, embarrassment, and strain if you plan ahead. When first-year teachers are asked which aspects of teaching bother them most, classroom control is almost invariably near the top of the list. Perhaps a major reason is that problems of control frequently erupt unexpectedly, and they often demand equally sudden solutions. If you lack experience, your shoot-from-the-hip reactions may be ineffective. Initial attempts at control that are ineffective tend to reinforce misbehavior, and you will find yourself trapped in a vicious circle. This sort of trap can be avoided if specific techniques are devised ahead of time. Having in mind several methods of dealing with trouble will prepare you for the inevitable difficulties that arise.

However, if you find yourself forced to use prepared techniques too often, some self-analysis is called for. How can you prevent so many problems from developing? Frequent trouble is an indication that you need to work harder at motivating your class. You might refer to the list of causes of misbehavior in the preceding section for some specific troubleshooting suggestions. Also, check on your feelings when you mete out punishment. Teachers who really like students and want them to learn consider control techniques a necessary evil and use them only when they will provide a better atmosphere for learning. If you find yourself looking for trouble or perhaps deliberately luring pupils into misbehaving, or if you discover yourself gloating privately or publicly about an act of punishment, stop and think. Are you perverting your power to build up your ego or giving vent to sadistic impulses?

Handbook Heading: Analyzing Feelings After Dealing with Trouble-makers

You will find an extensive list of *influence techniques* in the section that follows this discussion of general suggestions for maintaining classroom control.

2. Be prompt, consistent, and reasonable.

No attempt to control behavior will be effective if it is remote from the act that provokes it. For a troublemaker to comprehend the relationship between behavior and counterreaction, one must quickly follow the other. Don't postpone dealing with misbehaving pupils or make vague threats to be put into effect sometime in the future (such as not permitting them to attend an end-of-the-year event). By that time, most pupils will have forgotten what they did wrong. They then feel resentful and persecuted and may conclude that you are acting out of sheer malice. A frequent reaction is more misbehavior in an urge to "get even." (In such situations, guilty pupils are not likely to remember that you are the one doing the evening up.) On the other hand, retribution that is too immediate, that is applied when a student is still extremely upset, may also be ineffective. At such times, it is often better to wait a bit.

Be prompt, consistent, and reasonable when dealing with misbehavior

Being consistent about classroom control can save a lot of time, energy, and misery. Strictness one day and leniency the next, or roughness on one pupil and gentleness with another, invites all students to test you every day—just to see whether this is a good day or a bad day or whether they can get away with something more frequently than others do. Establishing and enforcing class rules is an excellent way to encourage yourself to be consistent.

Handbook Heading: Being Prompt, Consistent, and Reasonable in Controlling the Class

Harshness in meting out retribution encourages rather than discourages more extreme forms of misbehavior. If pupils are going to get into a lot of trouble for even a minor offense, they will probably figure they should get their money's worth. In the early days of Merrie England all offenses—from picking pockets to murder—were punishable by death. The petty thief quickly became a murderer; it was a lot easier (and less risky) to pick the pocket of a dead man and, since the punishment was the same, eminently more sensible. The laws were eventually changed to make punishment appropriate to the degree of the offense. Keep this in mind when you dispense justice.

3. Avoid threats.

If at all possible, avoid a showdown in front of the class. In a confrontation before the whole group, you are likely to get desperate. You may start out with a "yes, you will"—"no, I won't" sort of duel and end up making a threat on the spur of the moment. Frequently, you will not be able to make good on the threat, and you will lose face. It's far safer and better for everyone to settle extreme differences in private. When two people are upset and angry with each other, they look silly at best and completely ridiculous at worst. You lose a great deal more than a student does when this performance takes place in front of the class. In fact, a student may actually gain prestige by provoking you successfully.

Perhaps the worst temptation of all is to try to get back at the entire class by making a blanket threat of a loss of privilege or detention. It hardly ever works and tends to lead to a united counterattack by the class. One elementary school teacher had the reputation of telling her class at least once a year that they would not be allowed to participate in the Spring Play-Day if they didn't behave. By the time pupils reached this grade, they had been tipped off by previous students that she always made the threat but never carried it out. They behaved accordingly. Suppose, in a fit of pique, you tell your class that they must "all stay in forty-five minutes after school." What will you do when they start chattering in a chorus about bus schedules, car pools, music lessons, dentist appointments, and paper routes? You can usually avoid such nightmares by putting a stop to the problem before it begins to snowball.

4. Whenever you have to deal harshly with a student, make an effort to re-establish rapport.

Handbook Heading:
Ways To Establish Rapport

If you must use a drastic form of retribution, make a point of having a confidential conference with your antagonist as soon as possible. Otherwise, she or he is likely to remain an antagonist for the rest of the year. It's too much to expect chastised students to come to you of their own volition and apologize. You should set up the conference, then explain that the punishment has cleared the air as far as you are concerned and that they can start the next day with a clean slate. You shouldn't be surprised if a recalcitrant pupil doesn't respond with signs or words of gratitude. Perhaps some of the causes of misbehavior lie outside of school, and something you did or said may have been merely the last straw. Even if you get a sullen reaction, it is desirable at least to indicate your willingness to meet punished students more than halfway.

At the elementary level, you can frequently make amends simply by giving the child some privilege—for example, passing out paper or being hall monitor at recess. One teacher made it a point to praise a child for some positive action shortly after a severe reprimand.

5. Consider making occasional use of behavior modification techniques.

Many of the techniques that have been noted—particularly, stating rules, using techniques planned in advance, and being prompt and consistent—are used in a highly systematic fashion in the behavior modification approach to classroom control. In Chapter 7 you were acquainted with the techniques of behavior modification, including the suggestion that you follow this procedure when confronted by inappropriate behavior, as when two boys engage in a mild argument that stops and starts several times.

First, ignore the behavior. (It may extinguish because of lack of reinforcement.)

Second, remind the class that those who finish the assignment early will earn 5 bonus points and be allowed to see a film.

First ignore misbehavior, then stress rewards; use punishment as a last resort

Third, approach the boys and tell them (privately and nicely) that they are disturbing others and making life difficult for themselves. If they do not complete the assignment in the allotted time, they will have to make it up some other time.

Fourth, resort to punishment by informing the boys (in a firm but not nasty way) that they must leave the classroom immediately and report to the vice principal to be assigned to a study hall for the rest of the class period. Tell them they will have to complete the assignment when the rest of the class has free time.

Finish by pointing out that once the work is made up, they will be all caught up and in a good position to do satisfactory work for the rest of the report period.

The techniques just described are appropriate for secondary school students. The following behavior modification procedure for maintaining classroom control in the primary grades is recommended by Wesley C. Becker, Siegfried Engelmann, and Don P. Thomas:

Handbook Heading: Experimenting with Behavior Modification

1. Specify in a positive way the rules that are the basis for your reinforcement. Emphasize the behavior you desire by praising children who are following the rules. Rules are made important by providing reinforcement for following

them. Rules may be different for different kinds of work, study, or play periods.

Limit the rules to five or less.

As the children learn to follow the rules, repeat them less frequently, but continue to praise good classroom behavior.

2. Relate the children's performance to the rules. Praise behavior, not the child. Be specific about behavior that exemplifies paying attention or working hard. . . .

Relax the rules between work periods. . . .

3. Catch the children being good. Reinforce behavior incompatible with that which you wish to eliminate. Reinforce behavior that will be most beneficial to the child's development. . . .

4. Ignore disruptive behavior unless someone is getting hurt. Focus your attention on the children who are working well in order to prompt the correct behavior from the children who are misbehaving.

5. When you see a persistent problem behavior, look for the reinforcer. It may be your own behavior. (1971, p. 171)

6. When you have control, ease up—some.

It is extremely difficult, if not impossible, to establish a controlled atmosphere after allowing anarchy. Don't make the mistake of thinking you will be able to start out without any control and suddenly take charge. It may work, but in most cases you will have an armed truce or a cold war on your hands. It is far better to start out on the strict side and then ease up a bit after you have established control. Being strict doesn't mean being unpleasant or dictatorial; it simply means that all in the room are aware that they are expected to respect the rights of others.

Influence Techniques

In *Mental Hygiene in Teaching* (1959), Fritz Redl and William W. Wattenberg present a list of *influence techniques.* The list has been adopted as an organizational frame of reference for the following discussion. The sections headed "Supporting Self-Control," "Situational Assistance," and "Reality and Value Appraisal" are based directly on the list. All the subheadings in these sections are exactly as set forth on pages 348–363 of *Mental Hygiene in Teaching.*

Under each section specific examples are offered. Some are based on ideas noted by Redl and Wattenberg; some are the results of reports by students and teachers; some are based on personal experience. You might use the headings in

Signals such as staring at a misbehaving pupil are examples of influence techniques Redl and Wattenberg classify as "supporting self-control." (Junebug Clark/ Photo Researchers)

your Handbook. Pick out techniques that seem most appropriate for your grade level or that you feel comfortable about, and add other ideas of your own.

Supporting Self-Control

Students should be encouraged to develop self-control. This first group of suggestions is designed to foster that trait.

Signals   In some cases a subtle signal can put an end to budding misbehavior. The signal, if successful, will stimulate the student to control him- or herself. (This technique should not be used too often, and it is effective only in the early stages of misbehavior.)

Handbook Heading: Signals To Use To Nip Trouble in the Bud

Examples

Clear your throat.

Stare at the culprit.

Stop what you are saying in midsentence and stare.

Shake your head (to indicate no).

Say "Someone is making it hard for the rest of us to concentrate" (or the equivalent).

Proximity Control   Place yourself close to the misbehaving student. This makes a signal a bit more apparent.

Use supportive reactions to help students develop self-control

Examples

Walk over and stand near the student.

With an elementary grade pupil, it sometimes helps if you place a gentle hand on a shoulder or arm.

Interest Boosting   Convey interest in the incipient misbehaver. This relates the signal to schoolwork.

Examples

Ask the student a question, preferably related to what is being discussed. (Question such as "Herman, are you paying attention?" or "Don't you agree, Herman?" invite wisecracks. *Genuine* questions are to be preferred.)

Go over and examine some work the student is doing. It often helps if you point out something good about it and urge continued effort.

Humor   Humor is an excellent, all-around influence technique, especially in tense situations. However, remember that it should be *good*-humored humor—gentle and benign rather than derisive. Avoid irony and sarcasm.

Examples

"Herman, for goodness' sake, let that poor pencil sharpener alone—I heard it groan when you used it just now."

(Perhaps you have heard someone say, "We're not laughing *at* you; we're laughing *with* you." Before you say this to one of your pupils, you might take note that one second-grader who was treated to that comment unhinged the teacher by replying, "I'm not laughing.")

Situational Assistance

Handbook Heading:
Ways To Supply Situational
Assistance

Helping over Hurdles   Some misbehavior undoubtedly occurs because students do not understand what they are to do or lack the ability to carry out an assignment.

Examples

Try to make sure your students know what they are supposed to do.

Arrange for students to have something to do at appropriate levels of difficulty.

Have a variety of activities available.

Support from Routines   Trouble sometimes develops simply because students do not know what is expected of them. To avoid this in-limbo situation, it helps to establish a certain amount of routine, perhaps as part of the class rules (if you resort to such rules).

Examples

Establish a set pattern for getting started at the beginning of the day or period.

Make a specific routine of lining up for recess, lunch, and other activities.

At the beginning of gym classes (or the equivalent), where wild horseplay is at a maximum, establish a fixed procedure for taking roll (perhaps by having students stand on numbers painted on the floor), for determining activities to be participated in, and so on.

Nonpunitive Exile   Sometimes a student will get carried away by restlessness, uncontrollable giggling, or the like. If you feel that this is nonmalicious behavior and due simply to lack of self-control, ask the student to leave the room. (You may have recognized that what Redl and Wattenberg refer to as nonpunitive exile is the same as *time-out* described by behavior modification enthusiasts.)

Examples

"Herman, please go down to the principal's office and sit on that bench outside the door until you feel you have yourself under control."

Some high schools have "quiet rooms"—supervised study halls that take extra students any time during a period, no questions asked.

Use of Restraint   Students who lose control of themselves to the point of endangering other members of the class may have to be physically restrained. However, such restraint should be protective, not punitive; that is, don't shake or hit. This technique is most effective with younger children; such control is usually not appropriate at the secondary level.

Example

If a boy completely loses his temper and starts to hit another child, lead him gently but firmly away from the other pupils or sit him in a chair and keep a restraining hand on his shoulder.

Removing Seductive Objects   If certain objects or fellow students are too tempting for pupils, the wise thing to do is put temptation behind them.

Examples

If an elementary grade pupil gets carried away using a projector, a stapler, a paper cutter, or whatever, put it away for a while.

If high school students in a shop or laboratory course seem unable to resist the temptation to fool around with expensive equipment, lock it up or erect a barrier of some kind (even a cloth cover will do).

Anticipatory Planning   Some classroom situations are particularly conducive to misbehavior. If a certain activity seems loaded with opportunities for mischief, try to prepare the class ahead of time and emphasize the need for control.

Example

When an elementary school class is going to visit the local newspaper plant or the equivalent, stress the importance of not touching anything, keeping away from the machines, and paying strict attention to the guide.

Reality and Value Appraisal

Handbook Heading: Ways To Use Reality and Value Appraisal

Most of the techniques in the two preceding sections fall under the category of prevention. The following techniques involve prevention but also encourage more constructive behavior. As Redl and Wattenberg put it, "One of the goals of education is to enable people to increase the areas in which they can be guided by intelligence and conscience rather than by blind impulse, fear or prejudice" (1959, p. 358). The approaches presented here "appeal to children's sense of fairness and strengthen their ability to see the consequence of their actions" (p. 358).

Direct Appeals   When appropriate, point out the connection between conduct and its consequences. This is most effective if it is done concisely and if the technique is not used too often.

Examples

"We have a rule that there is to be no running in the halls. Herman forgot the rule, and now he's down in the nurse's office having his bloody nose taken care of. It's too bad Mr. Harris opened his door just as Herman went by. If Herman had been walking, he would have been able to stop in time."

"If everyone would stop shouting, we'd be able to get this finished and get out to recess."

Criticism and Encouragement   Sometimes it is necessary to criticize a particular student. It is preferable to do so in private, but often public criticism is the only possibility. (And it has the advantage of setting an example for other pupils.) In such cases you should do your best to avoid ridiculing or humiliating the student. Public humiliation may make a child hate you and school, counterattack, or withdraw. Because of the ripple effect, it may also have a negative impact on innocent students. One way to minimize the negative aftereffects of criticism is to tack on some encouragement in the form of a suggestion as to how the backsliding can be replaced by more positive behavior.

> **Give criticism privately, then offer encouragement**

Examples

If a student doesn't take subtle hints (such as stares), you might say, "Herman, you're disturbing the class. We all need to concentrate on this." It sometimes adds punch if you make this remark when your back is turned while you are writing on the board or helping some other student. (This is one way to show that you are with it.)

Act completely flabbergasted, as though the misbehavior seems so inappropriate that you can't comprehend it. A kindergarten teacher used this technique to perfection. She would say, "Herman! Is that you?" (Herman has been belting Lucy with a shovel.) "I can't believe my eyes. I wonder if you would help me over here." Obviously, this gambit can't be used too often, and the language and degree of exaggeration have to be altered a bit for older pupils. But indicating that you *expect* good behavior and providing an immediate opportunity for the backslider to substitute good deeds can be very effective.

Defining Limits   In learning about rules and regulations, children go through a process of testing the limits. Two-year-olds particularly, when they have learned how to walk and talk and manipulate things, feel the urge to assert their independence. In addition, they need to find out exactly what the house rules are. (Does Mommy *really* mean it when she says, "Don't take the pots out of the cupboard"? Does Daddy *really* mean it when he says, "Don't play with that hammer"?) Older children do the same thing, especially with new teachers and in new situations. The technique of defining limits includes not only establishing rules (as noted earlier) but also enforcing them.

Examples

Establish class rules, with or without the assistance of students, and make sure they are understood.

When someone tests the rules, show that they are genuine and that there *are* limits.

Postsituational Follow-up   Classroom discipline occasionally has to be applied in a tense, emotion-packed atmosphere. When this happens, it often helps to have a postmortem discussion—in private, if an individual is involved; with the whole class, if it was a groupwide situation.

Examples

In a private conference: "Herman, I'm sorry I had to ask you to leave the room, but you were getting kind of carried away."

"Well, everybody, things got a bit wild during those group work sessions. I want you to enjoy yourselves, but we practically had a riot going, didn't we? And that's why I had to ask you to stop. Let's try to hold it down to a dull roar tomorrow."

Marginal Use of Interpretation   Analysis of behavior can sometimes be made while it is occurring, rather than afterward. The purpose here is to help students become aware of potential trouble and make efforts to control it.

Examples

To a restless and cranky prelunch class, you might say, "I know you're getting hungry and that you're restless and tired, but let's give it all we've got for ten minutes more. I'll give you the last five minutes for some free visiting time."

The value of these techniques is that they appeal to self-control and imply trust and confidence on the part of the teacher. However, they may become ineffective if used too often, and that is why so many different techniques have been noted. The larger your repertoire, the less frequently you will have to repeat your various gambits and ploys.

Retribution

Handbook Heading: Using Retribution as Positively as Possible

When efforts at prevention and subtle control fail, you may occasionally have to resort to forms of retribution. If the misbehavior is an accomplished fact, you have no choice but to require the guilty party to suffer consequences. Such payment is part of education, too. In one sense, retribution is desirable in that it presumably teaches students that they cannot break rules of conduct with impunity. But there are many negative aspects to any form of punishment. The learning theory concept of generalization focuses attention on the major disadvantage: A punished child may come to associate hate and fear with all aspects of school and education. This suggests that you should make retribution as gentle as possible while still demonstrating that the misbehavior should not occur again. Here are some techniques to consider when you have no choice but retribution.

Making the Punishment Fit the Crime   This is one of the most commonly noted rules of retribution, but it is often difficult to put into practice. If you can think of compensating behavior that is directly related to the transgression, all the better.

Examples

If a boy has been playing around during class, it is appropriate to have him stay in during recess and do the work that had been assigned. (If he tells you smugly that by state law he has to have recess, just tell him he already *had* his recess.)

If a girl knocks over a vase of flowers during some horseplay, have her clean it up.

Withholding a Privilege   This is related to the point just mentioned.

Example

If repeated requests to hold down the chatter during study sessions go unheeded, enforce silence for a day or two. Emphasize that the privilege to exchange ideas with classmates will be reinstated when everyone has demonstrated control.

Detention   This time-honored technique is not easy to apply in a day of individualized scheduling, but it may be effective. It is usually unwise to require work on school subjects while the culprit is putting in time, however. A student forced to do math or reading in a situation loaded with guilt, anger, and unpleasantness may come to associate these feelings with academic matters.

Examples

If the second row of students from the window is fooling around instead of getting ready for recess, detain them three minutes after the rest of the class goes howling out the door.

An incorrigible talker might be asked to write a theme on the topic "Why Talking in the Class Disturbs Others." (Perhaps the talker really hadn't *thought* about it.) Having students write out sentences such as "I shall not talk in class" is ineffective in most cases. The writing is often carried out automatically, and the writer, while mechanically inscribing a whole row of *I*'s, may be thinking what a louse you are. For younger children, this can be a form of torture, especially if an unrealistic number of repetitions is required. One mother, for example, stayed up until midnight giving moral support to her second-grader as the boy laboriously wrote out *five hundred* "I will not talk in class" statements. The poor child had bleary eyes and writer's cramp and was in a state of nervous exhaustion by the time he finished. (The mother felt she had to go through with it once the task had been imposed by the teacher, lest the boy decide that his parents would intercede on his behalf whenever he got in trouble. At the end of the year she did tell the teacher what she thought of her.)

Punitive Exile   One of the techniques noted by Redl and Wattenberg was "nonpunitive exile." It may also be necessary to use what amounts to *punitive* exile. Pupils who deliberately misbehave and continue to disrupt the class—despite your efforts to get them under control—may have to be exiled in retribution. Recalcitrant pupils may be sent to a "quiet room" or to the principal's office or to any appropriate "solitary confinement" area. As with nonpunitive exile, it is usually desirable to set a time limit so students are invited to return once they have paid their debt to classroom society.

If you routinely send misbehavers out in the hall or to a quiet room and require them to stay there until the end of the period, you may actually encourage mischief. A pupil who is bored and wants a change of scenery may cause enough trouble to merit banishment—or escape. In other words, exile works as retribution only when what you are doing in class is reasonably interesting.

Private Conferences   If none of the milder techniques is effective or if milder techniques are tried and only arouse more hostility, it may be well to schedule a private conference. This is preferable to a confrontation before the entire class—not only for the sake of the pupil but also for your own protection. When you find yourself face to face with misbehavers, it is probably a good policy to let them have their say. Perhaps a student just lost control, regrets the action, and wants to make amends. For your part, you might simply explain why you had to insist that the behavior stop. It is helpful to finish such interviews on as positive a note as possible. Try to get across the point that you intend to let bygones be bygones and that you confidently expect better behavior in the future. (Some of the techniques noted under "Situational Assistance" apply here as well.)

Appeal to an Outside Authority   When defiance is open and the behavior is not cut short by the suggestion of a personal conference, it's probably time to obtain an arbiter in the form of the principal or vice principal. For example, a student whom you ask to go to a quiet room refuses. The student either implies or says directly or indirectly, "I won't go, and what are you going to do about it?" The wise course of action—regardless of your sex, size, and wrestling ability—is calmly to ask some member of the class to get the principal (or other authority designated for disciplinary control). Then go back to the lesson.

Try to avoid appealing to an outside authority unless all other measures have failed; in a sense, doing so is an admission that you can't handle the problem yourself. Yet you should face the fact that sometimes you will encounter such

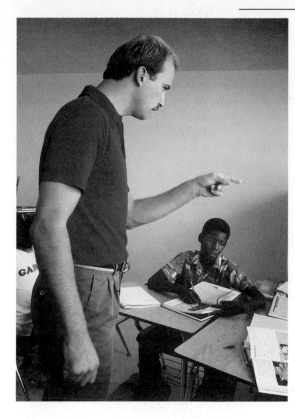

When confronted by a student, it is usually better to arrange for a private conference or appeal to an outside authority than to engage in a showdown in front of the class. (Bob Daemmerich Photos)

cases. There may be an impossible-to-avoid personality clash. Some pupils may be the victims of such disturbing experiences that they can't help themselves, or circumstances may simply conspire to get them out on a limb. It is then far better to get the troublemakers out of the room. A running battle kept up all period or all day makes everyone suffer and severely curtails learning. It is a good idea to find out who the responsible authority is as soon as you report for your first job; you will be more than a bit embarrassed if you send a pugnacious pupil to the principal only to have the culprit sent back two minutes later.

I-Messages and the No-Lose Method

As noted in discussing humanistic teaching techniques in Chapter 10, in *Teacher and Child* (1972) Haim Ginott offers a cardinal principle of communication: "Talk to the situation, not to the personality and character" (p. 84). Instead of making derogatory remarks about the personalities of two boys who have just thrown bread at each other, Ginott suggests that a teacher deliver an **"I-message"** explaining how he or she feels. Don't say "You are a couple of pigs"; say "I get angry when I see bread thrown around. This room needs cleaning." According to

I-message: tell how you feel about an unacceptable situation

Handbook Heading:
Using I-Messages

Ginott, guilty pupils who are told why a teacher is angry will realize the teacher is a real person, and this realization will cause them to strive to mend their ways. Ginott offers several examples of the cardinal principle of communication in Chapter 4 of *Teacher and Child*. In Chapter 6 he offers some observations on discipline: Seek alternatives to punishment. Try not to diminish a misbehaving pupil's self-esteem. Try to provide face-saving exits.

A different analysis of many of the same points Ginott stresses is presented by Thomas Gordon in *T.E.T.—Teacher Effectiveness Training* (1974). In *T.E.T.,* teachers are urged to use I-messages, and to resort to authority and punishment only when absolutely necessary.

Handbook Heading:
Speculating About Problem
Ownership

One procedure recommended by Gordon (to review points noted in Chapter 10) is for teachers to try to determine who *owns* a problem before they decide how to handle that problem. If a student misbehaves by doing something destructive (carving a desk top, for example), the teacher owns the problem and must respond by doing something to stop the destructive behavior. But if a student expresses anger or disappointment about some classroom incident (getting a low grade on an exam), that student owns the problem. Gordon suggests that failure to identify problem ownership may cause teachers to intensify difficulties unwittingly, even as they make well-intended efforts to diminish them. If a pupil is finding it difficult to concentrate on school work because his or her needs are not satisfied, the situation will not be ameliorated if the teacher orders, moralizes, or criticizes. According to Gordon, such responses act as roadblocks to finding solutions to student-owned problems because they tend to make the pupil feel resentful and misunderstood. The preferred way to deal with a pupil who owns a problem is to use what Gordon calls **active listening**. The listener is *active* in the sense that interest is shown and the talker is encouraged to continue to express feelings; the listener does *not* actively participate by interpreting, explaining, or directing. The listener *does* respond, though, by recognizing and acknowledging what the student says.

For teacher-owned problems—those that involve misbehavior that is destructive or in violation of school regulations—Gordon agrees with Ginott that I-messages are appropriate. Instead of ordering, threatening, moralizing, using logic, offering solutions, or commenting on personal characteristics, Gordon urges teachers to explain why they are upset. Proof of the effectiveness of I-messages takes the form of anecdotes reported in *T.E.T.* provided by teachers who used them successfully. A principal of a continuation school for dropouts, for example, reported that a group of tough boys responded very favorably when he told them how upset he became when he saw them break some bottles against the school wall. Almost invariably the anecdotes reported in *T.E.T* refer to the success of a teacher's first try at delivering an I-message. It seems likely that at least part of the success of the technique the first time it is used could be attributed to surprise or novelty. It is possible that extensive use of the technique might stir up rather than

In dealing with classroom conflicts, Thomas Gordon encourages teachers to use the no-lose method by which the teacher and students talk over a problem and resolve it in a mutually agreeable way. (The Stock Market/Henley and Savage)

calm down troublemakers. Instead of saying, "Gee! We never realized you felt that way!" they might say, "We're getting awfully tired of hearing about your troubles!"

Gordon urges teachers to try to resolve conflicts in the classroom by using the *no-lose method.* If either person in a conflict loses, there is bound to be resentment. If you tell a girl who is fooling around during a work period that she must settle down or stay after school, *she* loses. If you make a halfhearted and unsuccessful effort to control her and then try to cover up your failure by ignoring her and working with others, *you* lose. Gordon recommends that the preferred procedure is to talk over the problem and come up with a mutually agreeable compromise solution. He offers this six-step procedure for coming up with no-lose solutions, a procedure that is similar to techniques recommended by Leland Howe and Mary Howe (1975) for choosing class discussion topics (noted in Chapters 9 and 10) and by Gyorgy Polya (1957) for using heuristics (described in Chapter 9). The teacher and student(s) come to mutual agreement by following this procedure:

1. Define the problem
2. Generate possible solutions
3. Evaluate the solutions
4. Decide which solution is best

No-lose method: come to mutual agreement about a solution to a problem

5. Determine how to implement the solution

6. Assess how well the solution solved the problem (1974, p. 228)

To put this procedure into practice with an individual, you might approach a boy who is disrupting things during a work period and engage in a dialogue something like this:

You: You're making such a ruckus over here by talking loudly and shoving others that I can't hear the group I'm working with. It looks as if you are having trouble settling down. Any ideas about how we can both do what we need to do?

Pupil: I think this workbook junk is stupid. I already know how to do these problems. I'd rather work on my science project.

You: Well, suppose we try this. You do one page of problems. If you get them all correct, we'll both know you can do them and you should be free to work on your science project. If you make some mistakes, though, that means you need more practice. Suppose you do a page and then ask me to check it. Then we can take it from there. How does that sound?

Handbook Heading:
Trying the No-Lose
Method

To put the no-lose method into effect when the entire class is upset about something, it would probably be preferable to follow all six steps recommended by Gordon.

In certain situations Ginott's and Gordon's observations can be quite helpful. You might try to analyze what you say to pupils when you are upset to discover if you tend to mention character and personality instead of concentrating on the situation. If you find that you do criticize personal characteristics, make an effort to comment on the situation. You might also make an effort to determine who owns a problem before you decide how to deal with it. If a pupil is not behaving in the desired manner and appears to be unhappy or confused about it, you might try serving as an active listener. Encourage the student to talk about what is bothering him or her by serving as a sympathetic sounding board. In cases of defiant, disruptive, or destructive behavior, make occasional use of I-messages so that pupils learn that you have feelings that ought to be respected. And if you find yourself confronted by a hostile student or class, you might use the no-lose method to find a mutually agreeable solution to the problem.

Suggestions for Further Study

Classroom Management

Even though it was published in 1959, the second edition of *Mental Hygiene in Teaching* by Fritz Redl and William W. Wattenberg includes a particularly clear, concise, and well-organized analysis of influence techniques. Many of the techniques described have been used by teachers for years and will continue to be used as long as an instructor is asked to supervise a group of pupils.

More recent analyses of classroom control techniques can be found in *Building Classroom Discipline* (3rd ed., 1989) by C. M. Charles, *Any Teacher Can! Practical Strategies for Effective Classroom Management* (1984) by Joan C. Carson and Peter Carson, and *Comprehensive Classroom Management* (1986) by Vernon F. Jones and Louise S. Jones.

Discussions of classroom management that emphasize particular approaches or techniques can be found in the following books: James S. Cangelosi emphasizes the use of methods that foster student cooperation in *Classroom Management Strategies: Gaining and Maintaining Student's Cooperation* (1988); William W. Purkey and David B. Strahan (1986) emphasize the use of invitational learning in *Positive Discipline: A Pocketful of Ideas* (1986).

School Violence

If you would like information on how to reduce school violence through the use of behavior modification techniques, psychodynamic and humanistic interventions, and the teaching of prosocial values and behaviors, read *School Violence* (1984) by Arnold P. Goldstein, Steven J. Apter, and Berj Harootunian. *Victimization in Schools* (1985) by Gary D. Gottfredson and Denise C. Gottfredson describes research conducted at the Center for Social Organization of Schools at Johns Hopkins University on the nature and frequency of school violence and on possible solutions. Amalia J. Cuervo, Joan Lees, and Richard Lacey describe how modifications in instructional techniques, curricula, school organization, student involvement, school-parent relationships, and school-community relationships can reduce school violence in *Toward Better and Safer Schools* (1984).

Summary

1. Jacob Kounin, one of the early writers on classroom management, identified several effective classroom management techniques. Kounin emphasized the ripple effect, withitness, coping with overlapping activities, maintaining the momentum of a lesson, keeping the whole class involved in a lesson, using a variety of instructional techniques enthusiastically, focusing on the misbehavior of students rather than their personalities, and suggesting alternative constructive behaviors.
2. Researchers at the University of Texas found that in well-managed classrooms students know what they are expected to do and do it successfully, are kept busy with teacher-designated activities, and exhibit little confusion or wasted time. The classroom is marked by a work-oriented yet relaxed and pleasant atmosphere.
3. While school violence seems to have peaked between 1965 and 1975, it is still a problem. It is most likely to occur in inner-city junior high schools

with weak administrators. The most likely areas for violent incidents are stairways, hallways, cafeterias, and locker rooms. The safest areas are classrooms.

4. Possible explanations for misbehavior and violence, particularly among boys at the junior high and high school levels, include high levels of the male sex hormone androgen, a culture that encourages male aggression and independence, feelings of resentment and frustration over low levels of achievement, and difficulty in establishing a positive identity.

5. Other explanations for school violence focus on the characteristics and atmosphere of schools that are so large that they seem impersonal, that emphasize competition, that do not enforce rules fairly or consistently, that use punishment as a primary means of resolving conflict, and that offer a curriculum perceived as unimaginative and nonmeaningful.

6. Steps that classroom teachers can take to reduce school violence include providing students with well-conceived objectives, helping students set short-term goals, using instructional techniques derived from behavioral learning theories, teaching students how to use learning strategies, using a mastery approach, and allowing students to make some decisions about classroom rules and what is to be studied.

7. One school-wide program that may reduce violence and improve behavior is the Just Community. In a Just Community students are given responsibility for reducing undesirable behavior and increasing the frequency of desirable behavior.

8. Redl and Wattenberg first proposed their set of behavior management methods in 1959. These influence techniques are arranged by categories that roughly reflect a least direct to most direct ordering. The categories are: supporting self-control, situational assistance, reality and value appraisal, and retribution.

9. Haim Ginott suggests teachers use I-messages when responding to misbehavior. These are statements that indicate to students how the teacher feels when misbehavior occurs. The aim is to comment on the situation and not on the personality and character of the person.

10. Thomas Gordon also suggests that teachers use I-messages. In addition, he recommends that teachers determine who "owns" a problem, use active listening when the student owns the problem, and resolve conflicts by using the no-lose method. The no-lose method involves discussing problem behaviors with the misbehaving student and formulating a mutually agreeable compromise solution.

Key Terms

ripple effect *(650)*   active listening *(684)*
withitness *(651)*   no-lose method *(685)*
I-messages *(683)*

Discussion Questions

1. Can you recall any classes where you experienced Kounin's ripple effect? Since this phenomenon simultaneously affects the behavior of several students, would you consider using it deliberately? Why?

2. Do you agree with the argument raised earlier that school violence can be caused by a nonmeaningful, unimaginative curriculum? If so, what can you do to make the subjects you teach lively, interesting, and useful?

3. Haim Ginott and Thomas Gordon recommend that teachers speak to the behavior and not the character of the student when responding to misbehavior. How often have you seen this done? If it strikes you as a good approach that is not practiced often enough, what steps will you take to use it as often as possible with your own students?

chapter 14

BECOMING A
BETTER TEACHER

As you know from personal experience, some teachers are much more effective than others. Take a moment and think back to as many teachers as you can remember. How many of them were really outstanding in the sense that they established a favorable classroom atmosphere, were sensitive to the needs of students, and used a variety of techniques to help you learn? How many of them did an adequate, workmanlike job but left you bored or indifferent most of the time? How many of them made you dread entering their classrooms because they were either ineffective teachers or insensitive or even cruel in dealing with you and your classmates? Chances are you remember few outstanding teachers and you had at least one incompetent or tyrant (and perhaps several of them). You probably know from your experiences as a student that ineffective or vindictive teachers are often dissatisfied with themselves and with their jobs. It seems logical to assume a circular relationship in such cases: Unhappy teachers often do a poor job of instruction; teachers who do a poor job of instruction are likely to be unhappy.

If you hope to be an effective teacher who enjoys life in the classroom (most of the time), you will need to be well prepared and willing to work. You will need a wide variety of skills, sensitivity to the needs of your pupils, and awareness of many instructional techniques. Each chapter in this book was written to help you acquire these various skills, sensitivities, and techniques. You are also likely to need two other general abilities if you hope to function as an above-average, successful, satisfied teacher: the ability to cope with frustrations and the ability to benefit from experience and improve your skills as an instructor. This last chapter offers some suggestions you might use to enhance such abilities.

Coping with Frustrations

There are problems and frustrations in any profession or job, and teaching is no exception. If you hope to function effectively in the classroom, you will need to

690

By openly communicating, sharing ideas, and solving problems with their colleagues, teachers can relieve stress and improve their teaching skills. (Bob Daemmerich Photos)

learn to cope with the many problems that are an inevitable feature of public school education. Here is a list of suggestions on how to cope with frustrations. With the exception of points 10, 11, and 13, the statements in italics are exact quotations from *Mental Hygiene in Teaching* (1959) by Fritz Redl and William W. Wattenberg, pages 494-497.

1. *Develop self-awareness.* The better people understand themselves, the less likely they are to be overwhelmed by events they cannot control. Furthermore, those who understand and accept themselves are usually able to accept and understand others. If you feel that you might benefit from developing greater self-awareness, you might enroll in a college course intended to promote self-understanding.

2. *Recognize new possibilities in teaching.* If a "standard" technique for dealing with a problem is prohibited or not available to you, find a new and different way to do it.

3. *Evaluate dissatisfactions.* If you find yourslf dissatisfied with certain aspects of teaching, try to select those portions of the problem that *can* be dealt with and become a relaxed fatalist about the rest. (Confucius put it in the form of the familiar prayer: Give me the strength to change what can be changed, the courage to accept what cannot be changed, and the wisdom to tell one from the other.)

4. *Re-evaluate total load.* If you are inundated by work and pressure mounts, try to eliminate or reduce certain tensions. For example, if you are driven to the brink by having to grade term papers for five classes of thirty pupils each, don't assign term papers unless your teaching load is adjusted.

5. *Look for help on specific questions.* If you are hung up on a particular frustration, ask your principal, an older teacher, or a consultant for ideas. In some cases, all it takes is a little more experience or a different perspective to reveal a simple solution.

6. *Deliberately expose yourself to new experiences.* Anyone who is conscientious about teaching needs periods of rest and relaxation. Functioning as an inspirational instructor takes a lot out of a person. For this reason it may be wise to cultivate a noneducational hobby, take a nonteaching summer job or make the most of that three-month vacation.

7. *Seek satisfactions elsewhere.* If conditions in school block the achievement of psychological needs, make a deliberate effort to find satisfaction outside the classroom. For example, one high school teacher felt unhappy about the lack of overt acceptance by and admiration from his students (not because he was a poor teacher but because high school students often make it a point not to show admiration openly). He became the scoutmaster of a Boy Scout troop. Another way to satisfy partly frustrated needs is to develop a creative hobby.

8. *Talk it over with friends.* One purpose of psychotherapy is to provide catharsis—the release of tension. You can get much the same result by talking over your problems with others. There is obviously a limit to how much you can impose on any one person, but an occasional legitimate gripe will rarely strain relationships with a spouse, friend, or colleague, especially if you spread the gripes around and act as a reciprocal "therapist." If you are upset about something (the furnace at home went on the blink at 3:00 A.M.), talk about it, and warn the class that they had better look out for you that day.

9. *Stimulate group discussion.* A variation of the preceding point is "group therapy" sessions. Gripe sessions in a cafeteria or teachers' room are often an effective way to keep body and soul together, especially if there is an element of humor in them. (Looking for the humorous side of things is a fine, all-purpose method of dealing with frustrations in or out of the classroom.)

10. *Get physical release of tension.* When frustrations build up, you might indulge in recreational activities or in physical work to gain release.

11. *Avoid taking out your frustrations on the class.* A primary reason for seeking release of tension through creative hobbies, gripes, or physical activities is to avoid punishing your students. When you find yourself frustrated, it is natural to want to take out your anger on those thirty scapegoats trapped in your room, especially if they have done more than their share in contributing to your frustration. In a sense, your students are so many sitting ducks. The temptation to shoot them down can be almost irresistible. A certain amount of righteous indignation is probably a good thing for genuinely guilty pupils,

but too often an angry teacher is more at fault than the alleged provokers. If you are upset because of your own weaknesses or inabilities and compensate by bawling out the class or giving a spot quiz, the students will realize it. Frequently they will retaliate, and then you really *will* have some frustrations to cope with.

12. *Get professional help.* In some cases, personal problems are beyond the help that friends can give or are too extensive to be solved by any of the suggestions noted here. If you have reached this point, the sensible thing is to seek professional assistance. You should not regard the need for such help as an admission that you are a failure. Some frustrations may drive an individual to neurosis or psychosis. Individuals who recognize their need for help are often in better mental health than those who refuse to acknowledge the possibility.

13. *In extreme cases, execute a strategic withdrawal.* It sometimes happens that a teacher is caught in a bind. If you find yourself teaching in a school where you can see nothing but negative factors, it may be best to leave that field of forces. Unfortunate circumstances or personality conflicts may lead to an intolerable situation, in which case moving to a different school or a different district may be the sensible—rather than the cowardly—thing to do. If you discover, however, that your dissatisfactions are not with local conditions or people but that you simply do not enjoy teaching and that none of the preceding suggestions helps very much, it would be logical to look for a different kind of job. At stake is not only your own personal adjustment but also the well-being of your students.

Before suggestions that you might follow to improve your effectiveness as a teacher (and to avoid the necessity for resorting to the techniques just mentioned too often) are discussed, a few comments will be offered on consistency and control.

Consistency and Control

After making comprehensive observations of primary grade teachers over a period of time, Jere E. Brophy and Carolyn M. Evertson (1976) concluded: "For various reasons, most of them still unknown, many teachers are inconsistent from one year to the next in the degree of success they achieve in producing student learning gains, in the emotional responses they produce in students, and in their own emotional reactions and general behavior in the classroom" (1976, pp. 3–4). Brophy and Evertson further point out that new teachers, who often go through a process of trial and error when they first take over classrooms, are particularly inconsistent.

Teachers of primary school children affect not only academic achievement but also attitudes toward learning. (The Stock Market/Barbara Kirk, 1987)

In interpreting these conclusions, you should take note that Brophy and Evertson observed primary grade teachers. Teachers of the first, second, and third grades not only have the same group of students for the entire school year; they also supervise the initial learning experiences of those pupils. Thus, they influence not only academic achievement but also shape attitudes toward learning. It might be expected, therefore, that there would be quite a bit of variation between individual pupils and groups of pupils during the first years of school. It seems likely that teachers at the secondary level, who typically interact with several different groups of students for less than an hour a day during one report period, would not vary as much on measures of consistency. The subject and the primary instructional technique would also seem likely to influence the degree of variability from one year to the next. A high school teacher of a structured subject (such as math), for instance, who spent most class periods giving the same explanations, demonstrations, exercises, and tests year after year, would probably earn quite consistent ratings. A teacher of a course such as social studies, though, who invited each class to suggest topics to be studied and who made frequent use of discussion techniques, would probably vary in rated-effectiveness since the performance (and reactions) of each class would depend to a considerable extent on interactions between a unique group of students and the teacher.

If you expect to teach at the elementary level or plan to encourage student participation at the secondary level, you might prepare yourself for a degree of inconsistency. If you get off to a splendid start your first year in an elementary school, don't be surprised if things run less smoothly the next year. Conversely, if the first year turns out to be difficult, don't be discouraged. If you find that students in one section of a secondary grade course respond enthusiastically while those in another section seem sullen or hostile, recognize that variation is inevitable.

Differences in teaching effectiveness from year to year and from class to class may be inevitable, but that does not mean you cannot do anything about such variability. Perhaps the best way to put it is to say that you will have to work harder with some groups of students than with others. You should strongly resist the temptation to assume that some groups are simply going to be less responsive than others and that there is nothing you can do about it. You might use that assumption as an excuse for not putting out much effort. In their analysis of primary grade teachers, Brophy and Evertson concluded that those who were consistently effective perceived their job as interesting and worthwhile. They approached teaching with dedication and resourcefulness and took personal responsibility for what happened in their classroom. If they realized that things were not going well with a particular class, they experimented industriously with different techniques until they found something that seemed to work. Ineffective and inconsistent instructors, by contrast, thought of teaching as "just a job." They tended to react to unresponsive classes by blaming the situation on causes beyond their control. They were likely to offer rationalizations to account for lack of learning.

You may recall from the discussion of motivation in Chapter 11 that high-achieving students tend to attribute failure to lack of effort and resolve to try harder. Low achievers, by contrast, tend to attribute failure to lack of ability and assume that they have no control over what happens. You may also recall from discussions of *learned helplessness* in Chapter 3 that individuals who feel that they have no control over their own behavior are likely to experience depression. Therefore, if you aspire to be a high-achieving teacher and are eager to experience (at least occasionally) a sense of exhilaration and accomplishment rather than feelings of depression, you should assume that what happens in your classroom is up to you.

Brophy and Evertson make the point that "effective teaching involves *orchestration* of a large number of factors, continually shifting teaching behavior to respond to continually shifting needs" (p. 139). They also note that "the most successful teachers looked upon themselves as diagnosticians and problem solvers" (p. 45). Taken together, these two observations emphasize the point that to be consistently effective you are almost certain to need to use different approaches with different groups of pupils. You also will want to seek ways to improve your instructional skills.

The remainder of this chapter offers some suggestions you might follow to develop versatility and resourcefulness in teaching.

Improving Your Skills as a Teacher

There are a number of ways you can strive to become a more effective teacher. You might ask for students' suggestions or evaluations, use observation schedules, constantly use and revise your personal Handbook, or systematically analyze your technique by referring to the questions and suggestions for becoming a better teacher presented at the end of this chapter. Each of these will be discussed separately.

Student Evaluations and Suggestions

In many respects, students are in a better position to evaluate teachers than anyone else. They may not always be able to analyze *why* what a teacher does is effective or ineffective (which might be true of an experienced expert observer), but they know, better than anyone else, whether they are responding and learning. Furthermore, students form their impressions after interacting with a teacher for hundreds or thousands of hours. Most principals or other adult observers may watch a teacher in action for only a few minutes at a time. It makes sense, therefore, to pay attention to and actively solicit opinions from students. As a matter of fact, it will be virtually impossible for you to ignore pupil reactions. Every minute that school is in session, you will receive student feedback in the form of attentiveness (or lack of it), facial expressions, restlessness, yawns, sleeping, disruptive behavior, and the like. If you become aware that a particular lesson arouses either a neutral or a negative reaction, you may feel obliged, in self-defense, to seek a better way to present the same material in the future. If you find that you seem to be spending much of your time disciplining pupils, you may be driven to find other ways to teach.

In addition to analyzing the minute-by-minute reactions of your pupils, you may also find it helpful to request more formal feedback. After completing a unit, you might ask, "I'd like you to tell me what you liked and disliked about the way this unit was arranged and give me suggestions for improving it if I teach it again next year."

A more comprehensive and systematic approach is to distribute a questionnaire or evaluation form and ask students to record their reactions anonymously. You might use a published form or devise your own. In either case, a common format involves listing a series of statements and asking students to rate them on a five-point scale. Some of the published forms use special answer sheets that make it possible to tally the results electronically. One disadvantage of many rating-scale evaluation forms is that responses may not be very informative unless you can compare your ratings to those of colleagues. If you get an overall rating of 3.5 on "makes the subject matter interesting," for example, you don't know whether or not you need to work on that aspect of your teaching until you discover that the average rating of other teachers of the same grade or subject was 4.2. Published evaluation forms may not be very helpful unless all other teachers use the same rating scale. This may be possible in school districts that use a standard scale to obtain evidence for use in making decisions about retention, tenure, and promotion.

Another disadvantage of many rating scales is indicated by the phrase *leniency problem*. Pupils tend to give most teachers somewhat above-average ratings on most traits. Although leniency may soothe a teacher's ego, wishy-washy responses do not provide the information needed to improve pedagogical effectiveness. To get around the leniency problem and to induce pupils to give more informative reactions, *forced-choice* ratings are often used. Figure 14.1 shows a forced-choice rating form, the Descriptive Ranking Form for Teachers, developed by Don J. Cosgrove (1959). This form is designed to let teachers know how pupils perceive their skill in four areas of performance: (1) knowledge and organization of subject matter, (2) adequacy of relations with students in class, (3) adequacy of plans and procedures in class, and (4) enthusiasm in working with students. If you decide to use this form, you should omit the numbers in brackets that follow each statement when you prepare copies for distribution to students. On your own copy of the form, you should write in those numbers and use them to prepare your score in each of the four categories listed above.

To calculate your index of effectiveness in each category of the Descriptive Ranking Form for Teachers, assign a score of 4 to the phrase in each group that is ranked 1, a score of 3 to the phrase marked 2, and so on. Then add together the scores for all phrases identified by the parenthetical number 1, and do the same for the other sets of phrases. The cluster of phrases that yields the highest score is perceived by your students to be your strongest area of teaching; the cluster that yields the lowest score is considered to be your weakest. If you get a total of 30 points for all phrases indicated by the parenthetical number 1, for example, that means you ranked high in category 1 (knowledge and organization of subject matter). If you get only 12 points for phrases identified by the parenthetical number 4, you will need to work harder at being enthusiastic when working with students.

Quite often a homemade form that covers specific points regarding your personal approach to teaching will provide useful information. You might ask a series of questions about specific points (Were there enough exams? Did you think too much homework was assigned?). Another approach is to ask pupils to list the three things they liked best, the three things they liked least, and what they would

**Figure 14.1
The Descriptive
Ranking Form for
Teachers**

From Don J. Cosgrove,
"Diagnostic Rating of Teacher
Performance," *Journal of
Educational Psychology,* 1959,
50, p. 202. Copyright 1959 by
the American Psychological
Association.

This form consists of 10 sets of phrases which are descriptive of instructor performance. Each set is composed of four phrases. Please consider the instructor you have for this course. In each set of phrases, rank the phrases from 1 to 4 as they apply to your instructor. Give a rank of 1 to the phrase which most applies, and 4 to the phrase which least applies, using Ranks 2 and 3 for intermediate ranks. Every phrase must be ranked. There can be no equal ranks.

Set a   _____ Always on time for class [3]
        _____ Pleasant in class [2]
        _____ Very sincere when talking with students [4]
        _____ Well-read [1]

Set b   _____ Contagious enthusiasm for subject [4]
        _____ Did not fill up time with trivial material [3]
        _____ Gave everyone an equal chance [2]
        _____ Made clear what was expected of students [1]

Set c   _____ Classes always orderly [3]
        _____ Enjoyed teaching class [4]
        _____ Friendliness did not seem forced [2]
        _____ Logical in thinking [1]

Set d   _____ Encouraged creativeness [4]
        _____ Kept course material up to the minute [1]
        _____ Never deliberately forced own decisions on class [2]
        _____ Procedures well thought out [3]

Set e   _____ Authority on own subject [1]
        _____ Friendly attitude toward students [4]
        _____ Marked tests very fairly [3]
        _____ Never criticized in a destructive way [2]

Set f   _____ Good sense of humor [4]
        _____ Spaced assignments evenly [3]
        _____ Students never afraid to ask questions in class [2]
        _____ Well organized course [1]

Set g   _____ Accepted students' viewpoints with open mind [2]
        _____ Increased students' vocabulary by own excellent usage [1]
        _____ Students always knew what was coming up next day [3]
        _____ Students willingly worked for teacher [4]

Set h   _____ Always knew what he was doing [3]
        _____ Appreciated accomplishment [4]
        _____ Did not ridicule wrong answers [2]
        _____ Well informed in all related fields [1]

Set i   _____ Always had class material ready [3]
        _____ Covered subject well [1]
        _____ Encouraged students to think out answers [4]
        _____ Rules and regulations fair [2]

Set j   _____ Always managed to get things done on time [3]
        _____ Course had continuity [1]
        _____ Made material significant [4]
        _____ Understood problems of students [2]

suggest you do to improve the way a particular unit is taught. When you ask students to respond to questions like these, you usually not only get feedback about teaching techniques; you also get ideas you might use to improve your teaching skill. (On a rating scale, you may be rated below average on an item such as "Examinations are too difficult," but you may not know *why* you were rated low or what you might do to change things for the better.)

Observation Schedules

While your students can supply quite a bit of information that can help you improve your teaching, they cannot always tell you about technical flaws in your instructional technique. This is especially true with younger pupils, but even sophisticated graduate students in college may not recognize why certain teaching techniques are ineffective. Consequently, you may wish to submit to a detailed analysis of your approach to teaching. Several observation schedules have been developed for this purpose. *The Flanders Interaction Analysis Categories* (Flanders, 1970) is the most widely used teacher behavior schedule, but over one hundred others are described in the multivolume *Mirrors of Behavior* (1970), edited by Anita Simon and E. G. Boyer. As the title of the Flanders schedule indicates, it stresses verbal interactions between teacher and pupils. The following ten categories are listed on a record blank: accepts feelings, praises or encourages, uses student ideas, asks questions, lectures, gives directions, criticizes, pupil talk-response, pupil talk-initiation, and silence or confusion. A trained observer puts a check mark opposite one of these categories every three seconds during a period when teacher and pupils are interacting verbally. Once the observation is completed, it is a simple matter to tally checks and determine the percentage of time devoted to each activity. Then, if a teacher discovers that a substantial amount of time was spent in silence or confusion and that only a tiny fraction of interactions involved praise or encouragement, a deliberate effort can be made to change for the better.

Perhaps the biggest problem with such observational approaches is the need for a trained observer. But it would be possible to team up with another teacher and act as reciprocal observers if you feel that a detailed analysis of your teaching style would be helpful.

Using Your Handbook To Improve Your Teaching

In Chapter 1 the point was made that this book has been written to be used in three ways: (1) as a text for a course in educational psychology, (2) as a source of practical ideas on how to apply psychology to teaching, and (3) as a means for improving your teaching effectiveness. The opening chapter also pointed out two types of marginal notes: (1) Key Points, to be referred to in order to grasp the essence of a chapter and to prepare for exams, and (2) Handbook Headings, to be used in preparing for teaching and for perfecting instructional techniques. You

Successful teachers constantly analyze how students respond to classroom activities and assignments and strive to improve their effectiveness as instructors. The preparation of a personal Handbook and use of the Becoming a Better Teacher: Questions and Suggestions, should help you master and constructively modify your teaching skills. (Elizabeth Crews)

have probably referred to the Key Points already. If you expect to engage in student teaching in the near future, you may now find it valuable to refer to the Handbook Headings and to examine Becoming a Better Teacher: Questions and Suggestions. These two features were designed to complement each other, but they can be developed and used separately and independently.

Because of the nature of course work, it is probable that up to this point you have been asked to think of this book as a text. Your instructor may have asked you to concentrate on sections of the book that he or she felt were of greatest significance and/or which fit a particular sequence of courses in a teacher education program. Once course work is completed, however, you may wish to use this book—on your own—in two ways: (1) as the basis for developing a personal Handbook of teaching, and (2) to identify and compensate for weaknesses in instructional techniques.

The Handbook Headings offer a framework for you to use in developing your own set of guidelines for instruction. Before or during student teaching, you are urged to develop your own set of ideas about how to apply the information and techniques described in this book. If you take the trouble to put together your own concise Handbook, custom-tailored to fit the grade level and subjects you expect to teach, you should feel reasonably well prepared when you first take charge of a class. After a few weeks or months of experience, you might begin to make a systematic effort to analyze and improve your teaching technique. The information provided in Becoming a Better Teacher: Questions and Suggestions is offered as a means for achieving this goal. As noted in the opening chapter, these sections are based on points made in the text opposite Handbook Headings. They are designed to call your attention to specific aspects of your teaching technique and to stimulate ideas you might use to improve your instructional skills. To help you relate questions to appropriate sections of the text, each Handbook Heading printed in the margin is listed in Becoming a Better Teacher: Questions and Suggestions. Under each heading is a question you might ask yourself. The question format is used on the assumption that it is the most direct way to call attention to particular facets of instruction. Then at least one "answer" to the question is provided, written as if it were a specific suggestion you might make to yourself. These suggestions might be used in two ways: (1) as troubleshooting aids when you are confronted with a specific, identifiable problem and (2) as a basis for systematic-rotation evaluations. To put the latter procedure into effect, make it a habit during the first year of your teaching career to set aside at least a few moments at the end of each school day for examining the Becoming a Better Teacher questions for one chapter. If you feel that you might improve your teaching by concentrating on techniques highlighted by a particular question, plan a step-by-step campaign. The next day, peruse the questions for the next chapter, and so on. If you follow this procedure for a few weeks, you should systematically evaluate all aspects of teaching discussed in this book and also become thoroughly familiar with every section of your Handbook. Then, when you become aware of the need for improving some phase of instruction, you will know where to look for help, and you will have a good start toward devising your own step-by-step plan for solving a particular problem.

Suggestions for Developing a Personal Handbook

Perhaps the best way to begin to create your Handbook is to purchase a three-ring binder and a generous supply of lined paper. Then, as soon as possible after you complete this course (but definitely before you are scheduled to student teach), go through the chapters of this book and prepare your own personalized versions of the information and teaching suggestions that have been provided. You might also examine other books for supplementary suggestions. (Titles of books that provide practical tips for teachers on a variety of topics will be noted at appropriate points in the following guidelines.)

Once you have a general outline, you might insert additional teaching ideas you remember having observed, ask acquaintances to do the same, and observe effective teachers to pick up some of their particular tricks of the trade. Finally, use your Handbook to organize ideas you pick up during methods courses. If you follow most of these suggestions, you should have a source book of ideas on how to handle many of the teaching problems you are likely to encounter when you first take charge of a classroom.

Here are some guidelines you might follow as you begin to develop your Handbook, arranged with reference to each chapter of the text.

Chapter 2 Stage Theories of Development

Suggestions for making use of Erikson's description of psychosocial stages:

1. Under the heading "Stages Described by Erikson," describe the psychosocial stages that relate to pupils of the age level you expect to teach (pp. 45–45).
2. If you expect to be teaching high school students, record brief definitions and comments on *identity, sex roles, occupational choice, psychosocial moratorium, negative identity,* and *identity statuses* (pp. 46–53). Record points about each of these concepts that you feel might be of value when the time comes to try to understand how and why adolescents behave as they do.
3. Examine Suggestions for Teaching: Applying Erikson's Theory in the Classroom on pages 55–58. Select points that relate to the pupils you expect to teach and prepare your own summary. If you expect to teach preschool pupils, examine points opposite the Handbook Heading on page 55 (top). For points that relate to elementary or secondary school students, look opposite the Handbook Headings on page 56.
4. If you expect to be teaching any junior or senior high school course where you will have opportunities to work with students on an individual basis, you might examine *Skill-Streaming the Adolescent: A Structured Learning Approach to Teaching Prosocial Skills* (1980) by A. P. Goldstein, R. P. Sprafkin, N. J. Gershaw, and R. Klein. Summarize the techniques they recommend.

Suggestions for making use of Piaget's description of stages of cognitive development:

1. List and write your own definition of the basic principles of Piaget's theory: *organization, equilibration, scheme, assimilation, accommodation* (pp. 59–61).
2. Describe the Piagetian stages for the pupils you expect to teach. In most cases you should describe at least *two* stages since it is unlikely that pupils at any grade level will exhibit characteristics of only one stage. (Refer to the descriptions on pages 62–67.)
3. Summarize the educational implications of Piaget's theory for the age and grade level you expect to teach (pp. 68–71).
4. Examine Suggestions for Teaching: Applying Piaget's Theory in the Classroom (pp. 73–74). Select points opposite the Handbook Heading for the appropriate

grade level on page 73 or 74, and prepare your own summary. Leave room for additional points to be added later. If you will be teaching preschool or primary grade pupils, read *Young Children's Thinking* (1966) by Millie Almy, E. Chittenden, and P. Miller for additional suggestions. If you will be teaching elementary grade pupils, consult *Piaget for Teachers* (1970) by Hans Furth, *Thinking Goes to School* (1975) by Furth and Harry Wachs, or *Piaget for the Classroom Teacher* (2nd ed., 1980) by Barry Wadsworth.

Suggestions for encouraging moral development:

1. Prepare your own capsule summary of differences between the *morality of constraint* and the *morality of cooperation* (Table 2.1).
2. Prepare your own capsule summary of Kohlberg's stages of moral reasoning (Table 2.2).
3. Examine Suggestions for Teaching: Encouraging Moral Development (p. 87). Select points opposite the Handbook Heading: Ways To Encourage Moral Development that you think might help you foster moral development in the students you expect to teach. For more detailed suggestions, consult *Promoting Moral Growth* (1979) by Richard Hersh, Diana Paolitto, and Joseph Reimer, or *Moral Reasoning* (1976) by Ronald Galbraith and Thomas M. Jones.

Chapter 3 Age-Level Characteristics

Go through the section of this chapter that describes characteristics of the pupils you expect to teach. Prepare your own list of characteristics and describe how you might allow for each. Pay particular attention to sections opposite Key Points and Handbook Headings.

For additional information on specific topics, you might examine the following books:

Preschool and primary grade teaching: *Teachers of Young Children* (3rd ed., 1981) by Robert D. Hess and Doreen J. Croft

Handling differences of opinion, emotional outbursts, hostile behavior: *Teacher and Child* (1971) by Haim Ginott; *Teacher Effectiveness Training* (1974) by Thomas Gordon

Chapter 4 Assessing Pupil Variability

1. Under the heading "Criteria for Evaluating Standardized Tests," record your own brief definitions of the following: *reliability, content validity, predictive validity, construct validity, norms* (pp. 154–158).
2. Under the heading "Types of Standardized Tests," describe the nature of each of the following: *achievement tests, diagnostic tests, aptitude tests, individual tests, competency tests* (pp. 158–159; see also the Mid-Chapter Review on p. 177).

3. Under the heading "Types of Scores," record brief descriptions of the following types of scores: *norm-referenced, criterion-referenced, raw score, percentile rank, z score, T score, stanine score* (pp. 160–166; see also the Mid-Chapter Review on p. 177).

4. Under the heading "Intelligence Testing," record a brief definition of *intelligence* and state ways in which you can use the results of intelligence tests to improve student achievement.

5. Examine the Suggestions for Teaching: Using Standardized Tests (pp. 179–182), and prepare your own list of points to remember. Pay particular attention to the list of test-taking skills (pp. 179–180) to explain to your students before they take standardized tests.

Chapter 5 Dealing with Pupil Variability

1. Record your own brief description of the provisions of Public Law 94–142 (pp. 195–197). Be sure to describe these provisions: *development of an individualized education program, due process, protection in evaluation procedures, least restrictive environment* (including a definition of *mainstreaming*).

2. List characteristics of mildly retarded students (p. 208), and then outline teaching techniques summarized in the Suggestions for Teaching: Instructing Mildly Retarded Students (pp. 209–214). Include points noted under these Handbook Headings:

   Helping Mildly Retarded Pupils Deal With Frustration

   Combating the Tendency To Communicate Low Expectations

   Giving Mildly Retarded Students Simple Assignments

   Using Overlearning with Mildly Retarded Students

   Giving Mildly Retarded Students Proof of Progress

3. List characteristics of pupils classified as learning disabled (pp. 214–215), and then outline the points summarized in the Suggestions for Teaching: Instructing Pupils with Learning Disabilities (pp. 218–221). Be sure to note techniques under these Handbook Headings:

   Preparing Your Own Versions of IEPs

   Arranging the Classroom Environment To Facilitate Learning

4. List characteristics of emotionally disturbed students (pp. 222–223). Under the Handbook Heading: Activities and Materials That Encourage Cooperation (p. 225), note techniques for encouraging withdrawn students to interact with classmates.

5. Examine the Suggestions for Teaching: Instructing Gifted and Talented Stu-

dents on pages 235–239. Draw up your own list of guidelines, including points noted under these Handbook Headings:

Providing Horizontal and Vertical Enrichment

Individualized Study for the Gifted and Talented

Urging Gifted Students To Develop Creative Hobbies and Interests

6. Peruse the Suggestions for Teaching: Instructing Disadvantaged Pupils on pages 242–249. Draw up your own list of guidelines, including points noted under these Handbook Headings:

Ways To Teach Academic "Tricks of the Trade"

Using Productive Techniques of Teaching

7. Examine the Suggestions for Teaching: Promoting Multicultural Understanding (pp. 254–258). Draw up your own list of techniques for teaching students from diverse cultural backgrounds, including points noted under the Handbook Heading: Ways To Promote Awareness of Contributions of Ethnic Minorities.

Chapter 6 Devising and Using Objectives

1. Prepare your own capsule summary of the main headings of the taxonomies for the cognitive (pp. 270–272), affective (pp. 272–275), and psychomotor (pp. 275–277) domains.
2. Summarize Mager's suggestions for stating specific objectives (pp. 281–282).
3. Summarize Gronlund's suggestions for stating general objectives followed by lists of specific learning outcomes (pp. 282–285).
4. Print, type, or photocopy the lists of general objectives and specific outcome action verbs listed in Tables 6.1 (p. 285), 6.2 (p. 286), and 6.3 (p. 287).
5. Examine the Suggestions for Teaching: Using Instructional Objectives (pp. 296–309), and prepare your own list of procedures to follow in order to make effective use of instructional objectives.

Chapter 7 Behavioral Theories of Learning

1. Write a brief description of each of these basic principles of operant conditioning: *positive reinforcement, negative reinforcement, punishment, time-out, extinction, generalization, discrimination* (pp. 322–326).
2. Describe how and why you might set up a learning situation according to each of these reinforcement schedules: *fixed interval, variable interval, fixed ratio, variable ratio* (pp. 327–328).
3. Describe the nature and purpose of each of the following types of computer-

assisted instruction programs: *drill and practice, tutorial, problem solving, dialogue* (pp. 335–336).

4. Prepare a list of features commonly found in CAI programs that violate basic operant conditioning principles (p. 338). Prepare a second list that contains the features of a well-designed CAI program (p. 339).

5. Describe how you would use each of the following techniques to modify student behavior: *shaping, token economy, contingency contracting, extinction, time-out, response cost* (pp. 340–344).

6. Outline the four basic processes of observational learning (pp. 346–384).

7. Examine Suggestions for Teaching: Applying Behavioral Theories in the Classroom (pp. 352–368). Use the following Handbook Headings to organize your own list of applications. Refer to the examples following most points for specific ideas and techniques, selecting those that are most appropriate for the grade level and subject(s) you expect to teach.

Checking on Causes of Behavior

Ways To Supply Specific and Immediate Feedback

Ways To Supply Delayed Feedback

Ways To Supply Different Types of Reinforcement

Ways To Use Schedules of Reinforcement

Describing Terminal Behavior

Ways To Encourage Perseverance

Ways To Use Behavior Modification To Maintain Control

Chapter 8 Information Processing Theory

1. Write a brief description of each of the following structures: *sensory register* (p. 379), *short-term memory* (p. 382), *long-term memory* (p. 385).

2. Note factors that influence *recognition* and *attention* and ways that attending can be encouraged (pp. 380–382).

3. Describe how *maintenance rehearsal* (p. 383) differs from *elaborative rehearsal* (p. 383).

4. Describe how *organization* (p. 384) and *meaningfulness* (p. 384) help people store information in long-term memory.

5. Explain how *schemata* in long-term memory influence learning and recall (pp. 387–389).

6. Write a brief description of *metacognition* (p. 389) and explain its role in learning.

7. Prepare a list of *memory-directed tactics* and *comprehension-directed tactics* that you might help your students learn to use (p. 393).

8. Describe the components of a *learning strategy* and how you might help your students learn to formulate them (pp. 394–403).

9. Examine the Suggestions for Teaching: Helping Your Students Become Efficient Information Processors (pp. 405–417), and note procedures you might follow, including points relating to each of these Handbook Headings:

Techniques for Capturing Attention

Techniques for Maintaining Attention

Techniques for Increasing Attention Span

Ways To Use Chunking To Facilitate Learning

Organizing Information into Related Categories

Ways To Stress Meaningfulness

Ways To Teach Comprehension Tactics

Ways To Teach Learning Strategies

Chapter 9 Cognitive Learning Theories and Problem Solving

1. Briefly describe the significance of *structure* (pp. 425–426), the *spiral curriculum* (p. 426), and *discovery* (pp. 426–427) in Bruner's thinking about learning and teaching.
2. List and record an example of the various techniques Bruner developed for use in presenting the MACOS curriculum (pp. 427–428).
3. Examine the Suggestions for Teaching: Using The Discovery Approach in the Classroom (pp. 430–443), and prepare your own outline of ideas to try in your classroom. Include the following Handbook Headings in your own set of applications:

Ways To Arrange for Discovery To Take Place

Ways To Supervise Discovery Sessions

Techniques for Arranging Small-Group Discussions

Setting Up Projects and Contracts

4. Explain the relationship of *expository teaching* to *meaningful reception learning* (pp. 443–446).
5. Describe and provide an example of *well-structured problems* (p. 446), *ill-structured problems* (p. 446) and *issues* (p. 447).
6. List techniques you might use to improve students' skills on each of the following problem-solving steps (pp. 447–455):

Realize that a problem exists.

Understand the nature of the problem.

Compile relevant information.

Formulate and carry out a solution.

Evaluate the solution.

7. Explain the role of *intellectual skills* in problem solving (pp. 455–456).
8. Describe the conditions that lead to *positive transfer* (p. 470) and the conditions that lead to *negative transfer* (p. 470).
9. Describe the essence of *specific transfer, general transfer, vertical transfer,* and *lateral transfer* (pp. 470–471).

Chapter 10 Humanistic Approaches to Education

1. Briefly summarize the basic philosophies of education espoused by Maslow (pp. 481–482), Rogers (pp. 482–484), and Combs (pp. 484–485).
2. Summarize basic ideas presented by Gordon in *Teacher Effectiveness Training* (pp. 486–487), and note how you might determine problem ownership and use I-messages.
3. List techniques you might use to put into practice *invitational learning* as described by Purkey (p. 487).
4. Describe the essence of the *values clarification* approach (p. 489).
5. Refer to the Suggestions for Teaching: Using Humanistic Techniques in the Classroom (pp. 500–509), and prepare your own outline of procedures to follow. Include notes relating to each of these Handbook Headings:

Ways To Give Pupils Choices

Using Self-paced and Self-selected Styles

Ways To Communicate Interest in Pupils as Individuals

Ways To Help Students Develop Positive Feelings About Themselves

Ways To Set Up Values Clarification Sessions

Chapter 11 Motivation

1. Write brief summaries of the *behavioral* and *social learning* views of motivation (pp. 519–520). Then note some possible disadvantages of overuse of behavioral techniques (pp. 520–521).
2. Write a brief summary of the *cognitive* view of motivation (pp. 521–523). Then note limitations of this approach to motivating students (p. 523).
3. Record your interpretation of Maslow's *hierarchy of needs* (pp. 523–525). Then note educational implications of Maslow's theory (pp. 525–526) and possible limitations of such interpretations (pp. 526–527).
4. Note different ways that students may respond to success and failure (pp. 529–531).

5. Summarize findings regarding the impact of *competitive* and *cooperative* reward structures (pp. 532–536).
6. Summarize Brophy's argument about the significance of valuing learning for motivation (pp. 537–539).
7. Prepare your own version of the troubleshooting check list on pages 539–541, or note the page numbers on that list so that you will be able to turn directly to that section of the text when you want to try to identify possible causes of lack of student interest in learning.
8. Examine Suggestions for Teaching: Motivating Students To Learn (pp. 543–576). Use the following Handbook Headings to organize your own set of applications:

Ways To Make Learning Active

Ways To Promote Investigation

Ways To Make Learning Seem Adventurous

Ways To Make Learning Social

Ways To Make Learning Useful

Using Behavior Modification Techniques To Motivate

Ways To Arrange Short-term Goals

Ways To Analyze Motivation Problems

Ways To Satisfy Physiological Needs

Ways To Satisfy Safety Needs

Ways To Satisfy Belonging Needs

Ways To Satisfy Esteem Needs

Ways To Encourage Self-competition

Ways To Encourage Students To Set Their Own Objectives

Ways To Supply Positive Feedback

Ways To Permit Students To Direct Their Own Learning

Encouraging a Need for Achievement

Chapter 12 Measurement and Evaluation of Classroom Learning

1. Write your own definitions of *measurement* and *evaluation* (p. 584).
2. Describe the different types of *performance tests* and explain the purpose for using each one (pp. 587–589).
3. Describe the purpose of *written tests* and the various types of items that can be used in written tests (p. 589).
4. Prepare a list of the kinds of factors (such as attractiveness) that have been

found to influence teacher reactions to pupil behavior and performance, referring to the conclusions of Brophy and Good (p. 592) and Braun (p. 592). Then summarize guidelines to follow in efforts to minimize your own tendency to be influenced by such factors, using the Handbook Heading (if appropriate): Ways To Minimize Subjectivity.

5. Examine Suggestions for Teaching: Effective Techniques of Evaluation (that begins on page 593). Use the following Handbook Headings to draw up your own list of guidelines:

Outlining Units of Study

Being Considerate in Scheduling

Using a Table of Specifications

Guidelines for Writing Test Questions

Using Different Types of Test Items

Techniques for Evaluating Skills and Projects

Preparing a Detailed Key

Analyzing Test Items

6. Explain the rationale for using a *norm-referenced* approach to determining grades and summarize the procedures for doing so (pp. 621–630).
7. Explain the rational for using a *criterion-referenced* approach to determining grades and summarize the procedures for doing so (pp. 630–631).
8. Examine the suggestions for using a *mastery learning* approach (pp. 632–642). write a brief description of how you might proceed if you decide to use a mastery approach.

Chapter 13 Classroom Management

1. Draw up your own list of guidelines based on Kounin's *Discipline and Group Management in Classrooms* (summarized on pages 604–609). Use the following Handbook Headings:

Learning To Deal with Overlapping Situations

Learning How To Maintain Momentum

Ways To Keep the Whole Class Involved

2. Outline the characteristics of a well-managed classroom reported by University of Texas researchers (p. 656). Include points relating to this Handbook Heading: Planning How to Handle Routines
3. Summarize the reasons given for the occurrence of school violence (p. 666). Then make a list of suggestions for reducing school violence (pp. 666–669).

4. Examine the Suggestions for Teaching: Handling Problem Behavior (pp. 670–674), the section on Influence Techniques (pp. 674–675), and the discussion of I-messages and the no-lose method (pp. 683–686). Draw up your own list of classroom control techniques, using the following Handbook Headings:

Analyzing Feelings After Dealing with Troublemakers

Being Prompt, Consistent, and Reasonable in Controlling the Class

Ways to Establish Rapport

Experimenting with Behavior Modification

Signals To Use To Nip Trouble in the Bud

Ways To Supply Situational Assistance

Ways To Use Reality and Value Appraisal

Using Retribution as Positively as Possible

Using I-Messages

Speculating About Problem Ownership

Trying the No-Lose Method

Becoming a Better Teacher: Questions and Suggestions

The purpose of the following lists of questions and suggestions is to make it possible for you to engage in a systematic attempt to improve your teaching effectiveness after you have actually embarked on your career in the classroom. The points noted in these pages are presented in the form of questions and suggestions so that you can analyze your teaching style on a point-by-point basis. They are organized with reference to the Handbook Headings printed in the margins, the same headings that you have been urged to use as the basis for sections of your Handbook. The reasoning behind this dual use of Handbook Headings is that if you become aware of a weakness in your teaching technique as you examine the questions that follow, you will know exactly where to turn for specific ideas about how to overcome it (provided you have prepared a comprehensive personal Handbook).

When you first begin to teach, it is recommended that you spend a few minutes at the end of each school day referring to these questions and suggestions. If you follow a procedure of systematically working through the entire list, you will not only analyze many facets of your teaching style; you will also become familiar with where you can find leads to help you when you later encounter various kinds of teaching problems.

In some of the sections that follow, observational or other exercises are described. You might use these exercises to obtain information about certain types of pupil behavior or to plan group and individual instructional activities. If you are asked to assign grades for "citizenship" or "work habits," you might use the observational techniques described to make your evaluations as systematic and objective as possible.

Chapter 2 Stage Theories of Development

Ways To Apply Erikson's Theory (Preschool and Kindergarten)

Am I providing plenty of opportunities for younger pupils to develop a sense of autonomy? What else can I do to foster independence? Am I doing my best to minimize the emergence of feelings of doubt or shame? Suggestion: Check on how often I give children ample time to complete something on their own, how often I finish a task *for* a child.

With older pupils, am I making it possible for feelings of initiative and accomplishment to emerge? Do I make pupils feel guilty by imposing unnecessary restrictions or regulations? Suggestion: Keep a record of how much time I spend directing activities and how much time I permit pupils to engage in self-selected activities.

Ways To Apply Erikson's Theory (Elementary Grades)

Am I arranging learning experiences so that pupils can complete assignments successfully and in such a way that they acquire feelings of genuine accomplishment? What can I do to minimize feelings of inferiority on the part of those who don't do as well as others? Suggestion: Arrange learning situations so that pupils compete against themselves and frequently experience a sense of successful achievement. Use mastery learning techniques described in Chapter 12.

Ways To Apply Erikson's Theory (Secondary Grades)

What can I do to foster the development of a sense of identity? Do I take enough personal interest in individual students so that they feel they are being recognized as individuals? Suggestion: Keep a record of the number of times I recognize—say hello to, call on, smile at, talk with—each student in my classes. If I discover I have ignored some students, make it a point to address them by name and comment favorably on their work.

Is there anything I can do in the courses I teach to help students begin to think about occupational choice? Can I provide specific job skills, or should I concentrate on helping pupils get ready for college, not only by learning subject matter, but by becoming skilled students? Suggestion: Make a list of job skills—academic *and* nonacademic—I can teach in my classes.

Is it appropriate in the courses I teach to encourage analysis of sex roles so that each individual can develop a personal philosophy of how to deal with sex differences? Suggestion: Check to see if it will be appropriate to set up a discussion of male and female attitudes and achievement in the field of study I teach.

Should I explain the concept of *psychosocial moratorium* to students and point out that there is no reason to panic if they are not positive about occupational choice by the time they graduate? Suggestion: Point out that some of the famous people in almost any field of endeavor floundered around before they settled on that particular career.

How can I be tolerant of students who have chosen a negative identity? What can I do to avoid confirming a student's negative identity by reacting too harshly to impertinent or disruptive behavior? If I really have to put down a trouble-maker, do I try to give him or her a chance to do something praiseworthy immediately afterward? Suggestion: Keep a record of what I say and whom I say it to when I really criticize students. Then write out some guidelines for doing a more effective, positive job of handling the next incident involving a disruptive student. (Check Chapter 13 for ideas.)

Am I remaining aware of the fact that many of my pupils may be thinking in preoperational terms, that is, that they tend to think of only one quality at a time and are incapable of mentally reversing actions? What can I do to arrange learning experiences that stress only one thing at a time and also feature physical manipulation of objects rather than mental manipulation of symbols? Suggestion: Ask veteran teachers about teaching materials and techniques that stress manipulation.

Ways To Apply Piaget's Theory (Preschool and Elementary Grades)

What can I do to set up learning experiences so that pupils can learn through their own activities and also explain things to each other? Suggestion: Next week, set up some learning centers (tables with books, objects, and instructional materials in various areas of study and interest), and invite pupils to make and share discoveries.

How can I avoid having students acquire merely verbal learning (that is, memorizing statements that they do not really understand)? What can I do to encourage students to concentrate on concepts and ideas they thoroughly comprehend? Suggestion: Give pupils frequent opportunities to explain ideas in their own way.

Should I ask individual pupils to carry out some of the Piaget experiments so that I can estimate if they are thinking at the preoperational level and also give insight into how young children think? Suggestion: Pick out appropriate Piaget experiments that are described in Suggestions for Further Study (pp. 89–93) and obtain and prepare the necessary materials so that I will be equipped to evaluate how my students think.

When confronted by a tattletale or when discussing classroom rules, do I keep in mind that pupils of this age are moral realists and that they will need separate rules for different situations and tend to concentrate on consequences rather than intentions? Suggestion: If students get needlessly upset over minor rule infractions, point out that sometimes it is better to change the rules slightly, and go on to another topic.

What can I do to allow for the fact that most pupils shift from concrete to formal thinking around the sixth grade or so and that they will sometimes think one way, sometimes the other? Should I use some of Piaget's experiments or class exercises to estimate how many pupils are capable of formal thinking? Suggestion: Pick out appropriate Piaget experiments that are described in Suggestions for Further

Ways To Apply Piaget's Theory (Secondary Grades)

Study (pp. 88–93) and obtain and prepare the necessary materials so that I will be equipped to evaluate how my students think.

When students show that they are capable of formal thought, how can I teach problem-solving skills? Suggestion: Make a list of promising ways to teach problem solving after examining the section on that topic in Chapter 9, pages 447–455.

Should I avoid presenting far-out hypothetical situations in order to hold down the tendency for inexperienced formal thinkers to concentrate more on possibilities than realities? How can I encourage novice theorists to take into account realities? Suggestion: When selecting discussion topics, choose those that require students to deal with actual conditions and realistic problems and avoid those that more or less *force* far-out theorizing.

Ways To Encourage Moral Development

Am I taking into account differences between the moral thinking of younger and older pupils? Suggestion: Refer to Tables 2.1 and 2.2 on pages 63 and 77 of the text, or my own Handbook versions of those tables. Think about the kind of moral reasoning likely to be used by the pupils I teach.

Is it possible and appropriate for me—in the next few days—to introduce a classroom discussion of some aspect of morality? Suggestion: Refer to the techniques for arranging such discussions on page 87 of the text.

Chapter 3 Age-Level Characteristics

Active Games

Preschool and Kindergarten
What games and exercises can I use to permit pupils to be active in reasonably controlled ways? Suggestion: Ask veteran teachers for energetic but safe game ideas.

Riot-Stopping Signals and Activities

What signals can I use to gain immediate attention, even when the noise and activity level is excessively high? What activities and games can I use to calm down pupils when they begin to get carried away? Suggestions: Pick out some piano chords to use as an "Attention!" signal. Select two or three calming activities to use.

Allowing for Large Muscle Control

Am I requiring pupils to spend too much time working at finicky activities? Are the pencils, crayons, brushes, and tools we have in the classroom large enough, or do pupils seem to have difficulty manipulating them? Suggestion: Make an inventory of objects that are held in the hand, and check to see if some of them seem hard for children to manipulate.

Using Sociometric Techniques

Should I use sociometric techniques to become more aware of isolates? Should I try to help isolates develop skill and confidence in social situations by pairing them with popular children? Suggestion: Make lists of children I think are popular and those I think are isolates. Then ask children, individually, to tell me who they like best, record their choices on a target diagram, and compare the socio-metric responses to my predictions.

Am I exerting too much control over my pupils? If I keep insisting on quiet play, am I doing it primarily for my own convenience? Should I stipulate that once a child gets out some blocks, finger paints, or the equivalent, he or she must play with these materials for at least a specified period of time? How can I help children become conscientious about cleaning up after they have engaged in activities that involve equipment? Suggestion: Keep a record of the amount of time pupils spend engaging in particular self-selected activities, and note what they do when they switch from one activity to another.

How Much Control is Necessary?

Suggested Form for Activities Record Sheet

Activity	Pupil	Date and Time	Termination Behavior
Easel painting	Mary	4/12/86 9:35–9:45	Put messy brushes on easel tray and went over to join Nancy in doll corner.

Can I use the time-sampling technique to obtain information that may help me understand pupil behavior or plan learning activities? Should I obtain samples of social behavior, leadership behavior, quarrels, favorite activities, games? Suggestion: Carry out a time-sampling study of activities children engage in during free play. Perhaps use the results to plan rotation schemes or additional activities.

Using Time Sampling To Study Behavior

Suggested Form for Time-Sampling Record Sheet

Name	Painting	Blocks	Doll Corner	Workbench	Book Corner	Etc.
John A.						
Mary B.						
Etc.						

(Observe first child on list for ten seconds, put tally under appropriate heading, observe second child for ten seconds, insert tally, and so on. Wait ten minutes and follow same procedure. Keep a separate record for each day of the week. Wait two weeks and repeat procedure. Compare total tallies for children and activities.)

If pupils show a preference for war or gangster games, should I try to divert their attention to other activities? What kind of dramatic play *should* I encourage? Should I collect props and costumes to encourage students to engage in preferred forms of dramatic play? Suggestion: Make a list of props and costumes likely to lead to desirable forms of dramatic play. Get ideas for creative activities from

Encouraging Desirable Forms of Dramatic Play

books such as *An Activities Handbook for Teachers of Young Children* (4th ed., 1985) by Doreen J. Croft and Robert D. Hess.

Encouraging Girls To Achieve, Boys To Be Sensitive

Are there books in our classroom library that depict girls or older females as weak and submissive and destined to become only housewives? If so, should I dispose of them? Are there plenty of books that depict females engaging in a wide variety of careers? If girls in the class persist in playing with dolls, should I try to encourage them to engage in other activities? Suggestion: Carry out a time-sampling study to determine the proportion of girls and boys who engage in sex-stereotyped activities (for example, girls playing with dolls). (Use time-sampling form outlined above.)

Helping Pupils Understand Anger

The last time a pupil became angry about something or hit someone, or the like, did I simply intervene and punish, or did I try to help the child understand the behavior? Should I use Ginott's technique of taking the child aside and asking questions intended to help him or her realize why the angry outburst occurred, and, if possible, suggesting less destructive ways of letting off steam? Suggestion: Make a resolution to try Ginott's technique the next time I deal with an angry child.

Ways To Avoid Playing Favorites

Am I reacting more positively to some pupils than others and inadvertently causing jealousy and resentment? Do I respond more favorably to attractive, obedient students who show that they like me and less favorably to unattractive, troublemaking, or indifferent pupils? What can I do to be more positive to pupils I find difficult to like? Should I make a systematic effort to spread my smiles and praise around more equitably so that all pupils get approximately the same number of positive reactions? Suggestion: Keep a record of the number of times I respond positively to each child in the class. If some children don't have a check mark opposite their names after one week, make sure they do by the end of the next week.

Handling Sharing

Do all pupils get to participate in sharing? If not, how can I encourage shy children to gain some experience talking in front of others? Am I prepared in case someone starts to share the wrong things? Suggestion: Keep a record of sharing participation—who speaks up, what they say, how long they talk, how confident they are.

Suggested Form for Sharing Record Sheet

Name	Date	Topic	Duration	Attitude and Manner	Notes
Jane	10/14	Kittens	30 seconds	Spoke so softly it was difficult to hear what she had to say. Looked at floor whole time.	Encourage her to talk more in small-group situations.

Am I using techniques likely to lead my pupils to develop feelings of competence and self-confidence? How often and how successfully do I

interact with individual pupils?

show interest in what children say and do?

permit and encourage independence?

urge pupils to strive for more mature and skilled ways of doing things?

establish firm and consistent limits?

explain why restrictions are necessary?

show pupils that their achievements are admired and appreciated?

communicate sincere affection?

serve as a model of competence?

Suggestion: List these points on a sheet of paper, and try to keep a tally of the number of times I behave in the way described. Then concentrate on one or two points and make a deliberate effort to do a better job using that type of behavior.

Suggested Form for Analyzing Effectiveness in Encouraging Competence

Individual Interaction			
Name	Date	Time	Nature of Interaction
Jimmy	11/16	2 min.	Noticed Jimmy was standing in center of room sucking his thumb. Asked him if he had looked at any new books. Took him over to book corner and helped him pick out a book. Asked him to tell me about it later.

(Notes of this type could be jotted down immediately after interactions of various kinds. Similar records could be kept for other activities likely to encourage competence.)

Primary Grades

Am I forcing students to sit still for too long? What can I do to give pupils legitimate reasons for moving around as they learn? Suggestion: Keep a record of the amount of "seat time" pupils have to put in before they are given the chance to move around.

Am I encouraging pupils to engage in safe but strenuous games during recess? When I am on playground duty, do I remain alert for reckless play? Have I found out the procedure to follow if a child is injured? Suggestion: Keep a time-sampling record of recess activities.

Margin notes:

Encouraging Competence

Building Activity into Classwork

Safe but Strenuous Games

Enjoyable Team Games	At recess time, do students engage in frequent arguments about rules? If so, what team games might be used to arouse interest but minimize quarrels? Should I ask pupils for their favorite games or consult books describing team games of various kinds? Should I find out what teachers of other grades do during recess in order to avoid duplication of recess activities? Suggestion: Ask the class to suggest games they would like to play.
Handling Feuds and Fights	Am I alert for the possibility of feuds in the classroom? If I discover that some pupils seem to delight in antagonizing each other, what can I do to effect a truce? Have I thought about how to handle an honest-to-goodness fight? Suggestion: Keep a record of arguments and fights. If some pupils get into an excessive number of altercations, try to persuade them to find other ways to let off steam.
Avoiding Sarcasm and Extreme Criticism	Do I tend to use sarcasm with pupils who may take what I say too literally? Have I recently been excessively critical of individual pupils or the entire class? Have I ever ridiculed or publicly humiliated a pupil? If so, what can I do to prevent myself from engaging in such activities in the future? Suggestion: At the end of each day, analyze any extreme or critical statements I have made. (If I can't remember all critical remarks, make it a policy to write them down.) Ask myself if my anger was justified. Try to remember how the victim (or victims) reacted.
Spreading Around Responsibilities	Do I use a fair rotation scheme so that all pupils—not just favorites—get a chance to handle enjoyable responsibilities? Do I give pupils enough chances to help out? What other classroom responsibilities can I add to those already assigned? Suggestion: Ask the class to suggest ways to spread around enjoyable responsibilities. Keep a Responsibility Record to make sure every pupil gets a fair share of the most popular responsibilities.
Ways To Handle Wrong Answers	Have I used an effective technique recently for handling hopelessly wrong answers? If not, what should I say the next time this occurs? Suggestion: Ask veteran teachers how they handle wrong answers.

Elementary Grades

Helping Pupils Adjust To the Growth Spurt	Do any pupils seem to be upset about the timing of the growth spurt—fast-maturing girls or slow-maturing boys in particular? Is there anything I can do to help them adjust (for example, explain about the spurt, point out that things will eventually even out, urge them to engage in activities that do not depend on size or strength)? Suggestion: Pick out the three most mature and least mature girls and boys, and check to see if they seem bothered by their atypicality.
Encouraging Creative Expression	Do I give my pupils chances to engage in art and craft activities and to display their work? How can I encourage pupils to work at original craft and art projects? Are there ways I can encourage students to sing, act, dance, or play an instrument

if they want to do so before an audience? Suggestion: Consider setting up a Friday afternoon amateur hour.

Are there certain pupils who seem to lack social skills to the point that they offend others? Suggestion: Privately, and as subtly as possible, talk to such pupils about how what they do influences the reactions of others. Urge them to make an effort to take into account the feelings of others.

Ways To Promote Social Sensitivity

Have I given the pupils in my classes opportunities to participate in the formulation of class rules? Suggestion: Invite students to offer their ideas on class rules, but set up the discussion so that concrete thinking and moral realism are controlled. That is, don't ask them to supply *all* of the rules, and don't ask them to determine how rule violators should be punished.

Encouraging Participation in Rule Making

Am I treating girls as if they are more delicate and in need of protection than boys? Is there anything I can do to encourage girls to be more independent and less eager to win my approval? Suggestion: Keep a record of how I treat boys and girls and how often they ask for my approval.

Encouraging Girls To Be Independent

What can I do to allow for differences in cognitive style? Suggestion: Follow the procedure described in the Suggestion for Further Study titled Becoming Aware of Differences in Cognitive Style, pages 144–145.

Allowing for Differences in Cognitive Style

Junior High

Have I paid any attention to the behavior of late-maturing boys and early-maturing girls? Suggestion: Make it a point to pick out the least mature boys and most mature girls in the class. Observe them to determine if they seem to exhibit the sorts of behavior reported in Table 3.2, page 127. If late-maturing boys or early-maturing girls seem bothered, try to give them opportunities to gain status and self-confidence by succeeding in schoolwork or by taking on classroom responsibilities.

Helping Early and Late Maturers Cope

Is vandalism a problem in our school? Suggestion: Use techniques Rutter found to be associated with lower levels of vandalism. Show students I appreciate them, make my room as comfortable as possible, permit students to participate in making decisions, emphasize academic achievement, serve as a model to be imitated, function as an efficient class manager.

Ways To Reduce Vandalism

High School

Do some of the girls in my classes talk or act as if they have no control over their future lives? Suggestion: Urge girls to focus on academic and occupational goals that will open up a wide range of job possibilities. If girls (in particular) respond to

Helping Girls Acquire Feelings of Self-Control

failure by talking or acting as if they have no ability, use motivational techniques described in Chapter 11 to induce them to try harder the next time.

Helping Students Overcome Depression

Do some of the pupils in my classes seem extremely depressed most of the time? Suggestion: Make it a point to show such pupils that I care about them. Use teaching techniques to encourage them to work toward—and achieve—a series of personal, short-term goals.

Chapter 4 Assessing Pupil Variability

Using Standardized Tests

Am I going to need to administer any standardized tests to my students this report period? Suggestion: Find out if any tests are scheduled. A few days before any test is to be given, review the Suggestions for Teaching: Using Standardized Tests (pp. 179–182). Review those Suggestions once again before looking over test profiles and discussing scores with students.

Explaining Test-Taking Skills

Is a standardized test scheduled to be given in the near future? Suggestion: The day before the test is scheduled, explain test-taking skills to the class by covering the points noted on page 179.

Chapter 5 Dealing with Pupil Variability

Helping Mildly Retarded Pupils Deal with Frustrations

Do I pay enough attention to the kinds of frustrations faced by mildly retarded pupils? Suggestion: Make it a point to observe how mildly retarded children in class react when instructional activities tend to call attention to differences in learning ability. If the poorest learners in the group seem disappointed or upset, try to figure out ways to help them cope with inability to do school work as easily as others.

Combating the Tendency to Communicate Low Expectations

Do I tend to communicate the impression that mildly retarded students are not really capable of learning? Suggestion: Examine the list of tendencies and antidotes included under point 2 on page 210 If I recognize that I tend to react in some of the ways listed as tendencies, use the antidote suggested to combat that tendency.

Giving Mildly Retarded Students Simple Assignments

When I assign class work, do I take into account that mildly retarded pupils cannot cope with complex tasks? Suggestion: Prepare some cards that outline simple tasks that can be completed quickly, and ask children with retardation to work on such assignments when more capable students are involved with more complex tasks.

Using Overlearning with Mildly Retarded Students

Am I remaining aware that mildly retarded students may need to go over material many times to master it? Suggestion: Set up individual or small-group study sessions to expose mildly retarded pupils repeatedly to basic material. Try to introduce some variety into such drill sessions, but remember that pupils should be aware that they are learning the same material, even if it is presented in different ways.

Would some of my pupils be more successful academically if they were more sophisticated about study skills? Suggestion: Examine the examples of ways to teach academic tricks of the trade on page 244. Put some of the techniques described into practice as soon as possible.

Ways To Teach Academic "Tricks of the Trade"

Am I using teaching techniques with disadvantaged pupils that have been found to be productive? Suggestion: Examine the lists of most and least productive teaching techniques on page 246. Make a systematic effort to use productive techniques, and avoid those that do not seem to be effective.

Using Productive Techniques of Teaching

Do my students seem to be poorly informed about the contributions made to society by different ethnic groups. Suggestion: Implement the suggestions on p. 255 for increasing awareness of contributions of ethnic minorities.

Ways To Promote Awareness of Contributions of Ethnic Minorities

Have I set up lessons so that mildly retarded students will know that they have made at least some progress? Suggestion: Develop a chart or personal learning diary so that students can record tangible indications of progress as they complete assignments.

Giving Mildly Retarded Students Proof of Progress

Do any of my students need special kinds of instruction, even though they do not qualify as handicapped under PL 94–142? Suggestion: With the cooperation of the student, try preparing an individualized education program by noting objectives, describing teaching practices and assignments, and listing criteria for determining achievement.

Preparing Your Own Versions of IEPs

Do some of my students seem to have a particularly difficult time getting to work or persevering once they get started? Suggestion: Refer to the suggestions on pages 220—221 for arranging the classroom environment so that distractions are minimized.

Arranging the Classroom Environment To Facilitate Learning

Do any of my students keep to themselves even though classmates try to interact with them? Suggestion: Instead of lecturing or guiding a discussion, use simulations and games that require cooperation among participants.

Activities and Materials That Encourage Cooperation

Am I too busy to help withdrawn students become more outgoing? Suggestion: Have a high-achieving, outgoing student tutor a withdrawn student in a subject that gives the withdrawn student difficulty.

Getting Students To Initiate Interaction With a Withdrawn Child

Providing Horizontal and Vertical Enrichment	Have I been doing an effective job of supplying horizontal and vertical enrichment? Suggestion: In drawing up lesson plans, write down some horizontal and vertical enrichment ideas to use with pupils who finish assignments faster than others.
Individualized Study for the Gifted and Talented	Am I doing a conscientious job of planning individualized study projects for gifted and talented learners? Suggestion: The next time I ask students to work on a project, explain the contract approach, and invite gifted and talented learners (in particular) to discuss independent learning contracts with me individually.
Urging Gifted Students To Develop Creative Hobbies and Interests	Am I doing anything to encourage gifted and talented students who have extra study time on their hands to develop hobbies or interests in creative ways? Suggestions: Pick out pupils who always seem to finish assignments ahead of time or who have exceptional abilities in some area of interest. Urge them to convert a hobby or interest into a specialized field of investigation. At the elementary level, urge pupils to really get involved with a hobby. At the secondary level, encourage pupils to prepare projects for competitions of various kinds.

Chapter 6 Devising and Using Objectives

Ways To Use Instructional Objectives	Am I making effective use of instructional objectives? Suggestion: When planning teaching units, look over Mager's suggestions for stating specific objectives, and Gronlund's ideas on stating general objectives with specific learning outcomes. Then figure out the best way to state instructional objectives for each unit.
Using the Taxonomy of Cognitive Objectives	Have I consulted the Taxonomy of Educational Objectives: Cognitive Domain when drawing up lesson plans? Suggestion: The next time I plan a unit, refer to the headings and questions listed in the abridged version of the taxonomy for the cognitive domain presented on pages 270–272. Make an attempt to list the kinds of things I would like students to learn, using the headings of the taxonomy to organize them. Also, check the list of categories and specific outcome verbs in Table 6.1, page 285.
Using the Taxonomy of Affective Objectives	Am I making a systematic attempt to identify affective objectives? Suggestion: Look over the Taxonomy of Educational Objectives: Affective Domain (pp. 272–275), and list some habits and attitudes I should try to foster. Then describe specific ways I might encourage students to achieve those affective objectives. Also, check the list of categories and specific outcome verbs in Table 6.2, page 286.
Using the Taxonomy of Psychomotor Objectives	Am I being systematic about teaching psychomotor skills? Suggestion: Examine Suggestions for Teaching: Using Psychomotor Objectives (pp. 304–308) and use those ideas the next time I teach a skill. Also, check the list of categories and specific outcome verbs in Table 6.3, page 287.

Chapter 7 Behavioral Learning Theories

Did I do anything today that shaped undesirable forms of student behavior? Suggestion: The next time the class is listless or uncooperative or the next time a student is rebellious, analyze what I said and did before and after I noticed the behavior to try to determine if I inadvertently shaped it. If it appears that I *did* cause problems for myself, make a resolution to avoid making the same mistake again.

Checking on Causes of Behavior

The last time I asked the class to learn factual material, did I supply specific and immediate feedback? Suggestion: The next time I plan a lesson that requires students to supply many right answers, make it a point to arrange things so that feedback is frequent, specific, and immediate.

Ways To Supply Specific and Immediate Feedback

Am I taking into account that with meaningful material it may be preferable to supply delayed feedback? Suggestion: The next time I ask students to wrestle with "thought" questions, give them a chance to reason out, revise, and augment their answers before giving feedback.

Ways To Supply Delayed Feedback

Am I overusing certain types of reinforcement, thereby causing them to become ineffective? Suggestion: Make a list of dozens of different ways I can supply reinforcement. Then try to recall at the end of a day which ones I used and did not use in an effort to become a versatile rather than a mechanical reinforcer.

Ways To Supply Different Types of Reinforcement

Am I taking advantage of the impact of different schedules of reinforcement? Suggestion: When planning lessons, ask myself if I want spurts of effort (studying for exams) or steady output (continuous effort during a practice period), and plan to supply appropriate schedules of reinforcement.

Ways To Use Schedules of Reinforcement

Am I being systematic enough about describing precisely what students should achieve when they complete an assignment or a unit? Suggestion: The next time I draw up lesson plans, describe the terminal behavior and figure out what students will need to know or do in order to achieve it.

Describing Terminal Behavior

Am I taking advantage of the Premack principle (Grandma's rule)? Suggestion: Invite students to draw up their own reward menus, and then let them reinforce themselves after they have completed tedious tasks or tough assignments.

Ways To Encourage Perseverance

Is it feasible and appropriate for me to use learning contracts? Suggestion: During the next report period or when we start a new unit, explain the contract system, and ask if any students would like to work on individual projects instead of carrying out standard assignments.

Can I do a more effective job of controlling the class if I use behavior modification techniques? Suggestion: Pick out a common type of discipline problem (for example, two students scuffling), and plan how to handle it using behavior

Ways To Use Behavior Modification To Maintain Control

modification techniques. Then the next time that kind of trouble occurs, try out the planned techniques, and make any adjustments that seem necessary.

Chapter 8 Information Processing Theory

Techniques for Capturing Attention

Do I make sure I have everyone's attention before I present a lesson? Do I use innovative ways to present something new? Suggestion: Experiment with attention-getting techniques such as those described on pages 405–406. Spend a few moments when getting ready to present something new by trying to come up with a distinctive "grabber."

Techniques for Maintaining Attention

Am I able to maintain everyone's attention once I get it? Suggestion: Use a variety of teaching methods and materials—flash cards, board work, student teams, class projects, problems that require unusual forms of thinking—to keep interest and attention at high levels.

Techniques for Increasing Attention Span

Can my students learn to increase their attention span? Suggestions: Experiment with games such as those described on pages 407–408. Play two taped messages simultaneously and ask the students to listen to one while ignoring the other. Then see how well they can answer factual questions about the message they were supposed to be listening to.

Ways To Use Chunking To Facilitate Learning

Am I presenting hard-to-learn material in small enough chunks and in study periods of appropriate duration? Suggestion: Examine hard-to-learn material to see if it can be divided into chunks. Set up distributed study periods so that students can learn material in bite-size chunks.

Organizing Information into Related Categories

Are there sets of information my students need to learn that can be grouped into related categories? Suggestion: Examine text chapters and lesson plans, and look for ways to organize material that needs to be memorized into groups so that one item leads to an association with other items.

Ways To Stress Meaningfulness

Are my students searching for meaning as they learn or do they seem to resort to rote memorization? Suggestion: Give a brief explanation of elaborative rehearsal, and present students with a planned exercise so that they get practice elaborating on new information by relating it to what they already know. Have students tell each other how they searched for meaningful associations, and then urge them to use the same technique on their own.

Ways To Teach Memory Tactics

Do my students have difficulty recalling important information for discussions, oral presentations, and tests? Suggestions: Schedule a series of sessions on how to memorize. Explain how experts use memory aids, and give an example of each of the mnemonic devices listed in my Handbook. Whenever possible, supply mnemonics to help students learn. Ask students to develop mnemonics on their own, and ask them to share these with the rest of the class.

Do my students have difficulty understanding the meaning of what they read or of what I present in class? Suggestions: Schedule a series of sessions on how to study. Explain the purpose and mechanics of summarizing, self-questioning, and notetaking (see pp. 414–415). Provide opportunities for students to practice these skills on material they have been assigned to read. Give corrective feedback as needed. You might also prepare graphic displays of ideas like the concept maps in the Study Guide that accompanies this text.

Ways To Teach Comprehension Tactics

Are my students likely to benefit from use of learning strategies? Suggestion: Read the descriptions of learning strategies on pages 392–399. If it seems likely that my students might be able to formulate a strategy as described or a variation of it, explain the basic procedures and have them give it a try. After they have experimented with the strategy, ask them to discuss how it worked and how it might be improved.

Ways To Teach Learning Strategies

Chapter 9 Cognitive Learning Theories and Problem Solving

When I set up a discovery session, do I arrange the situation so that it helps students gain insight? Suggestion: The next time I plan a discovery session, think about how to present background information or otherwise arrange things so that students are likely to grasp new relationships.

Ways To Arrange for Discovery To Take Place

Am I doing an effective job supervising all-class discussions? Suggestion: Make up a check list of steps to follow in supervising discovery sessions that involve the entire class. Include such things as how to arrange desks and chairs, what sorts of questions to ask, a reminder to wait at least three seconds for students to respond, phrases to use when probing for more complete or revealing answers, and a strategy for calling on students so that everyone remains alert but no one feels threatened or ignored.

Ways To Supervise Discovery Sessions

Am I doing an effective job arranging small-group discussions? Suggestion: Make up a checklist of steps to follow in setting up and supervising small-group discussions. Include ideas on how to organize the groups and select a moderator and recorder, what to do while the groups interact, and guidelines for when to intervene.

Techniques for Arranging Small-Group Discussions

Should I give my students opportunities to engage in self-directed individual or small-group discoveries? Suggestion: Depending on the grade level or subject, experiment with project cards or the contract approach.

Setting Up Projects and Contracts

Chapter 10 Humanistic Approaches to Education

Ways To Give Pupils Choices

Am I giving my students plenty of opportunities to participate in making decisions and freedom to choose among alternatives? Suggestion: Try out the ten-step procedure recommended by Howe and Howe for permitting pupils to participate in planning a teaching unit.

Using Self-Paced and Self-Selected Styles

Should I introduce student self-direction by first using self-paced and then self-selected styles of learning? Suggestion: Set up a unit so that students can work at their own pace. Then set up a unit where students can choose from a variety of topics (perhaps presented on activity cards). If the activity cards work out, look for additional activities in teachers' journals and also ask pupils to make up activities to add to an "Independent Project File."

Ways To Communicate Interest in Pupils as Individuals

Am I communicating the feeling to students that I am interested in them as individuals? Suggestion: The next time I schedule a work period or exam, glance around the room and silently try to name every pupil in class. If I can't think of the names of some pupils, work at learning those names that afternoon. The next day make it a point to say something to all "unrecognized" pupils, partly to get practice in using their names, and partly to show them that I am aware of their existence and that I am interested in them as individuals.

Ways To Help Students Develop Positive Feelings About Themselves

Have I used any techniques recently to try to encourage students to feel good about themselves? Suggestion: Try out a values clarification strategy that encourages pupils to describe things they have done that they are proud of.

Ways To Set Up Values Clarification Sessions

Should I use any values clarification strategies during the next two weeks? Suggestion: Read the section on values clarification in Chapter 10 and/or one of the recommended books consisting of V.C. strategies, and pick out at least one to try out next week.

Chapter 11 Motivation

Ways To Make Learning Active

Am I giving my students enough chances to be active as they learn? Suggestion: Examine the examples of active learning on pages 544–545, and plan ways to use one or more of such techniques during the next few days.

Ways To Promote Investigation

Are there ways that I can give my students greater opportunities to *investigate?* Suggestions: Consider the possibility of setting up investigation centers in the room. Take the entire class to the library and have them select books in an area of interest. Ask the class to suggest possible field trips or guest lecturers.

Ways To Make Learning Seem Adventurous

Are there ways that I can legitimately and effectively use some "show biz" techniques in my classroom? Suggestions: As I plan each new unit, think about dramatic or unexpected ways to introduce it. Examine the techniques devised by

Cullum (pp. 546–548) to see if identical or similar activities might fit into lesson plans.

Am I giving my students opportunities to engage in social interaction as they learn? Suggestions: Have students team up and study for exams or prepare reports. Consider use of role playing or simulation games.

Ways To Make Learning Social

Am I making sure that my students are aware that what they are learning is useful or potentially useful? Suggestions: Frequently point out how what is being learned can be used. Devise class exercises that demonstrate the potential value of what is being learned.

Ways To Make Learning Useful

Am I making use of behavior modification techniques to help students stick with material that is not intrinsically interesting? Suggestions: Consider setting up a series of tasks so that students are aware of progress. Supply positive reinforcement in the form of verbal and written comments. Encourage students to use behavior modification techniques on themselves by following procedures similar to those described on pages 550–551.

Using Behavior Modification Techniques To Motivate

Am I expecting my students to work toward remote goals? Suggestion: Try developing the equivalent of a goal card, or use some variation of the personalized system of instruction.

Ways To Arrange Short-term Goals

Am I being systematic about analyzing motivation problems? Suggestion: Follow the procedures described on pp. 553–554. Make it a point to observe how students respond to assignments, and then speculate about causes of lack of motivation by referring to the troubleshooting check list on pages 539–541.

Ways To Analyze Motivation Problems

Am I taking into account the physiological needs of my students? Suggestions: List specific ways to make sure students' physiological needs are satisfied—for example, let students go to the bathroom as often as they (legitimately) need to. At frequent intervals, ask students if the room seems too cold or warm. Consider scheduling snack time, or urge students to have a snack between classes.

Ways To Satisfy Physiological Needs

Am I doing something that causes students to worry about their physical or psychological safety? Suggestion: Make up a list of safety-need dos and don'ts; for example, don't make students attempt any activity if they act apprehensive. Do make it a point to be sympathetic and supportive after students have had a bad experience.

Ways To Satisfy Safety Needs

Do my students give the impression that they feel welcome, relaxed, and accepted when they enter my classroom? Suggestion: Next month, schedule some sort of activity, such as a brief personal planning session, that gives me a chance to interact individually with every pupil in class.

Ways To Satisfy Belonging Needs

Ways To Satisfy Esteem Needs	Am I inadvertently putting down some of my students? Suggestions: Look for ways to play down public comparisons. Consider using the personalized system of instruction. Try to individualize assignments so that all students can improve.
Ways To Encourage Self-competition	Am I remembering the disadvantages of competitive reward structures? Suggestions: Have pupils keep private progress charts. Give recognition for good performance in a variety of activities. Follow the suggestions under the next two headings for encouraging pupils to set their own goals and finding a variety of ways to supply positive feedback.
Ways To Encourage Students To Set Their Own Objectives	Am I permitting my students to participate in setting individual objectives? Suggestion: Urge students to set goals for themselves by stating objectives in terms of a time limit, a number of proportion of correct responses, or a sample of actions. (Refer to the examples on pages 560–561.)
Ways To Supply Positive Feedback	Am I supplying plenty of positive feedback—in the most effective ways? When I use praise, do I use techniques that Brophy suggests are likely to be effective? Suggestion: Over a period of days, keep a record of how I use praise. Then analyze those praise responses with reference to the points raised by Brophy and the information summarized in Table 11.1 (p. 564).
Ways To Permit Students To Direct Their Own Learning	Am I being too dictatorial in determining what we will study and how we will learn it? Suggestions: Consider using the procedures for student-selected topics proposed by Howe and Howe (p. 567), the method for setting up a personal contract devised by Wlodkowski (p. 567), or the Check List of Prosocial Behaviors developed by Sorenson, Schwenn, and Bavry (p. 569).
Encouraging a Need for Achievement	Am I encouraging—or discouraging—my students to develop a sense of personal agency? Suggestion: Tell students who have just done poorly on some assignment that they *can* improve. Then encourage them to try harder by giving them a series of tasks of increasing difficulty and urging them to set their own goals. Consider attempting to strengthen feelings of self-worth by using techniques similar to those described by de Charms (pp. 574–576).
Ways To Use Modeling To Encourage Motivation To Learn	Am I setting a good example and calling attention to people who have benefited from diligent study leading to impressive achievements? Suggestions: Exude as much interest and enthusiasm as possible. Call attention to historical and public figures who have made significant contributions in various fields of study.

Chapter 12 Measurement and Evaluation of Classroom Learning

Ways To Minimize Subjectivity	Have I thought about ways to reduce the impact of such factors as the halo effect, cognitive dissonance, and projection? Suggestion: Consult the guidelines for reducing subjectivity on pages 592–593. Try out techniques that seem promising.

The last time I introduced a unit, did I explain what would be covered and tell students what they would be expected to do? Suggestion: The next time I plan a unit, make out a syllabus to be distributed the first day. Outline what will be covered, and explain how the grade will be determined.

Outlining Units of Study

Have I ever asked pupils for their reactions when I announce when exams will be scheduled or papers will be due? Suggestion: Each time I announce an exam or a project deadline, ask the class if there are any reasons I have overlooked that may make it difficult for them to meet those deadlines.

Being Considerate in Scheduling

Have I thought about using a table of specifications when I prepare exams? Suggestion: Look over the description of how to use a table of specifications on pages 598–601. If it appears that using such techniques will help improve exams in the subject(s) I teach, experiment with them when preparing the next exam.

Using a Table of Specifications

Have I examined the analysis of different types of test questions in Chapter 12? Suggestion: Read pages 605–613, and draw up my own list of guidelines for writing different types of test items. After writing the first draft of questions for the next exam, analyze each item with reference to the advantages and disadvantages listed in the item descriptions in the text. Use those points to improve the questions.

Guidelines for Writing Test Questions

Am I using a variety of test items on my exams? Suggestion: Analyze all recent tests I have given, and prepare a record of which types of items I have used. If I have overemphasized some types and ignored others, prepare a table of specifications for the next exam to make sure that I use a variety of items.

Using Different Types of Test Items

Am I going to need to evaluate skills for projects within the next few weeks? Suggestion: Before asking students to prepare projects or demonstrate their ability to perform a skill, plan how I will evaluate their productions or performance. Record techniques for evaluating projects and performance that I remember as fair and practical. Ask experienced teachers how they evaluate projects and performance.

Techniques for Evaluating Skills and Projects

The last time I corrected an exam, did I use a complete key? Suggestion: The next time I write exam questions, write a key that I can use in evaluating those questions. Then put myself in the position of a pupil, and check to see if the question clearly asks for the information listed in the key.

Preparing a Detailed Key

Have I analyzed the items on exams to weed out confusing or ineffective items and identify particularly good items? Suggestion: The next time I give an exam, ask students to help me identify good and bad questions. Do the same as I grade papers. Identify or record on index cards questions that seem to be particularly effective.

Analyzing Test Items

Making the Most of Mastery Learning

Have I considered using a mastery approach? Suggestion: Read the section on mastery learning on pages 632–635. Think about the possibility of using a mastery approach. If it will not be in conflict with school regulations, try out a mastery grading system some time this report period.

Chapter 13 Classroom Management

Learning To Deal with Overlapping Situations

Am I with it in terms of knowing what is going on in my classroom, or do I have too much of a one-track mind? Suggestions: Carry out a self-analysis of how I deal with simultaneous activities. Make it a point to look around the room continually as I carry out one activity and look for signs of incipient problems. Practice ways to handle more than one thing at a time. List some techniques to use to prove I'm with it: If I see two boys starting to shove each other just before I turn to write something on the board, tell them to stop as I write with my back turned. Start a sentence, insert a comment directed at the troublemaker, and go right on with the rest of the sentence.

Learning How To Maintain Momentum

Do I flip-flop from one activity to another or unnecessarily interrupt the flow of an activity? Suggestions: The next time I am tempted to interrupt what we are doing to comment on some unrelated incident or activity, fight down the impulse and keep things flowing. Also, make an effort to build momentum into class activities as I draw up plans for the day or period.

Ways To Keep the Whole Class Involved

Am I using techniques that tend to cause some members of the class to tune out? Suggestions: Make up a list of ways to keep everybody involved. Call on pupils in unpredictable order. Ask questions first, and then call on pupils. Ask several pupils to respond in quick succession. Have all pupils in the class respond to questions one way or another.

Planning How To Handle Routines

Have I made a concerted effort to anticipate and plan for how I intend to handle class routines? Suggestion: Ask an experienced teacher to describe typical classroom routines in our school and explain how he or she handles them. Then draw up my own detailed description of how I intend to manage my classroom.

Analyzing Feelings After Dealing with Troublemakers

How do I feel after I have to really put down a student? Suggestion: The next time I deal harshly with a pupil, make it a point to examine the emotional aftereffects I experience. If I am pleased and smug, should I be? If I am upset, what might I do to avoid experiencing similar emotional tension in the future?

Being Prompt, Consistent, and Reasonable in Controlling the Class

Am I being prompt, consistent, and reasonable in my efforts to maintain control of the class? Suggestions: Carry out a personal survey of how prompt and consistent I am as a disciplinarian. Perhaps ask the class to tell me in anonymous statements if they think punishments are reasonable.

The last time I sharply criticized a pupil, did I later make a move to effect a reconciliation? Suggestion: The next time I have to deal harshly with a pupil, make it a point to tell or show that individual that as far as I am concerned, bygones are bygones and I am not holding a grudge. Then try to give that pupil a chance to do something constructive.

Ways To Establish Rapport

Have I tried using a behavior modification approach to handle discipline problems? Suggestions: Write down and put into practice a series of steps to follow when dealing with classroom misbehavior. State rules or a description of what needs to be done in order to gain reinforcement. Perhaps invite pupils to prepare individual reward menus. Praise those who are doing what they should be doing. If negative behavior does not extinguish when it is ignored, point out unfortunate consequences that might occur if that behavior continues. At the same time, stress the desirability of completing the task and gaining reinforcement.

Experimenting with Behavior Modification

What signals might I use to communicate to incipient troublemakers that I am with it? Suggestions: Clear my throat. Pause a few seconds in midsentence, and stare at the misbehaving pupils. Move and stand near troublemakers. Direct a question at a pupil who is beginning to engage in disruptive behavior. Make a lighthearted remark about what is going on.

Signals To Use To Nip Trouble in the Bud

What techniques can I use to help potential troublemakers control themselves? Suggestions: Remind them of what they are supposed to be doing. Set up routines designed to minimize temptation. Send a pupil who seems on the verge of getting into trouble on an errand. Prepare the class and stress the need for control when a potentially explosive activity is imminent.

Ways To Supply Situational Assistance

How can I help pupils become aware of how their misbehavior regularly affects them and others? Suggestions: Take advantage of object lessons to illustrate why certain rules are necessary and logical. If a student must be criticized, follow it up with encouragement, conveying the idea that improved behavior is expected. Ask the class to help establish rules or at least talk about why rules are necessary and logical. After a tense and disagreeable experience, allow a cooling-off period, and then analyze what happened and why it should not happen again. Help pupils gain understanding of their own behavior when they show signs of losing control.

Ways To Use Reality and Value Appraisal

What are some things I can do to make punishment effective without causing negative repercussions? Suggestions: Try to make the punishment fit the crime. Withhold a privilege. Make cautious use of detention. Tell a disruptive student, "I want to have a conference at the end of the period (or day)." Find out what the school policy is for handling pupils who are so disruptive they must be sent out of the classroom.

Using Retribution as Positively as Possible

Using I-Messages

Am I applying Ginott's fundamental principle of communication, and am I using I-messages? Suggestion: Just after I reprimand pupils, jot down what I said. Then check to see if I criticized personality or character rather than the situation. If I *did* tell students they were lazy or sloppy or something similar, make a resolution to deliver an I-message the next time I face a similar situation—tell the student or the class how I feel about it.

Speculating About Problem Ownership

Have I ever tried to figure out who "owns" a problem before dealing with it? Suggestion: Starting tomorrow, try to classify the ownership of problems as soon as I become aware of them. If students are doing something disruptive or destructive, use an appropriate influence technique to handle it in an authoritative way. If the problem seems to be due to feelings of confusion, inadequacy, or incompetence, try active listening.

Trying the No-Lose Method

Am I trying to seek compromises when conflicts develop, or am I being too dictatorial? Suggestion: The next time I run into a conflict with an individual pupil or the class, try the no-lose method—define the problem, ask for and propose solutions, and come to mutual agreement about a solution.

Suggestions for Further Study

Coping with Frustrations

The frustrations you will need to cope with when you begin to teach will be similar to those teachers have faced for decades. Thus, even though *Mental Hygiene in Teaching* by Fritz Redl and William W. Wattenberg was published in 1959, it is still one of the clearest and most sympathetic discussions of ways teachers might cope with personal and professional problems they are likely to find.

Solving Problems

As you approach the end of your first year of teaching, you might find it of interest and value to read *Teaching Is Tough* (1980) by Donald R. Cruikshank and several associates. The book discusses common teaching problems under five headings: affiliation, control, parent relationships and home and community conditions, student success, and time. You would do well to postpone reading the book until after you have taught for several months because it contains a teacher problems check list that you can use to assess your skill at solving problems in each of the areas just noted and plan how to correct inadequacies. The book also outlines a twelve-step problem-solving process, and describes detailed techniques for handling each of the basic types of problems.

GLOSSARY

Accommodation Tendency to revise an existing scheme as the result of a new experience.

Achievement motivation Motive to achieve characterized by a desire to be successful; techniques designed to encourage students to strive to be successful.

Achievement test Standardized test designed to measure how much has been learned about a particular subject.

Acronym Mnemonic device made up of the first letter of a set of several words to be memorized.

Acrostic Mnemonic device made up of a sentence consisting of words that begin with the same first letter as a set of words to be memorized.

Adaptation Basic human tendency to adjust to the environment.

Adolescent egocentricism Tendency of adolescents to assume that their thoughts and actions are as interesting to others as to themselves.

Advance organizers Introductory materials that provide an organizing structure to help students relate new information to existing schemes.

Affective domain The domain whose taxonomy concentrates on attitudes and values.

Affective objectives Instructional objectives that stress attitudes, feelings, and values.

Agency Feeling on the part of individuals that they can control their own behavior (also called *personal agency*).

Androgyny Possessing both male and female characteristics.

Aptitude test Standardized test designed to supply an estimate of a student's potential ability in a particular area of study.

Assimilation Tendency to fit a new experience into an existing scheme.

Associative play Disorganized play, with no assignment of activities or roles.

Attribution theory Explanations of ways students respond to success or failure by attributing their performance to interactions between ability, effort, luck, and task difficulty.

Authoritarian parents Parents who lack warmth, make demands, and wield power, without taking into account the child's point of view.

Authoritative parents Parents who are confident in their abilities as parents and therefore provide their children with a model of competence.

Aversive control Students behave in a desired way in order to avoid having to do something disagreeable.

Behavioral learning theories Sets of principles based on observations of overt behavior.

Behavior disorder Term that is essentially synonymous with *emotional disturbance*. Preferred by many theorists because it calls attention to behavior that needs to be changed.

Behavior modification Technique of shaping behavior by reinforcing desirable responses, ignoring undesirable responses.

Chunking Memorization technique in which unrelated bits of information are grouped in some way.

Classical conditioning Form of learning first studied by Ivan Pavlov wherein a reflexive (or elicited) response becomes associated with a new stimulus (also called *Pavlovian conditioning*).

Cognitive domain The domain whose taxonomy stresses knowledge and intellectual skills.

Cognitive objectives Instructional objectives that stress knowledge and intellectual abilities and skills.

Cognitive style A marked tendency to repeatedly respond to problems in a particular way.

Cognitive theories Sets of principles proposed by psychologists to account for what happens in the minds of students as they learn.

Competency test Test designed to determine if individuals (such as potential high school graduates) possess minimum basic skills.

Competitive reward structure Classroom arrangement where only the best pupils earn rewards in the form of high grades.

Computer-assisted instruction Use of computers to present programs or otherwise facilitate or evaluate learning.

Confluent education Form of humanistic education stressing the flowing together of cognitive and affective elements.

Conservation Ability to recognize that properties stay the same despite a change in appearance.

Construct validity How accurately a test measures a particular attribute (or psychological construct).

Content validity How well the items that make up a test sample (or measure) a particular type of ability or understanding.

Contingency contracting Agreement that a teacher will supply a specified reward when a student completes a mutually agreed-upon assignment.

Convergent thinker Individual who tends to respond to questions and stimuli in predictable, conventional ways.

Cooperative play An organized form of play in which leadership and other roles are assigned; may involve some form of coordinated enterprise.

Cooperative reward structure Classroom arrangement where students are encouraged to help each other learn.

Criterion-referenced grading A student's performance is evaluated with reference to specified criteria or to that individual's previous level of performance.

Cumulative rehearsal A memory tactic in which a constantly changing set of items is repeated by continuously adding new items and dropping old ones.

Decentration Ability to consider more than one quality at a time.

Deficiency needs The lower needs (physiological, safety, belongingness and love, esteem) in Maslow's hierarchy.

Diagnostic test Test designed to identify specific academic strengths and weaknesses.

Disadvantaged pupils Pupils whose out-of-school experiences may fail to equip them for academic performance.

Discovery learning Form of instruction in which a teacher arranges the learning environment so that students can find their own answers.

Distributed practice Scheduling short study periods at frequent intervals.

Divergent thinker Individual who tends to respond to questions and stimuli in unpredictable, unconventional ways.

Egocentric thinking Assumption that others see things the same way; inability to imagine another's point of view.

Elaborative rehearsal Information processing techniques in which stored information is used to aid memorization. Facilitation of information transfer from short-term to long-term memory.

Emotional disturbance Condition characterized by chronic inability to learn, relate to others, or overcome depression (also referred to as *behavior disorder*).

Equilibration Tendency for children to seek cognitive coherence and stability.

Extinction Tendency for a conditioned response to disappear if not reinforced from time to time.

Extrinsic motivation Doing something to earn some sort of reward or because it is required.

Fear of failure An extreme degree of anxiety over the prospect of failure that motivates people to attempt to accomplish tasks that are either very easy or very difficult.

Fear of success Tendency of individuals to worry about being more successful than others because of fear of jeopardizing interpersonal relationships.

Fixed interval schedule Reinforcement supplied according to a fixed interval of time.

Fixed ratio schedule Reinforcement supplied according to a fixed pattern of responses.

Foreclosure type Adolescent who has unquestioningly endorsed the goals and values of his or her parents.

Frequency distribution Numerical or graphic record of scores earned by a class on one or more tests or graded assignments.

General objectives Objectives that describe the types of behavior students should exhibit in order to demonstrate what they have learned, accompanied by a sample of specific learning outcomes.

General transfer Transfer due to the use of the same cognitive strategies in working two tasks.

Generalization Tendency for a learned response to be aroused by any stimulus similar to a stimulus that was coupled with reinforcement (more specifically referred to as *stimulus generalization*).

Grade equivalent score Score on a standardized test that indicates level of performance with reference to average performance at different grade levels.

Growth needs The upper needs (self-actualization, knowing and understanding, aesthetic) in Maslow's hierarchy.

Growth spurt A period of unusually rapid physical growth between the sixth and ninth grades.

Heuristics Methods or techniques of problem solving.

Humanistic education Approach to instruction that stresses attitudes, values, personal fulfillment, relationships with others.

Identity Sense of psychosocial well-being produced by acceptance of one's appearance, clear goals, recognition from others.

Identity achievement type Adolescent who has made satisfying self-chosen commitments regarding sex role and occupational choice.

Identity diffusion type Adolescent who avoids thinking about goals, roles, and values.

Ill-structured problems Problems that are vaguely stated, have unclear solution procedures, and are subject to vague evaluation standards.

I-message A teacher explains how he or she feels regarding an unsatisfactory situation (recommended by Haim Ginott).

Individual education program (IEP) Specially planned program of instruction and evaluation designed for a particular handicapped child (as required by Public Law 94-142).

Individual reward structure A situation in which the rewards received by students are determined solely on the basis of each individual's accomplishments.

Information-processing theory Study of the ways sensory input is transformed, stored, recovered, and used.

Intellectual skills An ability to use rules to solve problems; composed of rules, concepts, discriminations, and associations.

Intelligence quotient (IQ) Score on an intelligence test (originally computed by dividing chronological age by mental age, with 100 representing average performance).

Interindividual variation Differences between individuals at a given point in time.

Intraindividual variation Differences within an individual over time and in different situations.

Intrinsic motivation Doing something for its own sake; the accomplishment of a task is its own reward.

Invitational learning Form of humanistic education in which teacher communicates to students that they are responsible, able, and valuable.

Irreversibility Inability to understand that one can return to the starting point of a sequence of mental or physical actions by performing the actions in reverse order.

Item analysis A quantitative method of determining the difficulty level and discriminating ability of multiple-choice items.

Keyword method Mnemonic device used to learn a foreign language word by forming a visual image or link with an English word.

Lateral transfer Transfer in which a previously learned capability is used to solve a similar problem in a different area.

Learned helplessness Feelings of helplessness and a lack of control over one's life, learned through experiences and from the reactions of others.

Learner-centered education An approach in which the teacher tries to be genuine and to establish a trusting, acceptant, empathetic attitude toward the student.

Learning More or less permanent change in behavior as a result of experiences.

Learning disabilities Disorders in basic processes that lead to learning problems not due to other causes.

Learning hierarchy The fixed sequence of associations, discriminations, concepts, and rules that must be learned to formulate and use a complex rule.

Learning strategy A general plan for improving one's ability to learn; comprised of metacognitive knowledge, strategic skills, and tactical skills.

Learning tactic A specific technique to memorize and/ or understand information to be learned.

Least restrictive environment Provision of PL 94-142 that directs school districts to place handicapped students in the most normal educational setting that the student's handicapping condition will allow.

Level of aspiration Tendency of individuals to set goals in an effort to succeed at the highest possible level while avoiding failure.

Long-term memory (LTM) Storehouse of permanently recorded information in one's memory.

Mainstreaming Policy of placing handicapped pupils in regular classes.

Maintenance rehearsal Information processing technique intended to help learners hold information for immediate use.

Massed practice Scheduling long study periods at infrequent intervals.

Mastery learning Technique of instruction whereby pupils are given multiple opportunities to master a series of exams, evaluated with reference to specified criteria.

Mean Arithmetical average of a distribution computed by adding together all scores and dividing by the mumber of scores.

Meaningful reception learning The integration of new ideas into existing knowledge schemes.

Median Middle score of a distribution.

Mental retardation Below average intelligence (defined by an IQ score of 67 or lower) accompanied by adaptive problems.

Metacognition Knowledge of how one's mind works; thinking about ways to improve one's ability to memorize and learn.

Mnemonic device Memory aid or system designed to improve recall.

Morality of constraint Moral thinking typical of children up to the age of ten or so: sacred rules, no exceptions, no allowance for intentions (also called *moral realism*).

Moriality of cooperation Moral thinking typical of children twelve years and older characterized by flexible rules, mutual agreements, allowance for intentions.

Moratorium type Adolescent who is suffering an identity crisis because of confusion or indecision about sex roles and/or occupational choice.

Motivation Arousal, selection, direction, and continuation of behavior.

Multicultural education Teaching practices that show understanding, acceptance, and encouragement for culturally diverse behavior and thinking patterns.

Negative identity Adopting forms of behavior opposite to those regarded as desirable by parents and most adults.

Negative transfer A situation in which prior learning interferes with subsequent learning.

Normal probability curve Theoretical distribution that takes the form of a symmetrical, bell-shaped curve.

Norm group A sample of individuals reflecting the larger population for which a test is intended; the norm group's scores serve as the standard of comparison for all other scores.

Norm-referenced grading A student's performance is evaluated by comparing it to the performance of others.

Observational learning Acquisition of a new form of

behavior as a result of observing another person benefit from using that behavior (also called *modeling*).

Operant conditioning Form of learning first studied by B. F. Skinner wherein a voluntary (or emitted) response is strengthened when it is reinforced.

Organization Basic human tendency to systematize and combine processes into coherent systems.

Parallel play Children play beside, but not really with, other children, perhaps using the same toys, but in an independent way.

Peg-word method Mnemonic device that involves associating a new item with a previously learned item.

Percentile rank Score that indicates the percentage of students taking a test who are at or below a particular raw score.

Perceptual centration Tendency to focus attention on only one characteristic of an object or aspect of a problem or event at a time.

Performance test A measure of how well people perform a particular skill or set of skills under more or less realistic conditions.

Positive transfer A situation in which prior learning aids subsequent learning.

Premack principle Students are allowed to engage in a self-selected activity after they complete assigned work (also called *Grandma's rule*).

Programmed instruction Form of instruction wherein material is organized into a series of small steps (frames) and feedback is supplied after each response.

Prosocial behavior Forms of behavior that involve understanding the needs and feelings of others, getting along with others, or functioning well in group situations.

Psychological androgyny Ability of an individual to assume masculine *or* feminine roles without difficulty or self-consciousness.

Psychomotor domain The domain whose taxonomy focuses on physical abilities and skills.

Psychosocial moratorium Period of delay of commitment or postponement of occupational choice.

Puberty The point in physical development when secondary sex characteristics appear and sexual reproduction first becomes possible.

Punishment A behavior modification technique that seeks to eliminate or suppress an undesired behavior by administering an aversive stimulus to an individual whenever the individual exhibits the undesired behavior.

Pygmalion effect Tendency for individuals who are treated as capable (or incapable) to act that way (essentially the same as *self-fulfilling prophecy*).

Reinforcement A behavior modification technique that seeks to strengthen a desired response by either presenting a positive stimulus after the behavior has been exhibited, or withdrawing an aversive stimulus after the behavior has been exhibited.

Reinforcement menu A behavior modification technique wherein students choose a positive reinforcer from a list of reinforcers whenever a desired behavior has been exhibited.

Reliability How consistent scores are if the same test is given to the same students a second time.

Scheme Organized pattern of behavior or thought.

Self-efficacy Feeling that one can successfully achieve a particular outcome (essentially the same as *agency* or *personal agency*).

Self-fulfilling prophecy Tendency for individuals to behave in ways they are expected to behave (essentially the same as *Pygmalion effect*).

Self-reinforcement Giving oneself a positive reinforcer whenever one's behavior meets or exceeds personal standards.

Sensory register Memory structure that holds information for possible processing.

Shaping Reinforcement of actions that move progressively closer to the desired result (or terminal behavior).

Short-term memory (STM) "Working" memory, or information temporarily stored in one's memory.

Skinner box Device developed by B. F. Skinner to study operant conditioning.

Social learning theory Form of behavioral learning theory attributing changes in behavior to observation and imitation.

Solitary play Children play alone, making no attempt to interact with others within speaking distance.

Specific objectives Objectives that specify the behavior to be learned, the conditions under which it will be exhibited, and the criterion for acceptable performance.

Specific transfer Transfer due to specific similarities between two tasks.

Spiral curriculum Teaching an idea in simplified form early in schooling and then reteaching it later in more complex form.

Spontaneous recovery The occasional reappearance of behaviors undergoing extinction.

Standard deviation Statistic that indicates the degree a particular score deviates from the mean of a distribution.

Standardized test Test prepared for nationwide use by a testing corporation which establishes norms by presenting a carefully selected set of items to a representative sample of students.

Stanine Score that indicates a pupil's position in a distribution divided into nine one-half standard deviation units.

Structure The basic or fundamental ideas of a subject and how they relate to each other.

Table of specifications Chart of types and numbers of test items to be included in an exam to ensure thorough and systematic coverage of a unit of study.

Target behavior A designated activity to be shaped through behavior modification (also referred to as a *terminal behavior*).

Task analysis Description of the elements or components of a task or skill.

Taxonomy Comprehensive classification scheme with categories arranged in hierarchical order.

Terminal behavior Desired result preselected by an experimenter or programmer who intends to shape behavior by applying operant conditioning principles.

Time-out Behavior modification technique in which undesirable behavior is weakened by temporarily removing positive reinforcement.

Token economy Reinforcing students through use of behavior modification procedures by supplying tokens (such as check marks) that can later be traded in for some reward.

Transfer Tendency for individuals to apply what they learn in one situation to other situations.

T score How far a raw score is from the mean in numerical terms, calculated by using a mean of 50 and a standard deviation of 10.

Validity How well a test appropriately measures what its users intend it to measure.

Values clarification Techniques of humanistic education designed to help students choose, prize, and act on their beliefs.

Variable interval schedule Reinforcement supplied after sporadic or unpredictable intervals of time.

Variable ratio schedule Reinforcement supplied according to a variable pattern of responses.

Vertical transfer Transfer in which a previously learned capability contributes directly to the acquisition of a more complex capability.

Vicarious reinforcement Imitating a modeled behavior that was positively reinforced in the expectation of receiving the same reinforcement.

Well–structured problems Problems that are clearly stated, can be solved using known solution procedures, and can be evaluated based on known standards.

Withitness Describes a teacher who demonstrates to students constant awareness of their behavior.

Zero transfer A situation in which prior learning has no effect on new learning.

Z score How far a raw score is from the mean in standard deviation units.

BIBLIOGRAPHY

Adelson, J. (1971). The political imagination of the young adolescent. *Daedalus, 100* (4), 1013-1049.

Adelson, J. (1972). The political imagination of the young adolescent. In J. Kagan & R. Coles (Eds.), *Twelve to sixteen: Early adolescence.* New York: Norton.

Adelson, J. (Ed.). (1980). *Handbook of adolescent psychology.* New York: Wiley.

Ahmann, J. S., & Glock, M. (1981). *Evaluating pupil growth: Principles of measurement* (6th ed.). Boston: Allyn and Bacon.

Ainsworth, M. D. S., & Wittig, B. A. (1972). Attachment and exploratory behavior of one-year-olds in a strange situation. In B. M. Foss (Ed.), *Determinants of infant behavior* (Vol. 4). New York: Wiley.

Almy, M. C., Chittenden, E., & Miller, P. (1966). *Young children's thinking.* New York: Teacher's College, Columbia University.

Alschuler, A. S. (1969). The effects of classroom structure on achievement motivation and academic performance. *Educational Technology, 9,* 19-24.

Ames, C., & Ames, R. (1984). Systems of student and teacher motivation: Toward a qualitative definition. *Journal of Educational Psychology, 76* (4), 535-556.

Anastasi, A. (1988). *Psychological testing* (6th ed.). New York: Macmillan.

Anderson, R. C. (1984). Some reflections on the acquisition of knowledge. *Educational Researcher, 13* (9), 5-10.

Anderson, T., & Boyer, M. (1978). *Bilingual schooling in the United States* (2nd ed.). Austin, TX: National Educational Laboratory.

Andre, M. E. D. A., & Anderson, T. H. (1978 79). The development and evaluation of a self-questioning study technique. *Reading Research Quarterly, 14,* 605-623.

Andre, T., & Phye, G. D. (1986). Cognition, learning, and education. In G. D. Phye & T. Andre (Eds.), *Cognitive classroom learning.* Orlando, FL: Academic Press.

Annis, L., & Annis, D. (1979, April). *A normative study of student's preferred study techniques.* Paper presented at the annual meeting of the American Educational Research Association, San Francisco.

Anthony, E. J. (1970). Behavior disorders. In P. H. Mussen (Ed.), *Carmichael's manual of child psychology* (3rd ed., Vol. 2). New York: Wiley.

Appleton, N. (1983). *Cultural pluralism in education.* New York: Longman.

Armbruster, B. B., Echols, C. H., & Brown, A. L. (1982). The role of metacognition in reading to learn: A developmental perspective. *The Volta Review, 84* (5), 45-56.

Asch, S. E. (1956). Studies of independence and conformity: A minority of one against a unanimous majority. *Psychological Monographs, 70* (9, Whole No. 416).

Atkinson, J. W. (1964). *An introduction to motivation.* Princeton, NJ: Van Nostrand.

Atkinson, J. W., & Litwin, G. H. (1960). Achievement motive and test anxiety conceived as motive to approach success and motive to avoid failure. *Journal of Abnormal and Social Psychology, 60,* 52-63.

Atkinson, J. W., & Raynor, J. O. (Eds.). (1974). *Motivation and achievement.* Washington, DC: Winston.

Atkinson, J. W., & Raynor, J. O. (1978). *Personality, motivation, and achievement.* Washington, DC: Hemisphere.

Atkinson, R. C. (1975). Mnemotechnics in second language learning. *American Psychologist, 30,* 821-828.

Atkinson, R. C., & Raugh, M. R. (1975). An application of the mnemonic keyword method to the acquisition of a Russian vocabulary. *Journal of Experimental Psychology: Human Learning and Memory, 104,* 126-133.

Atkinson, R. C., & Shiffrin, R. M. (1968). Human memory: A proposed system and its control processes. In K. W. Spence & J. T. Spence (Eds.), *The psychology of learning and motivation* (Vol. 2). New York: Academic Press.

Ausubel, D. P. (1963). *The psychology of meaningful verbal learning.* New York: Grune & Stratton.

Ausubel, D. P., Novak, J. D., & Hanesian, H. (1978). *Educational psychology: A cognitive view* (2nd ed.). New York: Holt, Rinehart & Winston.

Ausubel, D. P., & Robinson, F. G. (1969). *School learning: An introduction to educational psychology.* New York: Holt, Rinehart & Winston.

Ayllon, T., & Roberts, M. D. (1974). Eliminating discipline problems by strengthening academic performance. *Journal of Applied Behavior Analysis, 7,* 73-81.

Bachman, J. G., O'Malley, P. M., & Johnston, J. (1978). *Youth in transition: Vol. VI. Adolescence to adulthood: Change and stability in the lives of young men.* Ann Arbor, MI: Institute for Social Research.

Baker, K. (1985). Research evidence of a school discipline problem. *Phi Delta Kappan, 66,* 482-487.

Baldwin, A. L. (1980). *Theories of development* (2nd ed.) New York: Wiley.

Bandura, A. (1986). *Social foundations of thought and action: A social cognitive theory.* Englewood Cliffs, NJ: Prentice–Hall.

Bandura, A., Ross, D., & Ross, S. (1961). Transmission of aggression through imitation of aggressive models. *Journal of Abnormal and Social Psychology, 63,* 375-382.

Bandura, A., Ross, D., & Ross, S. (1963a). Imitation of film mediated aggressive models. *Journal of Abnormal and Social Psychology, 66,* 3-11.

Bandura, A., Ross, D., & Ross, S. (1963b). A comparative test of the status envy, social power, and secondary reinforcement theories of identificatory learning. *Journal of Abnormal and Social Psychology, 67,* 527-534.

Bandura, A., & Walters, R. H. (1963). *Social learning and personality development.* New York: Holt, Rinehart & Winston.

Banks, J. A. (1981). *Multiethnic education.* Boston: Allyn and Bacon.

Barth, R. (1979). Home-based reinforcement of school behavior: A review and analysis. *Review of Educational Research, 49* (3), 436-458.

Bartlett, F. C. (1932). *Remembering.* London: Cambridge University Press.

Bauer, G. L. (1985). Restoring order to the public schools. *Phil Delta Kappan, 66,* 488-490.

Baumrind, D. (1971). Current patterns of parental authority. *Developmental Psychology Monographs, 1,* 1-103.

Beck, A. T. (1970). *Depression: Causes and treatment.* Philadelphia: University of Pennsylvania Press.

Becker, W. C., Englemann, S., & Thomas, D. R. (1971). *Teaching: A course in applied psychology.* Chicago: Science Research Associates.

Bee, H. (Ed.). (1978). *Social issues in developmental psychology* (2nd ed.). New York: Harper & Row.

Bellezza, F. S. (1981). Mnemonic devices: Classification, characteristics, and criteria. *Review of Educational Research, 51,* 247-275.

Bem, S. L. (1975). Sex-role adaptability: One consequence of psychological androgyny. *Journal of Personality and Social Psychology, 31,* 634-643.

Bem, S. L. (1976). Sex-typing and androgyny: Further explorations of the expressive domain. *Journal of Personality and Social Psychology, 34* (5), 1016-1023.

Bennett, N., Jordan, J., Long, G., & Wade, B. (1976). *Teaching styles and pupil progress.* Cambridge, MA: Harvard University Press.

Berko, J. (1958). The child's learning of English morphology. *Word, 14,* 150-177.

Berliner, D. C. (1986). In pursuit of the expert pedagogue. *Educational Researcher, 15* (7), 5-13.

Berscheid, E., Walster, E., & Bohrnstedt, G. (1973). The happy American body: A survey report. *Psychology Today, 7* (6), 119-131.

Best, R. (1983). *We've all got scars.* Bloomington, IN: Indiana University Press.

Beyer, B. K. (1988). *Practical strategies for the teaching of thinking.* Boston: Allyn and Bacon.

Bjork, R. A. (1979). Information-processing analysis of college teaching. *Educational Psychologist, 14,* 15-23.

Blatt, M., & Kohlberg, L. (1978). The effects of classroom moral discussion upon children's level of moral development. In L. Kohlberg & E. Turcel (Eds.), *Recent research in moral development.* New York: Holt, Rinehart & Winston.

Block, J. H. (1971). Operating procedures for mastery learning. In J. H. Block (Ed.), *Mastery learning: Theory and practice.* New York: Holt, Rinehart & Winston.

Block, J. H. (1973). Conceptions of sex role: Some cross-cultural and longitudinal perspectives. *American Psychologist, 28,* 512-529.

Block, J. H. (1976). Issues, problems and pitfalls in assessing sex differences. *Merrill–Palmer Quarterly, 22,* 283-308.

Block, J. H., Efthim, H. E., & Burns, R. B. (1989). *Building effective mastery learning schools.* New York: Longman.

Bloom, B. S. (1968). Learning for mastery. *Evaluation Comment, 1* (2), Los Angeles: Center for the Study of Evaluation of Instructional Programs, University of California.

Bloom, B. S. (1976). *Human characteristics and school learning.* New York: McGraw–Hill.

Bloom, B. S. (1981). *All our children learning.* New York: McGraw–Hill.

Bloom, B. S. (1984). The two sigma problem: The search for methods of group instruction as effective as one-to-one tutoring. *Educational Researcher, 13* (6), 4-16.

Bloom, B. S., Englehart, M. B., Furst, E. J., Hill, W. H., & Krathwohl, D. R. (Eds.). (1956). *Taxonomy of educational objectives. The classification of educational goals. Handbook I: Cognitive Domain.* New York: McKay.

Borker, S. R. (1987). Sex roles and labor force participation. In D. B. Carter (ed.), *Current conceptions of sex roles and sex typing.* New York: Praeger.

Bower, G. H., Clark, M. C., Lesgold, A. M., & Winzenz, D. (1969). Hierarchical retrieval schemes in recall of categorized word lists. *Journal of Verbal Learning and Verbal Behavior, 8,* 323-343.

Bower, G. H., & Hilgard, E. R. (1981). *Theories of learning* (5th ed.). Englewood Cliffs, NJ: Prentice–Hall.

Boyer, E. L. (1983). *High school.* New York: Harper & Row.

Bracey, G. W. (1983). On the compelling need to go beyond minimum competency. *Phi Delta Kappan, 64* (10), 717-721.

Bracey, G. W. (1988). Selective retention. *Phi Delta Kappan, 69* (5), 379-380.

Brainerd, C. J. (1978). *Piaget's theory of intelligence.* Englewood Cliffs, NJ: Prentice–Hall.

Braithwaite, E. R. (1959). *To sir, with love.* Englewood Cliffs, NJ: Prentice–Hall.

Bransford, J. D. (1979). *Human cognition: Learning, understanding, and remembering.* Belmont, CA: Wadsworth.

Bransford, J. D., Sherwood, R., Vye, N., & Rieser, J. (1986). Teaching thinking and problem solving: Research foundations. *American Psychologist, 41* (10), 1078-1089.

Bransford, J. D., & Stein, B. (1984). *The IDEAL problem solver: A guide for improving thinking, learning, and creativity.* San Francisco: Freeman.

Brantlinger, E. A., & Guskin, S. L. (1985). Implications of social and cultural differences for special education with specific recommendations. *Focus on Exceptional Children, 18* (1), 1-12.

Braun, C. (1976). Teacher expectations: Sociopsychological dynamics. *Review of Educational Research, 46* (2), 185-213.

Brittain, C. V. (1968). An exploration of the bases of peer compliance and parent-compliance in adolescence. *Adolescence, 2,* 445-458.

Broadbent, D. E. (1958). *Perception and communication.* New York: Pergamon Press.

Brody, E. B. & Brody, N. (1976). *Intelligence: Nature, determinants, and consequences.* New York: Academic Press.

Bronfenbrenner, V. (1970). *Two worlds of childhood.* New York: Russell Sage Foundation.

Brophy, J. E. (1979). Teacher behavior and its effects. *Journal of Educational Psychology, 71,* 733-750.

Brophy, J. E. (1981). Teacher praise: A functional analysis. *Review Educational Research, 51* (1), 5-32.

Brophy, J. E. (1983a). Conceptualizing student motivation. *Educational Psychologist, 18* (3), 200-215.

Brophy, J. E. (1983b). Research on the self-fulfilling prophecy and teacher expectations. *Journal of Educational Psychology, 75* (5), 631-661.

Brophy, J. E., & Evertson, C. M. (1976). *Learning from teaching.* Boston: Allyn and Bacon.

Brophy, J. E., & Good, T. L. (1974). *Teacher-student relationships: Causes and consequences.* New York: Holt, Rinehart & Winston.

Brown, A. L., Campione, J. C., & Day, J. D. (1981). Learning to learn: On training students to learn from text. *Educational Researcher, 10* (2), 14-24.

Brown, G. I. (1971). *Human teaching for human learning: An introduction to confluent education.* New York: Viking Press.

Brown, R. (1973). *A first language: The early stages.* Cambridge, MA: Harvard University Press.

Broverman, I. K., Vogel, S. R., Broverman, D. M., Clarkson, F. E., & Rosenkrantz, P. S. (1972). Sex-role stereotypes: A current appraisal. *Journal of Social Issues, 28* (2), 59-78.

Bruce, M. G. (1988). Making the grade or marking time. *Phi Delta Kappan, 69* (5), 383-384.

Bruner, J. S. (1951). Personality dynamics and the process of perceiving. In R. R. Blake & G. V. Ramsey (Eds.), *Perception: An approach to personality.* New York: Ronald Press.

Bruner, J. S. (1960). *The process of education.* New York: Vintage Books.

Bruner, J. S. (1966). *Toward a theory of instruction.* New York: Norton.

Bruner, J. S. (1971). *The relevance of education.* New York: Norton.

Bruner, J. S. (1983). *In search of mind: Essays in autobiography.* New York: Harper & Row.

Bruner, J. S., Goodnow, J. J., & Austin, G. A. (1956). *A study of thinking.* New York: Wiley.

Bryson, J. E., & Bentley, C. P. (1980). *Ability grouping of public school students: Legal aspects of classification and tracking methods.* Charlottesville, VA: The Michie Company.

Burnett, C., Mendoza, G., & Secunda, S. (1975). *What I want to be when I grow up.* New York: Simon & Schuster.

Campbell, J., & Willis, J. (1979). A behavioral program to teach creative writing in the regular classroom. *Education and Treatment of Children, 2,* 5-15.

Canfield, J. T., & Wells, H. C. (1976). *100 ways to enhance self-concept in the classroom: A handbook for teachers and parents.* Englewood Cliffs, NJ: Prentice–Hall.

Cangeolsi, J. S. (1988). *Classroom management strategies: Gaining and maintaining students' cooperation.* New York: Longman.

Cantor, G. N., Dunlap, L. L., & Rettie, C. S. (1982). Effects of reception and discovery instruction on kindergartner's performance on probability tasks. *American Educational Research Journal, 19* (3), 453-463.

Carroll, J.B. (1963). A model of school learning. *Teachers College Record, 64,* 723-733.

Carroll, J. B. (1971). Problems of measurement related to the concept of learning for mastery. In J. H. Block (Ed.), *Mastery learning: theory and practice.* New York: Holt, Rinehart & Winston.

Carson, J. C., & Carson, P. (1984). *Any teacher can! Practical strategies for effective classroom management.* Springfield, IL: Thomas.

Carter, D. B. (1987). The role of peers in sex role socialization. In D. B. Carter (Ed.), *Current conceptions of sex roles and sex typing.* New York: Praeger.

Cartwright, G. P., Cartwright, C. A., & Ward, M. E. (1989). *Educating special learners* (3rd ed.). Belmont, CA: Wadsworth.

Case, R. (1975). Gearing the demands of instruction to the developmental capacities of the learner. *Review of Educational Research, 45* (1), 59-88.

Cassidy, J., & Johnson, N. (1986). Federal and state definitions of giftedness: Then and now. *Gifted Child Today, 9* (6), 15-21.

Cazden, C. (1968). The acquisition of noun and verb inflections. *Child Development, 39,* 433-438.

Chalfant, J., & Pysh, J. (1983). Teacher assistance teams. In C. Collin (Ed.), *Keys to success.* Monograph of the Michigan ACLD conference. Garden City, MI: Quality Printers.

Charles, C. M. (1972). *Educational psychology: The instructional endeavor.* St. Louis, MO: Mosby.

Chesler, M., & Fox, R. (1966). *Role playing methods in the classroom.* Palo Alto, CA: Science Research Associates.

Clausen, J. (1975). The social meaning of differential physical and sexual maturation. In S. Dragastin & G. H. Elder, Jr. (Eds.), *Adolescence in the life cycle.* New York: Wiley.

Coleman, J. C. (1980). Friendship and the peer group in adolescence. In J. Adelson (Ed.), *Handbook of adolescent psychology.* New York: Wiley.

Combs, A. W. (1965). *The professional education of teachers.* Boston: Allyn and Bacon.

Combs, A. W. (1981). Humanistic education: Too tough for a tender world? *Phi Delta Kappan, 62,* 446-449.

Combs, A. W. (1982). Affective education or none at all. *Educational Leadership, 39* (7), 494-497.

Combs, A. W., Avila, D. L., & Purkey, W. W. (1978). *Helping relationships: Basic concepts for the helping professions* (2nd ed.). Boston: Allyn and Bacon.

Combs, A. W., Blume, R. A., Newman, A. J., & Wass, H. L. (1974). *The professional education of teachers* (2nd ed.). Boston: Allyn and Bacon.

Conger, J. J., & Miller, W. C. (1966). *Personality, social class, and delinquency.* New York: Wiley.

Cook, L. K., & Mayer, R. E. (1983). Reading strategies training for meaningful learning from prose. In M. Pressley & J. R. Levin (Eds.), *Cognitive strategy research: Educational applications.* New York: Springer–Verlag.

Cooper, H. M. (1979). Pygmalion grows up: A model for teacher expectation, communication, and performance influence. *Review of Educational Research, 49* (3), 389-410.

Cormier, S. M., & Hagman, J. D. (Eds.). (1987). *Transfer of learning: Contemporary research and applications.* San Diego: Academic Press.

Cosgrove, D. J. (1959). Diagnostic ratings of teacher performance. *Journal of Educational Psychology, 50,* 220-224.

Covington, M. V. (1985). Strategic thinking and the fear of failure. In J. W. Segal, S. F. Chipman, & R. Glaser (Eds.), *Thinking and learning skills* (Vol. 1). Hillsdale, NJ: Erlbaum.

Cox, W. F., Jr., & Dunn, T. G. (1979). Mastery learning: A psychological trap? *Educational Psychologist, 14,* 24-29.

Craighead, W. E., Kazden, A. E., & Mahoney, M. J. (1981). *Behavior modification* (2nd ed.). Boston: Houghton Mifflin.

Craik, F. I. M., & Lockhart, R. S. (1972). Levels of processing: A framework for memory research. *Journal of Verbal Learning and Verbal Behavior, 11,* 671-684.

Cronbach, L. J. (1984). *Essentials of psychological testing* (4th ed.). New York: Harper & Row.

Cruickshank, D. R., & Associates (1980). *Teaching is tough.* Englewood Cliffs, NJ: Prentice–Hall.

Cuervo, A. G., Lees, J., & Lacey, R. (1984). *Toward better and safer schools.* Alexander, VA: National School Boards Association.

Cullum, A. (1967). *Push back the desks.* New York: Citation Press.

Daniels, S. (1967). *How 2 gerbils, 20 goldfish, 200 games, 2000 books, and I taught them how to read.* Philadelphia: Westminster Press.

Dar, Y., & Resh, N. (1986). *Classroom composition and pupil achievement.* New York: Gordon and Breach.

Dawe, H. A. (1984). Teaching: A performing art. *Phi Delta Kappan, 65* (8), 548-552.

deCharms, R. (1976). *Enhancing motivation: Change in the classroom.* New York: Irvington.

Dennison, G. (1969). *The lives of children.* New York: Vintage.

diSibio, M. (1982). Memory for connected discourse: A constructivist view. *Review of Educational Research, 52* (2), 149-174.

Douvan, E., & Adelson, J. (1966). *The adolescent experience.* New York: Wiley.

Doyle, W. (1983). Academic work. *Review of Educational Research, 53* (2), 159-200.

Duchastel, P. C., & Merrill, P. F. (1973). The effects of behavioral objectives on learning: A review of empirical studies. *Review of Educational Research, 43* (1), 53-69.

Duell, O. K. (1986). Metacognitive skills. In G. D. Phye & T. Andre (Eds.), *Cognitive classroom learning.* Orlando, FL: Academic Press.

Dusek, J. B. (1987a). *Adolescent development and behavior.* Englewood Cliffs, NJ: Prentice–Hall.

Dusek, J. B. (1987b). Sex roles and adjustment. In D. B. Carter (Ed.), *Current conceptions of sex roles and sex typing.* New York: Praeger.

Dweck, C. S., Davidson, W., Nelson, S., & Enna, B. (1978). Sex differences in learned helplessness: II. The contingencies of evaluative feedback in the classroom and III. An experimental analysis. *Developmental Psychology, 14*, 268-276.

Dweck, C. S. (1986). Motivational processes affecting learning. *American Psychologist, 41* (10), 1040-1048.

Dweck, C. S., & Bush, E. S. (1976). Sex differences in learned helplessness: I. Differential debilitation with peer and adult evaluators. *Developmental Psychology, 12*, 147-156.

Ebel, R. L., & Frisbie, D. A. (1986). *Essentials of educational measurement* (4th ed.). Englewood Cliffs, NJ: Prentice-Hall.

Edmunds, R. D. (Ed.). (1980). *American Indian leaders*. Lincoln, NE: University of Nebraska Press.

Edwards, A. J. (1971). *Individual mental testing, part I: History and theories*. Scranton, PA: Intext Educational Publishers.

Elkind, D. (1981). *Children and adolescents: Interpretive essays on Jean Piaget* (3rd ed.). New York: Oxford University Press.

Ellis, H. C. (1965). *The transfer of learning*. New York: Macmillan.

Ellis, H. C. (1978). *Fundamentals of human learning, memory, and cognition* (2nd ed.). Dubuque, IA: Wm. C. Brown.

Ellis, H. C., & Hunt, R. R. (1989). *Fundamentals of human memory and cognition* (4th ed.). Dubuque, IA: Brown.

Emmer, E. T., Everston, C. M., Sanford, J. P., Clements, B. S., & Worsham, M. E. (1984). *Classroom management for secondary teachers*. Englewood Cliffs, NJ: Prentice-Hall.

Endler, N. S., Rushton, J. P., & Roediger, H. L. III. (1978). Productivity and scholarly impact (citations) of British, Canadian, and U.S. departments of psychology. *American Psychologist, 33* (12), 1064-1082.

Epstein, C. (1980). Brain growth and cognitive functioning. In D. R. Steer (Ed.), *The emerging adolescent: Characteristics and educational implications*. Columbus, OH: National Middle School Association.

Erdelyi, M. H., & Goldberg, B. (1979). Let's now sweep repression under the rug: Towards a cognitive psychology of repression. In J. Kihlstrom & F. Evans (Eds.), *Functional disorders of memory*. Hillsdale, NJ: Erlbaum.

Ericsson, K. A., Chase, W. G., & Faloon, S. (1980). Acquisition of a memory skill. *Science, 208*, 1181-1182.

Erikson, E. H. (1963). *Childhood and society* (2nd ed.). New York: Norton.

Erikson, E. H. (1968). *Identity: youth and crisis*. New York: Norton.

Evans, J. (1985). *Teaching in transition: The challenge of mixed ability grouping*. Milton Keynes, UK: Open University Press.

Evans, R. I. (1967). *Dialogue with Erik Erikson*. New York: Harper & Row.

Everton, C. M., Emmer, E. T., Clements, B. S., Sanford, J. P., & Worsham, M. E. (1984). *Classroom management for elementary teachers*. Englewood Cliffs, NJ: Prentice-Hall.

Fagot, B. I. (1978). The influence of sex of child on parental reactions to toddler children. *Child Development, 49*, 459-465.

Fagot, B. I. & Leinbach, M. D. (1987). Socialization of sex roles within the family. In D. B. Carter (Ed.), *Current conceptions of sex roles and sex typing*. New York: Praeger.

Faw, H. W., & Waller, T. G. (1976). Mathemagenic behaviors and efficiency in learning from prose materials. *Review of Educational Research, 46*, 691-720.

Feather, N. T. (1980). Values in adolescence. In J. Adelson (Ed.), *Handbook of adolescent Psychology*. New York: Wiley.

Feingold, A. (1988). Cognitive gender differences are disappearing. *American Psychologist, 43* (2), 95-103.

Fernald, G. (1943). *Remedial techniques in basic school subjects*. New York: McGraw-Hill.

Feynman, R. P. (1985). *"Surely you're joking, Mr. Feynman."* New York: Norton.

First, J. M. (1988). Immigrant students in U.S. public schools: Challenges with solutions. *Phi Delta Kappan, 70* (3), 205-210.

Flanders, N. A. (1970). *Analyzing teacher behavior*. Reading, MA: Addison-Wesley.

Flavell, J. H. (1976). Metacognitive aspects of problem solving. In L. B. Resnick (Ed.), *The nature of intelligence*. Hillsdale, NJ: Erlbaum.

Flavell, J. H. (1979). Metacognition and cognitive monitoring: A new area of cognitive-developmental inquiry. *American Psychologist, 34* (10), 906-911.

Flavell, J. H. (1982). On cognitive development. *Child Development, 53*, 1-10.

Foster, D. W. (Ed.). (1982). *Sourcebook of Hispanic culture in the United States*. Chicago: American Library Association.

Frasier, M. M. (1987). The identification of gifted black students: Developing new perspectives. *Journal for the Education of the Gifted, 10* (3), 155-180.

Frederiksen, N. (1984). Implications of cognitive theory for instruction in problem solving. *Review of Educational Research, 54* (3), 363-408.

Furst, E. J. (1981). Bloom's taxonomy of educational objectives for the cognitive domain. *Review of Educational Research, 51* (4), 441-453.

Furstenberg, F. F., Jr., Lincoln, R., & Menken, J. (Eds.). (1981). *Teenage sexuality, pregnancy, and childbearing*. Philadelphia: University of Pennsylvania Press.

Furth, H. G. (1970). *Piaget for teachers*. Englewood Cliffs, NJ: Prentice-Hall.

Furth, H. G., & Wachs, H. (1975). *Thinking goes to school*. New York: Oxford University Press.

Gage, N. L. (1984). What do we know about teaching effectiveness? *Phi Delta Kappan, 66* (2), 87-93.

Gagné, R. M., (1965). *The conditions of learning*, New York: Holt, Rinehart & Winston.

Gagné, R. M., (1965). *The conditions of learning* (2nd ed.). New York: Holt, Rinehart & Winston.

Gagné, R. M., (1977). *The conditions of learning* (3rd ed.). New York: Holt, Rinehart & Winston.

Gagné, R. M., (1985). *The conditions of learning* (4th ed.). New York: Holt, Rinehart & Winston.

Galbraith, R. E. & Jones, T. M. (1976). *Moral reasoning*. Minneapolis, MN: Greenhaven Press.

Gall, M. D. (1970). The use of questions in teaching. *Review of Educational Research, 40*, 707-721.

Gallagher, J. J. (1975). *Teaching the gifted child* (2nd ed.). Boston: Allyn and Bacon.

Gallagher, J. J. (1985). *Teaching the gifted child* (3rd ed.). Boston: Allyn and Bacon.

Gallatin, J. (1980). Political thinking in adolescence. In J. Adelson (Ed.), *Handbook of adolescent psychology*. New York: Wiley.

Galton, F. (1890). Statement made in footnote to an article by J.M. Cattell, Mental tests and measurement, *Mind, 15*, 373.

Gardner, H. (1983). *Frames of mind: The theory of multiple intelligences*. New York: Basic Books.

Gelman, R. & Baillargeon, E. E. (1983). A review of some Piagetian concepts. In J. H. Flavell & E. M. Markman (Eds.), *Handbook of Child Development* (4th ed.): *Vol. III. Cognitive development*. New York: Wiley.

Getzels, J. W., & Jackson, P. W. (1962). *Creativity and intelligence*. New York: Wiley.

Gick, M. L. (1986). Problem-solving strategies. *Educational Psychologist*, *21* (1,2), 99-120.

Gick, M. L., & Holyoak, K. J. (1980). Analogical problem solving. *Cognitive Psychology*, *12*, 306-355.

Gick, M. L., & Holyoak, K. J. (1983): Schema induction and analogical transfer. *Cognitive Psychology*, *15*, 1-38.

Gilligan, C. (1979). Woman's place in man's life cycle. *Harvard Educational Review*, *49* (4), 431-446.

Gilligan, C. (1982). In a different voice: *Psychological theory and women's development*. Cambridge, MA: Harvard University Press.

Ginott, H. (1965). *Between parent and child*. New York: Macmillan.

Ginott, H. (1972). *Teacher and child*. New York: Macmillan.

Ginsburg, H. P., & Opper, S. (1988). *Piaget's theory of intellectual development* (3rd ed.). Englewood Cliffs, NJ: Prentice–Hall.

Glaser, R. (1976). Components of a psychology of instruction: Toward a science of design. *Review of Educational Research*, *46* (1), 1-24.

Glasser, W. (1969). *Schools without failure*. New York: Harper & Row.

Glasser, W. (1972). *The identity society*. New York: Harper & Row.

Gold, M., & Petronio, R. J. (1980). Delinquent behavior in adolescence. In J. Adelson (Ed.), *Handbook of Adolescent Psychology*. New York: Wiley.

Goldstein, A. P., Apter, S. J., & Harootunian, B. (1984). *School violence*. Englewood Cliffs, NJ: Prentice–Hall.

Goldstein, A. P., Sprafkin, R. P., Gershaw, N. J., & Klein, P. (1980). *Skillstreaming the adolescent: A structured learning approach to teaching prosocial skills*. Champaign, IL: Research Press.

Goldstein, H., & Seigle, D. M. *A curriculum guide for teachers of the educatable mentally handicapped*. Danville, IL: Interstate Printers and Publishers.

Goldstein, K. M., & Blackman, S. (1978). *Cognitive style*. New York: Wiley.

Gollnick, D. M., & Chinn, P. C. (1986). *Multicultural education in a pluralistic society* (2nd ed.). Columbus, OH: Merrill.

Good, T. (1982). *Classroom research: What we know and what we need to know* (R&D Report No. 9018). Austin, TX: University of Texas, Research and Development Center for Teacher Education.

Gordon, T. (1970). *P.E.T.: Parent effectiveness training*. New York: Wyden.

Gordon, T. (1974). *T.E.T.: Teacher effectiveness training*. New York: McKay.

Gottfredson, G. D., & Gottfredson, D. C. (1985). *Victimization in schools*. New York: Plenum.

Gottlieb, J. (Ed.). (1980). *Educating mentally retarded persons in the mainstream*. Baltimore, MD: University Park Press.

Gough, P. B. (1987). The key to improving schools: An interview with William Glasser. *Phi Delta Kappan*, *68* (9), 656-662.

Gould, S. J. (1981). *The mismeasure of man*. New York: Norton.

Grabe, M. (1986). Attentional processes in education. In G. D. Phye & T. Andre (Eds.), *Cognitive classroom learning*. Orlando, FL: Academic Press.

Gronlund, N. E. (1959). *Sociometry in the classroom*. New York: Harper & Row.

Gronlund, N. E. (1985a). *Stating behavioral objectives for classroom instruction* (3rd ed). New York: Macmillan.

Gronlund, N. E. (1985b). *Measurement and evaluation in teaching* (5th ed.). New York: Macmillan.

Gronlund, N. E. (1988). *How to construct achievement tests* (4th ed.). Englewood Cliffs, NJ: Prentice–Hall.

Grossman, E. J. (Ed.). (1977). *Manual on terminology and classification in mental retardation* (3rd ed.). Washington, DC: American Association on Mental Retardation.

Grossman, H. J. (Ed.). (1983). *Classification in mental retardation*. Washington, DC: American Association on Mental Deficiency.

Gruber, E., & Vonèche, J. J. (Eds.). (1977). *The essential Piaget: An interpretive reference and guide*. New York: Basic Books.

Gruneberg, M. M., Morris, P. E., & Sykes, R. N. (Eds.). (1978). *Practical aspects of memory*. New York: Academic Press.

Guerin, G. R., & Maier, A. S. (1983). *Informal assessment in education*. Palo Alto, CA: Mayfield.

Guilford, J. P. (1967). *The nature of human intelligence*. New York: McGraw-Hill.

Gutek, G. L. (1988). *Education and schooling in America* (2nd ed.). Englewood Cliffs, NJ: Prentice–Hall.

Hall, B. W., Villem, M. G., & Burley, W. W. (1986). Humanistic orientation and selected teaching practices among 1st-year teachers. *Journal of Humanistic Education and Development*, *25* (1), 12-17.

Hall, E. (1983, June). A conversation with Erik Erikson. *Psychology Today*, pp. 22-30.

Hall, G. S. (1904). *Adolescence: Its psychology and its relations to physiology, anthropology, sociology, sex, crime, religion, and education* (2 vols.). New York: Appleton.

Hall, R. V., Axlerod, S., Foundopoulos, M., Shellman, J., Campbell, R. A., & Cranston, S. S. (1971). The effective use of punishment to modify behavior in the classroom. *Educational Technology*, *11*, 24-26.

Halpern, D. F. (1984). *Thought and knowledge: An introduction to critical thinking*. Hillsdale, NJ: Erlbaum.

Hamachek, D. E. (1975). *Behavior dynamics in teaching, learning, and growth*. Boston: Allyn and Bacon.

Hammill, D., Leigh, J., McNutt, G., & Larsen, S. (1981). A new definition of learning disabilities. *Learning Disability Quarterly*, *4* (4), 336-342.

Harmin, M., Kirschenbaum, H., & Simon, S. B. (1972). *Clarifying values through subject matter*. Minneapolis, MN: Winston.

Hartshorne, H., May, M. A. (1929). *Studies in service and self-control*. New York: Macmillan.

Hartshorne, H., & May, M. A. (1930a). *Studies in deceit*. New York: Macmillan.

Hartshorne, H., & May, M. A. (1930b). *Studies in the organization of character*. New York: Macmilllan.

Hassett, J. (1984). Computers in the classroom. *Psychology Today*, *18* (9), 22-28.

Heckhausen, H. (1975). Fear of failure as a self-reinforcing motive system. In I. G. Sarason & C. Spielberger (Eds.), *Stress and anxiety* (Vol. 2). Washington, DC: Hemisphere.

Herndon, J. (1968). *The way it spozed to be*. New York: Simon & Schuster.

Herndon, J. (1971). *How to survive in your native land*. New York: Simon & Schuster.

Hersh, R. H., Paolitto, D. P., & Reimer, J. (1979). *Promoting moral growth: From Piaget to Kohlberg*. New York: Longman.

Hess, R. D., & Croft, D. J. (1981). *Teachers of young children* (3rd ed.). Boston: Houghton Mifflin.

Hess, R. D., & Shipman, V. (1965). Early experiences and the socialization of cognitive modes in children. *Child Development*, *36*, 869-886.

Hewett, F. M., & Taylor, F. D. (1980). *The emotionally disturbed child in the classroom: The orchestration of success* (2nd ed.). Boston: Allyn and Bacon.

Hiatt, D. B. (1979). Time allocation in the classroom: Is instruction being short changed? *Phi Delta Kappan, 61* (4), 289-290.

Higbee, K. L. (1979). Recent research on visual mnemonics: Historical roots and educational fruits. *Review of Educational Research, 49,* 611-630.

Highet, G. (1957). *The art of teaching.* New York: Vintage Books.

Hills, J. R. (1981). *Measurement and evaluation in the classroom* (2nd ed.). Columbus, OH: Merrill.

Hobbs, N. (1975a). *The futures of children.* San Francisco: Jossey–Bass.

Hobbs, N. (Ed.). (1975b). *Issues in the classification of children* (Vol. I). San Francisco: Jossey–Bass.

Hobbs, N. (Ed.). (1975c). *Issues in the classification of children* (Vol. II). San Francisco: Jossey–Bass.

Hoffman, L. W. (1972). Early childhood experiences and women's achievement motives. *Journal of Social Issues, 28* (2), 129-156.

Hoffman, M. L. (1980). Moral development in adolescence. In J. Adelson (Ed.), *Handbook of adolescent psychology.* New York: Wiley.

Hoge, R. D. (1988). Issues in the definition and measurement of the giftedness construct. *Educational Researcher, 17* (7), 12-16, 22.

Holyoak, K. J., & Koh, K. (1987). Surface and structural similarity in analogical transfer. *Memory & Cognition, 15* (4), 332-340.

Homme, L., & Tosti, D. (1971). *Behavior technology: Motivation and contingency management.* San Rafael, CA: Individual Learning Systems.

Hopkins, C. D., & Antes, R. L. (1985). *Classroom measurement & evaluation* (2nd ed.). Itasca, IL: Peacock.

Hopkins, C. D., & Antes, R. L. (1989). *Classroom testing: Construction.* Itasca, IL: Peacock.

Horner, M. S. (1968). *Sex differences in achievement motivation and performance in competitive and non-competitive situations.* Unpublished doctoral dissertation, University of Michigan, Ann Harbor.

Horner, M. S. (1970). Femininity and successful achievement: A basic inconsistency. In J. M. Bardwick, E. Douvan, M. S. Horner, & D. Guttman (Eds.), *Feminine personality and conflict.* Belmont, CA: Brooks/Cole.

Horowitz, F., & O'Brien, M. (1986). Gifted and talented children: State of knowledge and directions for research. *American Psychologist, 41* (10), 1147-1152.

Howard, E. R. (1981, Fall). *School climate improvement—Rationale and process.* Illinois School Research and Development.

Howe, L. W., & Howe, M. M. (1975). *Personalizing education: Values clarification and beyond.* New York: Hart.

Hyde, J. S. (1986). Gender differences in aggression. In J. S. Hyde & M. C. Linn (Eds.), *The psychology of gender.* Baltimore, MD: Johns Hopkins University Press.

Hyman, I. A., & D'Alessandro, J. (1984). Good, old-fashioned discipline: The politics of punitiveness. *Phi Delta Kappan, 66* (1), 39-45.

Illich, I. (1971). *Deschooling society.* New York: Harper & Row.

James, W. (1899). *Talks to teachers on psychology: And to students on some of life's ideals.* New York: Holt. (Reprinted in *The works of William James,* 1983, Cambridge, MA: Harvard University Press.)

Jamison, D., Suppes, P., & Wells, S. (1974). The effectiveness of alternative instructional media: A survey. *Review of Educational Research, 44* (1), 1-68.

Jenkins, R. L., & Hewitt, L. (1944). Types of personality structure encountered in child guidance clinics. *American Journal of Orthopsychiatry, 14,* 83-94.

Jensen, A. R. (1980). *Bias in mental testing.* New York: Free Press.

Jessor, S., & Jessor, R. (1975). Transition from virginity to nonvirginity among youth: A social-psychological study over time. *Developmental Psychology, 11,* 473-484.

Johnson, D. W., & Johnson, R. T. (1974). Instructional goal structure: Cooperative, competitive, or individualistic. *Review of Educational Research, 44,* 213-240.

Johnson, D. W., & Johnson, R. T. (1987a). *Learning together and alone: Cooperative, competitive, & individualistic learning* (2nd ed.). Englewood Cliffs, NJ: Prentice–Hall.

Johnson, D. W., & Johnson, R. T. (1987b). *A meta-analysis of cooperative, competitive, and individualistic goal structures.* Hillsdale, NJ: Erlbaum.

Johnson, R. E. (1975). Meaning in complex learning. *Review of Educational Research, 45* (3), 425-460.

Jones, M. C. (1957). Physical ability as a factor in social adjustment in adolescence. *Journal of Educational Research, 39,* 287-301.

Jones, M. C. (1957). The later career of boys who were early or late maturing. *Child Development, 28,* 113-128.

Jones, M. C. (1965). Psychological correlates of somatic development. *Child Development, 36,* 899-911.

Jones, V. R., & Jones, L. S. (1986). *Comprehensive classroom management.* Boston: Allyn and Bacon.

Kagan, J. (1964a). *Developmental studies of reflection and analysis.* Cambridge, MA: Harvard University Press.

Kagan, J. (1964b). Impulsive and reflective children. In J. D. Krumbolz (Ed.), *Learning and the educational process.* Chicago: Rand McNally.

Kail, R. (1984). *The development of memory in children* (2nd ed.). San Francisco: Freeman.

Kamii, C. (1984). Autonomy: The aim of education envisioned by Piaget. *Phi Delta Kappan, 65* (6), 410-415.

Karnes, F., & Collins, E. (1980). *Handbook of instructional resources and references for teaching the gifted.* Boston: Allyn and Bacon.

Kaufman, B. (1964). *Up the down staircase.* New York: Avon.

Kellett, M. C. (1980). *Memory power.* New York: Sterling.

Keller, F. S. (1954). *Learning: Reinforcement theory.* New York: Random House.

Kellogg, J. B. (1988). Forces of change. *Phi Delta Kappan, 70* (3), 199-204.

Kerr, M. M., & Nelson, C. M. (1983). *Strategies for managing behavior problems in the classroom.* Columbus, OH: Merrill.

Kiewra, K. A. (1985). Investigating notetaking and review: A depth of processing alternative. *Educational Psychologist, 20* (1), 23-32.

Kiewra, K. A. (1988). Cognitive aspects of autonomous notetaking: Control processes, learning strategies, and prior knowledge. *Educational Psychologist, 23* (1), 39-56.

Kindel, S., & Benoit, E. (1984, April 23). Hello, Mr. Chip. *Forbes,* pp. 132-136.

Kirk, S., & Chalfant, J. (1984). *Developmental and academic learning disabilities.* Denver, CO: Love.

Kirk, S. A., & Gallagher, J. J. (1989). *Educating exceptional children* (6th ed.). Boston: Houghton Mifflin.

Kirschenbaum, H. (1979). *On becoming Carl Rogers.* New York: Dell.

Kirschenbaum, H., & Simon, S. B. (Eds.). (1973). *Readings in values clarification.* Minneapolis, MN: Winston.

Kirschenbaum, H., Simon, S. B., & Napier, R. W. (1971). *Wad-ja-get? The grading game in American education.* New York: Hart.

Klatzky, R. L. (1980). *Human memory: Structures and processes* (2nd ed.). San Francisco: Freeman.

Klauer, K. (1984). Intentional and incidental learning with instructional texts: A meta-analysis for 1970 - 1980. *American Educational Research Journal, 21* (2), 323-339.

Klausmeier, H. J., Sorensen, J. S., & Ghatala, E. (1971). Individually guided motivation: Developing self-direction and prosocial behaviors. *Elementary School Journal, 71,* 340-350.

Kohl, H. (1967). *36 children.* New York: New American Library.

Kohlberg, L. (1963). The development of children's orientations toward a moral order: I. Sequence in the development of moral thought. *Vita Humana, 6,* 11-33.

Kohlberg, L. (1969). Stage and sequence: The cognitive-developmental approach to socialization. In D. A. Goslin (Ed.), *Handbook of socialization theory and research.* Chicago: Rand McNally.

Kohlberg, L. (1976). Moral stages and moralization: The cognitive-developmental approach. In T. Lickona (Ed.), *Moral development and behavior: Theory, research, and social issues.* New York: Holt, Rinehart & Winston.

Kohlberg, L. (1978). Revisions in the theory and practice of moral development. In W. Damon (Ed.), *Moral development: New directions for child development* (No.2). San Francisco: Jossey–Bass.

Kohlberg, L. (1985). The just community approach to moral education in theory and practice. In M. W. Berkowitz & F. Oser (Eds.), *Moral education: Theory and application.* Hillsdale, NJ: Erlbaum.

Kolb, D. A. (1965). Achievement motivation training for under-achieving boys. *Journal of Personality and Social Psychology, 2,* 783-792.

Kolstoe, O. P. (1970). *Teaching educable mentally retarded children.* New York: Holt, Rinehart & Winston.

Kounin, J. S. (1970). *Discipline and group management in classrooms.* New York: Holt, Rinehart & Winston.

Kozol, J. (1967). *Death at an early age.* Boston: Houghton Mifflin.

Krathwohl, D. R., Bloom, B. S., & Masia, B. B. (1964). *Taxonomy of educational objectives. Handbook II: Affective domain.* New York: McKay.

Krulik, S., & Rudnick, J. A. (1988). *Problem solving: A handbook for elementary school teachers.* Boston: Allyn and Bacon.

Kubiszyn, T., & Borich, G. (1987). *Educational testing and measurement* (2nd ed.). Glenview, IL: Scott, Foresman.

Kulhavy, R. W. (1977). Feedback in written instruction. *Review of Educational Research, 47* (2), 211-232.

Kulhavy, R. W., Schwartz, N. H., & Peterson, S. (1986). Working memory: The encoding process. In G. D. Phye & T. Andre (Eds.), *Cognitive classroom learning.* Orlando, FL: Academic Press.

Kulhavy, R. W., Yekovich, F. T., & Dyer, J. W. (1976). Feedback and response confidence. *Journal of Education Psychology, 68* (5), 522-528.

Kulik, J. A., Bangert, R. L. & Williams, G. W. (1983). Effects of computer-based teaching on secondary school students. *Journal of Educational Psychology, 75* (1), 19-26.

Kulik, J. A., Cohen, P. A., & Ebeling, B. J. (1980). Effectiveness of programmed instruction in higher education: A meta-analysis of findings. *Educational Evaluation and Policy Analysis, 2* (6), 51-64.

Kulik, J. A., & Kulik, C. L. (1984). Effects of accelerated instruction on students. *Review of Educational Research, 54* (3), 409-426.

Larsen, L. F. (1972). The influence of parents and peers during adolescence: The situation hypothesis revisited. *Journal of Marriage and the Family, 34,* 67-74.

Lerner, J. (1989). *Learning disabilities: Theories, diagnosis, and teaching strategies* (5th ed.). Boston: Houghton Mifflin.

Levin, J. R. (1982). Pictures as prose-learning devices. In A. Flammer & W. Kintsch (Eds.), *Advances in psychology: Vol. 8. Discourse process-*ing. Amsterdam: North–Holland.

Levine, D. U. (Ed.). (1985). *Improving student achievement through mastery learning programs.* San Francisco: Jossey–Bass.

Lickona, T. (1976). Research on Piaget's theory of moral development. In T. Lickona (Ed.), *Moral development and behavior: Theory, research, and social issues.* New York: Holt, Rinehart & Winston.

Little, J. K. (1967). The occupations of non-college youth. *American Educational Research Journal, 4,* 147-153.

Livson, N., & Peskin, H. (1980). Perspectives on adolescence from longitudinal research. In J. Adelson (Ed.), *Handbook of adolescent psychology.* New York: Wiley.

Lockwood, A. (1978). The effects of values clarification and moral development curricula on school age subjects: A critical review of recent research. *Review of Educational Research, 48* (3), 325-364.

Loftus, E. F., & Loftus, G. R. (1980). On the permanence of stored information in the brain. *American Psychologist, 35* (5), 409-420.

Long, J. D., Frye, V. H., & Long, E. W. (1985). *Making it till Friday* (3rd ed.). Princeton, NJ: Princeton Book.

Lorayne, H., & Lucas, J. (1974). *The memory book.* New York: Ballantine Books.

Luria, A. R. (1968). *The mind of a mnemonist: A little book about a vast memory.* New York: Ballantine Books.

Lynch, J. (1986). *Multicultural education: Principles and practice.* London: Routledge & Kegan Paul.

Maccoby, E. E., & Jacklin, C. N. (1974). *Psychology of sex differences.* Stanford, CA: Stanford University Press.

Maddox, H. (1983). *How to study.* New York: Ballantine Books.

Mager, R. F. (1962). *Preparing instructional objectives.* Palo Alto, CA: Fearon.

Magnusson, D., Duner, A., & Zetterblom, G. (1975). *Adjustment.* New York: Wiley.

Maier, N. R. F. (1930). Reasoning in humans. 1. On direction. *Journal of Comparative Psychology, 10,* 115-143.

Maker, C. (1982). *Curriculum development for the gifted.* Rockville, MD: Aspen Systems.

Manni, J. L., Winikur, D. W., & Keller, M. R. (1984). *Intelligence, mental retardation, and the culturally different child: A practitioner's guide.* Springfield, IL: Thomas.

Marcia, J. E. (1966). Development and validation of ego identity status. *Journal of Personality and Social Psychology, 3* (5), 551-558.

Marcia, J. E. (1967). Ego identity status: Relationship to change in self-esteem, "general adjustment," and authoritarianism. *Journal of Personality, 35* (1), 119-133.

Marcia, J. E. (1980). Identity in adolescence. In J. Adelson (Ed.), *Handbook of adolescent psychology.* New York: Wiley.

Marshall, S. P., & Smith, J. D. (1987). Sex differences in learning mathematics: A longitudinal study with item and error analysis. *Journal of Educational Psychology, 79* (4), 372-381.

Maslow, A. H. (1943). A theory of human motivation. *Psychological Review, 50,* 370-396.

Maslow, A. H. (1968). *Toward a psychology of being* (2nd ed.). Princeton, NJ: Van Nostrand.

Maslow, A. H. (1970a). *Motivation and personality* (2nd ed.). New York: Harper & Row.

Maslow, A. H. (1970b). *Religions, values, and peak experiences.* New York: Viking.

Maslow, A. H. (1970c). *New knowledge in human values.* New York: Harper & Row.

Maslow, A. H. (1971). *The farther reaches of human nature.* New York:

Viking.

Mastropieri, M. A., Scruggs, T. E., & Levin, J. R. (1987). Mnemonic instruction in special education. In M. A. McDaniel & M. Pressley (Eds.), *Imagery and related mnemonic processes*. New York: Springer–Verlag.

Matarazzo, J. D. (1972). *Wechsler's measurement and appraisal of adult intelligence* (5th ed.). New York: Oxford University Press.

Mayer, R. E. (1979). Can advance organizers influence meaningful learning? *Review of Educational Research, 49*, 371-383.

Mayer, R. E. (1984, April). *Learnable aspects of problem solving: Some examples*. Paper presented at the annual meeting of the American Educational Research Association, New Orleans.

McClelland, D. C. (1961). *The achieving society*. Princeton, NJ: Van Nostrand.

McClelland, D. C. (1985). *Human motivation*. Glenview, IL: Scott, Foresman.

McLaughlin, R. F. (1981). The effects of a classroom token economy on math performance in an intermediate grade school class. *Education and Treatment of Children, 4*, 139-147.

Mehan, H., Hertweck, A., & Meihls, J. L. (1986). *Handicapping the handicapped: Decision making in students' educational careers*. Stanford, CA: Stanford University Press.

Melton, R. F. (1920). Resolution of conflicting claims concerning the effect of behavioral objectives on student learning. *Review of Educational Research, 48*, 291-302.

Mercer, C. D., & Mercer, A. R. (1985). *Teaching students with learning problems* (2nd ed.). Columbus, OH: Merrill.

Mercer, J. R. (1975). Psychological assessment and the rights of children. In N. Hobbs (Ed.), *Issues in the classification of children* (Vol. 1). San Francisco: Jossey–Bass.

Mercer, J. R., (1977). *Labelling the mentally retarded*. Berkeley, CA: University of California Press.

Messick, S., (1976). *Individuality in learning*. San Francisco: Jossey–Bass.

Michaels, J. W. (1977). Classroom reward structures and academic performance. *Review of Educational Research, 47*, 87-98.

Miller, B. C., Higginson, R., McCoy, J. K., & Olson, T. D. (1987). Family configuration and adolescent sexual attitudes and behavior. *Population and Environment, 9* (2), 111-123.

Miller, G. A. (1956). The magical number seven, plus or minus two: Some limits on our capacity for processing information. *Psychological Review, 63*, 81-97.

Miller, G. A., Galanter, E., & Pribram, K. H. (1960). *Plans and the structure of behavior*. New York: Holt, Rinehart & Winston.

Miller, N. E., & Dollard, J. (1941). *Social learning and imitation*. New Haven, CT: Yale University Press.

Miller, P. H. (1983). *Theories of developmental psychology*. San Francisco: Freeman.

Miller, P. Y., & Simon, W. (1980). The development of sexuality in adolescence. In J. Adelson (Ed.), *Handbook of adolescent psychology*, New York: Wiley.

Mitchell, J. V., Jr. (1985). *Ninth mental measurements yearbook*. Highland Park, NJ: Gryphon Press.

Morgan, C. T. (1979). *How to study: Morgan & Deese's classic handbook for students* (3rd ed. rev.). New York: McGraw–Hill.

Morgan, M. (1984). Reward-induced decrements and increments in intrinsic motivation. *Review of Educational Research, 54* (1), 5-30.

Morgan, S. R. (1984). An illustrative case of high-empathy teachers. *Journal of Humanistic Education and Development, 22* (4), 143-148.

Morris, P. (1977). Practical strategies for human learning and remembering. In M. J. A. Howe (Ed.), *Adult Learning*. New York: Wiley.

Morris, R. B. (Ed.). (1961). *Encyclopedia of American history*. New York: Harper & Row.

Moss, H. A. (1967). Sex, age, and state as determinants of mother-infant interaction. *Merrill–Palmer Quarterly, 13*, 19-36.

Mueller, D. J. (1973). The mastery model and some alternative models of classroom instruction and evaluation: An analysis. *Educational Technology, 13* (5), 5-10.

Murphy, D. F. (1988). The just community at Birch Meadow Elementary School. *Phi Delta Kappan, 69* (6), 427-428.

Mussen, P. H., & Jones, M. C. (1957). Self-conceptions, motivations, and interpersonal attitudes of late and early maturing boys. *Child Development, 28*, 245-256.

Myers, C. R. (1970). Journal citations and scientific eminence in contemporary psychology. *American Psychologist, 25*, 1041-1048.

Nagy, P., & Griffiths, A. K. (1982). Limitations of recent research relating Piaget's theory to adolescent thought. *Review of Educational Research, 52* (4), 513-556.

National Advisory Committee on Handicapped Children (1968). *First annual report, U. S. Senate subcommittee on education of the committee on labor and public welfare*. Washington, DC: U.S. Government Printing Office.

Neisser, U. (1982). *Memory observed*. San Francisco: Freeman.

Newcomer, S., & Udrey, J. R. (1987). Parental marital status effects on adolescent sexual behavior. *Journal of Marriage and the Family, 49* (2), 235-240.

Nicholls, J. G. (1979). Quality and inequality in intellectual development: The role of motivation in education. *American Psychologist, 34*, 1071-1084.

Nicholson, G., Stephens, R., Elder, R., & Leavitt, V. (1985). Safe schools: you can't do it alone. *Phi Delta Kappan, 66*, 491-496.

Nickerson, R. S., Perkins, D. N., & Smith, E. E. (1985). *The teaching of thinking*. Hillsdale, NJ: Erlbaum.

Norman, D. A., & Rumelhart, D. E. (1970). A system for perception and memory. In D. A. Norman (Ed.), *Models of human memory*. New York: Academic Press.

Northway, J. L. (1940). A method for depicting social relationships obtained by sociometric testing. *Sociometry, 3*, 144-150.

Novak, M. (1971). Rise of unmeltable ethnics. In M. Friedman (Ed.), *Overcoming middle class rage*. Philadelphia: Westminster Press.

Nuttall, E. V. (1987). Survey of current practices in the psychological assessment of limited-English-proficiency handicapped children. *Journal of School Psychology, 25* (1), 53-61.

Nye, R. D. (1979). *What is B. F. Skinner really saying?* Englewood Cliffs, NJ: Prentice–Hall.

Offer, D. (1969). *The psychological world of the teen-ager: A study of normal adolescent boys*. New York: Basic Books.

O'Leary, K., & O'Leary, S. (Eds.). (1977). *Classroom management: The successful use of behavior modification* (2nd ed.). New York: Pergamon Press.

Ornstein, A. C., & Levine, D. V. (1989). *Foundations of education* (4th ed.). Boston: Houghton Mifflin.

Osgood, C. E. (1949). The similarity paradox in human learning: A resolution. *Psychological Review, 56*, 132-143.

Palincsar, A., & Brown, A. L. (1984). Reciprocal teaching of comprehension-fostering and comprehension-monitoring activites. *Cognition and Instruction, 1* (2), 117-175.

Paris, S. G., Cross, D. R., & Lipson, M. Y. (1984). Informed strategies for learning: A program to improve children's reading awareness and comprehension. *Journal of Educational Psychology, 76* (6), 1239-1252.

Paris, S. G., & Oka, E. R. (1986). Children's reading strategies, metacognition, and motivation. *Developmental Review, 6,* 25-56.

Parke, R. D., & Slaby, R. G. (1983). The development of aggression. In E. M. Hetherington (Ed.), *Handbook of child psychology: Socialization, personality, and social development* (Vol. 4). New York: Wiley.

Parten, M. B. (1932). Social participation among preschool children. *Journal of Abnormal and Social Psychology, 27,* 243-269.

Patterson, C. H. (1973). *Humanistic education.* Englewood Cliffs, NJ: Prentice–Hall.

Pauk, W. (1984). *How to Study in College.* Boston: Houghton Mifflin.

Peeck, J., Bosch, A. B. van Den, & Kreupling, W. J. (1982). Effect of mobilizing prior knowledge on learning from text. *Journal of Educational Psychology, 74* (5), 771-777.

Penfield, W. (1969). Consciousness, memory, and man's conditioned reflexes. In K. Pribram (Ed.), *On the biology of learning.* New York: Harcourt Brace Jovanovich.

Peskin, H. (1967). Pubertal onset and ego functioning. A psychoanalytic approach. *Journal of Abnormal Psychology, 72,* 1-15.

Peskin, H. (1973). Influence of the developmental schedule of puberty on learning and ego functioning. *Journal of Youth and Adolescence, 2,* 273-290.

Peterson, A. C., & Taylor, B. (1980). The biological approach to adolescence. In J. Adelson (Ed.), *Handbook of adolescent psychology.* New York: Wiley.

Peterson, L. R., & Peterson, M. J. (1959). Short-term retention of individual verbal items. *Journal of Experimental Psychology, 58,* 193-198.

Petri, H. L. (1986). *Motivation: Theory and research.* Belmont, CA: Wadsworth.

Phillips, J. L., Jr. (1981). *Piaget's theory: A primer.* San Francisco: Freeman.

Piaget, J. (1948). *The moral judgment of the child* (M. Cabain, Trans.). Glencoe, IL: Free Press. (Original work published 1932).

Piaget, J. (1952a). *The language and thought of the child.* London: Routledge & Kegan Paul.

Piaget, J. (1952b). *The origins of intelligence in children.* New York: International Universities Press.

Piaget, J., & Inhelder, B. (1956). *The child's conception of space.* London: Routledge & Kegan Paul.

Piaget, J., & Inhelder, B. (1969). *The psychology of the child.* New York: Basic Books.

Polya, G. (1957). *How to solve it* (2nd ed.). Princeton, NJ: Princeton University Press.

Power, C. (1981). Moral education through the development of the moral atmosphere of the school. *The Journal of Educational Thought, 15* (1), 4-19.

Power, C. (1985). Democratic moral education in the large public high school. In M. W. Berkowitz & F. Oser (Eds.), *Moral education: Theory and application.* Hillsdale, NJ: Erlbaum.

Premack, D. (1959). Toward empirical behavior laws: 1. Positive reinforcement. *Psychological Review, 66,* 219-233.

Pressley, M., Levin, J. R., & Delaney, H. D. (1982). The mnemonic keyword method. *Review of Educational Research, 52,* 61-91.

Privacy rights of parent and students (1975). *Federal Register, 40* (3), 1208-1216.

Purkey, W. W. (1970). *Self concept and school achievement.* Englewood Cliffs, NJ: Prentice–Hall.

Purkey, W. W. (1978). *Inviting school success.* Belmont, CA: Wadsworth.

Purkey, W. W., & Novak, J. M. (1984). *Inviting school success* (2nd ed.). Belmont, CA: Wadsworth.

Purkey, W. W., & Strahan, D. B. (1986). *Positive discipline: A pocketful of ideas.* Columbus, OH: National Middle Schools Association.

Quay, H. C., Morse, W. C., & Cutler, R. L. (1966). Personality patterns of pupils in special classes for the emotionally disturbed. *Exceptional Children, 32,* 297-301.

Raths, L., Harmin, M., & Simon, S. B. (1966). *Values and teaching.* Columbus, OH: Merrill.

Raudenbush, S. W. (1984). Magnitude of teacher expectancy effects on pupil IQ as a function of the credibility of expectancy induction: A synthesis of findings from 18 experiments. *Journal of Educational Psychology, 76* (1), 85-97.

Raugh, M. R., & Atikinson, R. C. (1975). A mnemonic method for learning a second-language vocabulary. *Journal of Educational Psychology, 67,* 1-16.

Read, D. A., & Simon, S. B. (Eds.). (1975). *Humanistic education sourcebook.* Englewood Cliffs, NJ: Prentice–Hall.

Redl, F., & Wattenberg, W. W. (1959). *Mental hygiene in teaching* (2nd ed.). New York: Harcourt Brace Jovanovich.

Reid, M. I., Clunies-Ross, L. R., Goacher, B., & Viles, C. (1981). *Mixed ability teaching: Problems and possibilities.* Windsor, UK: NFER–Nelson.

Rennie, S., & Grimstad, K. (1975). *The new woman's survival sourcebook.* New York: Knopf.

Resnick, L. B. (1987). Learning in school and out. *Educational Researcher, 16* (9), 13-20.

Reynolds, C. R., Gutkin, T. B., Elliot, S. N., & Witt, J. C. (Eds.). (1984). *School psychology: Essentials of theory and practice.* New York: Wiley.

Robinson, H. A. (1983). *Teaching reading, writing, and study strategies* (3rd ed.). Boston: Allyn and Bacon.

Rogers, C. R. (1967). Learning to be free. In C. R. Rogers & B. Stevens (Eds.), *The problem of being human.* Lafayette, CA: Real People Press. (Reprinted from S. Farber & R. H. L. Wilson, Eds., 1963, *Conflict and creativity: Control of the mind,* New York: McGraw-Hill)

Rogers, C. R. (1980). *A way of being.* Boston: Houghton Mifflin.

Rogers, C. R. (1983). *Freedom to learn for the 80's.* Columbus, OH: Merrill.

Rogers, D. (1972). *The psychology of adolescence* (2nd ed.). New York: Appleton–Century–Crofts.

Rohwer, W. D., Jr. (1984). An invitation to an educational psychology of studying. *Educational Psychologist, 19* (1), 1-14.

Rollock, B. (1988). *Black authors and illustrators of children's books.* New York: Garland.

Rose, T. L. (1984). Current uses of corporal punishment in American public schools. *Journals of Educational Psychology, 76* (3), 427-441.

Rosen, B. M., Bahn, A. K., & Kramer, M. (1964). Demographic and diagnostic characteristics of psychiatric clinic outpatients in the U.S.A., 1961. *American Journal of Orthopsychiatry, 24,* 455-467.

Rosenshine, B. (1976). Classroom instruction. In N. L. Gage (Ed.), *The psychology of teaching methods.* The 75th Yearbook of the National Society for the Study of Education, Part I. Chicago: University of Chicago Press.

Rosenthal, R. (1985). From unconscious experimenter bias to teacher expectancy effects. In J. B. Dusek (Ed.), *Teacher expectations.* Hillsdale, NJ: Erlbaum.

Rosenthal, R., & Jacobson, L. (1968). *Pygmalion in the classroom.* New York: Holt, Rinehart & Winston.

Rosenthal, T., & Zimmerman, B. (1978). *Social learning and cognition.* New York: Holt, Rinehart & Winston.

Rowe, M. D. (1974). Wait-time and rewards as instructional variables, their influence on language, logic, and fate control: Part one—wait-time. *Journal of Research in Science Teaching, 11,* 81-94.

Royer, J. M. (1979). Theories of the transfer of learning. *Educational Psychologist, 14,* 53-72.

Royer, J. M., & Cable, G. W. (1975). Facilitated learning in connected discourse. *Journal of Educational Psychology, 67,* 116-123.

Royer, J. M., & Cable, G. W. (1976). Illustrations, analogies, and facilitative transfer in prose learning. *Journal of Educational Psychology, 68,* 205-209.

Rubin, L. J. (1985). *Artistry in teaching.* New York: Random House.

Ruggiero, V. R. (1988). *Teaching thinking across the curriculum.* New York: Harper & Row.

Rutter, M. (1980). Changing youth in a changing society: *Patterns of adolescent development and disorder.* Cambridge, MA: Harvard University Press.

Rutter, M., Tizard, J., & Whitmore, K. (Eds.). (1981). *Education, health, and behavior.* Huntington, NY: Krieger. (Original work published 1970)

Rutter, M., Maughan, B., Mortimore, P., Ousten, J., & Smith, A. (1979). *Fifteen thousand hours: Secondary schools and their effects on children.* Cambridge, MA: Harvard University Press.

Sadker, M. P., & Sadker, D. M. (1982). *Sex equity handbook for schools.* New York: Longman.

Sameroff, A. J., & Chandler, M. J. (1975). Reproductive risk and the continuum of caretaking causality. In F. D. Horowitz (Ed.), *Review of child development research* (Vol. 4). Chicago: University of Chicago Press.

Sanders, N. M. (1966). *Classroom questions: What kinds?* New York: Harper & Row.

Saracho, O. N. (1982). The effects of a computer-assisted instruction program on basic skills achievement and attitudes toward instruction of Spanish-speaking migrant children. *American Educational Research Journal, 19* (2), 201-219.

Sassenrath, J. M. (1975). Theory and results on feedback and retention. *Journal of Educational Psychology, 67,* 894-899.

Saunders, M. (1983). *Multicultural teaching: A guide for the classroom.* New York: McGraw-Hill.

Scarr, S., Weinburg, R. A., & Levine, A. (1986). *Understanding development.* San Diego, CA: Harcourt Brace Jovanovich.

Scheirer, M. A., & Kraut, R. E. (1979). Increasing educational achievement via self-concept change. *Review of Educational Research, 49,* 131-150.

Schlaefli, A., Rest, J. R., & Thoma, S. J. (1985). Does moral education improve moral judgment? A meta-analysis of intervention studies using the Defining Issues Test. *Review of Educational Research, 55* (3), 319-352.

Schon, I. (1980). *A Hispanic heritage: A guide to juvenile books about Hispanic people and cultures.* Metuchen, NJ: Scarecrow Press.

Schunk, D. H. (1981). Modeling and attributional effects on children's achievement: A self-efficacy analysis. *Journal of Educational Psychology, 73* (1), 93-105.

Schunk, D. H. (1987). Peer models and children's behavioral change *Review of Educational Research, 57* (2), 149-174.

Seagoe, M. V. (1970). *The learning process and school practice.* Scran-ton, PA: Chandler.

Seagoe, M. V. (1975). *Terman and the gifted.* Los Altos, CA: Kaufmann.

Seligman, M. E. P. (1975). *Helplessness: On depression, development, and death.* San Francisco: Freeman.

Selman, R. L. (1976a). Social-cognitive understanding: A guide to educational and clinical practice. In T. Lickona (Ed.), *Moral development and behavior: Theory, research, and social issues.* New York: Holt, Rinehart & Winston.

Selman, R. L. (1976b). Toward a structural analysis of developing interpersonal relations concepts. In A. Pick (Ed.), *Minnesota symposia on child psychology* (Vol. 10). Minneapolis: University of Minnesota Press.

Shepard, L. A., Smith, M. L., & Vojir, C.P. (1983). Characteristics of pupils identified as learning disabled. *American Educational Research Journal, 20* (3), 309-332.

Shrable, K., & Sassenrath, J. M. (1970). Effects of achievement, motivation, and test anxiety on performance in programmed instruction. *American Educational Research Journal, 7,* 209-220.

Shulman, L. (1970). The hidden group in the classroom. *Learning and Development, 2* (3), 1-6.

Shulman, L. S. (1986). Those who understand: Knowledge growth in teaching. *Educational Research, 15* (2), 4-21.

Siegel, E., & Gold, R. (1982). *Educating the learning disabled.* New York: Macmillan.

Siegel, O. (1982). Personality development in adolescence. In B. B. Wolman (Ed.), *Handbook of developmental psychology.* Englewood Cliffs, NJ: Prentice–Hall.

Siegler, R. S. (1983). Information processing approaches to development. In P. H. Mussen (Ed.), *Handbook of child psychology: Vol. 1. History, theory, and methods (4th ed.).* New York: Wiley.

Simon, A., & Boyer, E. G. (Eds.). (1970). *Mirrors for behavior: An anthology of classroom observation instruments continued.* Philadelphia: Research for Better Schools.

Simon, S. B., Howe, L. W. & Kirschenbaum, H. (1972). *Values clarification: A handbook of practical strategies for teachers and students.* New York: Hart.

Simpson, E. J. (1972). *The classification of educational objectives: Psychomotor domain.* Urbana, IL: University of Illinois Press.

Simpson, M. L. (1984). The status of study strategy instruction: Implications for classroom teachers. *Journal of Reading, 28* (2), 136-143.

Simpson, R. L. (1962). Parental influence, anticipitory socialization, and social mobility. *American Sociological Review, 27,* 517-522.

Skinner, B. F. (1948). *Walden two.* New York: Macmillan.

Skinner, B. F. (1951). How to teach animals. *Scientific American, 185* (6), 26-29.

Skinner, B. F. (1968). *The technology of teaching.* New York: Appleton–Century–Crofts.

Skinner, B. F. (1976). *Particulars of my life.* New York: Knopf.

Skinner, B. F. (1979). *The shaping of a behaviorist.* New York: Knopf.

Skinner, B. F. (1983). *A matter of consequences.* New York: Knopf.

Skinner, B. F. (1984). The shame of American education. *American Psychologist, 39* (9), 947-954.

Skinner, B. F. (1986). Programmed instruction revisited. *Phi Delta Kappan, 68* (2), 103-110.

Slavin, R. E. (1980). Cooperative learning. *Review of Educational Research, 50* (2), 315-342.

Slavin, R. E. (1987a). Ability grouping and student achievement in elementary schools: A best-evidence synthesis. *Review of Educational Research, 57* (3), 293-336.

Slavin, R. E. (1987b). Mastery learning reconsidered. *Review of Educational Research, 57* (2), 175-214.

Slavin, R. E. (1988a). *Educational psychology: Theory into practice* (2nd ed.). Englewood Cliffs, NJ: Prentice–Hall.

Slavin, R. E. (1988b). *Student team learning: An overview and practical guide* (2nd ed.). Washington, DC: National Education Association.

Slung, M. (1985). *The absent-minded professor's memory book.* New York: Ballantine books.

Smith, D. D. (1989). *Teaching students with learning and behavior problems* (2nd ed.). Englewood Cliffs, NJ: Prentice–Hall.

Smith, M. L., & Shepard, L. A. (1987). What doesn't work: Explaining policies of retention in the early grades. *Phi Delta Kappan, 69* (2), 129-134.

Snow, R. E. (1986). Individual differences and the design of educational programs. *American Psychologist, 41* (10), 1029-1039.

Snowman, J. (1986). Learning tactics and strategies. In G. D. Phye & T. Andre (Eds.), *Cognitive classroom learning: Understanding, thinking, and problem solving.* New York: Academic Press.

Snowman, J. (1987, October). *The keys to strategic learning.* Paper presented at the annual meeting of the Mid-Western Educational Research Association, Chicago, IL.

Soar, R. (1973). *Follow Through classroom process measurement and pupil growth, 1970-71* (Final report). Gainesville, FL: University of Florida, College of Education.

Sonenstein, F. L., & Pittman, K. J. (1984). The availability of sex education in large school districts. *Family Planning Perspectives, 16,* 19-25.

Sorensen, J. S., Schwenn, E. A., & Barry, J. (1970). *The use of individual and group goal-setting conferences as a motivational device to improve student conduct and increase student self-direction: A preliminary study* (Tech. Rep. No. 520). Madison, WI: University of Wisconsin, Wisconsin Research and Development Center for Cognitive Learning.

Sorensen, J. S., Schwenn, E. A., & Klausmeier, H. J. (1969). *The individual conference: A motivational device for increasing independent reading in the elementary grades* (Practical Paper No. 8). Madison, WI: University of Wisconsin, Wisconsin Research and Development Center for Cognitive Learning.

Sorenson, R. C. (1973). *Adolescent sexuality in contemporary America: Personal Values and sexual behavior.* New York: World.

Spence, J. T. (Ed.). (1983). *Achievement and achievement motives.* San Francisco: Freeman.

Sprinthall, N. A., & Sprinthall, R. C. (1987). *Educational psychology; A developmental approach* (4th ed.). New York: Random House.

Stallings, J. A., & Kaskowitz, D. H. (1974). *Follow Through classroom observation and evaluation, 1972-1973.* Menlo Park, CA: Stanford Research Institute.

Standing, L. (1973). Learning 10,000 pictures. *Quarterly Journal of Experimental Psychology, 25,* 207-222.

Standing, L., Conezio, J., Haber, R. (1970). Perception and memory for pictures: Single trial learning of 2500 visual stimuli. *Psychonomic Science, 19,* 73-74.

Stephens, J. M. (1956). *Educational Psychology* (2nd ed.). New York: Holt, Rinehart & Winston.

Sternberg, R. J. (1984). Toward a triarchic theory of human intelligence. *Behavioral and Brain Sciences, 7,* 269-287.

Sternberg, R. J. (1988). *The triarchic mind: A new theory of human intelligence.* New York: Viking.

Stitt, B. A. (1988). *Building gender fairness in schools.* Carbondale, IL: Southern Illinois University Press.

Stronge, J. H., Lynch, C. D., & Smith, C. R. (1987). Educating the culturally disadvantaged gifted student. *The School Counselor, 34* (5), 336-344.

Strother, D. B. (1986). Suicide among the young. *Phi Delta Kappan, 67* (10), 756-759.

Sulzer–Azaroff, B., & Mayer, G. R. (1986). *Achieving educational excellence: Using behavioral strategies.* New York: Holt, Rinehart & Winston.

Surber, J. T., & Anderson, R. C. (1975). Delay-retention effect in natural classroom settings. *Journal of Educational Psychology, 67* (3), 170-173.

Suter, D. P., & Wolf, J. S. (1987). Issues in the identification and programming of the gifted/learning disabled child. *Journal for the Education of the Gifted, 10* (3), 227-237.

Swisher, J. F., Vickery, J. R., & Nadenichek, P. (1983). Humanistic education: A review of research. *Journal of Humanistic Education and Development, 22* (1), 8-15.

Taba, J., & Elkins, D. (1966). *Teaching strategies for the culturally disadvantaged.* Chicago: Rand McNally.

Tanner, J. M. (1972). Sequence, tempo, and individual variation in growth and development of boys and girls aged twelve to sixteen. In J. Kagan & R. Coles (Eds.), *Twelve to sixteen: Early adolescence.* New York: Norton.

Taylor, C. A. (Ed.). (1987). *Guide to multicultural resources.* Madison, WI: Praxis Publications.

Terman, L., & Oden, M. (1959). *Genetic studies of genius: The gifted group at mid-life. Thirty-five years' follow-up of the superior child.* Stanford, CA: Stanford University Press.

Thelen, H. A. (1960). *Education and the human quest.* New York: Wiley.

Thoma, S. J. (1986). Estimating gender differences in the comprehension and preference of moral issues. *Developmental Review, 6,* 165-180.

Thomas, J. W. (1980). Agency and achievement: Self-management and self-regard. *Review of Educational Research, 50* (2), 213-240.

Thomas, M. (1974). *Free to be you and me.* New York: McGraw–Hill.

Thorndike, E. L., & Woodworth, R. S. (1901). The influence of improvement in one mental function upon the efficiency of other functions. *Psychological Review, 8,* 247-261.

Thurlow, M. L., & Ysseldyke, J. E. (1979). Current assessment and decision making practices in model LD programs. *Learning Disability Quarterly, 2,* 15-24.

Tonemah, S. (1987). Assessing American Indian gifted and talented students' abilities. *Journal for the Education of the Gifted, 10* (3), 181-194.

Tresemer, D. (1974). Fear of success: Popular but unproven. *Psychology Today, 7* (10), 82-85.

Tresemer, D. (1977). *Fear of success:* New York: Plenum.

Triandis, H. C. (1986). Toward pluralism in education, In S. Modgil, G. K. Verma, K. Mallick, & C. Modgil (Eds.), *Multicultural education: The interminable debate.* London: Falmer.

Trubowitz, S. (1968). *A handbook for teaching in the ghetto school.* Chicago: Quadrangle.

Tulving, E., & Pearlstone, Z. (1966). Availability vs. accessibility of information in memory for words. *Journal of Verbal Learning and Verbal Behavior, 5,* 381-391.

Turnure, J. E., & Lane, J. F. (1987). Special educational applications of mnemonics. In M. A. McDaniel & M. Pressley (Eds.), *Imagery and related mnemonic processes.* New York: Springer–Verlag.

U.S. Committee for the White House Conference on Education. (1956). *A report to the president.* Washington, DC: U.S. Government Printing Office.

U.S. Department of Health, Education, & Welfare. (1978). *Violent schools-safe schools. The safe school report to the Congress* (Vol. 1). Washington, DC: U.S. Government Printing Office.

U.S. Office of Special Education and Rehabilitative Services (1988). *To assure the free appropriate public education of all handicapped children. Tenth annual report to Congress on the implementation of the Education of the Handicapped Act.* Washington, DC: U.S. Department of Education.

Valente, W. D. (1987). *Law in the schools* (2nd ed.). Columbus, OH: Merrill.

Van Hasselt, V. B., & Hersen, M. (Eds.). (1987). *Handbook of adolescent psychology.* New York: Pergamon Press.

Vargas, J. (1986). Instructional design flaws in computer-assisted instruction. *Phi Delta Kappan, 67* (10), 738-744.

Wadsworth, B. J. (1980). *Piaget for the classroom teacher* (2nd ed.). New York: Longman.

Wadsworth, B. J. (1989) *Piaget's theory of cognitive and affective development* (4th ed.). New York: Longman.

Walberg, H. J., Schiller, D., & Haertel, G. D. (1979). The quiet revolution in educational research. *Phi Delta Kappan, 61* (3), 179-182.

Walker, D. F. (1983). Reflections on the educational potential and limitations of microcomputers. *Phi Delta Kappan, 65* (2), 103-107.

Walker, J. E., & Shea, T. M. (1980). *Behavior modification: A practical approach for educators* (2nd ed.). St. Louis, MO: Mosby.

Wechsler, D. (1967). *Wechler Preschool and Primary Scale of Intelligence.* New York: Psychological Corporation.

Wechsler, D. (1974). *Wechsler Intelligence Scale for Children—Revised.* New York: Psychological Corporation.

Wechsler, D. (1975). Intelligence defined and undefined: A relativistic appraisal. *American Psychologist, 30* (2), 135-139.

Wechsler, D. (1981). *Wechsler Adult Intelligence Scale—Revised.* New York: Psychological Corporation.

Weiner, B. (1979). A theory of motivation for some classroom experiences. *Journal of Educational Psychology, 71,* 3-25.

Weiner, B. (1980). *Human motivation.* New York: Holt, Rinehart & Winston.

Weiner, B. (1986). *An attributional theory of motivation and emotion.* New York: Springer–Verlag.

Weiner, I. B. (1975). Depression in adolescence. In F. F. Flach & S. C. Draghi (Eds.), *The nature and treatment of depression.* New York: Wiley.

Weiner, I. B. (1980). Psychopathology in adolescence. In J. Adelson (Ed.), *Handbook of adolescent psychology.* New York: Wiley.

Werner, E. E., Bierman, J. M., & French, F. E. (1971). *The children of Kauai: A longitudinal study from the prenatal period to age ten.* Honolulu; University of Hawaii Press.

West, D. J., & Farrington, D. P. (1973). *Who becomes delinquent?* London: Heinemann.

Whimbey, A., & Lochhead, J. (1986). *Problem solving and comprehension* (4th ed.). Hillsdale, NJ: Erlbaum.

White, B. L., & Watts, J. C. (1973). *Experience and environment: Major influences on the development of the young child.* Englewood Cliffs, NJ: Prentice–Hall.

White, R. W. (1959). Motivation reconsidered: The concept of competence. *Psychological Review, 66,* 297-333.

Whitmore, J. (1987). Conceptualizing the issue of underserved populations of gifted students. *Journal for the Education of the Gifted, 10* (3), 141-153.

Wilen, D. K., & Sweeting, C. (1986). Assessment of limited English proficiency Hispanic students. *School Psychology Review, 15* (1), 59-75.

Willig, A. C. (1985). A meta-analysis of selected studies on the effectiveness of bilingual education. *Review of Educational Research, 55* (3), 269-318.

Wineburg, S. S. (1987). The self-fulfillment of the self-fulfilling prophecy. *Educational Researcher, 16* (9), 28-37.

Wingfield, A. (1979). *Human learning and memory.* New York: Harper & Row.

Wlodkowski, R. J. (1978). *Motivation and teaching: A practical guide.* Washington, DC: National Education Association.

Wolfgang, C., & Glickman, G. (1980). *Solving discipline problems: Alternative strategies for classroom teachers.* Boston: Allyn and Bacon.

Wong, B. Y. L. (1985). Self-questioning instructional research: A review. *Review of Educational Research, 55* (2), 227-268.

Wood, F. W., & Zabel, R. H. (1978). *Making sense of reports on the incidence of behavior disorders/emotional disturbance in school populations.* Unpublished manuscript, University of Minnesota, Minneapolis.

Woodring, P. (1957). *A fourth of a nation.* New York: McGraw–Hill.

Wright, H. F. (1960). Observational child study. In P. H. Mussen (Ed.), *Handbook of research methods in child development.* New York: Wiley.

Wynn, R. L., & Fletcher, C. (1987). Sex role development and early educational experiences. In D. B. Carter (Ed.), *Current conceptions of sex roles and sex typing.* New York: Praeger.

Yao, E. L. (1988). Working effectively with Asian immigrant parents. *Phi Delta Kappan, 70* (3), 223-225.

Yates, F. A. (1966). *The art of memory.* London: Routledge & Kegan Paul.

Yates, M. R., Saunders, R., & Watkins, J. F. (1980). A program based on Maslow's hierarchy helps students in trouble. *Phi Delta Kappan, 61* (10), 712-713.

Ysseldyke, J. (1983). Current practices in making psychological decisions about learning disabled students. In G. Senf & J. Torgeson (Eds.), *Annual review of learning disabilities: Vol. 1. A journal of learning disabilities reader.* Chicago: Professional Press.

Ysseldyke, J. E., & Algozzine, B. (1984). *Introduction to special education.* Boston: Houghton Mifflin.

Zelnick, M., & Shah, F. K. (1983). First intercourse among young Americans. *Family Planning Perspectives, 15,* 64-70.

Zelniker, T., & Jeffrey, W. E. (1976). Reflective and impulsive children: Strategies of information processing underlying differences in problem solving. *Monographs of the Society for Research in Child Development, 41* (5, Serial No. 168).

Zimmerman, B. J., & Blotner, R. (1979). Effects of model persistence and success on children's problem solving. *Journal of Educational Psychology, 71* (4), 508-513.

Zimmerman, B. J., & Ringle, J. (1981). Effects of model persistence and statements of confidence on children's self-efficacy and problem solving. *Journal of Educational Psychology, 73* (4) 485-493.

Zwier, G., & Vaughan, G. M. (1984). Three ideological orientations in school vandalism research. *Review of Educational Research, 54* (2), 263-292.

AUTHOR/SOURCE INDEX

SUBJECT INDEX

Ability groupings, evaluations of, 191–192; reactions against, 192–194; types of, 189–191

Abstract concepts, adolescence, 70–71; elementary grades, 65, 69; gifted students, 232; junior high grades, 132, 133; mnemonics and, 394; moral development and, 86

Abstracts, journals of, 28–29

Accommodation, Peaget's theory of, 59–60, 522

Achievement, acceptable, 305; attribution theory and, 530; effort and, 530, 574; evaluation of, see Evaluation; expectations and, 487, 496, 591, 631; factory school and, 487, 496; gender differences, 529; intelligence and, 169; modeling and, 349; motivation and, 537, 538, 572–576; need for, 527–529, 568–572, 728; objectives and, 291, 292–294; reducing violence and, 667; standardized assessment of, see Standardized tests; teacher expectancy and, 591 See also Tests

Achievement motivation theory, 527–532, 559–572, 574–576

Acquired immune deficiency syndrome (AIDS), 137

Acronym mnemonics, 394, 413

Acrostic mnemonics, 394, 413

Action verbs, instructional; objectives and, 283, 300, 599–600

Activities, building into classwork, 717; first class day, 660–661; motivating learning with, 544–545; preschoolers, 101; smoothness and momentum in, 651–653

Activity cards, 502

Adaptation, educational objectives for, 276; intelligence and, 169; Piaget's theory and, 59–60, 62

Administration, misbehavior and, 664, 682

Adolescence, career choices and, 50–52; cognitive development, 70–71; depression and, 138–140; egocentrism in, 71; emotional characteristics, 145; fundamental ideas and, 426; identity status, 52–54, 130; physiological aspects, 145; political thinking and, 133; role confusion in, 45, 46–50; sexual relationships in, 135–136; thought schemes, 62, 66–67 See also High school grades; Junior high grades

Advance organizers, 445

Adventure, learning and, 544, 546–548

Affective domain; taxonomy of objectives for, 272–275, 286, 303–304, 507–508, 722; learning and, 478–513

Age-level characteristics, see Development

Aggression, 223; gender differences in, 48, 105, 665; primary grades, 113; punishing, 227–228; social learning theory and, 348

Alcoholism, suicide and, 141

American College Testing Program (ACT), 159

Analogies, learning with, 412, 453

Androgyny, psychological, 49–50

Anger, helping pupils understand, 716; teacher's display of, 503–504 See also Aggression

Art, educational objectives for, 270

Artist, teacher as, 19–21

Assessment, see Evaluation; Tests

Assimilation, Piaget's theory of, 59–60, 522

Associations, memory and, 384

Attention, increasing, 724; information processing and, 381; mild retardation and, 208, 211; observational learning and, 346–347; sensory register and, 405–408

Attribution theory, 530–532, 535

Audiologists, 203

Audiovisual devices, 546

Authoritative parents, 109

Authoritarianism, adolescents and, 133–134; in parents, 109–110

Autism, 222

Aversive stimuli, 324

Behavior, 17–19; causes of, 354, 723; consequences of, 322; cultural factors, 42; desired, 322–324; Freudian view of, 42, 482; fundamental elements of, 320 321; prosocial, 569–571; self-awareness and, 107; social factors, 43, 46; strengthening, 340–342, 354–359; systematic sampling, 595; undesired, 324–325; weakening, 342–345 See also Behavioral theories

Behavioral scientists, teachers as, 6, 24–25

Behavioral theories, 318–373; classical conditioning, 318–319, 321–322; criticism of, 345; evaluation and, 585; misbehavior and, 673–674, 731; motivation and, 519–521, 727; operant conditioning, 319–345; social learning, 346–350, 519; teaching handbook and, 705–706; teaching suggestions, 352–368, 723–724; transfer of learning and, 469–472

Behavior disorders, 122, 222–223

Between-class grouping, 190, 191, 193

Bilingual Education Act, 249–250, 252

Binet-Simon scale, 166–167

Blind students, 200

Body of knowledge, understanding, 424–426

Book reports, as exam supplements, 633

Boredom, counteracting, 543–550

Boys, aggression and, 105; growth spurt, 116–117; moral development, 82; personality development, 54–55; time of maturity, 128 See also Gender differences

Careers, see Occupational choices

Central nervous system, learning disabilities and, 215

Central tendency, measures of, 622–623

Child labor laws, 188

Chunking, of information, 449–450, 724

Citizenship, National Assessment, objectives for, 279

Classical conditioning, 318–319, 321–322

Classroom atmosphere, businesslike, 662–663; motivation and, 517, 532–536,; 555–558; supportive, 662–663

Classroom management, 132, 648–689; analyzing techniques of, 650–657; control and, 715; Kounin's observations on, 650–655; teaching handbook and, 710–711; teaching suggestions, 658–663; University of Texas studies, 655–657

Client-oriented therapy, 482

Clinical teachers, 201

Cognitions, depression and, 140; metacognition vs., 389

Cognitive disequilibrium, 561

Cognitive development, see Development theories

Cognitive domain, age differences in, 613; educational objectives for, 270–272, 285, 294, 299, 600

Cognitive skills, learning transfer and, 470–471; modeling and, 349; optimal motivation and, 538; problem-solving and, 455, 465

Cognitive styles, differences in, 124–126, 144–145, 719

Cognitive theories, 484; information processing, 374–420; learning transfer, 472–473; motivation and, 521–523; problem-solving and, 422–477; teaching handbook and, 707–708; teaching suggestions, 725

College, admissions, 153; preparation for, 602–603

College courses, gifted students, 234

Cmpetence, development of, 109; encouraging, 717; innate drive for, 521, 522; tests of, 159

Competition, excessive, 559; fear of success and, 529; group, 533; individual, 532–533; mastery learning and, 637

Completion tests, 605

Comprehension, educational objectives for, 271–272; learning transfer and, 472–473; questions for, 414–415; self-questioning and, 397–398; tactics, 725

Compulsory attendance laws, 188, 189

Computers, computer-assisted instruction, 16, 320, 334–340, 362; information processing theory and, 376

Student Response Form

What do you think of this book? The authors and publisher would like to know what you think of this sixth edition of *Psychology Applied to Teaching.* Your comments will help us not only in improving the next edition of this book but also in developing other texts. We would appreciate very much if you would take a few minutes to respond to the following questions. When you have indicated your reactions, please send this form to: College Marketing, Houghton Mifflin Company, One Beacon Street, Boston, MA 02108.

1. On a ten-point scale, with 10 as the highest rating and 1 as the lowest, how do you rate the following features of *Psychology Applied to Teaching?*
   Overall rating compared to all other texts you have read _____
   Interest level compared to all other texts you have read _____
   Readability compared to other texts _____
   Clarity of presentation of concepts and information _____
   Value of the *Key Points* as a learning aid _____
   Helpfulness of *Mid-Chapter Reviews* _____
   Helpfulness of summary *tables* and *diagrams* _____
   Interest level and pedagogical effectiveness of the *illustrations* _____
   Usefulness of the *Suggestions for Further Study* _____
   Usefulness of the *Handbook Headings* and *Suggestions for Developing a Personal Handbook* _____
   Usefulness of *Becoming a Better Teacher: Questions and Suggestions* _____
2. Do you intend to sell this book _____ or keep it for future reference _____? (Please insert an X in the appropriate space.)
3. Have you used (or do you intend to refer to) *Becoming a Better Teacher: Questions and Suggestions* to improve your teaching effectiveness?
   Yes _____ No _____
4. Please turn to the table of contents and list here the numbers of all chapters that were assigned by your instructor.

   _____

5. If not all chapters were assigned, did you read any others on your own? Please indicate chapter numbers you read on your own.

   _____

6. Were there any topics that were not covered that you thought should have been covered?

   _____

7. Please indicate the number of each of the following types of exams that your instructor asked you to take:
multiple choice _____ short-answer _____ essay _____ oral _____ other (please specify) _____
8. Did your instructor give you the opportunity to compare your test answers to the answers provided by the person who wrote the questions?
Yes _____ No _____
9. Were you required to write a term paper _____ or complete some sort of term project? (Please specify the nature of the term project.) _____
10. Did you use the Study Guide? Yes _____ No _____
On a ten-point scale, how do you rate the usefulness of the Study Guide? _____

Did your instructor ask you to use the Study Guide _____ or did you obtain it on your own _____?
11. Are you attending a 2-year college _____, 4-year college _____, university _____?
12. What was your class standing at the time you took the course in educational psychology?
Freshman _____ Sophomore _____ Junior _____ Senior _____ Graduate _____
13. Is your college or university on the quarter system _____ or the semester system _____?
14. If you had the chance to talk to the authors of this book just before they started to prepare the next edition, what suggestions would you give them for improving *Psychology Applied to Teaching?*